In this second, revised edition

■   Clear explanations of essential logical concepts and
       distinctions

■   Comprehensive syllabus coverage

■   a controlled vocabulary with glossaries attached to each
       chapter

■   relevant, challenging, up-to-date examples

■   detailed case studies illustrating important points

■   exercises with answers

■   treatment of the material beyond the level of immediate,
       easy scepticism

■   ideas for discussion, presentations and essay writing

■   index of concepts

The Enterprise of Knowledge

A Resource Book for
Theory of Knowledge

Second Edition Revised

John L. Tomkinson

Anagnosis
Athens, Greece

Anagnosis
Harilaou Trikoupi 130
145 63 Kifissia
Athens, Greece
Website: www.anagnosis.gr

ISBN 960-87186-9-4
Second Edition, Revised

First edition published by Leader Books 1999
Reprinted 2001

© Anagnosis

2004

Photoset and printed by:
K. Pletsas - Z. Karadri O.E.
Harilaou Trikoupi 107
Athens
www.typografio.gr

PREFACE

"Boredom will always remain the greatest enemy of school disciplines. If we remember that children are bored, not only when they don't happen to be interested in the subject or when the teacher doesn't make it interesting, but also when certain working conditions are out of focus with their basic needs, then we can realize what a great contributor to discipline problems boredom really is. Research has shown that boredom is closely related to frustration and that the effect of too much frustration is invariably irritability, withdrawal, rebellious opposition or aggressive rejection of the whole show."

(Fritz Redl)

The Enterprise of Knowledge provides a broad introductory overview of the various types of human knowledge, the means by which that knowledge is acquired and communicated, and its reliability and limitations.

It is intended for use by teachers and students in the upper years of high school or the lower years of college, who require a framework for a general introduction to the entire spectrum of the problems of knowledge, for use in pre-university or first-year undergraduate interdisciplinary foundation courses. It is closely modelled upon the requirements of the course in the Theory of Knowledge of the International Baccalaureate (IB), and is offered as a resource book for that course, although, since it has been developed independently, it does not reflect the views of the International Baccalaureate Organisation (IBO); and, like all such texts, it is in no way endorsed by the IBO, the sole authority for determining the syllabus and requirements of that course.

Although the issues discussed are philosophical, and the book is largely a survey of questions in epistemology and in the various "philosophies of . . ." such as the philosophy of science and the philosophy of mathematics, no background in technical philosophy is presupposed or required. For this reason, the book may itself be used as an introduction to that subject, although one considerably less austere than is traditional, and one which is particularly suited to the needs of school students, who may not necessarily wish to go on to study philosophy at a higher level. The central issues of philosophy are addressed, at least in their most elementary forms, and the basic tools and distinctions necessary to the study of philosophy are introduced.

The main aim has been to present the more important and interesting issues, and to provide students with enough in the way of technical tools to consider them intelligently at an elementary level. This is done in the belief that these issues should not be left exclusively to the enjoyment of specialist students of philosophy. Nor should they be allowed to slip through the interstices of excessively rigid educational programmes, since they are the birthright of all students who are capable of reflective thought about the nature and limitations of the disciplines they are studying, and because awareness of these problems, and of the way in which they may be resolved, should be considered an essential prerequisite for any well-educated person.

The Philosophy of the Book

The title of the book was chosen to reflect the author's view that knowledge is justified true belief, and as such it is, beyond its most restricted levels, essentially a public matter. In addition, the study of the history of mankind reveals an ongoing process whereby the knowledge acquired by various distinct cultures has increasingly become incorporated into a single system, which is the common possession of mankind, like separate streams which feed into a single mighty river.

Knowledge which is of more than merely individual significance becomes the possession of the community when it is shared. The knowledge of each unique society has developed over the generations, until, in this age of globalization, it is shared with the worldwide community. This knowledge is not the *property* of anyone, not even of its individual sources. It is part of the common heritage of mankind. The knowledge which was used to put a man on the moon was not the exclusive property of NASA. Most of it was contributed by people who died without ever having known of NASA; people like Aristarchos of Samos, Nicholas Copernicus, Isaac Newton, and many more. Without their diverse contributions, NASA's achievement would hardly have been conceivable, let alone possible.

There is a single, simple value judgement underlying and permeating this text, and that is that, in general, knowledge is a good thing and ignorance is a bad thing. The Enterprise of Knowledge, with many roots but now a single trunk, requires certain special conditions for its healthy growth. The desirability of these conditions, and the undesirability of others which would impede the development of knowledge, constitute a second tier of values, which flow from the very nature of knowledge itself. Thus the initial commitment to knowledge authenticates the desirability of respect for reason and truth, and an open society with the free flow of information, and freedom to criticise anything and everything, including a culture's "sacred cows." The initial commitment to knowledge also authenticates the *un*desirability of all that leads to, or reinforces, ignorance: such as prejudice, dogmatism, ideological thinking, obscurantism and propaganda.

In addition, rather than leaving every issue considered hanging in the air, without resolution, a particular epistemological standpoint has been adopted on most issues and retained consistently throughout the book. In general, in relation to every issue of knowledge there is a naïve, unreflective viewpoint: that we know what we know, and that it is *obviously* true. This is the starting point of all of us until we begin to think critically. After that comes an initial scepticism, when we see through the naïve view. Making the move to this second level comes naturally to most students of pre-undergraduate and undergraduate age. Unfortunately, many proceed no further, and are left stranded, and often dissatisfied, on a level of scepticism almost as naïve as the realism they have abandoned. The tactics of the author in most cases is to go beyond this: to state and defend a position of qualified realism, which takes account of the problems of the naïve realist view, and of the initial and obvious criticisms levelled against it, yet seeks to move to a stage beyond. This should give students at this point in their education something substantial to think and argue about, and at the same time lead them beyond the level at which they would naturally come to rest.

Cultural relativism is firmly rejected and frequent reference is made on many occasions to the contribution to the Enterprise of Knowledge made by the ancient Greeks.[1] This is not to devalue other traditions, but is for two reasons. The first is that the author believes the contribution of the Greeks to the Enterprise of Knowledge is unique, in that Greece is the birthplace, so far as our records at present show, of the *self-conscious* cultivation of rigorous, critical thinking, and therefore of the development of *systematic* knowledge with a *critical* basis. The second is a consequence of this. Many of the problems which need to be considered on a course such as Theory of Knowledge have already found their most stark formulation, in simple non-technical language, in the literature of the ancient Greeks. This makes their discussion of these problems frequently an eminently suitable starting place for introducing them into the classroom.

Like all good education, and much more than most, Theory of Knowledge is likely, in practice, to be perceived in some quarters as inherently subversive, and the societies which adopt this standpoint may not always be the ones we expect. Two approaches to developing a resource book for worldwide use present themselves. One is to adopt a "safe," bland, watered-down, uncontroversial, lowest common denominator approach. The other is to face the issues squarely: to be challenging, up-to-date and relevant. In the second edition of this book, the latter alternative has been embraced wholeheartedly. Where ancient or traditional examples bring much-desired clarity to complex issues, and, despite being well-worn, are clearly relevant to current disputes, they have been adopted. Otherwise, examples have been chosen which raise what are controversial issues at the time of going to press.

If any problem arises because of conflict with local limits upon academic freedom, it should be born in mind that whatever noble sentiments schools, education authorities or examining boards may profess, the teacher on the spot is likely to be the one who will be called upon to "drink hemlock" to appease the offended. Therefore the classroom teacher needs constantly to be aware of the boundaries of what is permissible in education in his/her host school and country, and to choose carefully how subjects that may be locally controversial need to be approached, or even *if* they should be touched upon at all. Of course, if important issues cannot be considered in an open and critical manner in the classroom at this level, this raises the issue of whether any genuinely critical education is possible in such an environment, but that is another matter.

The Plan of the Book

The structure of this text does not exactly correspond to the famous TOK diagram. That is by the author's choice. It was clearly never intended that the TOK diagram should be accorded the status of "tablets of stone brought down from the mountain." The Teachers' Guide refers approvingly to "approaches using alternative structures," and specifically says: "It is left to teachers, if they wish, to design their courses within whatever frameworks they prefer." The framework adopted here is one which the suthor has found to work over the years. It also accords proper importance to what is the main problem of knowledge which students at this level face every day: To what extent should I accept the testimony of those recognised by society as authorities, and how, as a lay person and student, may I judge the value of the testimony presented by authorities (schoolteachers, university professors, textbooks, academic monographs, television programmes, newspapers, news magazines, newscasters, politicians, ministers of religion, etc., etc).

An introduction for the students is designed to assist them in making a quicker adjustment to this sort of course. The first two introductory chapters set the scene by introducing the key idea of the collective Enterprise of Knowledge (1), and an analysis of the concept of knowledge in relation to the knower (2). The second part of the book is concerned with the various sources of knowledge. Chapter three introduces a wide range of alleged sources, while the main foundations of knowledge: sense-experience (4), testimony (5) and reason (6), are each dealt with in detail in the following chapters. The next section deals with various "vehicles" of knowledge: the means by which knowledge is "manipulated," expressed and communicated in language (7), mathematics (8) and the arts (9).

In the largest section, the various areas of knowledge are covered. In the first chapter of this section, our everyday thinking is described, and compared with academic knowledge or (in the wide sense) scientific knowledge (10). The nature of our factual knowledge and the concepts of facts and explanation are analysed more closely in the next (11). There follow chapters on the chief areas of knowledge: the natural sciences (12), the human sciences (13) and history (14). We then turn to our knowledge of values, dealing specifically with aesthetic values (15), and then with ethics (16) and politics (17). The final section covers philosophy (18) and the contemporary challenges to the Enterprise of Knowledge (19). For those able or willing to consider such questions, a section on religion is added in an appendix.

Layout

The layout of the book has been developed in an attempt to be useful and student-friendly, without in any way contributing to the "dumbing down" currently fashionable in some circles and characteristic of much formal education today. In particular, the author firmly believes that students of pre-undergraduate and undergraduate age are perfectly capable of reading entire pages of text with no inessential illustrations whatsoever. The interest which excites the student should flow from the issues themselves, which are almost always best conveyed in words, rather than from any extraneous decoration offered to "sugar the pill." The tendency increasingly to treat older and more advanced students in a manner appropriate to young children does no long-term service either to our students or to society; and it is certainly no duty of the educator to collaborate with such "dumbing down." Instead, everything has been done to make issues, distinctions and arguments *clear* to readers as possible through the medium of language.

In order to assist the student to focus on the important issues, key terms are printed in bold type on their first significant appearance. In addition to being explained in context, definitions of each are provided in a glossary at the end of each chapter. This should be of particular use to international students and others not studying in their mother tongue. Exercises, suggestions for questions suitable for discussion are provided in each chapter as appropriate.

A research treatise would have a full apparatus of footnotes and references. But this is not a research treatise; it is a classroom tool. The ideas and arguments are what is important, not their sources. This is something which students on a course such as this need to be taught. Nevertheless, in coming into contact with these ideas and arguments, the student is stepping into the great stream of public debate which constitutes the Enterprise of Knowledge. It is a debate with a history, and the student should come both to feel and to understand his/her own place in the larger scheme of things by reference to prominent landmarks in it. For this reason, as also to assist orientation and reinforce the sense of the students' participation in the ongoing tradition, references have been made within the text to important contributors to the Enterprise by name.

The Need for Books

Courses such as the IB Theory of Knowledge are not subjects like others on the timetable, in which there is a large body of factual knowledge to be assimilated. They define "protected times and spaces" when the students can reflect upon their own knowledge, its nature and limitations. Ideally, they should be based in part upon, and in part flow from, the students' own firsthand experience as knowers. However, the students' firsthand experience is only a part of the picture. Much of their education is an initiation into the ongoing Enterprise of Knowledge, and that is an essentially social phenomenon. Moreover, reflection always requires something to reflect upon. In addition, reflection is something which can be done well or badly. It is part of the duty of a teacher leading a course such as Theory of Knowledge to assist the students to reflect well and productively upon their experience as knowers. There already exist tools to enable them do this:

these are the basic concepts and distinctions developed over the centuries by philosophers. Deliberately to fail to equip students to use these, on the grounds that it would somehow compromise the "authenticity" of their responses, would appear to be wilfully Philistine, educationally futile, and at best little more than romantic obsurantism.

No apology is offered for the size of this book. It is large. That is because it is a resource book, and needs to be of a decent size to contain a wealth of resources covering all aspects of the syllabus. To have these readily to hand, when required, in a convenient form i, in any case, preferable to hauling about masses of handouts of photocopies of magazine articles - or (more usually) photocopies of photocopies of magazine articles.

How this Book Can be Used by Teachers

The Enterprise of Knowledge is designed to serve as a basis for a complete course, the chapters forming a coherent sequence, each chapter forming a complete unit in itself. However, it has been written so as to allow for a flexible approach. Thus it is possible to use the book in a variety of ways, both by changing the order and by omitting some of the chapters. For example, some of the material in Chapter Eleven, *Facts and Explanations*, is quite technical, and might well be omitted if a less demanding approach is required.

Teachers can use this book in a variety of ways. Extracts from the text might be read by students before or during classes, in order to provide a springboard for more informed class discussion.

A standard procedure in such courses is to invite a guest speaker to make a presentation on a particular topic, expressing and arguing for his/her own standpoint. The speaker then retires, so that the students can feel free to be critical without embarrassment, while they try to assess the credibility of the speaker's position and the value of his/her arguments. It is not always possible to follow this procedure literally, and it is in any case very costly, in terms both of the speaker's time and the school's hospitality. *The Enterprise of Knowledge* can substitute as a visitor: one which the students can freely criticise, and return to at any time to re-examine, without anyone feeling the slightest embarrassment.

The book is written to be stimulating and provocative. As such, it can function as a target. Students using the book should be encouraged at any point to disagree with the author's position, if they so choose. Students at this level should be capable of reading, and working with, texts with which they harbour strong disagreements. This in itself should be considered a very important part of pre-undergraduate, or early undergraduate, education.

Experience has shown that many students who have grown up in traditions which rely heavily upon textbooks are bewildered by any course which does not present them with one, and consequently become insecure. Of course, they need to be weaned away from excessive reliance upon single printed sources of authoritative information. But if they have no book in their hands at all, they can simply become paralysed. For them, the possession of a book holds the promise that, in some manner at least, they hold their fate in their own hands. There is perhaps no better way to wean them from excessive reliance upon texts than to use one as a target in a course which encourages critical thinking.

Finally, *The Enterprise of Knowledge* can be treated as a quarry, or resource book, for the students' individual research in connection with oral presentations and essays.

Of course, no text should be allowed to *dominate* a course such as the IB Theory of Knowledge, or any other course intended to generate and foster critical thinking. But, as with all classroom aids, this can only be the responsibility of the teacher in the classroom.

Some teachers, particularly those unfamiliar with the material or approach, may choose to lean heavily upon a text for some time, until they "find their feet." Others, more experienced, may use it only when dealing with certain parts of the course, perhaps those parts where they feel particularly short of material, self-confidence, or personal interest. Others may reserve it for those occasions when the students get tired of their voice, or of their particular teaching methods. (Of course, there may be some blessed souls to whom this will never happen!) Others may use it simply as a resource book for private preparatory reading, individual research and reference.

Changes in the Second Edition

The author's aim in making changes in this edition has been to correct what was amiss, omit what has proved in practice to be of little use, replacing it with new material, and to bring the text up-to-date, both with changes in the IB Theory of Knowledge syllabus, and with recent developments on the world scene, which have made the desirability of an educated and critical citizenry an urgent priority.

- The plan of the text has been extensively recast
- Errors of various kinds have been corrected.
- Content which has been found in practice to be redundant or unhelpful has been removed, making way for new material.
- Some chapters have been almost entirely rewritten. This is particularly true of the chapters on Testimony, History, Politics, and the final chapter on contemporary challenges and threats to the Enterprise of Knowledge.
- The text has been brought up-to-date, to make it more obviously relevant to today's problems, and to stimulate more vigorous student discussion and participation.
- Control of vocabulary has been tightened.
- An index of basic concepts has been added.

About the Author

John L. Tomkinson comes from Stoke-on-Trent in the north-west Midlands of England. He was educated at the University of Wales, Lampeter, where he studied Philosophy and Theology, and the University of Keele, where he studied Philosophy, History and Education. He holds an MA and a PhD in Philosophy, and an MA in History.

An experienced British qualified and trained teacher, he has taught students from primary to undergraduate level, the latter in the University of Maryland, and has experience of the British and US systems of education, and also of international schools.

He began teaching General Studies and GCE "A" Level Logic in 1969, and IB Theory of Knowledge in 1989. Since 1985 he has been living in Athens, Greece, where he teaches IB Theory of Knowledge and History, and writes on various subjects.

CONTENTS

Areas of Knowledge

THINK

Acknowledgements

I am very grateful to the many people who were kind enough to offer criticisms of the first edition, together with suggestions for improvement. Particular thanks are due to my colleagues who teach Theory of Knowledge at the Moraitis School in Athens: Vassilis Kyrtatos, Tony Stevens and Elizabeth Paki; also to the coordinator, Spiros Molfetas, who always makes TOK a priority; and to Marcus deBaca, Chris Bowen, Agis Gallopoulos and Aris Karey.

Needless to say, the responsibility for all errors or omissions is entirely my own. Similarly, any and all views and opinions expressed in this book are entirely my own, and do not reflect those either of my colleagues or of the publishers.

Introduction

"The aim of education should be to teach us rather how to think, than what to think - rather to improve our minds, so as to enable us to think for ourselves, than to load the memory with thoughts of other men." (Bill Beattie)

This is a large book. But don't worry about it. The material in it is not here to be learned. It is here to assist and enable you to realise certain things about what you already know.

This course will be quite unlike anything you have experienced before. It is not a matter of mastering course material which the teacher will give to you in preparation for tests. It is a reflective course, in which you have the opportunity to think about what you have learned elsewhere, both in school and outside: to weigh it all up, to make comparisons and connections, to make some judgements of your own, and to consider some more fundamental questions than you have had the opportunity to deal with before. Although, hopefully, you will learn a lot on this course, its purpose is not so much to provide you with fresh information as to furnish you with new insights into the significance and limits of what you already know, to stimulate and encourage you to think, and to encourage you to think well.

The material in the various chapters will provide opportunities for class discussion. You may find some of the topics considered controversial, and you may already have very strong opinions about some of them. If you have something relevant to say, do not be afraid to say it. Do not feel that you need a high level of skill in debate before you can say anything. Skills are developed only by practice, and you will improve with practice. At the same time, it is pointless to feel that you have to make a contribution when you do not have anything worth saying. You should feel comfortable with that as well.

Just as you will expect others to listen to what you have to say, it is equally important that you listen carefully to what other people have to say. The rules of classroom debate are those of reason and politeness. Any view should be treated with as much respect it deserves. This will depend upon its clarity, and the quality of the evidence put forward to support it, or the arguments advanced to defend it. If you feel that there are problems with a position which is being discussed, then criticize it; even if it is one which the teacher is supporting - perhaps *especially* if it is one which the teacher is supporting.

Always express yourself clearly, precisely, and to the point. Avoid bringing up irrelevant issues as they slow things down. Argue forthrightly, but without hostility. It is not appropriate either to gloat if you, appear to score a point, or to burn with desire for revenge if someone appears to have scored a point over you. "Winning" and "losing" are not really appropriate terms to use about class discussion. "Personalities" and "feelings" are equally inappropriate. What is important is that discussion and argument allow us to see different sides of an issue. It is even a good practice, to improve your skills and gain insight, occasionally to play the "devil's advocate" by defending a position you do not agree with, or by attacking one you support. In that way, you will discover its strengths and weaknesses.

You may come across ideas and ways of looking at things which are very different from your own. Initially, some of these may seem strange, or even stupid. You *must* be open-minded enough at least to consider them. Most will have at least *something* to be said for them. Similarly you will read in this book, or hear in class, views which are familiar to you, but with which you deeply disagree. If you are not open-minded enough to listen to the other person's viewpoint, you will almost certainly not understand it very well. To understand an idea, even if you disagree with it, you must first undergo some suspension of disbelief, and consider what things would be like if it were true. This is not difficult; it is what happens when we read a novel or watch a film. If you do not really understand someone's point of view, you will not be in a very good position to criticise it effectively. In any case, if you are not prepared to listen to other people with whom you disagree, why should they listen to you?

Just as you are entitled to have your own views about the problems under consideration, others also have the right to *their* own opinions about them. This includes the author of this book. My purpose in stating my own views is not to convert you to my own way of thinking - I do not even know who you are - but to help you to make up your *own* mind on an informed basis. You should regard everything in this book as an opportunity for further reflection and argument, rather than as a final position to be accepted.

Because of the nature of the problems being considered, there are few final and definitive answers. Do not be dissatisfied if, after studying an issue, you find yourself unable to make up your mind which point of view is the correct one. Do not worry that you do not know "the answer." Perhaps no one does. Maybe there is no answer. What is important is not so much the conclusions you reach, but rather *that* you think about these things, and *how well* you think about them.

1. THE ENTERPRISE

"An educated mind is . . . composed of all the minds of preceding ages."
(Le Bovier de Fontenelle)

1. The Origins of the Enterprise

According to the seventeenth century philosopher Thomas Hobbes, the "natural" state of humanity before the appearance of civilisation was "poor, nasty, brutish and short." There are not many places on the earth's surface which are hospitable to human beings all the year round. Early man was exposed to all the elemental forces of raw nature: from scorching deserts and sodden marshes to terrifying mountains, trackless snowfields and reptile and insect-infested rainforests. He had to survive under the baking sun and in blinding snowstorms, in biting winds and under torrential downpours. For much of the time, he would have been in danger from excessive heat or cold, or from hunger, thirst, or drowning.

For hundreds of thousands of years our ancestors were engaged in a ceaseless battle against the elements in search of food, water and safety. The major concerns of our primitive ancestors would always have been to avoid predators, especially rival humans, to drink, eat, keep dry, warm (or cool), and care for their young. Any time left over would have been used for much needed rest and recuperation.

Practical Knowledge

As a part of this struggle for survival, early man sought to establish some control over his surroundings, to make his immediate environment as safe and comfortable as his meagre resources would allow. This is not an exclusively human trait. Other animals do this when they dig burrows or build nests, or when they mark off and defend territory. They establish this control with horn and hoof, beak and claw.

By contrast with most other creatures, man is physically slow and clumsy. Although a large animal, he lacks the bodily weapons, protective armour, and speed of many other species. Instead, man came to rely heavily upon his intelligence, and upon *knowledge*. *Homo Sapiens*, the gatherer of fruits, berries and roots, and hunter of animals, became also a hunter and gatherer of knowledge.

The knowledge possessed by our most distant recognizable ancestors would have been severely practical: how to build a shelter out of the materials available in the locality; which fruits and roots are poisonous; which insects bite; and so on. Even today, the desire for control over our environment to ensure our safety, ease and plenty, is still a major factor in the drive for **practical knowledge**.

Case Study: Ötzi

In September 1991 two hikers walking in the Alps came across a frozen corpse embedded in a glacier. That summer had been an unusually hot one. The ice had retreated further than usual, exposing the long buried and almost perfectly preserved corpse to the air. Luckily, it was spotted before it had deteriorated beyond recognition.

The body belonged to a man who had lived some five thousand years ago, which had been preserved in the ice since that time. Ötzi," as he was named by the scientists who studied his remains, provides a rare glimpse of our early ancestors, and allows us to learn something of the knowledge which they possessed. Although Ötzi had lived in a pre-literate society, he and his people already possessed quite sophisticated knowledge and skills.

He wore grass-lined shoes, a loincloth, leggings, a fur jacket, a cloak made of woven grass and a bearskin hat. He carried a basket, and a wooden-framed backpack with two compartments made of tree bark. One of these contained charcoal embers from a recent fire, insulated by maple leaves. A pouch containing small useful items was attached to his belt. He had with him various tools made of stone, wood, bone and deer antler. He was armed with arrows, a stone-bladed dagger with a wooden handle, and a stone axe. He also had a birch fungus which possesses antibiotic properties.

These various implements exhibit the practical knowledge and the skills of Ötzi's people. Traces of no less than seventeen different types of wood, each carefully chosen for the task for which it was most suited, were discovered among his gear. His axe blade was hammered to a degree of sharpness difficult to achieve even today; while it was fixed into a wooden handle, which had been carefully shaped to provide the best possible leverage when it was used.

Although he was well prepared for the cold, life must have been hard for Ötzi. He was only about thirty-five years of age when he died, yet he already suffered from swelling in some of his joints due to severe arthritis, which must have been very painful. These joints had been tattooed, perhaps in a futile attempt to charm away the pain. He had two recently broken ribs, and an arrow head embedded in his skull. He may have been driven from his village and killed by enemies, or he may have been attacked by strangers while travelling in the in the mountains.

Theoretical Knowledge

Despite early man's overriding need for drink, food, security and shelter, under the right conditions there must sometimes have been the opportunity to indulge in idle curiosity. This is not a distinctively human characteristic. As any pet owner knows, cats are inquisitive creatures; although, their curiosity is limited to particular things immediately before their eyes, such as moving balls of wool or mice. Some dogs cannot pass a gateway without checking out what is inside, or a low wall without putting their front paws on top to have a look at the other side.

But cats and dogs do not, as far as we can tell, bother themselves with *theoretical* problems. They do not wonder about the Origins of the Universe, or seek to discover the Meaning of Life. By contrast, a man might well ponder questions which have no practical significance whatsoever: such as how far away the stars are, or what causes lightning. These are theoretical questions, and in asking them, we seek **theoretical knowledge.**

2. Knowledge and Society

Human beings are social animals, and need other humans to survive. A few people choose live as hermits, totally cut off from human society. But even those who do, such as lighthouse-keepers and forest rangers, could not have survived entirely alone during their early childhood.

No one can survive in complete isolation from his fellow human beings from birth. Fish may hatch out of their eggs and swim on their way into life without ever being cared for by parents. But like most mammals, human young remain immature for far too long to stand any chance of survival alone from birth. For human babies there is simply no alternative to dependence upon parents: either upon natural parents or substitutes. Man must have evolved in family groups of some kind.

From what we know of indigenous peoples, isolated from the modern world and unaffected by modern technology, it seems that the gathering and hunting of food was usually a collective enterprise. Scouts would locate sources of food and report back to their group. Hunters would work together as a team to snare or bring down large animals.

The acquisition, storage and transmission of knowledge is no less a collective enterprise. Each man's individual knowledge may first have been confined within his own mind; but if it was not to be of only limited use, and to die with him, it would have to be shared with the others. The most useful knowledge of the tribe would have been passed on to the young; providing them with the skills and information necessary to survival. The transmission of this knowledge we would call their education.

In thousands of locations all over the inhabited world, early man was, for uncounted generations, engaged in the process of acquiring knowledge, sharing it with his fellows, and passing it on from one generation to the next. In this shared process we can see the roots of the great collective **enterprise** of knowledge.

Oral Tradition

Much tribal knowledge, steadily accumulated over many generations, would have been of value only within the neighbourhood of the people who had acquired it. It would have consisted of information about accessible resources, and the skills which had been developed for making use of them. If a tribe was, for some reason, forced to move into a new location with a different landscape and climate, with unfamiliar plants and animals, the process of building up a store of useful knowledge would have had to begin again almost from the beginning. Much of the former knowledge of the tribe, now useless, would be lost within two or three generations.

The ancestors of the indigenous peoples of Tierra del Fuego, on the southern tip of the continent of South America, may have crossed the Bering Straits to Alaska from Asia some 13,000 years ago, and then migrated southwards through the entire length of the American continent in stages. If we consider the various zones of climate and natural vegetation through which they people passed during their long wanderings, from icy tundra to tropical rain forests, we can see that the process of replacing old knowledge with new must have happened many times over.

Merely to retain important knowledge must have been a problem when the entire store of knowledge a people possessed had to be carried around in the memories of individuals. Memory is an unreliable method of storing information. People just forget. Old people might be expected to have the largest stores of knowledge, but memory tends to fail with advancing age.

All transmission of knowledge had originally to be accomplished by word of mouth. Knowledge would be handed down from one generation to another in the form of **oral tradition**. This was also used to preserve material which was not so much informative as entertaining. In this way, a people's store of knowledge would come to be mixed up with hunters' fabulous claims about "the one that got away," nasty stories about rival tribes, and jokes.

Among many groups, steps were taken to make the process of storing, transmitting and accessing the tribe's collective store of knowledge more reliable. Specialists were appointed to act as guardians of the tradition, and the responsibility of memorising the common store of knowledge was laid upon them. They became the "wise men." They developed great skill at learning by rote, and at reproducing efficiently what they had committed to memory. Various means were devised to assist the memory, by making the words to be learned more easily recalled. In this way poetry was developed. In time, apprenticeship systems were established, so that knowledge and skills could be systematically transmitted to new generations of specialists, who would, in their turn, be able to make what they had learned available to the tribe when it was appropriate. In such a society, a good student would have been one who remembered efficiently.

Stored Knowledge

The amount of knowledge that could be stored and passed on was dramatically increased with the invention of writing in the Near East some 6,000 years ago. For the first time, man was no longer dependant upon individual memory and oral tradition. With accessibility to written records it was possible to store much greater amounts of information than any individual could reliably remember. At the same time, the process of transmission was made much more effective.

Since the invention of writing there have been two types of knowledge: the knowledge that we carry around in our heads, and the knowledge that is stored in books. We can have access to knowledge by "looking it up." This has freed us from the burden of carrying around great masses of detailed information "in our heads" simply in order to avoid its being lost. We are free to forget, confident that if we ever need some particular item of information, we shall be able to find it.

In a literate society, an educated person is not one who remembers a lot, but one who is able to access and utilise information efficiently.

Dogma and Tradition

Ancient man was quite good at acquiring practical knowledge, since his immediate safety and well being depended upon it. He was unlikely to decide, say, that a particular species of fruit was safe to eat, when in fact it was poisonous. Mistakes of that kind soon dramatically reveal themselves as errors, and are very quickly corrected by the survivors.

When it came to matters of less immediate practical importance, matters of theoretical knowledge, early man was less successful. If it came to be thought that bolts of lightning were the weapons of a god who lived on a distant mountain peak, or that the sun spent each night sailing under the earth in a boat, those things would not, in the nature of things, quickly and clearly display themselves as errors. Ancient people could continue to hold such beliefs for as long as they wished, without any hint of their falsity impinging upon their minds. For this reason, the traditions passed down from generation to generation came to contain much that was false. A lot of this traditional material was very entertaining: tales of struggles with fearsome creatures, and the like — the ancient equivalents of *Batman* and *Star Trek*. Their value as entertainment was the source of much of their appeal.

Generally, ancient societies treated their stores of knowledge like all their other assets, as something to be jealously guarded and defended. What was handed down in the tradition of a particular society as its body of knowledge came to be valued as something precious: to be accepted, revered, and passed on unchanged to the next generation. Whenever an ethnologist asked the aboriginal Arunta people of Australia why they performed certain ceremonies, they would always reply: "Because the ancestors commanded it." Young people were everywhere pressured to accept without question the body of knowledge passed on to them by their elders.

We call this attitude towards knowledge "**dogmatic.**" Although this approach was effective in preserving the knowledge that had already been obtained, it tended to hinder, or even to prevent, the acquisition of new knowledge. The guardians of the tradition discouraged questioning and criticism, and stifled innovation. Thus in the great empires of the ancient world, such as those of ancient Egypt, Mesopotamia, Persia, India and China, men utilised such skills, and taught such knowledge as they possessed, with little *intellectual* progress for several thousand years. The enterprise of knowledge had reached a level plateau of development.

3. Rational Knowledge

The Triumph of Reason

The development of knowledge is, as we have seen, a collective enterprise. Once acquired, it is passed on to others, who in turn use what they have received as stepping-stones to further knowledge. But knowledge is not merely *passed on* in interaction with others, it is also actually *created* in interaction with others. In the cut and thrust of argument and debate, ideas are tried and tested. Old ideas may be shown to be inadequate, old ways of looking at things exposed as barren, and old theories discarded. New concepts may emerge, new perspectives come to be adopted, and new lines of thought are developed. In the traditional conservative empires of the ancient world, this was just not possible. Criticising the traditional ways and putting forward new ideas had come to be thought of either as foolishness or as wickedness.

It is no accident that the great intellectual breakthrough, when it occurred, took place among the Greeks of the sixth, fifth and fourth centuries BC. These gregarious people lived in tiny city-states, whose inhabitants valued their freedom. Each day the citizens would meet in the public areas of their small towns to gossip, and to debate about matters of immediate common concern. At the same time, they would also discuss anything else which took their fancy. In so doing, they felt at liberty to ask any questions, and to make any points, which occurred to them. Even more important, they also felt able to criticise any answers which they received. From such people, in the Greek cities of Asia Minor, on the islands of the Aegean, and in mainland Greece, the ideal of *rational, systematic* knowledge first emerged.

It began with speculations about the nature of the world among the Ionian Greeks during the sixth century, beginning with Thales of Miletus. It developed, and changed direction, with the famous conversations that Socrates held with the young men of Athens about ethics and politics during the fifth century. It achieved its full fruition in the systematic research of Aristotle into every field of human knowledge during the fourth.

According to Aristotle: "All men want to know." Actually, this is over-generous. People frequently prefer to accept ready-made dogmas. It is so much easier. Many students, if they were honest, would probably echo Montaigne: "There is nothing for which I would care to rack my brains, not even the most precious of knowledge." Thinking can be a very tiring activity. It is much easier to watch a movie or a basketball match. The fact that Aristotle thought that such a statement was true is an indication of the unique character of the Greeks of his day. This showed itself in several ways:

- The Greeks were insatiably *curious* about their world. Thales, Anaximander, Pythagoras, and Heracleitus all speculated about the nature and origins of the universe. Herodotus wanted to know about the ways of life and the customs of every other nation, and travelled extensively to find out for himself what these were.

- This curiosity resulted some remarkable *observations*. It was as though men were looking at the world for the first time with minds unclouded by dogma, and seeing it as it really is. The physicians of the medical school on the island of Cos compiled detailed case studies of the symptoms of their patients. Xenophanes of Colophon made a careful study of fossil remains in Sicily. Dionysius of Thrace laid the foundations of linguistics by classifying the various parts of speech. Aristotle investigated and classified many aspects of his environment: from the different species of sea creatures to the various types of government to be found in different human societies.

- Their approach to knowledge was *critical*. When Socrates questioned the young men of Athens, he systematically revealed to them the limitations of their own knowledge. He showed them that when they casually used words like "justice" and "truth", they did not really know what they were talking about.

- Above all, the Greeks recognised the *objectivity* of truth: that some things are simply true, regardless of what we may hope for or wish for; regardless of what is convenient or inconvenient for us; regardless even of what the authorities may insist upon. In the words of Hecataeus of Miletus, the oldest known historian in the world, "what I write is what I believe to be true." The ancient Greeks sought *objective truth*, even if it ran counter to their prejudices and undermined their interests. And having once glimpsed this ideal, they could not become blind to it again, as a character in Euripedes' drama *Hippolytus* testifies:

    "This is the truth I saw then, and still see.

    Nor is there any magic that can stain

    The white truth for me, or make me blind again."

- The ancient Greeks believed in the *rationality* of the universe. For other peoples the world was a terrifying place in which literally anything might happen, full of dark powers which needed to be propitiated by bloody sacrifices and precisely performed magical ceremonies. The Greek philosophers believed that the bewildering diversity of the world of our experience was underpinned by *cosmos*, a hidden order which controlled all appearances and made sense of them; yet which might show the world to be a very different kind of place from what we unreflectively think it to be. For Pythagoras, the key to this hidden order was mathematics.

- They believed in the power of human *reason* to discover and reveal this hidden order, and so make some sense of the bewildering complexity of the appearances of things.

Today we know that many of the theories, or hypotheses, of the ancient Greeks were uncannily close to the mark. Pythagoras' belief that number was the key to understanding the universe foreshadowed the power of mathematics to unlock the secrets of modern physics. In an age when most people thought that the heart was the seat of the intellect, Alcmaeon had realised that it was the brain which governs our powers of thought. Over a thousand years before the birth of Charles Darwin, Empedocles of Acragas suggested that mankind had evolved from lower forms of life in accordance with the principle of the survival of the fittest. Leucippus of Miletus taught that all matter is made up of tiny indivisible units, so anticipating the discovery of atoms and quarks. Democritus of Abdera developed this idea by seeking to explain all the objective qualities of things as caused by particles moving in space. Anaxagoras of Clazomenae explained the light of the moon as reflected sunlight. Anticipating Copernicus and Galileo by over a thousand years, Aristarchus of Samos held the sun, rather than the earth, to be the centre of the universe, and the stars to be unimaginably distant.

Of course, many of the other conclusions reached by the ancient Greeks are now known to have been mistaken. But even where their theories missed the mark, they remained fundamentally *rational*; wrong only because of the inadequate amount of information available to them at the time. What is important is not so much the particular answers which the Greeks suggested, but rather that they asked important questions, and sought *rational* means to secure answers to them.

Case Study: "The Sacred Disease"

Epilepsy is a disease in which a brain malfunction causes the sufferer temporarily to lose control of his bodily functions, when he may fall to the ground and shake uncontrollably. Called the "sacred disease" in ancient times, it was usually thought to be due to the invasion of the body of the afflicted person by a god or spirit.

Among the writings from the ancient medical school on the island of Cos is a small work on epilepsy called "The Sacred Disease." Surprisingly, the anonymous writer does not regard epilepsy as sacred at all, and pours scorn on those who prescribe magical therapies for it. He observes that if the patients get pain spasms on the right side, physicians blame the mother of the gods. If some faeces appears, and if it is rather thin, like that of birds, they attribute the condition to Apollo; while if the afflicted person foams at the mouth and kicks out with his feet, Ares is said to be to blame.

Instead of providing explanations in terms of the action of gods, the author of "The Sacred Disease" first carefully describes the symptoms, and then locates a natural cause in the brain. He suggests that there may be an excess of pressure in the blood vessels. He also observes that the condition is transmitted by inheritance. He concludes: "This disease seems to me to be in no way more divine than the others, but it has the same [type of] cause as every disease."

As an explanation of the causes of epilepsy, his account would today be considered inadequate. But while others sought explanation in myths, and a cure in magical spells, the physicians of Cos sought natural explanations, based upon the accurate observation of symptoms.

Factories and Treasuries of Knowledge

From an early date, libraries were created as storehouses of knowledge. The earliest belonged to the peoples of Mesopotamia and Anatolia: the Sumerians, Babylonians, Assyrians and Hittites, but mostly these contained business records. The world's first research institute was founded by Isocrates in Athens near the beginning of the fourth century BC. Its purpose was not merely to *pass on* knowledge, but also to *increase* the sum of human knowledge – a major function of universities today. This was followed shortly afterwards by the Academy of Plato, and later by Aristotle's Lyceum. It was in these Athenian schools, the world's first universities, that the earliest research libraries were set up.

Undoubtedly the greatest of all the libraries of the ancient world was that founded by the Ptolemies, the Greek rulers of Egypt after the death of Alexander the Great, in the city of Alexandria. There, a large body of scholars was permanently employed in translating into Greek all the significant known writings of the ancient world, so that they would be available for scholars from all over the world to study. The translations were made on standard-sized scrolls for convenient storage. By the first century BC, the library was said to have held more than 700,000 of them; and a complete catalogue, or list, of all the works in store was drawn up.

During the early years of the Christian era, many of the libraries of the ancient world were destroyed. The Christians destroyed an annexe of the library of Alexandria in 391. Then in 640 the leader of the Arab forces which had conquered that city ordered the burning of the main library, and did so in a way which signalled the temporary resurgence of dogmatism. Pointing to the ranks of scrolls and books, he posed a dilemma. If what they contained agreed with the *Qur'an*, the

Muslim scriptures, then they were unnecessary and useless. If what they contained did not agree with the *Qur'an*, then they must be false and wicked. Therefore, either they were unnecessary and useless, or else they were false and wicked. Either way, he concluded, they should be burned.

The libraries of Constantinople weathered the storm for many centuries more, until that city fell to the Turks in 1453. Learning in Western Europe was preserved through the Dark Ages only in the monasteries and cathedral schools, where monks laboured to copy ancient manuscripts. Unfortunately they frequently ignored, altered, or even wilfully destroyed, copies of many important works of which they disapproved, being interested only in those religious works which at that time enjoyed the approval of the Church authorities.

The Reawakening of the Enterprise

During the medieval period, few in Western Europe could read, while writing was considered to be a difficult craft which required the use of expensive materials, and which only trained specialists would venture to undertake. Since it was a laborious, time-consuming and expensive task to copy out books by hand, apart from those used for religious services, books were the costly possessions of a rich or privileged few. Even the most famous libraries of the Middle Ages contained tiny numbers of books by today's standards. A collection of two hundred volumes would have been regarded as a very large library indeed. Yet despite this bleak picture, with the rise of the medieval universities, such as Cairo, Bologna, Paris, Oxford, Cambridge, Salamanca, Prague and Vienna, the Enterprise of Knowledge survived.

Sometime before 1500, the invention of a printing press which used moveable type allowed the printing of copies of many different books with a minimum of cost and labour. At the same time, it was discovered how to make cheap paper out of rags. From that point onwards, books could be mass-produced at prices which the middle classes could afford, so that more people could read more books.

Members of noble families began to build up their own libraries, and in 1700 in South Carolina the first library designed for the use of ordinary people was opened. During the nineteenth century, public library services became available to all in many countries. Today governments support huge national libraries: such as the Bibliothèque National in Paris, the British Library in London, and the United States Library of Congress in Washington; while millions of people have access to public libraries in their own cities and towns.

Along with the spread of books there developed the idea that all men have the right to an education. This was gradually extended from a right to a basic training in literacy and numeracy, to the right to pursue education to whatever level a person is suited by his or her ability. In consequence, illiteracy came to be thought of no longer as the normal state of a human being, but as a special disadvantage, a cause of shame, and even an abnormality.

These developments have contributed to a vast acceleration in the rate of acquisition of knowledge, and a vast increase in the amount of knowledge stored and transmitted.

4. Knowledge in the Modern World

The "Knowledge Explosion"

In the past, a man might aspire to master for himself the entire range of significant human knowledge available within his culture. Aristotle, Leonardo da Vinci, and a few others were able to do this. In memory of the last period when this was still possible, we call someone who shows interests, talents and knowledge over a wide range of subjects a "Renaissance man." Another relic of this time has survived in the idea of an "encyclopaedia": a compendium of all worthwhile human knowledge in a manageable number of volumes.

As education has ceased to be an exclusive possession of privileged elites, so the rate of generation of new knowledge has increased. In this century, there has been a rapid expansion in the number of universities throughout the world. Each one employs people whose profession is nothing less than the development of knowledge through research and argument, and the transmission of the skills of acquiring and evaluating information and insights to new generations of scholars. It is frequently observed that of all the scientists who have ever lived, most are still alive today. But this is equally true of professional philosophers, mathematicians and historians. This has helped to create what Alvin Toffler has named the "knowledge explosion."

One consequence of this explosion of knowledge is an increasing need for specialisation, with the constant branching off of new disciplines from older studies. In the seventeenth century a man might master the whole of "Natural Philosophy" (what we today call "Science"). As the rate of acquiring knowledge increased, this came to be too much for a single person to cope with in a lifetime, and it became necessary to specialise in physics, chemistry or biology. Today each one of these is far too wide a discipline for any individual to master at its most advanced level.

Alvin Toffler points out that recent centuries have witnessed a corresponding acceleration in the number of books published. At the time of the invention of moveable type, about one thousand new book titles were appearing in Europe each year. In recent centuries, the rate of publication has doubled roughly every twenty years. By the mid-1960s it was approaching the rate of one thousand per day, and increasing.

Today, most research is first published in academic journals, which are sold only to university libraries. The number of these journals has increased so much during the present century that indexes and abstracts of their contents are published. These provide summaries of all the articles appearing in the journals on a particular subject during a given year, in order to enable the scholar to find what he needs out of the great mass of material available. Today there are several hundred such abstracts.

Librarians have been driven to seek more economical ways of storing information than printed books. Most recently computers have brought new dimensions to our ability to store, access, analyse and transmit data. They can be used not merely to store existing information, but also to extend our knowledge. They perform in a few seconds calculations which would take a man a year to work out. They may be used not only to store existing knowledge, but also to generate new knowledge.

New means of electronic communication now enable information to be transmitted with much greater efficiency than in the past. It is now possible for someone with a computer to communicate in seconds with data banks of information stored on computers anywhere in the world by means of the Internet, so that information stored on a single computer may be almost instantly available on the other side of the world.

Education for Today's World

The "knowledge explosion" affects everyone in school and college today. At the end of the nineteenth century, a young person might expect that the knowledge learned at school would equip him for a lifetime. Some change in his circumstances might require the addition of a little more, but that would be all. At the beginning of the twenty-first century no one can assume that he can acquire enough knowledge at school or college to suffice for the rest of his life. We need more and more to adopt a flexible approach towards knowledge. We need to be prepared to revise our opinions on all sorts of things in the light of new evidence. We need to be prepared to develop new skills at any period in life. Alvin Toffler points out that "The illiterate of the twenty-first century will not be those who cannot read and write, but those who cannot learn, unlearn, and relearn."

A Paradox of Education

Yet, despite this explosion of human knowledge, many people still cling uncritically to fantastic beliefs for which there is no good evidence at all, or which are wholly irrational. In the same apartment block we may find someone who is engaged in scientific research on the characteristics of earth tremors, with a view to being able, in time, to predict earthquakes; while next door lives someone who is convinced that the earth is hollow, and that there are space aliens living inside it. It is a strange paradox that the most sophisticated knowledge coexists today side by side with surprising **credulousness**.

During the 1980s, for help in making important decisions, the President of the Unites States of America could call upon the most advanced intelligence, scientific and technical resources ever available to a single man in history up to that time. Yet we learn that President Reagan frequently chose instead to rely upon the advice of his wife's astrologer.

Knowledge consists not in the mere collection of scraps of information, but in the skills involved in critical, independent thinking, and in the understanding which comes from such thinking. In today's world an educated person is not someone who "knows a lot," who carries around a lot of information in his memory bank, or someone who can boast complex technical skills. It is someone who has acquired the skills necessary for evaluating evidence and arguments, for making sound independent judgements about them, even, if necessary, against the view of the majority; and for placing new information in a wider perspective, so as to gain genuine insight and understanding.

Glossary

credulousness: a disposition to believe uncritically.

dogmatism: an attitude which demands that what is claimed as knowledge be accepted on authority and without criticism.

enterprise: a considerable undertaking of some kind.

rational knowledge: knowledge based upon open enquiry and subject to open debate and testing; as opposed to "protected" knowledge accepted on the basis of authority.

oral tradition: traditions which are handed down from generation to generation by word of mouth, i.e. not in written form.

practical knowledge: knowledge which is primarily acquired for some useful purpose.

theoretical knowledge: knowledge which is of no immediate practical value, but which is acquired simply because of a desire to know what the world is like, and how it works.

2. KNOWLEDGE AND THE KNOWER

It is the tragedy of the world that no one knows what he doesn't know — and the less a
man knows, the more sure he is that he knows everything." (Joyce Cary)

We all know what we mean when we use statements like "I have been waiting for a long time," and "It is time to start work." But if we are asked what time is, we are puzzled. And the more we think about it, the more puzzled we are likely to become. Words like "know" and "knowledge" are like this. We can use them successfully every day without getting puzzled, but if we are asked what it is to know anything, or what knowledge is, we are liable to become confused very quickly.

In order to think clearly about any important or difficult matter, it is a good idea first of all to do some mental house cleaning, putting the "furniture of our minds" in order. We need to make distinctions between ideas which may cause us some confusion if we are not clear about them from the start. For this reason, it is necessary to distinguish "knowledge" from several related words such as "belief," "awareness," and "certainty." Also, we tend to assume that if there is a single word for something, then there must be a single object of our thought which corresponds to it. We shall need to look very closely at "knowledge" in order to see whether there are different senses in which the word is used; and if there are, we shall need to distinguish them.

1. Knowledge and Belief

We all carry around with us a miscellaneous hodgepodge collection of beliefs, some are about individual people and places, while others are more general. A tiny sample of someone's beliefs might look something like this:

Fire burns.
I like chocolate ice cream.
Ottawa is a historic city.
Two of my friends work as waiters in a café.
Stealing is wrong.
If I am lucky, the topics I have prepared for the test will all turn up on tomorrow's paper.
My dog loves me.

Usually we express our beliefs in the form of statements, such as:

(1) My dog loves me.

When we wish to draw attention to the fact that what we are talking about is a belief, we may say:

(2) I believe that my dog loves me.

A belief such as (1) may be true or false. If my dog does love me, then my belief is true. If he does not, if he has been jumping about and wagging his tail deceitfully all these years just in order to get biscuits, it will be false. Just because someone *believes* something to be true, it does not follow that in fact it *is* true. We may be, and we very often are, simply mistaken. For the moment we may say that a belief is true if it corresponds with the facts, and false if it does not.

Grounds

One of the things which makes us rational is the extent to which we have good grounds for our beliefs. The **grounds** of our beliefs consist of the **evidence** or support we have for them. They are what would properly be offered in answer to the question "*Why* do you believe such and such?" The grounds of our beliefs are reasons we have for believing them to be true.

Unfortunately, many of our beliefs are groundless. We have no adequate reasons for holding them at all. We acquired many of the them before we developed any critical or reasoning faculties, or any ability to make our own independent judgements. Many have been "absorbed" from our social environment as a sponge soaks up water. These are the beliefs, outlooks and attitudes of the people among whom we live. For most people their most basic religious and political beliefs, attitudes and commitments will have been absorbed from their social environment in this way. How else could we explain, that those born in Christian countries tend to become Christians, while those brought up in Muslim countries become Muslims; that those born in the USA think that the USA is the greatest country in the world, while those born in France tend to award that prize to their own country? These are hardly coincidences.

Sometimes our real motive for believing something to be true is because it is in our interest for it to be so. For this reason, those dealing in heroin probably tell themselves that it does no real harm, while the director of a cigarette manufacturing company is likely to believe, against all the evidence, that smoking tobacco does not cause health problems. There is a lot of evidence that we are very good at believing what it is in our own interests to believe. We are also very reluctant to change our beliefs. Like an old pair of jeans or a favourite chair, they are ours, and we are comfortable with them.

Being a Rational Person

The influence of the society in which we live, together with the dictates of our own self-interest, are certainly reasons why we hold many of the beliefs we do. These are among the *causes* of our beliefs, the reasons *why in fact* we hold them, but they are not appropriate *grounds* for them. Grounds are reasons why we *ought* to hold beliefs. To the extent that we are rational beings, the reasons why we hold our beliefs are adequate grounds for holding them; to the extent that we are irrational, they are not.

Because we are accustomed to our beliefs, our usual way of looking at things, we feel uncomfortable if any of them are challenged, or exposed as groundless. In fact we may harbour unacknowledged suspicions that certain of our beliefs may be groundless. One sure indication of this is if we are irritated by the suggestion that they *might* not be true. Another indication of lack of confidence in our beliefs is if, when questioned about them, we do not try to defend them rationally, but content ourselves with asserting vociferously that they are "obviously true." It used to be obvious to many people that there is nothing shameful in ill-treating animals. Most educated people today would regard this belief as undoubtedly false.

Those of our beliefs which we consider to be particularly well founded, and which we do not expect ever to have to change, we call "knowledge."

2. The Varieties of Knowledge

In order to think clearly about knowledge we must take care to respect the language we use, and to look very carefully at what we can learn from the way we use the words "know" and "knowledge," in order to avoid being confused in our thinking. "Knowledge" is one of those difficult words which has several related, but distinct, meanings. Philosophers routinely distinguish three different types of knowledge. They do this by noting which words characteristically follow the verb "know" in a sentence in the English language.

Acquaintance

We frequently use the word "know" followed immediately by a direct object, e.g.

(3) I know David Beckham.

(4) I know Los Angeles.

(5) I know Megadeath's latest album.

This sort of knowledge claim implies some sort of direct acquaintance with the object known. For example, the claim that I know David Beckham implies that I have met him, probably quite a few times. I can recognise him under normal conditions, and I am acquainted with at least some of his habits, his likes and dislikes, and his character. The claim that I know Los Angeles implies that I have visited the city, probably quite a few times, and therefore I know what it is like. I can generally find my way around. I know where some of the more famous landmarks there are to be found, and so on. Similarly, the claim that I know Megadeath's latest album implies that I am familiar with the tracks, some of the lyrics, and the backing style.

Notice that although "know" is a strong word, there are no *precise* specifications for its use. Clearly, if I claim to know David Beckham on the strength of having seen several televised matches in which he played for Manchester United, and because I once spoke to a someone in a bar who claimed to know someone who once spoke to his cousin's girlfriend, then my claim would be considered to have no real basis. On the other hand, if I had been a classmate of his in school over several years; if I had spent a lot of time with him during that period and kept up the friendship since that time by telephone calls and occasional meetings, then the claim would be regarded as well-founded. But there is a very doubtful area in between, where some people would admit the validity of my claim to know David Beckham and others would think that claim too strong. Suppose, for example, that we had taken some of the same classes during one year at high school, and that I had spoken with him on several occasions during that period. On that basis, could I be said to *know* him? It is by no means clear.

Information

Frequently we use the word "know" followed immediately by a phrase beginning "that . . .":

(6) I know *that* David Beckham is married to a professional singer.

(7) I know *that* Los Angeles is a dangerous city to walk about in after dark.

(8) I know *that* Megadeath's latest album has eight tracks.

In each of these statements what I claim to know is not a person, a place, or an object, but a fact: the *fact* that David Beckham is married to a singer, that Los Angeles is a dangerous city to walk about in after dark, and that Megadeath's latest album has eight tracks.

This can also be expressed by saying that what we claim to know is the truth of a statement. The sentences above are claims to know the truth of the statements *that* David Beckham is married to a professional singer, etc. Thus this form of knowledge is called **propositional knowledge**.

Many languages distinguish between knowledge by acquaintance and propositional knowledge by having different words for them. French distinguishes between *connaître* and *savoir*, and German distinguishes between *kennen* and *wissen*.

Skills

Sometimes we use the word "know" immediately followed by a phrase beginning "how to . . ." for example:

(9) Jack knows *how* to write a computer software programme.

(10) Stella knows *how* to cook pancakes.

(11) Everyone should know *how* to give basic first aid.

In this case, "knowledge" consists of the ability to do something: it is the possession of a skill.

The Relationship between Acquaintance, Information and Skills

Although we have spent some time distinguishing these several forms of knowledge, they are all connected in complex ways.

If I can be said to know David Beckham (acquaintance) I must also, in addition, know at least *some* facts about him, e.g. that he is a British citizen (information). Although it may be true that at the time that I knew him, I did not pay much attention to him, because at that time he was not famous, and as a consequence, I know few facts about him. If I am genuinely acquainted with Los Angeles, then I should be able to formulate some true statements about it, such as that it has crime and pollution problems. But perhaps when I was acquainted with Los Angeles I was very young, and did not pay much attention to my surroundings. Yet, in either case it is inconceivable that I could claim *genuinely* to know David Beckham or Los Angeles, while at the same time being unable to say anything at all about them which is both true and non-trivial.

It would, however, be impossible to give a *precise* list of those propositions which I *must* know about them in order to be justified in claiming knowledge by acquaintance. Clearly some things would weigh more heavily than others. It would be odd to claim to know David Beckham, and yet not know that he played soccer for Manchester United, or to know Los Angeles and yet not know that it has a pollution problem. We would use such ignorance as evidence of a false claim to knowledge.

Although knowledge by acquaintance implies the possession of some propositional knowledge, having propositional knowledge of something does not necessarily imply acquaintance. An ardent fan who had never met David Beckham, but who had read everything written about him in the fan magazines, might well know many more true statements about him than someone who had known him briefly, but inattentively, by acquaintance.

Similarly, if I know how to drive a car, then I must have had some acquaintance with at least one car. In addition, I must know some things *about* a car, such as what the pedals and steering wheel are for, and so on. The exercise of a skill implies some acquaintance with whatever the skill is performed with, or upon, together with some propositional knowledge about those things. However, we are often in a position where we can successfully perform a skill, and yet are not able to articulate our moves in any great detail in terms of propositional knowledge.

Despite the connections between them, these three types of knowledge are very different, and whenever the words "know" or "knowledge" appear, we must be very attentive as to which of these three senses of the word is intended. When we use the word "knowledge" in connection with the Enterprise of Knowledge, the word is usually being used in the sense of "propositional knowledge."

What is Knowledge?

When knowledge is compared with belief, it is usually propositional knowledge which we have in mind. Both belief and propositional knowledge are characteristically expressed by use of "that . . ." phrases:

(12) I believe *that* England won the world rugby championship in 2003.

(13) I know *that* England won the world rugby championship in 2003.

Both propositions imply that we hold something to be true. In order to be justified in claiming that we know some statement to be true, the following conditions would have to be met:

- We hold the statement to be true; i.e. we *believe* it to be true. Propositional knowledge is a special type of *belief*. To *know* that England won the world rugby championship in 2003, I would have to *believe* that England had won the championship in that year.

- What we claim to be true actually *is* true. To be counted as knowledge, a belief must be a *true* belief. To know that England won the rugby championship in 2003, England would have to have won the rugby championship in 2003.

- If we claim to something to be true, yet we could not possibly have adequate evidence to support our claim, if we were just making a guess, then our claim to knowledge would not be allowed. That would remain the case even if we were lucky, and our claim turned out, by chance, to be true. In order properly to assert a claim to knowledge, we must have adequate grounds to *justify* that our assertion is true. To know that England won the rugby championship in 2003, I would have to have *adequate grounds* for my belief.

What actually *counts* as adequate grounds is by no means always clear. This is because "know" is a word like "old." It is not clear how old someone has to be to count as old, so it is not always clear whether a particular person should be described as old or not. The word is inherently vague because it lacks precise specifications. For the same reason it is sometimes arguable whether we really *do* know something or not. Nevertheless, we can say that propositional knowledge consists of true beliefs for which we have adequate justification.

PROPOSITIONAL KNOWLEDGE IS JUSTIFIED TRUE BELIEF

---

3. Knowledge and Certainty

The Quest for Certainty

We generally accept that our beliefs, however strongly held, *may* turn out to have been false. We may be persuaded into admitting that many of the beliefs we hold at present may turn out in the future to have been misleading. We may be similarly generous in admitting the falsity of many of our past beliefs. We may concede:

(14) I believed that it would rain heavily on Friday, but I was wrong.

But we would never admit this about what we claim to know. We never say:

(15) I knew that it would rain heavily on Friday, but I was wrong.

We never accept that our knowledge might be false. We are committed to our knowledge. We think that it cannot let us down. We are inclined to think that if we know something, then it *must* be so.

Technically, we would say that knowledge is indefeasible and certain. What we truly know is said to be **indefeasible** because it need never be revised. What we truly know is said to be **certain**, because we can rest assured that it is beyond any shadow of a doubt true. The catch, for there is one, turns out to lie in the qualification "what we *truly* know."

Case Study: René Descartes and the Quest for Certain Knowledge

In the seventeenth century the great French philosopher and mathematician René Descartes was disturbed by the number of things which he had learned during the course of his education, which he had later come to realise were not certainly true. He drew a **sceptical** conclusion from his realisation that much of what is claimed as knowledge is doubtful and uncertain. He decided that those things could not be matters of knowledge at all, but merely matters of opinion or belief. He began to think that most of our claims to knowledge are unjustified, and that " ... there [is] no body of knowledge in the world such as I had been led previously to believe."

He spent 10th November 1619 sitting beside a warm stove, plotting the systematic clearing away of all these beliefs falsely thought to have been knowledge, so that he could begin the construction of a body of genuine knowledge based upon what remained. He adopted the method of deliberately discounting anything about which there could be any doubt whatsoever. He thought that by this means he would be left with the indefeasible bedrock of knowledge which would provide the foundation upon which he could begin the construction of a body of truly genuine knowledge.

It would obviously be too lengthy a job to test each item of knowledge individually, so instead of individual items he chose to consider in turn the several general sources of our knowledge. Descartes thought that knowledge was of two sorts: that which is acquired through our senses, and that which comes to us from the exercise of our reason. He then demonstrated that there could always be some possibility of doubt about each, however unreasonable in practice that doubt might be.

He recalled that he had in the past once dreamed that he was sitting by the fire and writing, just as he was at that moment. That dream of course, was an illusion. But he noted that there was no special characteristic of the dream, evident from within the dream itself, which marked it as different from his waking experience, or as counterfeit, and which could be used to distinguish real sense-experience from dreamed sense-experience. Accordingly, he decided that it is impossible to prove beyond all possible doubt that any sense-experience is genuine. After all, however real his experiences might seem to him at any given time, he might always wake up afterwards and discover that he had been dreaming.

Descartes did not suggest that in fact he was dreaming, only that the mere *possibility* that he might have been dreaming, and in that state unable to distinguish dreaming from waking, renders all sense-experience open to some (admittedly extremely faint) suspicion. But that was enough for his purpose. Since knowledge must be above all possible taint of suspicion, he concluded that the everyday beliefs about the world which we obtain through our senses cannot count as knowledge.

He then went on to consider the knowledge which philosophers in those days believed that we came upon by the use of our reason. This consisted of so-called "rational truths": such as that the whole is greater than the parts; or that everything has a cause; or that two added to two makes four. Surely, even in a dream two added to two must make four!

Descartes had an even stranger argument to undermine our confidence in this type of knowledge. What, he mused, if there exists an all-powerful spirit with a strange sense of humour who has created us in such a fashion that when we were most certain that something cannot be false (such as that two added to two makes four) we are in fact deceived?

Descartes did not suggest that such a devious spirit actually exists, or that we are so deceived. He merely pointed to the fact that the bare possibility of such a situation demonstrates that it is just possible that we could be systematically deceived in our thinking, especially when we seem to understand things most clearly; and that this undermines the absolute certainty of our so-called "rational" knowledge.

If we exclude the things we think we know through our senses, and those which we claim to know on the basis of the exercise of our reason, what is left? Clearly, there can not be very much. In the end, all that Descartes could come up with to provide the foundation for the new body of genuine knowledge which he wished to build up was expressed in the famous statement: Cogito, ergo sum (I think, therefore I am). Whatever I may doubt, nevertheless there must be someone who does the doubting, (and therefore the thinking).

This strange set of arguments was the start of a three hundred-year quest to discover what, out of our alleged "knowledge," is actually known for certain. It was not an easy journey. The Scottish philosopher David Hume found good reasons to consider that, on the basis of this approach, even Descartes' Cogito failed to count as genuine knowledge. What Descartes did, however, was to concentrate our attention upon *method*. He made us see that if we are to understand the nature and limitations of our knowledge we must consider very carefully, the methods by which we acquire our knowledge.

"Knowledge" as an Achievement Word

Unlike Descartes, twentieth century philosophers have become very much aware of the many pitfalls into which language can lead us; and have generally realised that Descartes' quest, at least in the terms in which he understood it, was a mistake from the start.

In order to understand this, it is useful to look at the way we behave when our knowledge claims are revealed to have been false. We tend to say something like:

(16) I thought that I knew that Simpson would be found guilty, but as things turned out, I was wrong.

We never say:

(17) I *knew* that Simpson would be found guilty, but as things turned out, I was wrong.

We simply *do not allow* a knowledge claim to count as false. But this is not because we have indefeasible, certain and final truth. It is simply that when any knowledge claim which we have made turns out to have been false, we automatically downgrade it, or demote it, by re-labelling it as a mere opinion or belief. We never admit that the things we know may turn out to be wrong, but we do this by a sleight of hand. We take the line that if something we thought we knew to be true was not, it could never have been knowledge in the first place.

Descartes thought that if you had knowledge about something you could relax, content that you need never have to revise your views. When he realised that in practice we can never do that, he thought that the knowledge he possessed must not be the genuine article, and set out to identify precisely what the genuine article is, and he did not find much. Today, we can see that the problem is not that the knowledge he thought he had was not genuine knowledge, but rather that the term "knowledge" is used to refer to those beliefs which at any time are *thought* to be indefeasibly true. If those beliefs turn out to have been false all along, then we simply take back the label "knowledge."

The way that a philosopher today might put it is that "knowing" is an **achievement word**. It is used to indicate the successful outcome of an activity. It has a similar function to the word "win."

If we watch a race and note that Suarez came in first, we would say that he had won the race. If it subsequently transpired that during the course of the race the referees had disqualified him, then when we found out that this had happened, we would simply withdraw the title "winner" from Suarez. If questioned about our former judgement we would now say that Suarez had never been the winner of the race at all. The issue is whether the word "winner" was or was not correctly applied to the contestant we initially thought it should have been applied to.

When we claim to know, we are claiming that our minds have successfully got some sort of a handle on reality. If it turns out that we have not, we then withdraw our claim retrospectively and admit that there never had been any knowledge at all. Another way to put this is to say that:

(18) I know that Real Madrid will win the European Soccer championship this year

implies the truth of the statement

(19) Real Madrid will win the European Soccer championship this year.

If statement (19) turns out to be false, because Real Madrid is eliminated, then the original statement (18) would also turn out to have been false.

4. Individual Knowledge and Objective Knowledge

Like Descartes, we tend to think of knowledge as an essentially individual matter, as something which is "in someone's mind." However, that "someone" is necessarily a member of a community, sharing in its knowledge and perhaps contributing to it. Private experiences and insights may be shared with the community. In this way what was originally individual knowledge becomes the common property of a community, and may be preserved for future generations.

This knowledge is expressed in the form of propositions. It has the properties which it has independently of any *individual's* understanding of it. What is known may have implications which at present no single person realises. People may in the future use the information which we have in order to discover something essentially new. For this reason, the philosopher Karl Popper calls the knowledge which has become the possession of society **objective knowledge**.

It is knowledge in the sense of objective knowledge, the result a collective effort of individuals within their several societies, which we have in mind when we think of the great Enterprise of Knowledge.

Glossary

achievement word: a word which signifies the successful outcome of some activity.

certainty: the property of being true beyond all possible doubt.

evidence: grounds for holding something to be true in the absence of direct knowledge.

grounds: appropriate reasons for a belief.

indefeasibility: the property of being immune from being overthrown by future evidence.

objective knowledge: knowledge considered as the collective property of a community, expressed in propositions.

propositional knowledge: information; knowledge *that* something is, or is not, the case.

rational belief: belief based upon adequate grounds.

scepticaism: the inclination to question claims, to suspend judgement, to doubt.

3. The Sources of Knowledge

The degree of one's emotions varies inversely with one's knowledge of the facts - the less you know the hotter you get. (Bertrand Russell)

Knowledge may have several sources, although some of those which are sometimes claimed to be sources are suspect. Each will be considered here very briefly before examining the more important ones in greater detail.

Sense Experience

It is most immediately obvious that much of the knowledge we have of the world around us is provided by our senses. We are traditionally understood to have five senses: sight, hearing, touch, taste and smell. These are our individual "windows on the world"; the pathways along which information from and about the outside world enters our consciousness. **Sense-experience** provides us with our most immediate, vivid and personal knowledge of the world around us.

Testimony

For most of our information about the world beyond our own immediate sense-experience we rely upon the reports, the **testimony**, or the witness of others, either direct or indirect. This may be by someone directly telling us something we did not know, either directly on by means of the telephone, writing to us or sending us emails, printing newspapers or books for us to read, or broadcasting to us on radio or television. The one who tells us may be someone we know who is in our presence, or a stranger, only seen or heard via some instrument of communication.

In order to hear or to read the testimony of others, we need to use our senses of hearing and sight. But the new knowledge that we obtain from testimony is not simply a result of that sense-experience, rather the sense-experience is employed as a vehicle to convey to us the witness of others. What we actually see or hear: spoken words, marks on paper or even pictures on a screen, constitute the *medium* by which we come to know what we ourselves have not directly seen or heard.

Reasoning

Reasoning is an activity of the mind whereby we "think things out for ourselves." This takes place when we reflect upon the knowledge that we already have, which we have either learned directly from sense experience or indirectly through the testimony of others. We use our ability to reason to extend our knowledge by working out further truths.

In addition to these three noncontroversial sources of knowledge, there are several other alleged sources of knowledge which are much more doubtful.

Instincts

We know that other species are endowed with inborn **instincts** which warn them of danger, drive them to migrate, stimulate them into building nests at the appropriate time of the year, and so on. Given that man's evolution has also been driven by natural selection, and subject to similar forces as those which have led to the evolution of other species, it would be surprising if we were not also genetically equipped for survival by being furnished with instincts.

We do seem to have some instincts which develop in early childhood with the appropriate stimuli, e.g. the instinct to avoid potentially dangerous animals; to avoid dangerous environments and seek safe ones; to be able to monitor the moods and intentions of others, so as to predict their behaviour; to judge the effect of our actions upon others so that we can adjust our own behaviour accordingly. All of these inborn (i.e. not learned) abilities can be detected in young children.

However, instincts are not themselves knowledge. They are simply inherited patterns of behaviour.

Memory

Clearly, when we remember past experiences and information, if we remember correctly, we have knowledge.

But memory can tell us only what we *already* know by other means, such as sense-experience, testimony or reason. It cannot itself provide us with *new* knowledge. Of course, we may, after remembering something, by use of our *reason*, come up with new insights and new knowledge about what we have remembered.

Introspection

Introspection is said to result from the turning of our attention inwards, away from the external world, in order to focus upon our own individual inner consciousness. It is said that it is usually by introspection, for example, that we know that we are cheerful or sad. By introspection we are said to be aware of our own states of consciousness.

Usually today, both philosophers and psychologists prefer to think of acts of introspection as acts of *remembering* our mental states during the immediate past.

Intuition

Intuition is often proposed as the name of an immediate mode of awareness which is neither mediated by the senses nor explicable in terms of reason. Much is sometimes claimed for this mysterious faculty, e.g. "Intuition is clear knowing, without knowing how you know. It is the deepest wisdom of the human soul."

Unfortunately, supposed intuitions which people claim to have received have a habit of contradicting each other. When they do, there is no way of testing which is the genuine one; and when they do not, there is still no way of testing their genuineness. Since there is no way of testing them, they cannot be awarded the status of knowledge claims, since knowledge is *justified,* true belief.

The most charitable interpretation of claims to intuition is that some people are very good at picking up cues in other people's behaviour, and this enables them to make sound judgements. They may *claim* to know by intuition, but in fact, they are probably using sense-experience and reasoning, and rationalising their instinctive responses in particular situations. Much of the way in which we acquire our knowledge *can* seem mysterious to us, so we are inclined to explain it in "magical" ways.

Less charitably, claims to intuition may be attempts to justify claims to knowledge without being able to give any adequate explanation of how we came by it. In such cases, rather than face the fact that we have no justifiable claim to knowledge at all, we are inclined to invoke this mysterious faculty to account for it. Thus "intuition" is often simply an empty word which is used to cover up the fact that a knowledge claim is held on no justifiable grounds at all. It is a lazy, or even sometimes dishonest, alternative to seriously considering the basis (or the lack of any basis) of our knowledge claims.

A claim to know something "by intuition" is simply worthless.

Emotion

A new anti-intellectual fashion is to propose that the emotions function as a special source of knowledge. The supporters of this view rightly point out that throughout our daily lives we are continually heavily influenced by our emotions in making judgements, and that these judgements sometimes turns out to be for the best.

But this is woefully insufficient to justify the claim that the emotions may function as a *source of knowledge*. Whatever their origins, or the reasons why we hold them, our beliefs very often turn out to be correct, even though we could not justify them at the time. But unjustified beliefs which may turn out to be right are simply that - unjustified beliefs which may turn out to be right. They are not knowledge. Unjustified beliefs *cannot* be knowledge.

The view that our emotions provide us with knowledge is not only mistaken; it is very, very dangerous. Allowing our feelings to substitute for knowledge, apart from being a remarkably elementary mistake, risks licensing all our prejudices as knowledge. It is clear from his writings and speeches that Adolph Hitler felt a profound emotional revulsion towards Jews. He treated this not as an irrational prejudice, which distorted his perception of reality, but as an *insight* into reality, justified in some way by its emotional intensity - with horrific results in the Holocaust.

The exclusion of emotion from judgements of reality is a fundamental precondition of the advance of reason and the Enterprise of Knowledge. (Note, however, that emotions should not be confused with rational moral judgements, see Chapter Sixteen).

Extra-Sensory Perception (ESP)

Extrasensory perception is claimed to be another direct means of acquiring knowledge other than through the senses or by the use of reason.

The most ambitious claim of this kind is called **telepathy**, which is supposed to be the direct communication of one mind with another. In science fiction stories this faculty or power is frequently attributed to aliens. Extrasensory perception which is not telepathic, because the information is believed to come from some other source than directly from another mind, is termed **clairvoyance**.

Some people are fervent believers in the existence of ESP, while the overwhelming majority of philosophers and scientists are equally firm in their disbelief, on the grounds that there is no adequate evidence for its existence.

Inspiration

Inspiration refers to the belief that some ideas, especially particularly good ones, have somehow been "put into" our minds by some outside force.

Religious people sometimes claim special ways of acquiring knowledge of God or knowledge from God, by claiming inspiration for certain teachings, or books, or for themselves. These secifically religious ways of knowing will be surveyed in the appendix.

It is also sometimes said that a great work of art is inspired. This use of the term is a mere relic of the more ancient religious use of the term. Today such a claim is usually simply a rather misleading way of attributing greatness to a work of art.

There would appear to be three, and only three, main types of knowledge:
- Sensed knowledge, based upon our own sense perceptions.
- Reported knowledge, based upon the testimony of others.
- Inferred knowledge, based upon the use of our reasoning.

Each of these will be considered in some detail in the following chapters.

Glossary

clairvoyance: a supposed mysterious faculty of sensing something beyond the natural senses other than by telepathy.

extra-sensory perception: a supposed mysterious faculty of sensing something by means other than the natural senses.

inspiration: the supposed acquisition of knowledge from some external source by its being communicated directly into the consciousness

instinct: an inborn, and therefore unlearned, capacity.

introspection: the examination of ones own inner mental states.

intuition: a supposed mysterious faculty by which the mind apprehends knowledge directly other than through the senses or by the use of reason.

reasoning: the acquisition of new knowledge by the use of inference and the evaluation of evidence.

sense-experience: the acquisition of knowledge through the use of the senses.

testimony: the acquisition of knowledge on the basis of the witness of others.

4. SENSE EXPERIENCE

"There is more to seeing than meets the eyeball." (N. R. Hanson)

1. The Senses

Our Five Senses . . . and Others

As our "windows on the world" our five senses: sight, hearing, touch, taste and smell, are usually held to be the foundation of all our immediate knowledge of the world around us.

These senses depend upon sense-organs in our bodies, which are stimulated by various forms of energy in the outside world: radiant energy in the form of light and heat; mechanical energy in the form of sound and pressure waves; and chemical energy, detected by the senses of smell and taste. These stimuli are coded into nerve impulses, which are sent from the sense organs to the central nervous system. The nerve impulses are electrical signals, which vary in frequency according to the strength of the original stimuli. These excite certain specific areas of the brain, which act as receiving centres. Somehow, this excitation of an area in the brain results in our being aware of some aspect of the outside world.

Our various senses are not all of equal value to us. Of the traditional five senses, we usually rely upon the sense of sight more than any other, so that being blind is considered a much worse affliction than being deaf. This preference for sight is reflected in the languages we use. We have many words for qualities of things as we see them, but far fewer for qualities of things sensed by other means. However, if there is any doubt about what our other senses tell us, we tend to fall back upon the sense of touch for confirmation and reassurance.

Other animals have different preferences. The sense of smell is more important to dogs than sight. Although dogs may recognise people from some distance by sight, embarrassed visitors to houses where a dog is in residence will know that the animal is usually not satisfied until he has carefully sniffed each newcomer individually. This is because Dogs imprint things upon their memories not by staring, as we do, but by deliberate sniffing. And just as we carry visual maps of our environment in our heads in order to find our way around, so dogs probably have "smell maps" which enable them to navigate in their environment.

Frequently people ask the question "Is there a sixth sense?" In fact there is little mystery to this. Scientists say that we have several other senses. We simply do not *notice* that we have them, because we take them for granted.

A sense which is habitually taken for granted becomes evident to us when it goes wrong. In *The Man who Mistook His Wife for a Hat*, Oliver Sacks draws attention to the sense of proprioception, our awareness of the relative positions of the various parts of our own bodies, derived from receptors in the joints and muscle tendons. One of Sacks' patients suffering from Parkinson's disease developed a permanent list to one side by about twenty degrees, yet was quite unaware of it until he could see himself on videotape. His sense of proprioception had become distorted, so that he sensed that he was sitting or standing upright when in fact he was leaning to one side; and when he was upright it seemed to him that he was leaning uncomfortably towards the other side. This sense is affected by alcohol. A drunkard becomes ungainly because his perception of exactly where his limbs are situated is distorted. Hence as a test for drunkenness the police may ask a suspect to touch his nose with his extended forefinger, or to walk along a white line painted on the road.

We also have senses which provide evidence of bodily movement and heaviness, based upon sense organs in the muscle tendons and joints; senses of balance and rotation based upon sense organs in the inner ear; and inner senses, by which we can detect problems associated with internal organs by means of headaches, stomach aches, etc.

The Standard Model of Sense Perception

Understandably, when we seek to understand sense perception, we think primarily of sight. Today we think of the process of visual perception by analogy with the working of a camera. Light rays are reflected from the surfaces of objects in the outside world. Entering the pupil of the eye these are focused upon the retina, which acts as a screen. In this way an image of the external world is imposed upon the retina of the eye. The information this image contains is then conveyed, via the optic nerve, to the brain. The modification of the brain which is a consequence of this in some way results in our being conscious of aspects of the outside world.

Despite our partial understanding of this process, we tend to believe that through the sense of sight we have direct access to the outside world. We assume that other people with adequate eyesight looking at the same objects will have identical images formed on the retinas of their eyes, will have their brains stimulated in identical ways, and so will "see the same things" that we see. If we think about it at all, we tend to assume that similar processes takes place when the other senses are activated, and with similar results. We assume that the picture of the outside world which our senses provide us with is one which faithfully copies the world "as it really is." But this model of sense-experience is an oversimplified one which is, in some respects, very misleading. This can best be seen when we consider what happens when the process goes wrong.

2. When our Senses Mislead Us

Illusions, Hallucinations and Points of View

Although we are inclined to feel confident about what we are directly aware of through our senses, philosophers have drawn attention to the fact that we cannot necessarily trust the evidence of our senses to provide us with a true picture of the outside world.

What we perceive depends not only upon the input available to us from the outside world, but also upon the attention we pay to it.

- We may hear a crash in the distance as a motorcyclist, taking a bend too fast, swerves off a road and hits a tree, yet fail to hear the sound of a blackbird singing in the bushes nearby.

- A driver who follows a regular route to work may arrive at his destination and then realise, with alarm, that he cannot recall seeing part of the route he so recently followed.

Our powers of attention are limited, and some degree of concentration is demanded of us before perception takes place. In addition, we are selective about what we pay attention to. We regularly "tune out" unintrusive, recurrent noises, like the ticking of a clock. Regular stimuli tend to be ignored when we become accustomed to them, while something new is attended to immediately. Clearly this has survival value, since something which is new in our environment might be a dangerous predator and will need to be checked out; whereas something which has always been there, like a boulder or a tree, is unlikely to pose a danger to us.

What we perceive depends upon the conditions that obtain in our environment.

- A vase, which appears to be blue in a room illuminated by normal white light, will appear black if we exchange the white light bulb for a red one.
- A straight pole standing vertically in water, partly above and partly below the surface, appears to be bent, due to the refraction of light rays as they pass from one medium (water) to another (air) of differing density.

Thus "seeing a blue vase" and "seeing a bent post" are not simple matters of there being a blue vase or a bent post there to be seen.

What we perceive depends upon the relationship between the perceiver and what is perceived.

- Distant objects look smaller than those which are nearer, and the more distant they get the smaller they appear. The sun and moon appear to us as having the size of large balls, but we know them to be much larger.

The relative position of what is perceived and the perceiver in time, as contrasted with space, seems to alter not merely the shape of what is perceived, but its very nature.

- Because light takes approximately eight minutes to reach the earth from the sun, the sun which we appear to perceive now is in fact something which, strictly speaking, no longer exists, since it is the sun of eight minutes ago. Distant objects in the universe many millions of light years away, seen by means of long distance telescopes, may have entirely ceased to exist in the form in which we see them before the appearance of life on this planet.

What we perceive may depend upon the environment (in space and time) of the perceiver.

- In figure 1 the two central circles in each group are of the same size.
- In figure 2 the horizontal parallel lines are made to appear bent by the radiating lines in the background.

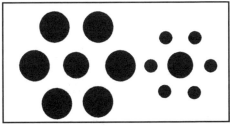

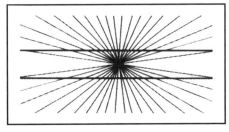

figure 1

figure 2

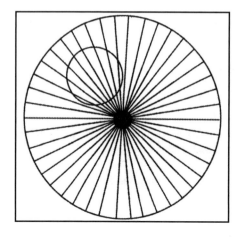

figure 3   *figure 4*

- Radiating lines, like the spokes of a wheel, distort our perception of the smaller circle in figure 3.
- In figure 4 the black squares lead many people to see dark grey dots in the grid between the squares.
- The afterimage of the sun we see on entering a darkened room is a consequence of the fact that we were a few moments previously looking at a very bright light source.

This dependence upon previous perceptions may lead us to apply opposite descriptions to the same stimulus.

- If the left hand is placed in a bowl of cold water and the right in a bowl of hot water, then both are simultaneously placed in a bowl of lukewarm water, the left hand will feel the lukewarm water to be hot, whereas the right hand will feel it to be cold.
- Someone who has just eaten something very sweet, followed by something normally perceived as moderately sweet, will perceive the latter to have a sour taste.

What we perceive depends upon the state of our sense organs, their health and sensitivity.

We have different thresholds of awareness. A poorly sighted person will see a less clearly outlined image than someone with better eyesight. The degree of our sensitivity may vary from one part of our body to another.

- A coin will feel larger to the tongue than to the back of the hand because the tongue is more sensitive to touch than the back of the hand.
- Illness may affect our sensitivity in odd ways.
- During a severe cold our food will seem to have lost its characteristic taste, or to have acquired a different taste.

What is perceived depends upon the general nature of our sense organs.

What we sense is determined by the structure of our sense organs. The German writer, Goethe, observed, "Were the eye not attuned to the sun, the sun could never be seen by it." Sense experience may be a very different experience for different species whose sense organs have evolved in different ways.

- Birds can detect ultraviolet wavelengths, and so see in colours not apparent to human beings. Their eyes may be able to see in more primary colours than we can discern, perhaps as many as eight. Birds which appear to us as dull in appearance, such as starlings or ravens, may appear to other birds in several very different brightly-coloured hues. Since many seeds have a waxy coat which reflects ultraviolet rays, whereas leaves and grass do not, the seeds birds eat would stand out conspicuously against their background. Similarly, small mammals which use their urine to mark their territory and trails may, in doing so, betray their presence to birds of prey, since the urine absorbs all ultraviolet light, rendering the stains visible to their predators.

- Some insects have all-round vision. That is why you cannot surprise a fly by stalking it from behind with a rolled-up newspaper.

    What is true of sight is also true of other senses.

- Humans can hear sound in frequencies of 20-20,000 cycles per second. Pigeons are sensitive within the 600-1,700 range, while grasshoppers respond to 28,000 cycles per second.

- Low-frequency vibrations are transmitted through the ground, and in some animals are "heard" through the body. Even humans, accustomed to going barefoot in desert areas, may be sensitive to the approach of people still over the horizon in this manner.

- Bats find their way about by echolocation, using sound to map out their environment. This is so finely tuned that they can detect changes in air currents caused by the flapping of an insect's wings, or an insect's footsteps.

- Rattlesnakes have a sense organ on their heads which is sensitive to infrared rays, and which will detect an animal several feet away by its body-heat.

- Certain fish in the muddy estuaries of South America form an electrical field around themselves. They can detect if this field is disturbed by obstacles in water too muddy for visibility.

    Had the human species evolved differently we might have had different sense-organs, and so we might have perceived the world very differently from the way in which, as a matter of fact, we actually do perceive it.

What we perceive depends upon the state of our brains.

    Sense-experience depends upon the brain as well as the sense organs themselves. When the chemistry of the brain is altered then strange sensory phenomena may result.

- Strange visual effects are reported by persons under the influence of hallucinogenic drugs, such as LSD.

- The brains of those who have the condition known as synaesthesia are somehow cross-wired, so that for some synaesthetes the sounds of words may be associated with colours, and for others with smells. For such people the word "dance" may be yellow and "drive" red. Other synaesthetes associate smells and tastes with colours, so that for them, the smell of baking bread may be orange, and the taste of almonds purple. A study tracking the flow of blood in the brains of synaesthetes who associate words with colours shows that when a list of words is read to them, blood flows to the part of the brain concerned with vision. This does not happen in normal people, suggesting to researchers that areas of the brain which are not normally connected have somehow become connected in the synaesthete.

    These curious features of sense-experience point to several conclusions regarding the knowledge of the world we acquire through the senses.

- We cannot justifiably claim that our senses give us a picture of the world which is infallible. We are prone to **illusions**, when our perception is distorted in some way, so that things appear to have properties which they do not really possess. Under some circumstances we may even have **hallucinations**, when we see things which are not there at all. For such reasons, we sometimes have to use one sense in order to correct another; as when we check the depth of the swimming pool by touch.

- The picture of the world which our senses give us is not constituted simply by data which we receive from outside. It is a complex product of many factors, including the relationship between the perceiver and what is perceived, the environment in which both exist, and the state and constitution of our own sense-organs and brains. What we sense is in part determined by the raw data which comes to us from the world around us, but also it is not *simply* a matter of what is in the world around us.

- The picture of the world which our senses give to us is not in any sense "complete." It is quite unaffected by colours we cannot see, sounds we cannot hear, aromas we cannot smell, and aspects of reality provided by senses we do not possess, even though these may be available to other creatures. Our picture of the world around is based upon a part of the possible data.

- We tend to objectify *our* picture of the world, as *the* picture of the world. We say that things "have the colour" which they normally appear to us to have, or "are" what colour they appear to be to us in white light. But our picture of the world is only one among many possible pictures. Had the human species evolved differently we might have had different sense-organs, and so we might have perceived the world very differently from the way in which, in fact, we actually do perceive it.

Delusions

There is worse to come. What we perceive depends not merely upon physical, chemical and biological factors, it also, to some extent, depends upon our own beliefs and expectations. There is now considerable experimental evidence that:

We tend to perceive what we expect to perceive.

These expectations we have may be the result either of our general cultural background, or our own individual past experiences.

- In an experiment, people were required to identify playing cards chosen from an apparently normal pack. When false cards, such as a red Ace of Clubs or a black Ace of Diamonds, were introduced, these were initially perceived by the subjects of the experiment as standard cards. Thus the red Ace of Clubs was mistakenly described as a red Ace of Hearts or a black Ace of Clubs. Only when the subjects of the experiment had been informed that there were strange cards in the packs which they were using did they begin to identify them correctly.

- An anchor-man on a BBC television program once announced that he had been to interview a giant in his home. As seen on the screen the man so described was clearly unusually large, although otherwise quite normal in proportion. His head almost touched the ceiling of the sitting room of his home, and it would have been necessary for him to stoop to pass out through the door. He appeared to be at least eight feet tall. Then the camera was pulled back to reveal that the "room" he had been standing in was a in fact stage set in which every item of its furnishings had been proportionally reduced in size. The "giant" was in fact a man of normal size. What was anomalous was not the large size of the man but the small size of the "room" and its furnishings. The date was April 1st.

Led by the expectation of seeing an unusually tall man, and faced with the disparity between the size of the man and everything else in the room, viewers initially "saw" a giant. When the cameras moved back to reveal other people standing around who were of the same size as the so-called "giant," and the furniture of the room disproportionately small in relation to them, the viewers then switched from "seeing" the man as a giant to seeing him as someone of normal size. At the same time, they switched from "seeing" the room and all the objects in it as normal-sized to seeing them as smaller than their usual size.

When the cameras moved back, viewers did not simply revise their beliefs about what they were seeing. There was a sudden switch in perception: from "seeing" a giant in a room of ordinary-sized objects to seeing a normally sized man in a room of unusually small objects.

We are likely to miss something, even if we are looking for it, if it turns up somewhere unexpected.

- After years of searching on various expeditions for an orchid thought to be extinct, a party of botanists in New Zealand finally noticed a specimen lying flattened under their groundsheet when they took down their tent after another unsuccessful search.

We tend to see what other people see, or say that they see.

Our perception may even be affected by our social situation.

- Psychologist Solomon Asch showed that people may be persuaded to report the length of a line as longer or shorter than it actually is and against the clear evidence of their senses, provided that the other subjects of the experiment all connive at saying that it is longer or shorter than they really know it to be. While some subjects may lie to conform their opinion to that of the majority, it seems likely that others, more suggestible, convince themselves that what everyone else says is so must in fact be so. Then they actually come to see it as so. The majority viewpoint affects their perceptions.

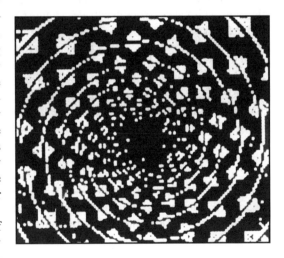

figure 5

Artists are well aware of the power of convention to influence our perception. They use rules of perspective in two-dimensional drawings to make us see a three-dimensional space which is strictly not there at all. A sense of movement may be suggested by a two-dimensional picture. Figure 5 looks like a vortex.

We tend to see what we want to see.

- An excited announcement by an expert birdwatcher over CB radio once led enthusiastic bird-watchers to flock from miles around to a field on the Isle of Scilly in the UK to witness the unusual appearance of a nighthawk, a rare visitor from North America. Only when scores of pairs of binoculars had been focused on the object of all this attention for some considerable time was it realised that it was, in fact, a patch of cow dung.

"Seeing As"

A lone traveller across a bleak moor in near-darkness may mistake a clod of grass for a crouching animal. On approaching nearer, he will see it for what it is. A young child lying fearfully awake in the near-darkness may perceive a robe hanging on a peg as a murderous intruder poised to spring upon her. When her mother enters the bedroom and puts the light on in response to her shrieking, the threatening "intruder" is instantly transformed into the familiar and harmless robe it really is. In each case a switch takes place between what was originally perceived, and what is subsequently perceived, to be the reality.

This sudden switch in perception can be seen by looking at pictures which are capable of more than one interpretation. Most famous is that of the white vase seen against a black background which switches to being two black faces in silhouette with a white space in between (figure 6). We tend to see first one then the other, but hardly ever both at the same time. Figure 7 may be seen as a duck facing left or as a hare facing right. Another famous ambiguous drawing (figure 8) may be seen either as an old woman or a young woman.

In all such cases, the drawing seems to switch from one to the other in front of our eyes. What seems to change is not so much our belief about what we perceive as the perception itself.

One way of explaining what happens has been to say that the observer has some sense-experience which is then subjected to a process of interpretation. We see a distant object approach in the sky and ask "Is it a bird, or is it a plane?" On receiving more detailed information as it gets nearer, noticing flapping wings, for example, we judge it to be a large bird.

On this account, we tend to think that the observer cannot be mistaken that he sees something, and that his seeing cannot itself be false. Any error must lie in the interpretation the observer places upon his experience, in the acts of judgement or the inferences which he makes *about* what he is seeing.

But we cannot usually distinguish the two,

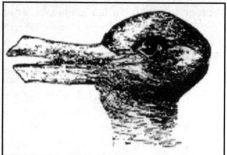

figures 6, 7 and 8

since we do not have access to an uninterpreted image on the retina of the eye. We do not possess an image of the black faces/white vase picture, which we then choose to interpret first as one thing and then as another. Rather we experience seeing the picture first as two black faces and then as a white vase, or *vice versa*. The frightened little girl first sees the robe hanging on the door as an intruder and then as a robe. Viewers to the BBC programme referred to above first saw the tall man as a giant in a normal-sized room, and then as a normal-sized man in front of an abnormally sized stage set.

Perception is not simply determined by the data provided by the senses. Perception involves the perceiver actively seeking for the best interpretation of the data. Thus perception involves going beyond what is immediately given to the senses. We seem to have some part in the construction of our experiences, and we construct them on the basis, in part at least, of our expectations. We then revise our opinion if those expectations are not fulfilled.

There is no great mystery in this. Ordinary expertise may alter what we see. The English poet and artist William Blake observed, "A fool sees not the same tree a wise man sees." While a university professor straying into an auto scrap yard might see only "parts of old cars," an auto-enthusiast might see a fascinating collection of interesting engine parts, carburettors, dynamos, and so on, including many rare and valuable items from veteran cars.

We contribute something to what we perceive through our senses. Perception is not simply a matter of recording, as on a blank page, the impressions we receive through our sense organs from the world outside, to be interpreted by us afterwards. Rather we order and process the incoming data as perception takes place. Thus, according to many philosophers *all seeing is seeing-as*.

This is supported by the little-known fact that we actually have to *learn* to see. We usually do this at such an early age, that we cannot remember doing it.

• In 1728 an English surgeon removed cataracts from the eyes of a thirteen year-old boy who had been born blind. It was recorded that, although the boy was intelligent, he could only gradually make sense of what his new power of sight brought to his attention. Initially he had no idea of distance, space or size, and could make nothing of two-dimensional representations of three-dimensional objects.

• The anthropologist Colin Turnbull, studied the lives of the pygmies who lived deep inside the rain forest of Zaire. One day, he took one of them to see the open plains, where the view stretched far to the horizon. When the pygmy first saw a herd of buffalo in the distance, he thought they were ants. He refused to believe that they were buffalo because they seemed so small. He had to learn to interpret visual perspective.

The Importance of Patterns

In *The Man Who Mistook His Wife for a Hat,* Oliver Sacks describes a man who suffered from a condition known as visual agnosia. As an unfortunate by-product of a routine operation, this patient could no longer recognise from sight anything complex around him, including people and places formerly familiar to him. His memory was intact. He could describe his house in words; but when faced with it, he could not recognise it. Yet he could spot a piece of fluff or dirt on a carpet and remove it. The problem was that he was unable to recognise patterns.

We naturally tend to organise what our senses detect into patterns. This is something which happens in the brain, not in the eye. Such a pattern is termed by psychologists a *Gestalt*. It is the *Gestalt* that we perceive. We perceive things only when they are ordered in patterns of some sort, and we experience the patterns as wholes. Thus we impose upon the world, as we perceive it, an order which is partly constituted by our own beliefs and expectations.

That this is so may be seen in several ways.

- We tend to see shapes that are not strictly present, if we consider the outlines actually presented to us. In figure 9 most people will immediately see a baby, although all that is actually present are geometrical shapes shaded in black.

In figure 10 we immediately see an inverted white triangle, although no triangle is actually there.

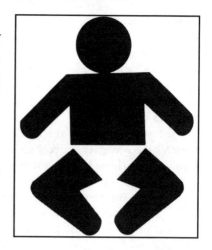

figure 9

- It is occasionally the experience of a foreigner who cannot speak the language of the country he is staying in that, while in a crowd, and aware of the unintelligible babble of voices all around him, a single intelligible phrase will suddenly detach itself from the surrounding noise and impose itself upon his attention. This will usually be a complete phrase, but one which will mean absolutely nothing out of context: perhaps "yellow tomatoes" or "the slow monkey." The visitor will look around to discover the source of this unexpected and remarkable phrase, making an effort to "tune in" to the surrounding conversations in order to detect the speaker of his own language. Usually it is soon apparent that there is none. The intelligible phrase seemingly came out of nowhere.

- The brain, searching for recognisable patterns, becomes desperate to find *some* intelligibility in the surrounding confusion of sounds. As soon as something remotely resembling a phrase in the known language is picked up, as soon as any sort of "fit" between the patterns of sound familiar to the foreigner and elements in the surrounding confusion becomes possible, the brain promptly makes the fit, and then proudly calls attention to it.

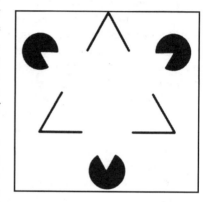

figure 10

- When we cannot quite recognise a pattern we can make sense of, we tend to become uneasy. This can be seen if we try to make sense out of figures 11, 12 and 13.

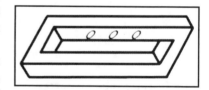

figure 11

This desire to resolve confusion into a recognisable pattern is the explanation of many apparently strange occurrences, like the cloud which appears to take the form of some familiar object, such as a castle in the sky, or a human face. It explains such recent religious apparitions as:

- an image of the Virgin Mary detected on the cement floor of a shower in the rear of an auto parts store in Progresso, Texas;

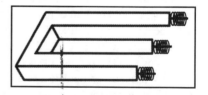

figure 12

- the face of Jesus seen in a tortilla by a woman in Lake Arthur, New Mexico;
- motorists who saw Jesus, covered in pasta and tomato sauce, on a billboard advertising Pizza Hut spaghetti in DeKalb County, Galvaston;
- viewers of CNN, who saw an apparition of Christ in a photograph of a six trillion-mile-long gas cloud taken by a space telescope;
- a Muslim schoolgirl living in Huddersfield, England, who sliced in half a tomato and found the messages in Arabic "God is great" on one side and Mohammed is the messenger" on the other, spelled out in the veins of the vegetable.

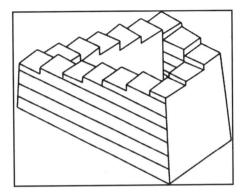

figure 13

The mind abhors formlessness, and where it is possible to impose a familiar form on what is really formless, the mind will do it. That is why Christians see the face of Christ or the Virgin Mary, while Muslims detect texts from the *Qur'an*, their holy book.

A false belief, caused by "seeing" a pattern in things which is not really there, is termed a **delusion**.

Case Study: The Canals of Mars

When men realised that the earth is not the unique centre of the universe, but merely one among many planets orbiting the sun, it was only a matter of time before they began to consider the possibility that human beings might not be the only intelligent form of life in the universe, but that on some of the other planets of the solar system intelligent life might also have developed.

Despite some significant differences from earth, the planet Mars seemed to be the most likely candidate. It is neither too near the sun, and so too hot for the development of life, nor too far away, and so too cold. It is also similar to the earth in that it has a day only slightly longer than twenty-four hours.

Accordingly, early astronomers expectantly trained their telescopes on the red planet. By modern standards, these were primitive instruments. But because Mars is Earth's neighbour planet it was possible to make out clearly two polar ice caps, together with dark areas that were thought to be oceans.

During the latter part of the nineteenth century the Italian astronomer Giovanni Schiaparelli was making observations when Mars was passing particularly close to the Earth, and saw a network of lines running between the icecaps and the oceans. They appeared artificially straight, and designed to transport water.

This sighting was later confirmed by the American astronomer, Percival Lowell. He believed that this indicated that there was intelligent life on Mars, and he followed up Schiaparelli's observations using more powerful telescopes. He recorded hundreds of what came to be called "canals". Lowell speculated that the Martian civilisation was more advanced than ours. He argued that it had probably already used up most of the available water on the planet, so that the survivors had to rely upon the water stored at the poles. He thought that the dark areas were not oceans but settled areas, irrigated by the canals that drew water from the ice caps.

These observations aroused considerable interest, and many astronomers directed their telescopes at the Martian surface. Many saw canals. Others saw patterns, although what they saw did not strike them as indicating canals. Some saw nothing like canals at all. Over the succeeding years, increasingly powerful telescopes were trained upon the planet, but fewer and fewer people saw canals. Then during the 1970s US and Soviet spacecraft orbiting Mars sent back to earth photographs of the planet's surface. These showed that the appearance of dark patches was caused by differences in the character of the rock of the Martian desert. Of the "canals", there was not the slightest trace.

They may have been illusions caused by clouds of dust in the atmosphere of the planet, or effects of the imperfections of the astronomers' telescopes, or even a consequence of optical fatigue, as tired astronomers peered into their instruments over long periods of time. It is much more likely, however, that the canals of Mars were simply a delusion, caused by the desire of Schiaparelli and Lowell to find traces of intelligent life. This may have generated expectations among some of those who tried to repeat their sightings, so that they in their turn "saw" canals, which simply were not there.

Occasionally, however, even today the canals of Mars resurface, as in a speech of then Governor George W. Bush in 1994: "Mars is somewhat the same distance from the Sun, which is very important. We have seen pictures where there are canals, we believe, and water. If there is water, that means there is oxygen. If oxygen, that means we can breathe."

3. What Our Senses Tell Us About the World

In view of these problems, the question must be asked: what do our senses, in general, tell us about the world around us? Three main positions emerge:

(16) We can only know what the world *seems* like to us; not how it *really* is.

We do not possess some pure sense of the external world and then subject it to interpretation. The existence of delusions shows us that thought and interpretation are themselves part of the process of perception. As the Immanuel Kant put it in his ponderous manner: "Without the sensuous faculty no object would be given to us, and without the understanding no object would be thought. Thoughts without content are empty, intuitions without concepts, blind."

We are necessarily constrained to perceive the world around us in certain ways that are predetermined by our membership of our species, our culture, and our individual past experience. We are determined, or constrained, to perceive the world in certain ways and not in others by our species because we have sense organs and brains of the type which we do have. We are predisposed by our culture and by our individual histories to see things in one way rather than another by the expectations with which these equip us.

We can never compare the world as we experience it with the world as it is, because only the world as we see it is available to us, therefore we are limited to viewing the world from the point of view of our own species, culture and past history.

This is the position philosophers call **perceptual relativism:** the view that and that there is no way of knowing objectively what the world is like in itself, only what it is like *to you or to me*.

Some philosophers have gone further, and argued that the problems associated with perception, together with our inability to compare our perceptions directly with the world itself in order to check their reliability, throw doubt upon whether there is any objective truth to be discovered about the world at all. They have argued that:

(17) It is beyond our power to know what the world is really like.

We can compare appearances and eliminate what is unusual. We can compare the data of different senses, where they conflict, and make a choice between them. Thus, as children, we confirm the depth of the paddling pool or by touch. However, when we do this we are comparing a representation of reality in vision with a representation of reality to touch, not a representation of reality with the objective external reality itself.

But if all that we can do is say how the world appears to us, we are condemned to live in a world of appearances. The truth about what the world is "really" like will necessarily always be beyond us. We never experience things-as-they-are-in-themselves, only the effects they cause upon our consciousness through the operation of our sense organs and brains. The "real" world, which lies behind its appearances, is forever unknown to us. This view is known as **perceptual scepticism**.

Despite the apparent force of these positions, there are arguments which suggest that both the sceptical and relativist positions are fundamentally mistaken, and that:

(18) We possess genuine knowledge of the world around us based upon our sense-experience.

Despite the phenomena of illusions, hallucinations and delusions, it is a fact that we cannot sense *absolutely anything at all*. What we sense is largely determined by what is out there to be sensed.

Various factors do with our sense organs and brains determine the limits of what we can sense. Others may interfere with the process of perception to determine the exact nature of the end product. But when this happens, it tends to happen predictably. We know that we can be misled by our senses, but we understand how and why it happens.

We may see what appear to be bent poles standing in water, but we know that they are not bent, and why they appear bent to sight. They do so because of perfectly understandable laws of nature which govern the refraction of light, which are explained clearly in every school textbook of physics. That such illusions occur does not mean that we cannot know whether the poles is straight, or that there are any poles there at all.

Similarly, during the psychological experiment referred to above, *some* people may see a red ace of clubs as a red ace of hearts. But the psychologist can explain what is happening, and once the error has been pointed out to us we pay attention to it and see what is there to be seen.

Illusions, hallucinations and delusions are minor glitches in a process which, on the whole, works very well. If it did not, we would never know for certain whether the objects we see were there at all. We would navigate the world like blind men, grasping at objects which do not exist, and stumbling over ones which do. This does not happen, and it does not happen because we generally know, using our sense-experience, what the world around us is like. Sense experience *generally* works, enabling us to move about the world successfully and so survive. And because our senses generally function successfully, we know that the world must be much as our senses picture it to us.

Moreover, it by no means follows that if we humans sense one set of phenomena and, say, dogs sense other sets of phenomena, that this somehow implies that the real world is not apparent to us. We humans focus our attention upon what we, with our distinctively human sense organs and brain, can see; while dogs, with their distinctively canine sense organs and brains, concentrate upon what they can smell. We may all be said to be more or less acutely aware of different aspects of a complex but common reality.

This view, that our senses generally give us knowledge of the world around, is known as **perceptual realism**.

Talking Point: The Strange Phenomenon of Blindsighting

Even if our senses are not complete and infallible guides to the outside world, we usually assume that we have privileged knowledge at least of what we ourselves actually sense. If I see a stick standing in water which looks bent, I may not be able to claim on the basis of that experience that

(1) There is a stick which standing in the water which is bent; but at least I can properly claim to know that

(15) I *seem* to see a stick which standing in water which is bent.

We usually assume that we have incorrigible knowledge of such things. Yet there may be problems even with this, suggested by the strange phenomenon of "blindsighting." A patient with this affliction responds appropriately to visual stimuli, while at the same time claiming to have no awareness of them at all. If a ball is thrown at a person with this condition, he will catch it. But if it is pointed out to him that he cannot both be blind and catch a ball, he will insist adamantly, and with every sign of total honesty, that he is truly blind and cannot see anything at all.

What this seems to show is that, in principle, it is possible for someone not to know, in some way not to be aware of, what he clearly perceives.

---

4. Observation

Problems of Observation

We depend for our survival upon observation. Precisely because of this, our powers have evolved in such a manner as best to ensure our survival, and not to provide us with accurate, detailed pictures of everything around us. We may be alerted by light footsteps behind us in the dark, but not to the colour of the shoes of someone approaching us in daylight.

Courtroom lawyers are very much aware that when it comes down to details, human beings can be very poor observers. Eyewitnesses to crimes are notoriously unreliable. Moreover, when we cannot recall something we ardently wish to remember, we are unfortunately inclined to fill the gaps in our memory using our imagination.

Observing is not straightforward matter of passively noting what happens in the outside world, and then accurately recording it. Observation requires our attention and effort. We need to know what, out of the multitude of aspects of our field of observation, we are supposed to be observing. The philosopher Karl Popper once demonstrated this by asking a class of students to take a pencil and paper and write down what they observed. Puzzled by the indefinite nature of his instruction, they soon asked him, in exasperation, exactly *what* they were supposed to be observing. We cannot simply observe; we must observe *something*. On the other hand, we must be careful to observe what is actually there, and not what we expect to be there or hope is there.

Good observation is important in a variety of contexts, both in everyday life and in academic research: from the witness of a crime using his observations to help the police apprehend, and the court to convict, a criminal, to observing the results of a scientific experiment. In such circumstances, it is important that the observations are both as accurate and unbiased as possible, and also accurately recorded.

How to Evaluate our own Observations

The amount of confidence we should place in claims to have directly observed something depends upon several factors:

- The environment at the time of the observation: Was it dark or light? Was there a blizzard or rainstorm? Was it misty or clear?

- The state of the sense organs of the observer: Do I have good eyesight? If I needed them, was I wearing my spectacles?

- The state of mind of the observer: Was I alert or sleepy? Was I under the influence of some narcotic substance, such as alcohol ? Was I composed, flustered or shocked at the time of the observation?

- The focus of attention of the observer: Was I attending to what I was observing, or was I preoccupied with something else? We are more likely to misinterpret what is on the edges of our field of attention than what our attention is directly focused upon.

- The experience and training of the observer: Have I been trained to observe what I was observing, and was I experienced at doing so?

- The dispassionate impartiality of the observer: Had I any strong interest in, or any predisposition towards, seeing one thing rather than another?

- The character of the observer: Am I generally honest with myself, or do I like to deceive myself and live in a world of make-believe? Do I allow imagination or wishful thinking to cloud my perception of reality?

- The memory of the observer: Do I correctly remember what I observed? There is experimental evidence to show that we are inclined to recall incidents which make us feel good and to repress those which make us blush with shame; that we remember what tends to support our beliefs, and that we are inclined to forget what counts against them.

- The amount of independent confirmation coming from other disinterested observers: Did anyone else present claim to have observed what I did? Under the circumstances ought they to have observed what I observed? If they did not, why not?

- The consistency of what was observed with our general knowledge of the world: Does what I observed fit in with what we know of the way the world works in general? If it does not, then we have to choose between my being mistaken or the world's being a very different place from the sort of place we thought it to be. Usually the former alternative is the most rational choice.

- The reliability of any record of the observation: Is the record clear and unambiguous? Was it made at the time of the observation or some time afterwards? If it was made afterwards, how long afterwards?

Talking Point: The Lonely Planet

Since visual, auditory, olfactory, gustatory and tactile sensations are events in the consciousness caused by external stimuli, it follows that the colours, sounds, smells, tastes, etc. which are elements in those sensations are also modifications of the consciousness of those who perceive.

Imagine a small planet in a distant region of space, hostile to life, not only beyond the reach of possible visit by life forms, but beyond the possibility of their viewing it by telescope, or even by photography from an unmanned space craft. There may be immense volcanic eruptions on that planet, outpourings of hot magma and exhalations of super-heated gases. But of one thing we can be assured: there will be no colours, sounds or smells. Explosions caused by pressure within the volcanoes will never produce a roar, however powerful they may be. The hot magma will never glow red, the gases will produce no stench. All these things: the colour of the magma, the sound of the explosions and the stench of the gases, are states of the consciousness of observers, and we have decided that there will never be an observer on this planet.

Sometimes it is argued that this view is incorrect. It is said that colour is the energy emitted from an excited object in photons, that sound is the vibration of air molecules, and that these things are present when no one is there to detect them, in much the same way that a radio station may broadcast even if no one tunes in to listen.

However, this objection misses the point. On an uninhabited planet there will be no colour; for colour is something in the mind of the person who sees. There will be no noise; for noise is something in the mind of the one who hears. There will be no odour without beings equipped with noses and minds; for the odour is in the mind of the one who sniffs.

Note that this dispute is not about the grounding in reality of our perceptions of colour, sound and odour, but about what the words "colour," "sound" or "odour" *refer* to.

Glossary

data: what is given in experience.

delusion: a firmly-held mistaken belief.

Gestalt: a pattern which enables us to grasp or to make sense out of some complexity.

hallucination: a distortion of sense-perception in which we appear to perceive things which do not exist.

illusion: a distortion of sense-perception in which things are perceived as having qualities which they do not possess.

perceptual realism: the view that in general our senses provide us with genuine knowledge of the world.

perceptual relativism: the view that we cannot say what the world is really like, only how it appears to you or me.

perceptual scepticism: the view that we cannot say what the world is really like at all, since we can never get behind the appearances, or representations, it generates in our consciousness.

5. TESTIMONY

"He that deceives me once, shame fall him; if he deceives me twice, shame fall me." (Scottish Proverb)

1. The Testimony of Others

Most of our knowledge is based neither upon our own direct sense-experience nor upon our reasoning about it. Instead, we receive it second-hand, from the **testimony**, or witness, of others.

Family and friends relate their experiences to us and pass on their judgements. Teachers initiate us into the shared knowledge of the community. Many of the various organisations we may belong to, such as political parties and religious groups, will furnish us with information and values. We are also bombarded through the various media of mass communication: newspapers, magazines, books, movies, radio and television broadcasts, and the Internet.

Sometimes, those who give testimony to us have themselves directly learned the truth of what they tell us from their own sense-experience and reasoning. More usually, however, they are passing on to us the testimony of others, so that we are learning third, fourth or nth hand.

As we have already seen, our own sense-experience is not immune from error and self-deception, and necessarily involves seeing the world from a selective and partial viewpoint. The mediation of information through others introduces further possibilities of error and deception. In judging the reliability of testimony, it is necessary to take account of all those circumstances which may invalidate our own observations, since they may also have operated upon those upon whose *original* sense experience the information is based. Then, in addition, we need to make judgements concerning the biases, honesty and reliability of our informants, and the distortions that may occur during the process of transmission of the information along the chain from one person to another.

The need for this can be seen clearly if we consider some common forms of false and misleading testimony.

False Testimony

Widespread "tall stories" told and retold in a hundred thousand workplaces, cafés and bars across the world, have become known as "**urban legends**." No one knows where they began, but they seem to gain currency because they touch upon general but unspoken fears. The following is one of the most widespread of the urban legends.

Case Study: The Vanishing Hitchhiker.

One dark and stormy night a lone motorist saw a forlorn young woman standing by the side of the road in a rainstorm and decided to give her a lift. The hitchhiker explained that her car had broken down. The driver lent the girl his sweater and dropped her off at her house. On passing the place next day, he knocked on the door, seeking to recover his sweater. It was opened by one of the girl's parents, who seemed to be expecting him. When the driver explained his purpose he was told that the girl had died some years before.

There are many variations of this legend. Sometimes the driver finds something the girl left behind in his car, and goes back to return it, thus learning the truth about her. Sometimes the driver is taken to the grave of the dead girl, where he finds the sweater he loaned her draped over the tombstone.

False testimony may sometimes pass through society with lightning rapidity, becoming both widespread and compelling. The American writer Mark Twain observed: "A lie can be all the way across the country before the truth can get its boots on." Such fast-moving and widespread false stories are known as rumours.

Rumours seem to spread more quickly during times of stress, or when the normal means of communication of information are no longer operating, especially during times of national crisis. It is clear that one factor which gives force to a rumour may be that people strongly wish, or fear, it to be true. Once it has become widespread we are tempted to believe it simply for that reason. Because humans are social animals, we tend to follow the herd instinctively. We justify this by saying: "There is no smoke without fire." And when someone shouts "Fire!" we move without waiting to check it out. Thus rumours are particularly dangerous because they can create panic. But however widespread a rumour is, however firmly it is believed, a rumour remains a rumour.

Because anyone with access to the Internet, however malicious, can post messages on it, and because anyone at all anywhere in the world, however credulous, can read them almost instantly, it seems likely that in the future the Internet will be the medium of transmission of many rumours.

When we have heard something from several different sources, it is difficult to credit the possibility that it may be false. What is repeated often enough gains credibility simply by being repeated, and so becomes generally thought of as "known." This is quite independent of whether or not there is any actual evidence it or not. Thus some things come to be generally accepted as true simply because they have been constantly repeated. Many pander to a common prejudice; e.g. that most of the crimes committed in a country are committed by foreigners. This is hardly ever true. It is constantly maintained that democracies do not start wars. This is obviously not true, since most wars since 1945 have been started by the USA. Of course, most of them are not called wars since if they were Congressional approval would be required to support them.

There are many "false facts" which tend to be repeated from person to person and book to book with such regularity that it is difficult to credit that they may not actually be true. They are often referred to as **pseudo-facts**. Some are harmless, such as the widespread belief, written in into many children's books on "the wonders of nature," that lemmings commit mass suicide. But some false impressions of reality can be very dangerous, since they may feed prejudice. In many countries it is firmly believed by large sections of the population that most crimes are committed by foreign immigrants. This is seldom true.

Case Study: False Beliefs relating to the Iraq War

In 2003, the Program on International Policy Attitudes, based at the University of Maryland, found in polls that a majority of US citizens held at least one of three mistaken impressions about the Iraq War, and that those contributed significantly towards popular support for the war. The three common misperceptions were:

* U.S. forces had found weapons of mass destruction in Iraq.
* President Saddam Hussein had collaborated closely with the Sept. 11th terrorists
* People in other countries either backed the U.S.-led attack upon Iraq, or were more or less evenly split between those supporting it and those opposing it.

Some sixty percent of Americans held at least one of those views.

The publicity put out by the Bush administration had clearly been a major factor in creating these false impressions. For example, President Bush claimed that Saddam had "trained and financed ... al Qaeda." The Vice-President and others in the administration frequently repeated such claims.

The study was able to correlate the frequency of misperceptions with the news sources consulted by the mistaken respondents. Eighty percent of those who relied on Fox News and seventy-one percent of those who relied on CBS, held at least one of the three misperceptions. The comparable figure for those who relied on newspapers and magazines was forty-seven percent, and for those who relied on the Public Broadcasting Service or National Public Radio twenty-three percent.

It was noted in explanation that the US media gave repeated and prominent air time to many reports that banned weapons *might* have been discovered in Iraq, but only modest coverage, if any, when those reports turned out to be wrong. The investigators also pointed out that much "reporting" actually consisted of mere repetition of government statements, with little consideration as to whether these were accurate.

The study also found that the false beliefs were persistent. At the end of the period during which the study took place, nearly a quarter of those polled still thought that banned weapons had been found in Iraq, and nearly half that there was clear evidence that Saddam Hussein had worked closely with the al-Qaida terrorists.

The Evaluation of Testimony

Clearly, it is clearly very important that we learn to evaluate the testimony of others effectively.

Discussion:

What would count as reasons for believing, or not believing, each of the following?

1. A good friend tells you that you missed your favourite movie on television last night.
2. Someone who hates you tells you that you missed your favourite movie on television last night.
3. Someone who hates you tells you that he saw a UFO land last night, and watched as tiny aliens emerged from the craft.

4. A good friend tells you that he saw a UFO land last night, and watched as tiny aliens emerged.

How to Evaluate the Testimony of Others

We need to consider the *character* of the person who communicates the information to us:
- Is he honest or dishonest? What is his past record?
- Is he liable to be mistaken or to get confused?
- Does he have a reasonably good memory?
- Has he any special interests, or motives for conscious deception? Has he an interest in, or any bias or predisposition towards, telling us one thing rather than another? Is he trying to sell us anything?
- Has he any special interests, prejudices or hang-ups, or any other motive for unconscious deception? e.g. the desire to please, to astonish, or to gain attention.
- Is he in a position to know what he claims to know?

We need to consider the *behaviour* of the *person* who communicates the information to us:
- Is his behaviour consistent with what he is telling us? i.e.. Is he behaving as though what he was claiming to be true is in fact true?

We need to consider the *language* used to inform us:
- Is it clear precisely what is being claimed?
- Is his language descriptive, or is it designed to be persuasive?

We need to consider the *content* of what is communicated to us:
- Does the testimony claim more than could have been observed, or reasonably inferred, by the person informing us, or by his alleged sources of information?
- Is the testimony consistent with, and confirmed by, other independent sources? (It is important that the other sources be genuinely independent to make the comparison of any value.)
- Is what is being communicated consistent with what we know of how the world works in general, or is it inherently improbable?

We need to consider the *source* of what is communicated to us:
- Is our informant communicating something he has witnessed himself, or is he merely passing on testimony he has himself received from others? If the latter, do we know where this testimony originated?
- If he is merely passing on testimony, do we know how far removed he is from the original source? When information is passed on along a chain of many persons the possibilities of mistakes, bias and dishonesty are multiplied.

2. The Bizarre, the Weird and the Wonderful

Some testimony is inherently incredible, because the claims it embodies are highly improbable. There are, however, different levels of improbability, as can be seen by comparing the following:
1. All the students in class handed in their assignments on time.
2. All the assignments handed in were of a very high quality.
3. A cow in Texas gave birth to a calf with two heads.
4. A cow in Texas gave birth to a lamb with two heads.
5. A farmer outside Boise, Idaho, was abducted by aliens, taken for a ride in a space vehicle, and then returned home unharmed.
6. A farmer outside Boise, Idaho, was abducted by aliens, taken for a ride in a space vehicle, and then returned home unharmed five minutes before he was abducted.

On the other hand, we should avoid being closed-minded; while some things are absolutely impossible or highly improbable, it is undoubtedly true that strange things sometimes do happen.

Case Study: The Giant Golden Turtle of the Hoan Kiem Lake

Many lakes are reputed to contain monsters. This was also true of the Hoan Kiem, a large rubbish-choked lake which occupies the heart of the Vietnamese capital. According to legend, a giant golden turtle rose from its waters in the mid-fifteenth century to snatch a magic sword from Emperor Ly Thai To, who had returned fresh from driving out Chinese invaders. Periodically the state press runs photographs of crowds gathered at the lakeside pointing excitedly at some fuzzy shape on the surface.

In December, 1996, the "South China Post" reported that doubters were confounded by the appearance of a very large and very old turtle with a one metre wide shell and a green and yellow head, about the size of a football. On one occasion, the creature came to within two metres of the shore, swivelling its head from side to side to show a great downcast mouth and peeling skin.

Although unlikely things do happen from time to time, we should each develop a "bullshit" detector, which warns us of the likely presence of rubbish. In particular, the rule should be observed that extraordinary claims require extraordinary evidence to support them.

DEVELOP YOUR OWN "BULLSHIT DETECTOR"

If I took my wallet to a soccer match in the back pocket of my jeans and later found that it was missing, it would not be rational to take the line that it had just "ceased to exist," since in our experience things do not cease to exist just like that. Nor ought it be considered that some property of the air had dissolved it: for the same reason. Nor should I blame tiny eight-legged aliens in invisible miniature spacecraft deftly picking my pocket. Such things are not consistent with what we know of the way things are. We need to be especially careful when someone tells us that something is so, which contradicts our most basic understanding of how the world works. What they claim may be strictly *possible*: but it is likely to be so very highly *improbable* that error or fraud is almost always a much better explanation.

Very often, the only way to support extraordinary claims is by searching around for "evidence" which is itself equally extraordinary. So that in order to believe in one extraordinary claim, we are required to accept many more. We should remember that the improbable added to the improbable is even more improbable.

**EXTRAORDINARY CLAIMS REQUIRE
EXTRAORDINARY EVIDENCE**

Case Study: Crop Circles

For a period of thirteen years, between 1978 and 1991 strange circular patterns appeared in the cornfields of southern England, caused by the bending of the stalks of ripe grain. UFO enthusiasts immediately saw them as evidence of landings by aliens in flying saucers, while New Age hippies claimed that the spots where the phenomena occurred exuded paranormal forces from the interior of the earth. Pat Delgado and Colin Andrews argued, in a book which sold more than 50,000 copies, that they were the products of "superior intelligence" - probably extraterrestrial.

Despite this wild theorising, since a large number of these circular patterns began to appear each year, genuine scientific interest was roused. A privately-funded Circles Effect Research Unit was set up under a physicist, Terence Meaden. This considered the hypothesis that whirling columns of air picked up electrically charged matter and flattened the crops. A team of Japanese scientists considered the possibility that ball-lightning, generated by microwaves in the atmosphere, was somehow responsible. They claimed to have created similar patterns by computer simulation in the laboratory, and their report was published in "Nature."

Then two men, David Chorley and Douglas Bower, came forward to explain how it had been done. The origin of crop circles lay in a practical joke conceived one evening in a public house. The pair decided to create a simple circle to convince people that a "flying saucer" had landed. Gratified by the sensation their work had aroused, they went on to produce between twenty-five and thirty circles each season, and began to attract imitators all over the world.

They were able to show how, armed only with a plank of wood, a ball of string and a wire threaded through the visor of a baseball cap to function as a sightline, they were able to create the patterns. One of the men would stand holding one end of the string, the other end of which, tied to a plank held parallel to the ground at knee level, was drawn across the surface of the crops. The weight of the grain was sufficient to ensure that most of the stalks were held down, creating the visible pattern.

When they read that enthusiasts were seeking government funding for research into the origin of the circles, they decided that it was time to come clean and admit every-thing. Predictably, the response of many of the crop circle enthusiasts was to argue that if some of the circles were hoaxes, not all could be conclusively proved to be such, therefore a genuine mystery remained. Some people are desperate for mystery at any price.

3. Authorities

Some testimony is presented to us along with the demand that it be treated as though it had a special claim upon our respect because of the authoritative source from which it originates. It comes along with a claim that we should pay special attention to what is said by this particular person on this particular subject; not treating it sceptically, or guardedly, as we would other testimony, but surrendering our independent judgement towards it.

Authorities are generally contrasted with **laymen**. We are all laymen in any fields where we do not ourselves have some special authority.

Traditional Authorities

Most human societies have been conservative and bound by their traditions. They have stressed the importance of showing particular respect towards those whose special status is recognised by custom. Traditional sources of authority include rulers and governments, their officials, religious leaders, teachers and parents. Deference towards them, and to their words, was thought to be a good thing in itself, and questioning them was considered to be either absurd or wicked.

To people brought up in a traditional society, the questioning of authority is always felt to be threatening. Elderly people reared under the tyranny of Stalinism in the countries of the old Soviet Union, can sometimes be heard reminiscing fondly about the certainties of those past days when there was no hubbub of debate, and no chorus of criticism of the government filling the newspapers. Instead, there was one authorised viewpoint which might never be openly criticised. And if anyone did attempt to upset the peace by dissent of any kind, there was a formidable array of policemen, courts, labour camps and executioners to deal with the threat. These people say: "At least you knew where you were with Stalin."

The growth of human knowledge has usually been in inverse ratio to respect for authorities of this kind. This is because the growth of knowledge depends upon the open discussion and free communication of new ideas, and upon the systematic testing of ideas to prove their worth. By contrast, traditional authorities do not welcome questioning or criticism of established viewpoints. They seek to control thought, and therefore society, in order to preserve their social and economic privileges. This is done by censorship, by demonizing criticism as "divisive," "disloyal," "heresy" or "revisionism," and by securing its punishment.

In a traditional society, information is the monopoly of a privileged few, who pass on to the majority only what it is absolutely necessary for them to know, or what it is convenient for the rulers to have them know or believe. Some beliefs are officially accredited, while others are condemned as unacceptable. Pressure is put upon people to conform by accepting the orthodox viewpoint and rejecting the heresies. Sometimes that pressure is very strong, and sometimes it can be fatal. Karl Popper has called such a society a **closed society**, since it is closed to the free spread of information.

A condition of the successful systematic development of knowledge is a society in which new ideas can be freely brought forward and openly considered and criticised. It is one in which ideas stand or fall on their own merits, not because of who supports or opposes them, or whether or not they conflict with established ideas. Such a society, where information flows freely, and where critical opinions may be stated openly, Popper has termed an **open society**.

Today most societies are partially open and partially closed. The success of the Enterprise of Knowledge depends upon resisting pressures to move towards a closed society and assisting all moves towards greater openness and the freer flow of information.

Intellectual Authorities

The danger to critical enquiry of authoritarianism is an obvious one. However, resting upon authority has many attractions. It removes uncomfortable feelings of puzzlement and intellectual stress, enabling us to rest secure in possession of "the Truth" without having to make any effort ourselves. Life as a rational autonomous individual can be confusing and tiring. People crave certainty so that they may give up their search for truth, confident in the belief that they are not missing anything desirable, since they have it already, handed to them, as it were, on a plate. Ideologies (see below Chapter Ten) provide for just such evasion of responsibility. The temptation to rely upon authority is an attractive one even for scholars, and they have sometimes fallen into the trap.

Case Study: The Authority of Aristotle

Aristotle was an intellectual giant. His approach to knowledge was always to look at the facts first, rather than selectively to seek support from them for theories already decided upon, as was the habit of many of his contemporaries.

He is said to have written one hundred and fifty philosophical and scientific treatises, of which thirty have survived. These were his lecture notes covering such varied subjects as philosophy, physics, astronomy, biology, medicine, ethics, political science and literary criticism. His scientific observations were broad but systematic, and his interpretation of them profound. He made many discoveries: e.g. that dolphins are mammals rather than fish; that the yolk of an egg is the nourishment for the embryo; that ruminants have chambered stomachs, and bees a social organisation. His observations in marine biology, made by a meticulous examination of the catches of local fishermen, were not improved upon until the twentieth century. He is responsible for originating and developing the study of logic, and achieved so much that, apart from a few minor adjustments, no major advances beyond his work were made until the nineteenth century.

It is not surprising that in Western Europe during the Middle Ages Aristotle was frequently called "the master of all who know." It was enough to quote Aristotle to settle almost any question which he had written about. Thus, paradoxically, the very success of this open-minded genius, who himself refused to defer to authorities, preferring instead to bow to the facts, became in itself a formidable obstacle to the growth of knowledge. For several hundred years he was simply too important to disagree with.

In consequence, when Aristotle got it wrong, as he did when he relied not upon his own observations but upon the general opinion of the people of his own day, scholars were reluctant to disagree with him. He thought that small insects were generated spontaneously from mud; and that earthquakes were caused by underground winds. He wrote that a woman contributed nothing to the generation of her baby except providing a place (her womb) for the father's sperm to grow in. He assumed that heavier objects fall faster than lighter ones. And for hundreds of years no one dared to disagree with those views. By the end of the Middle Ages, his very success, and the reputation this had generated, led to his becoming an impediment to the advance of knowledge.

The dangers of relying upon authority are obvious; but equally they are unavoidable. This is a consequence of the "knowledge explosion." Almost any field of study can now absorb a long lifetime of personal investigation. In order to check the accepted conclusions of experts in a single field, it takes years simply to acquire the background skills and knowledge necessary just to understand the problems, let alone to make informed judgements as to their solution. And even if we did have all the abilities necessary, and took the time and trouble, and even if we mastered all the necessary skills and acquire all the requisite background knowledge, to do this in one field of human knowledge, we should still need to rely upon the judgement of experts in all other areas.

Even experts have to rely upon other experts. The world famous biochemist relies upon the expertise of the astronomer for his knowledge of developments in astronomy; upon the expert psychologist for his knowledge of developments in psychology; and upon the expertise and skill of the pilot to land the plane which will take him to a conference he is to address on his own subject. All experts are laymen in all fields other than those of their own expertise. We are no longer able to manage without authorities, even if we wanted to.

It does not follow, however, that just because we have to rely upon the judgement of others for most of our knowledge, that we have to choose between blind faith or ignorance, between settling for knowing nothing which we cannot personally check for ourselves, or accepting anything which anyone chooses to tell us. There is a middle way, which involves making sound judgements about the reliability of those who claim to be authorities. We need to distinguish between testimony offered authoritatively which is liable to be trustworthy, and that which is liable to be misleading.

The ability to make such judgements is one of the most important skills needed in an educated person. It is a mark of an educated person that he is capable of making sound judgements about authorities, about which sources of information are deserving of respect, and which are not.

How to Evaluate Intellectual Authorities

- A claimed authority must be *identifiable*. It must be possible to identify exactly who the individual or individuals concerned were or are. Vague references to "all doctors," "many physicists" or "a leading brain surgeon" are inadequate.

  (1) Many doctors prescribe Craposan for heart, kidney, liver and brain disorders.

  Governments like to appeal to invisible authorities. They claim to have evidence supplied by intelligence agencies, which they cannot share with the public because it would compromise their operations and the safety of their agents. So we are supposed to take it on trust. This has been abused too often by unscrupulous politicians to have much credibility today.

- Authorities must be *genuine*. Appeal is sometimes made to authorities which are not genuine.

  Some anthropologists have claimed to have discovered a tribal people for whom the truth is thought to be whatever the majority of tribesmen declare to be true. In a less obvious form this may be true of any society, since we all tend to feel uncomfortable in differing from the group to which we belong, and feel the force of statements such as:

  (2) Everybody thinks that you are wrong.

  (3) Nobody believes that any more.

  Truth is not a matter of a democratic vote. If it were, then appeal to the majority would once have justified such universally held beliefs as that slavery is morally unobjectionable.

Antiquity does not necessarily imply authority. Appeal to custom, tradition and precedent, and in past ages used to have great power. This fallacy appears whenever, in response to a proposal to do something new, someone objects that it cannot be done because it has never been done before.

(4) *Headmaster*: I am afraid that your proposal is out of the question. Students at this school have never been allowed that kind of freedom before.

No doubt the students were aware of that fact. That is precisely why they were asking for an extension to their existing freedoms. What the headmaster needed was an argument to the effect that an extension of student freedom, of the type the students were seeking, would have been an undesirable change.

The converse of this, the appeal to what is modern and up to date, is more likely to be encountered today. It is assumed that whatever is new, modern, up-to-date or fashionable is most likely to be true. The most recent findings or the latest interpretation of something is to be preferred. Older experts have nothing to say to the student today. (5) See, dude, we're the new generation. We don't think the same. What you say: that's history. It's just irrelevant.

If knowledge grows cumulatively, then there is some sense in according a presumption of preference for the modern. However, the modern will one day be ancient. Since all authorities are open to the possibility that at some point in the future they will be shown to have been in error, it follows that no appeal to authority is sufficient to settle an issue finally and completely.

- He must be *competent*. We shall not usually be competent to judge this directly for ourselves. For this reason, we need to find out whether a claimed authority has been accorded recognition by colleagues and fellow-workers in his field of expertise.
  The award of titles and diplomas by universities and learned societies is designed to make this apparent. At each appropriate level the award of degrees (Bachelor, Master, and Doctor) is recognition that certain levels of proficiency in a subject have been achieved. At a higher level, distinguished professorial chairs, and awards like the Nobel prizes, are marks of approval bestowed by those generally considered competent to make such judgements. This is also true of the award of fellowships to learned societies, invitations to lecture in prestigious institutions, and publication in academic journals and by publishers of repute. Because such judgements are extremely important, governments usually regulate and monitor the institutions allowed to grant such awards. If they did not, anyone could set up a "College of Brain Surgery" or "Pilots' Academy" in a vacant building, and grant "diplomas" for a price. If this were to happen, we would rightly fear the operating table and the aeroplane flight.

- The expertise of the authority must be *relevant* to the matter in hand. Authorities are only authorities strictly within their own fields of expertise. It is reasonable to accept a distinguished biologist, a member of learned societies, holding a chair in a prestigious university, with a Nobel prize for his work on the diseases of the human eye, as a leading expert on the human eye. It would not be reasonable to assume that his thoughts on morality, history, politics, art, or how to fly an aeroplane, would necessarily carry any special weight beyond that of an educated amateur.
  Irrelevant expertise is frequently used in advertisements:

(6) Heart-throb rock superstar Jet Grunge recommends Grease-It medicated hair gel.

- The opinion of the authority must be *accurately represented*. If we are to accept an authority in his own field we must ensure that he really said what he is represented as having said, that he has not been misunderstood or misrepresented. It is what he *did* say that carries the weight of his authority; not something else that he did *not* say.

(7) After watching a very boring movie a film critic wrote: "This film was so bad that when I got caught in a traffic jam on the way home, I had a wonderful time, by contrast with the previous two hours I had wasted in the movie theatre,." The film company chose to quote from the critic's verdict in their advertisements the short phrase: "I had a wonderful time."

- The relevant authorities must be in *agreement*. Sometimes authorities are in disagreement among themselves. In such a case mere appeal to authority would be of no assistance in deciding between the rival viewpoints.

This situation is more likely at the most advanced levels of investigation, which may still be controversial. It is less likely when we come to better established ideas which have long been accepted. In the latter case, a lone voice, an isolated authority, should be treated with strong reserve. Disagreement between one authority and all the others may be because the isolated authority is out of date or eccentric.

- An authority should be *disinterested*. He should have no special interest in maintaining the particular point of view which he puts forward. Thus he should not be employed by the drug company promoting a product he is assessing. Similarly, he should not allow his religious, political or moral preconceptions and prejudices to influence his opinion.

- Authorities should be *honest*. There should be no hint of any attempt to deceive, say by manufacturing evidence. Authorities may sometimes be dishonest, and we need to be aware of that, and to develop means of detecting dishonesty.

Case Study: Sir Cyril Burt, IQ and the Missing Twins

When Sir Cyril Burt died in 1971, he was widely recognised as Britain's most eminent educational psychologist, whose studies of gifted and delinquent children, contributions to the development of factor analysis, and research on the inheritance of intelligence, brought him widespread respect. Within five years of his death, however, he was publicly denounced as a fraud, who had fabricated data to support his view that intelligence is genetically determined. Investigators had found reasons to doubt the integrity of his work and the authenticity of his results.

Burt had attempted to determine whether intelligence is inherited or the result of early environmental influences by studying pairs of identical twins separated from birth. These twins were ideal for his study, since they share a common genetic inheritance but were the products of different environments. If the IQ of these twins were highly correlated this would show that intelligence is inherited; if their IQs differed significantly, this would demonstrate that IQ is the result of environment. His studies showed a high correlation, supporting the view that intelligence is inherited.

> Two problems, however, were noticed with his research. The number of identical twins separated from birth must be very small, yet Burt always seemed to find fresh cases to investigate. Also, the correlations between IQ performance he recorded were always the same to three significant figures, which is highly unusual. On investigation, the research assistants who had actually administered the tests could not be found. They had never existed. The data they had supposedly collected had simply been manufactured to buttress Burt's claims that intelligence is inherited.

- The views of an authority consulted must be *coherent*. It would be quite irrational to accept an authority whose views were incoherent (i.e., which literally do not make sense, perhaps by being self-contradictory). In such a case, there would be no genuine position to accept. Of course, we are not entitled to regard a work as incoherent merely because *we* cannot understand it. But if an expert seems to say one thing at one point, and then subsequently asserts the opposite, that is, on the face of it, contradictory. It is up to the authority to demonstrate to us that, contrary to appearances, what he claims is in fact coherent.

Authorities should acknowledge the force of any evidence or counter-arguments which suggest that their theories are false. In this way, they acknowledge the *limitations* of their own knowledge.

Even then, the authorities can sometimes simply be mistaken. Although it is reasonable to accept the verdict of recognised authorities in their relevant fields, even if we have no comparable expertise in those fields ourselves, we should be aware that our respect should have its limits. Even experts are not infallible, and their errors may be difficult or impossible for non-experts to spot. To see the force of this we have only to consider the number of positions held by past authorities which are now known to be false: from the circularity of the planetary orbits to the existence of phlogiston. Again, the more well established a theory, the less likely it is that it rests upon some simple error or misunderstanding. But for this reason alone, no authority can be regarded as absolutely final. All positions accepted on authority are open to revision in the light of new evidence, either about the subject matter itself or about the reliability of the authority.

Famous Errors by Eminent Authorities

- "The abolishment of pain in surgery is a chimera. It is absurd to go on seeking it . . ." Dr. Alfred Velpeau (1839) French surgeon.
- "Rail travel at high speed is not possible because passengers, unable to breathe, would die of asphyxia." Dr. Dionysus Lardner (1793-1859) Professor of Natural Philosophy and Astronomy, University College, London.
- "Heavier-than-air flying machines are impossible." Lord Kelvin (1895) British mathematician and physicist.
- "Radio has no future." Lord Kelvin British mathematician and physicist (1897)

- "Everything that can be invented has been invented." Charles H. Duell, U.S. Commissioner of Patents (1899).
- "That the automobile has practically reached the limit of its development is suggested by the fact that during the past year no developments of a radical nature have been introduced." *Scientific American*, (Jan. 2, 1909).
- "Aeroplanes are interesting toys but of no military value." Marshal Ferdinand Foch (1911) Commander of French forces in World War I.
- "The foolish idea of shooting at the moon . . . appears to be basically impossible." A. W. Bickerton (1926) Professor of Physics and Chemistry, Canterbury College, New Zealand.
- "Stocks have reached what looks like a permanently high plateau." Irving Fischer, Professor of Economics, Yale University (Oct. 17th 1929) One week later the Wall Street Crash took place.
- "There is not the slightest indication that [nuclear] energy will ever be obtainable. It would mean that the atom would have to be shattered at will." Albert Einstein (1932) Just one year later, the atom was split.
- "I think there is a world market for maybe five computers." Thomas Watson, Chairman of IBM (1943)
- "That is the biggest fool thing we have ever done. The bomb will never go off, and I speak as an expert in explosives." Admiral William Leahy (1944) Advice to President Truman, when asked his opinion of the atomic bomb project.
- "[Television] won't be able to hold on to any market it captures after the first six months. People will soon get tired of staring at a plywood box every night." Darryl F. Zanuck (1946) Head of 20th Century-Fox
- "Space travel is utter bilge." Dr. Richard van der Reit Wooley, British Astronomer Royal (1956) The Russians put the first satellite in orbit around the earth during the following year.
- "There is no need for any individual to have a computer in their home." Ken Olson (1977) President of Digital Equipment Corporation
- "It's too early for a Polish pope." Cardinal Karol Wojtyla, (Oct 14th, 1978) Two days later, he was himself elected pope.
- "640K ought to be enough for anybody." Bill Gates (1981)

Scientists acan be so enthusiastic about their work that they are sometimes inclined to rush to announce their discoveries to the world, only to realise later that they had not discovered anything at all. During the last ten years, scientists have claimed to have found the genetic origins of intelligence, homosexuality, alcoholism, schizophrenia and manic depression. All these claims have been, in large part, retracted.

Appeal to authority may be a factor to be considered in evaluating a claim, but it can never be anything more than that. Nobody functions at one hundred percent efficiency all the time. We all have our "bad days," and that is true of experts no less than the rest of us.

The Authority of Print

Except for occasions when we are at school or university attending a lesson or lecture, most of us never personally meet or hear the authorities to which we defer. We come into contact with them only in print. Thus we need to be able to distinguish authoritative from non-authoritative sources in print, and to evaluate the authoritative sources.

First of all, it is important not to accept a printed work as an authority simply because it is printed. Incredible amounts of nonsense are printed each day. Among books published in the last twenty years are books which advance the claims that:

• The kings of France were descended from Jesus Christ;

• Humans are a genetically engineered race put on this planet by aliens from a twelfth planet in our solar system, called Nibiru, which orbits the sun in a vast elliptical path that brings it through the solar system once every 3,600 years.

• The moon has a surface gravity much like earth's, but NASA covered up that fact by using doctored televised transmissions of moon landings.

The very size of a written work may sometimes help blind us to the improbability of the ideas being proposed for our acceptance. For this reason, some authors pile up detail upon detail in order to distract our attention from the silliness of their central claims. An author trying to convince us that aliens landed on earth and conversed with our ancestors in ancient times, will move from ancient legend to ancient legend, from ancient city to ancient city, amassing a wealth of detailed "evidence," until we forget that no single piece is anything other than highly improbable, and become overwhelmed by the sheer mass of detail. We are led to forget that the improbable heaped upon the improbable is even more improbable.

> **THE IMPROBABLE ADDED TO THE IMPROBABLE IS EVEN MORE IMPROBABLE**

Some of the more incredible stories which appear in print are simply hoaxes.

In 1835 the *New York Sun* ran a series of articles supposedly reprinted from the *Edinburgh Journal of Science*. In these reports an astronomer, using a new, powerful telescope, reported the discovery life on the moon. Furry, winged, "moon men" had been spotted. "They averaged four feet in height, were covered, except on the face with short and glossy copper-coloured hair, and had wings composed of a thin membrane, without hair . . ." Needless to say, the *Edinburgh Journal of Science* did not report any such discovery, because it did not exist.

Others are planted as deliberate propaganda (see below). A frequently employed CIA device for "misinforming" US citizens is to plant unattributed lies or "black propaganda" in the foreign press. It is hoped that reporters searching the foreign newspapers for stories will pick them up and print them in the US press. John Stockwell, head of the CIA's Angola Task Force during the 1970s, admitted that he planted a phoney story in the African press about Cuban soldiers raping Angolan women. A few days afterwards, the story duly made its appearance in the headlines of the American press. Soviet propaganda agencies successfully convinced their people that the USA was a wasteland of rampaging, psychopathic criminals. During the 1980s they disseminated the idea that AIDS was originally a biological weapon perfected in US military laboratories which had accidentally leaked out into the general population, or had been deliberately set loose to infect and decimate the black population of the city ghettos. Much of the third world was persuaded that one or more of these stories was true. In Latin America, Soviet agents spread stories that the US was systematically abducting children in order to use their organs for rich US citizens who needed transplant surgery.

It is also important not to be impressed by what is in print because impressive words and phrases are used. **Jargon,** a special vocabulary, is properly used in order to make it easy to talk about difficult subjects. If used merely to be impressive it is often a smoke-screen for poor argument. The British philosopher, Bertrand Russell, once found himself lecturing in the USA on a subject which he had covered at Oxford under the title *Words and Facts*. He was told that Americans would not respect his lectures if he used monosyllables, accordingly he altered the title to *The Correlation between Oral and Somatic Motor Habits*. His American audience was duly impressed.

Equally, we should not be impressed by the mere presence of mathematical symbols or statistics. Some readers find such so overwhelmingly impressive as to paralyse their judgement entirely.

The business of being able to distinguish authorities in print is of great importance to students with papers to write. Marks will be lost if the bibliography contains material which is academically valueless because it is not intellectually respectable. Research students need to be aware of the different types of printed material available, and the level of authority each can be expected to carry. In research in science or history citations of works used, footnotes or endnotes, a bibliography and a reputable publishing company, are good indications of academic authority. But these are regularly imitated by the confidence trickster to give a spurious air of respectability.

HEADLINES WHICH CAN SAFELY BE IGNORED:
ALIENS KIDNAP LOCH NESS MONSTER
ELVIS PRESLEY SPOTTED IN SUPERMARKET IN STOKE-ON-TRENT
ANGELS DISCOVERED ON URANUS
GOAT FOUND SPEAKING EXCELLENT ENGLISH IN ARKANSAS

The Authority of Images

It has already been observed above that we are inclined to think that "seeing is believing." The force of any photograph or film record is much stronger, and therefore more authoritative, than the mere spoken or written word. We feel that "the camera cannot lie."

During the past century many photographs have been produced which purport to demonstrate the existence of various questionable entities, such as ghosts and unidentified flying objects. What these show quite clearly is that while the camera strictly may not be able to lie, the people who take and process photographs are very capable of deception.

It is becoming increasingly difficult to detect hoax photographs. In the past possible fakes were subjected to careful analysis in order to spot the hidden wire holding up a "flying saucer," or evidence like a shadow that would show that the object in the picture was not the size claimed, etc. Increasingly, more sophisticated computerised image processing is making it much easier to create a seamless fake photograph. Today, anyone equipped with an electronic scanner can scan an ordinary photograph, reproduce it in digital form in a computer, and then edit it in a variety of ways, producing results strikingly different from the original. With sophisticated, user-friendly image-editing software anyone can now create imaginative "photographs" at will.

Moving pictures are even more impressive to us than still photographs, and are therefore instinctively assumed to be a more authoritative and reliable record of the truth. But they may be as unreliable as still photographs, and for precisely the same reasons.

Case Study: The Alien Autopsy at Roswell

On August 28, and September 4, 1995, a controversial television program "Alien Autopsy: Fact or Fiction?" was aired on the Fox television network in the USA. It purported to depict the autopsy of the occupant of a flying saucer which had crashed in Roswell, New Mexico, in 1947, and showed close-up photographs of the "alien corpse." This "documentary" aroused considerable interest before being branded as a hoax by sceptics.

"The Roswell Incident" as came to be known, originated, on July 8, 1947, in an unauthorised press release from a public information officer at the Roswell Army Air Base, who reported that a "flying disc" had been retrieved from the ranch property of William Brazel near Roswell, New Mexico, where it had crashed. This came in the immediate wake of the first UFO sighting, a famous string of "flying saucers" witnessed by private pilot, Kenneth Arnold, on June 24, 1947. Just such sightings had long been anticipated by science-fiction magazines. The loosely expressed press release soon made headlines around the world. The young officer was reprimanded, and more precise information was then released. The unidentified flying object was a weather balloon, and photographs of its wreckage were distributed to the press.

In 1949 there appeared the first of a series of crashed-saucer hoaxes in a science-fiction movie, "The Flying Saucer," which allegedly contained actual footage of a captured spacecraft. An actor posed as an FBI agent and swore that the claim was true. The following year writer Frank Scully reported in his book "Behind the Flying Saucers" that the U.S. government had in its possession no fewer than three Venusian spaceships, together with the bodies of their occupants. Scully was fed the story by two confidence tricksters who were hoping to sell an oil-prospecting device which they claimed used alien technology.

Over the years, numerous rumours and hoaxes have claimed that saucer wreckage and the remains humanoids were stored at secret US Government facilities, for example at Wright Patterson Air Force Base, and that autopsies were carried out on alien corpses.

According to recently released Air Force files, the wreckage at Roswell in 1947 actually came from a balloon-borne array of radar reflectors and monitoring equipment launched as part of the secret Project Mogul, intended to monitor acoustic emissions from anticipated Soviet nuclear tests.

The alleged film of the alien autopsy revealed by Fox Television in 1995 was condemned by journalists and scientists for many reasons.

- There was no prior record of the existence of this film, which was attributed to an anonymous former government cameraman. It is difficult to see why the film should have surfaced when it did. No one had apparently cashed in on it decades ago, as they would have been likely to have done had it been genuine. Moreover, it surfaced despite the fact that mortal fear of repercussions from the government is supposed to have silenced all witnesses for decades.

- The film failed to agree with earlier alleged eye-witness testimony about the "autopsy." For example, informants had claimed that the Roswell creatures lacked ears and had only four fingers and no thumbs, whereas the film depicted a creature with small ears, five fingers and a thumb.

- Although the film was supposedly authenticated by Kodak, only the leader tape and a single frame were submitted for examination, not the entire footage. A Kodak spokesman told the UK "Sunday Times": "Sure it could be old film, but it doesn't mean it is what the aliens were filmed on."

- The film bore a non-military code description, which promptly disappeared after it was criticised as bogus.

- The claimed military status of the anonymous photographer was never verified.

- The "injuries" sustained by the "extraterrestrial" were inconsistent with an air crash.

- In one scene the "doctors" were dressed in white, hooded anti-contamination suits that could not have been for protection from radiation, since elsewhere they were shown examining an alien body without such suits. Nor were they for protection from unknown bacteria or viruses, since either would have required some type of breathing apparatus. It appears that the outfits served no purpose except to conceal the identities of the "doctors."

- Pathologists could not identify the internal organs removed from the bodies. While the alien seemed to have external organs much like ours, it seemed to have only amorphous lumps of tissue in its body cavities, and lacked definite internal organs.

- The "doctors" in the film used scissors like tailors, not like pathologists or surgeons. The forgers had not even bothered to use a group of actors trained in surgical instrument handling. They made no attempt to fake an autopsy, but slashed and cut at random.

- Special effects technicians noted that the alien figure was a dummy with a seam down one side. It appeared lightweight and "rubbery," and it moved unnaturally when handled, especially in one shot in which the shoulder and upper arm actually floated rigidly above the surface of the table, rather than sagging back against it as would have been expected.

- Many technical experts felt that the filming was done in such a way as to obscure the details of what was happening, rather than highlighting them; and that many of the parts of the autopsy that would have been difficult to fake had been deliberately avoided. At the most crucial moments, such as when the cranium was opened, the camera went out of focus, and the photographer usually positioned himself behind the actors so as to obscure the view.

Based on such objections, an article in the UK "Sunday Times" advised: "RELAX. The little green men have not landed. A much-hyped film purporting to prove that aliens had arrived on earth is a hoax."

Television executives have a responsibility not to mix entertainment with news documentaries in this way. Sensationalised and fictionalised accounts should not be presented as claims to fact in a way calculated to mislead the public.

Hollywood studios employ technicians in their "special effects" departments precisely in order to create illusions on the screen. The movie *Forrest Gump* shows what can be done by technicians in taking film of past events and inserting new images into them without this being obvious to the viewer. The central character, played by Tom Hanks, is shown holding conversations with several past presidents of the USA. After seeing this film, no one should be surprised at later being deceived by what appears to be genuine film footage of real events.

Authority on the Internet

With the development of electronic communications and the Internet, information is no longer the province of governments and commercial organisations, like the BBC, CNN, *The Times*, and *Le Monde*. Anyone can have a Web page, and can place on it whatever information, or misinformation, he wishes. This is certainly more democratic, and in some ways healthier, than when powerful organisations virtually monopolised all the media of communication.

But some of those organisations, although they represent government and commercial interests, may also exhibit some professionalism. They do not *usually* rush to propagate untrue rumours without making some attempt to check them out beforehand. By contrast, someone publishing his own web site, or posting to a usenet group or mail server, may have no understanding of the need to check information before publishing it. He may mischievously wish to spread false information deliberately, perhaps in order to strengthen support for his own political or religious views. Thus it is said that instead of information provided by experienced professionals, we may be faced with half-witted rumours passed on by random strangers.

With impressive web site presentation, the most unlikely material can be made to seem respectable. Edward Tenner, the author of *Why Things Bite Back: Technology and the Revenge of Unintended Consequences*, observes that one aspect of the computer age is the ability of almost anyone to prepare information which looks authoritative, with careful arrangement of texts and graphics. Tenner argues that people designing web sites sometimes "use graphics as a proxy for authority." We should remember that the most impressive graphics count for absolutely nothing when we are considering the reliability of the supposed information transmitted on a web site.

4. Propaganda

What is Propaganda?

Some testimony is deliberately and systematically contrived to distort the picture of the world we receive in the interests of some group or organisation. We call such deliberately manipulated testimony "propaganda."

Many people wish to convert others to their own beliefs and to influence their actions. Governments desire our obedience, co-operation and support, particularly when they are about to do something they think will be unpopular; political parties solicit our votes; special interest groups canvass our support; advertisers want our money; and religious groups our souls. All these organisations, some extremely wealthy and powerful, are out to convince us that their beliefs are true, that their programmes right, their causes just, their products the best. They may do this using all the media at their disposal: public speeches, posters, newspaper articles, books, movies, and radio and television advertisements and programmes.

If information is disseminated in a spirit of mutual seeking for the truth, in an open-minded manner, then there is no impediment to reason. But someone championing a cause may be so convinced of the justice of his case that he seeks to convert others to his viewpoint by any means available, while being unprepared to engage in genuine dialogue.

Propaganda is communication in which considerations of truth and reason are subordinated to effectiveness of persuasion. The aim of the propagandist is to govern or control our beliefs and desires, and hence to control our actions. Even in its mildest forms, propaganda is an attempt at mind and behaviour control.

Propaganda and Truth

To call something "propaganda" is not thereby to imply that it is not true. It is to imply that truth has been subordinated to other, non-rational considerations. Truth may be conveyed by propaganda, but that is not the point. Propaganda may be used to convey a fabrication of lies; but more usually it is a mixture of truth and falsehood, since a complete set of lies will be easy to detect, and crude propaganda is usually ineffective. The most effective propaganda messages contain a substantial amount of truth. It is precisely this element of truth which gives the propaganda its credibility, and helps us swallow the fabrications which are associated with it.

The point of propaganda is not *what* is conveyed, but *how* it is conveyed. If considerations of strict fidelity to truth are subordinated to those of success in persuasion, we have propaganda.

Governments have used propaganda since ancient times to convince us of their power and legitimacy. Totalitarian governments, which seek to control the thought, attitudes, speech and action of their people, have used all available means to achieve those ends: speech, writing, architecture, sculpture, music, ceremonial, and so on. This is evident in many of the surviving relics of past civilisations, from the pyramids and great palaces of ancient Egypt to the columns and domes of papal Rome. Religious organisations and cults engage in systematic mind-control. In capitalist societies, propaganda is most often, and most obviously, encountered in the form of commercial advertising.

In modern times, the manufacture of propaganda has been organised as never before, and placed on a scientific basis. The findings of the social sciences and psychology are marshalled to improve and refine the art of propaganda. For example, in order to assess their effectiveness, slogans and advertisements used in advertising and election campaigns are pretested on sample groups before being used on the public.

Democratic governments may use propaganda to manipulate public opinion to gain support for something which the public would not otherwise wish to do. In the most extreme case, that would be to justify attacking a section of the population, or the people of another country. In war, propaganda is used to maintain the morale of one's own population and lower that of the enemy, and to justify war crimes, sometimes in advance.

The Abuse of Language

Propaganda is always accompanied by the deliberate misuse of language. This is one of the most reliable indications of its presence. The American Nobel prizewinner Toni Morrison observed: "There is . . . rousing language to keep citizens armed and arming; . . . stirring, memorializing language to mask the pity and waste of needless death; . . . diplomatic language to countenance rape, torture, assassination; . . . the language of surveillance disguised as research; of politics and history calculated to render the suffering of millions mute; language glamorised to thrill the dissatisfied and bereft into assaulting their neighbours; arrogant pseudo-empirical language crafted to lock creative people into cages of inferiority and hopelessness."

Propagandists use words which trigger associations with others which have the power to evoke the desired thoughts and emotions, positive or negative. Words like "liberty" "security," "democracy," "flag," "patriotism" and "nation" typically provoke positive feelings; while "terrorist" or "death" will provoke negative emotions. In his book *Words that Sell,* Richard Baylan lists such words for every aspect of marketing a product, from the initially attracting the attention of the prospective customer to the close of the deal.

Such words as these are examples of **coloured language**: language which does not merely refer to something but which also induces or conjures up an attitude towards it. By using a particular word, we not only refer to something, but we also express approval or disapproval of it. Because the use of such language arouses strong emotions, we may slip from noting that the speaker is expressing his personal approval or disapproval to accepting his judgements.

In the media, labelling with coloured terms is extensively used to insinuate approval or disapproval. Approval is suggested by "a vigorous defence policy," "a staunch ally," and "a healthy economy." Disapproval is conveyed by referring to "evil ones" and "those who hate freedom."

Sometimes the context and manner in which a word is used implies a positive or negative judgement. A word which should be positive may even be used in such a way as to make it appear negative. An "activist" is someone prepared to do something about what he believes in. Citizens prepared to take an interest in political matters and play a political role are precisely what a healthy democracy needs. Since it is always used in a negative way, it is implied that a good citizen is one who is not interested in politics, and is prepared to leave these things to his betters. Today there seems to be a concerted effort to use the label "activists" to denigrate someone's position in order to dissuade ordinary citizens from taking any political action at all, thus rendering them powerless.

Language may be deliberately used to mislead or deceive, to distort or to hide the truth rather than to convey it. Following George Orwell's "doublethink" in "nineteen Eighty-Four," Christopher Ricks and Leonard Michaels have coined the term "doublespeak" to refer to language which has these functions.

One important effect of **doublespeak** is to deny what is happening, or to deny any responsibility for it. George Orwell observed: "In our time political speech and writing are largely the defence of the indefensible . . . political language is designed to make lies sound truthful and murder respectable, and to give an appearance of solidity to pure wind." For this reason, language may also be directed not merely at raising, but also at lowering the emotional temperature, as a means of concealment.

We very readily accept that totalitarian states may twist language in their propaganda. The following examples are all taken from the Western Media.

• The *Christian Science Monitor* (6/2/87) referred to Indonesian head of state, General Subandrio Suharto of Indonesia as a "moderate leader, while the *Economist* described him as "at heart benign." Yet he came into power on the wave of an outburst of organised terrorism that resulted in the slaughter of between half a million and a million people, mostly landless peasants. But Suharto was a "staunch U.S. ally" who brought "stability" to Indonesia, although running a notoriously corrupt regime infamous for its human rights violations. In this manner, the Western press toned down criticism of a genocidal criminal.

• Sometimes the speaker unwittingly gives the game away himself. In explaining the frequently used phrase "coalition of the willing" to describe those states supporting the US invasion of Iraq in 2003, General Colin Powell, (in an interview on Fox News, March 9th, 2003) said:

> **"Doublespeak"**
>
> Ministry of Defence = War Department
> police action = invasion
> air support = bombing
> incontinent ordinance = bombs that miss their target
> friendly fire = firing upon allied troops mistakenly (This is used not only to avoid stating
>   that once more *we* have killed some of our own men, it is also used as a way of
>   avoiding admitting that the enemy has inflicted some damage on us).
> collateral damage = civilians we have "incidentally" killed or injured
> elimination of undesirable elements = imprisoning or killing dissidents
> strategic withdrawal = retreat
> liberation = occupation
> ethnic cleansing = genocide
> human shields = civilians near to enemy forces (when *we* are bombing)
> diehard remnants = people resisting occupation by *our* troops
> fanatical or suicidal resistance = fighting back against *our* troops
> staunch ally (e.g. the UK) = client state which does everything we require of it
> targeted killings = government sponsored murders carried out by its accredited agents or
>   soldiers
> controlled landing = brought down by enemy fire
> acting in self-defence = the most powerful state in the world is attacking another country
> fanatics = people who oppose *our* occupation of *their* country.
> anti-American = anyone who opposes the policy of the current US Government

"Let me just say that there are a number of nations in the world that are fully supporting our efforts, and you heard a number of them speak at the Security Council the other day: Spain, the United Kingdom, Bulgaria, Italy, Portugal, the newly independent nations of the former Soviet Union. [...] *And they do it in the face of public opposition.*" [Italics inserted]

• Norman Solomon writes: "Searching the Nexis database of U.S. media coverage . . . I found several dozen stories using the phrases 'Israeli retaliation' or 'Israel retaliated.' During the same period, how many stories used the phrases 'Palestinian retaliation' or 'Palestinians retaliated'? One. Both sides of the conflict, of course, describe their violence as retaliatory. But only one side routinely benefits from having its violent moves depicted that way by major American media. The huge disparity in the media frame is a measure of the overall slant of news coverage."

• Minorities are frequently identified by association as a class when reporting crime. Muslims are frequently identified by religion, as in "Muslims Convicted in World Trade Centre Case," (Associated Press), and "Islamic violence" (*New York Times*). Yet you would never hear terms like "Jews convicted" or references to "Christian violence." Similarly we often hear of Muslim fundamentalists and Muslim fanatics, but much more rarely of Jewish fundamentalists or Jewish fanatics, Christian fundamentalists or Christian fanatics. Yet they are at least as active, influential and dangerous.

• Leaders who serve U.S. interests are invariably labelled "moderates" by the U.S. mass media. Any evident immoderate behaviour tends to be overlooked.

• Notice how 'alleged' is automatically used for all reports of carnage caused by Western forces, but not of others. When it appears that our airmen or soldiers have "allegedly" committed an atrocity, wait for the following sequence: "We don't know what happened"; "something happened but we don't know what, we must check to find out"; "it is likely that an enemy missile was the cause of the explosion"; "the enemy are firing on their own people to make it look as though our troops are committing atrocities."

•   Most important is the labelling that *never* happens:

Phrases You Will NOT Hear or Read in the US Media

US aggression	The US secret police
US terrorism	fanatical Christians
US imperialism	fanatical Jews
US nationalism	Christian extremists
US concentration camps	Israeli terrorism

God-Making

One of the most common forms of propaganda in the news is distortion of the truth in an attempt to build up the personality, character and abilities of a leader, attributing to his actions always the very of motives. This was a prominent function of fascist propaganda in the 1930s in building up the public perception of the "Leader," Mussolini or Hitler. Similarly, Stalin was the subject of a personality cult which went to extremes to glorify him. But it is sometimes used, to a lesser extent, in democratic countries.

Case Study: "The President's Vision"

At a time when he clearly had no policy concerning the Israeli-Palestinian dispute, except support whatever Israel was doing, President George W. Bush took to referring to his "vision" for the Middle East. This was immediately reinforced by other government officials and spokespersons, who would refer to "the president's vision" in awed tones, as though to some secret revelation of the truth received from above. So much was to be expected. But very quickly, supposedly independent news reporters and announcers began to parrot it, e.g. on CNN.

National emergencies have frequently been used to refurbish a politician's public image, but few have been remade as quickly and completely as George W. Bush following the terrorist attack of September 11th. The President's entire political past disappeared as the USA set itself to create, in its imagination, "the President it always really wanted":

The President's eloquence was compared to that of Churchill. "When he said 'Let's roll' at the end, I think there is a bit of Churchill in that . . ." (Chris Matthews on Larry King Live) *Newsweek's* Howard Fineman described Bush as "eloquent," "commanding" and "astute." "From where does George W. Bush - or Laura, for that matter - draw the strength for this grand mission, the ambitious aim of which is nothing less than to 'rid the world of evildoers'?"

Falsehoods

Wise propagandists know that outright lying is risky, and therefore to be avoided wherever possible in sophisticated propaganda. However, when omission and distortion prove to be inadequate to their purpose, and when the truth is too far from what it is acceptable to say, propagandists may resort to outright lies. Sometimes they cannot resist, since they probably expect to get away with it. The most extreme case of such a lie would be the lie to justify going to war to attack another nation.

Case Study: A Fictional Military Build-Up

When US President George H. W. Bush ordered American forces to the Persian Gulf, to reverse Iraq's 1990 invasion of Kuwait, one of the reasons given was that an Iraqi attack upon Saudi Arabia was imminent. Citing top-secret satellite images, Pentagon officials estimated that up to 250,000 Iraqi troops and 1,500 tanks were poised on the border, threatening vital US oil supplies.

The *St. Petersburg Times* in Florida acquired two commercial Soviet satellite images of the same area, but could find no sign of Iraqi troops anywhere near the Saudi border - only empty desert. On several occasions, a *Times* reporter contacted the office of Secretary of Defence (now vice president) Dick Cheney, for an explanation. He was simply told: "Trust us." To this day, the Pentagon's photographs of the Iraqi troop buildup remain classified.

The fictional atrocity story, often used in wartime, is an especially dangerous case of lying, because it makes the hearer justified in feeling self-righteous indignation towards the enemy, and so is liable to licence atrocities of imaginary revenge.

Case Study: Babies Torn from their Incubators

In Autumn 1990, members of Congress and the US public were moved by the tearful testimony of a fifteen-year-old Kuwaiti girl, Nayirah, before a congressional committee. She described how, as a volunteer in a Kuwait maternity ward, she had seen Iraqi troops storm into the hospital and take the incubators, ripping out of them some three hundred babies, and throwing them "on the cold floor" to die.

No less than seven Senators referred to the story during a subsequent debate on the motion for war, which passed by just five votes. In the following weeks, President Bush referred to the incident no less than five times, comparing these "ghastly atrocities" with those of Hitler.

However, reporters who sought to confirm the story after the war could not, and doubts began to arise about its veracity. Later, it was learned that Nayirah was in fact the daughter of the Kuwaiti ambassador to Washington, and had no connection whatever to the Kuwait hospital. She had been coached by senior executives of the biggest advertising or public relations company in the world, which had a contract worth more than $10 million with the Kuwaitis to "project the case for war."

Case Study: The Weapons Inspectors "Expelled" from Iraq

John Diamond wrote in *USA Today* on 8th August 2002, that "Iraq expelled UN weapons inspectors four years ago and accused them of being spies." This was taken up and repeated by many in the US Government, including President George W. Bush, over a long period of time, as evidence that Iraq had wilfully resisted UN efforts to disarmam Iraq.

But in fact Iraq did not "expel" the weapons inspectors. They were withdrawn by Richard Butler, the head of the inspection team, in anticipation of a military attack on Iraq by the USA. The facts were reported at the time in the very same newspaper, *USA Today* on 17th December 1998: "Russian Ambassador Sergei Lavrov criticized Butler for evacuating inspectors from Iraq Wednesday morning without seeking permission from the Security Council."

President George W. Bush himself exposed the falsity of this claim when he declared, in the presence of UN Secretary General Kofi Annan, that the invasion of Iraq was justified because he had given Saddam Hussein "a chance to allow the inspectors in, and he wouldn't let them in." He continued, "And, therefore, after a reasonable request, we decided to remove him from power."

The *Washington Post,* in its report of the speech, appended the following comment: "The president's assertion that the war began because Iraq did not admit inspectors appeared to contradict the events leading up to war this spring: Hussein had, in fact, admitted the inspectors, and Bush had opposed extending their work because he did not believe them effective." *The New York Times* failed to mention the president's remark at all in its report on the speech.

Case Study: Iraq and its Weapons of Mass Destruction

At the Nuremberg War Crimes trial in 1946, Herman Goering explained: "Why of course the people don't want war. Naturally. That is understood. But, after all, it is the leaders of the country who determine the policy and it is always a simple matter to drag the people along, whether it is a democracy, or a fascist dictatorship, or a parliament, or a communist dictatorship. Voice or no voice, the people can always be brought to the bidding of the leaders. That is easy. All you have to do is tell them they are being attacked, and denounce the peacemakers for lack of patriotism and exposing the country to danger. It works the same in any country."

The Lie

Before the Iraq War, the world was given repeated warnings by prominent members of the US and British governments about the dire threat posed to the world by Iraq's weapons of mass destruction. We heard reports of growing Iraqi stockpiles of the most vicious weapons devised by mankind, weapons that could be slipped easily to Saddam Hussein's "allies" al-Qaida. We heard of Iraqi unmanned aerial vehicles that could fly over the continental United States, raining death from chemical and biological weapons. We were even warned about Iraqi nuclear bombs, and frightened by the prospect of mushroom clouds drifting over US cities.

To take but a few examples:

• "Simply stated, there is no doubt that Saddam Hussein now has weapons of mass destruction." (Dick Cheney, US Vice-President, August 26th, 2002)

• "Right now, Iraq is expanding and improving facilities that were used for the production of biological weapons." (George W. Bush, US President, Speech to UN General Assembly, September 12th, 2002)

• "We know for a fact that there are weapons there." (Ari Fleischer White House Press Secretary, Press Briefing, January 9th, 2003)

• "25,000 liters of anthrax ... 38,000 liters of botulinum toxin ... materials to produce as much as 500 tons of sarin, mustard and VX nerve agent ... upwards of 30,000 munitions capable of delivering chemical agents ... several mobile biological weapons labs ... thousands of Iraqi security personnel ... at work hiding documents and materials from the U.N. inspectors." (George W Bush, State of the Union Address, January 28th, 2003)

• "We know that Saddam Hussein is determined to keep his weapons of mass destruction, is determined to make more." (Colin Powell, US Secretary of State, Remarks to UN Security Council February 5th, 2003)

• "We have sources that tell us that Saddam Hussein recently authorized Iraqi field commanders to use chemical weapons - the very weapons the dictator tells us he does not have." (George W Bush, Radio Address February 8th, 2003)

• "Intelligence gathered by this and other governments leaves no doubt that the Iraq regime continues to possess and conceal some of the most lethal weapons ever devised." George W Bush, Address to the US People, March 17th, 2003)

• "We are asked to accept Saddam decided to destroy those weapons. I say that such a claim is palpably absurd." (Tony Blair, British Prime Minister, March 18th, 2003)

• "Well, there is no question that we have evidence and information that Iraq has weapons of mass destruction, biological and chemical particularly . . . all this will be made clear in the course of the operation, for whatever duration it takes." (Ari Fleisher, Press Briefing, March 21st, 2003)

• "There is no doubt that the regime of Saddam Hussein possesses weapons of mass destruction. And . . . as this operation continues, those weapons will be identified, found, along with the people who have produced them and who guard them." (Gen. Tommy Franks, Press Conference, March 22nd, 2003)

• "Saddam's removal is necessary to eradicate the threat from his weapons of mass destruction." (Jack Straw, British Foreign Secretary, April 2nd, 2003)

• "I think you have always heard, and you continue to hear from officials, a measure of high confidence that, indeed, the weapons of mass destruction will be found." (Ari Fleischer, Press Briefing, April 10th, 2003)

• "We'll find them. It'll be a matter of time to do so." (George W Bush, Remarks to Reporters, May 3rd, 2003)

• "I'm absolutely sure that there are weapons of mass destruction there and the evidence will be forthcoming. We're just getting it just now. (Colin Powell, Remarks to Reporters May 4, 2003)

- "We never believed that we'd just tumble over weapons of mass destruction in that country." (Donald Rumsfeld, Fox News Interview, May 4th, 2003)
- "I'm not surprised if we begin to uncover the weapons program of Saddam Hussein — because he had a weapons program." (George W Bush, Remarks to Reporters May 6th, 2003)
- "Before the war, there's no doubt in my mind that Saddam Hussein had weapons of mass destruction, biological and chemical. I expected them to be found. I still expect them to be found." (Gen. Michael Hagee, Commandant of the Marine Corps, Interview with Reporters, May 21st, 2003)
- "But for those who say we haven't found the banned manufacturing devices or banned weapons, they're wrong, we found them." (George W. Bush, Interview with TVP Poland, May30th, 2003)
- "You remember when Colin Powell stood up in front of the world, and he said Iraq has got laboratories, mobile labs to build biological weapons ...They're illegal. They're against the United Nations resolutions, and we've so far discovered two... And we'll find more we apons as time goes on. And we'll find more weapons as time goes on." (George W. Bush, Press Briefing, May 30th, 2003)

Forged "Evidence"

Lies sometimes need to be backed up with evidence; and since they are lies, the evidence has to be manufactured.

A key piece of evidence that Saddam Hussein had an active nuclear weapons program turns out to have been fabricated. Documents offered as evidence that Iraqi officials had sought to obtain uranium in Africa were judged forgeries after careful scrutiny by UN and independent experts. Mohammed El Baradei, director general of the International Atomic Energy Agency (IAEA), told the UN Security Council that the claim, made by the president in many speeches and repeated by Secretary of State Colin Powell, that Iraq had tried to purchase high-strength aluminium tubes to use in centrifuges for uranium enrichment, was baseless.

The faked evidence as a series of letters between Iraqi agents and officials in the central African nation of Niger. The documents had been given to the UN inspectors by Britain and reviewed extensively by U.S. intelligence. The forgers had made relatively crude errors, such as using names and titles that did not match up with the individuals who held office at the time the letters were supposedly written.

A British "intelligence dossier" that purported to describe Iraqi efforts to evade UN weapons inspectors was largely taken from twelve-year-old PhD thesis. The author said: "Had they consulted me, I could have provided them with more updated information." Other parts were taken from several other identifiable sources. It is not so much that the "intelligence dossier" was copied from the Internet, as that what was claimed to be up-to-date "intelligence" was not.

Not only was the report not what it claimed to be, but the figures contained in it were altered to support the case for war. Thus a passage describing Saddam Hussein's militia as 15,000 strong was changed to make it 30-40,000. This raises the question of how many other figure were tampered with in similar fashion.

The Aftermath

The behaviour of administration officials after the non-appearance of the weapons of mass destruction is instructive.

Some, ever hopeful, continued to argue that Saddam did have weapons of mass destruction, and they would, one day, be found: "We are learning more as we interrogate or have discussions with Iraqi scientists and people within the Iraqi structure, that perhaps he destroyed some, perhaps he dispersed some. And so we will find them." (George W Bush, NBC Interview April 24th, 2003) The only problem was that Iraq is a country as big as California, as we were constantly reminded, and it might take a long, long time. The hope, presumably, was that people would just forget about it, so that undue embarrassment could be avoided.

Another response was: "They sent them to Syria." It was not explained how the Iraqis could have exported such massive weaponry across the border under the gaze of U.S. spy satellites and other detection devices.

Then they pounced upon the discovery of a biological agent in the possession of an Iraqi scientist. What they had found was not the tons of weaponry that Powell promised in his speech to the United Nations. It was one vial of the B strain of botulinum, not the more deadly A strain. It did not contain botulinum toxin, the actual nerve agent, only the fairly common botulinum bacteria that *could* produce the toxin. The vial had been given to the Iraqi scientist for safekeeping in 1993, and had remained untouched in his refrigerator at home ever since.

Sometimes, the lie was simply denied. Donald Rumsfeld, at a hearing of the Senate's appropriations subcommittee on defence, May 14th, 2003 said: "I don't believe anyone that I know in the administration ever said that Iraq had nuclear weapons." This could be compared with Dick Cheney's: "We believe he has, in fact, reconstituted nuclear weapons." (NBC's Meet the Press, March 16th, 2003). Again, Condoleeza Rice, on NBC's "Meet the Press," on June 8th, 2003, stated "No one ever said that we knew precisely where all of these agents were, where they were stored." This could be compared with Donald Rumsfeld: "We know where they are. They're in the area around Tikrit and Baghdad and east, west, south and north somewhat." (ABC Interview March 30th, 2003)

Another response was to assert that failure to discover the weapons did not really matter, since the war had never really been about weapons of mass destruction at all; it was a humanitarian action to get rid of a cruel dictator and to bring the benefits of freedom to the Iraqis.

Perhaps the most honest response was "For bureaucratic reasons, we settled on one issue, weapons of mass destruction (as justification for invading Iraq) because it was the one reason everyone could agree on." (Paul Wolfowitz, Vanity Fair interview, May 28th, 2003)

The behaviour of US forces is also instructive. They occupied the Iraqi National Monitoring Directorate, the archive containing all the information about Iraq's weapons systems, for a full two weeks, and then pulled out, after which looters were allowed to go in and destroy everything. It did not look as though they were seriously searching for anything. In fact if weapons of mass destruction had gone missing, the US government and military would have been desperately keen to locate them, and they obviously were not.

The Facts

We now know that fears of Saddam Hussein's weapons of mass destruction were not grounded in reality. The Iraq Survey Group, a team of 1,200 inspectors headed by David Kay, found none of the chemical or biological weapons that had been named by top U.S. officials before the war, nor any of the specific equipment, such as mobile laboratories and unmanned aircraft, they had accused Saddam of hiding. David Kay, the head of the Iraq Survey Group, grudgingly reported to Congress that he had found no chemical or biological weapons, not even a program to produce them. He had found no Iraqi program to develop nuclear weapons. He had found no evidence of unmanned aerial vehicles capable of spreading biological or chemical weapons.

We now know, if we did not know beforehand, that the leaders of the "Coalition of the willing" also knew. Iraqi general Hussein Kamel a son-in-law of the Iraqi dictator who hd defected to the West, had brought with him secret documents on Iraq's weapons programme when he had fled Iraq.

These secrets were repeatedly referred to by George W Bush and his officials as "evidence" that Iraq still had large quantities of deadly weapons of mass destruction, and that only war could disarm them. The Blair government echoed this. In a dramatic presentation to the UN Security Council on February 5th, the US Secretary of State Colin Powell stated that the truth about Iraq's nerve gas weapons "only came out after inspectors collected documentation as a result of the defection of Hussein Kamel, Saddam Hussein's late son in law".

But when a transcript of the United Nations debriefing of Hussein Kamel was obtained by *Newsweek*, it was seen to contradict almost everything Bush and Blair had said about the threat of Iraqi weapons. Kamel had categorically told them: "All weapons - biological, chemical, missile, nuclear - were destroyed." *Newsweek* reports that the CIA and MI6 were told this; and that Blair and Bush *must* have been told the truth.

In a book based upon his diaries, published by the *Sunday Times*, former British Foreign Secretary, Robin Cook, reported that when he spoke with Blair two weeks before war started, Mr. Blair privately admitted that Saddam Hussein had no weapons posing a "real and present danger." He added that Mr. Blair had appeared prepared to go to war regardless of any progress made by UN weapons inspectors.

On October 7th, 2003, Australian Prime Minister John Howard was censured by the Senate for misleading the public in sending Australia to war with Iraq. The motion noted that no evidence had yet been produced by Mr. Howard to justify his claims that Iraq possessed stockpiles of biological chemical weapons that justified going to war, and attacked Mr. Howard for failing adequately to inform Australians of intelligence agency warnings that a war with Iraq would actually *increase* the likelihood of a terrorist attack. A Green Party senator said that Mr. Howard had been involved in an unprecedented deceit of the nation and deserved censure, while Senate Opposition leader John Faulkner said that Mr. Howard had been "loose with the truth."

Of course the lie was evident to many before these damaging revelations. North Korea admits to having WMDs, and has been treated with "kid gloves." No country prepared to use WMDs would have been invaded. The weakness of the Iraqi military was well-known to the Bush administration. During the Gulf War, not a single US or Allied armoured vehicle was destroyed by enemy fire. The Gulf War hd been a one-sided massacre. General Schwarzkopf estimated that 100,000 Iraqi soldiers had been killed, (he would not estimate civilian deaths). US pilots joked about "duck shoots" and "turkey shoots." Three mechanised brigades used snow ploughs mounted on tanks and earth moving equipment to bury (sometimes alive) thousands of Iraqi soldiers in more than seventy miles of trenches. When Bush and Blair rushed to war, allegedly because of the imminent threat from Saddam's WMDs, refusing to wait for the results of UN weapons inspections, they knew that what they were doing was quite safe.

During the Iraq War, many lies put forward had remarkably short lives. They ranged from "a camouflaged chemical weapons factory," "a Scud missile inside a factory," "Scud missiles fired on Kuwait," "uprising in Basra," "a column of one thousand vehicles making its way South," "it wasn't our missile," to "Syria is supplying night vision equipment."

Jacques Ellul, in his book, *Propaganda*, states that for propaganda to be effective, it must have the ability to drown out everything else. US Government propaganda was quite ineffective outside the USA because there are still alternative information channels; including the Internet, which has become a very important alternative news source.

Dr. Josef Goebbels (Nazi Minister of Propaganda) stated that, paradoxically, to be effective propaganda, all news should be as accurate as possible and credible. The large body of truth which is transmitted is what gives gives credibility to the entire message, and so to the element of falsehood or distortion which is smuggled in with it. The rapid succession of lies used in the Iraq War breached this rule. It may have been done in the belief that the public has virtually no memory, therefore falsehood after falsehood will leave the desired inpression, whereas if the exposure of the falsehoods is played down, the desired impression will be left in the minds of the public. . Others believe that the authors of this propaganda made fatal the mistake of listening to their own voices, and so came to believe their own falsehoods.

Unfortunately, we have to conclude that, despite some constitutional "checks and balances" and protective laws, there is no trick of dishonest argument that some government leaders will not use to persuade us to assent to what they wish to do in our name; or which some politicians will not use to win a vote; which some missionaries will not use to "save" a soul; and which some salesmen will not use to sell a second-hand car. The more aware we are of the nature of propaganda, the various devices and tricks used to convince and persuade us, the better able we shall be to detect it, and the less vulnerable we shall be to its power. It is not only in dealing with claims of the bizarre, the weird and the wonderful that we need to keep our "bullshit" detector switched on. We need it in dealing with the statements of statesmen, politicians and salesmen of all kinds as well.

Unfortunately, we also need it in our reading of the news.

**WHEN YOU LISTEN TO POLITICIANS ON THE TELEVISION
KEEP YOUR "BULLSHIT DETECTOR" SWITCHED ON**

5. The News

"We are bombarded by strange paradoxes that pop up on our television screens, and then disappear without a chance for proper reflection and gestation — only the contradiction, hypocrisy, and idiocy are left behind to enrage us." (V. D. Hanson)

What we learn about contemporary events comes to us in the form of "news" by means of the media of mass communication: television, newspapers and news magazines, radio and the Internet. The picture we have of major contemporary events: who threatens us, who supports us, is provided by the news media. On a more profound level, the mass media determine our world-view. Through endless repetition they determine what is regarded as normal and where the boundaries of acceptable debate lie. For this reason, the media have the power to shape public opinion. This power can be seen in the following incident.

Case Study: The Great Martian Invasion Panic

When Orson Welles was asked by the American broadcasting company, CBS, to produce a weekly hour-long radio drama, he adapted Bram Stoker's "Dracula." Succeeding plays were based upon works by Chesterton, Dickens, Dumas, and Galsworthy. A dramatisation of H. G. Wells' novel "War of the Worlds" was planned for Hallowe'en. A futuristic tale, this depicted a Martian invasion of the Earth. In order to create greater realism for its East Coast US audience, the setting of the story was moved from Victorian England to contemporary America, and the drama was presented in the form of a succession of "radio news broadcasts." The play began with what was apparently the interruption of a music program to inform listeners that an alien had landed in New Jersey, and thereafter newsreaders described the terrifying story as it unfolded.

Welles feared that the adaptation was insufficiently dramatic, and still harboured misgivings about it when the broadcast went on the air. He need not have worried. Although listeners had been clearly informed at the start of the program that they were listing to a fictional radio drama, thousands who tuned in late to hear this believed the USA was under alien attack.

Panic soon followed, with many citizens loading their pick-up trucks with supplies of food, their children, grandma, the dog, and their guns, and then heading for the hills. Much of the population of a large stretch of the East Coast fled to the mountains to escape imminent destruction by extraterrestrial invaders.

When we read news in print, in newspapers and news magazines, we can digest in detail, and more critically, the implications of what we are being told. What news in print offers in depth, however, compared with the television news, it lacks in vividness and immediacy. Television news has a speed of delivery, an immediacy and a force which the other media lack. Of all the means of news delivery, it is now by far the most important. Because it presents images, the television news has even greater power to shape our view of the world around us, and our outlook towards it, than the radio. *CNN* actually boasts about this, with its slogan "The power of *CNN*."

For most of us television news broadcasting provides our prime source of information about the outside world. On the small screen in our homes we sometimes witness current events as they happen, and as these are explained to us by the presenters. During news broadcasts, the screens in our homes seem to function as windows through which we look out onto the wider world. For this reason, we need to devote some attention to television news as a source of knowledge. The reality, however, is not so simple. To media professionals, the belief that the news is our "window on the world" is known as the **Transparency Fallacy**.

A mature citizen, taking a conscientious and active role in civic affairs, needs to be well informed about current events, to act on the basis of knowledge rather than inculcated belief. Only in this way can his/her participation in democracy be intelligent and well-directed. Therefore, the citizen needs to be able to make sound judgements about the news, and particularly the television news.

In order to evaluate the television news it has to be realised that what we see on our television sets is the result of a long and complex process of preparation. In order to assess the reliability of the picture of the world which the news bulletins give to us, we need to understand something of that process, and of the people involved in it.

The news is not simply an account of what is happening in the world. An uncountable number of things happen every day, which never get onto the news, nor should they. The news is always based upon a *selection* of the stories available on any given day. Only what is important and/or generally interesting counts as newsworthy. Judgements have to be made about what is of long-term importance and interest to the viewers.

A useful exercise, which reveals the judgements made in creating the news we see, is to compare the relative time and prominence given to disasters involving multiple deaths from various parts of the world. How many accidental or criminal deaths of ordinary people do there have to be for them to be mentioned on the television news? One may be sufficient for local, or even for national, television in the area covered by reception. Local news is considered important by the viewers, and this is known to the programme-makers. In a distant continent, a very large number may not rate sufficient. Generally the higher the level of material culture, or the richer a society, the more likely it is that the disaster will be noted. Poor, illiterate or politically powerless people count for less on the news than richer, articulate citizens of western democracies.

The medium of visual images itself often takes over the act of choice. Action pictures are much more impressive than mere words. The choice of news items will usually include any images of fires, floods, earthquakes and plane crashes which are available, since they are dramatic. Professionals say: "If it bleeds, it leads." One of the most dramatic stories ever, in this sense, was the destruction of the Twin Towers in New York.

Everyone is aware of the practice by which governments with totalitarian ambitions have censored and distorted the news transmitted to their people. Authentic pictures of Soviet tanks on the streets of Prague surrounded by hostile jeering crowds during the invasion of that country in 1968 were shown to Soviet citizens on television. But the sound track which accompanied them was one of cheering crowds, producing a quite false and misleading impression of the reception the Red Army had received.

What is less well known is the degree to which control and even censorship, often of very subtle kinds, is exercised in the West. In some countries this is by direct government control, and in others by economic censorship: "The owners/shareholders/advertisers would not like it."

News is sometimes deliberately hidden from our gaze. The Falklands War was kept off television screens by the British government, assisted by the extreme isolation of the theatre of war in the South Atlantic. Similarly, many people had the illusion of watching the Gulf War as it was happening on CNN. In fact CNN generally showed set piece press briefings by military commanders and their publicity staff, and carefully edited film, mostly of individual "smart bombs" exploding on target. There was certainly little sign of the Iraqi civilian casualties of US bombing. Following the Iraq War of 2003, the Bush administration has censored images of dead American soldiers and their coffins returning from Iraq, as well as barring access to Iraqi hospitals to journalists hoping to estimate the number of civilian deaths.

The news bulletins which we see on the screen have been created by a team working under a producer. Judgements of relevance and significance have been made by the members of that body; decisions have been made about which topics to include and exclude; which sections of film reports to use; and of what sort of commentary to add. We need to know about the preferences and prejudices of the production team before we can judge how accurately their work reflects what we would consider an impartial picture of what is happening.

The people who make such decisions are called **gatekeepers**, because they decide what to take notice of, what to record, and exactly how it should be recorded and presented. In the process, they also decide what should *not* be take up or passed on, or *how* it should *not* be presented. In order to appear on our television screens, or on the pages of our newspapers, information and pictures alike must pass through the hands of many gatekeepers.

These gatekeepers are crucial to the process of newsmaking, for their choices of what is to feature on the news will determine what the public thinks is happening in the world. Unless a citizen is very well-read and up-to-date with current events, he/she will tend to assume that what does not appear in the news bulletins is not happening; or if it is, there are no new developments; or those developments are not worthy of notice.

> **WE TEND TO ASSUME THAT WHAT WE DO NOT SEE ON THE NEWS IS NOT HAPPENING, OR IS NOT IMPORTANT**

Present at the events as they happen, or more usually interviewing the witnesses afterwards, are the news reporters and cameramen. They may decide on the spot whether to ignore a story, which details to note, and which to pass on. This is the first and lowest level of gatekeeping.

We tend simply to assume a certain expertise in those who report in an apparently knowledgeable manner from foreign places, and therefore we accord them a certain authority. Yet the well-respected Peter Jennings of ABC News admitted on CNN's "Larry King Live" that when he first went to report on events in the Middle East he had no idea of the simple geography of the region. "I had to learn that I was in Beirut, and that Syria was over there…"

When the reporter gathers information about a story, he does not passively take down whatever people tell him. He actively seeks out information by asking questions. The questions he asks, and the type of information he is seeking, will be determined by his own preconceptions about what happened; about what is important about it.

Any story written up by a reporter will be told from some particular point of view. The choice of point of view adopted by the reporter will determine how the story is told, and how the public understands what is going on. In general, that point of view should be determined by what happened, not by the reporter's preconceptions or prejudices. But news reporters are only human, and they inevitably bring to a situation their own preconceptions, and these may influence heavily what they write. Professionals tell a story about a reporter who went out to the Belgian Congo (now Zaire) when the Europeans were being forced to vacate the country because of a popular uprising. On his arrival at Lusaka airport, he saw a group of Belgian women awaiting evacuation. He rushed up to them and shouted: "Has anyone here been raped and speaks English?" He already knew what story he wanted to get. In his mind, perhaps even in his notebook, the story had already been written, before he had arrived in the country he was supposed to be reporting on.

Even the cameramen who record events as they happen do not passively await events, recording everything that passes before their camera lenses. They already have an idea of what they want to shoot, and from what angle.

Once the material is back in the newsroom or newspaper office, it will be edited for presentation to the public. The editorial process is one of selection and rewriting. It is also one of gatekeeping. Here a choice of film material will be made, which will determine which, out of all the relevant footage available, is to be aired. Choice of footage can alter completely the impression the public gets of what happened. Suppose that there has been a political demonstration, accompanied by some violence, and the footage includes the following:

> demonstrators marching down a road;
> some vague scuffling;
> a demonstrator hitting a policeman over the head with a banner;
> several heavily armed policeman beating and kicking an unarmed demonstrator.

Which will be shown? Whatever is chosen for viewing will come to stand for the entire march in the minds of the viewers. If the viewers see only a demonstrator hitting a policeman over the head with a banner, they will come away with the impression that the marchers were violent thugs looking for trouble with the police. If they see only the police beating up a lone unarmed marcher, they will come away with the idea that the police were intent on causing a disturbance themselves, and intimidated and assaulted the peaceful demonstrators. Since a single image can be expected to stand for the entire event in the minds of viewers, their impression of the demonstration conveyed by the news programme will be determined, not by what actually happened on the streets, but by the choice of footage to use; a choice that has been made in the newsroom.

> **A SINGLE IMAGE MAY COME TO STAND FOR**
> **AND TO CHARACTERISE,**
> **AN ENTIRE EVENT FOR THE VIEWERS**

The *order* in which the footage is shown is also very important. If the shot of the demonstrator hitting a policeman over the head with a banner were to be shown *before* the policemen beating up the lone marcher, viewers will conclude that the marchers were provocative and violent, and that the police were forced to respond. If the shots are shown in reverse order, it will be assumed by the viewers that police violence provoked at least one marcher to respond in kind. In order to give the viewers an accurate idea of what actually happened, the order in which the footage is shown will need to reflect the order in which the events occurred. But the editors may not actually know which came first. They may not care. Or they may know but not care, since they may have their own ideas about "what really happened", and the impression they wish to convey

The commentary written to accompany the images, written in the newsroom, will frequently determine how the public interprets what is seen on the screen. Those who engage in the editorial process act not merely as gatekeepers, but also as interpreters, effectively letting through one interpretation of events, and blocking others.

> **OUR IMPRESSION OF EVENTS DERIVED FROM THE NEWS**
> **IS LARGELY CREATED IN THE NEWSROOM**

Also important is the **framing** of the news, the way it is presented: the amount of exposure it receives; how close to the lead story it appears; the tone of presentation: sympathetic or slighting; and the accompanying visual and sound effects."

The appearance of the studio from which the newsreaders broadcast, including the newsreaders themselves, has not come about by accident. It has been deliberately designed to create an impression of some kind. Since the news is supposed to be informative, the intention of the designers is frequently to convey sincerity and authority, to convince us that what we are hearing is reliable, and that what we are seeing is the truth. For this reason, the newsreader may wear formal clothes, adopt a serious, authoritative expression, gaze straight at the camera, and adopt a smooth, confident delivery with a detachment intended to signify impartiality, and an impersonal voice. The point of this is to convince us that the content of the broadcast is not mere personal opinion, but objective truth. Michael Parenti notes (in "Methods of Media Manipulation," in *20 Years of Censored News* by Carl Jensen & Project Censored) that television commentators, newspaper editorialists and columnists often adopt "an aura of ... authoritative ignorance, as expressed in remarks like 'How will the situation end? Only time will tell.' Or, 'No one can say for sure.' (Better translated as, 'I don't know; and if I don't know then nobody does.')" The easiest way to do this is by "palming off trite truisms as penetrating truths. Newscasters learn to fashion sentences like 'Unless the strike is settled soon, the two sides will be in for a long and bitter struggle.' And 'The space launching will take place as scheduled if no unexpected problems arise.' And 'Because of heightened voter interest, election-day turnout is expected to be heavy.'"

A more informal approach is to use two news readers who obviously like each other and interact well. This conveys the impression that the news organisation is made up of "nice people" like ourselves, who can be trusted, and who would never knowingly deceive us.

These choices about what the include and exclude, and how to present what to include, can be influenced by the prejudices of the proprietor of the company which is making the programme. The mass media of communication are expensive to set up and run. To launch a television station requires considerable capital. This is needed to employ the necessary technical experts, to purchase the expensive equipment required, etc. Thus, like most valuable products, in a capitalist society, television and radio broadcasting and large-scale newspaper ownership are necessarily the prerogative of huge corporations and wealthy billionaires. This means that the news media in most countries are overwhelmingly in the hands of the wealthy and powerful.

For non-governmental news channels, the news is not broadcast to inform people, but to make money for the owners and shareholders of these companies. This money is obtained from advertisers, so that the influence of advertisers will be taken into account in deciding what goes into the news. It is difficult to see how a commercial station would go out of its way to give due prominence to stories which showed their financial sponsors or major advertisers in a bad light. That is perhaps why we learn so little on the news, for example, about the inhuman conditions under which many of the products which we buy are manufactured in developing countries.

This is a distinctively capitalist form of censorship, exercised not by governments but by commercial companies and their wealthy owners, directors and shareholders. Censorship does not have to be government imposed, and it does not have to be crude and direct to be effective. On the contrary, the less crude it is the more effective it is likely to be. Indirect pressure exercised by special interest groups may be very effective in slanting or "deselecting" news coverage.

Moreover, since the operation of capitalism gives all the advantages in the marketplace to those who already enjoy them, in proportion to the extent to which they already enjoy them, those with the greatest capital and assets are able to use their greater resources to undercut their competitors. This leads inevitably to the development of vast monopolies.

For this reason, that pluralism of the media in capitalist countries, which is supposed to guarantee its diversity and freedom, is an illusion. Although there may be many competing television channels, and many newspapers and magazines, in any particular country, most of these may be in the ownership of a few large monopolies.

In 2000, twenty corporations around the world owned almost all the major media. Bagdikian's *The Media Monopoly* shows that just a half-dozen corporations now control most of the US media. CBS is owned by Viacom; NBC and CNBC by General Electric; the MSNBC Network by GE and Microsoft; ABC by the Disney Co.; and the Fox network by Rupert Murdoch's News Corporation. CNN is owned by the world's largest media conglomerate, AOL-Time Warner. Moreover, Bagdikian points out that we should not think of these corporations as "six," since they are interrelated in complex ways. "They own each other's stock, cooperate in joint ventures, and divide profits from some of the most widely viewed programs on television, cable and movies."

This is not a problem limited to the USA. In Australia, right-wing billionaire Rupert Murdoch controls seven out of twelve daily newspapers and seven out of ten Sunday newspapers. In the towns, he controls two-thirds of the daily newspapers and three-quarters of the Sunday newspapers. Another billionaire, Kerry Packer, controls most magazines, together with the dominant commercial television network. In Italy, the richest man in the country, billionaire Silvio Berlusconi, owns the three most important television channels, national newspapers and the largest publishing house. As Prime Minister, he also controls the three state television channels. As controller of ninety percent of Italian television, in 2003, he had a law passed which removed remaining restrictions on his right to own any other form of media in Italy

Public opinion exerts some influence upon the news transmitted. Newsreaders know that they can get away with expressions of prejudice if they coincide with a general public sentiment. In strongly nationalistic countries, expressing approval of extreme nationalist sentiments or actions will not be considered improper. Disapproval of unpopular minorities or foreign countries may be conveyed by facial expressions and tone of voice, so reinforcing existing prejudices.

This is one of the reasons why generating a sense of fear and "war fever" is important. If the country is threatened or at war, then the "pack mentality" takes over, and criticism of the government becomes disloyalty, and arouses tremendous hostility. Hitler used the burning of the *Reichstag* to enact laws which deprived people of freedom. Just after the events of September 11th, the Bush administration came up with the phrase "War on Terror." Suddenly, US news channels began to use the phrase over and over again. To many viewers of CNN, it appeared that the presenters had been told to use the term as many times as possible, or had offered a bonus to whoever could use it on air more times than anyone else. (It was also displayed in lurid colours on the screen, in case anyone watching was deaf.) This effectively united the country against a mysterious foreign enemy, and effectively deflected criticism from the government for many months.

On most channels, news time is limited, and many important events receive no coverage at all. Yet the news may report on "celebrities'" private lives, or even the birth of an animal in a zoo. These will be defended as of interest to the viewers. In this way, news coverage becomes mere entertainment. In this way it is easier to use up the time available without having to mention embarrassing developments, or without going into the stories covered so much depth that the viewers may begin to entertain doubts about the angle from which they are being presented.

Censorship

Totalitarian regimes have sometimes employed agents to work their way through television and radio scripts and newspapers to ensure that nothing slips through which might upset the leadership, embarrass the government, or compromise the party line. Mussolini used to do the job himself. Words or phrases may be changed, images vetoed, or entire stories excised before publication. Publishing houses and broadcasting companies which publish material which the leader, party or government does not like may be closed down, and their proprietors and staff intimidated, injured, imprisoned or even killed.

Except in wartime, citizens of democracies, which are thought of as "open societies" where information flows freely, are usually confident that nothing is being kept from them. But this, unfortunately, is not true. An investigation of the contents of news bulletins and newspapers will reveal that some things are effectively hidden or half-hidden.

For several years "Project Censored," based at Sonoma State University, in the USA, published an annual list of the most important news stories that the national media had failed to develop, or in some cases, failed to report at all, during the previous year. Their listing for 1998 included reports on: the finding that pollution contributed to human aggression; how twenty-one US states offered immunity to powerful corporations from penalties for violating environmental laws; how big business was systematically seeking to control the universities and colleges of the USA; a threat to the Columbia River Basin from an army plan to burn nerve gasses and toxins in Oregon; a conspiracy by US paper companies to crush the Zapatista rebels in Mexico; how blood tests had exposed the cause of the Gulf War syndrome; that law-enforcement officials were selectively targeting elected black officials for special surveillance; Russian plutonium lost over South America; and the Clinton administration's aggressive worldwide promotion of US arms sales.

The Thatcher and Blair governments, in the UK, have been particularly aggressive in attacking civil servants who inform the public what their government is doing. In an off-the-record briefing to correspondents on Dec. 3, 1986, Bernard Ingham, then the Prime Minister's press spokesman said: "There is no freedom of information in this country; there's no public right to know. ... Bugger the public's right to know. The game is the security of the state-not the public's right to know.'"

Censorship in the Western world is not usually the result of some special intervention, whereby someone from outside steps in to forbid publication or broadcasting. It is built into the news gathering and editorial processes, where decisions are made about what gets covered and how. Censorship is a function of the gatekeepers.

Washington reporter James Deakin described, in *Straight Stuff,* the process by which knowledge of the permissible limits on discussion is passed down to the reporters who go out, gather and report the news: "Their editors were salaried employees.... The reporters knew this. They tried sporadically but they could not demonstrate a full-scale alternative to the official line. And they knew that if they somehow succeeded in doing this, they would find it virtually impossible to get it into print. So they did not try too hard… It was what you call an atmosphere, a climate." In "Nineteen Eighty-Four," George Orwell wrote about the conditioned reflex of stopping short, as though by instinct, at the threshold of any dangerous thought. It includes the power of not grasping analogies, of failing to perceive logical errors, of misunderstanding the simplest arguments if they are inimical to the prevailing ideology, "and of being bored or repelled by any train of thought which is capable of leading in a heretical direction." Today's dominant news media are very good at doing this without any external censor looking over them.

Recent events affecting US media include the following:

- A columnist for the *Oregon Daily Courier*, Dan Guthrie, was fired for writing a column that criticized Bush for "hiding in a Nebraska hole" in the aftermath of the September 11th attacks.
- The city editor of the *Texas City Sun* was fired after writing a column critical of Bush's actions the day of the attacks. The paper's publisher made an apology and wrote an editorial headed "Bush's Leadership Has Been Superb."

- On September 17th, Bill Maher, host of *ABC*'s "Politically Incorrect," criticised Bush's characterization of the September 11th hijackers as "cowards"; pointing out that the label could more plausibly be applied to the U.S. military's long-range cruise missile attacks on than to the hijackers' suicide missions. Major advertisers dropped their sponsorship, and several stations dropped his show. Commenting on this at a news briefing, White House spokesman Ari Fleischer said: "There are reminders to all Americans that they need to watch what they say, watch what they do, and this is not a time for remarks like that; there never is." The White House's transcript of Fleischer's remarks omitted the phrase "watch what they say," in what officials later called a "transcription error."

- Robert Fisk reported in 2003 about a new *CNN* "Reminder of Script Approval Policy" which requires that all reporters preparing scripts have to submit them for approval. Everything that originates outside Washington, LA (Los Angeles) or NY (New York), including all international bureaus, has to go to script editors in Atlanta for approval. They can insist on changes.

During the Yugoslav and Iraq wars, foreign media criticizing the US position, or giving alternative versions of what was happening from that put out by the US and allied governments, were attacked as liars and anti-American. These attacks could be physical. In Yugoslavia, the Serbian Television station was deliberately bombed by the USAF. In Afghanistan, the local headquarters of Al Jazeera television, one of the stations most critical of Bush, were destroyed. In Iraq, its offices were bombed, and staff killed. When independent journalists began to reveal too much about the behaviour of US and British forces in Iraq, a US tank fired a direct hit into the Palestine Hotel, which killed and wounded journalists. At first, an army spokesman said that shots had been fired from the lobby of the hotel and that the tank had returned fire. But the tank had shot at the fifteenth floor.

The most common form of media misrepresentation is omission. Sometimes the omission includes not just vital details of a story but the entire story itself, even stories of major importance that might reflect poorly upon the powers that be. A major problem for the citizen is to know when he is *not* being informed about something because censorship is operating. It is difficult to know what you are not being shown or told, because you do not see or hear about it. There are, however, some ways in which the intelligent citizen can detect censorship, and working out if we are being presented with a fair and appropriate picture of events, merely on the basis of what can be seen, heard or read.

"Burying" the News

It is sometimes possible to discover a "missing story" because the media, unwilling to face the charge that they have omitted a story entirely, slip in briefly and unobtrusively, so that, if challenged, they can say that they have covered it. Thus a story which, by any standards, ought to be a major news event may be smuggled in the small print, mentioned briefly, and then it unaccountably disappears. We hardly ever notice that it has disappeared, if we ever even noticed it was ever there in the first place.

Case Study: US War Crimes during the Korean War

Faced with the increasing demand at home and abroad for a thorough inquiry into an incident in the south Korean village of Rogun-ri in July 1950, during the Korean War, the U.S. and South Korea formed a joint investigation body to probe reports of a massacre of

---

civilians by US forces there. The fifteen- month-long investigation produced a report which conceded that panicky and poorly trained American troops shot at civilians who were huddled under a bridge for shelter between July 26th and 29th, 1950. But the Pentagon claimed that there was no firm evidence that the soldiers were actually ordered to kill the civilians. There followed an expression of regret by President Clinton, which studiously avoided any acknowledgement of responsibility. A spokesman for relatives accused Washington of seeking to cover up similar killings by US troops during the war. Since 1999, information about another one hundred and sixty similar attacks on civilians has surfaced.

The Korea Truth Commission on U.S. Military Massacres of Civilians, the International Action Centre and Veterans for Peace, a veterans' group in the U.S. set up a Tribunal in New York formed of a panel of distinguished judges. Evidence presented to the Tribunal included eyewitness testimony and documentary accounts of massacres of thousands of civilians. Abundant evidence was presented concerning criminal conduct, including the systematic levelling of most buildings and dwellings in the north by U.S. artillery and aerial bombardment; widespread atrocities against civilians and prisoners of war; the deliberate destruction of facilities essential to civilian life; and the use of illegal weapons (biological and chemical warfare) against the people and the environment of northern Korea. Documentary and eyewitness evidence was presented showing mass rapes, sexual assaults and murders. The final judgment of the Court demanded that the U.S. government make full disclosure of all information about war crimes committed in Korea, and condemned the refusal of the U.S. Government to grant visas to a delegation from North Korea, charging that this was clearly designed "to prevent them from telling their story to the world."

This, you would imagine, would have been one of the major stories of 1999-2001. Yet few would have noticed it in their news bulletins. It was briefly "mentioned" by CNN in passing one day, while the "International Herald Tribune" carried several small paragraphs low down on an inside page. They had "done their duty" by mentioning it, yet had also contrived successfully to bury it.

Occasionally a guest being interviewed may refer to something which has never been mentioned on the news, but which was so important that it clearly ought to have been.

Case Study: An Unnecessary War

During the lead up to the Falklands War in 1982 the Peruvian Government offered a peace plan for a negotiated settlement, which was mentioned at the time in the media only dismissively. On May 13th of that year, Edward Heath, a former Prime Minister, remarked during an interview that the Argentinians had accepted it virtually as it stood, asking only for three very minor amendments, so insignificant that they could not possibly be refused. But Prime Minister Thatcher had rejected them out of hand. That was the only reference to this incident on British news bulletins, and Thatcher got the war that she so obviously wanted. Had it not been for that particular statement, it would not be apparent today that the war was unnecessary.

Case Study: News as Soporific

The issue of *Time* magazine for October 27th, 2003, contained a very important article by Johanna McGeary entitled "Danger Around Every Corner" about the perils facing US occupation troops in Iraq.

A graph listed the body count for US servicemen since President Bush had declared an end to "major combat operations." It analysed the tactics and nature of the resistance, and pointed to possible adverse developments in the future. It was an article which contained information which many US citizens would consider of vital public concern, as were other articles in that same issue, one which brought great credit to this journal as a making a serious contribution to in-depth news coverage.

Yet this important story was not allowed to feature on the front cover of the issue. Instead, an article on the alleged benefits of meditation: "Just Say Om" was chosen. Illustrative diagrams inside, under the heading "Calming the Mind," suggest that it was decided not to alarm the US public by troubling them about the body count in Iraq unless they were strong enough to open the magazine and choose to read the article inside. The public passing the newsstands needed instead some soporific tocalm their minds, lower their heart rate, and reassure them that all was well.

News is often a soporific. UK residents should note the calm, reassuring tones habitually used by news readers there. It says: "Bad things are happening, mostly abroad of course; but the authorities have the situation in hand, so you can go back to sleep - or the soccer match - or the soap opera."

Absent Historical Context

One of the chief forms of censorship on the media is the frequent absence of any historical context to explain ongoing news stories. Usually, news people will explain this by reference to the lack of time or space available in which to provide proper contexts. So much which is newsworthy happens each day that it is impossible to provide in depth retrospective analyses of contemporary problems. This is not generally convincing, because while there may be some genuine problem on television or radio, these do provide some in depth coverage, particularly of those events which the powers-that-be want explained in context. Moreover, considering many of the "human interest" stories included in the news, it is clear that time could be found.

CNN, for example, is very aware of the importance of background. At the time of going to press, Zane Vergee tells us several times a day: ""We show people *why* a present situation is happening; *why* a story is important to *you*." Alas, they frequently do nothing of the sort. A result of lack of context is that viewers and readers fail to understand certain stories, and so are inclined to dismiss them. It is hard to avoid the suspicion that the resulting uninterested incomprehension is precisely what such coverage is intended to achieve.

One of the most appalling running news stories is that of the ongoing struggle between Palestinians and Israelis. Yet the viewer might wait a very long time for the full background to this bitter and long-lasting dispute to be presented.

Case Study: A People Twice-Dispossessed

Almost every day we hear,in passing, that Palestinians have been killed by the Israeli army, or occasionally, and with much more outrage, that a number of Israelis have been killed by a Palestinian suicide bomber. Sometimes explanatory reference is made to the year 1967, as if the problem was created by Israeli occupation of the West Bank and the Gaza strip. Yet we never seem to be informed about the real background to this dispute, or informed that the Palestinians are not fighting to retain their land, but the poorest part of it, from which they were previously driven. Nor, when we hear Israeli government spokesmen denouncing "terrorism," are we ever reminded that the state of Israel was founded on a wave of terrorism, and that at least one of its chief terrorists became prime minister.

The origins of the intractable Israeli-Palestinian problem go back to the end of the nineteenth century. At that time, Palestine was part of the Ottoman Empire, and the Jews numbered about 10,000 out of a general population of 350,000.

During the 1880s there was a wave of anti-semitism in Russia and elsewhere. The founder of Zionism, Theodore Herzl became convinced that the Jews needed a homeland of their own. He approached various leaders and was offered land in Argentina and Uganda. At the first Zionist Congress in Basle in 1897, Eastern European Jews demanded what they called their "ancestral lands" in Palestine. Some of them had recently settled there, and their religious beliefs encouraged them to think that they had a special right to occupy it. In *The State of the Jews* Herzl wrote of a future Jewish state in Palestine: "For Europe, we would constitute a bulwark against Asia down there, we would be the advance post of civilisation against barbarism."

The idea that the Jews might settle in Palestine was a typical nineteenth century romantic nationalist fantasy. The last dispersion of the Jews had taken place in 133-5 AD. Had any other book than the Old Testament been cited as the reason for demanding to colonise land last occupied nearly two thousand years previously, it would have been dismisssed out of hand.

Herzl also wrote of the Palestinian people to be displaced: "We shall endeavour to encourage the poverty-stricken population to cross the border by securing work for it in the countries it passes through, while denying it work in our own country. The process of expropriation and displacement must be carried out prudently and discreetly." The Zionists crafted the misleading slogan: "a land without people for a people without land," and in a typical example of doublespeak, began to call the settlers "sons of the land," and the indigenous inhabitants aliens and foreigners.

Following extensive lobbying in the UK, in 1917 the government promised the Zionists a Jewish Homeland in Palestine in the Balfour Declaration. The protests of local people were simply brushed aside. In 1919 Balfour wrote: ". . . we do not even propose to consult the inhabitants of the country" and stated that Zionism's hopes for the future "are much more important than the desires and prejudices of the 700,000 Arabs who presently inhabit Palestine."

During the period of the British mandate, Jewish settlements grew steadily by the systematic buying up of land, using money from abroad, with which local people could not compete, and which left them homeless. This led to disturbances and outbreaks of fighting between settlers and local people. Immigration increased with the rise of Adolph

Hitler, provoking another rising in 1936, which was put down by the British. The settlers refused to mix with the local population, and began to demand the establishment of a Jewish state occupying all of Palestine, and unlimited right of settlement to all Jews.

After 1945 the numbers of Jewish refugees seeking to go to Palestine swelled. In order to enforce their demands for a Jewish state, terrorist activities were conducted against both the British and the Arabs, led by Irgun and the Stern Gang. Their most spectacular atrocity was the blowing up of the King David Hotel, the British military headquarters in Jerusalem, in which ninety-one people lost their lives.

Under pressure from the USA, in 1947 the British handed the problem over to the newly-founded United Nations Organisation, and announced the imminent withdrawal of all their troops from the country. The United Nations produced a compromise plan which divided Palestine into two halves: an Arab Palestinian state, and a Jewish state.

As soon as the British withdrew, fighting between the Arabs and Jews began. The Jews declared a state of Israel, and surrounding Arab states, declared war on it. Swedish diplomat Count Folke Bernadotte, the UN mediator in Palestine, negotiated a truce, which soon broke down. Bernadotte, a man who had saved thousands of Jews during the Second World War, was assassinated by members of the Stern Gang, one of whom, Yitzhak Shamir, was later to become prime minister of Israel.

Poorly armed, poorly led and poorly coordinated, the Arabs failed to recover the land taken by the Jews, who adopted a deliberate strategy of expulsion encouraged by several massacres. Most of the Palestinian villages that fell under Israeli control, about half of the villages in the country, were razed to the ground, and their inhabitants forced to flee. Some cities such as Beir al-Sab' (BeerSheba) were entirely cleared of their original inhabitants. Hundreds of Palestinians were summarily executed. This war left perhaps a million Palestinians living in terrible conditions in refugee camps in Gaza and the West Bank. Egypt took control of Gaza and Jordan the West Bank.

In 1956 the Israelis collaborated with the British and French in an attack upon Egypt after Nasser nationalised the Suez Canal. In 1967 they launched a pre-emptive attack on neighbouring states, capturing Gaza and Sinai, the West Bank and the Golan Heights. Israel then ignored a United Nations order to return the occupied territories. In 1964, the Palestine Liberation Organisation was founded as a resistance movement to recover their independence and their lost homeland. In 1973 Egypt tried to recover its lost territory, but failed.

In 1974 "Gush Emunim" (the block of the faithful) a fundamentalist movement which believes that Israel should be exclusively Jewish within its most extensive ancient borders, was established. Its members believe that they are living in the Messianic age, and that anything less than the total elimination of all non-Jews in "the promised land" is God's punishment because some Jews have become westernised and seculararised.

In 1978-9, under pressure from the USA, the Egyptians made a peace with Israel to recover the Sinai Peninsula. Palestinian freedom fighters operated against Israel from the Lebanon, provoking an Israeli invasion of that country in 1982. The UN Security Council demanded that Israel withdraw, but was ignored. Under Israeli control, right-wing Lebanese Christian forces were allowed to enter the Palestinian refugee camps of Sabra and Shatilla, where they massacred between four and eight hundred Palestinian civilians.

By the Oslo Agreement of 1973, Israel and PLO agreed to mutual recognition. It was agreed that Israel would withdraw from the West Bank and Gaza, and the PLO would renounce terrorism and recognise Israel's right to exist. The Israelis withdrew from a small area given up to Palestinian sovereignty, another area dceded only to Palestinian civil control, and retained total control over a third part of the country. They did not dismantle settlements, instead, they increased and expanded them. So Palestinian groups did not renounce their goal of destroying Israel, and continued to finance and sponsor resistance activities.

In 1975, the United Nations formally recognised Zionism as a form of racism. At the Camp David Agreement, the leadership of the PLO decided to compromise and accepted the right of Israel exist, in effect accepting the loss of most of their own homeland. The occupation and settlements continued, and the first *Intifada*, or popular resistance, began in 1987. In 1995 Israeli prime minister Yitzhak Rabin, who had decided to move in favour of "compromise," was assassinated by a right-wing Israeli. Since then, things have gone from bad to worse. In March 2002, Saudi Prince Abdullah proposed a peace plan, according to which Israel would withdraw from the occupied territories in return for Arab recognition. It was not taken up.

It seems clear that the Israelis have no intention of simply withdrawing from the territories they have occupied. Having obtained half of their land from the Palestinians in 1948, they would appear, since that time, to have been about the business of taking the rest. The Israeli government has siezed over seventy per cent of the land on the West Bank and thirty per cent of Gaza, usually the best land, and have taken total control over Palestinian water resources. New settlements have been made in Palestinian territory by religious extremists, guarded by the Israeli Army. These, and the roads built to connect them, further split up Palestinian territory.

Since 1967, more than an eighth of the population of the West Bank and Gaza have been imprisoned, many for periods of up to twelve years, with no charges being brought against them, often for years at a time. Palestinian prisoners are routinely subjected to psychological torture, or forms of physical torture that do not leave visible marks. Interrogations are conducted to expose the victims weaknesses, to undermine their resistance, induce fear and degradation, and to recruit informers. The death squads of Shin Beth, the Israeli secret police, murder at will. In addition to "official" oppression, Israeli settlers on the West Bank constantly harass the Palestinians, uproot their olive trees, destroy their property, and commit murders with impunity.

With the destruction of the economy, Palestinian farmers have had no alternative but to work for Israelis in menial jobs at rates of about half the pay of Jewish workers in comparable jobs. Palestinian workers are forbidden to sleep near their work places, and are forced to travel an average of one hundred kilometres a day, forbidden to set up labour unions, and forced to pay part of their salaries into a fund held by the Israelis, for which they provide no accounts, and from which no Palestinian has ever received any benefits.

The Israeli Army periodically blockades the West Bank, and closes universities and schools for extended periods. Democratic institutions have been subjected to systematic destruction. The last municipal elections were held over twenty years ago. The Israeli government dismissed the elected representatives and replaced them with Israeli officials.

Palestinian municipal leaders have been systematically dismissed, exiled or assassinated. Up to 1991, more than a thousand leading Palestinians have been exiled.

Every detail of day-to-day life is subject to bureaucratic controls, creating enormous psychological pressures. The simplest matters, like harvesting the olives on one's own land, must be approved by Israel's military regime. The constant threat of harassment curfews, arbitrary arrest, road blocks and murder, plague Palestinian daily life, and have forced the population to retreat behind closed doors as darkness falls. People have been forbidden to go to the seaside, to pray in holy places, or to take walks in the mountains. The few places of entertainment have closed down.

These measures, which seem to echo those taken against Jews in Nazi Germany during the 1930s, have generated a climate of fear, anxiety, depression and frustration. Simply to go on living under these conditions demands a high degree of personal courage. Today, Israel's policy seems to be to convince Palestinians that they have no rights or security in their own land, and to make life so unendurable for them that emigration would be the only way out. Not surprisingly, many have opted for that solution.

Now a wall is being built around the West Bank, snaking deep into Palestinian land, incidentally destroying several important archaeological sites. The Israeli plan is clearly that any Palestinian settlement which remains will be inside what are effectively "reservations" *within* Gaza and the West Bank.

It is a paradox that the people whose land Israel has occupied, and who have been so mistreated for such a long time, and who are now struggling for their freedom, are regarded by US president George W. Bush and many US citizens as "terrorists" like al Qaeda. It is also a paradox that Zionists react to all criticism of their excesses by accusing their critics of anti-Semitism. It is clearly not in the interests of the Jewish people, many of whom disagree profoundly with what is being done in their name in Palestine, that their Zionist brethren should "muddy the waters" in this way.

The News as Propaganda

The use of news as propaganda by a democracy can be seen clearly in its employment during the Cold War, a period of mutual hostility and "warfare by any other means", including psychological warfare. The principles which governed US anti-Communist propaganda were explained by agents of the United States Information Agency (USIA), which ran the CIA funded radio station, the *Voice of America* to Leo. Bogart, and published in his *The US Information Agency's Operating Assumptions in the Cold War*

The policy of the USIA was not to confront the claims of Communist ideology directly: "the hard-hitting and anti-Communist approach just doesn't pay off. The more subtle you do it the better it does. The US always comes off better when it does something in an educational way rather than in a horn-tooting way." The reasons given for this include the rather surprising confession that "USIA will be beaten if it engages the Communists in direct combat." Instead, the USIA should create the impression that Communism is undemocratic, impracticable, aggressive, alien, a deadly menace to our most cherished values and institutions, yet also, at the same time, profoundly ridiculous. It was certainly successful in the USA, for American public opinion is almost entirely summed up by this view of Communism. Moreover, "We could state a Soviet position only as a prelude to a rebuttal."

The USIA was to work to create a favourable disposition towards the USA, so that when things happened that threw the USA into a bad light, there would be less desire to believe them. So, the USIA set itself to oppose such popular negative stereotypes as that the USA is an undemocratic, stratified class society, abusive of racial minorities; that Americans are a barbarous people, lacking in culture; and that US policy is imperialistic, and geared to the use of force. In order to counter these impressions, the *Voice of America* was consistently to present US citizens as cultured, generous and altruistic people, who sincerely desire the freedom of all the other peoples of the world; that the USA is a peaceful, democratic, classless society, where the various races live harmoniously and happily together; and that the US economy is the most successful in the world.

Today governments and military forces employ public relations managers, popularly called "spin doctors," to "manage" the news for them. They give advice on when and how to make announcements, so as to create the best possible impression of themselves and their work. They seek to **spin** the news, that is, so to manage it that the desired "angle" or interpretation of events they wish people to accept is adequately conveyed to the public. They systematically trumpet government achievements, while doing their best to play down, excuse or hide, government failures. Thus a "spin doctor" in Downing Street is reported as saying on September 11th, 2002, following the attack on the two towers in New York, that any really bad news the government had should be released immediately. The implication was that at that time no one would notice it.

When trying to understand what is really going on in the world, you have to take account of the work of the spin doctors, and allow for the fact that the news, as presented to you, has been through a long process of "doctoring" so as to generate certain impressions and reinforce certain beliefs and attitudes.

> ## IN ORDER TO UNDERSTAND THE NEWS
> ## YOU WILL NEED YOUR "BULLSHIT DETECTOR"

In their book *Manufacturing Consent*, Noam Chomsky and Edward Herman propose a Propaganda Model as the best way to understand the Western media generally: " ... they serve to mobilize support for the special interests that dominate the state and private activity, and that their choices, emphases, and omissions can often be understood best, and sometimes with striking clarity and insight, by analysing them in such terms."

News Media as "Fronts" for Government Agencies

Newspaper reporters sometimes actively work for, and may actually be paid by, government espionage and intelligence organisations.

In 1991, Richard Norton-Taylor of the *Guardian* revealed the existence of some ninety UK journalists and broadcasters, many in senior positions, in the pay of the CIA. In 1985 *The Observer* exposed a secret process the headquarters of the BBC World Service whereby the names of applicants for editorial jobs were routinely passed on to MI5 for "vetting." Journalists with a reputation for independence were refused employment because they were not considered "safe." This practice had been going on for forty years.

Many journalists willingly act as agents for intelligence organisations for no pay at all, but simply because they feel flattered to be employed by them. In his autobiography, *News from the Front*, ITN newscaster Sandy Gall boasted of his MI6 contacts, and of the work he did for them.

> **IT HAPPENED IN THE PAST,**
> **AND WE DID NOT KNOW ABOUT IT;**
> **WE HAVE NO REASON TO SUPPOSE**
> **THAT IT IS NOT HAPPENING NOW.**

Of course it is a problem when *our* reporters act on behalf of *their* espionage agencies. When the *Times* of London, reported, in 1994, that Richard Gott, editor of the *Guardian*, had accepted trips from the Soviet Embassy in London, it protested: "The Gott affair has resurrected the pernicious doctrine of moral equivalence between the West and the Soviet Union. It has been suggested that Mr. Gott's links with the KGB were no different to reporters' contacts with Western intelligence. The two are not the same. Many British journalists benefited from CIA or MI6 largesse during the cold war; none was supporting a totalitarian regime devoted to the overthrow of their own country. . .". Journalist John Pilger points out that the comment that many British journalists were paid by the CIA and MI6 during the cold war is itself "an astonishing admission."

The "Staging" of News Events

Events are frequently deliberately "staged" in order to create the right effect on the television screen. Among recent examples are the following:

* The famous toppling of the statue of Saddam Hussein when US forces occupied Baghdad was designed to bring back memories of previous popular uprisings in Eastern Europe. This contrived media event was staged just opposite the Palestine Hotel where the international media were based. CNN warned viewers in advance that "something" might happen, and cameras were trained on the statue for some time before about fifty Iraqis appeared, led by one of their number jumping up and down with improbable glee, and followed by what looked like a larger number of journalists and cameraman. They later tried to tear down the statue, but had to give way to US troops with tanks and armoured vehicles who just happened to be in the vicinity.

  A famous wide angled shot of this event reveals that at most around two hundred people were present in a largely empty square: and most of those were journalists, while the square was cordoned off by US forces, presumably to prevent the arrival of any genuine Iraqis, whose responses might not be predictable, from interfering and spoiling the effect. The BBC website at least had the honesty to report that "dozens" of Iraqis were involved. In a remarkable twist, it was reported that a US flag placed on the face of the statue by marines was the very flag which had been flying over the Pentagon on September 11 when it was attacked. This wild *non sequitur* was a deliberate and obvious attempt to reinforce the impression that the US attack upon Iraq and the attack of September 11th upon the US were somehow connected.

* When George W. Bush declared combat operations over, he was flown onto the deck of the USS Abraham Lincoln to do so, his small S-3B Viking jet making a tailhook landing. Although he did not actually pilot the aeroplane, he emerged from it dressed in a full-combat "Top Gun" flight suit to deliver his speech. With the sea as his backdrop, Bush announced that the United States and its allies had prevailed against Saddam Hussein. The landing was widely televised and received extensive media coverage throughout the day.

  Soon pertinent questions were being asked about this performance. Since a simple helicopter arrival would have been sufficient, as the ship was lying some forty-eight km off San Diego, why did he have to arrive by jet? Why, indeed, not wait for the ship to dock? Why fly out at all? Navy officers had slowed and turned the ship when land became visible from the deck to preserve the illusion of being out at sea. White House Press Secretary Ari Fleischer said that the president had arrived that way because he wanted "to see an aircraft landing the same way that the pilots saw an aircraft landing. He wanted to see it as realistically as possible." Democrats on the House of Representatives Appropriations Committee said that the cost of the presidential photo-opportunity could top a million dollars: including delaying the USS Lincoln, an extra day of air patrols, keeping the crew at sea, presidential security and flying Bush to the ship.

Double Standards

One sure way to detect bias and propaganda in the media is by identifying the application of double standards.

Case Study: Civilian Passenger Planes Shot Down by Military Action

One night in 1983, a Korean passenger airliner, KAL007, flew off course, deep into Soviet territory above sensitive military installations. A Soviet interceptor plane shot it down. The Soviets claimed that they believed it to be a military aircraft on a spy mission.

The Western press condemned the downing of the plane as an outrage. The "New York Times" editorial was headed "Murder in the Air", and asserted unequivocally that "There is no conceivable excuse for any nation shooting down a harmless airliner." Other editorials used phrases like "wanton killing" and "reckless aerial murder." Television coverage followed suit. The most famous news presenter in the USA, Dan Rather, called it a "barbaric act."

Five years later, on July 3rd, the USA shot down an Iranian airliner, Iran Air flight 655, killing 290 people. The circumstances were very different. The Iran Air jet was not overflying a sensitive area of the USA during the night. It was shot down in broad daylight on the far side of the globe from the USA, well within its approved commercial airline route, over international waters in the Persian Gulf.

Yet no equivalent outrage was evident on this occasion. The "New York Times" editorial said that "while horrifying, it was nonetheless an accident," and concluded, "The onus for avoiding such accidents in the future rests on civilian aircraft: avoid combat zones, fly high, acknowledge warnings." Many reports expressed sympathy not for the dead passengers and their families, but for the "plight" of the man who had shot the plane down, Capt. Will Rodgers III of the U.S.S. Vincennes, whose picture appeared in the newspapers with headlines like "Captain's Anguish" ("Newsday") and "Captain's Agony" ("New York Post").

A greater crime than the actual shooting down of the airliner seemed, to many US journalists, to be the reluctance of the Iranian government to simply forget about it and say nothing. They claimed that the Iranian government would be eager to exploit the event for propaganda advantage. Tom Fenton on CBS Evening News complained that the Iranians seemed intent on making sure the event would not slip from the world's front pages. "Times" correspondent R.W. Apple, Jr. headlined his analysis of the event "Military Errors:

The Snafu as History." (5/7/88) He observed that "the destruction of an Iranian airliner . . . came as a sharp reminder of the pervasive role of error in military history."

When the other side does it, it is a "barbarous crime," deserving universal condemnation. When we do it, under circumstances which have even less excuse, it is merely a "tragic error" about which it would be unreasonable to complain.

Limiting the Range of Debate

Censorship frequently functions by restricting any debate to views which are within what are considered by the authorities to be acceptable limits. This has the double advantage of imposing censorship of unacceptable opinions, while maintaining the appearance of fostering debate, and of giving equal airtime to opposing points of view. A "contest" is set up between speakers representing different points of view, but the speakers chosen will not cover the entire spectrum, only the range of views considered acceptable.

The right wing of discussion is usually represented by a committed supporter of right-wing causes, someone who calls for significantly change in the *status quo* in a reactionary direction. The left wing of the debate is often represented by a centrist who supports maintaining the status quo, and only very rarely a genuine radical. Speakers representing opposition to the established viewpoint will tend to be rather moderate, toned-down, weak, or ineffectual.

Gore Vidal testified: "I was made aware of the iron rules in 1968, when William F. Buckley, Jr., and I had our first live chat on ABC at the Republican convention in Miami Beach. Buckley Junior's idea of a truly in-depth political discussion is precisely that of corporate America's. First, the Democrat must say that the election of a Republican will lead to a depression. Then the Republican will joyously say, Ah Hah, but the Democrats always lead us into war! After a few minutes of this, my attention span snapped. I said that there was no difference at all between the two parties because the same corporations paid for both, usually with taxpayers' money, tithed, as it were, from the faithful and then given to "defence," which in turn passes it on to those candidates who will defend the faith. . . Although my encounters with Buckley Junior got ABC its highest ratings, I was seen no more at election times. Last year, Peter Jennings proposed to ABC that, for old times' sake, it might be a good idea to have me on. "No," he was told. "He'll just be outrageous.""

During the Vietnam War there was a lively debate in the US media between "doves" and "hawks" over the rights and wrongs of the war. This was supposed to be an indication of the open and free nature of the US media. The hawks would argue that if we persevered, we could win. The doves would protest that we could not win, even if we tried. It would costly too much, and it would involve a lot of killing. Both sides, however, doves hawks, would agree that the USA had a right to be in South Vietnam, and that it had got itself there for the very noblest of reasons..

Anyone who thought that the USA was not defending South Vietnam, or democracy and freedom, but was engaging in a ruthless imperialist war, was barred from the debate. For this reason, there was no genuine debate over the ethics of the war, whether it was right or wrong, only about the tactics, whether it was convenient and desirable, or inconvenient and undesirable.

Unfair Balancing

In addition to the above, other means may be found of "loading the scales" in what is given all the appearance of a fair debate.

- The two sides may not be accorded equal prominence. "One study found that on the most liberal of the mainstream media, right-wing spokespeople are often interviewed alone, while liberals appear less frequently, and almost always paired against a conservative. Radical views are normally shut out entirely.

- Because a standard context, or no context at all, is needed to present the generally accepted view of some particular problem, significant time is required by a speaker with views not usually expressed in order to present an alternative viewpoint in a convincing manner. But news programmes usually have small time slots for interviews, so that there is insufficient time for alternative views to be convincingly expounded. The usual reason given for this, that the public is incapable of sustained attention on any topic for more than a few minutes, suggests a contempt for the public on the part of media managers.

- A spokesman with a thick accent may be chosen to represent an unpopular viewpoint. The majority of viewers will not be watching very attentively. They are probably doing other things at the same time. If something is difficult to follow they will tend to "tune out" for a while, so they will simply fail to hear his arguments. During the NATO bombing of Serbia, the Serbian position was usually represented by someone with a thick accent, whose English was difficult to follow without a real effort. Then, one day on *CNN*, a speaker appeared representing a Serbian group in England. A longtime UK resident, he spoke with no detectable accent, and in addition, he was a devastating controversialist, who questioned the presuppositions of the NATO position very effectively. We never saw him again.

- The bias of the media may be detected in the difference between the attitude of the interviewer to each interviewee. One may be treated with respect, even servility, and an understanding approach to his difficulties. By contrast, a hostile attitude may be adopted towards the other speaker, who may be interrogated abruptly, and constantly interrupted in mid-sentence in a hostile manner. The irrelevant answers of one speaker may be heard out respectfully, while the other is curtly reminded to "answer the question."

Inconsistencies

The presence of inconsistencies is an indication of propaganda. The inconsistencies may be in the supposed facts as reported.

- US military spokesmen make a point of assuring the world, during attacks on other countries, that meticulous care is always taken to avoid hitting civilian areas by the use of very sophisticated "smart technology." Yet some missiles have failed even to land in the country at which they were aimed. Missiles in the Kossovo campaign landed in Bulgaria. Missiles in the Iraq War managed to fall in Iran, Saudi Arabia and Turkey. If they cannot find a country properly, it seems a little overambitious to claim that these missiles can avoid civilian casualties.

- During the Iraq War some places were "liberated" several times. Thus Basra was "secured," followed by an admission that though the British had indeed "secured" it, they hadn't actually captured it. The US Marines who were said to have "secured" Nasiriyah several days before they "captured" it.

- The author recalls seeing on CNN recently a spokesman for the US administration explaining how lucky the Iraqis were that Saddam Hussein had been overthrown by the "Coalition of the willing." In illustration, he pointed out that Iraqi citizens had no longer to fear "the knock on the door in the middle of the night." It would have been very effective - except that within two minutes we saw US soldiers kicking in the doors of Iraqi houses in the middle of the night. Of course, they were searching for evildoers; but no doubt Saddam's men would have said the same. In any event, the terrified children hiding behind their mothers while shouting armed soldiers forced their father to lie on the floor while they bound his hands and dragged him away "for questioning" would be hard pressed to see the difference.

The News as a Means of Social Control

Walter Lippman said in 1921 that the art of democracy requires "the manufacture of consent." Noam Chomsky has taken this up to explain the function of the news media in the USA today. In some states the powerful are able to control the people by the use of brute force. In others, supposedly democracies, they cannot do this for it would give away the illusion of "rule of the people by the people and for the people"; so they must achieve their aims by controlling what the people think, so that they freely consent to the controls on behaviour which, in totalitarian states, are imposed by force. This "manufacture of consent," is what George Orwell called with more English bluntness "thought control."

It has proved very successful. The majority of US citizens today probably accept whole-heartedly that the USA is the freest country in the world (although they probably know little about any other), governed only by laws made by the citizens themselves. They believe that in their electoral process they have a genuine choice between real alternatives. They rarely stop to consider how limited their choice, usually between two alternatives; and how "safe" for the powers that control US political life this choice is; or the mechanisms by which this restriction of the political agenda has been achieved. Gore Vidal wrote that "The corporate grip on opinion in the United States is one of the wonders of the Western world. No First World country has ever managed to eliminate so entirely from its media all objectivity - much less dissent."

How to Watch the News Intelligently

- Look out for "coloured language."
- Look out for selective treatment of events.
- Look for "missing" or "buried news."
- Look out for missing background.
- Look for inconsistencies in the news presented.
- Look for lack of balance in treatment of events and speakers
- Look for propaganda presentations under the guise of reports
- Look for value judgements in the newscasters' asides, tone of voice or demeanour.
- Ask why the studio is decorated in the way it is.
- Ask why the newscaster(s) dress and speak in the way they do.
- Ask what message the computer generated graphics and musical background are intended to convey.
- Look for attempts to bully criticism of standard viewpoints into silence as "unpatriotic"; e.g. "Are you accusing the President of the United States of . . . ?"

Glossary

authority: someone recognised to have considerable knowledge and expertise in a field, and so someone whose judgement will be reliable and capable of settling questions.

closed society: a society in which the transmission of information is rigidly controlled, and in which criticism of established views is forbidden.

coloured language: language which does not merely refer to something but which also induces a positive or negative attitude towards it.

consistency: lack of internal coherence.

evidence: the data on which a judgement or conclusion might be based or probability established.

gatekeepers: those who decide what news of events and developments is released to the public in news broadcasts, and the "spin" that is put upon it.

hearsay: what one does not know directly, but only by being told by others.

jargon: a specialist or technical vocabulary.

layman: one who can claim no special authority or expertise in some field.

open society: a society in which the transmission of information is not controlled or impeded, and in which criticism of established views is freely allowed.

propaganda: organised persuasion by some group in which considerations of truth and rationality are subordinated to effectiveness of persuasion.

pseudo-facts: commonly held false beliefs.

rumours: stories of doubtful accuracy which spread quickly and widely.

spin: putting an emphasis on a story that is favourable to government or corporate sponsors and acceptable to the owner of the media organisation concerned, so that it leaves the public with an impression of what is happening that is acceptable to them.

urban legends: widely recounted and believed but false stories.

6. REASON

"He who cannot reason is a fool; he who will not is a bigot; he who dare not is a slave."

(W. Drummond)

1. What is Reasoning?

A school prize was awarded in the Greendales School each year for the student in the senior grade who had gained the highest overall marks in all subjects. The headmaster of the school happened to pass Duncan in the corridor one day when it was empty, and told him in confidence that although the results had not been officially published, he had won the prize. Later that day Duncan happened to read in the newspaper that a millionaire who had been born in the city had decided that year to award an extremely valuable prize for the student in the senior grade with the highest overall marks in all subjects in all the schools in the city, and that the prize was going to a student in the Greendales School.

We now know what Duncan also then discovered, that he had won the valuable prize to be awarded by the millionaire. But how? His award had not been announced. Duncan "put two and two together," as we were able to do. He took two separate pieces of information he had been given:

(1) Duncan had won the prize awarded in the Greendales School that year for the student in the highest grade who had gained the highest overall marks in all subjects.

(2) A prize had been awarded by a millionaire for the student in the senior grade with the highest overall marks in all subjects in all the schools of the city, and that prize was going to a student in the Greendales School.

From these facts we were able to reasoned a third, namely that:

(3) Duncan had won the prize awarded by the millionaire.

Aristotle said: "Man is a rational animal." He has a capacity to reason, a power to connect items of information, learned from direct sense-experience or through the testimony of others, and draw from them new conclusions, so extending his knowledge and understanding. This is something which we do all the time, at every level from casual everyday thought to highly complex academic work. If someone discovers one hour before shop closing time that there is no milk in the refrigerator, he may reason that if he wants milk in his tea, he had better go out and get some before the shops shut, i.e. within the hour. The detective reasons that since there was no sign of forcible entry from outside and no alarms were activated, the bank was robbed by, or with the help of, one or more of its own employees equipped with all the necessary keys and the codes needed to disarm the alarm system. These are both examples of reasoning.

It is important to note that not all of our thinking is reasoning. Much of the time a person is simply reacting to his environment. He observes that:

(4) It is cold this morning.

(5) There is no more coffee in the packet.

(6) What a pity I forgot my brother's birthday yesterday.

(7) Wow! The European basketball final is being played off later today!

It is only when a person reflects on his experience that reasoning comes in. He starts to reason when he says to himself:

(8) If I go out I will have to put a coat on because it is cold outside.

(9) If I want some coffee, I will have to go out to the supermarket.

(10) I had better get something for my brother's birthday, or he will make a fuss and my parents will be angry with me.

(11) I want to see the European basketball final. I will be able to watch it on the television.

The processes of reasoning involved, spelled out in the example below, are often below the level of consciousness.

(12) I forgot my brother's birthday yesterday

He will be upset about it.

When he gets upset he makes a fuss.

When he makes a fuss, this upsets my parents.

My parents will probably be angry with me.

Only if it is difficult or complicated, or if our conclusions are challenged, do we become aware of the processes of our reasoning. Then we begin to think reflectively. We start to think *about* our thinking. This is what we shall be doing in this chapter.

Efficient Reasoning and Logic

Reasoning is an activity, and like any activity which is directed towards some end, it can be done well, so that the end is likely to be achieved, and achieved efficiently, or badly so that it is not.

We can reason in a vague, muddled and shallow way, never settling for any length of time on any single issue, but darting here and there as the fancy takes us. People who habitually think like this are said to have "butterfly minds." They flit from one point to another, considering any issue only very briefly, without absorbing anything or making any real progress. They are rather like someone slumped exhausted in an armchair at the end of the day, idly zapping through the television channels with the remote control, taking in only vague impressions. By contrast, we should aim to think clearly, focusing upon the relevant and important points at issue, and making an effort not to drop them until some genuine progress has been achieved.

The difference between being able to reason well and reasoning badly is an important one. In everyday thought it is usually considered to be one of the most important differences between intelligence and stupidity. In order to think critically and reason well, it is necessary to focus our attention upon the processes of reasoning itself, which are usually transparent to us. Only in this way can we analyse the quality both of our own reasoning and that of other people.

Generally, some attention and training is required in order to improve performance in any activity if it is to be done well. There is no reason to suppose that reasoning is any different. There are normally three ways in which we improve a skill. Firstly, we need to know some facts about the goal which we are aiming for, and we need to know what is necessary to perform the skill well. Then we need some practice in attempting to achieve that goal. The name for the body of knowledge about reasoning, the exact ends to be achieved and the means of getting there, is **Logic**. Logic is the study of the principles of sound reasoning.

A special logical vocabulary enables us to think more precisely about our reasoning: "argument," assumption," "inference," "conclusion," "criterion," "evidence," "relevance," "prejudice," credibility," "ambiguity," "objection," "support," "bias," "justification," "contradiction," "consistency," "thesis." We are in a better position to assess the efficiency of reasoning, both our own, as well as that of others, when we can use this vocabulary with accuracy and ease.

Arguments

The reasoning for or against a particular position or thesis is called an **argument**. In every-day speech we often use the word "argument" for a dispute or verbal contest, for arguments *with* other people; but the word is also used for a set of statements which might be used to support or attack someone's position. In this case we are not interested directly with arguments which people *have with* other people, we are concerned with arguments which people *present to* others. These are used when attempting to establish or argue that something is true, or when attempting to show that something which someone else has claimed, and perhaps argued to be true, is in fact false. In this sense, argunemnst are used to make out a case for something, or to attack a case that someone else has made.

Since the purpose of putting forward an argument is to persuade other people, arguments usually have two sides to them: a logical aspect and a rhetorical aspect. Logic concerns those features of an argument which should convince any rational person to the extent that he is genu-inely rational. **Rhetoric** is concerned with personal appeals to the people to whom we are actually presenting the argument, such as appeal to the hearers' special interests and prejudices, the use of personal charm to persuade, and "window dressing." Clearly, the rhetorical aspect dominates in propaganda. In serious academic work the rhetoric should usually be either suppressed or ignored as irrelevant. Effective rhetorical devices are usually effective impediments to reasoning. That is precisely why they are used, deliberately to befuddle our powers of reasoning.

Arguments, considered from a logical point of view, are sequences of statements which are linked together in such a way that some of them provide the support for others. We infer one statement from another or from several others. **Statements** are distinguished from other types of sentence, such as questions, commands or exclamations, in that they assert that something is or is not the case.

Exercise 6.1

Which of the following sentences are statements?
1. Put the meat in the oven.
2. Is the meat cooked yet?
3. The meat is cooked.
4. Good heavens!
5. The table is ready.

Like all sentences, statements can only appear in some particular language: Spanish, Russian, Chinese, etc. When reasoning we are not really concerned with the statements as such, since we are interested in what it is that the statement asserts rather than in what we use to make the assertion. The content of a statement will be the same whatever language is used. When we wish to talk about the content of a sentence which is used to make a statement, we call it a proposition. A proposition is what is asserted by a statement.

Several statements which are synonymous will express the same proposition, e.g.

(13) Some students hate school.

(14) Some students are haters of school.

(15) School is hated by some students.

This is true of statements in different languages which have the same meaning:

(16) The dog is dead

(17) Le chien est mort

and (18) Der Hund ist tot.

These all express the same proposition. Logic is language-neutral. For this reason, if an argument is sound in one language, it will be sound in all; if it is unsound in one language, it will be unsound in all.

A single statement in a particular language which is ambiguous, i.e. which means more than one thing, may be used to express two different propositions. The statement:

(19) Castles are sometimes captured without difficulty

may express two propositions, one about fortresses and one about chess pieces.

Assertion and Entertainment

In argument we **assert** a proposition. That is to say we put it forward as true. In using it we implicitly affirm its truth.

It is not always necessary to do this. We may simply **entertain** a proposition. To entertain a proposition is merely to notice it, to hold it before one, to consider it without commitment as to its truth or falsity. The numbered propositions used as examples in this book are not being *asserted*, they are merely being *entertained*, or presented as useful examples.

It is a mark of an educated person that he is able to entertain propositions independently of belief in their truth. Indeed, it is a good practice in debate not merely to entertain entire standpoints, but actually to argue for them as an exercise in reasoning. This is called "playing the devil's advocate."

Inference

Propositions are either true or false. Arguments are constructed out of propositions which are related to each other in such a way that the truth of some of them constitutes grounds for accepting the truth of others. We are able to infer the truth of some propositions on the basis of the truth of others. The process of thought whereby we pass from one or more statements to others, on the grounds that we think that if the former are true then the latter may be, or must be, true is called **inference**. The former propositions are premises, and the latter conclusions. We are said to *infer* a **conclusion** from its **premise** o premises.

The grounds for passing from the premises to their conclusion is that there is some relationship between the two, such that if the former is true, it is likely (or certain) to be true, that the latter will also be likely (or certain) to be true. The premises are said to *imply* the conclusion. When we make an inference from premises to conclusion in an argument we do so on the basis of the **implications** of the premises. We draw out those implications to establish the truth of the conclusion. When we draw out the implications of premises in this way, we are said to infer a conclusion.

Inference and Implication

Never confuse the words "implication" and "inference" by using "imply" for "infer." Inference is a process of thought whereby a supposed truth or truths (the premise(s)) is used to obtain another truth (the conclusion) by use of reason. People infer. They infer correctly if their inference is based upon the implications which exist between propositions. Even where there are genuine implications, inferences may not actually be drawn, because nobody may ever actually bother to draw them.

Implications are logical relationships which hold between propositions, such that if the former (premise(s)) are true, the conclusion is likely to be, or must be, true. They justify the making of inferences. Implications are not made by us; they are discovered. The process of inferring is that of tracing the relationships of implication between propositions. Implications may be there without anyone seeing them or without anyone actually making inferences on the basis of them.

The word "imply" is also used loosely in everyday speech to mean "express indirectly" or "hint," as in "What are you implying?" This should be avoided in serious work in order to avoid confusion.

Indications that a conclusion is being inferred from premises are words like "therefore," "consequently," "hence," and "it follows that." Indication that a conclusion has been inferred from its premises is given by "because" "since" and "for the reason that."

Exercise 6.2
Which of the following are arguments? In the case of those which are arguments, pick out the conclusion.
1. Foreign students have a harder time at college than those who are studying in their own country, because they have to cope with learning to survive in a strange environment as well as managing their studies.
2. An artist's work is an extension of his personality.
3. Although the police announced a reward for information leading to the arrest of the terrorists, no one came forward.
4. Customers benefit from advertising because it brings to their notice the variety of goods available in the shops and helps them make their choice of what to buy.
5. If governments use tax money to help support theatres in danger of closing down, then they should also use it to help sports clubs in financial difficulties.

Arguments can be sound or unsound. A **sound argument** is one in which good grounds are provided for accepting the conclusion. An **unsound argument** fails to provide this. Sound arguments have rational force:

> "You cannot help paying attention to . . . arguments if they are good. If it were testimony, you might disregard it . . . Testimony is like an arrow shot from a longbow; the force of it depends on the strength of the hand that draws it. Argument is like an arrow shot from a crossbow, which has equal force though shot by a child." (Samuel Johnson)

Most of the essays which students write as assignments or in examinations should take the form of the presentation of an argument or arguments. The student presents the evidence for particular points of view, usually arguing that one position is preferable to the others, and giving reasons why this is so.

Fallacies

There are many barriers to sound reasoning. We may be tired, distracted or prejudiced. In addition to studying what we must do to reason soundly, the study of examples of poor reasoning is valuable because it helps us to be able to recognise, and therefore to avoid, the more common pitfalls. These are called "fallacies."

In everyday language, a fallacy is a widespread false belief. e.g. "It is a fallacy that mirrors attract lightning." But in logic a **fallacy** is a mistake in reasoning. It is used in particular for an unsound form of argument which is so deceptive that it is frequently mistaken for a sound form. These fallacies are usually given names, so that we can learn to recognise and avoid them. Fallacies may be used unintentionally when the person presenting them reasons badly, or they may be used as rhetorical devices with the deliberate intention of creating the *impression* of winning a dispute.

There are many ways in which arguments can fail, and so there are many fallacies which we can commit in constructing them. Many have traditionally been given names, but there is no universally accepted classification. You will be introduced to many more of the most important. Among those most commonly met with in everyday conversation are those due to irrelevance.

2. Relevance

The first characteristic of efficient reasoning is that we must think clearly, and in any argument we must see clearly what the point at issue is, and stick to it for as long as is necessary to deal with it. The clear thinker sorts out in his mind which of the ideas which have occurred to him are relevant to the point at issue, and which are irrelevant. The former he marshals for use; while the latter he dismisses. It is the mark of a weak thinker to allow his mind to wander so that he is distracted by irrelevant matters and loses sight of the point.

Fallacies of Irrelevance

The following are the more common fallacies of irrelevance (ways of being irrelevant):
Ignoring the Point: In serious argument we attempt either to establish our own position or to undermine someone else's. These are precise goals, and precise methods are required in order to achieve them. Our argument must be on target or, as logicians say, "to the point." If it is not, it will be irrelevant, and we shall have committed the general type of fallacy traditionally called "ignoring the point." No amount of irrelevant material, however brilliant or entertaining, should be regarded as carrying weight if it is not relevant to the matter in hand. We should treat someone using an irrelevant argument just as the man on the gate at a soccer match would treat someone who tried

to get through the turnstiles with tickets for a music concert.

If conclusions are drawn, or apparent rebuttals offered without even the appearance of any attempt at relevance, it is said that the irrelevant point a *non sequitur*, that it "does not follow."

Red Herring: This is the name for any simple attempt at diversion of the argument from its proper point by distracting the hearer in some way.

(20) *Boy*: Did you go to the dance with Peter last night?

Girl: Do you know that your eyes flash when you lose your temper? It makes you look very handsome.

Humour and ridicule may be used very effectively in order to distract people from the point to which they ought to be attentive. We can best be on our guard against it by ourselves being clear what the real point at issue is, and by warning our opponent to "stick to the point" if he strays.

Man of Straw: Finding it difficult to attack an opponent's reasoned and reasonable views, we may attribute to him more extreme and unreasonable views than the ones which he in fact holds. Precisely because these positions are more extreme and unreasonable, they will be more vulnerable to attack. Instead of attacking our opponent's true position, we set up a weak "man of straw," and then attack and demolish this easier target. When we do this, people may be deceived into thinking that we have demolished our opponent's original position.

(21) *Father*: Since the examinations are drawing near, I think that from now on you ought to start doing some regular revision in the evenings.

Son: If you expect me to do nothing but turn myself into a zombie, working round the clock twenty-four hours a day for the next few months, never going out anywhere, never having any pleasure at all, then I think you're expecting too much.

Appeal to Force: Force is not usually presented as an argument, it is used *instead* of an argument. But if the threat of force is presented in the guise of an argument, then this fallacy has been committed. It is not force itself, but the *threat* of force, which is used.

(22) *Boss*: We can't raise your pay by a higher rate than the rate of inflation. That would be socially irresponsible.

Teacher: But you have consistently raised the fees you charge students by a higher rate than the rate of inflation.

Boss: Look! If you don't like working here, you can always go somewhere else, you know.

At first sight this may appear to be a simple diversion, but there is an implied threat in the boss' words.

Appeal to Undesirable Consequences (*argumentum ad consequentiam*): Someone points to the disagreeable consequences of holding a particular position as evidence that it must be false.

(23) You cannot accept the truth of the Theory of Evolution, because it were true, then we would have descended from monkeys and apes.

Appeal to sentiment: The argument may be directed not against an opponent's position but towards his sentiments, such as pity, hatred, envy, patriotism, etc.

(24) Oh! But you can't fail my daughter. If this "fail" grade stands it will ruin her career for life. We have already made great sacrifices for her education.

Argumentum ad Hominem (Argument directed towards the man): Argument is directed towards the opponent rather than the opponent's position or arguments. This may take several forms:

It may be merely abusive:

(25) "There ought to be limits to freedom. We're aware of this [web] site, and this guy is just a garbage man, that's all he is."

Sometimes an argument is based upon the assumption that what discredits an opponent also discredits his argument. Sometimes an opponent is discredited as hypocritical or inconsistent in his behaviour. This does not destroy the force of any argument he uses. (If his *argument*, as opposed to his *behaviour,* were to be found inconsistent, then it would be discredited.) To draw attention to the bad character of a witness in a trial is to cast doubt upon his general trustworthiness, and therefore upon the value of his evidence. Similarly, to cast doubt upon the character of someone standing in an election to some office is to provide evidence of his unsuitability as a candidate, although it will count for nothing against any arguments or policies he is advocating. Thus when George W. Bush said, in explaining his educational policy:

(26)   "You teach a child to read, and he or her will be able to pass a literacy test."

we are entitled to wonder whether the speaker is qualified to preside over US education policy.

Argument from Ignorance: Sometimes called the "**argument from silence**", this involves the assumption that if something has not been shown to be true we can assume that it is false, or if it has not been shown to be false we can assume it to be true. The assumption is, of course, false. Merely because something has not been shown to be true (or false) does not entail that it is false (or true).

(27) I believe that flying saucers exist. After all, no one has ever proved beyond doubt that they every single claimed sighting is a fiction, or figment of someone's imagination.

Argument from the Possibility of Truth or Falsity: It is equally fallacious to argue from the mere possibility of the truth of a proposition to its truth, or from the mere possibility of the falsity of a proposition to its falsity. Most propositions, if true, could have been false, and if false, could have been true. In addition to the mere possibility of truth or falsity, some argument or evidence is required to establish the *actual* likelihood of a proposition's truth or falsity.

(28) It is possible that ghosts might exist, so I am justified in believing in them.

Dissolving into Incoherence: This involves saying something in which the sense breaks down completely.

(29) "We want our teachers to be trained so they can meet the obligations, their obligations as teachers. We want them to know how to teach the science of reading; in order to make sure there's not this kind of federal – federal cufflink." (George W. Bush)

Exercise 6.3
Identify the fallacies of relevance in the following:

1. If the company pays off all of the claims against it for negligence, it will become bankrupt and have to close down.
2. Since scientists cannot prove that global warming will happen, we can safely assume that it will not.
3. We should disregard what Smith says about conservation. He has shares in the logging industry.
4. We hope you will accept our recommendations. We spent several months and a lot of resources working on them.
5. You should get back home by ten - if you want to go out on Saturday evening.
6. "Well, I think if you say you're going to do something and don't do it, that's trustworthiness."

3. Vacuity

In order to establish some position by rational means we need to support it with adequate argument and sufficient evidence. This support must be something *other* than what we are attempting to establish, since nothing can be support for itself.

Fallacies of Vacuity

Fallacies of vacuity involve the opposite error to the fallacies of relevance. We stick to the point, but we do so too closely, in that rather than providing evidence for the conclusion we merely repeat our "conclusion", or assert it more vociferously, as though the conclusion could stand as evidence for itself.

Mere Assertion: Sometimes called the *argumentum ad nauseam*, this is the simple repetition of a proposition as a substitute for evidence or argument to support it. Simply to state your view is not to argue for it, however forcefully you state it, and however many times you state it.

(30) "See, I believe in the power of the people. I truly do. I do."

Begging the Question: Repetition is sometimes disguised. We may advance a proposition in support of itself, so that the "evidence" for our conclusion is merely the conclusion itself, but it is presented in disguise by the use of synonymous words or phrases.

(31) "A low voter turnout is an indication of fewer people going to the polls."

We may state a proposition in tendentious terms, "building into it" the conclusion we desire to establish. In this way we hope to put a ready made conclusion into our hearer's mind. This form is dangerous because it relies upon our reluctance to question a positive assertion that is presented in a forceful manner. This is often done by prefacing statements requiring supporting arguments with such epithets as: "It is clearly true that..."; Let's face it . . ."; "Without question . . ."; "I don't have to remind you . . ."; "Let us be honest . . ."; and "I'm not telling you anything you don't already know, but. . ."

(32) Everyone knows that communism is dead.

(33) Surely no one today would doubt that communism is dead.

(34) It would be futile to deny that communism is dead.

(35) Anyone who sincerely examines the state of the world today will admit that communism is dead.

Tautology

This involves asserting that X is X.

(36) "If we don't succeed, we run the risk of failure."

(37) It's no exaggeration to say the undecideds could go one way or another."

(38) "It's very important for folks to understand that when there's more trade, there's more commerce."

Tautologies may sometimes plunge into total incoherence:

(39) "A Key to foreign policy is to rely on reliance."

Arguing in a Circle: "Begging the question" may be disguised by a series of intermediate steps.

In his book, *A Soldier's Way*, US Secretary of State General Colin Powell recalls his arrival at his first post in Vietnam during the war. He was sent to a remote fortified base on the Laotian border called Shau. When he arrived he could not understand why a base had been erected in such a vulnerable position, and he made enquiries about it from the Vietnamese officer he had been designated to assist.

(40)   "Very important post," he was assured.

          "But what is its mission," he asked.

"Very important post" came back the reply.

"But why is it here?"

"Outpost is here to protect airfield."

"What is the airfield here for?"

"Airfield here to supply outpost."

This prompted Powell to recall the soldiers' rueful refrain: "We're here because we're here, because we're here, because we're here . . ."

Poisoning the Well: Without offering any support, we deliberately exclude all evidence against our own position from a particular source.

(41) I wouldn't listen to anything he says about it. He's a psychiatrist, and they're all mad anyway.

Examples of this fallacy can be very close to the *argumentum ad hominem*, but here we are concentrating upon the making of an assumption which favours the desired conclusion by removing from consideration what may count against it, and doing this without justification.

Argument by Redefinition: One of the proponents in an argument redefines a key term in order to *appear* not to lose it.

(42) All politicians are dishonest. The expression "honest politician" is a contradiction in terms."

A regular sign of the presence of this fallacy is often the appearance of the words "real," "true" and "genuine."

Double Bind: Two alternatives are presented, both leading to an objective desired by the presenter. This provides his audience with an illusory freedom of choice between two possibilities, neither of which is really an option that they would genuinely wish to take.

This works because, while perfectly capable of resisting a single suggestion which we do not wish to take, we are inclined, if offered alternatives, simply to choose the least objectionable.

The effectiveness of this fallacy can easily be seen in the behaviour of small children. A child told to go to bed at 8:00 pm. is likely to object; but one offered the choice of going to bed at 7:30 pm. or 8:00 pm. is likely freely to opt for 8.00 pm.

Complex Question: A variant of Double Bind involves the building of assumptions into apparently open questions, so that to answer the question at all is to commit oneself to a questionable assumption or action.

(43) How do you account for the fact of extraterrestrial visits to earth?

The question

(44) Why has communism failed?

carries the assumption that it has.

Surprisingly this fallacy sometimes turns up in examination questions:

(45) Was Alexander the Great an insane megalomaniac or a military and political genius?

When faced with complex questions we may attempt to show that the alternatives do not exclude each other, and can be held simultaneously; we may show that the alternatives are not exhaustive, and that there is a third possibility; or we may simply refuse to accept either or both of the alternatives offered.

Complex question is also used to limit our choice of action:

(46) *Shopkeeper to customer hovering near something*: "Cash or credit card?"

Deliberate Ignorance: A point of view is clung to despite contradictory evidence, so that the person holding it becomes irrational. The sign of this is such phrases as "I don't care what you say. . ." or "Don't try to confuse me with arguments . . ." This is the ultimate form of begging the question.

(47) I don't care what anybody says. No one will ever convince me that smoking causes cancer.

An attitude of superiority may be adopted towards contrary evidence or arguments in order to avoid meeting the threat they constitute. This is a way of disguising deliberate ignorance.

(48) "I will never apologise for the United States of America – I don't care what the facts are."

(49) "I stand by all the misstatements that I've made."

Exercise 6.4

Identify the fallacies of vacuity in the following:

1. It is clearly beyond dispute that Palmer is the better candidate for the job.
2. Where did you hide the money?
3. No school ought to seek to control the dress of the students because control over the way that students dress has nothing to do with a school.
4. Miracles cannot possibly occur, since they are temporary suspensions of the law of science, and if we were ever to come across such an occurrence we would simply reassess our understanding of the law broken so as to account for the anomaly.
5. Will you take it now, or shall I have it delivered?

---

5. Closed System Reasoning and Open Reasoning

Human reasoning always appears in one of two basic forms: closed system reasoning and open reasoning.

Closed system reasoning is thinking which is abstract and isolated from the real world. This may best be understood by considering the following simple puzzle:

"Kirk, Miller and Pierce were born, although not respectively, in Kingston, Milton and Pirehill. Today they live, again not respectively, in Keston, Mereville and Painton. For each of them, the first letter of his surname, place of birth and present place of residence are all different; and none of them has ever lived in the same city as any of the others. Also, Kirk has never been to Painton. Find out where each of them was born, and where each now lives."

In solving such problems, the best strategy is usually to eliminate what is impossible and then take what is left.

We are told that Kirk has never been to Painton. Since his place of residence and the first letter of his name must be different, he cannot live in Keston. Therefore he must live in Mereville. Since his name, place of residence and place of birth all begin with different letters, he must have been born in Pirehill.

We now know that Miller cannot have been born in Pirehill. But he cannot have been born in Milton either, because of its initial letter, so he must have been born in Kingston. Since the initial letters of his name, place of birth and residence must all be different, he must live in Painton. Pierce, therefore, must have been born in Milton and he must live in Keston.

This is clearly an artificial puzzle. No one would consider attempting to solve this problem by using the telephone directory, or by ringing friends he might have in those towns to see if they knew anyone going by these names. The problem is intended to be solved entirely by the application of reason to what is given. Moreover, it is assumed that the data was correct and final.

We do not need to worry about whether Pierce has possibly moved from Keston since the puzzle was constructed.

Although the puzzle appeared to be about three people born and resident in certain towns, it is not really about people at all. Neither the people not the towns have any individuality. All that matters is the initial letter of their names. The puzzle could have been expressed as follows:

Kos, Mos and Pos were born, not respectively, in Ka, Ma and Pa. Today they live, again, not respectively, in Ke, Me and Pe. For each of them, the first letter of their surname, original and new places of residence are all different, and none has ever lived in the same city as any of the others. Kos has never been to Pe. Find out where each of them was born, and where each now lives.

Closed system thinking is characteristic of games, such as chess and draughts. It is also characteristic of mathematics. Thinking takes place within a rigidly defined set of parameters or limits. For example, in chess all movement is limited to a field of eighty-four squares. The pieces can only be those which are traditionally used, and they can only move in the ways laid down by the rules of the game. A threatened pawn can never take refuge by slipping off the board for a while, or leapfrog its attacker to avoid capture. An opportunistic player can never get in several extra moves between his opponent's moves. The possibilities are rigidly circumscribed. This is not to say that closed thinking is necessarily simple. The possibilities presented by the game of chess, artificially limited though they are, are sufficient to allow the exhibition of immense intelligence, foresight and skill by chess masters.

By contrast, **open system reasoning** is part of, and open to, or at least resembles, the world in which we all live. Consider the following problem:

Maria thinks: "Shall I do my homework now, or shall I leave it until later? If I do it now I shall get it over with, but the shops will close in an hour or so, and I would like to go to buy a birthday card for my father today. But if I go to the shops, and Penelope invites me to her apartment later, as she said she would if her parents go out for the evening, than I shall still have my homework to do."

In this case, the future is not circumscribed in the way it is in a chess game. Maria could decide to go to the shops, but fail to find a suitable birthday card for her father, and so gain nothing by her journey. She might stay at home and get her homework done, and then find that Penelope's parents decide not to go out after all, or that even if they do, Penelope may fail to invite her around for the evening. The homework may turn out to be unexpectedly difficult, so that even if Maria starts early, she may not finish it in time to go out later. News of the death of one of Maria's distant relatives, or a sudden unexpected thunderstorm and power failure, may disrupt everything.

This sort of reasoning lacks the relative certainty that is encountered in closed system reasoning. Yet despite this contrast, some thinking about the real world is very much like closed system thinking. When reckoning up our change in a shop, we pay attention only to the rules of arithmetic. This is true even if we decide to overlook a mistake, or tip the storekeeper.

When an electrician comes to repair the television, he understands how it works, and the conditions which are necessary for it to work properly. He has to locate the reason why, in the case of a television which has broken down, it does not work. By following the chain of causes and effects in the electrical system, he may be able to locate the problem using closed system thinking. But he may be thrown off balance by some unusual combination of problems, or by the unusual interference of something from outside the system itself, such as a dead mouse. Here his experience of what happens when television sets fail to work properly, will help locate the problem.

It is always necessary to be aware whether we are dealing with closed system reasoning, or open reasoning.

6. Consistency

The heart of all reasoning lies in consistency. This is particularly obvious in the case of closed system reasoning, which is entirely determined by consistency.

Someone may rationally hold a set of beliefs only if they are **consistent**. We say that a set of beliefs is consistent if all the propositions which express those beliefs can be simultaneously true. Sets of beliefs are **inconsistent** if one of them cannot be true with the others because it contradicts them, or has consequences which contradict them. Someone who holds inconsistent beliefs is irrational. There can be no argument with someone who, upon discovering the inconsistency of his beliefs, does not seek to render them consistent by changing them.

Inconsistency and Inconstancy
Someone may be a fanatical supporter of Manchester United throughout one season, and of Manchester City in the next. This may be inconstant, but it is by no means inconsistent. Someone may prefer the steak from the restaurant menu on one occasion and the salmon on another. This may be different, but it is not inconsistent. The consistency we are interested in is consistency of beliefs, not consistency of preference.

The idea of consistency depends upon **contradiction**. We are all familiar, in a rough and ready way, with the idea of opposites. If I assert that the dinner is burned, and you claim that it is not, we have both taken up opposite standpoints. The proper term for this sense of "opposite" is "contradiction." In English we usually express the **contradictory** of a proposition by adding "not" to the sentence in the appropriate position, or by putting "it is not the case that" in front of it.

The essential point about propositions which are contradictory to each other is that they are **logically incompatible**, in that they cannot both be true. At least one of them must be false. A proposition "p" and another proposition "it is not the case that p" between them exhaust the possibilities. Thus if one is true the other must be false, and if one is false the other must be true. Thus if we consider:

(50) The toast is burned

and   (51) The toast is not burned

Since nothing can be both true and false at the same time, for someone to hold the views expressed by both (50) and (51) at the same time would be to hold as true the proposition:

(52) The toast is burned and the toast is not burned

which is simply **self-contradictory** and *cannot* be true.

The objection may be raised that some people prefer their toast to be cooked longer than others, and that what counts as the toast's being burned will vary from person to person. Undoubtedly, this is true. This problem arises because of the inexactness of our everyday speech. Once we have adopted specifications for what counts as the toast's being burned, then it should be possible to decide, in any given case, whether the toast is actually burned or not.

Consider the two propositions:

(53) The dog is lying inside its kennel

(54) The dog is not lying inside its kennel.

Suppose the dog to be lying half inside and half outside the kennel. Both (53) and (54) would appear to be true, but also, for the same reason, both would also appear to be false. Once more, once we specify exactly what constitutes the state of affairs referred to as "the dog being in its kennel" the problem is solved. Suppose we decide that to count as being in its kennel all of the dog's body, including its nose and paws, have to be clearly under cover, then if the dog is lying half inside and half outside (53) is false and (54) is true.

In "tightening up" our language in this way we are clearly moving away from open-system thinking and towards creating the conditions for closed-system thinking.

Incompatible Propositions and **Incompatible Beliefs**

A proposition and its contradictory, such as (53) and (54) are **logically incompatible**. But note that the following pair are not logically incompatible.

(55) I believe that the dog is in its kennel.

and   (56) You believe that the dog is not in its kennel.

Both may be true at the same time without contradiction. My believing one thing and you believing another is not an incompatible state of affairs, even if our respective beliefs are *themselves* incompatible. It would, however, be **inconsistent** for *a single person* to hold incompatible beliefs, such as (53) and (54).

Exercise 6.5

Which of the following pairs of propositions are logically incompatible, i.e. both could not be true at the same time.

1. a. Seville is in Spain.
    b. Seville is not in Spain.
2. a. I believe that Great Britain should be in the European Union.
    b. You believe that Great Britain should not be in the European Union.
3. a. I believe that Great Britain should not be in the European Union.
    b. Great Britain should be in the European Union.
4. a. I believe that Great Britain should be in the European Union.
    b. I do not believe that Great Britain should be in the European Union.
5. a. On Mondays, Wednesdays and Fridays, I prefer my coffee with sugar.
    b. On Tuesdays, Thursdays and Saturdays, I prefer my coffee without sugar.

Conclusive Arguments

When, if the premise(s) of a properly constructed argument are true its conclusion must also be true, we have a conclusive argument. The truth of the conclusion is certain, relative to the premises. In conclusive reasoning we infer from the premise or premises of an argument that its conclusion must be true.

Deduction

Conclusive arguments are almost always **deductive arguments**. These are arguments which move from the more general to the less general. That is to say we assert in our conclusion less information than is asserted in the premises, (or no more information than is asserted in the premises). Since the conclusion of a successful deductive argument follows necessarily from its premises, the form of implication found in deductive arguments is a very strong one, called **entailment.** To say that proposition p entails proposition q is to say that the truth of proposition q follows necessarily from the truth of proposition p.

Entailment

All propositions entail the truth or falsity of some other propositions. The proposition

(57) Julian is older that Jeremy

entails the truth of the proposition

(58) Jeremy cannot be Julian's father,

and the falsity of the proposition

(59) Jeremy is not older than Julian.

Proposition (59) is entailed by (57), that is to say, if (57) is true then (58) is true. By contrast, (59) contradicts (57), that is to say if (57) is true (59) must be false. The falsity of (59) is entailed by the truth of (57).

Although the truth of (57) is evidence for the truth or falsity of some other propositions, its truth leaves the truth of most other propositions undetermined, e.g.

(60) Julian is Jeremy's father.

Since (58) asserts that Julian is older than Jeremy it is certainly the case that (60) might be true. On the other hand Julian and Jeremy might equally well not be related at all. The truth of (57) has no implications for the truth or falsity of (60), leaving it undetermined. Even if (60) happened to be true, that truth could not be determined on the basis of the truth of (57), for not every male is the father of every other male younger than himself. More information that is given in (57) would be required to determine the truth of (60).

Exercise 6.6

"The Olympic Games of 1996 were held in Atlanta, Georgia, USA"

On the basis of that proposition alone, and not of any knowledge which you may happen to have, which of the following can be determined to be true, which can be determined to be false, and which cannot be determined with respect to truth or falsity at all? (Remember, you are not being asked which propositions you *know* to be true or false, but which could be determined entirely on the basis of the truth of the proposition above.)

1. The Olympic Games of 2000 were held in Sydney, Australia.
2. The Olympic Games of 2000 were held in the Southern Hemisphere.
3. The Olympic Games of 2004 are to be held in Athens, Greece
4. The Olympic Games of 2000 were not held in Cairo, Egypt.
5. The Olympic Games of 1996, in Atlanta, Georgia, were marred by a terrorist incident.
6. Every Olympic Games other than those of 1996 have been held in some venue other than Atlanta, Georgia.
7. The closing ceremony of the Olympic Games of 2000 was held in London.
8. The Olympic Games of 1996 were held in Georgia.

The inference from the truth (or falsity) of a single proposition to the truth of falsity of another is the very simplest form of argument, with a single premise and a conclusion.

Validity

The secret of efficient and successful use of deductive reasoning is the ability to distinguish valid arguments from those which are invalid. An argument is **valid** if (and only if), when the premises are each true, the conclusion must also be true. To put it another way, an argument is valid if and only if there is no way the conclusion could be false without at least one premise also being false.

The term "valid" refers to arguments, not to propositions or statements. Validity concerns the relationship between the premises and the conclusion, and not the actual truth-values of the component statements. That is, it has to do with which combinations of truth-values of premises and conclusion an argument will permit, not with which combinations actually do occur.

The essence of deduction lies in the need to avoid inconsistency. If it would be inconsistent to hold the premises of an argument to be true and also to hold its conclusion to be false, then that argument is said to be **valid**. If not, it is invalid. In a valid deductive argument the truth of the premises *entails* the truth of the conclusion.

Some valid arguments do not contain any true propositions at all, and some invalid arguments are composed entirely of true propositions. All that an argument's being valid tells us is that when and if all of the premises of this argument are true, then the conclusion is guaranteed to be true. If an argument is valid, if you make sure that the premises are true you can be sure that the conclusion will also be true. If you start with false premises, however, there is no telling where the argument may take you. In this way, valid deductive arguments are rather like computers. The value of what comes out depends upon the value of what was put in. As computer experts say "Rubbish in, rubbish out."

Truth and **Validity**

These terms are sometimes confused. Truth is a property of propositions; validity is a property of arguments.

A deductive argument is valid only if, if the premises are true, then the conclusion must be true. This is because the truth of the premises *entails* the truth of the conclusion.

It does not follow from this that the conclusion of a valid deductive argument must be true. If the premises are false then the conclusion may also be false. The value of validity lies in the relative security we have that *if* the premises are true *then* the truth of the conclusion is guaranteed.

Form

It was the Greek philosopher Aristotle who first made the surprising discovery that what an argument is about, i.e. its subject matter, has nothing directly to do with its validity or invalidity; that the validity of an argument depends upon its **form** or structure.

"The design of a car," "the program of a concert," "the pattern of a dress," "the plans of a building," and "the blueprint of a new aircraft" are all phrases which stand for the way things are put together. They refer to the arrangement of their parts relative to each other and to the whole. They refer to the underlying *structure* which gives unity to something. This structure need not be something deliberately designed. The structure of a snowflake is very complex and elaborate, and yet it occurs without human intervention.

The notion of form may be seen more clearly if we consider that a single entity may change its form yet retain its identity, as when a caterpillar turns into a butterfly. When something loses its form completely, in so doing it loses its identity as a distinct entity, as when a snowman melts, or the audience at a concert disperses at the end of the performance.

A common form may be discerned in things of very different types. We may abstract a common aspect of form from, say, the months of the year, the signs of the zodiac, the apostles of Jesus and the mythical labours of Hercules. In this case, we have isolated their common form of "twelveness."

A structure, which need not necessarily be a physical object, is made up of elements. These elements may be related together in different ways. The character of a thing may be changed dramatically without adding to or subtracting from any of its elements, but simply by rearranging them, i.e. by altering the relations holding between the elements. The words "tea", "ate," and "eat" are each composed of exactly the same elements, but these stand in different relations to each other, creating different entities. Form consists of the relationship which the several elements within a whole have with each other.

Arguments also have form. The form or structure of a building may be contrasted with the material out of which it is made. The form of an argument is contrasted with its subject-matter, what it is *about*. Two arguments may have quite different subject matter but the same skeleton or form. This can be seen if we look at two examples of a type of argument called by logicians the **hypothetical syllogism**:

(61)   If William Shakespeare wrote *Hamlet*, then he was a great writer.
         William Shakespeare did write *Hamlet*.
         Therefore, William Shakespeare was a great writer.

(62)   If Justin was behind the bicycle sheds at break, then Justin is the killer.
         Justin was behind the bicycle sheds at break.
         Therefore, Justin is the killer.

Each argument consists of a conditional or hypothetical statement asserting what would be the case if something else were the case. This is followed by an assertion that the stated condition is in fact fulfilled; and then the conclusion drawn that its consequent is also fulfilled. By eliminating those words which provide the subject matter of the argument and replacing them with the symbols p and q, we can expose the common form of the two arguments above to be:

$$\text{If } p \text{ then } q$$
$$\underline{p}$$
$$\text{therefore } q$$

The initial hypothetical proposition asserts that if p obtains then q will also obtain. (Note that this statement does not assert that p in fact does obtain, only that *if p* obtains *then q* also obtains). The second premise asserts that p does in fact obtain. The conclusion is then drawn that q also in fact obtains. What p stands for is called the **antecedent**, and what q stands for is called the **consequent**.

Aristotle's discovery was that if an argument form gives us an invalid argument on one occasion, then any argument of that form will also be invalid. If an argument form gives us a valid argument on one occasion, then any argument of that form will also be valid. Since there are only a limited number of different forms, called "moods," for each type of argument, this is extremely useful information to have.

The fact that a deductive argument is valid does not necessarily mean that we can be confident that its conclusion is true. This is because valid deductive arguments can be built up with one or more false premises.

(63) All fungi are poisonous. (false premise)
         Mushrooms are fungi. (true premise)
         Therefore mushrooms are poisonous. (false conclusion)

The conclusion of this argument happens to be false, but *if* the premises had been true, the conclusion would have been true, so the argument is perfectly valid.

A true conclusion can be validly derived from false premises.

(64) All birds can fly. (false premise)
Bats are birds. (false premise)
Therefore bats can fly. (true conclusion)

The only possibility ruled out by the validity of a deductive argument is the drawing of a false conclusion from true premises.

Clearly validity is not very useful by itself. In order to have a **sound** argument we must have a valid argument the premises of which are also known to be true. Only a sound argument guarantees the truth of its conclusion.

Valid Arguments and Sound Arguments

A deductive argument is said to be valid only if, if the premises are true, then the conclusion must be true. It is said to be sound if, in addition to being a valid argument, its premises are also true. Thus the truth of the conclusion of a sound argument can be relied upon.

Hypothetical Syllogisms

We have already come across examples of the simple species of argument known as the hypothetical syllogism (examples (11) and (12)). Arguments of this kind may appear in four different forms, or moods. Two are valid and two invalid.

Note: In setting out the forms of these arguments the symbol "~" is used to show the negation of a statement. e.g. If "p" stands for "Penny is watching television" then "$\sim p$" stands for its contradictory, "It is not the case that Penny is watching television" or "Penny is not watching television."

Affirming the Antecedent:

We have already met the argument:

(65) If William Shakespeare wrote *Hamlet*, then he was a great writer.
William Shakespeare did write *Hamlet*.
Therefore, William Shakespeare was a great writer.

This has the form:

If p then q

p

therefore q

We recognise the validity of this argument intuitively. It is a basic law of Logic known as **Modus Ponens**.

Affirming the Consequent:

(66) If Kit was driving under the influence of drink, then he would drive erratically.
Kit was certainly driving erratically.
Therefore, Kit was driving under the influence of drink.

If p then q

q

therefore p

Affirming the consequent (q) will not justify asserting the antecedent (p). Kit may have been driving erratically for some other reason, such as that he was in a temper, or ill.

Following the crash of TWA 800 when taking off from Kennedy Airport on July 17, 1996, killing all 230 people on board, the *New York Times* reported that the plane had been blown up by a bomb. The newspaper had learned that investigators had found microscopic traces of a chemical explosive, and using this form of argument, the staff had concluded that this evidence proved that the plan had been blown out of the sky. The reporters reasoned as follows:

If a bomb was used to blow up a plane, then some detectable bomb residue would have been left.

<u>Bomb residue was found.</u>

Therefore the plane was blown up.

But finding residue alone does not prove that a bomb blew up the plane, because there might be some other explanation for the residue, as there was in this case. It turned out that the plane had previously been used in a training exercise for bomb-sniffing dogs. The newspaper had fallen victim to the fallacy of "**affirming the consequent**." This fallacy ignores the possibility that the consequent had some other cause than the antecedent stated in the argument. This mood is invalid, and therefore that all arguments of this form are invalid.

Denying the Antecedent:

(67)   If Aubrey has been shot through the heart, he will die.
<u>Aubrey has not been shot through the heart.</u>
Therefore Aubrey will not die.

If p then q

$\underline{\sim p}$

therefore $\sim q$

Denial of the antecedent (p) will not justify denial of the consequent (q). If a man is shot through the heart, he will die. But if he is not shot through the heart, it does not follow that he will not die, for there is more than one possible cause of death. His wife may have hired a hit man to have him run down while crossing the road, or an aeroplane may crash onto his office. Arguing in this manner involves committing the fallacy of **denying the antecedent**.

Denying the Consequent:

(68)   If Aubrey is shot through the heart he will die.
<u>Aubrey has not died.</u>
Therefore Aubrey has not been shot through the heart.

If p then q

$\underline{\sim q}$

therefore $\sim p$

This is clearly a valid form of argument. It is a law of Logic known as **Modus Tollens**.

Affirming the antecedent and denying the consequent are both valid moods, while affirming the consequent and denying the antecedent are invalid.

Exercise 6.7
Give the mood of each of the following hypothetical syllogisms and say whether or not it is valid. Explain your answers.
1. If that man sitting at the corner table is Bill Gates then he is very rich. It is not Bill Gates, so he is not very rich.
2. If the bus drivers were on strike he would have been late. He was not late, therefore the bus drivers were not on strike.

3. If he is guilty he will avoid my eyes. He is not avoiding my eyes, therefore he is not guilty.
4. If the particles in this rock sample have a biological origin, then there was once life on Mars. The particles it appears, do not have a biological origin, therefore there has never been life on Mars.
5. If popular sayings are always true then it will always be raining in Manchester. It is not always raining in Manchester, therefore popular sayings are not always true.

Proof

What we want most of all is certainty, and arguments which will extend our range of certainty. That is, we desire sound arguments. An argument may be formally valid and yet useless, because one or more of its premises is false. Validity in an argument is necessary if it is to be useful, but by itself, it is not enough. To be really useful, or sound, a deductive argument must both be formally valid and also have known true premises.

This is the strongest form of argument, and is known as a proof. A **proof** is an argument such that any rational person should find completely convincing. Thus anyone who is offered a proof and refuses to recognise its force is, to that extent, behaving irrationally.

Of course, someone may determine, in advance, not to accept *any* arguments in favour of some particular position, however strong they might be. Such a person may say "You can't prove that to me, whatever you say." But this does not in any way detract from the force of the argument being presented. It merely reveals the stubborn irrationality of the person who refuses to accept its rational force.

By contrast, someone may find a poor argument convincing. This may indicate either that the argument is dressed up in a convincing manner, and this camouflage is not detected; or that the hearer is predisposed for some reason to accept the argument; or that he is simply incapable of judging its true worth. A proof may not be very persuasive to those who fail to understand its rational force. It may be presented in a very dry and unattractive way; yet in spite of this, it loses nothing of its rational force.

We should take great care how we use the word "proof" in essays. Always think carefully before claiming, or demanding a proof. It may not be appropriate in the context.

Convincing Someone and Proving Something

Someone has convinced someone of something if, as *a matter of fact*, he has brought that person to believe it to be true. Someone has proved something if he has presented arguments of such logical force that *any rational person* would see that it was true. Thus to prove something is to provide arguments which *ought* to convince us that something is true, although whether we are actually convinced or not will depend upon how rational we are.

Conviction is a matter of the psychology of each individual. Proof is a matter of logic, and is the same for everyone, whether he realises it or not. This contrast might be expressed by saying that conviction is a subjective matter; while proof is objective.

The Value of Deductive Reasoning

The strength of deductive reasoning is that it is conclusive. It is conclusive because in a valid deductive argument the conclusion never goes beyond the premises. The conclusion is true since the premises are true, so that there would be a contradiction in asserting the premises to be true but denying the truth of the conclusion.

But in this case the truth of the conclusion is already asserted in the premises. If you know the premises to be true, in a sense, you already know the truth of the conclusion. The argument is thus worthless because it begs the question. Consider following the valid deductive argument:

(69)   All drunkards are irresponsible.

<u>Brett is a drunkard.</u>

Therefore, Brett is irresponsible.

How could we know that all drunkards are irresponsible? Presumably, we would find out in some way. But in order to be able to claim something about all drunkards we already need to know about Brian and his drinking habits. Setting up the syllogism and then drawing the conclusion seems an unnecessary effort.

All deductive arguments are subject to this sort of circularity. No deductive argument can ever be used to prove anything essentially new, for we should always need to know the truth of the conclusion before we could know the truth of the premises. Accordingly, some logicians have argued that the deductive arguments are not a method for acquiring new knowledge, but rather a method for displaying the consequences of what is already known. Deduced conclusions are just restatements of truths contained in the premises

Deductive arguments are valuable, however, precisely because they do this. They help us to organise the information which we already possess; and they help us to make clear to ourselves its implications. Although those implications may not be logically novel, indeed - they cannot be, they may be psychologically novel. We may not realise the implications of what we already know or believe; the process of making deductions lays those implications bare for us. Our conclusions may be new *to us*, because we had not previously thought through the logic of our beliefs, even though they contain no more than the information contained in the premises. The information we possess is cast in new form, a form which may give us new insight and suggest new applications, since the deductions from even a small set of premises are not at all obvious, and may take years to understand.

Exercise 6.8

Is each of the following true or false:

1. Some valid arguments are sound.
2. The premises of a valid argument must be true.
3. An argument with a false premise is invalid.
4. The premises of a valid argument guarantee the truth of its conclusion.
5. All invalid arguments are unsound.
6. The conclusion of a valid argument is always true.
7. The premises of a sound argument are always true.
8. The conclusion of an invalid argument is always false.
9. Some sound arguments are valid.
10. Some unsound arguments are valid.

7. Analogy

What is Analogy?

When we draw an analogy between things we indicate one or more respects in which they are similar. Analogies may be drawn between "things" or relations. For example analogies have been drawn between the processes of teaching children and caring for plants, the function of the heart and that of a pump, the structure of the solar system and that of the atom.

Strictly speaking, analogical language is ambiguous, but usefully so. Aristotle noted that some terms are systematically ambiguous. Thus John Brown may be healthy, John Brown's urine may be healthy, and the diet of the country folk may be healthy; but each is healthy in quite different ways. John Brown's "health" refers to the state of his constitution. His urine is "healthy" in the sense that it is a *sign* of health in him; while the diet of the country folk is said to be "healthy" in that it might tend to be a *cause* of health in John Brown and other country people. The term "constitution" is used with systematic ambiguity of John Brown, his urine and the diet of the country folk.

These ambiguities lie in "dead" metaphors, buried in our vocabulary. The English language preserves analogies between the head of a body, the "head" of a page, the "head" of a stream, the "head" of a pass and the "head" of an organisation.

This is because analogy is a fundamental method of thinking. It is used to make our descriptions more lively and picturesque in figures of speech. An explicit analogy is known as a **simile;** e.g.

(70) "The new students have taken to this course like ducks to water";
while an implicit analogy is called a **metaphor;** e.g.

(71) "When the lesson was cancelled there was a flood of complaints from the students." These figures of speech, based upon analogy, appear in great works of literature. But they are also scattered throughout our everyday speech as clichés: e.g.

(72) With the examinations coming up our backs are against the wall. You must change your tune, turn over a new leaf, pull your socks up, put your hands to the plough, your shoulders to the wheel, and your noses to the grindstone.

Argument by Analogy

In an argument based upon analogy known similarities between two (or more) things are used as a basis for concluding that the two things are also alike in other respects. Their form is of the type:

a has the characteristics *W, X, Y* and *Z*.
b has the characteristics *W, X* and *Y.*
Therefore it is probable that *b* also has the characteristic *Z*.

Such an argument can never be conclusive. Even if it has force, the premises may be true while the conclusion is false, because the conclusion does not follow necessarily from the premises. At best such arguments point to the probability, or the likelihood, that their conclusion will be true, e.g.

(73) Children are like puppies. They have to be domesticated - trained how to behave - otherwise they will grow up wild, uncontrollable and dangerous to others.

Many of our everyday inferences are made on the basis of analogy. If we have found the food at a particular restaurant to be tasty in the past, then we tend to expect that it will be so in the future by analogy.

Misleading Analogy

Arguments by analogy are strengthened by number of relevant similarities between the things compared, and weakened by the number of significant differences between them. There are at least *some* similarities between any one thing and anything else. What counts are *relevant* or *significant* similarities and differences. Sometimes an argument from analogy may be based upon a comparison which is erroneous or misleading; significant differences between the objects being ignored, while the similarities which give the analogy credibility may be insignificant.

When she was British Prime Minister, Margaret Thatcher was fond of comparing her government's financial and economic policies to those of a prudent housewife controlling her household budget. She claimed to be directing the economy of the country in the light of lessons she had learned during her childhood as a grocer's daughter, and in a manner of which any prudent housewife would approve. But there is probably little genuine similarity between the economy of a modern nation state and that of a private household. Differences of scale of this magnitude usually entail profound differences of kind.

(74) It is true that keeping taxation down will starve resources to the social services. And it has to be accepted that the homeless and unemployed will undergo some suffering as a consequence. But remember: "you can't make an omelette without breaking a few eggs." Causing human suffering cannot appropriately be compared to "breaking a few eggs."

Discussion: Evaluate the following analogical arguments:
1. One of women's most distinctive functions is the care of children. This so true that societies in which men, rather than women, nurture small children are altogether exceptional. Since those who are ill, infirm or senile resemble children in many ways, not merely by being physically weak and helpless, but also by being psychologically dependent, it is clear that women are especially qualified for nursing duties. Therefore girls should be directed towards careers in nursing and the caring professions.
2. People should not allow pornographic material into their homes since it would be like serving contaminated food to their families.
3. "If you cut up a large diamond into little pieces, it will entirely lose the value it had as a whole; and an army divided up into small bodies of soldiers loses all its strength. So a great intellect sinks to the level of an ordinary one as soon as it is interrupted and disturbed, its attention distracted and drawn off from the matter in hand: for its superiority depends upon its power of concentration – of bringing all its strength to bear on one theme, in the same way as a concave mirror collects into one point all the rays of light that strike upon it." (Arthur Schopenhauer, *On Noise*).
4. "I'm a uniter, not a divider. That means when it comes time to sew up your chest cavity, we use stiches as opposed to opening it up." (George W. Bush to David Letterman on *Late Night with David Letterman* (01.03.00) referring to Letterman's recent open-heart surgery).
5. It is dificult to see why some people make such heavy weather of reconciling the truth of the Bible with the findings of modern science. If you have received a message which warms your soul and gives you hope of eternal life, why should you bother about the shape and colour of the envelope it arrives in, or whether it has a stamp on the outside?

8. Generalisation

All our observations are necessarily restricted by the limits of our individual experience. Yet we constantly reach beyond our experience in the claims we make by generalisation. The process of generalisation moves from "all observed instances of x are y" to "all instances of x are y." This form of reasoning, from the particular to the general, or the less general to the more general, is technically known as **induction**. Inductive reasoning has the form:

x_1 is an instance of C and has the property P
x_2 is an instance of C and has the property P
x_3 is an instance of C and has the property P
Therefore, it is probable that all instances of C have the property P

The premises of such an argument establish the truth of their conclusion only with some degree of probability, greater or lesser, and never with total certainty. The conclusion of an inductive argument is always liable to be overthrown by the occurrence of a single contradictory instance.

Case Study: The Inductivist Turkey

The philosopher Bertrand Russell tells of a turkey who noted that from the first day of his arrival at the turkey farm he was always promptly fed at 9.am. Being a careful thinker, he did not jump to conclusions, but made careful observations of the time of his feeding on the different days of the week and under all the different weather conditions. Finally, after considering all the evidence available to him, he was driven to the conclusion that he could rest content, in the confident expectation that every day he would be fed at 9.am.

He was not disappointed until Christmas Eve when, instead of being fed, he had his throat cut.

Reliable and Unreliable Generalisations

Despite this problem, everyone makes generalisations. People sometimes say: "You should not generalise." But that is just silly. That statement itself is a generalisation. Generalisation is absolutely unavoidable, since we all have an overriding need to know more about the world than can be learned from our own individual experiences.

All classification is based upon generalisation. We have found that characteristics of things appear in recognisable bundles, and we attach a name to a bundle of characteristics, generalising it as a permanent feature of the environment. In the future we expect to see characteristics in those same bundles, and in general we are not disappointed. For this reason, all language is based upon generalisation. The use of simple words like "house," "mouse" and "sing" all embody generalisations concerning bundles of characteristics. If something which is not itself an object of our experience is described by using any of these words, then we expect that it will have characteristics of certain types and within certain ranges.

Without generalisation we could not function, because we would not be able to rely on our past experience. If we could not reason that because the floor of our bedroom has supported our weight in the past, it is probably safe to get out of bed this morning, we could never get anything done at all. Thinking well does not involve avoiding generalisations. If we think that we can do that, we are simply deceiving ourselves. Thinking well involves avoiding *hasty* and *ill-founded* generalisations.

The judgement of inductive arguments is not usually a clear-cut matter. It is never possible to state precisely what amounts to "enough instances" to ground a reasonable generalisation. But the strength of an inductive argument is increased if observations are taken in a wide variety of times, places and circumstances in order to ensure that they are typical of the widest range of instances. The wider the observations, the more confidence we can place in the generalisation. Again, "how wide" depends upon the objects being generalised about.

Copper sulphate crystals are rather boring, predictable things, which have a few predictable characteristics and which behave in a few predictable ways. Dogs, on the other hand, have more, and more complex, characteristics. They have a wider range of behaviour, and may behave in much less predictable ways than crystals. Thus two or three cases of observing the characteristics of copper sulphate crystals will usually suffice to ground a wide generalisation. If we have observed copper sulphate crystals turn white when heated in a normal atmosphere on several occasions, then that is sufficient to establish that copper sulphate crystals probably always turn white when heated under similar circumstances; and we can comfortably rest upon this conclusion.

But if you wish to know what happens to a dog in a garden when you open the gate and walk inside, you will need to make a lot of observations of different dogs under different circumstances to establish any useful generalisations at all. One dog may ignore you; another may approach to be petted; a third may hide round the back until he has worked out what you are up to; while yet another may decide to stand and fight. More disconcertingly, the *same* dog that one day rolls over on its back to be tickled *may,* on another occasion, due to some unfathomable whim of his own, decide to bite you.

Copper sulphate crystals never opt to turn pink or yellow instead of white on a whim. Unlike dogs, copper sulphate crystals are not subject to passing irrational moods and fancies which lead them to do strange and unpredictable things. The dog may one day decide to bring home some useless piece of junk, say an old coat, simply because he has taken a fancy to it. Copper sulphate crystals never surprise us in that sort of way. Human behaviour is even more complex and unpredictable than that of dogs.

These differences are extremely important in the methodology of the various sciences. Psychologists have to be much more tentative about their judgements than zoologists, and zoologists than chemists.

Since a single contradictory instance is enough to overturn an inductive argument, most effort should be focused upon seeking out instances which do not fit in with the general pattern. A fairly exhaustive search will increase the reasonableness of the generalisation, and therefore the degree to which we are justified in relying upon it.

Fallacies of Generalisation

Inadequate Generalisation: Inadequate generalisation is generalisation based upon inadequate evidence. Either too few cases have been observed, or they have been observed over too narrow a range of possibilities, or conflicting cases have not been sought for, or they have been ignored. People generalise about the inhabitants of other countries based upon a very few instances, or about the countries themselves, on the basis of a couple of weeks spent in a resort during a summer vacation. It is on the basis of such inadequate generalisations that people make such judgements as that people abroad are not as polite or truthful as we are.

A particular form of inadequate generalisation is when our choice of instances upon which to base our conclusion is selective.

Selective Treatment of the Evidence: The philosopher Francis Bacon described this approach as one of counting the hits and forgetting the misses; as when a chauvinistic patriot boasts the number of Nobel prizewinners his country has nurtured, as an example of its superiority to other nations, but is silent on the number of serial killers it has also fostered. This sort of reasoning lies behind much belief in clairvoyance and fortune-telling.

These are the sort of generalisations that have got the process a bad name. But inadequate generalisations are examples of poor thinking not because they are generalisations, but because they are inadequate. People should not say "You should not generalise." They should say: "You should not generalise thoughtlessly or recklessly."

Discussion: Are the following generalisations weak or strong. Explain your judgement, identifying any fallacies of generalisation you detect.

1. I have a pain in my stomach. People who have cancer of the stomach get pain in their stomachs. Therefore, I must have cancer.
2. To see how people will vote in the next election we polled thirty passers-by in Ekali. This shows conclusively which party is going to sweep the polls.
3. The fruit on the top of this box looks fresh, so the entire box must be fresh.
4. Marcia has had thirteen accidents in the last six months, yet she insists that it is just a coincidence and not her fault at all.
5. Italians are all thieves. At Bari I hadn't been off the ferry boat more than an hour when I found that my pocket had been picked.

How to Evaluate Arguments

- What is the proponent of the argument arguing for? What is his conclusion? Is it clear and unambiguous?
- Are his arguments relevant?
- Are his arguments conclusive or inconclusive?
- What type of argument is he using, deductive, inductive, by analogy? Is it the right sort of argument to establish his conclusion?
- Does his argument turn upon any vagueness or ambiguity?
- Are his arguments vacuous?
- Are there any illicit appeals to authority?
- Is the use of language emotive or persuasive rather than cool and rational?

If he is using an argument from analogy:

- Are the things compared relevantly similar, or not?

If he is using an inductive argument:

- Is there enough evidence to support his conclusion?
- Have a sufficient range of examples been considered?
- Has any attempt been made to seek for counter-examples?

If he is using a deductive argument:

- Are the premises of his argument true?
- Is the argument formally valid?

Glossary

analogy: a similarity between two things.

argument: a set of propositions in which some (the premises) provide grounds for holding others (the conclusion)

argumentum ad hominem: an argument directed at an opponent, rather than at an opponent's own argument or position.

assumption: a statement supposed to be true without proof or demonstration; an unstated premise or belief.

complex question: a question with built -i assumptions designed to limit possible responses

conclusive argument: an argument which, under certain circumstances, guarantees the truth of its conclusion.

deduction: a form of argument based upon inference from the universal to the particular, or from the more general to the less general.

form: the structure, pattern or arrangement of the elements within an argument, together with the ways in which they are related together.

generalisation: an inference from the particular to the general, or from the less general to the more general.

hypothetical proposition: a proposition of the form "if. . . then. . ."

hypothetical syllogism: a syllogism composed of a single hypothetical proposition and two categorical propositions.

inconclusive argument: an argument which can never guarantee the truth of its conclusion.

induction: a form of argument based upon generalisation, from the particular to the general, or from the less general to the more general, as a consequence of which the premises are inadequate conclusively to support the conclusion.

logic: rational thinking; the analysis of the standards of rational thinking.

logical necessity: the relation between two propositions such that the assertion of one together with the denial of the other involves a logical contradiction.

man of straw: an artificially vulnerable position falsely attributed to an opponentin argument as easier to attack than his real position.

metaphor: an implicit comparison.

middle term: the term which appears in both premises of a categorical syllogism.

non-conclusive argument: a species of argument in which the truth of the premise(s) is by itself insufficient finally to establish the truth of the conclusion.

proposition: what is entertained or asserted by using a statement sentence.

proof: a valid deductive argument with known true premises.

quantifier: a word or words which indicate the distribution of one of the terms of a proposition.

red herring: an attempt at diversion from relevance in argument

self-contradictory: a complex truth functional proposition is self-contradictory if it cannot be true for any truth values of the elementary propositions of which it is composed.

simile: an explicit comparison.

sound argument: a valid argument with premises known to be true

statement: an assertion that something is, or is not, the case.

tautology: a proposition of the form "*x* is *x*"

validity: the property of an argument such that if its premises are true its conclusion must be true.

7. LANGUAGE

"Language is the dress of thought." (Samuel Johnson)

Consider the following sentence:

(1) Three hundred and twenty two pink rabbits with blue tails chased the drunken police-men down the highway.

It seems highly likely that this is the first time that this sentence has ever been used in the entire history of the world. Yet not only was I able to create such a unique sentence, but you are immediately aware of what it means. With only a finite number of words and a limited set of grammar rules we can create an indefinite number of sentences referring to an indefinite number of states of affairs.

Through the medium of language, we can be informed about people, places and situations which we ourselves have never directly experienced. A traveller can tell us about a road accident he was involved in near his home, or his journey to the source of the Nile, and although we were not present we can, because of the power of language, to some extent share in his experiences. We can lie and create fiction. We can speculate about what might have been if history had taken a different turn. We can depict states of affairs which are possible, but which have never existed. We can consider daily life in ancient civilisations, or conditions in distant parts of the universe. We can describe times and places which we could not possibly experience. We can conjure up imaginary worlds which are, in some ways, unlike any which, as far as we can tell, have ever existed or ever will exist, like the "Middle Earth" created by J. R. R. Tolkein in *The Lord of the Rings*.

This facility is unique to humans. Animal communication systems consist of a finite number of calls with such specific meanings as "danger," or "the danger is past." Bees use a simple analogue system, in which each of a number of characteristics in their "dance" can be varied along a continuous scale to communicate some information. The overall direction of the dance tells in which direction the food is located, and the vigorousness of the bee's wiggling tells how much food is to be found there. By contrast, there is no theoretical limit to the number of words that can exist in human languages.

No group or tribe of human beings has ever been "discovered" which lacks this talent. Every human society has at least one language which they use to communicate with each other. It is these languages which function as the primary vehicles for our knowledge.

1. The Functions of Language

Language is the chief vehicle of knowledge. It is the principal means by which we crystallise, express, reflect upon, store and communicate our knowledge. Although we usually think of language as used to communicate information, this is only one of many functions which it can be called upon to perform. It may be used to:

- Express feelings and emotions. e.g. "Gosh!" "Oh, bother!" Many expressions of this type are unprintable.
- Inform others about what the world is (or might be) like, by asserting (or entertaining) that such and such is or is not the case. e.g. "It is snowing outside."
- Direct others in an attempt to control our environment in some way, usually by means of simple questions, requests, commands or warnings. e.g. "Can you tell me where I can find a good book shop?" "Leave me alone."
- Infer or draw conclusions from premises or evidence, and so reason about things. e.g. "If Andrew ditches his girl friend, then he will not have a partner for the school dance."
- Evoke or conjure up moods, feelings and emotions, a sense of place, time or situation. Much travel writing is of this kind. "In the fading light of the setting sun the buildings of the distant city took on a purplish hue."
- Establish or maintain interpersonal contacts, and to maintain social cohesion by conveying a sense of "togetherness." Greetings and social chat build up social bonds. e.g. "Yo, dude!" "How are you? Lovely day, isn't it?"
- Add dignity to a person or an occasion, usually by the adoption of a formal style. This includes the language of important documents, charters, awards, etc. e.g. "Elizabeth the Second, by the grace of God, of the United Kingdom of Great Britain and Northern Ireland, and of all her other territories and possessions beyond the seas, Queen, Head of the Commonwealth, Defender of the faith, etc.: Be it known that We . . ."
- Perform certain kinds of acts which actually change things in some way by the mere act of uttering or writing of words. "**Speech acts**," which include pronouncements by referees and umpires during games, the making of promises and agreements, declarations of war, peace and surrender, writing out cheques, etc. are recognised as changing circumstances by their mere performance. e.g. "I, Julian, take you, Davina, to be my lawful wedded wife . . ."
- Mislead, or distort the truth; as in lying or propaganda.
- Play or entertain others. We are intended only to be amused or engaged, not to take any truth claims etc. seriously. We may tell entertaining stories or jokes.
- Although language is so useful, there are some things which it does very badly. Try, for example, to express in words how to tie a reef knot, or exactly what you do when you drive a car. Tying a reef knot and driving a car are much easier, once you know how, than describing in words the precise sequences of actions which need to be performed. This is true of most skills, when we have learned them. In the following chapters we shall consider whether some information is better conveyed in other ways than in ordinary language, for example by the use of mathematical symbols, or by using the techniques of the fine arts.

Language may be used to reinforce social differences and buttress social privilege. If some dialects are regarded as superior and others as inferior, then language will be used to enable prospective employers to discriminate in favour of privileged groups and against "outsiders," effectively barring them from important and lucrative posts.

The social dimension of language may lead to pretentiousness, e.g. calling the janitor a plant manager or environmental technician, the garbage collector a refuse disposal operative, or glass fused silicate.

Talking Point: Is Language Male-Dominated?

Feminists have argued that our languages both reflect and reinforce male dominance.

God is always treated as male - as father and king, rather than mother and queen - despite the fact that believers assert that God is above gender divisions. Feminists also point to the use of female animal terms to refer disapprovingly to women, e.g. "bitch," "cow" and "vixen." Only if a woman is described using the male or sexless term "fox," is it a mark of approval. The current American slang term "you guys" is now used sexlessly, but this is by elevating the woman to the status of honorary male, since no one uses "ladies" or "you girls" in a similar gender-neutral sense, because males would feel humiliated if addressed in this way.

- Language may also be used to conceal or mislead, as we have seen in connection with propaganda.

Case Study: "Torture-lite"

An article in *Atlantic Monthly* written by Mark Bowden, entitled "The Art of Interrogation: A Survey of the Landscape of Persuasion," discusses what he calls the "civilized" methods of breaking people down" used by the US military when interrogating suspect terrorists and others. He argues that "A method that produces lifesaving information without doing lasting harm to anyone is not just preferable; it appears to be morally sound." He is not prepared to call such interrogation methods "torture." He reserves that word for "the more severe traditional outrages," and uses "coercion" to refer to what he calls " torture lite, or moderate physical pressure."

Bowden lists the methods of "moderate coercion" carried out by the U.S. military as: "sleep deprivation, exposure to heat or cold, the use of drugs to cause confusion, rough treatment (slapping, shoving, or shaking), forcing a prisoner to stand for days at a time or sit in uncomfortable positions, and playing on his fear for himself and his family."

Bowden asserts that these tactics, "although excruciating" for the victim, "generally leave no permanent marks and do no lasting physical harm." In fact, these are forms of torture that do lasting psychological harm to the victim, and can lead to a lifetime of nightmares, depression, and suicidal tendencies. The purpose of avoiding the use of the term "torture" would appear to be, quite simply, to avoid having to say that, at the beginning of the twenty-first century the US military uses torture.

2. By What Right is our Language "Corrected"?

In learning how to use our language, we are constantly having our vocabulary, grammar syntax and spelling corrected by our teachers and others. As children, we were told to speak "correctly": that a particular word was not being correctly pronounced, or was being used in the wrong context. Students' written work is, as a matter of course, regularly marked by teachers' corrections of grammar and spelling in accusatory red ink. To understand the authority anyone can claim to guide and correct our language, we first need to investigate how languages develop.

What Counts as a Language?

There are usually reckoned to be about three thousand languages. This figure is necessarily approximate because the term "language" is a vague one. It is not clear what counts as a language and what counts as a dialect or a local version of a language. A dialect speaker from Bristol, in England, may fail to understand a dialect speaker from Glasgow in Scotland; yet both will consider that they are speaking the same English language. By contrast, a Dane who has never learned any foreign languages at all may be able to understand someone from Southern Norway speaking the language they both call Norwegian. There is complete understanding between speakers of Serbian and Croatian and between Czech and Slovak. Understanding of slow speech is possible between Spanish and Portuguese. Comprehension is difficult, but not impossible, between Polish and Serbian.

What counts as a different language usually depends on political considerations: whether the speakers of each live in a separate nation-state, each with its own separate territory, government and flag. Mandarin and Cantonese, which are mutually unintelligible, are usually referred to as dialects of Chinese because they are both spoken within the boundaries of China, a single nation state under a single government with a single flag.

Where Have the Different Languages Come From?

Linguists, have noted that the various languages spoken throughout the world can be classified according to similarities in their vocabulary and grammar. These similarities are held to be evidence of common origins. (Languages are essentially made up of sound patterns which are uttered and which are listened to. Written language is a quite distinct, and much later, development. For the moment we shall be thinking only about spoken language.)

The interrelationships between languages and language families have been detected by considering large numbers of native words.

The languages which are spoken today have not only evolved to be what they are, but they are still in a continuous process of evolution. They are constantly undergoing change. This development is a slow one, so slow that we do not normally notice it, but the change can be can be seen clearly over a long stretch of time. If we compare the English of Shakespeare, of Charles Dickens, and of today's edition of The Sun, the differences are obvious. When the differences become great, we may speak of one language evolving into another, such as Latin into Italian, Spanish, Portuguese, French and Rumanian.

Many factors contribute to this process of change. Languages whose speakers live in contact with each other develop common features, especially in the way in which words are pronounced and the way in which words are put together in sentences (syntax), by unconscious imitation by the speakers of one language of speakers of the other. The French spoken by Frenchmen born near the German border comes to sound to non-French speakers, on first hearing, rather like German.

This effect is particularly important when people who have spoken one language come to speak another, perhaps after conquest by foreigners speaking a different language. The new language may be affected by the language which is given up. The earlier tongue, although it has been replaced, exercises a hidden influence over the newcomer, and modifies it, especially in its pronunciation. The influence of lost languages helps to explain why Latin developed in Gaul (France) into French, in Iberia into Spanish, Catalan and Portuguese, in Italy into Italian, and in Dacia into Romanian. In each area the development of Latin was influenced in different ways by the different languages it replaced.

Over the course of time difficult sounds and combinations of sounds which may require an effort to distinguish or pronounce will tend to be discarded. There are many complicated clicking sounds, difficult to make and to difficult to distinguish from each other, which are found in the languages of aboriginal peoples, but which have disappeared from most developed languages. A range of these clicks may be heard as used by N!Xau, the Kalahari bushman who starred in the movies The Gods must be Crazy. Of all these clicks, only the simple "k" sound remains in most modern languages. In English the initial hard consonants "k" and "g" in words like "knife," "knit," "gnash" and "gnaw" are difficult to pronounce separately when the speaker was in a hurry. For this reason they have disappeared from modern pronunciation.

Words may be shortened for convenience: frequently used polysyllables being sometimes reduced to monosyllables. Thus "omnibus" has already become "bus", and the noun "telephone", is in the process of becoming "phone."

Grammar also becomes simplified as analogy is used to eliminate irregularities. This is one of the most important factors in the evolution of English from Anglo-Saxon, so that the language has lost, among other things, all the original case endings except the "s" of the genitive. Complications and irregularities tend to disappear as the sheer weight of errors in students' work overwhelms their teachers.

Primitive languages have few words for abstract ideas, even at a low level of abstraction. In effect, this makes them much more complicated and unwieldy to use than more highly developed languages. The aborigines of Tasmania had no unique word for a tree, only words for gumtrees, wattle trees, etc. The Zulu of South Africa have words for "red cow," "white cow," etc., but none for "cow."

Primitive languages are extremely complex, but this is because of their low level of abstraction. Their complexity does not make the language subtle, since a large vocabulary is required to say the simplest things. Primitive languages are simply less efficient than more highly developed languages. That is why they are called "primitive."

Old words drop out of use when they are no longer needed, and new words are coined or borrowed to serve new needs. Many words for medieval farm implements dropped out of use with the development of new agricultural machinery during the industrial revolution. That revolution, and more recently the invention and development of computer technology, have spawned masses of new words, from "locomotive" to "modem."

Written Language

Written language is secondary to the spoken language, and a much later development. Aristotle said: "Speech is the representation of the experiences of the mind, and writing is the representation of speech." With the invention of writing, a new dimension was added to linguistic behaviour. Script is both a means of communicating at a distance through space and time, and also a means of information storage and retrieval superior to the memory.

Although there are about 6,700 languages on earth at the moment (two hundred of these almost extinct) only some 2,500 have ever been reduced to writing. Of these, all but about two hundred and fifty have only parts of the Bible in writing, with perhaps a grammar and a dictionary in addition, produced by Christian missionaries.

The script in which a language is written down and the language itself are quite independent of each other. The resemblances of one language with another which are used by linguists to determine relationships which indicate common origins, are totally independent of the scripts which are used to express those languages, which may have a quite separate history of development behind them. Unrelated or only distantly related languages may share the same script; while closely related languages may use quite different scripts. The Latin script is now used for languages quite unrelated to the one for which it was originally adapted, and it is now employed to put into writing languages with origins as diverse as English, Turkish, Swahili and Malay-Indonesian. By contrast, Serbian and Croatian are almost identical in speech, but the Catholic Croats use the Latin alphabet while the Orthodox Serbs use the Cyrillic script, which is adapted from the Greek.

There are two fundamentally different ways of expressing language in writing, which can be distinguished as "thought-writing" and "sound-writing." Thought-writing uses ideographs. A single sign is used to represent an idea, concept or word. Sound-writing uses alphabets, in which a single sign represents a sound, or group of sounds.

The first script was probably a form of picture writing. Its main advantage is that since meaning is displayed in picture form it should, theoretically at least, convey meaning without having to be learned. We should be able to recognize what a sign or pictogram refers to by its appearance. International road signs are pictograms. Moreover, they are independent of the language, no translation should be necessary from one language to another. Any speaker of any language should, in principle at least, be able to read pictograms written by speakers of any other language whatsoever, just as motorists speaking any language may instantly understand the international sign for "no overtaking." Moreover, writing many centuries old should be readily understandable today without having to learn the old forms of the language.

However, pictograms inevitably become conventionalised. That is, over a long period of time, the signs come to diverge further and further from the original pictures. This happens because, with constant use, writers inevitably develop ways of "cutting corners" in their writing, and these alterations come to be recognised and accepted in practice. From being an imitation of nature, the sign comes to be a conventional symbol.

Conventions

Conventions are "ways in which we do things," where they could have been different. It is a convention in Britain to eat holding the knife in the right hand and the fork in the left. It is also a convention to use the convex side of the fork to carry food to the mouth. These are not commandments given to the British by God. There is nothing in the nature of things which necessitates that the knife and fork should be used in this way. In fact it is actually more convenient to use the fork as a spoon to carry food to the mouth than to use it in the conventional way. It takes a high degree of skill and dexterity, together with considerable experience, to keep peas from falling off the back of the fork while it is in transit to the mouth, and the British have to acquire these things. People in other countries do it differently anyway.

But if you do not eat this way, in Britain at least, people will probably think that you are ignorant and that you do not know how to behave "properly," or that you are deliberately being offensive, and then they will take offence. If you were to explain that you just do it differently from everyone else, they will probably think that you are weird. In any case, you will be the loser.

Conventional rules have no validity independently of our expectations and customs, but even so, they must not be treated lightly or with contempt, for the one who does so is likely to suffer for it, if only by social ostracism.

In addition, adaptations have to be devised to express things which cannot be "pictured": abstract ideas such as "goodness" and "hope", and those small but important functions such as plurality or alternation (either . . . or . . .). When conventions are devised for these functions, different conventions will come to be adopted in different places and at different times, and these will have to be learned.

In this way the pictures gradually becomes less and less universally recognisable, and evolve into conventional signs which can only be understood by someone who has previously learned their meanings. This has happened to Chinese script. It may be possible to see the picture hidden in a conventionalised Chinese ideogram when it is pointed out to us by someone who can read Chinese, but it cannot usually be recognised unaided. Someone who is ignorant of the Chinese language cannot read Chinese script simply by recognising the ideas pictured in the signs. Moreover, in time the ideograms come to be used for words, rather than the ideas the words stand for. Additionally, as the ideograms develop differently in different geographical regions, the script will come to differ from place to place, and from language to language, and so the script (like the spoken language) will develop into mutually unintelligible forms which will need to be translated.

Ideographic script has further disadvantages. A vast number of signs are necessary, one for each basic idea or word, and these are a great burden on the memory when they have become conventionalised. It is necessary to know a minimum of 2,000-4,000 ideograms for elementary Chinese and as many as 50,000 for a proper appreciation of the literary language. Each ideogram has to be learned separately. A reader confronted by a new word is usually quite unable to read it, since there is nothing to link what is on the paper to the sound of the corresponding spoken word.

Around 1700 BC, workers or slaves under Egyptian rule in the Sinai Peninsula came into contact with Egyptian hieroglyphic symbols. They adopted some of the symbols to write down the consonant sounds of their language, Proto-Canaanite. They chose pictorial Egyptian symbols (like ox-head, house, etc.) to use as signs for the sounds. The Phoenician alphabet evolved from the Proto-Canaanite during the 12th century BC, and most of the alphabets used today are descended from this, although they may look very different today.

Sometime between 1200 and 900 BC, the Greeks modified the set of signs to suit the sounds in their own language, and also adapted some letters to represent the vowel sounds, so creating the first genuine alphabet. A version of the Greek alphabet used on the island of Euboea was transmitted to the Etruscans of central Italy, and so on to the Romans and most of the Western world. Later, saints Cyril and Methodius of Thessaloniki adapted the Greek alphabet to express the ancient Slavic language. The result is the Cyrillic script, used today by the Russians, Serbs, Bulgarians and others.

Such aids to reading as spaces to separate the words, punctuation and accents, are later developments to aid efficient comprehension.

Alphabets have great advantages over ideograms. Fewer symbols are required, usually between twenty and fifty, so that the system is more efficient. Unlike ideograms, sound-script is necessarily tied to a particular language. However, it should be possible to use an alphabet with just the small effort of learning which symbol corresponds to which sound in the spoken language. Since, ideally, one letter should correspond to one sound, and vice versa, a reader should be able to pronounce a word correctly when he sees it in written form for the first time. Likewise, he should be able to spell correctly a word which he has heard but has never before seen written down.

This is generally true of some languages, such as Italian, which are called phonetic languages for this reason. But it is by no means true of many others, particularly English and French. This is because the spelling of these languages came to be standardised some time ago, with the development of printing. As we have seen, the spoken language is in a constant state of change and development, and this includes pronunciation. By contrast, written forms of the language tend to remain fixed. The one-to-one correspondence between letter and sound broke down over a period of time and can no longer be automatically relied upon. For this reason spellings now just have to be learned.

A thoroughgoing simplification of the spelling would make English easier to learn, both for native speakers and for those learning English as a foreign language. However, a reform of the spelling could never be a final answer to these difficulties. The crucial problems lie in the nature of language and the relationship between the spoken language and the script used to represent it. The ancient Romans used to say: Verba volent, scripta manent (words fly, writing remains). Language inevitably changes over a period of time, so that either the spelling would have to change with it, or the reformed spelling would in time cease to be phonetically accurate. Sooner or later we should inevitably find ourselves with the original problem once again.

Standards of Language Use

We are now in a position to deal with the question: who decides what counts as a mistake in English, or in any other language? Why are some usages castigated as errors? On what grounds are our spelling, grammar, and syntax corrected by our teachers? Clearly, in one sense these questions have a simple answer. Our parents and teachers learned how to use the language correctly from their own parents and teachers, and so on. But how does *anybody* know what counts as right or wrong? Parents and teachers act as authorities on the language. But on what basis do these authorities make their judgements? They cannot be made entirely on the basis of other authorities. There must be some *reasons* why some usages are correct and others incorrect. It is *these* grounds, which justify the judgements of authorities, which we need to locate.

Some people like to talk as though there is some sort of absolute standard with which all our usage may be compared, and by which it may be judged, and that this standard holds whatever people actually do. Parents and teachers are said to be justified in correcting our language because they know the rules, and how to apply them. Those who argue in this way assume that there are rules of pronunciation, grammar, and spelling which exist "by themselves," independently of how people actually use language. They provide a fixed point of reference against which all language use may be judged. They prescribe what you "ought" to do. You "ought" to obey the rules of grammar, etc. If you do not, your usage will be incorrect, and you will have fallen into error. This will be true however many people are in error, and however frequently they err.

Failure to understand the essentially evolutionary nature of language may lead to what is sometimes called the **etymological fallacy**, the view that an earlier meaning of a word must in some sense be the "correct" one. Thus the "real" meaning of "nice" must be "fine" or "precise", and the real meaning of "naughty" is "evil", because those were the meanings which those words carried in past centuries.

For some languages there are institutions which are authorised by governments to control the processes of linguistic change. The Académie Française, was founded by Cardinal Richelieu in 1634 to "give our language certain rules, and to render it pure, eloquent, and able to deal with the arts and sciences." Since that time the Académie has acted as a high court, deciding "officially" exactly what is, and what is not, correct French. Every forty years or so the Académie produces a revised edition of an official dictionary. In between editions it issues advice, warnings and judgements. The academicians are recognised as setting the standards for good usage through-out the French-speaking world.

This has been compared to the behaviour of the legendary Danish King Canute, who had his throne carried down to the seashore, where he tried to use his royal authority order the waves of the incoming tide to turn back. He got his feet wet. The author of the first English dictionary, Dr. Johnson, observed that: Academies have been instituted to guard the avenues of the languages, to retain fugitives and to repulse invaders; but their vigilance and activity have been in vain; sounds are too volatile and too subtle for legal restraints, to enchain syllables and to lash the wind are equally the undertakings of pride, unwilling to measure its desires by its strength."

Nevertheless, this view is popular because it is seems clear and simple, and people like things to be clear and simple. People like to be able to say: "This is right and that is wrong; and that is all there is to it." However, reality is not usually so simple. Behind this position there is a false analogy between the traditional popular view of the rules of morality and the rules of language. According to the traditional view of morality, God has laid down what is right and wrong, and that is all there is to it. To disobey is simply to sin. Stealing would be no less wrong even if everybody in the world actually stole. According to this view something similar is true of language. We could all be speaking incorrectly, and probably are; but despite that fact, the rules remain the rules.

This conservative view probably developed out of the dominance over the minds of scholars in past centuries of the fixed grammars and vocabularies of Classical Greek and Latin. But those grammars were only fixed because the languages were studied as though they were dead, fixed for all time in their ancient forms. In fact Ancient Greek never died out, it just evolved into Modern Greek; while Latin is alive and flourishing today in the forms of French, Italian, Spanish, Catalan, Portuguese and Romanian.

It is clear from what we have seen of the constantly changing nature of language that there can be no absolute standard by which any usage can be judged; and to suppose that there could be is simply to fail to understand what language is.

Basing their ideas upon the nature of language and how it develops, many linguists today take a radically opposite view from the one we have been considering. They argue that language is what people actually speak or write, and nothing more. A language is not what someone, however learned, thinks it ought to be. On this view grammar lays bare the regularities which lie behind what people actually say or write, it does not, and could not, impose regularities upon them. On this view there are - strictly speaking - no errors in language behaviour at all, only deviations from the statistical norm.

From this point of view there would seem to be no point in teaching spelling and grammar. People will communicate with each other because they need to; and how they do it, well . . . that is just up to them. In that case the student with the red marks on his misspellings might protest to his teacher "My spelling is not wrong, it is just different. This is how I do it, and that's all there is to it."

This approach fails to take account of the fact that in order to communicate efficiently we all depend upon shared conventions. If I decide to use the word "yes" for those circumstances in which other people use the word "no", and *vice versa*, the result will be a serious failure to communicate and considerable confusion, and I shall suffer on account of it.

A compromise view recognises that rules of grammar and pronunciation are not fixed and immutable, independent of what people actually do, and that at any given time some of them are in a process of change. Yet it also recognises that effective communication depends upon the observance of rules. According to this view, "correct," when applied to speech or writing, means "in accordance with the rules which are conventionally accepted at the present" and nothing more. But since the main purpose of language is communication, and since this depends upon the shared use of conventions, those conventions must, generally, be observed. If we do not observe them we shall merely irritate and confuse those with whom we are trying to communicate."

Part of the force of prescriptive views is derived from the fact that social prestige attaches to some uses of the language and is absent from others. Since social discrimination is likely to lead to loss of opportunities for employment and advancement, that in itself is adequate reason for parents to pressure their children, and for teachers to guide their students, to observe the conventions in force at the time. Not to do so would be to disadvantage them. This is not because these conventions are in some way objectively "correct," independently of the actual behaviour of the language-using community, but rather that the language-using community expects such behaviour, and failure to conform to the conventional rules will usually lead to misunderstanding, censure and discrimination. If two people are applying for the same job, and one observes the conventions of speech and writing while another disregards them then, all other things being equal, it is likely that the one who observes the conventions will get the job. Also, examinations test, among other things, awareness of the conventions. To the extent that he disregards the conventions a student will score low in his examinations, and so lose those opportunities which are opened up by educational qualifications.

3. The Language Barrier

Language is not only a means of communication, it is also a barrier. If two people both speak the same language, they can communicate with each other and exchange ideas. If they speak different languages, and do not have a language in common, communication is difficult. The ancient Greeks mocked all non-Greek speakers as "barbarians," an attitude which the philosopher Max Black expressed as: "Here's someone who talks differently. Let's throw a stone at him."

The existence of languages which we do not understand limits the number of people to whom we can listen, speak, read and write with comprehension. If someone's native language has few speakers, and if that is the only language he understands, then he is very limited, not only in the number of people he can efficiently communicate with, but also in the opportunities he has for a successful and prosperous life. Some two thousand living languages are each spoken by just a few thousand people. Those born into a large language community are, by contrast, very fortunate. About ten languages are spoken as first languages by half the population of the world. According to the *Ethnologue* (1996) these are:

1. Mandarin Chinese	885,000,000	
2. English	322,000,000	
3. Spanish	266,000,000	
4. Bengali	189,000,000	

5. Hindustani	182,000,000
6. Portugese	170,000,000
7. Russian	170,000,000
8. Japanese	125,000,000
9. German	98,000,000
10. Wu Chinese	77,175,000

Anyone who could speak the first six of these languages could speak to half the people on earth.

Language Differences

Languages differ not merely in their vocabularies but also in the way they are constructed. Since all the languages most westerners are likely to learn to use are similar in structure, we tend to assume greater similarities among languages than is the case. When we branch out into unfamiliar regions, the differences are more marked. The vocabularies of different languages reflect the interests and concerns of the native speakers. These may be very different from our own. This leads to great differences from the languages we know in the range of their vocabularies. Aboriginal languages have no words to stand for the technical vocabulary of computers, but many for their local *flora* and *fauna*. Thus, according to Peter Farb, the Masai of Kenya have seventeen words for cattle, while the Ifugeo of the Philippines have twenty words for rice. By contrast, some languages fail to distinguish what we distinguish. Thus the Koyas of India have only one word to refer to the unfamiliar phenomena of dew, fog and snow.

Case Study: Quechua - The Language of the Incas

Quechua is the most widely spoken Amerindian language, with over eight million speakers in Peru, Ecuador, Bolivia, and Chile. It is the language of the Incas. In English we have borrowed the words "cocoa," "condor," "guano," "Inca," "jerky," "llama," "pampa," "puma" and "quinine" from Quechua.

This language has many features strange to speakers of Indo-European languages:

- No distinction is made between "he" and "she"; yet "we" meaning "we and you" is distinguished from "we" meaning "we but not you."
- Particles are attached to nouns to signify the attitude adopted towards the statement uttered, in order to indicate:
    personal knowledge: "I know it for a fact."
    hearsay knowledge: "or so I've heard."
- There are also particles attached to verbs to show that an action is:
    for someone else's benefit
    for the actor's own benefit
    futile, or of little importance
    unusual, out of the ordinary
    important or urgent
    lamentable, or to be regretted
    not the responsibility of the speaker.

Being able to use all these particles correctly is regarded as an important sign that someone knows the language well.

Many languages "divide up" the world in ways different from European languages:

- The Apaches of North America divide up some parts of the human body in a different way from English, having single words for hand and arm, for thighs and buttocks, and for chin and jaw.
- English-speakers have only one word, "uncle," covering both a father's brother and a mother's brother. In many other languages there are different words for these relations, and it would be necessary to know which was being referred to before choosing which word to use for a person we call an uncle.
- Many languages fail to distinguish between certain colours which are distinguished in English. Many West African languages fail to distinguish blue and green, and the East African language, Kiswahili, does not distinguish between red and brown. The Shona of Zimbabwe have one word, *cipsuka*, for the colours red and orange. While an English-speaker needs to decide whether an object he is talking about is red or orange, a Shona-speaker can leave this undetermined.

Many languages have grammatical features which are surprisingly different from those of the languages familiar to most people reading this book:

- Hebrew has no verb tenses to show past, present and future action. Only ongoing and completed actions are differentiated.
- In Japanese, adjectives have tenses, which are shown by changes of the word endings, just like verbs: distinguishing e.g. "is red" from "was red".
- In Nootka, spoken by Indians on Vancouver Island, Canada, there are special grammatical features for talking to different classes of people. If the person being spoken to is unusually big or fat the speaker adds *aq-* to the verb stem before any other suffixes. There are other affixes for addressing those who are lame, children, unusually short adults, those with eye defects, left-handed persons, circumcised males, etc.

Translation

Because of these differences it may be difficult, or even impossible, to translate some sentences from one language to another.

- Firstly, there may be no simple word or set of words in the one language which would reproduce the exact sense of the original. There is no expression in English corresponding to the Danish expression *"Tak for mad,"* which is used exclusively by guests or members of a household after a meal, for conveying thanks to their hostess.
- There is sometimes more than one word in one language for a single word in another, so that a distinction made in one language is difficult to render in another.
- The French greetings *"Ca va?"* and *"Hallo"* may both be translated by the English "Hello". But the first French greeting is made face to face, while the second is used when answering the telephone. This distinction will be lost in any simple translation into English.
- In Italian and German the word for "yes" is frequently repeated: *"Si, si, si."* *"Ja, ja."* A single *si* or *ja* would often sound brusque. By contrast, in Tagalog (Filipino) repetition is used for *de*emphasis, and so produces the opposite effect. A direct translation from a language where repetition signified emphasis into Tagalog would produce the opposite effect to the one intended.

There may be no feature in the culture which lies behind the one language which corresponds to the cultural features referred to in the original. Under those circumstances, a straight translation might prove misleading. "Bathroom" and its equivalents in English, Finnish and Japanese do not stand for places which are alike, either in their furnishings or purpose.

Ideological differences also create problems for translators. "Democratic" is understood in liberal western democracies as meaning that a people choose their government in multiparty elections. In communist states the same term was understood to mean rule by the working class, through the vanguard of the working class movement, the Communist Party. This was held to be incompatible with multiparty democracy. Thus the statement "Our country has a democratic form of government" would have meant one thing to an English citizen, while its literal translation into Russian would have meant quite another thing to a Soviet citizen.

Sometimes, in order to translate a sentence from one language into another we need more information than is provided in the original sentence. As the Tasmanian aborigines had words for various types of tree, but no word for a tree as such, it would be impossible accurately to translate the simple sentence "He sat under a tree" into their language. We would first need to make a decision as to what sort of tree was referred to, and we might have no information on which to base a decision.

Usually, these problems can be circumvented, although with some difficulty and inelegance of expression, perhaps using long circumlocutions and awkward grammatical constructions.

Universal Grammar

These differences raise the question as to whether or not all languages have a single basic structure (depth grammar). According to Roger Bacon: "In substance, grammar is one and the same in all languages, but it may vary accidentally." Is there a "universal grammar" which underlies all languages, or not? The American linguist Noam Chomsky has argued that there is.

Recent studies have demonstrated that many features are common to all languages. These are said to constitute a Universal Grammar, a basic blueprint for language, within which variations occur. The linguist Steven Pinker compares this with the body plan found among all the animals within a given *phylum*. The same parts can be distorted in different species, in the way that a bat's hand functions as a wing and a seal's as a flipper; visible differences concealing a common structure. In the same way, a universal grammar may lie concealed within the various languages by surface variations and by differences of vocabulary. According to Noam Chomsky, from a Martians'-eye point of view, all humans speak the same language. This universal grammar is a "generative grammar," in that it allows us, on the basis of a few sentences we have heard, to understand, and construct, an infinite number of new sentences using a finite vocabulary.

Chomsky also maintained that much of the structure of human language is inborn in the brain, so that a baby has only to learn the vocabulary and the structural parameters of his native language - not how language works. There is good evidence for this view. Young children may learn to talk remarkably well from what would sometimes appear to be a very inadequate exposure to language. It can be shown that babies acquire some rules of grammar that they could never have "learned" from what was available to them, if the structure of language were not "built-in." In addition, the structure of language on different levels seems to be associated with particular parts of the brain, since it can be lost by injury to those areas. There are also some unexpected structural similarities between all known languages. This issue is still hotly debated among linguists.

Even if language is in some sense instinctive in humans, like the songs of birds, what is inherited is a basic structure. The language that is actually spoken depends upon the young learning particular forms and patterns of speech from their parents and other adults, leaving us with the problem of communication across language barriers, and raising the question whether there ought to be a universal language for all mankind.

Is a Universal Language Possible or Desirable?

Although there has never been a truly universal language, there have been some periods when a single cultural area did share a common language, or when all those who travelled or who were educated shared a common language: Greek in the eastern parts of the Roman Empire and in the Byzantine world, Latin in the western Roman Empire and in medieval Western Europe, and Arabic in most of the Islamic world.

In Western Europe the universality of Latin broke down with the development of writing in the modern forms of the language — French, Catalan, Spanish, Portuguese, Italian, etc. Its demise was hastened by the division of the Catholic Church at the Reformation. Even so, there was still a clear need for a universal language, and the prestige of France during the eighteenth century secured for that language the status of being the recognised language of diplomacy. As such it came to be used by the representatives of all Western governments when dealing with each other.

Several attempts have been made to create a universal language artificially. The French philosopher, René Descartes, saw the need for a language which would be simple enough to be learned by everyone without much effort as a second language. It would be absolutely regular and logical, totally lacking in unpredictable idioms. Everyone would learn his mother tongue together with the new, international language, and in this way, everyone would be able to communicate with everyone else.

Many artificial languages have actually been created, such as Volapuk and Interlingua ("Latin without the grammar"). Some artificial languages have been the product of whimsy or were designed for entertainment. J. R. R. Tolkein, created several languages for the different creatures which feature in his books, *The Hobbit* and *The Lord of the Ring*. More recently, fans of *Star Trek* have developed Klingon, a language spoken by creatures of that name in the television series.

By far the most important of the languages created with serious purpose is Esperanto, invented by Dr. L. L. Zamenhof, a Russian-Polish Jew, and published in 1887 under the pseudonym "Dr. Esperanto," meaning "one who hopes." This name was adopted for the language itself which is said to have about two million speakers today. Esperanto has a consistent and logical grammar, said to consist of only sixteen rules. There is a direct correspondence between written and spoken language: for each letter there is one and only one sound, and all letters are pronounced. Most of the vocabulary was taken from European languages. It is now spoken around the world, and some children of Esperantists are said to have learned it as a native language. Unfortunately, it has features which some see as quite unnecessary complications, such as male and female gender for nouns. Also, some argue that its dependence upon European models robs it of its claim to universality. In any case, since there seems little chance that most people will ever learn it, it has only added to the babel of languages it was intended to replace.

A common language would clearly be of practical benefit to all. It would save a lot of time and expense in translating the speeches of delegates at international conferences, in translating documents for international treaties, trade contracts, etc. It would prevent the misunderstandings which can sometimes arise when the parties to negotiations and agreements use translators and translations. It would remove barriers of communication between peoples and facilitate international travel, so that anyone could travel anywhere and be immediately understood. It would be a boon to international tourism. It would enable students theoretically to study in any country of the world, and enable researchers to read the work of authorities in their subject of any nationality. In these ways, it would enable the rise of a truly international academic community. Moreover, the literature of every country would be economically available in translation to anyone, whatever his own native language.

It could be argued that such a language ought be an artificially created language, like Esperanto. Only an artificial language could be simple enough to reduce the effort of learning it to a minimum. Moreover, because of national rivalries and jealousies, only an artificial language would be universally acceptable.

However, the idea that an artificial language could gain universal acceptance is probably wildly unrealistic, as the evidence of the history of Esperanto shows. Only an existing language could gain that position. It would do so by becoming a language which it would be socially and economically limiting not to know. Then it would gain its position without any decision of governments being necessary, simply in virtue of the law of supply and demand. Ambitious parents would insist that their children become proficient in it. An existing language, moreover, already has its grammars, dictionaries, and its teachers in existence.

If an existing language were to develop, Mandarin Chinese, as the most popular language spoken on earth, would appear at first sight to be the most promising candidate. However, since Chinese is not written in an alphabetical script, it would be onerous to learn and difficult to use mechanically.

The second candidate, by the same measure, would be English. The spelling is notoriously difficult. Some expressions are idiomatic and often quite illogical, for example, the many difficult phrasal verbs. Moreover, in the Third World, English is still sometimes associated with American and British imperialism.

Despite all that, it does have many advantages. The second most frequently spoken language in the world, in every inhabited continent there is at least one country where English is already an official language. It is the language of the world's dominant superpower. It uses the Latin alphabet, which it shares with the speakers of many other major world languages, e.g. Spanish, Portuguese, French and German. It is the language of science and technology, since most higher level scientific publications are in English. It is already the international language of aviation, used by air-traffic control all over the world to talk to pilots. It is becoming the language of global communication in finance, tourism and the Internet. It is the language which carries the most prestigious and dynamic popular culture, e.g. in popular songs and films.

English has some useful features which would make it suitable as a universal language. It has little unnecessary grammar. It can be successfully used with a small vocabulary. Ogden and Richards, who invented "Basic English," calculated that a core of eight hundred words could be used to define all the other words in the dictionary. This is partly due to the versatility of those difficult phrasal verbs. Due to its history it has a very rich vocabulary with many near-synonyms. This makes it a very expressive language. It has a considerable vocabulary of scientific terms based upon Greek and Latin which it shares with most other languages, making learning the vocabulary easier. Moreover, access to English makes available an incomparable treasury of literature spanning a thousand years and several continents.

Despite these advantages, it would be impossible to get the nations to agree to accept English as a universal language. Nevertheless, it seems that English is already evolving into a universal language by a natural process. During the last decade of the twentieth century the former satellite states of the Soviet Union in Eastern Europe very quickly dropped the obligation imposed upon them by Soviet rule to teach Russian as the second language in their schools, and turned to English to replace it. When the use of English has become so widespread that ignorance of it is a distinct disadvantage in life, it will have effectively become the world language.

This development might, however, be considered undesirable, in that it might lead to the disappearance of first languages, which many argue would be a cultural impoverishment of human civilisation.

Language and the Limits of Thought

Most of our knowledge comes to us encoded in a language. This language may to some extent determine the nature and limits of our knowledge. The nineteenth century diplomat and philologist Wilhelm von Humboldt said: "Man lives with the world about him, principally, indeed exclusively, as language presents it."

Language may not simply be a means of describing and explaining how the world is, it may also assist in the very structuring of our experience itself. According to Benjamin Whorf, "We see and hear and think as we do mostly because of our language community." He argues that:

"We cut up nature along lines laid down by our native languages. The categories and types that we isolate from the world of phenomena we do not find there because they stare every observer in the face; on the contrary, the world is presented in a kaleidoscopic flux of impressions which has to be organised by our minds — and this means largely by the linguistic system in our minds. We cut nature up, organise it into concepts, and ascribe significances as we do, largely because we are parties to an agreement to organise it in this way — an agreement that holds throughout our speech community and is codified in the patterns of our language."

He goes on to say that we are not conscious of what we are doing, and we cannot avoid doing it in the way that we do, because we are constrained by our language to do it one way rather than another. He goes on to argue that people whose native languages have markedly different grammars will see the world in different ways, and attend to markedly different aspects of it.

This sense in which we "live in different worlds" is not merely a matter of how we chop the world up. Some experiences are said actually to depend upon our language. The characteristics of the language will determine which features of things we select to focus our thought upon. But beyond that, it is argued that our experiences do not come to us independently of language. The philosopher Ludwig Wittgenstein argued that a great many of our experiences would actually be impossible without language.

Whorf maintained: "Observers are not led by the same physical evidence to the same picture of the universe unless their linguistic backgrounds are similar or can in some way be calibrated." What we count as reality is to some degree dependent upon our language. Accordingly, "We see and hear and think as we do mostly because of our language community." The structure and vocabulary of the language determines what can and cannot be said, and therefore thought, by its speakers. Language thus becomes something like a system of railway tracks along which, and only along which, our thoughts must run. As the philosopher Ludwig Wittgenstein put it: "The limits of my language are the limits of my world." This view is known as **linguistic relativism**.

One consequence of its being true would be that the elimination of a language would involve the elimination of a unique way of looking at the world. When Europeans arrived in North America, there were several hundred different language groups spread over the continent. Now only about one hundred and fifty survive. Nearly all of these are spoken by a few dozen old people, even in tribes that still number in the thousands. The younger generation of Native Americans prefer to speak English. In consequence, in fifty years time, the number of these languages will have declined to a mere handful. These losses are not merely losses of another language; they are losses of insights into human experience, distinctive "ways of looking at things" developed by the experience of countless generations of language-speakers in their particular environment. These "ways of looking at things" embody knowledge, which will be lost to the mainstream culture when the language dies.

4. Language and Reality

(1) Heavy, black clouds mean that rain is on its way.

(2) Holes in the cabbage leaves mean that the caterpillars have been eating them.

(3) The ringing of a bell means the end of class.

(4) The word "death" means the end of life.

(5) He was engaged in a quest for the meaning of life.

The above are all examples of meaning in its most general sense: when one thing makes us think of another. People sometimes talk about the *real* meaning of a word, as though this is something which lies around waiting to be discovered. It may have been misplaced or lost because of our slovenly misuse of language, but can somehow be recovered by careful investigation.

This way of talking stems from the common ancient view that our words have some sort of necessary link with what they stand for in the world. It was believed that in some sense words represent the "essences" of things, what they *really* are; while the structure of grammar in some way reflects the "grain" or "structure" of reality; and that is how language works.

In order to express this sense of a necessary connection between words and things, it was sometimes claimed that the words of human languages are gifts to mankind from the gods, who alone could have known the true, secret names of things.

This belief in a necessary connection between words and things explains some strange features of past cultures.

• Much ancient magic was based upon the belief that someone who knows the right words, and utters them correctly, can command the things those words refer to because of the strength of the connection between words and the things which they represent. A spell frequently consisted of the recitation of words describing or commanding some desired effect, which were thought to have the power, merely by themselves, to bring about that effect.

• In some cultures people were very reluctant to divulge their names to strangers, fearing that knowing their name would give the stranger some sort of "handle" or power over them. In order to avoid this danger, at least one tribal people adopted the practice of giving all children two names: a "false" name by which they were publicly known, and a "true" name known only to their closest family and kept secret from everybody else.

Since we now know much about how languages develop, this view that there is a necessary connection between language and reality is no longer acceptable. If it were true, we should all be using the same language, or perhaps approaching the same language as our knowledge increases. In any case, it is absurd to suppose that there is a necessary connection between, say, "being a dog" and the very different words "dog" (English), *pes* (Czech), *kutya* (Hungarian), *kalb* (Arabic), *mbwa* (Swahili); while there is no such connection between "being a dog" and the words "cat," "kill" or "sophistication."

Words as Symbols

We learn from experience that some things are the signs of others, for example, that yawning is a sign of tiredness, because the one is found to accompany the other. For this reason, when we see the one we immediately think of the other. Seeing someone yawn makes us think of tiredness. It may even make us feel tired ourselves. In communication, we deliberately take advantage of this association of ideas. We associate a **sign**, the word "tiredness," with the feeling of being tired. Seeing the sign makes us think of what it signifies. When x is deliberately used as a sign of y in order to bring y to mind, then x is said to be a **symbol** of y. Words are symbols because they represent things to us by deliberate design, and are understood to do so by the community.

The modern view is that natural language is an arbitrary and conventional code of symbols, which have no "real" or necessary connection with the things they refer to in the world. The symbols used in language are **arbitrary** because each one could have been different. But for the accident of history, dogs could equally have been referred to in English as *werps* or *zints*. There is nothing in the symbol "dog" which makes it any more suitable to perform the function that it in fact does perform than *werp* or *zint*. The symbols of language are **conventional** because the English-speaking community does, as a matter of fact, refer to dogs as "dogs".

Arbitrary and Conventional

Something is **arbitrary** if it could have been different. Something is **conventional** if that is the way we do it in our society. We follow a convention, a customary way of doing things.

In western societies we usually greet each other with a handshake. Things need not have been like that. Had the course of history taken a different turn we might have greeted each other in some other manner, perhaps by holding up our hands with palms extended outwards in a salute, or by rubbing noses. Because the act of greeting might have been performed in a different way, the handshake is *arbitrary*. Yet in our society, the custom has grown up that we do, in fact, greet each other with a handshake. That is the custom or convention. For that reason, the handshake is *conventional*. Thus the handshake is both an arbitrary and a conventional form of greeting.

Because it is *both* arbitrary *and* conventional, language may be compared with money. The paper which makes a banknote is virtually worthless in itself. The banknote has value only because society has decided to treat it as valuable. Banknotes have no intrinsic value, (no value "in themselves"), they only have value because we can exchange them for things which do have intrinsic value, things that we do want for themselves, like chocolate bars or sneakers. Similarly, the symbols of language do not mean anything by themselves, in virtue of some special character possessed by the words themselves. They have meaning only because *we choose* to give them meaning as a society, and they mean what we, collectively, choose them to mean.

This does not mean, of course, that *I* can successfully use words to mean anything *I* wish, any more than I can choose to regard a dollar bill as worth a million dollars and get away with it. Language is a social phenomenon.

Relics of the Ancient View of Language and Reality

Today, no one would seriously wish to defend the ancient view that there is some mysterious connection between particular words and what those words stand for; yet we frequently still behave as though such a connection did exist. The ancient view of the relation between language and reality, although discarded, lingers on in some of the ways we think and act today, and lies behind some of our less rational behaviour.

Most societies have forbidden words, words which may not be uttered or written because of their close association, in our minds, with what they stand for. It is as though the mere use of these words brings us into contact with the dangerous or unpleasant reality which is somehow present in the words themselves. For this reason, there are many words which could not be used in this book, even if anyone had wanted to use them, because they are not printable.

- Religious belief is a source of taboos. In ancient times it was believed that a god, hearing his name uttered, might sit up and take notice. If he had been disturbed lightly or thoughtlessly the god might become irate, with disastrous consequences for the mortal who had thereby insulted him. Today light or irreverent use of the name of God, or of other religious figures, is called blasphemy.

Many **circumlocutions**, or indirect forms of expression, are used to avoid having to refer to unpleasant things with which we do not wish to come into contact.

- In our society, we often avoid mentioning death. For this reason there exist a variety of roundabout ways of referring to death without actually having to say that someone is dead. Instead, he is "sleeping," "deceased," "defunct," "fallen," "no more," "bereft of life," "asleep in the Lord," "with the saints," "under the sod," "pushing up daisies." He has "croaked," "departed this life," "gone to a better place," "gone to kingdom come," "gone to glory," "kicked the bucket." He has been "called home," "gathered to his fathers," "released from suffering," "with the angels," "gathered to the Lord," "born into a better world," etc., etc., etc.

Many difficulties with language could be avoided if we distinguished *using* words from *mentioning* them.

Use and Mention

It is one thing to *use* a word in a sentence and quite another to *mention* it in order to talk *about* it. In this book we have had reason to consider many words which we have not actually used. A few paragraphs above the words "bathroom," "lavatory" and "toilet" were mentioned, but they were not *used*. No one wrote "I am going to the bathroom." We were not thinking about bathrooms (lavatories/toilets) but about the *words* "bathroom," "lavatory" and "toilet." We were using the *names* of those words, rather than the words themselves.

Of course the name of a word is itself a word, and looks identical to the word it names, and this is likely to cause some confusion. In order to make it clear that words are being mentioned rather than used, that we are *considering* the words rather than *using* them in making statements, (i.e. that we are using the *names* of the words rather than the *words themselves)*, the usual convention has been followed of enclosing them in quotation marks viz.: "bathroom," "lavatory" and "toilet." The difference can clearly be seen by comparing the examples below:

(6) Blue is a colour

(7) "Blue" is a four-letter word.

It would be quite wrong to say:

(8) Blue is a four-letter word

or   (9) "Blue" is a colour.

Blue is a colour, whereas "blue" is the name of the word which stands for that colour. Blue is not a word and "blue" is not a colour.

Some Real Connections between Words and Reality?

Although we have seen that there is no real connection between words and what they represent, onomatopoeic imitate sounds in nature, e.g. "bow-wow," "cuckoo," "buzz," "crack," "bang," "bubble," "thunder."

It is sometimes objected that there are no genuinely onomatopoeic words, since different languages represent sounds in nature differently, e.g. "whisper" in English appears as *flusken* in German, *chuchoter* in French, *hviske* in Danish, and *susurar* in Spanish. The noise characteristically made by a dog, in English *bow wow*, or *woof*, is *ouah ouah* in French; *au au au* in Portugese; *gav* in Greek, *bup bup* in Chinese; *wanwan* in Japanese; and *gonggong* in Malay-Indonesian. The sound of the cock crowing, which is *cock-a-doodle-do* in English, is *cocorico* in French; *ki-kiriki* in Greek; *kukurikuuuu* in Hungarian; and *ake-e-ake-ake* in Thai.

Yet these words, although different, do all do reproduce the sounds they refer to. The words represent a choice from a *range* of sounds, those made by large angry dogs and small querulous dogs, for example. Also, our speech organs can imitate the same sounds in many different ways.

5. Classification

Sense and Reference

The mathematician and philosopher Gottlob Frege distinguished two fundamentally different functions of words as **reference** and **sense**.

He demonstrated the difference between these terms by means of an example. The planet Venus appears twice nightly in the sky as a bright point of light near the moon. It first appears after dusk, before fading from view, then again it reappears just before dawn. Many ancient people did not realise that these two points of light in the sky, visible at different times, were appearances of the same body. Consequently, they called the bright star which appeared beside the moon after dusk the "Evening Star," and the point of light which heralded the dawn they called the "Morning Star." We now know that the terms, "Evening Star" and "Morning Star" refer to the same object, the planet Venus. Both phrases *referred* to the same body, the planet Venus, and so they had the same reference. But the terms "Evening Star" and "Morning Star" clearly have different *senses*, or different meanings, since the former means a bright body which appears in the evening sky, while the sense of the latter means a bright body appearing before the dawn.

Because the terms "Morning Star" and "Evening Star" have the same reference but different senses or meanings this example allows us to see clearly the difference between **reference** and **sense**. But the same distinction between sense and reference may be made in the function of most terms. The sense of "moon" is that of a satellite of a planet, while its reference consists of our own Moon, the moons of Mars, the moons of Jupiter, and so on.

When we consider the meaning of words, it is usually the sense of the words we are thinking about. But there are some words, **proper names**, which are used in such a way that their reference is the most important aspect of their meaning. These are expressions which are primarily intended to refer to individuals, while their sense, if they have any, is of little importance e.g. Tony Blair, Stoke-on-Trent, August, the Andromeda Galaxy, Olympic Airways, Apollo 16.

Although in origin many of these terms were descriptive, personal proper names now carry little meaning because their origins have been forgotten. The name "George" is in origin a Greek word meaning "farmer," but hardly anyone who gives that name to his son today is aware of that. Usually we choose names because of their associations. Babies are given the names of people admired by, their parents: relatives or media stars. Or a name is chosen simply because its sound gives the parents pleasure. In using someone's name, we do not usually have in mind any residual meaning or associations that the word may carry. We simply use it as a label. Proper names function like labels.

General Terms

The idea that words function rather like labels has only limited value. Proper nouns form only a small part of any language. If we ask what common nouns or other parts of speech, such as verbs, and adjectives, label we soon run into difficulties. Such words designate classes. Classes are the result of our classifying things.

When faced with any sort of practical or intellectual activity, an initial process of "sorting out" is usually necessary. This process of sorting is what logicians call "**classification.**" Many would consider our ability to order nonidentical things into classes to be the foundation of human thought.

This process is at one extreme very crude and at the other highly sophisticated. A fruit picker may use two categories when gathering in the crop, viz. "good" and "bad," i.e. "worth the labour of picking" or "fit only to be ignored." On the other hand, a botanist will use the most subtle and sophisticated systems of classification to make sense out of the myriad varieties of plant life.

All classification involves some degree of **abstraction**. In grouping things in accordance with their possession of certain characteristics which we regard as significant, we necessarily ignore many others. In classifying plants merely as, say, edible or inedible, we ignore their many other characteristics.

The degree of sophistication necessary for classification depends upon one's purpose. It can be a matter of great importance to get the level right. Suppose yourself to be a reporter in a war-torn country taking shelter from battle in a ruined house. Suddenly a soldier from one of the warring factions bursts into your hideout, his automatic weapon held ready to fire. He may classify people he meets in the war zone as either allies, enemies or neutrals, in the which case you will be recognised as a neutral when you yell "Press!" and hold up your press card. On the other hand you may be unlucky, and the soldier who bursts in may be operating with a cruder system of classification containing only two groups: "friend" or "foe"; and he may be inclined to assume that anyone not obviously fitting into the former category must belong to the latter. In that case, you might be in serious trouble.

Classes

Classification involves mentally grouping individual things together, or forming notional (i.e. not physical) collections. The widest name for such a group is a **set**, and the individuals in the set are its elements. The individuals grouped together in a set may be collected quite arbitrarily. I may form a set out of, say, Clarence, Clarence's dog, Clarence's dog's bone and the Eiffel Tower. It is not clear what use it would be to form such a set, and most of the sets which we do form are of elements or individuals which share some common characteristic, e.g. red things, or dental surgeons. Such sets as these, we call classes.

A **class** is a set, or group of things, which is distinguishable because all the members of the group possess some significant characteristic in common. A class is determined by naming a characteristic; and any characteristic may determine a class. We name a class by referring in words to those characteristics which determine its membership; e.g. "rodents," "whole numbers between nine and forty-one exactly divisible by five," or "one-eyed policemen."

For convenience, "**term**" is used to refer to the words which define a class, however many words are necessary to define it, and in whatever language they appear. Thus "left-handed sailors who are fluent in ancient Persian" is a single term. Similarly, "football", *Fussball* (German) *calcio* (Italian) and *jalkapallo* (Finnish) also express a single term, since they all signify the same class defined by the same property and having the same members. These words are different in their different languages, but a single class is referred to by using them. Thus systems of classification are language-neutral; they are unaffected by the language used to express them.

The property which all the members of a class have in common is called its **class-property**. It is in virtue of their possession of the class-property that the members of a class *are* its members. These class-properties may be natural or acquired. The class-property "being a cow" is a natural property. Cows have it without anyone doing anything about it. The characteristic "having crossed Antarctica alone" is an acquired one. It has to be earned.

The individuals which form a class are termed its **members**. Classes may have a determinate membership, one which can, in principle, be counted. e.g. "The class of whole numbers between five and sixteen." In practice it may be impossible to perform the counting operation since the actual membership may be constantly changing, e.g. "the class of squirrels." Since squirrels are being born and dying in different places all the time no final count is ever possible. But it is in principle possible to know what counts as a squirrel and what does not, and the number of squirrels, however quickly it changes, is finite.

Some classes have an indeterminate membership which cannot be counted even in principle. This is because the membership is either indefinite or inherently vague. "The class of whole numbers" is an indefinite one, since there is an infinite number of whole numbers. "The class of kind old ladies" is inherently vague, since it is not clear exactly what is to count as being either kind, or old (or even, perhaps, a lady).

These two forms of indeterminacy are different in an important respect. While we cannot list all the members of the class of whole numbers, we are nevertheless sure when we come across an individual whether it is or is not a member of that class. Thus if, for the first time in my life, I come across the number 456,396,108, I know immediately that it is a whole number. By contrast, no sharp line can be drawn to distinguish between ladies who are old and those who are not, and between ladies who are kind and those who are not. In addition, no attempt to draw a line by defining one of these terms very precisely will command general assent. The attempt to do so would be absurd. The concepts "kind" and "old" are inherently vague, and that is all there is to it.

Some classes are necessarily one-membered classes, e.g. "Presidents of the United States currently holding office." Some are empty classes, having no members at all, e.g. "pink elephants stoned on orangeade." A class, the members of which are all contained within another class, is termed a **subclass** of that in which all its members are contained, e.g. "The class of sweaty socks" is a subclass of "the class of socks." A complement class, or negative class, may be formed by considering everything of a particular type which is *excluded* from a particular class because it does not have the class-property proper to it; e.g. "Things which are *not* red," "things which are *in*edible," and "the *im*mortals."

Clearly, if we are talking about things which are not red, we are only considering coloured things. "Coloured things" is called the **universe of discourse**. The original class and its complement class together make up the universe of discourse. In Figure 7.1 "P" represents a particular class, "~P" is its complement class, and "U" the universe of discourse.

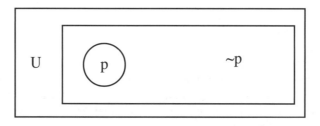

Figure 7.1

Exercise 7.1
Which of the following classes are indefinite, inherently vague or neither of those?
1. intelligent students
2. whole numbers between six and eight
3. fractions
4. ants
5. movie stars
6. pebbles
7. basketball players
8. liars
9. hundred dollar bills
10. members of the Edinburgh Golf Club

These operations result in tables of classification or division which display the relationships of the sub-classes within a class in the form of the branches of a tree.

Relatively speaking, at any particular level the higher class is called the genus, while the lower classes are called its species. (These terms are used in a special sense in the biological sciences, where the most complex and sophisticated systems of classification have been developed in order to cope with the more than 1,500,000 different species of living things known to man.)

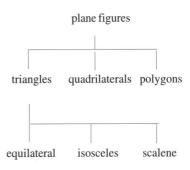

figure 6.2

How to Build a Table of Classification

The logical process of classification or division can be rendered useless or inefficient if it is done badly. In order to avoid this, certain rules of procedure have been drawn up by logicians:
• At each stage of a table of classification or division the co-ordinate classes (those on the same level of division) must be mutually exclusive. Two classes are mutually exclusive if the co-ordinate classes exclude each other and so share no members. If this rule is not observed some of the members of the genus will appear in two or more co-ordinate species, resulting in cross classification or cross division.
• At each stage of a table of classification or division the co-ordinate classes must be collectively exhaustive. Two classes are collectively exhaustive if all the members of the genus are included in the species. If this rule is not observed some of the membership of the genus will not appear at all in the species.

In order to ensure that these rules are not broken, it is necessary that:
• At each stage only one principle of classification or division is used.
• No steps must be omitted in the process of classification or division.

Relativism

In general, systems of classification reveal classes of things we have decided to create. Systems of classification would seem, therefore, to tell us more about the intentions and purposes of the people who draw them up, rather than about the world they are supposed to categorise. Some philosophers have argued that this is all that they can do. This last position is another form of relativism.

In general, systems of classification are designed by reference to the purposes of their creators, and therefore *in general* they can only tell us about those purposes. But this is not *always* true. We can, indeed, create any system of classification we choose; and the ones we do choose to create will undoubtedly reflect our needs, wishes and intentions. But *one* of those needs will be to help us understand what the world is like. And in relation to this end, not *any* system of classification at all will do.

If we are to classify what is actually in the world in such a way that we can come to know it and successfully deal with it, then we have got to pay attention to the similarities and differences between things which are actually out there. *Scientific* classification, in particular, is created with the intention of reflecting the way things are objectively.

In fact, while there are some differences, classifications in natural history are remarkably similar from culture to culture, and tend to be based upon similar criteria. Despite radically different forms of language and conventions, the same species tend to be distinguished from each other, and related to each other, in the same ways. This is due to the fact that what is being classified are the same aspects of the same world using the same basic principles. The differences are usually found with respect to life-forms which are comparatively unfamiliar or inaccessible.

While systems of classification are necessarily relative to purpose, if that purpose is knowledge and understanding of the world, then our systems of classification will only be useful to the extent that they pick out significant similarities and differences which are actually present in the world.

Case Study: The classification of Dolphins

Dolphins appear, to the casual observer, to be a species of fish. They are stream-lined, good swimmers and live in the sea. They look rather like sharks. But the zoologist knows that, unlike fish, they are warm-blooded; they nurse their young with milk, and they have lungs and hair. Despite appearances, dolphins are closer to man than sharks.

Once the zoologist classifies the dolphin with man as a mammal, he will expect to see that it will have a certain bodily structure: red blood cells without nuclei, a four-chambered heart, a nervous system of a certain type, and so on. Investigation shows that this is so.

For this reason, the scientific classification of the dolphin as a mammal is not a matter of arbitrary choice at all. It depends upon what is really out there in the world, it refers back to the world, and it helps us to make good predictions about the world.

Many of our systems of classification are not scientific, however, and they may embody our false beliefs and prejudices. Unfortunately, we tend to assume that the world will conform to our systems of classification, and become uneasy when it does not. This is particularly true when people fail to conform to our expectations by failing to behave as we expect them to behave.

- People sometimes get unaccountably enraged when they cannot immediately decide on the sex of a young person on the basis of hair length, dress or use or non-use of jewellery or cosmetics. Very short hair on a girl or earrings on a boy may provoke irrational wrath or scorn. This is because their simple classification systems are being undermined by the untidy way in which people actually behave. This lies at the basis of homophobia, prejudice against homosexuals. Even in the West, girls wearing trousers were once regarded as outrageous, while men wearing skirts will be thought outrageous even today.

- All human beings like to think of living things as being either alive or dead. We like to feel that everything is one thing or the other, and we do not like the boundary between the two to be challenged. That is one reason why we tend to be fearful of such ideas as ghosts, and why notions such as "the undead" or "the living dead" can be used to such effect by the writers of horror films.

  But this division is, in reality, not a clear one. It only appeared so when our knowledge was limited and our medical skills primitive. Even then people pronounced dead would sometimes "come back to life" before burial. Because doctors were so poor at detecting death, some individuals developed a chronic fear of being accidentally buried alive. Today the borderline is becoming less and less clear as scientific knowledge and medical technology improves. For example, it is not clear into which class we should put people who are brain dead, some of whose bodily functions can be kept going on life support machines. These situations raise serious ethical questions.

Dichotomy

One special form of classification, that of **dichotomy**, sometimes gives rise to terrible problems. Any universe of discourse can be divided neatly into two mutually exhaustive and collectively exhaustive classes: a single defined class together with its complement class, the latter containing everything within the universe of discourse which is *excluded* from the original class because it lacks the class-property proper to that class, e.g. humans and non-humans.

Dichotomy is a technically faultless form of classification, but has been criticized as it is not of much practical use. At each level of classification the complement class is undefined in its extent, except insofar as its members fail to possess the single characteristic on the basis of which the division is being made. This makes dichotomies rather uninformative. There is no guarantee that all the classes named actually have members.

Surprisingly, dichotomy can be an extremely dangerous practice. It leads to what is sometimes called the fallacy of "**black-white thinking**." This way of thinking is characteristic of the zealot and fanatic, and is illustrated by the following urban legend:

Case Study: A Jewish Doctor in Northern Ireland

The province of Northern Ireland in the United Kingdom was long a byword for religious bigotry. Both Roman Catholics and Protestants engaged in savage acts of terrorism and brutality against members of the rival community.

One dark night a Jewish doctor answered a call from a sick friend who lived outside the town, and drove out to into the countryside to visit him. Travelling down an unlit lane, dark figures stepped out of the shadow of the hedgerows, and motioned him to stop the car. They were masked and armed, and he knew they would not hesitate to shoot.

He braked, and nervously wound his window down.

"Are you a Catholic or a Protestant?" a large figure with a rifle dressed in battle fatigues demanded. The others gathered around expectantly.

The doctor breathed a sigh of relief. To have answered either way would have been dangerous, for it was not clear whether the men were Catholics or Protestants, and a wrong answer might have meant death. But the doctor was not a party to this dispute.

"I'm a Jew," he replied.

But his masked interrogator was not to be put off: "Are you a Catholic Jew or a Protestant Jew?"

Now the doctor knew that he was in real trouble.

People who insist on dividing everything into two diametrically opposed classes usually label one of these "good" and the other "evil." Everything which is not in the "good" class is thought to be "evil," and is liable to be treated as such. This outlook is called **Manichaean** after an ancient religious teacher who taught that there were two gods, one good and one evil, and that everything in the universe was subject to one or the other, and so was either "good" or "evil." This dangerously simplistic way of thinking has formed the justification for the worst examples of bigotry and persecution in history.

The most famous spokesman for such an outlook today is President George W. Bush of the USA, who declared: "I see things in black and white. I'm not about nuancing." He said of the entire human race, all seven billion of us," You're either with us, or you're with the terrorists." He has denounced regimes which act independently of US direction, and refuse to play along with US policy as an "axis of evil." This has the effect not only of demonizing regimes which are out of favour with the White House, it has the converse effect of whitewashing regimes in favour. Thus Saddam's Iraq and North Korea were members of the axis of evil because they "had weapons of mass destruction" and Iran because it was trying to obtain them; whereas Israel and Pakistan, which had them, are "good guys."

6. Clarity

If we are to think efficiently and communicate successfully, we must pay attention to the meaning of what we say or write, and so aim for clarity in our thought and expression. We should try to be as lucid as possible in conceiving and articulating what exactly it is that we are thinking, talking or writing about.

The more clearly, and accurately a statement is formulated, the easier and it is to establish whether it is true or false. Given a clear statement of an issue, and prior to evaluating conclusions or solutions, it is important to recognise what is required to settle it. And before we can agree or disagree with a claim, we must understand it clearly. It makes no sense to say "I don't know what you mean, but I oppose it, whatever it is."

If two people are to have a meaningful discussion, it is necessary that they speak the same language. This means that both participants use the same words with the same meanings. If two people have a dispute about democracy, but both mean different things by "democracy," then they are not going to get very far. If they have a discussion about communism, and one mean by "communism" what the other means by "socialism," then they will not get very far either. These confusions tend to arise because of the vagueness or ambiguity of the words we use.

Vagueness

Many of the words we use are **vague**, or lacking in precision.

The meaning of a word may be **indeterminate**, so that it is not possible to say conclusively whether the word is applicable in some cases or not. There are clear cases when a word is applicable and clear cases when it is not, and there is a "grey area" where there is some doubt. Terms like "easy" and "difficult," "dark" and "light" shade into each other.

Vagueness often arises simply because of the way the world is. It is full of properties which exhibit magnitudes or qualities on continua which shade indefinitely into each other, like the colours of the rainbow. We have to accommodate our language and behaviour to that fact. What exactly counts as "bald"? Clearly some states do and clearly some do not; but in the grey area in between there is no hard and fast line to be drawn.

Very often the location of this difficult area on the continuum between the two extremes is relative. What is small for an elephant is not necessarily small for a mouse; what counts as slow for a hare is not slow for a tortoise. It is thus not possible to specify in advance exactly to which circumstances a word may apply.

Vagueness is not *always* undesirable. Teachers sometimes behave as though precision is always necessary, and is in all circumstances to be preferred to vagueness. It is easy to see why. After many years spent in combating vagueness, and trying to get students to be more precise where precision *is* required, they come to behave as though vagueness is *always* due to sloppy thinking. What is required, however, is that we be as precise *as is appropriate*.

Fallacies of Clarity

Much argumentation is rendered confused and fruitless because of lack of clarity. Judicious lack of clarity can be deceptive, deliberately or otherwise, in its effect.

Unclear Conclusion: The value of much argument is undermined because the person advancing the argument is unsure what his own position is. Sometimes someone may alter the meaning of his conclusion, and therefore shift his position, during the course of an argument.

Meaningless Claim: Assertions are made which are unverifiable because they contain words or phrases which are unclear in any ordinary context.

(6) Sounds of the Nineties. The world's most popular tunes on one record. A fabulous offer. This is the perfect Christmas gift.

What constitutes a "perfect Christmas gift?" Surely nothing is quite perfect! What is very suitable (or "near-perfect") for Aunt Mabel, who likes embroidery, will be quite unsuitable for young Kevin, who is into karate.

(7) "Doseyourself" contains extra strength.

Extra than what? Extra than nothing?

Slippery Slope Arguments: In the case of terms where there is no clear dividing line between possession of a property and not possessing the property, or between the possession of one property as opposed to another, there is no point at which it is possible to say that at some particular point someone will possess or not possess a particular property; e.g. that with one more hair a person will count as having a beard, or with one less will count as bald. From this it may be improperly concluded that there is no real difference between having the property and not having it, or between having the one property as opposed to the other.

Such arguments may be used to claim that there is no difference between sanity and insanity, being an amateur or being a professional, or between the abilities of those who pass examinations and those who fail them.

There are cases where it is not clear where a line can be drawn, but where nevertheless a line should be drawn. The law will often require that a line be drawn, and the effect of a legal case may be to draw such a line for the future. Suppose, for example, in a particular country the police can search a vehicle for drugs without a warrant, but require a warrant to search a dwelling house. Then suppose they search a mobile home, a caravan in which someone is living, and their right to perform the search is challenged in the courts. The court will rule whether a caravan constitutes a dwelling or vehicle for purposes of police searches. The line drawn will affect future police behaviour and the outcome of future court cases.

Questions about where to draw the line may be of great moral and social importance, e.g. What counts as murder? Killing enemy soldiers in war? Judicial execution? Abortion? Killing in self-defence? Causing death by wilful negligence?

Hair-Splitting: This is the demand for more precision than is reasonable given the subject matter and its importance. Pointing out to your mathematics instructor, who is about to teach a theorem in Geometry that his drawing of a triangle on the blackboard is not really a triangle, since its sides are not perfectly straight lines, would be true, but it would not help the teaching of the theorem.

Incomplete Terms

A lot of confusion is caused by the use in conversation and argument of **incomplete terms**, that is, terms which require some specification before we can make sense of them. It is easy to repeat the saying:

(8) Honesty is the best policy.

But what does the assertion *mean*? Honesty is the best policy for those who are honest, or for those who have dealings with those who are honest, or for everybody? It is by no means clear. It is not clear because the term *best* needs some specification before we can understand the proposition: "best for whom?"

Students often assert that:

(9) Hitler's recorded speeches are an unreliable source of historical data.

It is clear what they mean, and why they say such things. Hitler made promises in his speeches that he did not keep: "We have no more territorial claims in Europe," etc. It was unwise for those who heard his speeches to believe what he said. But that does not mean that his speeches are historically useless. They provide valuable information about, for example, what Hitler wanted the public to believe that his intentions for the future were, the way politics was conducted during the 1930s, the nature of Nazi propaganda, etc. They are a *very* useful source of historical data.

The problem is that the *unreliable* needs specification before we can evaluate the claim.

Discussion: In each case below the incomplete terms have been italicised. Explain the problems of interpretation they raise.

1. It is *dangerous* for young people to be allowed to question government policy.
2. Our party has a *progressive* policy.
3. It is *desirable* for private companies to be allowed to provide educational resources for schools.
4. More freedom in the classroom is clearly *better* than the imposition of dicipline.
5. Bethoven's "Ninth Symhony" is too *long*.

Ambiguity

Ambiguity is found whenever a single word may have more than one unrelated meaning, e.g. "rook" which may refer to a black bird or a chess-piece. This might be better expressed by saying that there are two different words which share a common form in the language.

Discussion: Compare in detail what you each mean by the following words or phrases:

1. education
4. conscience

2. democracy
5. progress

3. freedom
6. activist

Fallacies of Ambiguity

These are committed when a plurality of meanings is used to derive an unwarranted conclusion.

Equivocation: A word or phrase which has more than one meaning is used in an argument in such a way that the argument depends upon a shift from one meaning to the other during the course of the argument. When this happens people are at cross purposes and there is no true meeting of minds.

(10) Joe is mad at his children. Since people who are mad should be committed to mental asylums, Joe should be committed to a mental asylum.

Examples may arise when using relative terms:

(11) Since an elephant is an animal, a small elephant must be a small animal.

They may also occur when using theory-laden terms such as "democracy" or "natural."

(12) Since this is the Peoples' Republic of North Korea, the inhabitants must enjoy individual freedoms here.

Accent: Ambiguity may arise out of the varying stress which may be laid upon the pronunciation of a statement. In this case, the meaning is changed by altering which parts of a statement are emphasised. If the success of an argument depends upon such a shift, then a fallacy in reasoning has been committed.

(13) A: "I'm not going to give any more to your charity this year."

B: "Fine, I'll put you down for the same as last year."

Amphiboly: Ambiguity may arise on account some fault in the structure of a sentence, due to careless or ungrammatical phrasing.

(14) The waiter served the coffee with greasy hands.

Composition: This is the incorrect attribution of the characteristics of the parts to an organised whole, or the assumption that what can be said distributively can also be said collectively. One form of the fallacy of composition is to conclude that a property shared by the parts of something must apply to the whole.

(15) Every player in the Moscow Dynamo team is a star player, therefore Moscow Dynamo is a star team.

Another form of this fallacy is to conclude that a property of a number of individual items is shared by a collection of those items.

(16) A car uses less petrol than a bus, so it will cause less pollution than a bus. Therefore cars are less environmentally damaging than buses.

Division: This is the converse of composition, and involves the incorrect attribution of characteristics proper to the organised whole to the several parts, It assumes that what can be said collectively can be said distributively. The first form of this fallacy is to assume that a property of some thing must apply to its parts. For example:

(17) The New York Yankees are a star team, therefore all their players are star players.

Another form is to assume that a property of a collection is shared by each individual.

(18) Locusts can destroy a forest. Therefore, this locust can destroy a forest.

Exercise 7.2
Identify the fallacies of vagueness or ambiguity in each of the following.

1. The end of life is happiness. Since death is the end of life, death is happiness.
2. If South Vietnam falls to the Communists, so will the other states of south-east Asia, and before you know it the Red Flag will be flying over Hollywood.
3. A: Stephen is mad with his wife because she has crashed their car.
   B: If he is mad he should see a psychiatrist.
4. Because the human brain has the property of consciousness, each individual neural cell must have this property also.
5. You should not punish careless drivers, since no hard and fast line can be drawn between careless driving, and driving which is not careless.
6. Alice told her mother she was a fool.
7. Conventional bombs did more damage in the Second World War than nuclear did bombs did. Therefore, a conventional bomb is more dangerous than a nuclear bomb.
8. Enforced payment of income tax is a deprivation of freedom. Since to be deprived of freedom is to become a slave, anyone compelled to pay income tax is a slave.
9. Save water and waste paper.
10. Jimmy must be good at school; his teacher said that he had improved his performance from last year.

If it is a mistake to fail to be clear when clarity is required, it is of course equally foolish to demand clarity where vagueness is required. As we have already seen, some of our words are inherently indeterminate. "Rich" is indeterminate because there is no specification of what counts as qualifying as rich, e.g. having an annual income in excess of $500,000 a year, having an income in the top ten per cent of the nation to which you belong, etc. It is not clear when a stream becomes big enough to qualify as a river or when a pool becomes a lake in terms of average volume of water, or when a copse becomes a wood in terms of land surface area.

7. Definition

What is Definition?

The proper response to most of the fallacies above is to appeal to a definition. In seeking precision in our thought, we frequently resort to definitions. We all know where to find definitions — in dictionaries — but what exactly are they? According to the *Oxford English Dictionary* the word has two basic meanings. It may refer to a statement of what a thing is, an explanation of the essential nature of a thing; or it may refer to a statement of the meaning or significance of a word or expression.

The first meaning is based upon the ancient view of the relationship between words and things as necessarily connected. Definition was seen as putting into words the essential nature of things, as encapsulating in words what they *really* are. The philosopher Spinoza said that a "true definition . . . expresses . . . the nature of the thing defined."

We are still sometimes tempted to ask what the *real* meaning of an important word is; not what people *think* it is, but what it *really* is. Today we should say that this idea, that somehow the essence of real things may be caught and imprisoned in words, involves an outmoded "magical" understanding of the nature of language.

Today definition is understood in the second sense, in the words of John Stuart Mill as "A proposition declaratory of the meaning of a word." It is simply a concise report of the conditions under which a word happens to be used, i.e. the conventions which govern its use. Since the conventions change, from time to time dictionaries need to be updated. Some conventions fall into abeyance, others are modified, and new conventions appear.

Heuristic and Objective Definitions

There are many reasons why we may wish to use definitions.
- We may wish to teach someone the meaning of a word and so increase his vocabulary.
- We may desire to reduce or eliminate vagueness. We know the meaning of a word in a rough way, but we are not quite sure of the limits of its use.
- We may need to eliminate ambiguity. A word may have several meanings, and a definition may be used to indicate which specific meaning is intended in some particular context.
- Disputes may have arisen because different people are using a term in different ways. There is no genuine disagreement about the facts, only a verbal confusion. In these circumstances a definition will clear up which usage is at fault.

These purposes fall into two clearly distinguishable groups. We may wish to:
- teach someone how a word or expression is used;
- specify precisely the parameters or limits within which it is used.

In the former case, in order to teach successfully, we need to take account of what the person we are teaching already knows. The purpose of the definition will not be served if the person who is being taught does not understand what we are saying. On the other hand, anything which does help him to understand will be useful. In this case we need to employ a **heuristic definition**.

By contrast, when attempting to specify the parameters of a word as precisely as possible, say for serious academic work, we are only concerned with accuracy, to be "spot on." In this case, if someone reading what we have written does not understand, we would say that he should try something simpler. His failure to understand is not our problem. In such a case, we seek an **objective definition**.

Methods of Defining

There are many ways to teach how a word is used, and so to convey its meaning to others. **Ostensive Definition:** The meaning of a word is often taught to young children by pointing, or some other gesture indicating examples of the word being defined.

However there are many problems associated with the use of this method. Firstly, all gesture is ambiguous. When someone points to a house in order to teach a child the meaning of the word "house" he might, strictly, be drawing attention to the building, to its type, to its style, to a particular part of it, or to its purpose. What he is pointing at is clear only if you already know the meaning of the word "house." Any individual indicated could be used to indicate many different classes. Pointing at Bill Clinton could be taken as referring to an example of the classes: "man" (human being), "man" (male human being), "US citizen," "politician," "Democrat," "husband," "father," "ex-president," "someone accused of perjury," etc. Moreover, simple physical limitations confine the use of this method to objects which are near at hand. You cannot point to the ocean when you are standing in the middle of a desert. Empty classes and abstract terms cannot be indicated using this method, since in these cases there is nothing to point at.

Denotative Definition: A second method is to list the individual membership of the class, which the word refers to, until the hearer realises what the individuals listed are examples of; e.g. "Rover, Rex, Lassie and Prince are dogs." A variant is to list the subclasses of the class; e.g. "Poodles, dachshunds, collies and spaniels are dogs." These methods properly qualify only for heuristic definition because they are inexact. They merely indicate what sort of thing a word stands for.

Synonymous Definition: More serious attempts at definition include citing a synonym, giving another word having the same meaning as the word being defined. This is the stand-by of small dictionaries, which have little space for anything else. Some words, however, simply have no exact synonyms, and many words which appear synonymous are in fact only near synonyms, such as "fire" and "conflagration." (The second word would only be used for a substantial blaze.)

Regular Definition: Giving a rule for the use of the word to be defined is sometimes possible, e.g. "'I' is used by each language speaker to indicate himself." This is useful for words which have syntactical functions, (those which help put a sentence together).

Analytical Definition: Perhaps the most satisfactory method of giving a definition is that which involves providing an analysis of the meaning of the term. Aristotle worked out a method for doing this by using concepts associated with tables of classification. We think of a word as referring to a class. We indicate the genus to which that class belongs, and also that property which distinguishes the class from all other co-ordinate classes of the same genus. For example, "A triangle is a plane figure bounded by three sides." "Plane figure" (i.e. figure on a two-dimensional surface) is the genus, while "bounded by three straight lines" is the differentiating characteristic (distinguishing triangles from quadrilaterals, pentagons, hexagons, etc.).

Traditionally called definition *per genus et differentiam*, this was for long regarded as the only "proper" method of definition, and it is still in practice extremely useful.

However, some words are notoriously difficult to define in this way; e.g. "dog." We can easily find its genus: "mammal"; the problem arises when we seek a single differentiating characteristic which all dogs (including huskies, alsatians and poodles) have, but which other mammals (including wolves, dingoes and foxes) do not have.

(3) *Student*: I am really making an effort this year. I have increased my study time by one hundred per cent.

A one hundred percent increase on ten minutes work a week would not be an impressive improvement, nor likely to achieve very much.

Frequently comparisons are made between statistics which have been arrived at by different means, and therefore which are not strictly comparable.

In 1987, the Italian government claimed that its economy had overtaken that of Britain, something which was seen as a national triumph in Italy and as a national humiliation in Britain. The Italian Government statisticians had suddenly "discovered" an additional 16% of gross national product (GNP). This represented the "black economy" the sum total of illegal or undeclared economic activities conducted. The figures for the United Kingdom included nothing for the black economy which, while no doubt less than that of Italy, would not have been entirely nonexistent. Clearly, to compare the GNPs of countries makes no sense where the figures are arrived at in different ways. Moreover, the new Italian figure was meaningless anyway. The trouble with undeclared economic activity is that, since it is undeclared, there is no reliable data about it. The Italians simply plucked a figure out of the air and announced a triumph for Italian enterprise. Comparisons are only relevant if made on the basis of the same populations.

Irrelevant Statistics:

Statistics may be quite unobjectionable in themselves, but they may be used to support some quite irrelevant conclusion. This is most prominent in what is sometimes called the **Naturalistic Fallacy**. This is an important fallacy of ethical thinking. It is committed when we confuse what is statistically "normal," i.e. falling within a certain range of frequency, with what is "right"; and if we assume that what is statistically unlikely, extreme or abnormal, is *for that reason* morally abnormal and objectionable. This leads to the prejudice that unusual behaviour must be morally wrong or blameworthy simply because it is unusual, and demands unthinking conformity to the majority line. There is no necessary connection between statistical normality and moral rectitude.

How to Evaluate Statistics

We should consider the *data* upon which the statistical findings are based.
- Is the data correct? Can this be checked?
- Is the data adequate? Is the sample of an adequate size and nature?
- Have the data been manipulated? Is the sample the only one considered, or have previous samples been rejected as obtaining the "wrong" results?

We should consider the *presentation* of the statistics.
- Are the statistics vague, e.g. unspecified averages?
- Are the statistical operations applied to the data appropriate?
- Are the statistical findings presented in a way which deprives them of meaning?
- Are the statistical findings presented in a way which distorts their significance? e.g. distorted graphs.

We should consider the *use* made of the statistics.
- Are the statistics truly relevant to the matter in hand?
- Are statistics being compared truly comparable?
- Are the statistics being employed properly and appropriately?

How to Construct an Analytical Definition

Like most things, analytical definition can be done well or badly. Traditionally rules have been set out for avoiding the pitfalls. The following are based upon the nature of definition. Observance of them will ensure that your definition is a good one. When the rules are broken the faulty definition is said to involve a fallacy. The breaking of each rule involves a separate fallacy.

The first set of rules ensures that the definition functions adequately as an objective definition:

- The defining phrase must not be wider than the expression being defined. If it were, too much would be included in the definition; e.g. "A shoe is a covering for the foot." This would include socks, and so commit the fallacy of being too wide.
- The defining phrase must not be narrower than the expression being defined. If it were, the definition will cover too little; e.g. "A shoe is an outer covering for the foot made of leather." This would exclude shoes not made of leather, such as plastic or canvas shoes. It would involve the fallacy of being too narrow.

Other rules are designed to ensure that the definition succeeds heuristically, i.e. that people will be helped to understand by referring to it.

- The defining phrase must not contain any expression that occurs in the expression being defined, or any expression that could be defined only in terms of the expression being defined.

If it does, the definition will fail because the term to be defined is effectively used in its own definition. Famous examples of this fallacy include: "Life is the sum of the vital functions," and "Truth is veracity in thought and act." Such fallacious definitions are said to be circular.

- The defining phrase should not be expressed in obscure language, since what is obscure cannot be explained by what is equally obscure.

Obscurity is relative, however. What is obscure to a layman may not be to a specialist. "A dynatron oscillator is a circuit which employs a negative-resistance volt-ampere curve to produce an alternating current" may be obscure to a layman, but it is helpful to a student of electrical engineering. However, Dr. Johnson's famous definition of a net as "anything made with interstitial vacuities" probably helps no one.

- The defining phrase should not be expressed in figurative language.

The use of figurative language may be amusing, or even illuminating, but it cannot provide a clear example of what the word being defined means; e.g. "A wedding ring is a matrimonial tourniquet designed to prevent circulation." A figurative definition is inadequate in serious work.

- If the expression being defined is affirmative, then the defining phrase must also be affirmative.

The defining phrase is supposed to explain what the word being defined is, not what it is not. The definition "A couch is neither a bed nor a chair" is unacceptable for that reason. However, if the word being defined is negative in meaning, this must be expressed in the defining phrase, e.g. "baldness is the state of not having hair on one's head." The sense of many apparently positive terms is actually negative, e.g. "indissoluble," "immortal," and "invisible."

Exercise 7.3

Comment upon or criticise the following, considered as objective definitions:
1. Architecture: frozen music. (Goethe)
2. Politics: the art of the possible. (Bismarck)
3. Religion: a sense of the Beyond.
4. A point: that which has no parts and no magnitude. (Euclid)
5. Poetry: rhymed speech.

Some Special Types of Definition

Stipulative Definition: Stipulative definition is the assignment of meaning to a new word or words. It is most commonly found in the sciences and technology, where new usage has to be stipulated because something new has been discovered or invented for which no name exists; e.g. "radium," "telephone," "modem." Occasionally a new term is invented in science to avoid the intrusion of emotive associations of familiar words, e.g. Spearman"s "g-factor" for general intelligence.

Sometimes a word in current use is given a new meaning, totally unrelated to that which it has in everyday speech. The very unlikelihood of the usage is itself a guarantee against confusion. Thus the object used to move the cursor on a computer screen is called a "mouse." Perhaps the most striking example of this form of stipulation is the names given by physicists to the quarks, the ultimate particles out of which everything is made. They are listed in six varieties or "flavours" as "top," "bottom," "up," "down," "charmed" and "strange"; each of which occurs in one of three "colours": "red," "green" or "blue."

A stipulative definition cannot be true or false, it can only accepted or rejected by the community it is intended to assist.

Precising Definition: A precising definition is a special kind of stipulative definition, which involves assigning of a more precise usage to a term already in general use. Precising definitions are used in all branches of science, allowing the words to be usefully employed, while avoiding the vagueness and imprecision of common speech.

Some Precising Definitions

Current: the rate of flow of electrical charge. (Physics)
Acids: substances that give off hydrogen ions. (Chemistry)
Altitude: the angle measured from the horizon to a celestial object. (Astronomy)
Fault: a fracture along which a relative displacement has occurred. (Geology)
Labour: all human resources which can be used in the production of goods and services. (Economics)
Drive: an aroused condition of the organism based upon deprivation or other noxious stimulation. (Psychology)

Operational Definition: In the sciences, a word is sometimes defined, for purposes of research, by reference to an operation, such as an experiment. This is in order to give precision to the research. e.g. Someone investigating the consequences of stress would need first of all to define what, for purposes of his research, constituted stress. It might, for example, be defined in terms of liability to absences from school, or work due to sickness during a particular period of time. Aggression in children might be defined in terms of the number of aggressive acts observed to have been initiated on a school playground during a specified period.

Theoretical Definition: This is the attempt to characterise a term in such a way as to explain what it stands for in terms of a particular theory. A theoretical definition is not merely a matter of explaining the use of a word. It is an attempt to assert the truth of a theory about what the word stands for. It is a special form of persuasive definition, not slipped in order to pre-empt proper consideration, but presented as a succinct expression of a particular viewpoint. Since they embody claims about the world and the way it is, these definitions may be true or false.

Some Theoretical Definitions

Heat: the vibration of molecules.
Clouds: buoyant masses of visible water droplets or ice crystals.
Justice: the interest of the stronger.

Persuasive Definition: This is a form of theoretical definition. Persuasive definitions are attempts to persuade or influence attitudes by the apparent act of explaining the meaning of a word. If the definition is accepted, then a theory has also been accepted. Persuasive definitions are a tool of the propagandist.

(19) "Abortion is a chance, at last, for all children everywhere to be truly wanted and loved within their families, and is a basic right of all citizens."
Persuasive definitions may be negative as well as positive:

(20) "Abortion is the murder of defenceless human beings, the denial of basic human rights to the weakest and most vulnerable of our citizens, and the encouragement of promiscuity among our spoiled and irresponsible young people."

Persuasive definition is a regular tool of those engaged in propaganda.

Case Study: "Weapons of Mass Destruction"

During 2003 the US and UK governments accused Saddam Hussein of having "weapons of mass destruction," and of being an unsafe person to hold them because he had "used them on his own people". This was a reference to the gassing of Iraqi Kurds. The main reason for the US/British attack on Iraq revolved around this concept of "weapons of mass destruction" (WMDs) which were identified as nuclear, chemical and biological weapons." This definition was the justification for going to war. It seems a simple definition, but in fact it is not.

The essence of the charge was not that Saddam Hussein had WMDs. This is important. If we consider nuclear weapons alone, the USA, USSR, China, UK, France, Israel, India, Pakistan and North Korea all have nuclear weapons. Nor was it that he had WMDs and had used them before. That would invite the retort that the USA had used them before, since the USA used nuclear weapons on no less than two occasions against Japanese cities in 1945.

In order to give the charge credibility, chemical weapons had to become weapons of mass destruction. Now chemical weapons have been used by many states: Germany, France and the UK in the First World War and Italy against the Abysinnians. Napalm was devised by the Americans and supplied to the Greek Air Force to use against Communist resistance fighters in the Greek Civil War, and was so successful that it was used extensively in Vietnam. Agent Orange was used in Vietnam to defoliate the forests in a form of "ecological warfare." But chemical weapons, terrible though they are, awere not usually referred to as WMDs.

But if chemical weapons became WMDs, since few people know about the Greek Air Force's use of napalm against its own citizens, Saddam Hussein's use of gas against Iraqi Kurds could be made to appear *uniquely* monstrous. The purpose of the exercise was to devise a charge which would fit the regime of Saddam Hussein, and *only* the regime of Saddam Hussein. The crime was defined to "fit" the criminal, and not the criminal identified by reference to the crime.

Further inconsistency can be seen in that US and British forces used depleted uranium shells against Iraq, ignoring a UN resolution which classifies *them* as illegal WMDs. Depleted uranium contaminates the land, causes cancer and other health problems among all who come into contact with them, including birth defects in children. In addition, many people consider the cluster bombs now lying all over Iraq in their thousands much more dangerous to civilians than poison gas, which quickly disperses. Small children will be picking them up for years to come.

Exercise 7.4

Classify the following definitions as stipulative, precising, operational, persuasive or theoretical. Any particular example may fall into each of several categories.

1. "A cynic is a man who knows the price of everything and the value of nothing." (Oscar Wilde, *Lady Windermere's Fan*)
2. "Political power, properly so-called, is merely the organised power of one class for oppressing another." (Karl Marx and Freidrich Engels, *Communist Manifesto*)
3. By "demonstrating a pattern of aggressive behaviour" I mean having hostile bodily contact with playmates on the schoolyard at least four times during the period of one week.
4. "By 'good' I understand that which we know for certain is useful to us." (Baruch Spinoza, *Ethics*)
5. A democrat is someone who loves liberty.

8. Meaning

Although we are all able to use the word "meaning" without much trouble in everyday contexts, it is not clear to philosophers precisely what it means to say that words and sentences are endowed with meaning. The word "meaning" can itself mean many different things.

We have seen that words are arbitrary and conventional symbols for things. But how does this work? Philosopher John Searle has pointed out that over three centuries ago Descartes asked the basic question in philosophy: "What is knowledge, and how is it possible?" But he continued by saying that if you take that question very seriously, it leads eventually to an even more fundamental question: "How does the mind represent the world at all?" i.e. "What is meaning?" Thus he takes the basic question of Philosophy to be "How do mental states represent, and how do they have this remarkable capacity to make objects represent?" Or, to put it another way: "How can a mere object or noise stand for something in the world?"

Meaning as Labelling

A very primitive view of the nature of meaning, but one which we seem naturally disposed to accept before we think deeply about the problem is that words are labels for things. The word "dog" functions in some way as a label for dogs. Many stories about the beginning of the world found in ancient mythologies have the creator god "naming" all the things he has created, i.e. attaching verbal labels to them, by which they were afterwards to be known. To know the meaning of a word is to know what it stands for.

Immediately we start to think about this theory, its simplicity is seen to be deceptive. Proper names label, but it is not clear exactly what a common noun like "dog" labels. Is it all dogs, or "doggie nature," and if the latter, what exactly is that? And what would words like "either," "similar" or "Ouch!" label?

Moreover, the objects a word stands for cannot be its meaning, since two words may refer to the same thing but have different meanings. We have already distinguished the *sense* or meaning of a word from its *reference*. Words which are primarily referential may be said to act as labels, i.e. proper names. But these are a very small fraction of the words we use. Moreover, the objects a word stands for cannot be its meaning, since two words may refer to the same thing but have different meanings.

Meaning as Picturing

According to the philosopher Ludwig Wittgenstein in the *Tractatus Logico-Philosophicus*, the structure of language "mirrors" or "pictures" the structure of the world. An arrangement of points in a diagram represents a possible arrangement of things in the world. Propositions are constructed out of words in the same way that diagrams are constructed out of points. In this way, propositions are diagrams of reality, and on this view, to know the meaning of a word is to entertain in one's mind an appropriate mental image.

This may seem convincing until one asks what it can mean to say that propositions are *pictures* of reality. It is not at all clear. Moreover, this supposed "explanation" would only cover propositions which may be used to assert statements of fact.

Meaning as Use

Wittgenstein himself later rejected this idea and turned instead to an attempt to explain meaning in terms of the use of language. He argued that words function as we wish simply because they are tools which we use. The meaning of an expression is nothing more than the rules which govern its use in the language. For a word to have a meaning in a language there must be some group of speakers who use it in accordance with certain rules. For a person to know the meaning of a word is for him to be able to identify the rules which govern its use. In the case of many of our words, these rules identify the word with classes of objects in the world.

Ludwig Wittgenstein used the concept of a "language game" to explain this. He said that one could imagine a tribe whose language consisted only of requests. Members of the tribe make requests and the other members either comply or refuse. Human language as it exists in reality is more complex; it is a combination of a great many language games. Yet the principle of meaning, according to this theory, is the same: the meaning of a word is the function of its employment in such games. Thus to Wittgenstein the question "What is a word?" is analogous to the question "What is a piece in chess?" and should receive a reply in terms of the moves which can be made with it in playing the language game.

Meaning as Encoded Thought

More generally philosophers have considered that words have meaning in virtue of their power to "stand for," or "represent," what they signify. These are vague notions, but Steven Pinker explains this in terms of its relation to a "language of thought" which he terms "mentalese." He argues that we generally use language in order to communicate with other people when we wish them to attend to what we are attending to in thought. Speech is essentially the expression of that thought. Saying something involves encoding thought, which is in "mentalese," in a natural language. Understanding what someone says is decoding speech or writing back into "mentalese."

9. Language and the Limits of Knowledge

Does All Thought Necessarily Take Place in Language?

The traditional "common sense" view of this is that we first think, and then express our thoughts in language. This has two implications, firstly that thought is quite independent of language, and secondly that language depends wholly upon thought.

The usual picture we have of the process of speaking is that we first think of what we are going to say, and then express those thoughts in words. The ideas we have when we think may be put into words. These words in some way "contain" those ideas. When we wish to communicate our thoughts to someone else, we use language as a vehicle to "carry" them to the other person, who hears them. This recipient then "extracts" the meaning from the words he hears, so that the idea of the original thinker becomes present in his own mind.

On this view language functions rather like the telephone. We first speak into the telephone, the sound waves are converted into electrical impulses and carried along the wires, and then at the other end the electrical impulses are converted back into sound waves once more.

This way of looking at the relationship between thought and language is based upon common sense, and is implicit in the language we use. But in this century it has been called by some philosophers the "Language Myth", since there is evidence which suggests that this picture is incorrect. The relation between language and thought may be much closer than we normally imagine. In consequence, it has been argued that without language we cannot think at all in any "higher" sense, and consequently that all our knowledge must be "carried" by and in our language.

- How often have you said something hurtful "without thinking," to a parent in a state of anger or other high level of emotion, and immediately regretted it? When recalling what happened it seems as though the words "just came out." After such an incident we are liable to resolve that in future we shall "think before we speak." This suggests that speech is not always previous thoughts put into words, since on such occasions we are not conscious of any previous thoughts.

- A child who learns to read first "reads aloud" by speaking out the words on the page. Only later, when pressured by his teacher, does he learn to read silently: first without making a noise and then without even moving his lips. Silent reading is a skill which has to be learned, and has only comparatively recently developed. There is considerable evidence that until modern times, it was the possession of an admired few. This in turn suggests that silent thought is a skill developed by internalising audible speech.
- When thinking deeply about some complicated matter we tend to do so in words. On such occasions, even the articulate adult will find the muscles of his voice box vibrating slightly. This suggests that speech is not voiced thought, but that thought is sub-vocal speech.
- Someone may be so absorbed in his thoughts that he begins to speak them out loud without realising what is happening. Only when someone says "What did you say?" does he become aware of what has happened. In such cases, we seem to have glimpsed the tip of an iceberg: and that speech, which we normally do not vocalise, has on this occasion "slipped out."
- This close connection between language and thought is also found in true sign languages. Oliver Sacks describes an old deaf lady he saw on Martha's Vineyard:

> "This old lady, in her nineties, but sharp as a pin, would sometimes fall into a peaceful reverie. As she did so, she might have seemed to be knitting, her hands in constant complex motion. But her daughter, also a signer, told me she was not knitting but thinking to herself, thinking in Sign. And even in sleep, I was further informed, the old lady might sketch fragmentary signs on the counterpane -– she was dreaming in Sign."

Such considerations as these have seemed to many to undermine our traditional picture of the relationship between words and thoughts. Clearly this does not apply to such primitive states as being aware of heat or pain, only to conceptualising those things, to saying to oneself "I am hot" or "I am in pain." These are things which we do *after* we have pulled our hand out of the fire or jumped out of the path of a falling meteorite.

On this view, language is not externalised thought; thought is internalised language. If this view were true, then thought would necessarily be in language, and there would be no true thought without language. From this it would follow that if something could not be said in a particular language, then it could not be thought in that language either. According to Hans Reichenbach: "If you can't say it, you don't know it." Because he had no word for "tree," a Tasmanian aborigine would not only not be able to say in his language, "Hesat under a tree," he would not even be able to think it. And if he could only speak his mother tongue, "He sat under a tree" would be something which would be for him literally unthinkable.

George Orwell feared that totalitarian governments would fashion this power to influence language in their own interests as a tool of their despotism. He envisioned a new language, called "Newspeak," deliberately created out of English in order to control the minds of the population:

There is certainly evidence that language influences attitudes. When interviews were given to bilingual Japanese women who had gone to live in San Francisco after marrying US servicemen, each woman was interviewed twice, once in Japanese and once in English. It does seem that the women gave responses which were socially conditioned, conservative and traditional when approached in Japanese, and more independent and liberal when interviewed in English.

However, the view that thought and language are one is insupportable.

- It is possible to show experimentally that those who cannot use language can nevertheless think. This is something quite familiar to anyone who has a baby in the family, or a pet dog. Particularly useful are those cases of people who have been born deaf, and who have not been taught any language, including any sign language, for a long time.
  In *A Man Without Words* Susan Schaller recounts the story of Idelfonso, a twenty-seven year old Mexican illegal immigrant in Los Angeles. He was deaf and had never been taught any sign language. Schaller taught him, and so was the first person who was able to communicate with him through language. Idelfonso was then able to tell her of his life before he possessed language, and to put her in touch with other languageless adults. They showed many signs of complex abstract thought. They handled money, played card games, repaired locks and performed elaborate pantomimed narratives for each other.
- Experiments have demonstrated that on occasion we may all think visually rather than in language. Roger Shepard devised an experiment in which letters of the alphabet were displayed at various angles to the perpendicular. Mixed in with these were mirror images of the same letters, similarly displaced. The participants had to press one button if the letter was the right way round, and another if it was a mirror image. Study of the response time suggested that the subjects were revolving the images by visual imagination, since those letters furthest from the vertical took longest to respond to. The subjects were not mentally manipulating descriptions in words, since there was no correlation between length of verbal descriptions of the shapes and length of response time.
- Many skills which we perform automatically, once they have been learned, are very difficult to describe in words, e.g. how to tie knots, how to drive a car. They are usually taught by imitation. We first watch someone do it, and then try it ourselves, correcting our mistakes as we go along. When we do think about such things, we usually do so visually. That is why we need a diagram to repair complex machinery. We could perform some of these skills quite adequately without language at all.
- Many successful people have claimed that some of their most creative thinking involved visual imagery. Galton, Poincaré and Einstein all claimed that their most creative thinking was nonverbal. Michael Faraday said that he visualised the lines of force which he postulated for magnetic fields as tubes passing through space. Albert Einstein is quoted as saying: "I rarely think in words at all. A thought comes, and I may try to express it in words afterward."
- We all sometimes find ourselves wishing to say or write something, but not quite knowing which are the appropriate words to use to express precisely our exact thoughts. We feel that we have knowledge which we cannot express in words, and therefore which we cannot communicate.
- We coin new words to express thoughts for which our existing vocabulary is inadequate, which shows that our thought runs ahead of our vocabulary.
- If language and thought were the same thing, then to be able to say something would be to know it. Yet we all know the difference between saying something which we understand and mere parroting. It would be difficult to explain the phenomenon of ambiguity, where we may mean different things by the same sentence, and may even be aware of that possibility. The fact that the same sentence can mean two different things shows that words and thoughts are different. The same words can express different thoughts. Moreover, we can express the same thought in different words.
- Even more devastating to the claim that thought depends upon language, if thought and language were one and the same, it is difficult to see how we could lie successfully.
- Steven Pinker points out that when we remember something, we usually remember the

substance or gist of it, not some form of words. For there to be a substance or gist, different from the particular words which are used to express it, shows that thought is not reducible to words.

This evidence clearly shows that we do not need to think in any language in order to think. It does not show, however, that we do not need representations of some kind to think to a sophisticated degree. The higher level thinking which is not done in words is either, for deaf people, accomplished in Sign, or using visual images. Although not part of a language, the visual images are essentially representations.

Steven Pinker maintains that we think in a language of thought, which by its structure in some way represents reality, and which he terms "mentalese." However, it would appear that thought at any sophisticated level is always hidden from us behind a further representation of some kind, either visual or verbal.

A Second Look at Language and the Limits of Thought

Clearly, the evidence suggests that language is not necessary for thought. Moreover, the conclusions drawn by Whorf and others that language constitutes and limits the world we experience and live in, do not seem to follow from the evidence they presented.

- If we really did live in different worlds from those speaking a different language, so that we shared neither the words we use nor the experiences of the world they designate, then translation from one language to another would simply be impossible. Whereas we know that while, at times, it may be difficult, it is not impossible.
- Much of the vocabulary of different languages does serve to pick out the same things, qualities and processes in the world. Words in nearly all languages will pick out such things as "tree," "dog," "star," "water," and so on. Other words, however, do not so much pick out what is out there as organise it, and organise our relations with it. Thus we classify as "polite" or "impolite" what we in our society and culture regard as acceptable or unacceptable behaviour. But here again, the differences are conspicuous only against a pervasive background of agreement. In some societies it may be polite to belch after a meal to show respect to one's host; while in others that would be considered impolite. But in all societies consideration for others and sensitivity to their needs will be considered polite, while stealing from one's host or violently attacking members of his family will be considered unacceptable.
- Much is made of the fact that people speaking different languages break up the colour spectrum in different ways. However, where a language is lacking a colour word which we possess, so that one word does for two of our colours, it will be found that the two colours stand side-by-side on the colour chart. Thus West African languages fail to distinguish blue and green. But no language ever uses a single word for colours which are distant from each other on the continuum, such as red and blue, while distinguishing others in between them. Language forces us to break into separate sections what is in reality a continuum. When this happens, the boundaries drawn will inevitably be rather arbitrary, and they will be drawn in different places by different peoples. But the fact that we divide the continuum in slightly different places from some other group does not entail that we "see" the world differently from them. Once qualifications are used further to describe the colour range, indirect means will prove adequate to show that distinctions which we make in one language can be made in the other, although perhaps with less attention being automatically drawn to them by the vocabulary used in one language than in the other.
- Different people are interested in different features of the common world, and that leads to the

need to develop specialist vocabularies. When I venture inside my computer I see "electronic-looking bits and pieces," whereas the computer specialist sees such things as mother boards, SIMM sockets, microchips, VGA cards, and so on. He needs a special vocabulary to do what he does, I simply need the telephone number of the technician in the after-sales service department of the store where I bought my computer. The technician and I both live in the same world. The computer technician simply pays closer attention to some things which I am happy to ignore, and possesses knowledge of which I am ignorant; and to do that he needs a vocabulary which I do not require.

People speaking different languages may tend to pay attention to slightly different aspects of their environment. They may tend to focus upon and articulate slightly different aspects of the world. But it is clearly the common world in which we all live which is being attended to by means of language. We all have to live in the same world, although we may attend to different aspects of it, and view different aspects as of different importance. But it is not our language that chains us to some particular viewpoint, it is our environment and our way of life. It is because we have the environment that we do have, and because we live in the way that we do, that we pay attention to some things rather than others. It is this which determines how we chop up things with our language. Our way of life determines our interests and concerns, and these in turn determine our outlook, and what we want to talk and think about. Life determines language; language does not determine life.

Languages are instruments which we use to describe our world and to interact with each other. To be successful, our language must be adapted to the world in which we live, and to the society in which it is used. That is why inhabitants of the Brazilian rain forest need many names for the flora and fauna of their region, and lack the terms necessary for the practice of computer technology; while the computer technicians of Silicon valley possess that vocabulary but lack words to deal with the flora and fauna of the Brazilian rain forest. Our world is not constrained by our language; our language has to be conformed to our world. Similarly, to be of use, a language has to express those relationships which are important in a society or it will be inefficient. If it matters whether an uncle is a maternal or paternal uncle, say for purposes of the discharge of important social responsibilities or inheritance, then that distinction will be marked in the language of that society. If that difference is not important, then it will not be marked. But the social reality is not created by the language used; the language used conforms itself to social realities.

This view, that language conforms to the real world, rather than that the experienced world we live in is a product of our language, may be called **linguistic realism**.

The philosopher Max Black has asserted that all languages are equally adequate and fit for the purposes for which they were intended, which sounds democratic and fair, but how could he know that to be true? Certainly some languages may be better instruments for describing aspects of the world than others. The languages of the Amazon Indians will be very effective at describing the world the speakers of those languages have lived in for millennia. They would not be well adapted for describing the world of the computer engineer in Silicon Valley. But because of the great changes taking place in the world of the Amazon Indians, and the comparatively sudden irruption of Westerners into their lives in the form of mineral prospectors and settlers, their language may not be well-adapted to their way of life for much longer.

We may be liable to be influenced in our thought by manipulation of language, as George Orwell feared, but the power of language over us has severe limits. We seem to be quite capable of noticing when governments and others are trying to influence our thought by sly choice of language, and of taking measures to avoid being unduly moved by it. In fact excessive use of language in this way simply leads to general cynicism. Television advertisements have to race to be one step ahead of our scepticism if they are to be at all effective. Political Broadcasts only reinforce the prejudices of those already disposed to believe what they see and hear.

Yet although language may not be necessary for thought, it may certainly assist or hinder its efficiency in different ways. For example, it has been shown that memory is strongly influenced by language. When subjects were shown plastic squares in many different colours, they tended to remember best those colours for which there was a clear identifying word in the language. Those that had to be described indirectly were recalled less efficiently. Certainly, without language of some kind we are condemned to isolation and barred from participation in the Enterprise of Knowledge.

10. Non-Verbal Language

In interpreting the significance of what is said to us we take account not merely of what is said, but also of the way in which it is said: volume, intonation, stress, accent and speed, any supporting gestures, and the demeanour of the speaker.

Our speech is also often associated with supporting gestures. This is especially true in Mediterranean countries, where a speaker's hands are rarely still. In addition, the way we stand and hold ourselves may convey hesitancy, hostility, servility, good will, and so on. We call these forms of nonverbal communication **body language**.

When we communicate over the telephone misunderstandings sometimes arise because we cannot see each other's facial expressions and gestures. It is difficult to know whether some-one intends what he says to be taken literally or whether he is being ironical. A similar problem arises over the Internet, where people communicate using the written word. In order to avoid misunderstandings a code of "smileys" has been devised which serve as substitutes for tone of voice and bodily signs. The happy face ": -)" implies that what was said was intended to be understood humorously, and that no offence should be taken. The sign "; -)" is used to imply sarcasm, on account of the wink it depicts.

We also use a variety of bodily signs to supplement our language which are purely conventional, and may differ from culture to culture. Nodding the head up and down usually signifies assent, while shaking it from side to side conveys dissent. In Greece, however, assent is signified by tilting the head downwards, and dissent, by tilting it upwards. In Britain putting the thumb and forefinger together to form a circle indicates that something is very good. In France the same gesture indicates worthlessness, while in Sardinia it is profoundly insulting. Like ordinary language, such signs are also subject to processes of evolution. Some gradually disappear, while new gestures appear and gain acceptance.

There are sign languages which are genuine nonverbal languages used by the deaf which have vocabularies of thousands of words, and grammars as complex and sophisticated as those of any verbal language. These true sign languages are distinct from hybrids, such as Signed English, which is a word-for-word signed equivalent of English, and other artificial languages invented to bridge the gap between genuine sign languages and spoken languages.

American Sign Language (ASL) has a grammar which relies on space, hand shapes, and movement in three dimensions. Particular facial movements, such as raising and lowering the eyebrows and pursing or clenching the lips provide information about relative clauses, create questions, and add adverbs. Bellugi and Klima explain, in *The Signs of Language*, that sign language has a visual drama unavailable to speech. The "listener," is like the audience at a play, watching the action unfold before his eyes. When a foreign signer goes to another country and learns the native form of sign, he usually signs with an identifiable accent.

We also learn much from other people through their unconscious body language, as when we learn that somebody is bored because he yawns. Unintentional signs of our thoughts, attitudes and intentions may be detected by facial expression, eye contact, dilation of the pupils of the eye, bodily posture, sweating, etc.

These signs may also differ from culture to culture, and because they are not under conscious control, they may be the cause of serious misunderstandings.

Some body language seems universal. The stoop of deference before a superior is probably found in all cultures. The reason for this is that many of the "signs" we read are inborn responses, like the tendency of a dog to fawn and lower its head or roll over onto its back. Some researchers claim to have detected a number of emotions which are always expressed by the same distinctive facial features and grimaces: happiness, anger, fear, disgust, and surprise. Others dispute their universality, arguing for example that while some facial movements, such as smiling, may be universal, their significance may vary from culture to culture. Perhaps the most reasonable position is that there are universal grimaces, but their significance may be culturally modified.

Obviously someone who is aware of such unconscious communication and can use it has to his advantage in dealing with other people. If we suspect that someone may be intending to deceive us, say a second-hand car salesman or a politician, then it may be useful to look at his body language rather than listen to what he is saying. The religious leader Martin Luther used to advise his followers to watch a person's fists rather than his mouth, implying that body language may be a more reliable indication of a speaker's intentions than what he says.

So-called body language, if truly unintentional, is not properly language, since it is natural rather than conventional. The stances and gestures of body language function as signs in the way that clouds are a sign of rain, rather than in the way that the word "rain" is a sign of rain.

Glossary

accent, fallacy of: ambiguity arising out of the ways in which a sentence might be stressed.

ambiguity: the quality of conveying more than one meaning.

arbitrary: could have been otherwise.

body language: non-verbal means of communication using bodily stance and expression.

circumlocution: an indirect way of saying something.

class: a set which is defined by the common characteristic shared by its members.

class member: one of the individual things which makes a class.

class property: the property which all the members of a certain class, and only the members of that class, have in common.

classification: the process of grouping individuals into classes.

complement class: the class formed by excluding all individuals possessing a specific property.

composition, fallacy of: the incorrect attribution of characteristics proper to the parts to an organised whole.

conventions: ways of doing things which have come to be accepted.

complement class: a class formed from all those individuals which do not possess some specific property.

concept: the object of our thought, or idea, when we are thinking. It is used when that idea is complex, puzzling or difficult in some way.

definition: a statement the meaning of a word.
denotative definition: defining by citing members or sub-classes of the class the word stands for.
dichotomy: a form of classification/division in which a universe of discourse is divided between a class and its complement class.
division, fallacy of: the incorrect attribution of characteristics proper to an organised whole to the several parts.
element: one of the individual things which makes up a set.
etymological fallacy: the argument that an earlier meaning of a word is, simply in virtue of that fact, its "correct meaning."
heuristic definition: teaching someone the meaning of a word.
incomplete terms: terms which require further specification if we are to make sense of them in any particular context.
indeterminate terms: a term such that that it is not always possible to say conclusively whether it is applicable in any particular case or not.
linguistic realism: the view that our language is determined by our needs and by the world we experience around us, as are our thoughts; and not vice versa.
linguistic relativism: the view thatthe way we experience the world is in large part determined by our language.
logical division: the process of grouping the members of classes into sub-classes.
objective definition: a statement of the precise limits or parameters of the use of a word.
operational definition: defining a word, for purposes of research, by reference to some specific operation.
ostensive definition: defining by pointing.
precising definition: a definition which proposes a new, more limited and precise use of a word already in use.
proper name: a word or words which are intended to refer to one and one only individual.
reference: a function of language which involves picking out an individual or individuals.
sense: meaning.
set: a collection of individual things.
sign: something which disposes us to expect or recall something else.
slippery slope, fallacy of: an argument that since there is no clear division between having one property and another along a continuum, there is no difference between having one property and the other.
stipulative definition: a definition which proposes the creation of a new word for some new concept or class of objects.
splitting hairs, fallacy of: demanding greater precision than the subject-matter warrants.
sub-class: a class all of the members of which are contained within another class.
symbol: something deliberately employed as a sign of something else.
theoretical definition: the characterisation of a word in terms of explain what it stands for in relation to a particular theory.
universe of discourse: a class taken together with its complement class.
vague: not clearly, precisely, or definitely expressed or stated; not sharp, certain, or precise.

8. MATHEMATICS

"If a teacher makes a mistake when working on the blackboard, and a member of the class points it out, the teacher has no alternative but to correct it. He is subject to the same rules as his pupils, and these are not the rules of an authoritarian hierarchy but of a shared structure of concepts. In mathematics, perhaps more than any other subject, the learning process depends on agreement, and this agreement rests on pure reason."

(R. Skemp)

1. Mathematical Propositions

In many ways, Mathematics an unusual discipline:

The assertions of mathematics, such as "2 + 2 = 4" are usually held to be uniquely certain and unquestionable. For this reason Mathematics has been called "the science of making necessary conclusions."

It might be thought that mathematical truths are derived from, and based upon, sense experience; that they are about things in the physical world. Certainly we come to learn basic arithmetical truths, such as "2 + 2 = 4" by counting groups of things, both separately and together, and then comparing the results. A child may learn his first mathematical truths by manipulating coloured counters or blocks. The teacher first teaches him to count, then shows that by adding two counters to two counters, that four is obtained. Thus the young child learns by experience that the statement "2 + 2 = 4" is true.

But arithmetic is not simply *"in the facts,"* it is something which we *apply to* the facts. If mathematical truth were simply a matter of conformity to the empirically known facts, we could not explain several characteristics of mathematical propositions:

- **We know mathematical propositions to be true independently of any particular experiences.** No one ever checks empirically his calculation that 364,112 + 112,364 = 476,476 by counting objects of those numbers separately, adding them together, and then counting them to see what the result is. The truths of mathematics seem to be justifiable independently of our sense-experience. The technical term to describe this independence of any particular experiences is to say that they are known **a priori**. We say that mathematical propositions are a priori propositions.

- **Mathematical truths are immune from the chances and contingencies of the passage of time.** It is assumed that if 2 + 2 = 4 today, then it will everywhere be so, and that it will always be so;

and that there will never be a need to check whether that result still obtains under differing circumstances. The term used to describe this property of mathematical propositions is that they are **necessary** propositions. If true, they are necessarily true.

- **The contradictory of a mathematical statement is necessarily false.**

We can see that "2 + 2 = 3" is not only false, it is necessarily false. It could not have been true. If they are false, mathematical propositions are necessarily false.

Numbers and **Numerals**

It might be argued that if we were to use the numeral "3" to stand for the number we now refer to using the symbol "4," then "2 + 2 = 3" would indeed be true. This is so, but that proposition would not be what *we* mean by "2 + 2 = 3," it would be what *we* mean by "2 + 2 = 4." Always distinguish numbers and the numerals we use to represent them. Numerals are ways in which we represent numbers. The same number might be represented by different numerals; e.g. the number four may be represented by the numerals "4", "11$_{base three}$" or "IV."

Mathematical reasoning also seems uniquely strong, and is the proper home of proof. Several different methods of proof are used in mathematics:

- Logical Deduction: Existing mathematical propositions, each of which must either have been previously proved, or be evident without proof, are used to deduce, by valid logical argument, new mathematical propositions.
- Complete Induction: A form of inductive reasoning which covers all the particular instances, and so is able to guarantee the truth of the conclusion.
- *Reductio ad absurdum*: The mathematician assumes the opposite of what he is trying to prove and derives a contradiction from it, showing his original assumption to be absurd. The logical form of the argument is: [(~p ? q) & ~q] ? p ; This is a variation of the *modus tollens*.
- Construction: Objects asserted to exist are exhibited or constructed.

2. Mathematical Systems

If we say that knowing a mathematical truth requires that we be able to prove it, then our proofs must have some firm basis on which to build. It is not possible forever to rest upon positions that have been previously proved. Ultimately, mathematical proofs must consist of inferences from propositions assumed to be true without themselves being proved. Such original "foundation" propositions are called **axioms**. Aristotle saw the necessity for this when he said: "It is not everything that can be proved, otherwise the chain of proof would be endless. You must begin somewhere, and you start with things admitted but indemonstrable. These are the first principles common to all sciences which are called axioms or common opinions."

The first people to attempt to set out proofs in mathematics systematically were the ancient Greeks.

The Geometrical System of Euclid

Many ancient peoples had been able to lay out the foundations of buildings accurately, and so manipulate lines and plane figures. The ancient Greeks added two new characteristics to this process:

- They abstracted the essentially *mathematical* factors from the associated circumstances.
- They *generalised* the solutions so as to cover all examples of the same type.

Many mathematicians provided proofs of relationships which always hold between lines and shapes. Sometime around 300 BC Euclid gathered these together and arranged them in such a way that each theorem could be proved by means of rigorous deductive logic from previous theorems.

As we have seen, there had to be some assumptions required to provide the premises from which the theorems could be proved, and which were never themselves proved. Euclid managed to reduce these to a bare minimum of five unproven assumptions or axioms and five postulates, which were held to be so obviously true as to be **self-evident** and not themselves requiring proof. The result was a system of interrelated propositions, each of which could be regarded as true because each could be proved by deduction from the axioms and postulates, or by deduction from propositions already proven from the axioms.

Euclid's Assumptions

Axioms:

1. Things that are equal to the same thing are equal to each other.
2. If equals are added to equals, the sums are equal.
3. If equals are subtracted from equals, the remainders are equal.
4. Things that coincide with one another are equal to one another.
5. The whole is greater than its parts.

Postulates:

1. It is possible to draw a straight line connecting any two points.
2. It is possible to extend a straight line indefinitely in any direction.
3. It is possible to draw a circle with a given centre through a given point.
4. All right angles are equal to each other.
5. Given a line 1 and a point P not on 1, there is only one line m in the plane of P and 1 that passes through P and does not meet 1.

The axioms are general logical rules, whereas the postulates are what defines the field (what the system is dealing with). Today that distinction would not be made, and the postulates would also be called axioms.

The reduction of a subject matter or theory to a set of minimum basic assumptions is called **axiomatization**. The **deductive system** resulting from Euclid's axiomatization of Geometry provided a model or paradigm of the ideal form of knowledge which was to have great influence for over two thousand years. This is because:

- It is based upon axioms which are held to be self-evident, and therefore to be themselves absolutely certain truths.
- It involves arriving at other truths which are no less certain than the axioms since they are derived from them in the most rigorous manner possible by a process of deductive proof from the axioms themselves, either directly or indirectly (from other theorems in turn themselves derived from the axioms).
- It is possible within a system to follow a precise and finite step-by-step procedure, called an **algorithm**, to solve problems.
- It is a most economical system, since, in the words of Isaac Asimov: "Never before was so much constructed so well from so little."

Despite the fact that Euclid did not specify the rules of logic by which the deduction of theorems could be made, so that his system was incomplete, the necessity and certainty apparently found in Mathematics made it, for most philosophers, an ideal model or paradigm for knowledge. There is a story that over the entrance to his academy Plato placed the words "Let none that is ignorant of geometry enter here."

Euclidean geometry was later supplemented by Aristotelian Logic, which enabled us to grasp the principles of deduction by which the new theorems are derived from previous ones. Understood in this light, Euclid's Geometry continued to provided the pattern for knowledge until in the eighteenth century. At that time, the philosopher Spinoza, in his *Ethics*, attempted to deduce all significant knowledge from a few basic axioms, allegedly self-evident, precisely in the manner laid down by Euclid.

Counterintuitive Mathematics

Despite its prestige, mathematicians were always unhappy with Euclid's fifth axiom, which is of a different character from the others. Many times they tried to prove it from the other four, so as to show it to be a mere theorem, but without success.

In the process of trying to prove the necessity of the Fifth Postulate concerning parallel lines by a *reductio ad absurdum*, the mathematician Lobachevsky substituted a different axiom: Given a line 1 and a point P not on 1, there are at least two lines in the plane of P that pass through P and do not meet 1. Lobachevsky had produced a new version of geometry, with new theorems, such as that "All triangles have the sum of their angles less than two right angles" and "The larger the triangle the smaller the sum of the angles, and the smaller the triangle the larger the sum of the angles." Lobachevsky's geometry can be regarded as describing a two dimensional surface with negative curvature, i.e. the interior of the surface of a sphere in two dimensions.

Later Reimann changed the Fifth Postulate in a different way to read: Given a line 1 and a point P not on 1, there are no lines in the plane of P that pass through P and do not meet 1. But in order to maintain the consistency of the axioms he had to change Postulate One to "Two points may determine more than one line"; and Postulate Two to "All straight lines are finite but un-bounded." The new theorems which result from this include "All straight lines are circles" and "The sum of the angles of a triangle always add up to more than two right angles, and the sum increases with the size of the triangles." His geometry may be thought of as describing a two dimensional surface with positive curvature, the outside of a sphere in two dimensions.

There are other differences between these geometries. In Euclidian geometry only one line can be drawn parallel to another through a point outside the first line. In Lobochevskian geometry at least two lines can be so drawn, whereas in Riemannian geometry none can. In Euclidian geometry parallel lines are always equidistant from each other, in Lobachevskian geometry there are never equidistant, while in Riemannian geometry there can be no parallel lines at all.

Logical Systems

The development of these new systems of geometry showed that Euclid's system was not unique. His axioms were not uniquely self-evident. More than that, it showed that a mathematical system has a value quite independent of the truth of its axioms.

This draws attention to the feature of mathematical thinking as essentially closed-system thinking using a limited number of rules and presuppositions, as opposed to open-thinking, which has to take account of what actually happens in the world. Such closed systems of thought are insulated from reality.

Mathematical systems, such as the geometries of Euclid, Lobochevsky and Riemann, are a species of logical systems.

A **logical system** is the most abstract form of system, requiring only:

- Some primitive symbols:
    - variables, e.g. "x", "y", "z."
    - constants, e.g. "~," "&," "=."
    - logical punctuation, e.g. "( )."
- Some formation rules which determine which combinations of primitive symbols are permissible. An allowable combination is a "well-formed formula" (wff).
- Axioms, or initial assumptions, in the form of wffs.
- Rules of procedure, allowing the derivation, by deduction, of new wffs (theorems) from the axioms or from previously derived theorems.

Once such a system has been specified, we are free to derive theorems from the axioms. Although the initial specifications of the system are arbitrary, everything that follows from that point follows by necessity, entailed by the axioms. The character of the theorems is not a matter of choice. Because the axioms in such a system do not have to be true, indeed, they may correspond to nothing real at all, they and the theorems derived from them may be counterintuitive.

The geometrical systems we have considered above are examples of logical systems. Georg Cantor demonstrated that Set Theory was such a system; while Giuseppe Peano axiomatized ordinary arithmetic. Peano adopted three undefined terms: "number", "zero" and "successor, and five axioms, and set out to derive all the truths of arithmetic from them.

Peano's Axioms of Arithmetic

- 0 is a number.
- The successor of any number is a number.
- No two numbers have the same successor.
- 0 is not the successor of any number.
- If P is a property such that (a) 0 has the property P, and (b) if a number n has the property P, then the successor of n has P.

Using these axioms, Peano was able to deduce, in principle, the series of integers as theorems.

How Mathematicians Evaluate Proofs

- Is the proof of *valid deductive* form.
- Is the proof as *economical* as possible in the number of axioms used and the number of steps required to reach the proof. If one proof refers to four axioms, while another proof of the same theorem in the same system uses only two, then the latter is more economical. If one proof takes twenty-five steps while another takes a mere five steps, then the latter is more economical.
- Is the proof *elegant*? Some proofs delight by the ingeniousness with which they achieve their end as economically as possible. Some mathematicians talk of such a proof containing some sort of twist or surprise in order to achieve this. These are said to be elegant proofs.

Recent Mathematical Proofs

- Fermat's conjecture that if n is a natural number such that n > 2, then there are no non-zero integers x, y, z such that xn + yn = zn.
- The Four-Colour Theorem, which states that four colours will be sufficient to colour the countries on any plane map such that no two adjacent countries have the same colour.

Incompleteness in Systems

One problem with considering the integers as part of a system is that the series is infinite. Goldbach's Conjecture states: "Every even number above two is the sum of two prime numbers." This has been proved for thousands of pairs, but since there seems to be no *reason* why every even number has to be the sum of two primes, there remains the theoretical possibility of a contradictory instance. The only solution would be some proof which would demonstrate that any even number simply *has* to be the sum of two primes, whatever that number happens to be. Such a proof has not yet been discovered.

Later, Gödel demonstrated that a mathematical theory, such as the arithmetic of natural numbers, cannot be completely derived from a finite set of axioms: in any such system, some propositions can be neither proved nor refuted. This is called the **Incompleteness Theorem**. If a formal system is incomplete, then there exist statements within the system which can never be proved to be valid or invalid.

Inconsistency in Systems

In 1902 Bertrand Russell discovered a paradox in Cantor's set theory: "In a library there are many books, some of which are catalogues of books or even catalogues of catalogues. And a catalogue may well list itself, too. Now consider the catalogue of all catalogues that do not list themselves: does it list itself or not?"

Later, Kurt Gödel demonstrated that the consistency of any formal axiomatic system cannot be proved in that system, but only in a meta-system, which in turn can of course again not prove its own consistency. He showed that in any system S, it is possible to formulate an expression which says "This statement is unprovable in S." If such a statement were provable in S, then S would be inconsistent. Hence any such system must either be incomplete or inconsistent. Gödel's proof depends on a self-reference paradox.

Some Self-Reference Paradoxes

- "All Cretans are liars . . . One of their own poets has declared so." (The Liar Paradox of Epimenides)
- This statement is false. (Eubulides' Paradox)
- Adjectives can be divided into "autological" ones which are self-descriptive, such as "pentasyllabic," and "heterological" ones, i.e. words that do not describe themselves, like "bisyllabic." Is "heterological" heterological? It would seem that the word "heterological"' is heterological only if it is not. (Grelling's Paradox)
- The barber of Seville shaves all Sevillians who do not shave themselves. Does the barber shave himself or not? (The Barber Paradox, attributed to Bertrand Russell)
- The set of all sets which are not members of themselves is neither a member of itself nor not a member of itself. (Russell's Paradox)

---

3. What is Mathematics About?

Mathematics as essentially the study of logical systems. The certainty available in mathematics derives from the strict application of deductive logic to clearly defined terms and unambiguously formulated propositions. It is certain that, if the deduction has been carried out faultlessly (and this is something which can be checked) then the theorems follow necessarily.

The application of the techniques of deductive logic allow us to see what is concealed in the collective assertion of the axioms. The theorems assert nothing *logically new*, although they may, as a matter of fact, be surprising to us because we were unaware of the implications of the axioms.

This certainty is purchased at a cost. It is only a relative certainty. The theorems are true *if and only if* the axioms from which they are derived are collectively true. In the words of Charles P. Steinmetz: "Mathematics is the most exact science and its calculations are capable of absolute proof. But this is so only because mathematics does not attempt to draw absolute conclusions. All mathematical truths are relative, conditional." However, since the axioms are not factual propositions making claims about the world, Bertrand Russell observes that mathematics is also "the only science where one never knows what one is talking about nor whether what one said is true."

Arithmetical statements, for example, may be said to be "true" relative to the axioms of the system in which they are used. They appear to apply to the world simply because we apply the system of arithmetic to model some aspects of the world. The "fit" is so good that we find the process of doing arithmetic useful. But this "fit" is limited. Two raindrops and two raindrops running down the car windscreen do not make four raindrops when they come together, they make one large raindrop. Two exotic fish added to two more exotic fish in the aquarium may only make four fish for a very few moments only, if one pair immediately eats the other. Two rabbits added to two other rabbits in a hutch may soon make many more rabbits than four.

Mathematics and Reality

If mathematical thought consists of manipulating the elements of logical systems, is it *about* anything at all? What are the objects of mathematics, such as numbers and shapes? Are they real things?

It soon becomes clear to the student of even Euclidian geometry, as it was to the Greeks, that the points, lines and shapes of Geometry are not points lines and shapes such as may be come across in the real world. The points have no magnitude, the lines have no width, and the shapes are always perfect. Such perfection is simply not found in the real world. No triangle in the world of sense-experience has its angles equal exactly to two right angles, because no triangle in the world of sense-experience is bounded by perfectly straight lines. By the definition of a triangle as a plane figure bounded by three straight lines this is to say that the triangles we observe in the world of sense-experience are not real triangles anyway. They are imperfect approximations to the true triangles with which geometry deals.

Clearly, the objects of mathematics are not material objects, like tigers and trees. They are not even material objects of a very shadowy or insubstantial kind, like clouds or rainbows. They do not exist in any place, and they are unchangeable, or immutable. They were not created and they will never disappear. They exist independently of space and time.

Mathematical Platonists argue that the objects they study are objectively real, and inhabit "The region of absolute necessity, to which not only the actual world, but every possible world must conform."

They point out that mathematical objects (numbers, shapes) possess those characteristics which they do possess quite independently of us. We do not invent them. We discover them, just as the ancient Greeks discovered that the square on the hypotenuse of a Euclidian right-angled triangle is equal to two right angles. They may have characteristics yet to be discovered, or even characteristics which no one will ever, as a matter of fact, get around to discovering. We must accept what characteristics they possess. Platonists believe that mathematical truths are not merely about the way our world is, they argue that they are about the way any possible world must be.

By contrast, **mathematical conceptualists** take the line that, as Einstein put it: "Mathematics deals exclusively with the relations of concepts to each other without consideration of their relation to experience."

Mathematical intuitionists argue that mathematical objects are products of our mental operations. They are constructed by us, and have only those properties which we recognise them as having. Thus for intuitionists there can be no properties of mathematical objects which they possess independently of us and which we may never discover. To grasp the meaning of a mathematical statement is to know what mental construction would constitute a proof of it. If there is such a proof, then the statement is true. For intuitionists, numbers are the product of processes such as counting, usually thought of as sets. All the properties of numbers, the relations which hold between them and the operations which can be performed with them, are considered to be properties, relations and operations of sets.

Mathematical formalists argue that there are no mathematical objects at all. Mathematics consists essentially in formulae: axioms, definitions and theorems. There are rules which we use to derive one formula from another, but these formulae are not *about* anything at all, they are just sequences of symbols. Such formulae may be applied to the real world and so be *interpreted* as saying things about the world which may be true or false, but of themselves they are neither true nor false. Mathematical formulae have neither meaning nor truth-value in themselves. Thus according to David Hilbert: "Mathematics is a game played according to certain simple rules with meaningless marks on paper."

Why is Mathematics so Useful?

Russell objected that theories which denied the objective reality of the objects of mathematics can not account for the way in which we find mathematics so useful in our understanding of, and manipulation of, the real world.

Since the time of the Pythagoras it has been a fundamental assumption of scientific thought that the world is amenable to mathematical treatment. Pythagoras discovered, probably by measuring the lengths of the strings of a musical instrument, that the chief musical intervals are expressible in simple numerical ratios. From this he surmised that in number lay the key to understanding all the complexity and diversity of the universe.

Even if mathematics can be thought of as a game, in which sets of axioms are invented, and the systems that can be derived from them deduced and investigated, the results frequently turn out to be of practical utility. Alan Watts says: "The mathematician does not ask whether his constructions are applicable, whether they correspond to any constructions in the natural world. He simply goes ahead and invents mathematical forms, asking only that they be consistent with themselves, with their own postulates. But every now and then it subsequently turns out that these forms can be correlated, like clocks, with other natural processes."

The US philosopher mathematician A. N. Whitehead expressed wonder at this applicability of mathematical abstractions to the real world:

"Nothing is more impressive than the fact that as mathematics withdrew increasingly into the upper regions of ever greater extremes of abstract thought, it returned back to earth with a corresponding growth of importance for the analysis of concrete fact . . . The paradox is now fully established that the utmost abstractions are the true weapons with which to control our thought of concrete fact."

In this sense of wonder he is echoed by Einstein: "How can it be that mathematics, being after all a product of human thought independent of experience, is so admirably adapted to the objects of reality." Examples of the development, for purely theoretical reasons, of Mathematical systems which later found employment in modelling aspects of reality include the following:

- Kepler used the mathematics of the ellipse in his work on the planetary orbits.
- Galileo used the mathematics of the parabola in his study of projectiles.
- Newton invented the calculus, and then discovered its application to bodies moving in space in his Theory of Gravity.
- Bernhard Riemann devised his system of non-Euclidian Geometry during the nineteenth century, and it was applied to space by Einstein at the beginning of the twentieth century in his Theory of Relativity.
- The Norwegian mathematician Sophus Lie developed a form of algebra during the nineteenth century which scientists were to use during the twentieth to develop the theory of quarks, the ultimate building blocks of matter.

If we consider mathematical propositions as mere definitions, or derived from definitions, this problem of the "fit" between the real world the various systems of mathematics does not seem to be a genuine one.

The German writer Goethe suggested that mathematical truths are simply disguised definitions, true in virtue of the meaning of the terms used:

"Mathematics has the completely false reputation of yielding infallible conclusions. Its infallibility is nothing but identity. Two times two is not four, but it is just two times two, and that is what we call four for short. But four is nothing new at all. And thus it goes on and on in its conclusions, except that in the higher formulas the identity fades out of sight."

Carl G. Hempel points out that from this it follows that:

"The propositions of mathematics have, therefore, the same unquestionable certainty which is typical of such propositions as "All bachelors are unmarried", but they also share the complete lack of empirical content which is associated with that certainty: The propositions of mathematics are devoid of all factual content; they convey no information whatever on any empirical subject matter."

Having chosen to define an unmarried man as a bachelor, we should not be surprised to discover that in the real world those to whom we attach the term "bachelor" turn out to be unmarried. The mystery of the fit of mathematics to the world is nothing more than a much more complex instance of this same process.

Mathematics as a Language

Mathematics has many points of similarity to a language. We use it as a vehicle for our thoughts. Using Mathematics we organise, express and communicate our knowledge. And we do so using conventional signs.

Using the language of Mathematics, we gain a great facility for precision. As a language, however, mathematics does not say very much about reality. Bertrand Russell pointed out that it is very abstract: "Ordinary language is totally unsuited for expressing what physics really asserts, since the words of everyday life are not sufficiently abstract. Only mathematics and mathematical logic can say as little as the physicist means to say."

4. Applied Mathematics

Mathematics is applied to the world by being given physical **interpretations**, or acting as a model of some aspect of the physical world.

Mathematical theories are used to **model** the world by functioning as simplified representations, by making certain assumptions about a given situation and abstracting from its objective complexity. Deductions made on the basis of the theory are then treated as predictions about the aspects of the world being modelled. If the predictions are correct, then the model is established as a useful one. If not, then another model is sought.

Measurement

What is Measurement?

By means of measurement, we quantify the continuous properties of things.

The process of **direct measurement** involves comparing two bodies having the same quality, one calibrated in standard units. The property of the thing to be measured is compared with the same property of the standard scale of measurement, in such a way that a number and a unit are determined as the measure of that quantity. Thus to say that a rod is three metres long is to compare the rod with a standard metre ruler, and to observe that the rod is exactly three times longer than the metre ruler.

Sometimes we cannot physically make such a comparison. Instead we have to rely upon **indirect measurement**. In this case we rely upon an observed correlation between two different qualities, showing that one is dependent upon the other. We can measure quantitative changes in one quality by marking the quantitative changes in another. Thus we measure temperature by comparison of the length of a column of mercury with the units of length marked on the glass tube. This can be done in virtue of a law which has the implication that the rate of expansion and contraction of the mercury is in direct proportion to the rise and fall of the temperature.

Standards of Measurement

Measurements are made by comparing the property to be measured with a standard. The standard will be given in units, which must be specified together with the numerical value of the quantity. We may measure a length in miles, yards and feet, or in kilometres and metres. To say that the length of something is, say 34.5, is meaningless. We need to know 34.5 *what*? inches? metres?

A **standard of measurement** should have two qualities:
- Accessibility: it should be conveniently available for making comparisons.
- Invariance: it should never vary in respect of the quality of which it constitutes a standard.

These two often conflict. In everyday life and in the earlier stages of a science, accessibility is the more important, but as science develops in sophistication invariance becomes more significant.

Until the eighteenth century units of measurement were not well standardised. Many different units were used: hands, cubits, leagues, gills, pecks, pints, stones, tons, etc. To make matters worse, the value of the same unit might vary from place to place. Today only two systems are in wide use, the International System of Units (SI), based upon the French metric system adopted as a consequence of the French Revolution, and the older British System, now no longer officially used in the UK, but still in use in the USA

During the 1790s the French Academy of Sciences set out to establish a single standard of length, the metre, based upon one ten millionth of the distance between the earth's equator and either of the poles. Their estimates were out by about 0.023%. This did not matter as the metre was quickly established, for practical purposes, as the length of a platinum rod made to that assumed length. This, rather than the fraction of the distance between the equator and the poles, effectively became the standard metre. In 1889 the metre was more precisely defined as the distance between two lines engraved on gold plugs near each end of a bar of platinum-iridium alloy kept at a constant temperature of 0^0C at the International Bureau of Weights and Measures in Paris. For convenience, twenty-nine identical bars were sent to laboratories around the world.

These standard metres, **calibrated**, or carefully copied from, the original rod in Paris, were themselves used to calibrate other measuring rods. Thus, theoretically, every measuring rod using units based upon the metre has been calibrated, directly or indirectly, with the standard in Paris. This is done using microscopes and dividing engines.

By the end of the nineteenth century the metre had also been defined in terms of the wavelength of light. This method was adopted by international agreement in 1961 as 1,650,763.73 wavelengths of an orange light emitted by the gas krypton 86. The length of the standard metre bar was measured by comparison with these wavelengths, so that the new standard should be as little changed from the old one as possible in order to avoid practical problems, (all metre rulers suddenly "becoming inaccurate"). Since all atoms of a given species are identical and emit light of the same wavelength, the standard is both accessible and invariant. Krypton-86 was chosen because its wavelength is sharply defined, and the isotope can be obtained easily and cheaply.

Error

While counting may be precise, no measurement is absolutely precise. Uncertainty arises from various sources. Mistakes may arise from blunders made by the person measuring, such as faulty reading of the scale, faulty calculation, or faulty transcription of the reading. Errors proper are more significant inaccuracies due to the limited accuracy of any measuring instrument other than the original standard, or the limited ability of anyone to read a measuring instrument accurately.

Errors are of two types: random errors and systematic errors.

Random errors occur both above and below the true value, and are caused by:
- Imperfections in the senses of the observer.
- The insensitivity of the measuring instrument.
- Changes in the physical property being measured, e.g. changes in the length of the object measured or of the measuring instrument due to expansion and contraction caused by changes in temperature.

Random errors can be detected by repeating measurements, and can be compensated for by calculating their mean.

Systematic errors are caused when the measurements recorded by an instrument are systematically above or below the true values. These are caused by:
- Incorrect design, working or calibration of the instrument, e.g. a slow stopwatch.
- Persistently incorrect operation of the instrument, e.g. by delay in starting a stopwatch.
- Persistent incorrect reading or interpretation of the instrument, e.g. because of the angle from which the stopwatch is viewed.

Systematic errors cannot be detected simply by repeating measurements, nor can they be compensated for by taking an average. They can be revealed and corrected by varying the operator, the instruments used, and the conditions under which the measurements are taken.

Because of the inevitability of error, records of measurements should be accompanied by an indication of **estimated uncertainty.**

What Can be Measured?

Galileo said: "Measure what is measurable, and make measurable what is not so." This begs the question as to what is properly measurable. It is clear, however, from what we have already considered, that a property must have certain characteristics to be measurable. For a quality to be measured:

- Things possessing that quality must be such that they can properly be ordered, i.e. the quality must be intensive.

- It must make sense to say that the thing possessing the quality being measured has a certain number of units of the quality.

- It must be possible to obtain general agreement about the number of units of a property a thing possesses.

- It must make sense to manipulate the units mathematically. Measurements are subject to such operations and addition, subtraction, multiplication and division. For this to be possible it must make sense to apply to them the laws of arithmetic.

When all these conditions are fulfilled, we are said to have an **extensive quality**. An extensive quality is one which it makes sense to try to measure.

Thus it must be possible sensibly not only to say, comparing some property shared by two individuals, that one is "greater than" or "more than" the other, but that one is "five times greater than" or "seven and a half times greater than" the other. Moreover, it must be possible to say that if, by some standard, we have two units and three units of some property, then with both added together we would have five units.

Beauty, by contrast, is intensive; for while it is possible to rank things in order of greater or lesser beauty, it is does not make sense to assign numbers to beautiful objects in respect of their beauty. On the other hand, mass is extensive since objects can be ordered in relation to greater or lesser mass, numerical values can be attached to the masses without absurdity, so that it makes sense to perform calculations with them.

Discussion: Can we properly say any of the following?
1. You and I each have a problem; between us we have two problems.
2. Your problem is much worse than mine.
3. Your problem is five times worse than mine.
4. If I take on your problem as well as my own, my problems are worse than they were before.
5. If I take on your problem as well as my own, my problems are six times worse than they were before.

There are two views of the nature of the properties which are measured. The *realist* view is that there are objective physical quantities which exist independently of our measuring them. By contrast, the *conventionalist* view is that the meaning of every physical magnitude consists simply in certain numbers being ascribed to physical objects. Until the conventions have been established whereby the ascription is made, measurement statements have no meaning. On this view there is no such thing as a physical quantity apart from a conventional system of measurement. The length of a body is *nothing more than* a reading on a ruler, its temperature is *nothing more* than a reading on a thermometer.

The realist view would seem preferable to the alternatives, since:

- It seems absurd to suppose that roads had no length, precipices had no height, and that there were no fluctuations in temperature or variations in light intensity until some conventions for measuring them were established. Measurement does not usually generate awareness of the strength of properties measured, it merely makes that awareness more precise and renders the properties more convenient to handle.
- As science has developed, more accurate methods of measurement have been developed. This looks like an attempt to obtain more and more precise estimates of the magnitude of real physical properties which they possess independently of our measuring them.
- Very different methods may be devised to measure magnitudes of the same property. Hence it seems absurd to suppose that the strength of a property is nothing more than the means used to measure it.

However, what *counts* as a property may depend upon our theories. At one time coldness was considered to be a distinct property with the opposite characteristics to heat. Nowadays coldness is regarded simply as the absence of heat, just as darkness is understood to be the absence of light.

Measurement and Reductionism

Scientists have been led to focus exclusively, wherever possible, upon those properties which are conveniently measurable, those qualities of things that possess quantitative aspects. Originally this was because of the immense prestige of mathematics as providing certain knowledge, but later a consequence of the success of the procedure.

Early scientists, such as Kepler and Galileo, initiated a tradition of confining their researches to those properties of things which were measurable, such as size, weight and speed of motion, and ignored those others, such as colours and odours which were not. The former came to be termed **primary qualities**, and the latter **secondary qualities**. Inevitably, Kepler came to consider the secondary qualities not merely as less important for his particular inquiries but also as generally less important than the primary qualities. Galileo went far beyond this, and asserted that while primary qualities have an objective existence in the external world, secondary qualities are subjective, depending for their existence upon our sense-experience.

Thus insofar as science deals with some aspect of reality, it tends to do so only by means of its measurable properties. In this way science may appear to legitimise a view that only the measurable aspects of things are significant or objective. This is a form of reductionism.

Later, with the development of the human sciences, in order to achieve for their studies the status of physics, many of the leaders in those fields sought to import mathematics into their work through measurement, even though some of the qualities they dealt with were not extensive. If properties are "measured" which it does not even make sense to talk of measuring, the result will necessarily be nonsense.

Statistics

Reasoning about large numbers of things is very difficult because we find it difficult to pay attention to the complex evidence, and to give each item of evidence its proper weighting. Instead what is striking, or close to us, or in accordance with our desires or prejudices, is usually given greater weight than it deserves. Most people feel greater trepidation when travelling by aeroplane than by automobile. Yet it can be shown statistically that the most dangerous part of an aeroplane journey is the drive to or from the airport. But while a rare plane crash kills many people and hits the headlines, more common automobile accidents do not. Moreover, most of us *feel* safer in a car than in a plane because we are closer to the ground. We feel that in an emergency there is something that we could do to save ourselves; while in an aeroplane we feel helpless. Yet, per travelling mile, many more people die in motor vehicles than in aeroplanes.

US citizens were warned by the State Department about travelling in parts of Europe after some terrorist incidents during the mid-1980s. Many Americans heeded this warning, because what they saw on their television screens made them feel that in that part of the world they might be in significant danger of violent death from terrorist action. But because of the much higher level of violent crime in the USA than in Europe, they were actually in much greater danger staying at home.

In order to avoid these psychological impediments to the proper assessment of evidence, mathematical analysis should be applied to the figures in preference to vague, impressions. This **actuarial** approach is adopted by insurance companies to calculate premiums. The discipline of the treatment of information about classes of things or populations, where each is associated with a set of possible outcomes, is called **statistics**.

Fallacies of Statistical Reasoning

Statistics are, however, no less capable of abuse than any other form of presenting data. The presence of numbers may give them a spurious appearance of authority and accuracy. For that reason, we lump together "lies, damned lies and statistics." Problems may arise with the data, the nature of the statistics employed, or the presentation and employment of the statistics.

Problems with the Data

Incorrect Data: The figures which make up the data may simply be wrong. A study in *Newsweek* in 1994 showed that reports of the numbers of women claiming to have been killed by their husbands or boyfriends in the USA was 4,000 according to the Centre for Women's Policy Studies, and 1,400 according to the FBI's Uniform Crime Report.

Discrepancies as large as this may arise because:
- Interest groups may exaggerate the size of problems in order to mobilise public opinion for change. The Centre for Women's Policy Studies is a feminist group, intent upon giving maximum publicity to the damage women suffer at the hands of men.
- Questions may be ambiguous or misunderstood. Adler also cited a 1992 poll which purported to show that 22% of Americans thought the holocaust, the attempted extermination of the Jews by the Nazis, may not have happened. If true, this would revealed amazing ignorance. But there was a confusing double negative in the question which people had been asked, and a reworded questionnaire subsequently found that only 1% held this view.
- People questioned may distort the truth. There are some things people do not like admitting to. They may lie. An investigator who asks people if they have ever been dishonest is not likely to be told the truth by anyone who is dishonest.

Meaningless Data: Questionable assumptions may be made in arriving at the figures.

In a survey of the number of homeless in the USA conducted in 1987, three hundred and eighty-one soup kitchens and shelters in twenty large cities were investigated: a small and probably unrepresentative fraction of the total. In those places a random sample of people was questioned. The data was then "adjusted," for example, by adding in the children, who were not counted directly. The very questionable assumption was then made that the rate of homelessness in small cities was one third what it was in the big cities. It was further assumed that from one fifth to one third of the homeless had been missed out altogether, and a final range of 400,000 to 600,000 was arrived at for the nation as a whole. When referring to the study those who commissioned it chose to quote only the upper figure.

- Some things may be inherently difficult to define. Asked if they have ever been the subject of domestic violence, different people who had experienced what would to the outside observer appear to be the same sort of behaviour from their spouses might respond differently. What *counts* as violence to one person may not be considered worth mentioning by another. Such a question might rather reveal the proportion of spouses who *feel* that they have been subjected to domestic violence. Other matters inherently difficult to define, and so to quantify, would include "date rape" and racial and sexual harassment.

Inappropriate Quantification: Numbers may be used where their application is inappropriate, so that the result is meaningless. Many rating systems are inherently flawed for this reason. It is quite reasonable for someone to say that he found one movie more entertaining than another, or much more entertaining than another. It makes sense for a single person to rank or order movies in order of preference. But to rate films as *generally* entertaining is a much more dubious practice. To describe one movie as "twice as entertaining" as another is nonsense. To award one hotel or resort "five marks out of ten" and another "ten out of ten" is equally nonsense. It just does not make sense to use numbers in this way in reference to inherently unquantifiable properties.

Statistically Inadequate Samples: Inadequate samples may be used to obtain the data, with the result that the effects of chance are increased.

- **Small samples** may be very untypical of the whole.
- **Biased Sample:** Surveys may be large enough, but inadequately representative of the population as a whole. The data may be skewed because the sample was biased. Since people often vote by social class, to attempt to predict the outcome of an election by using data obtained in an area dominated by one social class would be to skew the data in one direction rather than another. All telephone surveys skew the data in favour of those classes who own a telephone, excluding the poorest section of the population.

  Samples must reflect proportionately, in their composition, all the relevant differences found in the general population. It is sometimes very difficult to find out what these factors are, and very costly to ensure a balanced sample when they are known.

Problems with the Nature of the Statistics

Misunderstanding the Nature of Averages: This can best be illustrated by the astonishment of US President Dwight D. Eisenhower, who expressed alarm on discovering that fully half of all US citizens had IQs below average.

Confusion of Averages: Many investigations result in the production of a statistical average. Averages are used to highlight or measure the central tendency of the scores which comprise the data. This can be done in several ways.

- The **mode** is the figure which occurs most frequently in the data. This highlights the central tendency of the scores in relation to frequency of occurrence.

- The **median** is the figure which is midway between the highest and lowest scores, the fiftieth percentile. This highlights the central tendency of the scores in relation to their total spread.
- The **arithmetic mean** is the total sum of the scores in the data divided by the number of scores. If the spread of scores does not approximate to a normal curve of distribution, the arithmetic mean can be misleading.

  The average wage of people employed in a school was found to be high, but then it was discovered that the teachers all received low pay, while a small number of administrators were very well paid.

False Interpolations: False estimates may be made of unknown variables which lie between known variables simply by running a line representing the trend between two known points. The acceptability of interpolations will vary depending upon the number of known points and their stability.

Problems of Presentation

Data may be represented pictorially in the form of **graphs**. Most types of representation are based upon two axes or straight lines, one vertical and one horizontal, both of which are marked off in scales of measurement. Histograms or bar graphs are a method of presenting data frequency distributions for discrete variables, such as attendance in class on different days of the week. Frequency polygons may be created by joining up points on the graph in order to display the frequency of continuous variables, such as the rise or fall of a patient's temperature. Pie charts may be used for both types of variable. Here a circle represents the total frequency, with separate sectors representing the frequencies of individual readings, the areas of the sectors being proportional to the magnitude of the frequency it represents.

Misleading Graphs: Graphs may be portrayed in a deliberately misleading manner:

Since the units chosen along the axes are arbitrary, it is easy to distort the graph so as to give a false impression of the significance of the data. By stretching the scale on the vertical axis a small difference can be made to appear large. Similarly, by squeezing the units of measurement on this axis, differences can be minimised. In order to minimise the possibility of distortion and misrepresentation a convention is often observed that the height of the vertical axis should be three-quarters the length of the horizontal axis.

Figure 9.1 shows the annual percentage pass rate in a school for public examinations in Mathematics.

Figure 9.1

1997	1998	1999	2000	2001	2002	2003
72%	74%	75%	74%	76%	78%	80%

Over the last seven years there was a slight but definite improvement. This is displayed in the graph to the right. However, it is difficult to see the changes because, relative to the total results, they are so slight. What the graph chiefly shows is not so much the improvement as the lack of significant variation in the results

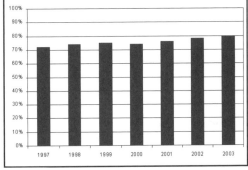

Figure 9.2

A frequent practice is to chop off the bottom and very top parts of the graph. This has a distorting effect, making any differences appear much greater than they really are. This is useful for governments and companies wishing to boast of significant improvements where there are none to speak of. (Figure 9.3).

Figure 9.3

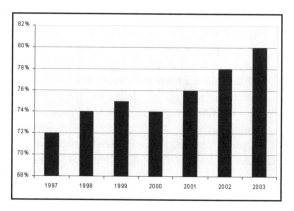

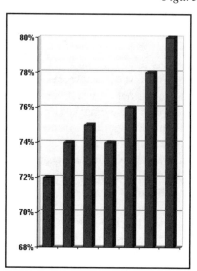

Three-dimensional pictographs add a dimension with increase of volume, so that a ratio of two to one will appear as eight to one. This magnifies the differences even more. (Figure 9.4)

Figure 9.4

If solid figures of some sort are substituted for the columns, the degree of distortion may appear even more impressive.

Problems arising out of the Employment of Statistics

False Extrapolations: Trends may be projected in a mechanical way to forecast the future without taking account of the fact that circumstances alter. The very publication of a prediction may itself influence the future.

Discussion: How might the following predictions affect future behaviour?
1. Traffic on the coast road is expected to reach record volume over the coming weekend.
2. At the present rate of sale, all tickets for the cup final will be sold my tomorrow evening.
3. Recent history shows that the government increases the tax on luxury goods during August.
4. More people are arrested for driving while under the influence of alcohol over the Christmas holiday period than at any other time in the year.
5. Most motoring accidents occur during the early hours of the morning.

Improper Comparisons

Statistics may be provided which imply a comparison but which do not provide one of the two terms of the comparison. For this reason, they are meaningless.

Some Recent New Applications of Mathematics

In recent years new branches of Mathematics have been developed to model specific types of situation.

- Game Theory involves applying mathematics to game-like situations, such as business and war, where:
  - Participants compete against each other.
  - They do so to maximise some property which defines "winning."
  - There are positions of uncertainty.
  - There are only a limited number of options available.
  - It is necessary to predict the actions and responses of others, when they are also predicting one's own actions and responses.

  Game theory is used to choose the best possible strategies to follow in given situations.

- From its name, Chaos Theory appears to do the impossible and make sense out of what has no reason in it. But the name is misleading. Chaos Theory is used to model situations which are so complex that they *appear* to us simply as disordered. Many phenomena were so complex that the use of mathematics to understand them was not practical, e.g. turbulence in the flow of water. It was assumed that such phenomena followed strict mathematical laws, but that their complexity forbade any accurate prediction. Chaos theory allows scientists to see patterns where none were discernible before.

Some physical systems seem to behave unpredictably despite their apparent simplicity, and despite well-understood physical laws governing their behaviour. These systems are ones which show a very high degree of sensitivity to initial conditions, and to the way in which they are set in motion. Thus the movements of the balls in a pinball machine are precisely governed by well-understood physical laws, and yet the final outcome is unpredictable. Using chaos theory, while it is impossible to predict exactly what will happen, it is in general possible to model the overall behaviour of such a system, focusing on the order inherent in it. Chaos theory has been used to analyse such complex physical systems as human population growth, the behaviour of epidemic diseases, stock market trends, the turbulent flow of fluids, irregularities in heartbeat, plasma physics, and the motions of groups and clusters of stars.

Glossary

actuarial: an approach to statistics using mathematical analysis.

algorithm: an explicit and finite step-by-step procedure for solving problems.

asymmetrical relationship: a relationship such that if it holds between p and q, then it cannot hold between q and p.

average: a value that is supposed to give the most typical score of a range of scores, either the mean, median or mode.

axiom: a proposition the truth of which is assumed and subsequently used in a mathematical system as a basis for the deduction of further propositions which will be true of the axioms are true and if the deductions are valid.

axiomatization: the process of deriving all the propositions of a system from a few undefined terms together with a few fundamental basic propositions which taken are accepted beyond question within the system, by a process of logical deduction.

calibration: the checking of measuring instruments with a conventional standard.

closed-system thinking: thinking within an artificially circumscribed context, so that the number of factors to take account of is determined in advance.

deductive system: the formalisation of a subject by using deduction to derive the truths of that subject undefined terms and axioms.

deviation: whether data scores are spread out or bunched.

direct measurement: directly comparing the property to be measured with a scale.

estimated uncertainty: an explicit limit of precision of measurement.

extensive magnitude: different numerical values can be assigned to different positions on t he ordering, such that the ordering is preserved when ordered by the relation "greater than".

frequency table, a table of data listing on one line all the possible outcomes of the variable, from the smallest to the greatest, and on another the relative frequency of each occurrence.

graph: a geometrical representation of a function.

indirect measurement: relying upon a correlation between the property to be measured, which cannot be measured directly, and another property which can be measured directly, and measuring that property.

intensive magnitude: a magnitude which can be ordered.

intransitive relationship: a relationship such that if it holds between p and q and between q and r, then it cannot hold between p and r.

law of large numbers: outcomes which are the result of chance will increasingly approach what the calculus of probability predicts as the number of outcomes approaches infinity.

logical system: a set of axioms, and rules of inference for generating theorems from the axioms.

mathematical conceptualists: those who believe that the objects of mathematics are simply concepts.

mathematical formalists: those who believe that, properly speaking, there are no mathematical objects at all, only   strictly meaningless axioms, definitions and theorems.

mathematical intuitionists: those who believe that the objects of mathematics are products of our mental operations, having only those properties which we recognise them as having.

mathematical model: an interpretation of a logical system.

mathematical Platonists: those who believe that the objects of mathematics are somehow real, although not to be located in the external world.

measurement: a means for the quantification of the continuous properties of things.

naturalistic fallacy: a confusion between what is statistically normal and what is right.

non-symmetrical relationship: a relationship such that it holds between p and q, then it may or may not hold between q and p.

non-transitive relationship: a relationship such that if it holds between p and q and between q and r, then may or may not hold between p and r.

paradox: from premises generally accepted as true, a conclusion is validly deduced which is either self-contradictory or conflicts with our profoundly held beliefs.

postulate: an assumption held to be self-evident.

primary qualities: the quantifiable qualities of things.

random errors: errors made either side of a true reading.

scale of measurement: a standard of measurement against which some property of other things can be measured.

secondary qualities: qualities of things thought not to be quantifiable.

statistics: the discipline of the treatment of information about classes of things or populations, where each is associated with a set of possible outcomes.

symmetrical relationship: a relationship such that if it holds between p and q, then it must hold between q and p.

system: a system of deduction of new propositions (theorems) from axioms by a defined set of rules of deduction.

systematic errors: errors of measurement which consistently skew the reading in one direction rather than another.

theorem: a proposition in a mathematical system which is validly deduced from axioms or from other propositions validly deduced from the axioms.

transitive relationship: a relationship such that if it holds between p and q and between q and r, then it must also hold between p and r.

9. THE ARTS

"I must study politics and war that my sons may have liberty to study mathematics and philosophy. My sons ought to study mathematics and philosophy, geography, natural history, naval architecture, navigation, commerce and agriculture in order to give their children a right to study painting, poetry, music, architecture, statuary, tapestry, and porcelain." (John Adams)

1. What is Art?

Before we can consider art as a medium for the manipulation, expression and communication of knowledge, we shall need to consider the prior question: What is art? At first glance this does not seem problematic. Most people would agree that the following are famous examples of works of art:

- The painted ceiling of the Sistine Chapel in the Vatican Palace, showing the creation of the world, by Michaelangelo.
- The *Ninth* or *Choral Symphony*, by Beethoven.
- The statue of Hermes with the child Dionysos by Praxiteles in the museum of Olympia, Greece.
- The play *Hamlet*, by William Shakespeare.
- Chartres Cathedral in France, designed and erected by a host of unknown architects, craftsmen and labourers.

But there is no consensus about some other objects which have been proposed as works of art by art authorities and galleries, and which have been bought and sold as such.

- A reproduction of the Mona Lisa with a beard and moustache added, entitled L.H.O.O.Q., which read in French becomes "She has a hot ass," by Marcel Duchamp.
- Fire bricks arranged in a rectangle and entitled *Equivalent VIII*, by Carl André.
- A pear shaped urinal entitled *Fountain*, chosen, neither designed nor created, by Marcel Duchamp.
- Canvases "painted" by a chimpanzee.

The Nature of Art

It seems clear that today there is no generally accepted definition of "art," so that the meaning of the term is a matter of some controversy. From that it follows that there is no clear and generally accepted standard by which we may judge something to count as a work of art. From this it does not follow, however, that any talk about art is futile.

Discussion: Which of the following situations may result in something which can appropriately be called a "work of art"?

1. I skilfully copy a painting which is a recognised work of art. I do it so well that only an expert could tell, after very careful examination, which was the original. Is the copy art?
2. I create a software program for my computer so that I can generate random sounds. Many people find one sequence, which I have recorded, very striking. Is this art?
3. I photograph a famous painting, and then mass produce copies of it. Are the copies art?
4. I collect various objects from a garbage heap, empty tin cans, cereal packets, used tea bags, etc., and arrange them for exhibition under the title "The Throwaway Society." Is this art?
5. I drape large yellow plastic sheets over the town hall, so as to cover it completely. Is this art?
6. I place my pet mice in shallow trays containing paint of different colours, then encourage them to run around over a large sheet of paper. I call the result "Joy." Is the result a work of art?
7. I have just watched the latest episode of my favourite soap opera. It was very entertaining. Is that a work of art?
8. I get drunk and vomit over my canvas, let it dry out, and then refer to it as "a revolutionary and iconoclastic stance towards art." Is the result a work of art?

The following explanations of the term have been suggested:

"Art" is a Meaningless Term: Some have effectively argued that the term has no clear meaning at all. According to Marshall Macluhan "Art is anything you can get away with", i.e. if you can sell it to somebody as art, then it is art.

Family Resemblance: While no clear definition can be provided, all works of art exhibit a quorum of overlapping resemblances, although no single one which all share in common.

Institutional Christening: A work of art is an artefact which belongs to a type or genre which, within some particular society, is called art by the appropriate authorities. If an artefact is displayed in an art gallery then the activity which produced it is art. Of course many instances of the same type may be refused admission, but that may be merely because they are considered to be bad examples of the art form – and that is another story.

Significant Form: In his *Art*, Clive Bell argued that all genuine works of art bring about a special aesthetic emotion in their audience. This is evoked by the presence of significant form in the work of art. This significant form is a matter of the relation of the parts within the whole, and is therefore a matter of form or structure: shapes, colours, textures, etc., rather than subject matter.

Some people are better at art appreciation than others because they are better able to detect significant form.

Historical Account: In difficult circumstances it is frequently useful to examine the history of a word, to establish what a word meant at some time in the past when its meaning was more clear, and then move on from there.

"Art", in the widest sense, was essentially skill. Something made by art was chiefly distinguished from something produced by nature. A work of art is an "artifice," it is "artificial." An "artefact" is something which did not exist in nature and which has been produced by the exercise of human skill and workmanship. The Irish dramatist Oscar Wilde tried to tried to draw attention to the artificiality of art by wearing a green carnation, since a green flower is rare in nature, and a green carnation unknown.

For this reason it simply generates confusion to pass off as art:

- natural objects, things which have no skill expended upon them at all;
- objects which are largely the product of accident, e.g. dadaistic poems, where the words are cut up, picked out at random from a box, and strung together to form a "poem"; "paintings" which are the result of random splashes of paint on canvas.
- So called "ready-mades," objects simply taken by the artist and presented as works of art, such as Duchamp's bottle-rack and urinal.

Such objects, may sometimes be interesting curiosities, capable of making people ask themselves important questions, and they may even, on rare occasions, be worthy of public display; but it is simply confusing to refer to them as works of art.

In the Dewey Decimal System of classification, used widely to classify books in libraries, arts may conveniently be divided into two categories: **useful arts** and **fine arts**. The useful arts are often called crafts: e.g. agriculture, engineering, cookery, medicine, carpentry. They are usually performed for the sake of some practical end or goal which is other than, or extrinsic to, the performance of the skill itself. Thus plumbing is carried out in order to have a controlled convenient water supply and sewage disposal systems, while automotive engineering is practised to maintain and repair cars so that they function as we wish them to. The hydraulic engineer does not fit pipes so that we can admire them, but to carry liquids. The farmer does not grow crops in order that we should admire his skill, but to produce food. Useful arts are generally valued not for themselves, but for the practical services they offer to us.

The fine arts include painting, sculpture, music, photography, story writing, athletics. Fine arts are generally performed with no extrinsic or utilitarian goal in mind. We value either the performance of the art or its immediate product, for itself. Because fine arts are generally valued in and for themselves, we say that they have **intrinsic value**.

Intrinsic and Extrinsic Value

An activity has extrinsic value if it is valued not for itself, but for something else which the performance of the activity achieves. Thus building a house would normally be an activity performed not because it is enjoyable or worth doing in itself, but in order to get a house built. It is the house which is built which is valued, and for which the work was performed.

An activity has intrinsic value if it is valued and performed not for some extrinsic end, but simply for itself. Usually chess players play chess not to pass the time or to win prizes, but simply because they enjoy playing chess and for no other reason.

The distinction between useful arts and fine arts is not an absolute one. In reality there is a continuum between the useful arts and the fine arts, stretching between arts whose purpose is entirely utilitarian and arts whose purpose is entirely aesthetic, decorative or recreational.

Some of the details of what we now consider to be fine arts had, and may still have, a practical value. The bases and capitals of columns helped to diffuse the load they bore on to the masonry above and below them. The cornices and pediments of windows protected the facades of the buildings from the erosive effects of rainwater.

Some arts are difficult to place, e.g. ceramics, although usually particular examples or artefacts will fall clearly on one side of the divide rather than the other. The manufacture of cheap sanitary equipment will be a useful art, while the production of expensive, individually hand-painted vases will be an exercise in fine art.

Sometimes we may take up an unusual stand, and value the product of one of the useful arts for simply for itself, as when we admire the sheer craftsmanship which went into making a very ordinary chair. We may occasionally value one of the fine arts for something extrinsic which it achieves, as when we value fine paintings as investments.

Sometimes the distinction between useful and fine arts has been presented as one between activities which are carried out for sordid gain, and activities performed under the noble inspiration of a disinterested love of art. But the matter of any money paid to the artist is irrelevant to this distinction. Some of the noblest examples of fine art have been created in return for payment. Leonardo da Vinci and Michaelangelo, Raphael and Bernini, did not work for the sheer love of art, they were paid for their work, no less than a hydraulic engineer or surgeon. Some works of fine art undoubtedly have been created without thought of payment. But then a plumber or vegetable gardener may occasionally enjoy the luxury of exercising his particular skills without payment, just for the pleasure of doing a job well. The British wartime leader Winston Churchill notoriously spent much of his time when out of political office building a wall on the estate of the Duke of Marlborough, presumably for the opportunity of solitary relaxation out of doors.

2. The Aesthetic Purpose of Art

The question "What is art for?" can easily be answered in respect of the useful arts. They are performed for the extrinsic ends which alone usually justify the effort involved in performing them. Farming is generally carried out for the production of food, cooking to make food palatable, electrical engineering to bring us the benefits of electric power. The question only becomes interesting, and more difficult, when asked about the fine arts. e.g. What is opera for? What is soccer for? What is novel-writing for?

Sometimes the products of the fine arts may be adapted as useful arts for some practical purposes. A photograph taken for the pleasure of taking it may be used by the police in order to help them arrest a criminal or locate a missing person. Art is also frequently used as propaganda. Aside from such practical considerations as these, the fine arts are frequently said to have the following, not necessarily mutually exclusive, purposes:

- To "hold a mirror up to nature" or draw our attention to significant aspects of reality.
- To express emotions.
- To exercise, express, and give form to, the imagination by the creation of something essentially new.
- The communication or teaching of some truth or moral purpose.
- To provide a wholesome environment in which good citizens can grow and develop. Plato based this upon his, not unreasonable, belief that people tend to be assimilated to their environments. Like chameleons, people will take on the moral "colour" of their surroundings. Surrounded by good works of art people will become better. Surrounded by evil, unwholesome or unhealthy works of art people will become corrupted and emotionally and spiritually impoverished.
- To create what Clive Bell called "significant forms" which have aesthetic value or beauty, e.g. balance and harmony.
- To create artefacts with a primary intention of addressing the aesthetic consciousness. Thus James Joyce defined art as "the human disposition of sensible or intelligible matter for an aesthetic end."

3. Aesthetic Experience

At the heart of the nature of art lies the **aesthetic experience**. This is something which also permeates everyday life.

- Jason has just bought a poster of his favourite pop group, and he is going to pin it to the wall of his bedroom. He spends some time trying to fix it in the position where it will look best.

- The chief constable is going to a dinner at the Freemason's Lodge. He spends some time beforehand choosing the right tie to go with his suit and the occasion.

- When he went on holidays to Crete, the first thing that Harry did was to go to the top of a cliff on the edge of the village where he was staying to look out over the sea. He was disappointed to find that the villagers had apparently been tipping their household refuse, old refrigerators and broken furniture over the edge for several years.

- When people in Upper Snetterington complained about an auto scrap yard on the edge of the town the local council advised the owners to build a tall fence around it to hide it from view.

All of these are examples of aesthetic interest. The purely aesthetic interest may be mixed up with other factors which are not strictly aesthetic. Jason may wish to avoid being criticised by his mother for making his room "look a mess." The chief constable wants to "cut a figure" at the Freemasons' dinner, and Harry may be ecologically sensitive so that he deplores pollution. The people of Upper Snetterington may be concerned that an eyesore on the edge of their town would cause a decline in the value of their property. But in each case it is primarily the *appearance* of something which is being attended to.

Our interest in these things involves aesthetic evaluation. This may be positive, negative, or anything in between; and to express this range we use words like "beautiful," "ugly," "interesting," "boring," "fitting," "unfitting," "striking" or "banal."

This aesthetic attention may be directed towards both natural objects and the creations of man. We may pay attention to the beauty of objects in the natural world, such as a sunset, a snowscape, or a woodland glade. Some natural objects, such as the Grand Canyon or Victoria Falls are as admired and as famous as any works of human artifice. The chief and obvious difference between the two is that a work of art has been deliberately fashioned by man, whereas nature is "just there."

The elements necessary for an aesthetic experience stimulated by a work of art are:

- an artist or performer;

- a medium in which the artist works. This will include the materials and techniques they employ; as well as the conventions of the society in which they operate, particularly as these relate to the art form;

- the "work of art" created: whether an object or performance;

- a public, audience or spectators, to appreciate the work.

There are sometimes problems identifying some of these elements.

Who is the Artist?

In some cases it is not clear who the artist responsible for a work of art actually is. In the case of an opera, for example, many people come together to make a performance possible: director, producer, conductor, stage designer, costume designer, orchestra, singers, stage hands, etc. Arguably, any one of them could ruin the performance. All could significantly change what was originally in the mind of the composer.

Talking Point: The authority of the artist

Does the artist have a special authority in explaining and interpreting his work, or can his audience see things in his work of which he himself would have been unaware? Was Shakespeare as clever as the critical literature makes him out to have been?

What is a "Work of Art"?

By using the term "work of art," it is implied that the object in question is both a product of some endeavour and also a good example of its type.

The concept of a work of art, however, is a difficult one in many ways. We all know what is meant by the phrase, but when we try to be precise about exactly *what* it refers to, it is sometimes not at all clear exactly what the work of art actually is. This can be seen by considering several examples.

Case Study: "The Mona Lisa," a portrait painting by Leonardo da Vinci.

Leonardo da Vinci's painting, the Mona Lisa, is an object displayed in the Louvre Museum in Paris. Visitors can see it on display there.

Postcard prints of the original are sold in the shop attached to the Louvre. While the postcards may be works of art in their own right on account of the quality of the photography, Leonardo's creation is unique. Looking at the photographs is not looking at Leonardo's work of art, it is looking at photographic copies of his work, which is a different thing altogether.

Yet even in looking at the original in the Louvre there is a problem. Because of changes in the chemistry of the surface of the painting, visitors do not see exactly what Leonardo's contemporaries saw. For example, small cracks around the mouth are said to have changed subtly the character of the famous smile. Therefore when we view the canvas today, we do not see what the artist presumably intended us to see.

Nevertheless, despite the fact that our Mona Lisa is not exactly Leonardo's Mona Lisa, it is clear what we are referring to when we identify the work of art.

The photographs of the Mona Lisa, although not the original work of art, and not even photographs of the original work of art in the strict sense of that term, may be yet considered subsidiary works of art in their own right, as examples of the photographer's art. Moreover, since they reproduce an apprximation of the original, we can appreciate something of the original by looking at them.

Despite all the difficulties noted above, it is clear what the *Mona Lisa* is, and when someone refers to it, we know what they are talking about or writing about. In many other cases, however, this is not at all clear. There are problems with the identification, or **individuation**, of many works of art. As long as we do not think carefully about them, we know what people are referring to when they talk about them, but when we focus our attention upon some works of art, they seem to dissolve before our eyes.

Case Study: A copy of "The Grapes of Wrath," a novel by John Steinbeck.

I possess what is called a "copy" of this novel. But reading my copy of *The Grapes of Wrath* is not like looking at copies of the Mona Lisa. In reading my copy of the novel I am reading the novel. Each individual who reads a copy of *The Grapes of Wrath* is similarly confronted directly by the novel. Yet, paradoxically, if every person in a class of twenty-five has his own copy, it does not follow that there are, in the class, twenty-five works of art. Through my copy of the novel I am face to face with the novel itself, although the novel itself is identical with no single physical thing.

When I looked at a copy of the *Mona Lisa* I could only say that I had seen a copy of the painting, not the painting itself; but when I read my copy of *The Grapes of Wrath* I can justifiably claim to have read the novel itself. Yet there is no "original novel" kept in some library which is the novel, of which all others are merely copies, not even the original manuscript written by the author and sent to his publisher, although that may be a relic of the author which a keen collectors might wish to obtain.

According to the Italian philosopher Benedetto Croce, the work of art proper exists only in the mind of the artist, and the physical artefact is only an effect of real the work of art.

This is seen as unsatisfactory as soon as we notice that we can identify any work of art only in and through a performance, a book, a score, or a canvas. Otherwise we should have to say that the world might contain an uncountable number of great works of art whose only defect is that they have never actually been transcribed in some medium. The physical embodiment of a work in sounds, language, scores, or other inscriptions is a fundamental a part of it, since only from this can it be identified at all.

Richard Wollheim, in *Art and Its Objects* argues that works of art are "**types**" and their embodiments "**tokens**." This distinction is borrowed from the US philosopher and logician C. S. Peirce, who argued that the letter 'x,' for example, is neither identical with any particular token of it (such as the one printed on this page) nor distinct from the class of such tokens. Peirce therefore calls the letter x a type. A type is a formula for producing tokens. The letter "x" is uniquely identifiable even if we only ever come face to face with its tokens.

This would seem to make sense of examples like the novel, which is known only in its tokens. But in some fields of art, the work seems to be a unique physical object, e.g. the Mona Lisa, to which the distinction does not apply.

Moreover, the simple distinction between type and token does not entirely remove the confusion concerning works of art which could be described as tokens. Consider the following:

Case Study: The Recording of a Performance of *The Mastersingers of Nürnberg*, an opera by Richard Wagner.

I have recordings of this work on compact disc and videocassette. But recordings are hardly the work itself, their quality depends upon the type and quality of the recording, something very different from the performance. The recordings are of a live performance in

---

the Festspielhaus built by the composer himself at Bayreuth especially for the performance of his own operas. The conductor is Horst Stein with the orchestra of the Bayreuth Festspielhaus. The singers include Bernd Weikl, Siegfried Jerusalem and Mari Anne Häggander with the chorus of the Bayreuth Festspielhaus. The performance is directed by Wolfgang Wagner, the conductor's grandson. All these people, and many others I have not named, such as the stage designer the costume director and the lighting director, made a contribution to the total performance. So when we praise this opera as a work of art, is the performance the work of art?

There are three problems with this approach. Is it the opera as created by these people? If so, what about other productions of this opera? Are they distinct works of art? They may be very different. Some performances are in modern dress, in others the music is conducted at a faster or slower tempo, and so on. Even each separate performance with this conductor, orchestra, singers etc. may be very different. Moreover, some features of any modern performance, those connected with the lighting, for example, could not have been conceived by Richard Wagner, the composer.

So is the work of art Wagner's score and libretto? A mere score is not an opera, it is a book. Is it the first performance of the opera? That took place in Munich in 1868, and no living person has seen it. Is it some ideal in Wagner's mind? That, no one has ever seen or heard, or ever will.

It seems clear that the piece of music which is the work of art is distinct from all its performances, although perhaps each of these may be considered as subsidiary works of art in their own right.

4. Art as a Vehicle of Knowledge

Although both natural objects and works of art are appropriate subjects of aesthetic experience and judgement, it makes no sense to seek to "understand" a natural object. It makes sense for someone to confess that he does not understand a work of art, such as Pablo Picasso's painting *Guernica* or T. S. Eliott's poem *The Wasteland; while* it does not make sense to admit to being unable to understand, Ayer's Rock or the Grand Canyon. This suggests that a work of art may function as a vehicle of communication.

The arts may be used for many of the functions for which language can also be employed. They may:

- express feelings and emotions;
- Evoke or conjure up moods, feelings and emotions, a sense of place, time or situation;
- inform others what the world is like;
- maintain social cohesion by conveying a sense of "togetherness." Nationalistic music or music at concerts may build up and cement a social identity.
- add dignity to a person or an occasion. Arts, such as architecture, painting, and music have traditionally been used to dignify kings and courts, their dwellings, persons and actions.
- play, or entertain others. It should not be forgotten that we sometimes use language merely in order to engage, amuse, divert or entertain, and such use of language may be strictly nonsensical. Much art that would otherwise appear difficult to consider as language, such as pure music and abstract painting, may be compared to language which is used merely to entertain by its sound.

Art as a means of Expression

It is certain that art can function as a means of expression. In the case of literature or opera there is no problem in understanding how this can be so, because those arts employ ordinary language. But it is not so easy to see what the nonverbal arts, such as pure music, abstract painting, or architecture can be said to express, or how they could accomplish this. In *The Language of Music* the British musicologist Deryck Cooke argues that all music functions as a language, but that concepts may not be expressed in this language, only feelings.

According to some philosophers, the expression of feelings is the proper sphere of art, just as philosophy, science, and other disciplines are the proper spheres for the expression of ideas.

Art as a Means of Communication

If works of art are capable of functioning as vehicles of expression, and if they can be understood as such, then they are capable of communicating what has been expressed. If a work of art communicates, then in some sense art functions rather like a language, through signs and symbols.

There is a difference between the literary and the non-literary arts. Literary arts use varieties of ordinary languages to express and convey meaning. Since the medium of literature is words, and words are conventional vehicles of meaning, literature has meaning in a way that the other arts do not. Similarly, the actions of actors on stage in drama and opera may be said to have meaning in the same way that signs and body language have meaning. But in those senses, mere shapes, colours and musical notes do not have meaning.

What Does Art Communicate?

In the case of verbal arts this is usually clear. There is disagreement between the **referentialists**, who hold that nonverbal arts, such as music, can and do refer to meanings outside themselves, and the **formalists**, who maintain that art just "means itself."

Reality: Many people have held that art may "hold up a mirror to nature." By focusing our attention upon, and guiding our understanding of, some aspect of nature we are induced to concentrate upon it and reflect upon it.

In order to do this, art does not need to be crudely imitative of life. As George Moore put it, "Art is not nature. Art is nature digested . . ."

Feelings: If art can express feelings, then it can communicate them. This must be especially true of music.

Ideology: Rulers, churches and political parties have clearly all used the fine arts to impress and to indoctrinate their followers and to intimidate their opponents. The palaces of ancient kings were used to impress their subjects with the immovable strength and power of their rulers, and the futility of even thinking about revolt. The massive cathedrals of the Middle Ages, which dwarfed the towns which clustered around them, were designed in part to exhibit to all in material form the grandeur and power of the church. Paintings on the walls and carvings over the doors of countless churches across the length and breadth of Christendom depicted the blessings of heaven which those who conformed to the church's dictates could expect as their reward after death, and even more the graphically, the punishments in hell awaiting those who disobeyed.

The Christians used their art to glorify God and save souls. Marx would have had art used in the service of the class struggle. All are, as stated in more general terms by Walter Pater, expressing their own specification of the function of living the good life. Modern fascist and communist states have produced massive granite monuments designed to exhibit their strength and to intimidate and cow opposition. All these would have been dwarfed if the plans of Albert Speer, the architect of Hitler's "Thousand Year Reich," had ever been implemented.

Morality: According to Plato, the purpose of art should be to make us better citizens. **Didactic** literature is explicitly used teach morality. This is exemplified in works such as *The Pilgrim's Progress* by John Bunyan.

Most works of literature were not created primarily to teach a moral lesson, yet they may do so incidentally. They allow the reader to deepen his moral insight by reflecting on other people's problems and conflicts. The reader can view such situations with detachment and learn from them without himself having to undergo the experiences of the characters in the book. By reflecting on these situations under circumstances which favour a more cool, rational and objective stance than would be possible if the reader were himself immersed in the circumstances depicted in the book or movie, he is enabled to acquire experience second-hand, and to be guided in his reflections upon this so as to make his own moral decisions more wisely in his turn.

Morality depends upon our ability to stand in someone else's shoes, to see things from their point of view. This involves the exercise of the imagination. Literature stimulates and develops the imagination, carrying the reader beyond the confines of his own small world, and enabling him to share the experiences of others distant in space, time, class, and culture.

That art may function in many ways like language is clear; *how* it does is another matter.

Literature

Literature, as the primary verbal art, is an especially rich means of expression and communication, usually able to handle ideas with greater precision than any other of the arts.

Fiction is essentially untrue on the pedestrian, literal level, yet it may be a vehicle of important general truths about the human condition. The skill of the author is to present the truths he wishes to communicate to us in such a powerful way that we will be:

- identify with one of the characters, and so
- undergo some proxy experience;
- comprehend the insights the author wishes to convey through those experiences;
- enjoy the experience of reading the novel.

What those insights are depends upon the author and the *genre*.

- For the "New Critics," *poetry* is a means of communicating feelings and thoughts that can not be expressed in any other kind of language. The language of poetry differs from everyday language and from the language of science and philosophy, but it communicates equally important knowledge. This is done by employing the associative values of words, symbolism, metaphor, and imagery.
- *Romantic novels* usually convey insights into interpersonal relationships, such as: everyone is capable of forgiveness, some effort may be needed to make a relationship work after the first flush of attraction has worn off.
- *Science fiction* novels may take some development in society and point to what will happen if it is allowed to continue unchecked, e.g. the development of computer technology; the development of new means of surveillance and invasion of personal privacy by the authorities; the generation gap; the drug culture; the rise in crime. They may point to possibilities which may develop in the future, such as nuclear blackmail by terrorists; a new, deadly and fast-spreading epidemic; the collision of a large comet with the earth. Science fiction novels frequently function as the "warning nightmares" of society.

In general it may be observed that the arts are a powerful medium of expression and communication, even if we do not always understand *how* this works. An insight which might take a moment to express literally and seem trite in speech may strike us as the profound truth about the human condition it is when it is conveyed through the medium of, say, opera. By contrast, the arts are usually a heavy and blunt instrument, incapable of expressing or communicating clearly very precise or finely differentiated thoughts.

Glossary

aesthetic attention: attention paid to the valued appearance of something.

art: the production of something intended to be an object of aesthetic attention by human skill and workmanship.

didactic art: having the purpose of teaching something.

extrinsic value: a value not for itself, but as a means to something else.

fine arts: arts which are performed for an end intrinsic to themselves.

formalism: the view that art has no meaning outside itself.

individuation: specifying the criteria by which we can determine whether we have, or do not have, an instance or individual of a particular type.

intrinsic value: a value of something simply for itself.

high art: socially prestigious forms of art.

popular art: forms of art which are not socially prestigious and which are associated with the masses.

referentialism: the view that non-verbal arts, such as music, can and do refer to meanings outside themselves.

token: a copy of or performance of some other object or event.

type: a uniquely identifiable object or event.

useful arts: arts which are performed for some end extrinsic to themselves.

10. EVERYDAY KNOWLEDGE

"Rarely do we find men who are willing to engage in hard, solid thinking. There is an almost universal quest for easy answers and half-baked solutions. Nothing pains some people more than having to think." (Martin Luther King, JR.)

1. Characteristics of Everyday Thinking

Our everyday thinking is frequently of very poor quality.

- It is frequently *vague* and inexact: "I met whatshisname in town the other day."
- It is often *disorganised*. We carry around items of information which are not integrated into any general scheme of things.
- For this reason, our thinking is frequently *inconsistent*. The inconsistencies may pass unnoticed and unremarked. Young children may believe that their Christmas presents come both from their parents and from Santa Claus. A parent may assure her young child not to worry because God is always there and will take care to keep her safe from all dangers, and at the same time will warn her not to play near the road, since she might get injured or killed by a vehicle.
- It is *uncritical*. We tend to take our own habitual view of things as the truth, without considering the grounds of our beliefs or the limitations of our ways of knowing. When faced with evidence against our beliefs we tend to cling onto them, and to defend them regardless. Much of our reasoning consists in seeking justifications for going on believing as we already do.
- We tend to be dominated by the **conceptual system** of the *group,* the assumptions, attitudes, beliefs and outlook of nation, class, church, etc.
- We tend to be *partial* in collecting evidence in support of our existing viewpoint, while systematically ignoring any evidence which may count against it. Indeed, we are not likely to be influenced by incoming information if it does not correspond to deeply held beliefs. If our horoscope in the newspaper turns out to make a correct prediction, we are impressed. We forget all those times when it did not. This selectivity lies at the basis of superstition.
- We are prey to wishful thinking. We tend to believe what we wish to believe, or what it is convenient for us to believe. We prefer to force the evidence to fit our prejudices rather than use the evidence to determine our opinions.

An important way in which to run reality checks on our perceptions and beliefs is to compare them with those of others. But we often seek out people who agree with us, or selectively choose literature supporting our belief. If the majority doubts us, then even if only part of a minority we can collectively work to dispel doubt and find certainty. We can invoke conspiracies and cover-ups to explain an absence of confirmatory evidence. We may work to inculcate our beliefs in others, especially children. Shared beliefs can promote social solidarity and even a sense of importance for the individual and group.

- We allow *emotion* to influence us, rather than dealing with issues calmly and coolly.
- We are mostly concerned with *practical* problems and their solution.
- We are prejudiced towards the idea of *control*, always preferring to look at things as though they were, or could be, under our control in some way. This wish lies behind the superstitions of the gambler, who believes that he can influence the outcome by wearing his lucky shirt or by carrying his rabbit's foot. It is also the reason why interviews are popular as a means of choosing people for places in college or work, when almost all the studies done on the subject show the method to be quite useless in predicting future efficiency or success. At least, when interviewing people we *feel* we are in control.
- We tend to *generalise too hastily* from our own limited experience. After only one or two bad experiences we immediately draw an unwarranted general conclusion. This is a consequence of the power, well-known to psychologists, which first impressions have over us.
- We are in a rush either to accept or to reject proposed positions, even if we have inadequate evidence to support a reasonable judgement. Our discomfort with a state of suspended judgement is expressed in the phrase "sitting on the fence." The philosopher Bertrand Russell wrote: "Man is a credulous animal and must believe something. In the absence of good grounds for belief he will be satisfied with bad ones." We are reluctant simply to reserve judgement.
- We tend to black or white thinking. That is to say that we like to divide everything into two mutually exclusive classes: good and evil, right and wrong. Religious people do this directly, by claiming to be fighting for the Lord against Satan. Anyone who opposes them must, they are inclined to argue, be doing the devil's work. Communism was demonized in the USA after the Second World War.
- We tend to exclude or even to *persecute* those who do not conform in our set ways of thinking and to accepted societal norms of thinking. Irving Janis has studied the dangers of group conformity in connection with several US foreign policy disasters such as Pearl harbour, the Bay of Pigs invasion of Cuba and the Vietnam War, and its avoidance in others, such as the Cuban Missile Crisis. He showed how the pressure for conformity with the group, or **"groupthink,"** led to the group response becoming increasingly less flexible and intelligent as a general opinion of the members coalesced.
- Everyday thinking is under some circumstances highly unstable. This may be seen in the phenomenon of the **moral panic**, a collective hysteria, which is nowadays usually generated by the mass media. These may be whipped up following some particularly grizzly or tragic crime. Sometimes they are deliberately generated by politicians hoping to capitalise on fears, or by newspaper reporters hoping to increase sales of their product. Today moral panics usually relate to terrorism, crime, sex or narcotics.

Among past famous moral panics are the anti-Semitic pogroms once common in Europe; the Witch burnings at the end of the Middle Ages; and the *Grande Peur* or "Great Fear" which accompanied the Revolution in France, when villagers all over the country became agitated at the totally false rumour that the King was sending armed men to attack them.

- Sometimes we do not want to know. We prefer *ignorance*, since we hope "Ignorance is bliss." Matthew Arnold said that, "The mass of mankind will never have any ardent zeal for seeing things as they are."

2. Prejudice

Why do people argue illogically? Sometimes it is lack of skill, or we are just not paying attention to what we are doing. But sometimes the reason is much more sinister. Our reasoning may be systematically perverted, either by ourselves or by others. This may be due to anxiety, guilt or wishful thinking. This makes us prejudiced.

What is Prejudice?

While someone may be perfectly capable of reasoning correctly about the chances of a coin falling heads or tails upwards, or whether it is likely to rain soon, he may be less capable of straight thinking about, say the level of taxes which should be paid by peoples of different income groups or the reliability of the Bible. Peoples' reasoning ability is frequently distorted in favour of, or against, some particular position. When those particular subjects come up for discussion, people become less rational than they normally are. This is because of prejudice.

Prejudice is a form of irrationality. It is one of the main causes of faulty or unsound reasoning. It consists of judging an issue or holding an opinion on it *before* examining the evidence for it; or *independently* of examining the evidence; or even of wilfully holding an opinion *against* the clear balance of the evidence. It is the attitude of mind which expresses itself as: "Don't bother me with the evidence. My mind is made up." The essential point is this ignoring of the evidence in adopting or holding to a standpoint. When we are prejudiced, our judgements are biased. They are not fair, impartial or disinterested.

Prejudice is not necessarily negative. We may be unfairly biased or prejudiced *in favour of* a particular point of view, idea, group, institution or practice. People are frequently prejudiced in favour of people from, or arguments in the interest of, their own country, social class, or religion.

It is important to be clear that prejudice is not a matter of holding certain currently unpopular views which are usually labelled as prejudices, e.g. that foreigners are the cause of all our troubles, or that women or blacks are inferior. It is a matter of the *way* in which our beliefs are held. If someone were to hold a belief usually described as an indication of prejudice, but to hold it on good grounds, and only on account of the worth of those grounds while fairly taking into account alternative points of view and giving them due consideration, then holding that belief would not *of itself* indicate prejudice. Prejudice is not a matter of *which* beliefs are held; it is about *the grounds* on which they are held, and the *manner* in which they are held.

Nor is prejudice a matter of the strength of our beliefs. We are not necessarily prejudiced if we hold beliefs strongly, as opposed to tentatively. We all believe very strongly that fire burns, and are instantly prepared to act upon that belief. This is not a prejudice, however strong our belief may be, because we have ample evidence for its truth. It is a mark of prejudice when we hold views firmly when there is *no good reason* to do so.

As a matter of fact, however, our prejudices will usually be views which we do hold very firmly. We are firm about them precisely in order to cover up for the lack of adequate grounds we have for believing in them. Prejudices are usually held dogmatically and asserted strongly, even violently, in order to compensate for an uncomfortable, underlying feeling we have that they have no adequate rational foundation. For adequate grounds, we substitute bluster and emotion. Thus prejudices are rarely held *coolly*. If such views are to retain their hold over us, and we want them to, then it must be in virtue of their emotional force rather than by cool reason.

In really bad cases of prejudice the afflicted person may seem, in one sense, more rational than normal. Used to having his odd, or obviously false, views attacked by those around him, he becomes practised at defending them. This will give him the *appearance* of someone using logic effectively and thinking more deeply than usual. But it will soon become apparent that his thinking is not straight when it is observed that, despite an appearance of rationality, he allows no evidence or argument to count against his view. He behaves like the psychotic who is paranoid, suffering from the delusion that people are "out to get him." Evidence of overt hostility is cited in support of his case. Evidence of friendliness and good will, or even of lack of interest or concern, is interpreted as slyness and subtlety on the part of the enemy to reduce his vigilance and so trap him unawares. Evidence so treated becomes irrelevant, since the theory is going to be held whatever the evidence happens to be.

Someone under a delusion, a false picture of reality, may reason well, if he has a logical mind or training, but only in support of his delusion. What he will not do, is apply his abilities or training *critically* to his delusion. This he protects. He protects it from others by his ability in debate. He protects it from himself by being careful never to examine it critically, and by never facing evidence and arguments that might undermine it, and assessing them fairly.

There is no sharp line to be drawn between those who are mentally ill and those who are sane. There is a continuum between the two extremes, and many people lie in an area on that continuum, where it is not easy to say whether they are sane or not — sometimes entire nations appear to get into this state. They believe that some different racial group is undermining their lives and well-being, when it is not, or that the answer to every significant question is written in a book they have, or that people from outer space keep on kidnapping them in order to conduct experiments on them. All prejudice involves a mild form of delusion.

Why We Become Prejudiced

Prejudice usually has one of several causes:

- We are not disposed to alter our *habitual* way of looking at things. The conventions, customs, beliefs and habits of the societies to which we belong: nation, church, social class, sexual orientation, peer group, profession, political party, clubs, etc. are something we identify with. They define our personality against the rest of the world. They help us know who we are. We feel challenged when they are threatened.
- When we have made up our minds we are reluctant to admit that we were wrong. It offends our pride.
- Prejudice is often a cover for *self-interest*. Much of our so-called reasoning consists in trying to find excuses to continue to believe what we want to believe, in spite of evidence that we are wrong. This process is called **rationalisation**.

    Certain strategies are typically used by us to maintain our prejudices against evidence:

- We consider evidence *selectively*, avoiding what does not fit in with our prejudices and seeking out what fortifies them. At the same time we actively consider arguments, the true purpose of which is not to establish the truth, but rather to support the view or position we happen to hold. We insist upon telling ourselves that this is all right because what we happen to believe is the truth anyway.
- We shall notice evidence and arguments which support our own viewpoint and fail to notice those which count against it. Our memories are very selective, and they tend to retain what supports our prejudices and to lose what does not. Aware of this, Charles Darwin used to keep

a notebook in which he recorded everything which counted against his conclusions so that he would not simply forget them.

- We may be unable to avoid some evidence and arguments which count against our prejudices, either because they are so prominent or powerful or because people will not let us forget them. Our judgement of these will tend to be unfair. We will not give them due consideration. We will seek reasons, often very superficial reasons, to dismiss them without detailed examination. This leads to **special pleading**. We apply inconsistent standards to evidence, allowing evidence or arguments which support our prejudices and disallowing the same when they do not. Thus someone who does not work but lives off unearned, inherited income may argue that welfare cheques for the poor should be stopped because they will make them idle. Another will argue against abortion on the grounds that it is never right for us to take human life, while at the same time supporting a strong armed forces and the death penalty. Special pleading is faulty reasoning because it is inconsistent.
- We commonly *rationalise* when we do not get something we want. We tell ourselves that we never wanted it anyway, because it was not worth having. Thus when someone turns you down for a dance, you say "He/she was such a bore anyway. That was a close shave." Sometimes we decide to make the best of a situation we cannot change, and so re-describe reality to convince ourselves that it is all for the best. Excuses often involve rationalisation: "It wasn't my fault I failed the test. The room was too stuffy. It was not properly lit. I think I had influenza too. Anyway, the teacher is no good."
- One of the most potent buttresses of prejudice is the use of **stereotypes**. These are ready-made, mental impressions or pictures which govern the way we react to the world. We are usually provided with them by society. Thus Frenchman are romantic, black people are good at sports but not at intellectual activities, homosexuals are weak and effeminate, red-haired people are quick-tempered, etc. When our thinking is dominated by stereotypes, we overlook an individual's unique qualities by viewing him only according to our rigid preconceptions.
- We may go into *denial* mode, and just refuse to accept the facts and face up to the truth.
- We may allow ourselves to be *distracted*, so as to avoid facing the truth. Better to go to the soccer match or to watch the television and forget all about it.

The Consequences of Prejudice

The consequences of prejudice can be very serious - even fatal.

- We may fail to see the truth even though it is staring us in the face because we think we already "know" it.
- We may close ourselves off from whole dimensions of life and experience unnecessarily because we think we "know" them to be worthless, dangerous or evil, like the fourth century North African bishop, Saint Augustine, who warned Christians against Mathematics: "The good Christian should beware of mathematicians . . . The danger already exists that the mathematicians have made a contract with the devil to darken the spirit and to imprison man in the bonds of hell."
- Prejudice makes people stupid, for prejudice is a matter of turning away from reason, insofar as we keep reason from us we become stupid. The more prejudices we have and the stronger their hold over us, the more stupid we become. Two quotations show the extremes to which this can lead. The first is from an address made to King Ferdinand VII of Spain by the Rector of the University of Cervera on the occasion of a royal visit: "Most Catholic Majesty . . . Far be from us the dangerous novelty of thinking." The second is the response of a Spanish Civil War general to an argument from a Liberal intellectual: "Down with intelligence!"

- Prejudices allow us to be manipulated by others. They are like buttons they can press to get a desired response. Propagandists systematically appeal to their hearers' prejudices.
- We may be influenced to act unjustly or with cruelty, to persecute people who are different from us, or who have different ideas from us, because we think they are wrong, inferior or evil. Most historical persecutions have been perpetrated by people who believed themselves to be right. This led them to do things they would probably never otherwise have considered; e.g. medieval persecution of religious dissenters, the Nazi attempt to eliminate all Jews, Gypsies, and homosexuals by systematic genocide.

A life cocooned in prejudices is a life spent in an intellectual dream-world. We assume that our own opinions are automatically and obviously right, while those of other groups are equally obviously wrong or wicked, and we refuse to countenance any alternative. We should always be prepared to consider the possibility that we are wrong, and that the other person is right. But to say that is not to say that there is no such thing as truth, or that truth is always relative. Nor does it follow that we should never have definite views of our own, or be prepared to stand up for them, or subject other peoples' views to objective scrutiny, and, if appropriate, argue against them.

How to Detect Prejudice in Oneself

- Do I genuinely believe the things I am saying to be true?
- Do I avoid considering the rational foundations of my own beliefs?
- Do I engage in special pleading?
- Do I find myself inventing "explanations" to square the facts with my general view of reality?
- In arguing for my beliefs, am I am arguing in my own interest? If so, is this merely a coincidence?
- Do I genuinely try to understand the other person's viewpoint, or am I content to see it in terms of a stereotype?
- Do I genuinely consider the merits of the arguments for the other side, or do I shut my ears to them or fend them off?
- Do I argue to establish the truth, or to win for the Cause?
- Do I deliberately resort to unfair tactics, such as illicit appeals to authority, ignoring the point, aggression or ridicule?

Open-Mindedness and Truth

The more we are aware of the nature and causes of prejudice, the better able we are to spot it in others and guard against it in ourselves.

It is not sufficient to argue against our opponents simply by asserting that they are prejudiced, that their views are mere rationalizations. We must argue that their views are wrong by attacking the grounds of those views themselves directly. The truth arises out of the clash of opinions, when we are forced to defend our own positions, attack those of others, and then reflect upon what happened with open minds.

3. Ideological Thinking

We crave *ideologies*, ready-made systems of knowledge, which will provide us with a complete picture of reality or "The Truth." Ideologies are framework theories which determine and limit thought. They provide a description of reality, and an explanation of how things came to be as they are. They also provide a set of fundamental unquestionable values, which determine how we should act, and what we should aim for. They determine what questions can be asked, and what sort of answers are permissible. Questioning them is not normally considered permissible by their supporters. Instead, they are frequently held and asserted with strong emotional commitment, and fiercely defended from attack by the supporters of rival systems in a partisan manner. Followers of political ideologies are usually concerned in debate to score points over rivals rather than reach the truth dispassionately.

Most ideologies are systems of religious or political belief, and will be covered as such in the chapters on Politics and Religion, and govern our everyday life, but they can also slip into academic thinking.

Because these ideologies provide an entire framework of thought, many of the most familiar judgements and practices in a society are determined by, and assume the truth of, a particular ideological viewpoint, even though the members of that society may not generally be aware of it. This is because the assumptions upon which they are founded are so widely accepted within a particular society that no one questions them. Yet they may be assumptions, and they are often highly questionable.

Possessing the Truth in such a "package" relieves people of the burden of confronting the limitations of our knowledge, and the difficulty of making choices with imperfect knowledge. In effect, they relieve us of the burden of freedom. This avoidance of choice by placing ourselves under the control of a system, the French philosopher Jean-Paul Sartre calls **bad faith**. It explains the popularity of many dogmatic religious and political movements which claim to have "all the answers." Many people seem to need an ideology to live comfortably. They depend upon outside sources for their thinking, and have not yet reached the point where they can rise above ideology to think independently.

Yet ideological thinking is inferior thinking. It is today the major source and support for old-fashioned pre-rational dogmatic thinking. It is narrow-minded, and blind to anything that veers from what the ideology permits. It is opposed to reason. The inner logic of an ideology is usually designed to fit comfortably around its underlying assumptions. Ideologies usually depict a binary world, starkly divided between good and evil, right and wrong. It demands little from its adherents beyond loyalty, praising and supporting the "good guys" and condemning and opposing the rivals.

But ideologies immunise us against reality and conscience. They influence our perceptions, the way we see the world. They reassure their adherents that their beliefs are right and their actions justified, even altruistic, especially when they seem not to be.

Something of the power of ideologies over us can be explained by the psychological theory of **Cognitive Dissonance**. People try to make sense of the world by looking for consistency among their experiences, and turning to other people for confirmation. If there is some inconsistency between a person's experiences and beliefs or actions, as will usually be the case when under the influence of an ideology, this will set up an unpleasant internal state called cognitive dissonance. This will trigger an attempt to restore cognitive consistency by reinterpreting the situation so as to minimize whatever inconsistency may be there. According to the Theory this is because people try to reduce any perceived inconsistency among various aspects of knowledge, feelings and behaviour whenever possible.

Case Study: Faithful Beyond Disproof

Psychologist Leon Festinger was fascinated by the story of a nineteenth century religious movement in the USA, which several times issued prophesies about the end of the world on particular dates, its forecasts being conclusive disproved each time, yet which was able both to keep its followers and recruit new ones in spite of that.

Festinger managed to find a tiny religious cult in Chicago which was awaiting the end of the world on a specific date in the near future, and decided to study it to see what happened. The founder of the sect announced that she had received a messsage from the "Guardians" of outer space that on a certain day the end of the world would come. At that time, the Great Lakes would flood Chicago. Only true believers, the members of the cult, would be saved by being picked up by the Guardians in flying saucers. On appointed doomsday, the members of the sect expectantly awaited the predicted cataclysm. When it did not occur, the leader of the sect received another message: To reward the faith of the faithful, the world had been saved. Joy broke out. Paradoxically, while some left the sect, most of its members became more committed than ever before. Many of them went out and recruited more followers. Given the failure of the unambiguous prophecy, the opposite might have been expected. The falsification of a predicted event should have led to a loss of faith. But it did not.

It seems that by abandoning his belief that there are Guardians, a person who had once held this belief would have to accept a painful dissonance between past beliefs and actions and present scepticism. The believer's prior faith would now appear foolish. Some members of the sect had given up their jobs or spent their savings; such acts would have lost all meaning and value without belief in the Guardians. The dissonance would have been intolerable, but it was reduced by belief in the new message. The cult members could now think of themselves not as fools, who had thrown everything away for a silly belief, but as loyal members of a select few, whose faith had saved the world from destruction.

Since disbelief in any cause to which you have committed yourself involves admitting the worthlessness of all your previous sacrifices on its behalf, and since this would involve considerable cognitive dissonance, it is usually easier to find some excuse to go on with the commitment. Thus ideologies which demand sacrifices, such as religious sects, are particularly able to hold on to their adherents.

Festinger uses another example to make his theory clear. A habitual smoker who learns that smoking is bad for health will experience dissonance, because this knowledge is dissonant with the fact that he continues to smoke. He could reduce the dissonance by changing his behavior, by ending the habit of smoking, which would be consonant with the cognition that smoking is bad for health. Alternatively, he could reduce dissonance by changing his cognition about the effect of smoking on health, and come to believe that smoking does not have such a harmful effect on health at all, again eliminating the dissonant cognition. He might look for positive effects of smoking, and decide to believe that smoking reduces tension or keeps him from gaining weight. Or he might decide that the risk to health from smoking is negligible, compared with the danger of road accidents. He might also decide that the enjoyment he gets from smoking is too valuable a part of his life to give up. All of these are strategies for reducing cognitive dissonance while continuing to smoke. Since tobacco is habit forming, this is the option most smokers will choose.

How to Detect Ideological Thinking

We must suspect ideological thinking when we come across the following:

- The belief that a particular outlook (theory, creed) is *sufficient* by itself to answer all the significant questions about some major aspect of reality;
- The desire to *protect* one's beliefs, and an unpreparedness to consider seriously alternatives or criticisms, or to admit any possible conditions which would serve to falsify them.
- The desire to *convince* rather than reach the truth openly; therefore a preparedness to resort to propaganda.
- The belief that all alternative views and/or criticisms are *disloyal* or stupid; and therefore a willingness to use force, if that were feasible, to secure agreement.
- The views you defend seem designed to *justify* existing privileges and injustices.

Critical Thinking

In our everyday life we cannot initially avoid thinking on the basis of, and within the limitations of, the viewpoint of our society. But we do not need to be passive in our acceptance of whatever irrational beliefs and false authorities society provides us with. We can learn to think for ourselves by gradually developing the critical skills, and the insights which will follow from the exercise of them, to enable us to exercise sound, independent judgement.

How to be a more Rational Person

- Do not oversimplify and so distort what you are trying to understand. In particular, try not to see everything in terms of "black or white."
- Monitor your own thinking. Be self-critical, correct your own mistakes, and so become capable of self-improvement.
- Distinguish facts from interpretations, opinions, judgements or theories.
- Think and express yourself clearly and without vagueness or ambiguity. Do not confuse concepts or get side-tracked from the point of a discussion by irrelevant issues.
- Cultivate a cool and unemotional approach to thinking, so as not to be diverted by irrational feelings and emotions.
- Be aware of and articulate the assumptions behind your own thinking and reasoning, and the values and principles upon which your judgements and actions are based. Do not allow preconceptions to cloud your consideration of the evidence.
- Become aware of the strengths and limitations of your reasoning, its appropriateness and effectiveness, and how much it can be used to support.
- Recognise the different levels of reliability of your various sources of information, and the nature and the limitations of those sources.
- Become capable of considering a subject in some depth, not getting fatigued and giving up or being content with merely a shallow understanding, but pursuing inquiry to the level of fundamentals.

- Recognise the strengths of alternative viewpoints and arguments levelled against your own position. Put yourself in the position of an opponent and see things from his point of view. In this way become able to understand alternative points of view, and the reasons why they are adopted.
- Value and strive for consistency. Seek to iron out inconsistencies in your beliefs, and especially between your beliefs and your practices.
- Do not allow your thinking to be constrained by the limits of conventional disciplines. Think across the barriers of the disciplines, and use your insights in one area to illuminate others.
- Do not uncritically accept the views of your own society on all points. Be capable of independent judgement.

By contrast with everyday knowledge, **academic knowledge**, today usually created and acquired in universities, or in association with universities, is precise, self-aware, systematic, takes into account alternative viewpoints and possibilities, and is achieved by sustained rigorous, critical thinking.

Glossary

academic Knowledge: bodies of rational, systematic knowledge, built up using critical methods.

bad faith: relying upon the uncritical acceptance of some system of knowledge to evade difficult choices.

cognitive dissonance: a theory that our behaviour is frequently governed by the need to reduce the mental dissonance caused by incompatible beliefs and practices.

conceptual system: the assumptions, attitudes, beliefs and outlook of our group though of as a whole.

consistency: propositions or beliefs are consistent if they can both be true.

groupthink: our tendency to conform our thinking to that of the group(s) to which we belong.

incoherent proposition: a proposition such that we do not know what it would be like for it, and any propositions entailed by it, to be true.

inconsistency: propositions or beliefs are inconsistent if they cannot both be true, so that the truth of one implies the falsity of the other.

opinion: a statement of belief or feeling.

prejudice: holding opinions independently of, or without regard to, the evidence.

rationalisation: the process of finding excuses to believe what we want to believe.

special pleading: the application of inconsistent standards to evidence, allowing evidence or arguments which conform to our prejudices, while disallowing what does not.

stereotypes: ready-made fixed mental impressions or pictures which govern the way we react to people.

11. Facts and Explanations

"The degree of one's emotion varies inversely with one's knowledge of the facts — the less you know the hotter you get." (Bertrand Russell)

1. Empirical Knowledge

What Are Facts?

As Damien was left his office building and stepped into the street outside one morning, he heard what sounded like three gunshots. A man in a black overcoat directly in front of him suddenly groaned and fell to the ground. A woman who happened to be passing by involuntarily put her hands up to her face and screamed horribly. With his own safety uppermost in his mind, Damien quickly glanced in the direction from which the sound of gunshots seemed to have come, and saw a man with gun. He also noticed in the background several men standing about with clipboards in their hands. Then he saw the sound equipment, the cameras and the cameramen. The "victim" got up and dusted himself off. Damien recognised his face as one he had seen many times on the television.

We place great value upon facts. But what were the facts in this case? Clearly, a movie was being shot. But if we had stopped the narrative at the end of the first paragraph, things would have seemed very different. It is likely that the reader's understanding of the facts changed shortly after reading the beginning of the second paragraph.

Facts are not data. *Data* is what our senses bring to us. Facts are the data interpreted by theories. Facts carry a lot more implications than the data they interpret. The data is instantly interpreted by us using schemata or patterns based upon our learned general ideas about the world. In other words, we never really have access to uninterpreted data.

But it does not follow from this that we can successfully interpret the data just anyhow. Some facts are more theory-laden than others. Strictly speaking, the observation that a man is falling to the ground is itself an interpretation of the data. After all, the figure that Damien observed falling to the ground might have been a woman cleverly disguised as a man - or a lifelike dummy. But that is less theory laden than the assertion that someone had just been shot. And that in turn is less theory laden than the proposition that someone had just been murdered.

When new data was introduced, the interpretation that a man had been shot was discarded in favour of an interpretation of the scene in terms of a different kind of shooting - a television programme was being filmed. The new interpretation was *forced* by the new data. Although we do not have access to uninterpreted data, our interpretations, and therefore our observations, are nevertheless *constrained by* the data.

When the data is compelling, and this is supported, where appropriate, by consistency with what others say they observed and with the way we know things work in general, then we believe ourselves to have grasped what is going on. When we can justify our belief claims, and they are true, we have knowledge. *What* we know, we call "the facts." We use the term "facts" of states of affairs which actually obtain in the world, or have obtained. Thus **facts** are states of affairs which obtain now, or which have obtained in the past.

Statements of fact must be distinguished from reasoned judgements and personal preferences. We can distinguish these quite easily, since each is characteristically used to answer different kinds of question:

- Those with one right answer (factual questions) e.g. What is the melting point of copper?
- Those with better or worse answers (well-reasoned or poorly reasoned answers) e.g. What were the causes of the First World War?
- Those with as many answers as there are different human preferences (a category in which mere opinion rules) e.g. Which ice cream ought we to have after dinner: the chocolate or the strawberry?

Only the third kind of question is a matter of mere opinion. The second kind is a matter of reasoned judgement: we can rationally evaluate answers to the question (using objective standards such as relevance, clarity, and consistency).

When questions that require better or worse answers are treated as matters of personal preference, then a tendency uncritically to assume that everyone's opinion is of equal value inevitably asserts itself, and we can expect to hear the assertion that everyone has a right to his own opinion. This demonstrates a failure to understand the difference between offering legitimate reasons and evidence in support of a view and simply asserting that view to be true.

Factual knowledge obtained through our senses or those of others, claims to which would be justified by reference to sense-experience, is called **empirical knowledge**. Since we have to wait upon the way things actually turn out in order to know what the world is like, this knowledge is also called *a posteriori* knowledge, "knowledge after the fact," knowledge which necessarily waits upon events.

Most of the subjects on school and university curricula are matters of fact at their most elementary level. A good student knows the "right answers." Later, we graduate to more advanced studies which are matters of reasoned judgement, where there are no "right answers" only answers of better or poorer quality.

Exercise 11.1

Is each of the following merely an opinion, a judgement, or a fact?

1. Animals need water in order to survive.
2. The isthmus of Corinth is cut by the Corinth Canal.
3. It was fortunate that no one was drowned when the ferryboat sank.
4. Bordeaux is not the capital city of France.
5. *Lawrence of Arabia* is one of the best films ever made.
6. Vanilla ice cream is better than strawberry.
7. Real Madrid is a good soccer team.
8. Many foreign tourists express their appreciation of French cuisine.
9. Thai cuisine is superior to Italian cuisine.
10. Intelligence is an inherited characteristic.

Evidence

When claims to empirical or *a posteriori* knowledge are challenged, **evidence** is required to support them. The one who makes a claim by asserting some proposition is the one who is obliged to provide evidence for its truth.

Evidence may be direct or indirect. We have **direct evidence** when we have perceptual knowledge of something ourselves, or reliable testimony of perceptual knowledge of it. We have only **indirect evidence** when we lack direct evidence and have to use reason to infer the truth. In courts of law evidence of this type is called **circumstantial evidence**. Either there are no eyewitnesses or the eyewitnesses disagree, so we have to work out what happened, making judgements about it.

When we are doing academic work, the standard of thinking we employ in marshalling evidence must be much better in quality than is normal in everyday life. We must be:

• clear

• precise

• consistent

• rigorous

• We must be aware of the nature and limitations of the methods we are employing.

• We must use arguments based upon what we know of the circumstances, and use our powers of inference.

Circumstantial evidence is strong when the facts not only point in one direction, but when they are such that they could not reasonably be thought to point in any other direction.

It is important to note that failure to find evidence is not itself evidence of anything and should lead only to uncertainty.

Because of the problems associated with perception and testimony, empirical evidence can yield only probability, although this may be sufficient to establish a conclusion beyond reasonable doubt. Most of our lives are lived, from moment to moment, on the basis of probability.

Discussion: Indicate the *kind* of evidence required to support the following statements:

1. There is an underground railway network in London.
2. Metals expand when heated.
3. There are one hundred centimetres in a metre.
4. A triangle has three sides.
5. I feel sick.
6. There is ice on the surface of the moon.
7. Heat consists of the vibration of particles.
8. Alexander the Great was buried in Alexandria, Egypt.
9. All brothers are males.
10. I have appendicitis.

Reasoned judgements are conclusions reached by an individual based on premises which can either be facts or opinions. It is well-reasoned judgements which advance our knowledge.

2. Explanation

Academic knowledge has two purposes: to describe the world and to explain it.

Description and Explanation

W hen we describe something, we say things about it which are true, and which might allow someone to identify what we are talking about. Descriptions serve a similar function to photographs.

By contrast, something is explained when we have not merely established *that* it is so and what it is like, but when we understand *why* it is so, when we have established the *reasons* why it is so.

Explanations

The request for an explanation may mean many different things and require many different kinds of response. Someone may be asked to explain:

- The meaning of a word: e.g. Explain the meaning of "psychosomatic." This is done by providing a definition.
- The meaning of a passage: This requires a paraphrase in simpler language.
- How to play a game: e.g. Explain how to play chess. This requires a summary of the rules of the game.
- How to accomplish a task: e.g. Explain how to get a driver's license. This requires instructions on how to perform a complex series of actions.
- An apparently puzzling act: Would you explain why you took a long and indirect route to get to your holiday destination? This requires a statement of motives.
- An apparently morally unacceptable action: Explain why you stole the answers to the test. This requires some sort of moral justification, or plea of mitigating circumstances.
- Some occurrence or class of occurrences: Could you explain why moths are attracted to flames? This requires an explanatory hypothesis or theory.

Although all these requests for explanation require a different response, what all the appropriate responses have in common is that they make what is explained in some way understandable, so that the intellect is able to get some sort of handle on it.

The term "explanation" is ambiguous. It might refer to the act or process of explaining, or to what is created by such an act, i.e. to the process of creating an explanation or to the product which is the result of that process.

We very much desire explanations. We are not very fussy about what counts as an explanation, or whether it is likely to be true, but an explanation of some sort we absolutely *must* have. This accounts for much mythology. Like Rudyard Kipling's *Just So Stories*, which provide whimsical explanations for prominent features of various animals, (How the Elephant got Its Trunk, etc.), myths provide easily understood pseudo-explanations for things for which we have no genuine explanation.

We are lazy and become impatient with long or complicated arguments and explanations, unless they are entertaining. We want things sorted out briefly or we would rather have nothing to do with them at all. We have been encouraged in this laziness by the mass media. We have been conditioned by television to expect frequent commercial breaks, so that politicians now talk to us in "sound bites" rather than in fully developed arguments.

Context-Relative and Context-Independent Explanation

There are two fundamentally different purposes in explanation, which require different approaches to the process of providing explanations, and different ways of judging whether an explanation is adequate or not.

Explanation typically takes place when someone wishes to make some subject matter intelligible to someone else by accounting for it in some way. Explanations are made to specific persons at specific times and places and within particular contexts. In order to succeed in making explanations, we must take into account the previous knowledge of those for whom they are intended. In order to induce the desired understanding, it is necessary to ensure that the content of the explanation can be understood by those for whom it is intended. Our explanations are necessarily relative to the contexts in which they are made.

Such explanations are regarded as successful when the one to whom the explanation is given expresses satisfaction, and shows evidence of having understood what is being explained. These are sometimes called heuristic explanations.

By contrast, those engaged in science, and in other serious academic disciplines such as history, aim to produce explanations which are objective, in that they are independent of any particular context. Their usefulness does not depend upon whether any specific audience is capable of understanding them on some particular occasion. They are not aimed at explaining some particular matter x to individual y on occasion z, but to explain some matter x to any audience capable, in principle, of understanding them. Such explanations are not context-relative.

This form of explanation is not oriented towards particular individuals for whom it is intended, but towards the subject matter being explained. Objective, or context-free explanations are not judged by their power of inducing understanding in those to whom they are made, but rather in the adequacy with which they account for what is being explained, i.e. their completeness, strength and elegance. Consequently while context-relative explanations elucidate the unfamiliar in terms of the familiar, context-free explanations usually explain the familiar in terms of the unfamiliar.

Such context-independent explanations are sometimes required in non-academic contexts, e.g. in a court of law. After a road accident the court will not wish merely to receive an account of what happened which seems illuminating to the people present, but one which provides a correct and adequate account of the reasons why the incident occurred.

This distinction between types of explanation is similar to that between "proof" as a convincing or persuasive argument, and "proof" as a logical demonstration.

Causes

The most common form of explanation is in terms of causes. Some event, or class of events, is explained as the effect of a particular cause, or type of cause.

We very often find ourselves trying to work out what makes something happen, to apprehend the causes either of particular events or of particular types of event. Our interest can range from questions like why my car would not start in the morning to whether food additives cause cancer.

When we say "x causes y," we are claiming at least the following:

- Whenever x occurs, y occurs.
- If x did not occur but everything else were the same, then y would not occur.
- There is no third event z that is the cause of both x and y.

It would seem at first glance that a cause is necessarily something which precedes its effect in time, but this is not so. Causes may be contemporaneous with their effects. A book resting upon a cushion is the causes of the configuration of the cushion it is resting upon.

Theories of Causation

But what is a cause? There are several different theories.

Regular Concomitance: The view of the philosopher David Hume was that a cause is an "object precedent and contiguous to another, and where all the objects resembling the former are placed in a like relation of priority and contiguity to those objects that resemble the latter."

This is at present the dominant view of causation in the science. Thus:

"To say that the electric current causes a deflection of the magnetic needle means that whenever there is an electric current there is always a deflection of the magnetic needle. The addition in terms of always distinguishes the causal law from a chance coincidence." (Hans Reichenbach, in The Rise of Scientific Philosophy)

Despite its general acceptance, this theory presents insuperable difficulties.

It fails to distinguish between causality and mere concomitance. The difference between the two is highlighted by the "direction" of the cause-effect relationship, and which is absent in cases which are nothing more than concomitance. This directionality is not temporal, since the cause is supposed to *produce* the effect, which is precisely why to cite the cause of an event is to *explain* it.

Necessary and Sufficient Condition: According to John Stuart Mill causes are to be found among the antecedents of an event, in the necessary and sufficient conditions for its occurrence.

Necessary Conditions and Sufficient Conditions

A **necessary condition** is one in the absence of which the effect never occurs. Thus a source of electrical power is a necessary condition for the lighting up of a light bulb. A **sufficient condition** is one which, when it occurs, the effect occurs. Thus the switching off of the light is a sufficient condition for a light bulb's going out.

Note that the presence of an electricity supply is necessary for the bulb being illuminated, but it is not sufficient. The light has to be switched on, and the bulb has to be in working order, etc. The presence of an electricity supply is a necessary, but not a sufficient, condition for the illumination of the bulb.

Note also that while switching off the light is a sufficient condition for the bulb's going out, it is not a necessary one. The bulb might go out because of a power cut, or the bulb itself might fail.

According to John Stuart Mill, those antecedents usually considered as causes are those such that:

• The effect cannot happen unless the antecedent happens; i.e., the antecedent is a necessary condition for the production of the effect.

• If the antecedent happens the cause must happen; i.e. the antecedent is a sufficient condition for the occurrence of the effect.

Exercise 11.2

Identify the relationship between the following pairs as one of the following:

          necessary condition, but not sufficient condition

          sufficient condition but not necessary condition

          necessary and sufficient condition

          neither necessary nor sufficient condition

1. success in school / success in later life
2. drinking a solution of arsenic / death
3. lack of food / hunger
4. increase in the supply of money / inflation
5. systematic revision / success in the examination

Perhaps a better way of expressing this position is to say that a cause is an event or state of affairs by producing or preventing which we produce or prevent that which is said to be its effect.

Some philosophers think that we actually observe causal activity. There is more in the phenomenal world than sense data, for example grouping and proximity. We are not faced with an aggregate of unrelated sense data in our visual field. We perceive relationships between the various elements within it. If we see a brick shatter a window we see the effect actually produced by the power of the cause. It is the moving brick which causes the shattering of the window. We see the effect being brought about by the action of the cause when we see the brick shatter the window.

Causal connections are not necessarily general as Hume's account assumed. R. Harré and E. H. Madden point out in *Causal Powers*, causes are the particular manifestations of the capacities of particular things. Causation is a datum of experience, and is not to be explained or explained away by reducing it to something else. Since it is a primary constituent of experience causation is to be explained only in terms which are effectively circular. For an individual, to cause something is to originate, create produce, induce or bring it about.

Since causes bring about their effects we may speak of the effects being dependent upon their causes. This dependence may be of several types, depending upon whether the change in the world which a cause produces is merely an alteration of something or the bringing into existence of something new. Individuals may owe to other things not merely their states but also their very existence itself. Citing a cause of this type explains not merely *how* the effect exists, but *that* it exists.

Chance and Coincidence

We tend to feel very uneasy when confronted by explanation in terms of chance or coincidence.

When we say that something happened "by chance" we usually mean that there were several contributory causes, each of which in itself was insignificant or unremarkable, all of which happened to coincide to produce a result which could not, in practice, have been predicted.

We are particularly disturbed by such explanations when the consequences are very serious for us. In such cases we seek a single cause as momentous as the consequences, and are very unsatisfied if all we can find is the coincidence of a multitude of insignificant causes.

Case Study: Peter and a Small Patch of Oil on the Road

Peter, his parents' much loved eighteen-year old son, was a pleasant, well-adjusted and outgoing young man. He was intelligent, achieved high grades in school, and was on the honour role. He had already been accepted to read medicine at a good university, and his family and school had great hopes for his future as a doctor. Good at several sports, Peter was popular with his neighbours and classmates alike, and never had the least trouble finding a date for a Saturday night dance.

One morning Peter's mother asked him to step out to the neighbourhood supermarket to get some milk, which she had forgotten while shopping. Crossing the road outside his home he stepped on a tiny, and almost invisible, patch of oil, left from the leaking sump of a delivery vehicle which had been parked there for a few minutes the previous day. The sole of his shoe, which was fairly, although by no means dangerously, smooth, came down at just such an angle, and with just the required force, to cause him to slip. Because of the angle at which his body was poised at that moment, he overbalanced and fell over. Unfortunately for him, he was too surprised to reach out his hands, and fell at just that angle which would allow his head to strike against the corner of a low brick wall in front of a garden. The corner of the wall was not worn down at that point, and the contact of his skull with the corner of the wall caused serious brain damage, from which he died almost instantly.

Peter' parents and friends were distraught. They did not know how it could have happened, but the police made a very thorough investigation, and were able to explain everything to his parents.

At first Peter's parents blamed themselves for not making their son change his shoes for a better pair before going out. His mother blamed herself for a while for sending him out to fetch the milk. Then they blamed the delivery van driver for leaving the tiny patch of oil on the road; then the council for not properly maintaining the surface of the pavement; then the owner of the garden for having a low wall with a dangerously sharp edge. Then, realising the futility of all this Peter's mother decided that God loved her son so much that he could not wait for him to join the angels, and so had "called" him to himself unexpectedly early. Meanwhile, his father began to get interested in astrology, and wondered whether it was all a matter of unavoidable fate, written in the stars.

The cause of Peter' death is easy for us to understand, it is nothing more than the coincidence of several factors, each in itself quite unremarkable. Every day such things happen as people wearing smooth-soled shoes, walking on oily patches, even slipping, and occasionally hitting their heads. For all those things to happen in just the way that will result in a death is very unfortunate, but that is all that there is to it. For Peter' parents, who loved their son and had nursed him through his childhood illnesses, who were proud of how he was developing, and who had great hopes and ambitions for his future, such an explanation was emotionally unacceptable. It would have seemed to deprive his death, and therefore his entire life before that, of any meaning.

Yet such events happen all the time. One soldier walks uninjured through a minefield while his friend who happens to step on a hidden land mine and is horribly maimed. A strong and apparently perfectly healthy young person happens to choke on a piece of food at dinner one day, and is dead within seconds. Under such circumstances we are very reluctant to say: "It was just an unlucky chance coincidence of factors – and that is all that there is to it."

Fallacies of Causal Reasoning

Magical Thinking: We think magically when we attribute causal connections where none could possibly exist.

During a soccer match Gerald found himself wishing that the striker on the visiting team, who looked likely to win the match almost single handed, would be injured and so have to leave the field. Shortly after that, he was injured and was taken off in an ambulance. Gerald then found himself wondering guiltily, "Was it my fault?"

Our brains and nervous systems are the products of millions of years of evolution. But natural selection selects not for the acquisition of knowledge, but for reproductive success. A small animal in tall grass which detects a rustling, and which has learned that this occasionally signals the presence of a hungry predator, may wonder if there really is a predator this time, or if a gust of wind caused the grass to rustle. If the animal hangs around debating the issue, or waits for conclusive evidence before doing anything, then it will probably have a short life. The animal which responds to the rustle in the grass by instantly running away is much more likely to survive.

For this reason, our brains are wired so as to make hat are strictly unfounded assumptions on the basis of a single association of two significant events, such as touching a hot stove and feeling pain. Such significant associations produce a lasting effect on us, while non-pairings of the same two events are not nearly so influential. If a child were to touch a stove once and be burned, and touch it again without being burned, the association between pain and stove would not automatically be unlearned. This is important for survival.

This instant jumping to conclusions underlies much of the errors we make. Humans are very poor at accurately judging the relationship between events that only sometimes occur together. For example, if we think of Uncle Harry, and then he telephones us a few minutes later, this might seem to demand some explanation in terms of telepathy or precognition. However, we can only properly evaluate the co-occurrence of these two events if we also consider the number of times that we thought of Harry and he did not call, or we did not think of him but he called anyway. But these latter circumstances, the non-pairings, have little impact on our learning system.

The world around us abounds with coincidental occurrences, some of which are meaningful but the vast majority of which are not. This provides a fertile ground for the growth of fallacious beliefs. We readily "learn" that associations exist between events, even when they do not. We are all even more prone to error when rare or emotionally laden events are involved. We have to work to overcome such magical predisposition, and we never entirely manage to do this.

Confusion of Association and Causation: Hume's theory of causation failed, as we have seen, because it failed to distinguish causation from concomitance. Our causal thinking sometimes does this, as when we just assume that a fall in the stock market must be due to some event or development going on at the time, such as stalled Palestinian peace negotiations or a scandal in the White House. There may in any given instance of association be a causal connection, but mere association is not enough, of itself, to establish this.

The Latin phrase ***post hoc, ergo propter hoc*** (after that, therefore because of that) names the fallacy of supposing that what follows something must have been caused by it. It is a particularly common special case of the fallacy of confusing causation with association.

The classic example was given by the philosopher John Stuart Mill. Soon after a church steeple had been built on the coast, quicksands developed. The villagers concluded that the quicksands had somehow been caused by the building of the steeple.

Notoriously, medical doctors benefit from this fallacy. Most of the everyday illnesses humans get will go away without medical treatment. Today, people tend to resort very quickly to the doctor, and he prescribes some treatment. When the patient has recovered it is usually assumed that this must have been due to the treatment the patient received.

Sometimes we can have evidence that establishes more than just correlation in presence, yet still not have enough to show causation.

(1) Our patients only get those red spots when they have a fever of 102^0 or more. So the fever must be causing the spots.

Here there is an underlying disease that is causing both the spots and the fever. The spots and the fever are both symptoms of the disease, which is their underlying cause. So knowing that x and y are correlated both in presence (when there is fever there are spots) and in absence (no fever, no spots) may not be enough to prove that x is the cause of y. We might be ignoring a common cause.

In order properly to explain one event by reference to the other, it is necessary to establish some necessary connection between them.

Single Cause: We frequently find ourselves seeking for the cause of some phenomenon because we have made an unfounded assumption that there is a single cause of the effect we seek to explain.

(2) Widespread poverty in South America is caused by the greed of large landholders. If we got rid of the rich, money-grubbing upper-class leeches, we could eliminate poverty entirely.

Confusion of Cause and Effect: Another source of possible error in looking for causes is the problem of confusing cause and effect, and assuming the effect to be the cause, or *vice versa*. This can sometimes be subtle and hard to spot.

For instance, it is common for young patients of a certain form of schizophrenia to come from families with certain distinctive, problematic relationships between the members. This might lead researchers to believe that the family structure is the cause of the schizophrenia. But this might be a case of confusing cause and effect: it might be that the families of young schizophrenics take on a peculiar form because of the effects on family relationships of the presence of a child with early symptoms of the condition.

A tribe in the South Pacific believed that having lice was a cause of good health. They had correctly observed that healthy people all had lice, while people in poor health did not. So there was a correlation between the presence of lice and being in good health. The reason was that lice find healthy people better hosts. They have a body temperature they like and a good blood supply. So rather than the presence of lice being the cause of health, it was the good health of those who had lice that was encouraging the lice.

Anecdotal Evidence: An anecdote is an especially memorable story. People sometimes try to either support or cast doubt on causal claims with a well-chosen anecdote. This may be entertaining, but of little logical force.

(3) They say smoking causes lung cancer, but I don't believe it. My uncle Michael smoked three packs a day, and he died on his eighty-fifth birthday, when a shark got him swimming off the coast of Fiji.

We all know that one example does not either prove or disprove a generalisation, yet many people find this sort of evidence persuasive. Anecdotes are persuasive because they are easy to remember, and they may be very striking or humorous. If, in addition, the conclusion is something we want to believe (that smoking will not cause us health problems), then the attraction of an anecdote can be all but irresistible.

Exercise 11.3
Identify the fallacy of causal reasoning in each of the following:
1. I took Dr. Adamson's new cold cure, and within three days I was cured. It really works!
2. An examination of the statistics shows that lung cancer causes tobacco smoking.
3. It is useless to expect human beings to behave morally, since we are all merely apes who have come down from the trees.
4. On the only day I ever crashed my car it was a Tuesday, so I know that Tuesdays are unlucky.
5. Do you realise that by leaving the lights on your balcony switched on all night you are contributing to global warming?
6. During the 1980s the West had tough and bellicose leaders as far as relations with the Soviet Union were concerned in Ronald Reagan and Margaret Thatcher. Some years after that the Soviets Union came to an end. The only reason for this can be because the West had such tough leaders.
7. Ancient Rome fell because its leaders were corrupt.
8. I have to confess my guilt. I hoped my wife would have an accident with the car to prove myself the better driver, and she did. I did not realise that my ill will could be so deadly.
9. George was late for the plane which crashed. It must be his destiny to be preserved for some future great work.
10. Drinking milk definitely leads to heroin use. A new government report based on a study of over five hundred hard-core narcotic addicts shows that one hundred per cent of the addicts had drunk milk before taking heroin.

3. Some Other Forms of Explanation

Covering Law Explanations, are the sort of explanations frequently said to be characteristic of science.

From a scientific law and a set of initial specific conditions which shows that law to be applicable, the resultant specific state of affairs to be explained is deduced. The laws themselves are similarly deduced from laws of wider application. This is sometimes called the "Covering Law" model of explanation. A reversal of the process of deduction allows for prediction, with which this form of explanation is said to be symmetrical.

Enthusiasts of this view used to claim that all true scientific explanations must be of this form. They would rewrite all other types of explanation in deductive-nomological form. Causal explanations were said to be covering law explanations with the relevant law omitted because it was to well known to bother to state.

The success of the enterprise of rewriting all scientific explanations according to this pattern seems to depend upon nothing else than the well-known fact that it is easy to construct, from a given conclusion and one given premise, a valid syllogism. Thus given something to be explained E, and antecedent conditions used by someone to explain it C, the enthusiast supplies a covering law to the effect that "Whenever C obtains E obtains." The three propositions are then presented as a reduction of the original explanation to the deductive-nomological type.

Most objections to this theory focus upon its identification of prediction with explanation.
- Firstly, prediction requires only a correlation, whereas explanation requires something more. We may predict successfully without in any way being able to understand why our predictions work. Newton's Theory of Gravity enables us to predict such diverse phenomena as the planetary

orbits, the behaviour of the tides and the trajectory of missiles. Yet no mechanism was provided by Newton to account for the phenomenon of gravity, and he was unable to counter the objection of his contemporaries that he was proposing ghostly action acting instantaneously at a distance without any medium to carry the force. Newton's Theory predicts, yet fails to explain, the motion of bodies.

▪ Similarly, we may explain without being able to predict. Darwin's Theory of Evolution could explain the multiform appearances of living things by natural selection, but is unable to predict how things will turn out in the future.

▪ The main problem with this approach is that it relies upon Hume's analysis of causation as mere correlation. Genuine explanation requires some mechanism intervening between cause and effect to account for the interaction.

Statistical Explanations

Statistical explanations are like covering law explanations, except that the law is replaced by a statistical generalisation. Since that is all it is, there can be no strictly deductive relation between the law and initial conditions on the one hand, and the specific situation being explained on the other. The former simply render the latter probable to some degree. The degree will depend upon the strength and reliability of the original generalisation.

Genetic Explanations

In a genetic explanation a sequence of facts is cited leading up to the event to be explained, so as to describe the evolution of the phenomenon. We try to understand things by reference to their history and evolution, by examining a chain of connected developments by which they came to be what they are today.

Genetic explanations are common in history, geology and biology. Although they stress the uniqueness of the phenomena being explained, they do imply some degree of generality.

Great care has to be taken with these explanations to avoid the fallacy of *post hoc ergo propter hoc*.

The Genetic Fallacy is an attempt to reduce the significance of a movement or a state of affairs *merely* to a proposed account of its origins or earliest antecedents.

(4) Our great nation cherishes freedom today because many of the founders of the republic were men who prized freedom more than life itself.

Functional Explanations

Phenomena may sometimes be explained by demonstrating the role they play in the functioning of some system.

We are familiar with systems in everyday life. The body is said to contain a digestive system. Cars have ignition systems. Buildings have heating and air conditioning systems. Cities have transport systems. States have educational systems, legal systems and systems of government. What such diverse systems all have in common, in virtue of which they are called systems is:

▪ They are all complex phenomena with many parts, but betraying some degree of unity or integration.

▪ They all have some structure or organisation which creates the integration. This provides for connections or links between the several units or parts of the system.

▪ There is some movement or transfer of material or information from one part of the system to another.

▪ This movement requires some sort of impetus or motive power. This may be material, such as the input of heat energy in a heating system, or immaterial, such as the desire for qualifications in an educational system.

▪ The system functions as a whole. The various parts function together, in virtue of the organisation, to produce some end which could not be achieved by the parts separately.

A system is different from a machine in that a machine is nothing more than the sum of its several parts, and these determine the functioning of the whole; whereas in a system the whole determines the functioning of the parts.

Feedback is the return of part of a system's output in order to change its input. Positive feedback increases the input. Negative feedback diminishes it, and so slows the functioning of the system down or stops it entirely. An example of positive feedback would be a "growth economy" in which profits are fed back into the system by being invested in the economy in order to produce further profits. An example of negative feedback would be the Watt steam governor. A pair of weights fly outwards caused by centrifugal force if the engine races. This operates a valve which then reduces the input of fuel. Positive feedback is inherently destabilising.

In feedback processes, certain elements may play a key role as regulators of development. In systems which develop, change is allowed to take place, but only in a certain direction. **Feedback mechanisms** cumulatively reinforce the direction of change.

In certain processes of development, a sudden change may be triggered. When the cumulative effect of positive feedback reaches a critical level, a sudden and possibly dramatic change of state ensues. These critical levels are termed **thresholds**.

Systems need to maintain their structure and organisation despite the throughput of material, or they will break down. Thus the system of the human body is regulated in respect of temperature by numerous feedback mechanisms. If the regulation fluctuates wildly we feel ill. If that fluctuation is not controlled, the system breaks down, and we die. The equilibrium of a steady state must be maintained, and to do this the system must have a capacity for self-regulation. **Negative feedback** mechanisms dampen down change which may threaten the structure of the system. These sense some development which may affect the survival of the system and effect a change in its operation so as to eradicate the risk.

Purpose and Intention

In attempting to understand some state of affairs we may consider aspects of a situation actually present during our experience of it, or we may range backwards in time in search of causal factors. The fizzing of a freshly opened bottle of cola may be explained either in terms of the physics and chemistry of the processes of fizzing, or reference may be made to events in the past, such as the bottling process and the opening of the bottle.

But in addition to these explanations, the desire for a full understanding of the situation might lead us to consider the future, as well as the past and present. A proper understanding of the opening of the bottle and its fizzing would include reference to the reasons why people manufacture and sell bottles of cola, why people buy them and open them. In short, we need to know what cola is *for*.

This reference to the future does not exactly parallel the references to the past or present. Those are to an actual past and present, to what has actually happened or to what is actually happening. The reference to the future is not to observable future events, about which only forecasts can be made, but to an idealised future. Bottles of cola are manufactured and sold primarily in order to make a profit for the shareholders of the company, but this can only happen if people wish to drink cola. Without understanding that people like sweet, fizzy drinks we cannot really understand why the drink fizzes. Without understanding that the person opening this bottle of cola now is thirsty, and is motivated by the aim of slaking his thirst, we can not fully understand the situation. Of course the drinker's thirst may not actually be quenched. Just before the lips of the bottle reaches his lips, he may be felled by an assassin's bullet, so that the bottle falls to the ground, smashes, and its contents gush away. But that would not be relevant to understanding why the bottle was opened. It is the future aimed at, the future towards which actions in the past and present are oriented, that is relevant to explaining the present.

An agent's purposes, intentions, motives, desires, etc., may be cited in explanation of his actions. These are very common in everyday life and in courts of law. Behaviourists would regard these as scientifically inadmissible because they refer to hidden inner mental states. Thus the form of a statue is explained by reference to the aims, intentions and motives of the sculptor who made it. According to Alisdair Macintyre:

"When we ascribe an intention, purpose or motive to someone; we do more than assert a tendency to behave in a particular way or a pattern in their actions. What more we do is brought out by distinguishing between statements about causal properties and statements about the dispositions of human beings . . . The evidence required to justify the assertion that 'salt is soluble in water' is simply that it has so dissolved; whereas the evidence required to justify the assertion that 'Smith is ambitious' is always more than that he has behaved in an ambitious fashion. The relevant difference between salt and Smith, between things and people, is perhaps no more than that people can talk about their behaviour. For it always makes sense to say that Smith seems to be ambitious, because he behaves in certain ways, but that he may not in fact be ambitious; it would be nonsense to say of salt that it has dissolved and would therefore seem to be soluble but might not be."

Motives are the drive which lies behind purposive actions of individuals. They are ascribed to intelligent individuals. They are end-directed, since people are motivated to perform acts *in order to* achieve some goal. They are usually complex. An act typically has more than one motive, and motives of more than one kind. Some are more important and potent than others. Although some may be subconscious, they are often a matter of deliberate conscious choice.

There can be no direct evidence of the operation of a motive. Motivation must be inferred from signs such as the subject's professions, his behaviour compared with our own and other peoples' general behaviour, etc.

Apparently unique, motives nevertheless have some general features, as Ernst Nagel points out: "But if mere proof were that a given factor was one circumstance under which an individual performed some particular act does not establish the claim that the factor was a *reason* why the individual acted as he did, how then can a historian warrant his imputation of a causal role to the factor? . . . The historian can justify his causal imputation by the assumption that, when the given factor is a circumstance under which men act, they generally conduct themselves in a manner similar to the particular action described in the imputation, so that the individual discussed by the historian presumably also acted the way he did because the given factor was present. In short generalisations of some sort are required in historical explanations of individual actions."

The clearest sorts of situation to be explained by reference to the future are those which are the results of conscious human endeavour. These are, however, not the only such situations. It would hardly be possible to understand the desperate attempts of the spider to crawl out of the bath without taking into account, in general terms, what would happen to the spider if it failed, i.e. its being drowned, and what would happen if it succeeded (i.e. its being able to obtain sustenance and preserve its life). This is not to claim that the spider is able to make conscious decisions based upon an assessment of the future probabilities. It is rather to claim that without reference to ideal future situations, such states of affairs as the behaviour of the spider in the bath cannot be understood.

Such end-directed states of affairs are common in the natural world. The structure and development of a developing seed or growing plant can only be properly appreciated as related to the form of the mature plant towards which it is tending, and which, given no internal or external impediment, (e.g. genetic disorder or drought) it will achieve. On the face of it, the suitability of reference to an ideal future in explanation is a distinctive characteristic of living things or of the artefacts of living things.

What is characteristic of such things is the presence of goal-directed activity. This is something which we are very good at spotting. It usually does not take long for us to decide whether the stones which people are throwing in our direction are being thrown at random or are intended to strike a definite target. Explanations in terms of purpose are called **teleological explanations**.

Reasons

The word "reasons" unfortunately has rather confusing several overlapping uses. The demand for reasons may simply be a demand for an explanation. The "reason" required for something happening may be its cause. Your reason for doing something may be your motive in doing it. On the other hand, your reason for believing something may be your grounds for believing it to be true. In the sense in which reasons provide a special form of explanation they are the grounds for my beliefs, the intellectual justification for believing what I do. In a rational world the reasons for my holding a belief would explain why I hold it, but in reality this may not always be true since I may be irrational in holding the beliefs that I in fact hold.

---

4. Models

Analogies can be used better to understand a difficult topic. In some cases, they can lead us to look at a topic in a new way — one which may lead to new insights which prove valuable to our understanding. (e.g. comparing the mind to the activity of a computer).

Systematically applied analogies are called models. In everyday language the term *model* has several distinct but related meanings: replica, type, ideal, something for display, etc.

Models are representations of something else. They are simplified pictures or maps of some complex aspect of reality which reproduce those features of the reality modelled which we consider to be important, i.e. its structure, organisation, how it functions, etc. This simplifies a very complex reality, allowing us to think more clearly and efficiently about it, describe it, and understand it better. They help us to do these things because they avoid the confusing detail of reality.

In **isomorphic models** every element, state, relationship and process in the original is mapped and reproduced in the model. More usually we have to make do with **homomorphic models**, which are less perfect representations of reality.

Static models represent things which are not systems, or they focus upon structure of a system rather than the processes which go on inside it. **Dynamic models** represent the processes which operate within systems.

Where the mapping is isomorphic, the model may be an exact replica. But usually only parts which are of concern to the investigator are mapped, so that the model may not look like what it represents. In such cases the model is simpler than the original.

The purpose of construction of such models may be:

- To remind us what something is like;
- To make the original modelled available to us, e.g. by reducing or enlarging the scale.
- To discover further information about the original modelled, e.g. the model of an aeroplane in a wind tunnel. To deal directly with the original may be costly, inconvenient or simply impossible.

Elements within a homomorphic model may be treated only in terms of what enters it or leaves it, without reference to its internal structure or working. Such a model is called a **black box**.

Theoretical models are not physical constructions. They are descriptions of something A in terms of something else B, made in virtue of an analogy between A and B, which is based upon their shared characteristics.

They are created:

- To *describe* some aspect of the world we find it difficult to grasp with the mind, either because it is so complex or because it is in some way beyond our immediate experience.
- To *investigate* some aspects of the behaviour of the original by using the model, e.g. computer models of the earth's climate
- To *explain* some aspect of the world.
- To *direct* our procedures

Today in the West medicine is dominated by the "disease" model of illness. According to this model, sickness is caused by the invasion of the body by sickness-causing agents: bacteria, or viruses. Treatment is by physical intervention from outside in the form of the administration of drugs or surgery. This may be contrasted with more traditional holistic models, which treat sickness as some sort of imbalance or lack of harmony within the organism, possibly a lack of harmony within the mind. Use of these models suggests that treatment should involve obtaining the co-operation of the sufferer in locating the cause of disharmony and imbalance and restoring proper harmony and balance. It could be said that the disease model has been vindicated by its success.

Models such as the Ptolomaic and Copernican models of the universe may have the status of laws or theories in science.

Models are by their nature only approximations to the complex realities they stand for. Thus the use of one model does not rule out the use of others. Of the structure of the atom, Robert Oppenheimer said:

"There is a place for many approaches to the system [of the atom], none of which completely exhausts the subject. You need to think of more than one approach, and you need to carry it out, in order to find out everything you can find out."

Since mapping is, properly speaking, a mathematical transformation, models may be expressed in mathematical notation. These are called **mathematical models**.

Dangers in the use of Models

However useful a model may be, it remains a simplification of the truth. Lecomte du Nouy said: "The human brain craves understanding. It cannot understand without simplifying; that is, without reducing things to a common element. However, all simplifications are arbitrary and lead us to drift insensibly away from reality."

In choosing one structure to represent some aspect of reality rather than another the model-builder is highlighting some factors and relationships, while casting others into the shadows. The model will be a good one insofar as the more important factors and relationships are highlighted, and the less important consigned to oblivion. But if the more important factors are ignored and the less important illuminated, the model will be misleading.

We are sometimes inclined to confuse our models with the whole truth. When this happens, our use of our models becomes rigid:

• When we hold one model, we become so attached to it that we are sometimes not prepared to countenance the use of another model to throw light upon the same phenomena.

• We fail to look beyond the model to the reality we are investigating, and so the model blinds us to aspects of that reality which the model cannot illuminate.

• We may bring *a priori* commitments to models of a certain kind to a subject to which they may be ill-suited and misleading.

• We may confuse the model with reality, and so ask meaningless questions. People sometimes wonder what the expanding Universe is expanding into. This question is suggested by the popular model of the Universe as a curved object embedded in a higher dimensional space into which it is expanding, understood in terms of an expanding balloon. It is helpful for some purposes to think of the Universe this way, but everything that we measure is within the Universe, and we see no edge or boundary of expansion. Thus the Universe is not expanding into anything that we could ever observe, and whether it is or not is beyond any hope of observation, checking or measurement. The balloon analogy is just a model that is introduced to help us think about a curved space, but it does not entail that there is some extra-dimensional space which the Universe is expanding into.

5. Adequate and Inadequate Explanations

Some General Fallacies of Explanation

Misdirected Explanation: We need to explain what is true. If some state of affairs does not actually obtain, then any explanation why it does is misdirected and redundant.

King Charles II, famous for his sense of humour, once asked the members of the Royal Society to explain to him why a fish weighs more when it is dead than when it is alive. The learned members came up with various ingenious explanations for this strange phenomenon. When they had finished king pointed out to them that *what* they were explaining with such skill and virtuosity was simply not true.

***Ad hoc* Explanations:** Other explanations are vacuous because "occult qualities" are created on an ad hoc basis to "explain" some particular phenomenon. Leibniz objected to those who refer to such qualities: " . . . which they imagined to be like little demons or goblins capable of producing unceremoniously that which is demanded, just as if watches marked the hours by a certain horodeictic faculty without having need of wheels, or as if mills crushed grains by a fractive faculty without needing anything resembling millstones." In this way, the doctor in Molière's play *La Malade Imaginaire,* explains that opium puts people to sleep on account of its "sleep-producing power." An *ad hoc* explanation is merely an exercise in verbal sophistry.

Animistic Explanations: It seems natural for human beings to provide animistic or supernatural explanations of natural events.

The Greeks were the first people to attempt systematically to exclude supernatural phenomena from the process of explanation. The usual ancient explanation of an earthquake was that it was caused by the struggling of giants imprisoned under the earth. Aristotle suggested that the cause of earthquakes was caused by masses of air trapped underground trying to escape. This required the existence of no race of giants to be especially postulated simply to explain this particular phenomenon. Moreover, although incorrect, it must have seemed reasonable to anyone who had witnessed or heard reports of the currents of air released from the volcanoes or through the sulphur craters to be found in various places around the Mediterranean.

How to Provide Adequate Explanations

The following questions should be asked of any explanation:

- Has the constitution of the phenomenon being explained been analysed and its essential component parts delineated, together with their relations with each other?
- Has its part in a wider system been recognised, together with the function it performs within that system?
- Have we located and specified its causes?
- Have we given an account of its origins?
- Have we stated the purpose (if any) for which it was designed?
- Have we made any comparisons with other things which may illuminate it and make it easier to comprehend?
- Have we chosen the explanation requiring the fewest assumptions. (Occam's Razor)

Levels of Explanation

Frequently it seems that organised systems may produce some effect which seems to be in some way greater than the parts themselves. Thus the motions of matter may produce life, neural functions may produce consciousness, and arrangements of sounds may produce beauty. This property of things is called **emergence**.

The phenomenon of emergence leads to different descriptions of the same thing when it is being considered at different levels. A **level of description** is a field of discourse in which the characteristic descriptions contain distinctive sets of concepts which are related to each other, and which refer to distinctive aspects of the subject matter. Thus on the level of material object language we might expect to come across such terms as *object*, *mass* and *motion*. On the level of living things such distinctive concepts as *growth*, *reproduction* and *sickness* appear. On the level of moral consciousness, we meet *obligation*, *duty* and *blame*.

These different levels of description are not mutually incompatible. The existence of these different levels of description underlines the need for different levels of explanation. The different levels of explanation are not incompatible as such.

6. Necessity

Since empirical knowledge is *a posteriori*, i.e. since it depends upon what actually happens in the world, the way in which things actually turn out, it always makes sense to suppose that things *might* have turned out differently.

For this reason the propositions which express empirical knowledge are always such that their truth value could have been different from what it is. If they turn out to be true, they could have been false. If they turn out to be false, they might have been true. Such propositions are called **contingent propositions**. We never know whether such a proposition is actually true or not unless we have some evidence about the state of the world upon which to base our judgement. We must wait upon the facts.

By contrast, there are some propositions which, whether true or false, could not have a truth value other than the one which they do have. If they are true, they are necessarily true, and if they are false they are necessarily false. These are called **necessary propositions**.

Necessarily false propositions are either self-contradictory or incoherent.

Coherence and Incoherence

The philosopher Richard Swinburne explained a **coherent proposition** as one such that someone who understands it could, in principle, know what it would be like for it, and any proposition entailed by it, to be true. As an example of a coherent proposition which is known to be false he cites:

(4) The moon is made of green cheese.

Despite its silliness, we know what it would be like if the moon were to be made of green cheese. We know what sort of tests we could apply to check the claim. We know how we should have to behave in order to behave appropriately if it were true. We can envisage the sort of problems its truth might cause, and the sort of problems which its being true might be used to resolve.

By contrast, an **incoherent proposition** is one such that we do not know, in principle, what it would be like for it to be true, e.g.

(5) Beauty is triangular.

Necessary Truth

Most necessarily true propositions, and perhaps all, are true either in virtue of their meaning or of their logical form. They are either true by definition or because they are tautologies.

Proposition (6) below is true in virtue of a definition, in virtue of the language we use.

(6) Bachelors are unmarried men

We have collectively resolved to adopt the convention that the word "bachelors" will designate all unmarried men and only unmarried men. In virtue of this convention, (3) will be necessarily true.

Note that the apparently similar, but very different, proposition:

(7) "Bachelor" means "unmarried man"

states a fact about the English language which might have been different from what it happens to be, and is, therefore, a contingent proposition. This is because its subject is not bachelors but the English word "bachelor," as is indicated by the use of inverted commas.

Proposition (8) below is a tautology, true in virtue of its logical form (p is p):

(8) A cockroach is a cockroach; (said by a friend who wants to introduce you to his pet.)

(9) Either the bank is open or the bank is not open.

(10) All brown cows are brown.

The fact that a proposition is true in virtue of its logical form may be disguised, e.g.

(11) When people are out of work, unemployment results. (US President Calvin Coolidge)

Propositions of the form of (10) may appear disguised in the form of statements of class inclusion:

(12) All dolphins are mammals

(since dolphins will be defined as "mammals plus x," where x is what distinguishes dolphins from all other mammals, its distinguishing characteristic.)

Tautologies may be useful in clarifying what we mean by the words we use, and as rhetorical devices, but they must never be confused with statements of empirical fact. Usually, they are a sign that a "bullshit detector" is urgently required, e.g. in political speeches.

Propositions which are true in virtue of language or logic express **conceptual truths,** not truths about the world. Their truth is found by analysing the propositions themselves, rather than by looking outside them for evidence of their truth. To deny the truth of such a proposition is to involve oneself in self-contradiction.

> e.g. (13) "All I was doing was appealing for an endorsement, not suggesting you endorse it." (George H. W. Bush)

Such propositions are necessarily true, i.e. true without possibility of revision. They are said to be known to be true *a priori*, that is, independently of any evidence. A consequence of this is that they are empty of empirical content. They tell us nothing directly about the world.

When we reason that things are true because there is evidence for their truth, ultimately someone's sense experience, we are reasoning empirically. When we argue that something is true because it ought to be true or it just has to be true, and cite no evidence grounded in sense-experience, we are arguing aprioristically.

Exercise 11.4

Are the following contingent, necessarily true or necessarily false?
1. Some bachelors are married.
2. Tokyo is the capital city of Japan.
3. Pigeons are mammals.
4. Kim drew a four-sided triangle on his examination paper.
5. This computer could not have been made of chocolate.

---

7. *A priori* Knowledge

Empirical knowledge, knowledge of the world justified ultimately by reference to sense-experience, is contrasted with *a priori* **knowledge**.

The main problem with a priori knowledge is that it is not clear how it can be about the world, as opposed to about the relations between our ideas, considered in abstraction from the world. In the past, thinkers often preferred *a priori* knowledge since it expressed necessary truths, which they felt have a better claim to be considered knowledge than mere empirical knowledge, which depends upon the way things actually happen to turn out, and which is always contingent upon events. As a result, a lot of their thinking was "building castles in the air."

The Greek philosophers of Alexandria were inclined to aprioristic thinking. One day two philosophers were travelling along a road with a donkey and its Egyptian driver. They were arguing about how many teeth a donkey had, and used various abstruse *a priori* arguments to the effect that it *must* have so many. When the driver could stand this no longer, he yanked open the donkey's mouth, counted them, and told them. The philosophers were appalled at such crudity.

Case Study: Why Jupiter Cannot Have Four Moons.

Consider the following argument advanced by the Florentine astronomer, Francesco Sizzi, arguing against Galileo's discovery of four moons of Jupiter. It is based upon the generally accepted notion at the time that the human being (the microcosm) was a living image of the universe as a whole (the macrocosm.)

"Just as in the microcosm there are seven 'windows' in the head (two nostrils, two eyes, two ears, and a mouth), so in the macrocosm God has placed two beneficent stars (Jupiter, Venus), two maleficent stars (Mars and Saturn), two luminaries (sun and moon), and one indifferent star (Mercury). The seven days of the week follow from these. Finally, since ancient times the alchemists have made each of the seven metals correspond to one of the planets; gold to the sun, silver to the moon, copper to Venus, quicksilver to Mercury, iron to Mars, tin to Jupiter, lead to Saturn.

From these and many other similar phenomena of nature such as the seven metals, etc., which it were tedious to enumerate, we gather that the number of planets is necessarily seven ... Besides, the Jews and other ancient nations as well as modern Europeans, have adopted the division of the week into seven days, and have named them from the seven planets; now if we increase the number of planets, this whole system falls to the ground ... Moreover, the satellites are invisible to the naked eye and therefore can have no influence on the earth, and therefore would be useless, and therefore do not exist."

From the way in which this astronomer is arguing, it is clear that the knowledge which is being claimed is not dependent upon any specific astronomical observations, but is independent of any particular experience.

A priori knowledge is expressed in propositions which can be known to be true or false independently of any experience of the object of knowledge or of any phenomena causally connected with it. Logic and mathematics are the areas of *a priori* knowledge, since the truths of logic and mathematics are either tautologies, definitions, or the result of deductions from them. By contrast, modern science achieved its successes precisely by turning away from *a priori* reasoning towards an empirical approach to knowledge.

Formal logic was invented in Classical Greece and integrated into a system of thought by Aristotle. It was, for him, a tool for finding truth, but it did not prevent him from making profound errors. Many of the scientific conclusions he came to were wrong.

Aristotle understood that logic can be used to deduce true consequences from true premises. He failed to realise that we may have no absolutely true premises, except ones we define to be true, such as "2+2=4." Aristotle thought that the mind contains some innate and absolutely true knowledge which can be used as premises for logical arguments. As we have seen, the conclusions of valid deductive arguments do not represent new truths. Thus neither logic nor mathematics can reveal new truths about the world.

It is important to achieve the appropriate balance between the two approaches to knowledge. The ancients believed many things which were just not true, not on the basis of wrong evidence, but by ignoring the evidence in favour of what they thought *must* be the case. The British philosopher, Bertrand Russell, expressed this with characteristic pungency when he observed: "Aristotle maintained that women have fewer teeth than men; although he was twice married, it never occurred to him to verify this statement by examining his wives' mouths." In this he resembled the philosophers on the road with the Egyptian donkey driver (above).

Case Study: Aristotle's Theory of Physics

Following Aristotle, it was believed by most ancient scholars that all objects tend naturally towards their proper place in the universe. This place was defined by reference to the element or form of matter of which a thing was composed: earth, air, fire or water. All physical objects were believed to be formed from a combination of these elements. Heavier objects were considered to have more weight than lighter objects because they have a greater proportion of the heaviest element, earth, in their composition. They naturally tend towards the proper place for earth, the lowest level in the universe. The greater the proportion of earth, the heavier they are, the greater their tendency downwards, and so the faster they will fall. From this it follows that heavier objects fall faster than lighter objects.

It was not until Galileo, according to an ancient story, conducted an experiment to see whether this was actually the case by dropping balls of different weights down a chute and timing their fall, that it was discovered that all fall at the same velocity.

The ancients had been thinking aprioristically, whereas Galileo, the early modern scientist, was thinking empirically.

The ancient Greeks had a story about a brigand named Procrustes who lived near the borders of Attica in the time of Theseus. It was his practice to offer unsuspecting travellers the use of his on bed. Then during the night the size of the sleeping traveller would be "adjusted" to fit the size of the bed. Whatever overhung the edges was chopped off. If the unfortunate traveller was too short for the bed, he was stretched until he had become the correct fit. Those who adopt an aprioristic approach towards the truth tend to chop it down to size, or to stretch it out to fit their preconceptions. Outside all but very narrow limits, an *a priori* approach to knowledge tends to be an indication of mere prejudice. It ensures that the facts will be "adjusted" to fit a **Procrustean bed**.

Glossary

ad hoc **explanation:** a purely verbal formula which has the appearance of explaining some thing but which does not because it was contrived only for that purpose.

animistic thinking: thinking based upon the attribution of consciousness, desires, will, intentions, etc. to inanimate objects.

a posteriori **knowledge:** knowledge which can be established only through observation.

a priori **knowledge:** knowledge which is independent of observation.

black box: a model treated only in terms of what enters it or leaves it, without reference to any internal structure or working.

category mistake: a confusion of logical types.

cause: an agency which effects some change.

circumstantial evidence: indirect evidence.

coherent proposition: a proposition such that we know what it would be like for it, and any propositions entailed by it, to be true.

conceptual truth: a truth which is such in virtue of language or logic.

consistency: propositions or beliefs are consistent if they can both be true.

contingent proposition: a proposition such that, if true, they could have been false, and if false, they could have been true.

conventionalism: the view that the hypotheses and laws of science are condensed descriptions of phenomena, without any explanatory value.

data: what is immediately given to the senses.

description: a verbal portrait of something.

dynamic model: a model which represents the processes which operate within a system.

emergence: the appearance of new properties of systems of things not found in their several parts.

empirical: relying or based on experience rather than on theory or meaning.

empirical knowledge: knowledge based directly or indirectly upon the evidence of experience.

empirical truth: truth which are so in virtue of the state of the world, as evidenced ultimately by sense experience.

evidence: information provided by sense-experience or testimony for the truth (or falsity) of some empirical proposition.

explanation: an account of something

explanatory model: useful descriptions of some less well-known x in terms of some better known y, made in virtue of an analogy between them, and used to explain x.

facts: isolated pieces of information about nature; states of affairs which obtain in the world.

feedback: the return of part of a system's output in order to change its input.

functional explanation: an explanation of something in terms of the part it plays in

homomorphic model: a model in which not every element, state, relationship and process in the original is mapped and reproduced in the model

incoherent proposition: a proposition such that we do not know what it would be like for it, and any propositions entailed by it, to be true.

inconsistency: propositions or beliefs are inconsistent if they cannot both be true, so that the truth of one implies the falsity of the other.

isomorphic model: a model in which every element, state, relationship and process in the original is mapped and reproduced in the model.

level of description: a field of discourse in which the characteristic descriptions contain distinctive sets of concepts which are related to each other, and which refer to distinctive aspects of the subject matter.

magical thinking: thinking based upon improperly attributed causal connections.

mathematical model: an explanatory model expressed in mathematical notation.

necessary condition: a condition in the absence of which the effect never occurs.

necessary proposition: propositions which, whether true or false, cannot have any other truth value than the one which they do have.

negative feedback: feedback which diminishes input, slowing down or stopping entirely the functioning of the system.

objective explanation: an explanation which accounts for something, regardless of whether, as a matter of fact, people find it intelligible or convincing.

opinion: A statement of belief or feeling.

positive feedback: feedback which increases input.

post hoc, ergo propter hoc: the fallacy of supposing that if *y* follows *x*, then *y* is caused by *x*.

pragmatic explanation: an explanation which serves to make something intelligible to someone.

Procrustean bed: an *a priori* standard to which you force the facts to conform.

self-contradictory proposition: a proposition which, if true, would be false; and if false, would be true.

static models: models which represent things which are not systems, or which focus upon structure of a system rather than the processes which go on inside it.

sufficient condition: a condition such that when it occurs, the effect occurs.

Symmetry Thesis: the view that there is a perfect symmetry between explanation and prediction so that each is a reverse of the other.

tautology: a proposition which is true in virtue of its logical form, and hence tells us nothing specific about the world.

teleological explanation: explanation in terms of purpose.

threshold: a critical level triggering a sudden change in the state of a system reached as a result of the cumulative effect of positive feedback.

12. THE NATURAL SCIENCES

"Truth in science can be defined as the working hypothesis best suited to open the way to the next better one." (Konrad Lorenz)

1. What Scientists Do

Descriptive Science

The early stages of a science involve getting to know better that aspect of the world which is its subject matter. This involves making more systematic observations, and more precise and accurate records of those observations, than is customary in everyday life, and then reducing what has been observed to order by systematic classification.

Until recently there was little more than mapping the heavens that could be done in astronomy. In the field of biology the process of mapping and classifying the various species of living things is still by no means near completion. Scientific advance may still take the form of simply discovering some hitherto unknown phenomenon, recording it, classifying it, and beginning the process of seeking to understand it. Since our immediate environment has been well-explored, such discoveries more and more tend to take place further afield, in the depths of the oceans or in the vastness of space.

Case Study: The Living Worlds of Ocean-Bed Hydrothermal Vents

In 1977 two geologists descended 8,200 feet into the ocean near the Galapagos Islands. They were looking for a deep-sea hot spring or hydrothermal vent, which they had predicted would be found along rifts in the earth's crust, where the tectonic plates are drifting apart, and where volcanic activity is likely to occur. It was thought that lava would well up through these rifts, forming new crust, and heating the water that percolates down through cracks in the rock. Hydrothermal vents would then spew this hot water back into the ocean. As expected, they found their first vent, an area about one hundred meters across, where water streamed out of cracks in the ocean bed at a temperature of 60°F.

At the same time, they also made a completely unexpected discovery: The hot vent was jammed with living creatures. "Reefs of mussels and fields of giant clams . . . along with crabs, anemones, and large pink fish." Both the ten-inch clams and the blind crabs scuttling about were porcelain white, in stark contrast to the otherwise barren black basalt of the newly formed ocean floor surrounding the vent. The most common creature to inhabit this strange world was six-foot long white tubeworm that extended feathery, bright red plumes from the top of its tube.

Oceanographers have since mapped a hitherto unknown world of hydrothermal vents extending north to south through the Atlantic and Pacific Oceans. As the tectonic plates separate, lava flows in between them creating new sea floor at a rate of several inches per year. The newly formed crust is a dark, glassy lava that cracks as it cools. Seawater percolating down through those cracks may be heated to temperatures up to 700^0F. The water is superheated rather than boiling, because the pressure is so great at the depths where vents are found.

All the vents are home to a great diversity of life, including more than two hundred and fifty known species of free-living bacteria and about three hundred newly described animal species.

Problems Generate Scientific Investigations

Scientific inquiry usually arises as a response to a problem of some kind. These problems may be practical, concerned with how to achieve some end: e.g. How to find a cure for AIDs, how to devise a cheaper, non-polluting fuel for automobiles; or they may be purely theoretical, concerned with how to understand some phenomenon of nature, such as the ability of some animals to migrate year after year over vast distances to the same precise locations.

As we have seen, scientists may still make spectacular discoveries through observation of the world around. Seeking to understanding these may itself raise problems.

Case Study: Sea Worms without Mouths, Guts or Anuses

The discovery of animal life in ocean hydrothermal vents raised the puzzling question about what the creatures discovered there could be living on at that depth. Most living things get their energy from sunlight. Plants depend directly on the sun for their energy, and animals eat plants or plant-eating animals, and so depend indirectly on the sun. But there is no sunlight in the black depths of the ocean. More puzzling still is the strange fact that the giant tubeworms discovered at the hydrothermal vents had neither mouths, guts, nor anuses.

This question was answered in 1980, when a Harvard graduate student, Colleen Cavanaugh, had a bright idea that turned out to be correct. The water spurting from hydrothermal vents is full of hydrogen sulphide and other energy-rich compounds. Before the discovery of the ocean vents it was already known that sulphur springs found on land are home to bacteria, which obtain their energy by oxidising the sulphide in the water by a process of chemosynthesis.

The hydrothermal vents teem with sulphide-oxidising bacteria, which grow in thick, white-to-yellow-to-pink mats that cover all the hard surfaces around the vents, from rocks to clam shells to tubeworm tubes. Occasionally blooms of these floating bacteria become so dense they create the appearance of a blizzard. Many of the creatures living at the vents eat these sulphide-oxidising bacteria: the first known animals to depend on chemosynthesis rather than photosynthesis for their ultimate source of energy.

But what of the large mouthless, gutless, giant tubeworms? Obviously they could not eat bacteria. The initial assumption was that they were absorbing tiny particles of food through their skin. This method of "eating" had originally been proposed for their relatives: hair-sized tubeworms that also lack mouths and guts. First found in 1900, these are so small that they could theoretically absorb all the food they need through their skin. The giant tubeworms, however, are too big to obtain enough nutrients using this method, because their surface area relative to their body size is much smaller.

The mystery was solved when Cavanaugh was watching the curator of worms at the Smithsonian Institution give a public dissection of a giant tubeworm that had been sliced like a salami. When he reached the trophosome, an organ of then-unknown function that extended along seventy-five percent of the length of the tubeworm, he mentioned that he had seen sulphur crystals in the organ.

At this point, Cavanaugh realised that the tubeworms might have symbiotic relationship with sulphide-oxidising bacteria. She obtained a sample of tissue and, with the help of other biologists, showed that the tubeworms did harbour bacteria inside their trophosome cells. In fact, bacteria comprised the bulk of trophosome tissue. Other researchers subsequently showed that the trophosome contained enzymes characteristic of sulphide-oxidising bacteria which are not found in animal cells.

Symbiosis is a partnership that can result in two (or more) species surviving in an environment where neither could manage alone. In this case, the tubeworm obtains a source of food in the nutrient-poor depths of the ocean; although it is not yet clear whether the tubeworms live on bacterial excretions or dead bacterial cells. In return, the bacteria get a supply of sulphide. A tubeworm collects the compound using its red plumes, and transmits it to the bacteria via sulphide-binding proteins in its blood.

Ironically, although these symbioses were first found at deep sea hydrothermal vents, biologists have since discovered that they exist in more than a hundred species of marine invertebrates, including the tiny tubeworms originally thought to subsist on food absorbed through their skin. All these animals live in sulphide-containing environments such as mudflats, sewage outlets and sediments containing petroleum.

The choice of which problems scientists actually work upon tends to be dictated by the financial resources made available by government grants or private corporations, and also upon the availability of the means to perform the research, e.g. access expensive equipment. Preparedness to fund research may depend upon social, political and economic factors. Governments may support research on pollution control, for example, but would oppose research on racial differences in IQ test performance, because this might be socially divisive. Big business may be reluctant to finance research on finding a cure for a disease, if the results would not produce significant profits. Economic, social and political considerations are all interrelated in complex ways.

The Generation of Hypotheses

Having studied the problem, including everything available written on it, a scientist must propose a "candidate" solution, or **hypothesis**. (The term "hypothesis" carries has several meanings. In ordinary language it may refer to a groundless assumption, a hunch, a prediction, a proposed theory. Here it refers to a candidate, or provisional, scientific law or theory.)

A researcher will first study the general field, and all similar past research. The dominant theory in any particular field of science usually plays a major role in suggesting to a researcher what is relevant to his investigation and what is not.

This need for background knowledge, and the dominance of existing theory, explains why discoveries frequently seem to be made in different parts of the world at more or less the same time. Both Hooke and Newton arrived at the concept of gravity more or less simultaneously. In this way, we can also see that the insights of each generation are built upon the understanding reached by the previous generation of investigators as part of the collective Enterprise of Knowledge.

Although hypotheses are usually suggested by the accepted theory which dominates a particular branch of science, in the early stages of a particular field of study there may be no generally accepted theory, or the currently-dominant theory may not provide any clues. The philosopher John Stuart Mill sought to provide a series of rule-of-thumb methods which can be tried out in such circumstances, known as Mill's Methods.

Mill's Methods

The Method of Agreement: "If two or more instances of the phenomenon under investigation have only one circumstance in common, the circumstance in which alone all the instances agree, is the cause (or the effect) of the given phenomenon."

$$a\,b\,c\,d \text{ occur together with } w\,x\,y\,z$$
$$a\,e\,f\,g \text{ occur together with } t\,u\,v\,z$$

Therefore, a is the cause (or the effect, or an indispensable part of the cause) of z

In a case of food poisoning, if it turns out that all the patients ate the hamburgers at a particular fast food restaurant on the previous evening, then a hypothesis that the hamburgers were cause of the poisoning is suggested.

The Method of Difference: "If an instance in which the phenomenon under investigation occurs, and an instance in which it does not occur, have every circumstance in common save one, that one occurring only in the former; the circumstance in which alone the two instances differ, is the effect, or the cause, or an indispensable part of the cause, of the phenomenon."

$$a\,b\,c\,d \text{ occur together with } w\,x\,y\,z$$
$$b\,c\,d \text{ occur together with } w\,x\,y$$

Therefore, a is the cause (or the effect, or an indispensable part of the cause) of z.

If the those people who went to the fast food restaurant and did not eat the hamburgers did not get food poisoning, we should conclude that a causal relationship existed between the hamburgers and the food poisoning.

The Joint Method of Agreement and Difference:

It is better, wherever possible, to use both of these methods in conjunction with each other. In a case of food poisoning, if the hamburgers are suspected since all those afflicted ate them, then if all those who did not eat them did not get food poisoning, this makes a hypothesis that the hamburgers were responsible much more likely.

The Method of Concomitant Variations: "Whatever phenomenon varies in any manner whenever another phenomenon varies in some particular manner, is either a cause or an effect of that phenomenon, or is connected with it through some fact of causation."

$$a\,b\,c\,d \qquad\qquad w\,x\,y\,z$$
$$2a\,b\,c\,d \qquad\qquad wx\,y\,2z$$
$$4a\,b\,c\,d \qquad\qquad w\,x\,y\,4z$$

Therefore, a and z are causally connected.

This method is widely used in everyday life, for example in order to judge the effectiveness of advertising is judged by fluctuations in sales figures.

The Method of Residues: "Subtract from any phenomenon such part as is known by previous inductions to be the effect of certain antecedents, and the residue of the phenomenon is the effect of the remaining antecedents."

$$a\,b\,c\,d \qquad\qquad w\,x\,y\,z$$

b is known to be the cause of y

c is known to be the cause of x

d is known to be the cause of w

Therefore, a is the cause (or the effect, or an indispensable part of the cause) of z.

The higher radioactivity of uranium ores than the pure uranium extracted from them led the Curies to analyse the residues in search of the source of the radio-activity. It was found that a large part remained with the sulphite of barium. From this a further substance was extracted which was more than a million time s more active than uranium. This substance, ultimately responsible for most of the unaccounted for radioactivity in the uranium ores, was called radium.

Despite the usefulness of such methods, the production of hypotheses remains essentially a creative process. The philosopher Karl Popper wrote: " . . .there is no such thing as a logical method of having new ideas, or a logical reconstruction of this process. My view may be expressed by saying that every discovery contains 'an irrational element' or a creative intuition . . ." Thus it is not possible to provide rules for the creation of hypotheses.

This is demonstrated over and over again in the history of science, by the number of scientists who have made important discoveries and advances in their subject, who have told us that their ideas occurred to them in the most inconsequential of ways.

Although background knowledge is indispensable to appreciate them when they occur, hypotheses may actually arise from reflection upon everyday common-sense knowledge, or even from the folk tradition so frequently despised by " educated" people.

Case Study: Edward Jenner and Smallpox

Throughout history, smallpox has been one of the deadliest scourges suffered by mankind. It was a disease which killed the unlucky and disfigured, and sometimes blinded, those fortunate enough to survive an attack. Traces of it can be found in the mummies of ancient Egypt, and it remained among the deadliest of diseases to afflict humankind until modern times.

It had long been widely noticed that someone who contracted a mild form of this disease seemed to be immune from any later and more serious infection. It was also known that the injection of matter from the sore of someone with a mild infection might develop resistance to the disease in those who were well, but it was a very risky practice. Sometimes the injected person was given the disease in a form which was not mild enough, and this would sometimes prove fatal.

Then the English physician Edward Jenner became aware of a countryside tradition in Gloucestershire, England, that milkmaids who contracted the similar but harmless disease called cowpox would afterwards be immune from smallpox. Jenner decided to test a popular hypothesis that contracting cowpox would ensure immunity from smallpox. He not only closely observed sixteen people who had naturally contracted the disease, but also contrived that others should deliberately contract cowpox by vaccinating them with infected material. The results were positive.

Although preachers rushed to condemn the practice of vaccination as interfering in the ways of God, and taught that those who had been vaccinated would develop some of the characteristics of cows, such as horns and tails, it was quickly recognised that Jenner had discovered a method to prevent the disease. The Emperor Napoleon had the French army vaccinated; while Thomas Jefferson wrote to Jenner saying that: " . . . future nations will know by history only that the loathsome smallpox has existed, and by you has been extirpated." This prophesy came true in 1977, when the United Nations World Health Organisation issued the statement that the last known case of smallpox had been located and isolated.

Sometimes, hypotheses *seem* to arise as a consequence of chance occurrences and accidents. However, only a well-prepared mind can so appreciated the significance of such an event that he is able to use the insight it gives him to generate a useful scientific hypothesis.

Case Study: Alexander Fleming and the Discovery of Penicillin

In 1908 Alexander Fleming wrote a thesis in which he described all the defences against bacterial infection which were then known. These included the patient's own natural resistance to infection, vaccines, antiseptics, and some antibacterial agents which successfully overcame specific bacteria. In 1909 he administered salvarsan to patients. This was a chemical discovered by Paul Erlich to have the power to kill the bacteria which caused the disease syphilis, the nineteenth century equivalent of AIDs. During the First World War Fleming worked in France, where he observed the inadequacy of existing antiseptics to prevent the infection of war wounds.

Then in 1922 he investigated the source of the body's natural resistance to bacteria, in order to discover its secret. Having a cold at the time, he added some of his own mucous to a bacteria culture, and observed that it killed the surrounding bacteria. He isolated the chemical lysozyme as responsible.

Thus he had a thorough knowledge of the background of the problem he was studying when, in 1928, a chance incident occurred which was to provide a medical breakthrough. In 1928 spores of penicillium mould floated onto one of his culture plates, killing all the bacteria around it. This is the common green-grey mould is frequently seen growing on oranges. He said: "I had often seen such contamination before. But what I had never seen before was staphylococci undergoing lysis around the contaminating colony. Obviously, something extraordinary was happening. With the background that I had, this was more interesting than my staphylococcal research, so I switched promptly." The result was the development of penicillin.

The contamination of the culture plate was accidental, but no mind could have been more prepared for the accident when it happened. He added: "But for my previous experience it is likely that I should have simply thrown the plate away, as many bacteriologists had done before me."

The Formulation of Hypotheses

In the formulation of hypotheses, precision is important. The more precise a hypothesis is formulated, the more easy it is to test, and to know whether it has, or has not, failed the test. Precision is achieved through clear thinking and careful expression, by the use of technical terms, and mathematics.

The advantage of using mathematics in science lies in its usefulness as a tool of reasoning. Herbert Simon wrote: "Mathematics has become the dominant language of the natural sciences not because it is quantitative - a common delusion - but because it permits clear and rigorous reasoning about phenomena too complex to be handled in words."

By formulating a hypothesis in mathematical terms, a scientist is able to make a precise, rather than a vague, prediction, allowing for a much more precise testing. A prediction which merely says that "Φ will increase" is compatible with more possible hypotheses than one which says that "Φ will increase x-fold within a period of y." Thus incorrect hypotheses can be eliminated and discarded much more efficiently, and results compatible with several different hypotheses are avoided.

The Testing of Hypotheses

Most hypotheses in science are so general that they cannot be tested directly. Instead, particular consequences are deduced from the hypothesis, and these are checked by systematic observation or experiment.

Systematic Observation: The casual observations characteristic of everyday knowledge are inadequate for scientific study. In science, observation must be genuinely systematic.

Observation may take place in the field, i.e. in uncontrolled circumstances, or in the laboratory, i.e. under controlled circumstances. Observation in the field is valuable for the investigator who wants to know how things normally interact with each other, for example in the Earth's ecological system, or in animal or human societies. In some branches of science, such as vulcanology and natural history, field work is essential. Ideally, however, the factors to be investigated are studied in the artificial isolation of the laboratory.

Scientific Instruments: The process of observation may be improved and extended by the use of scientific instruments. These extend the range of possible observation beyond the limits of the human senses in many ways:

- Distance: e.g. Using radio telescopes, it is possible to detect objects approximately ten billion light years away.
- Magnitude: e.g. Microscopes are limited by the size of the wavelengths they detect. Thus ordinary optical microscopes get fuzzy as they begin to detect very small objects, since the light waves tend to go around them. The best optical microscopes can magnify an object 2,000 times and detect two dots 1/5,000 of a millimetre apart. Ultraviolet light has shorter waves than visible light, and these can distinguish two dots 1/10,000 of a millimetre apart. The electron microscope, using smaller waves still, can magnify an object two million times.
- Wavelength, e.g. infrared detectors, x-ray machines;
- Precision, e.g. measuring instruments such as thermometers.

    Scientific instruments also allow us to record our observations for future reference, e.g. using photo detectors and video cameras. By such means we are no longer limited to trying to recall experiences which may at the time have been fleeting, or difficult to interpret.

Mathematical Analysis: Mathematical analysis of the data of observation provides the most precise and systematic use of this method.

Case Study: The Discovery of the Planets Neptune and Pluto

The existence of the planet Neptune was first predicted using mathematical arguments based on Newton's laws of gravity, and then confirmed by observation.

The planet had actually been observed and recorded by Galileo in 1613, and later by several more astronomers, but without being recognised as a planet. Its discovery did not come from such chance observations, but resulted from a mathematical analysis of the deviation of Uranus from its predicted orbit.

Bouvard, director of the Paris Observatory, had published accurate tables of the orbits Jupiter and Saturn, and in 1808 decided to produce the tables for Uranus. However, he could not make all the observations fit the corrected predictions, even after taking the gravitational influence of the other planets into account. He published his tables of Uranus in 1821, but wrote: " . . . I leave to the future the task of discovering whether the difficulty of reconciling [the data] is connected with the ancient observations, or whether it depends on some foreign and unperceived cause which may have been acting upon the planet."

Several astronomers, including Le Verrier, decided to investigate these irregularities in the motion of Uranus, in order to find out whether they could be attributed to the gravitational attraction of an undiscovered planet which lay beyond it; and if possible determine its orbit, and seek to locate it.

Le Verrier first showed that the influence of Jupiter and Saturn could not explain the observed position of Uranus, and that the only possible explanation for its behaviour must be the influence of another planet with an orbit further out from the Sun. He gave some details of a possible orbit of this hypothetical body, with a position for it for the beginning of 1847, and estimates of its mass and diameter.

Le Verrier wrote to the German astronomer Galle at the Royal Observatory in Berlin on 18 September, asking him to search for the "new planet" at the location he had predicted. It took Galle less than thirty minutes to locate a "star" not on their map. They had found the missing planet, and confirmed it the following night by observing it had moved relative to the fixed stars. Galle wrote to Le Verrier on 25th September, with the news: ". . . the planet of which you indicated the position really exists." Once the orbit of Neptune had been worked out sufficiently well, the records were searched to see if it had been recorded earlier. It was discovered that it had, but it had been mistaken for a faint star.

Unfortunately, the planet Neptune itself did not follow the orbit computed for it, even after taking the gravitational attraction of all the other known planets into account. Also, both Uranus and Saturn were still slightly out of place when the mass of Uranus was taken to account. Percival Lowell, an American astronomer, analysed the data mathematically, and predicted the existence of a further planet beyond the orbit of Neptune, which must be responsible for these discrepancies.

A search was begun at the Flagstaff Observatory in the USA in 1915, and for two years the area of the sky in which the new planet was predicted to be located was photographed. Nothing was found. Lowell redid his mathematical analysis and again photographed the area of the sky where his predictions showed that the planet would lie. There are images of Pluto on those plates, but they are faint and were not recognised.

It was not until January 1929 that Clyde W Tombaugh was able to write: " . . . on the afternoon of February 18th, 1930, I suddenly came upon the images of Pluto! The experience was an intense thrill, because the nature of the object was apparent at first sight." The planet was photographed every night from then on to confirm the observation, and on 13 March 1930, the one hundred and forty-ninth anniversary of the discovery of Uranus, an announcement was made. The name Pluto was given to the new planet.

Experiment

Experiment is by no means confined to the science laboratory; it is something we do in our everyday life. But of all the things which scientists do, it is perhaps justly the most well-known, for reliance upon experiments has been the key to the success of modern science.

Experiment provides the firm foundation in empirical reality which gives science much of its strength. Mere observation, by itself, is very liable to be rendered valueless by the interference of factors which affect what is being observed without our knowledge. Experiment involves active interference in the phenomena under investigation, controlling it in some way to increase the systematisation and sophistication of the process of observation. It is based upon the idea that we can establish causal connections between phenomena by manipulating them. It is assumed that we can confirm any particular causal connection by controlling and manipulating the possible cause so as to influence the effect.

Ideally, the experimenter isolates the phenomena he wishes to investigate in a laboratory. Then he abstracts a single variable factor from a complex situation for closer inspection and manipulation. (A variable is a phenomenon which undergoes observable change.) The variable controlled by the investigator is called the independent variable ("a" in Mill's Methods). Manipulating the independent variable will produce a further change in the situation, which will be observed, if possible measured, and recorded. This second factor in the situation which changes is called the dependent variable ("z" in Mill's Methods).

Case Study: Marijuana and Memory

Subjects arriving at a laboratory were apparently all treated in the same way by being given a biscuit, and then by being asked to memorise a list of unrelated words. One week later they returned to the laboratory where, once again, all were treated in the same fashion by being asked to recall those words. Each subject had been treated in exactly the same fashion, except that some had been given biscuits with 5 milligrams of THC, the active ingredient of marijuana, others 10 milligrams, others 15 and others 20 milligrams. Except for the dose of THC, all other conditions were held constant. The dose of THC was thus the independent variable.

Their retention was measured as a percentage of words from the lists recalled. This was the dependent variable. The results showed that retention decreased rapidly with small amounts of THC. It is clear that the taking of marijuana adversely affected efficiency of recall.

It is frequently necessary to preserve a second variable in order to compare it with the main control variable. If, for example, a new medicine is alleged to cure a disease thirty percent of the time, we must make sure that a control population, taking a dummy sugar pill, called a **placebo**, which as far as the subjects know might be the new drug, does not also experience spontaneous remission of the disease thirty percent of the time. This is called a **control experiment**.

It is sometimes difficult to secure conditions under which we can be reasonably certain that the two situations being compared differ in one relevant respect only, so that in practice there can be great difficulties involved in applying this method carefully.

Case Study: Disposing of Spontaneous Generation

Since ancient times men have believed that small creatures are spontaneously created under certain circumstances. In particular, dead bodies were thought to give rise to the worms and flies which seemed inevitably to appear in them.

With the development of empirical science, several experiments were conducted which seemed to confirm this theory. During the seventeenth century, the Belgian Jean-Baptiste Van Helmont covered up a pile of old clothes and wheat for some time, then uncovered it, and discovered it to be crawling with rats. He concluded that old clothes and wheat gave rise spontaneously to rats. Similarly, a German, Athanasius Kircher, made a pile of dead flies covered in honey, and "discovered" that these gave rise to live flies.

An Italian Francesco Redi gathered a collection of animal remains, including dead pigeons and snakes, pieces of veal and the heart of a lamb, and enclosed them in an airtight box, making this a controlled experiment. No grubs, flies or rats appeared, showing that the creatures thought to have been spontaneously generated were lured to the remains rather than generated in them.

Redi's use of Mill's Method of Difference fell upon deaf ears however, since, with the discovery of the microscope, which revealed a hitherto unknown world of tiny creatures, then called animalcules, belief in spontaneous generation received a new lease of life. The British scientist, John Needham, heated a flask of vegetable juice to kill the animalcules in it, poured the juice into a test tube, and let it sit. After a while animalcules could be found in it once more.

The Italian scientist, Lazarro Spallanzani, thought that the animalcules had been introduced in the air, so he repeated the experiment, but sealed the test tube in which the juice was stored after being heated. No animalcules appeared. When Spallanzani declared that he had disproved spontaneous generation, Needham argued that by sealing the test tube he had merely prevented animalcules which would have been generated from breathing. His experiment proved nothing.

The issue was finally settled by French scientist, Louis Pasteur, who repeated the experiment in a flask with a long curved neck, which would keep out the animalcules but allow in some air. When none appeared in the flask, but some showed up at the bottom of the curved part of the neck, it became clear that they were introduced from outside. Spontaneous generation was not happening.

Unfortunately, extraneous influences, known as **uncontrolled variables**, may affect the outcome of an experiment. Thus the researcher has to ensure, as far as possible, that they are excluded. In addition to the convenience of having everything required to hand, this is what laboratories are for. They serve as shields against the intrusion of unwanted extraneous variables in the experimental situation.

However, perfect shielding of an experiment is never entirely possible. Every ordinary laboratory is unshielded from such effects as the earth's magnetic field and cosmic radiation. But all uncontrolled variables which *may* have an effect upon the issue of an experiment are excluded, insofar as these can be identified. The assumption is then made that they have been identified, and that this shielding has been successful, so that all the relevant causal factors except the one under investigation are known and accounted for, and held constant, and so do not affect the outcome of the experiment. Thus Galileo's law of falling bodies discounts the effect of air resistance, and assumes that the bodies are falling in a vacuum. Similarly mechanical laws assume no effects of friction, which would disturb the outcome of forces operating upon moving bodies in the real world, and so disturb the calculation of forces. These qualifications are called **ceteris paribus clauses**.

The Evaluation of Experimental Research

Publication of the results is an essential part of science, since experiments and their results have to be replicated by other workers in the field. Experimental research is systematically subjected to the evaluation of the rest of the international scientific community. This may be by:

- Attempting to repeat the experiment. This is the most important method.
- Assessing the significance of the experiment – exactly what it tells us.
- Assessing the experimenter's honesty.
- Assessing the experimenter's competence.

The assessment of the value and significance of experiments may be a complex and difficult matter. In order for this to be simplified, procedures are standardised and experiments accurately reported.

Case Study: Cold Fusion - Did It Happen or Did It Not?

Nuclear fusion is the process by which the nuclei of hydrogen elements combine to form helium in the interior of the sun, releasing immense amounts of energy. The opposite process to nuclear fission, it could be used to generate nuclear energy without the constant danger of the process spinning out of control. It is generally thought that nuclear fusion will take place only at temperatures as high as those in the interior of the sun. In order to produce such temperatures huge heat-generating machines, called tokamaks, have been constructed at great cost.

Then in 1989 two eminent physicists, Stanley Pons and Martin Fleischmann, announced that they had succeeded in inducing nuclear fusion in their laboratory, merely by passing an electric current through two electrodes in a solution of heavy water.

They claimed they had seen bursts of energy from their apparatus, one of which had burned a four-inch hole in a concrete floor, something which could not be explained simply as a by-product of a chemical reaction. They had also detected nuclear radiation, although not as much as would have been expected under the circumstances.

Instead of following regular procedure and publishing their claims in the scientific press, Pons and Fleischmann called a news conference and announced their discovery to the world. The reaction of the scientific community was mostly sceptical, if not downright hostile.

If Pons and Fleischmann had been successful, they would have discovered a very cheap, pollution-free and safe way of obtaining nuclear energy from seawater. They would certainly be awarded the Nobel prize, and could have expected to become immensely rich through the commercial application of their discovery.

Initially several other laboratories claimed to have achieved the same results themselves. Then they began to explain that these results were due to faulty equipment or mistakes in measurement. According to the physicist Frank Close, in "Too Hot to Handle," there was in fact no evidence of nuclear fusion. Pons and Fleischmann had been mislead by their enthusiasm.

Since then some laboratories claimed to have replicated their original results, although they are not entirely consistent. Most scientists insist that the apparently positive results were due to nothing more than sloppy laboratory work, and that the announcing of the "discovery" was overhasty.

Common Flaws in the Treatment of Evidence

Just there are regular pitfalls in ordinary reasoning, so there are predictable errors which are made in the assessment of scientific evidence.

Subjective Measurement: There are occasions when a study or experiment must rely on the measurement of a subjective experience: such as whether a patient feels better or worse after taking medication. But subjectivity is notorious for introducing errors into results. For this reason scientists seek to eliminate this subjective element as much as possible. It is considered better to measure the effect of a medicine through chemical or physical analysis or other objectively measured symptom than through patient report. It is thought better to count light flashes with a photo-detector than with one's eyes.

Case Study: René Blondlot and N-Rays

At the beginning of the twentieth century the French scientist René Blondlot claimed to have discovered a new ray, which he called the N-ray, after Nancy, the name of the town and university where he lived.

N-rays were allegedly a form of radiation emitted by all substances except green wood and certain treated metals. In 1903, Blondlot claimed he had generated N-rays by placing a hot wire inside an iron tube. The rays were allegedly detected by a calcium sulphide thread, which glowed slightly in the dark when the rays were refracted through a prism of aluminium. According to Blondlot, the N-rays were invisible except when they hit the treated thread. Blondlot moved the thread across the gap where the N-rays were thought to come through and when the thread was illuminated, it was said to be due to N-rays. Dozens of other scientists confirmed the existence of N-rays in this manner in their own laboratories.

"Nature" magazine was sceptical of Blondlot's claims, since laboratories in England and Germany had not been able to replicate his results. So, the physicist Robert W. Wood of Johns Hopkins University as sent to investigate. Wood suspected that N-rays were nothing more than a delusion, so he surreptitiously removed the prism from the N-ray detection device. Without it the machine was not supposed to be able to work. Yet, when Blondlot's assistant conducted the next experiment, he "detected" N-rays. Wood then unobtrusively replaced the prism, but the assistant saw him and thought he was removing it. So the next time Blondlot tried the experiment, the assistant claimed that he could not see any N-rays. But he should have seen them, since the equipment was then in full working order. He had seen N-rays when he should not have seen them, and he did not see them when he should have seen them.

It was clear that the scientists whose work supported Blondlot's conclusions had deceived themselves into thinking they were seeing something, when in fact they were not. They saw what they wanted to see, not what was actually there. Blondlot and his followers suffered from what Martin Gardner calls "self-induced visual hallucinations."

Small Differences: When only minute differences are observed between the test sample and the control sample, the results of an experiment should be regarded with suspicion. Such a result suggests that a different experimental design is called for, or that tighter controls should be enforced, or that other possible hypotheses should be investigated.

Tighter Controls Change the Results: If tightening the controls in an experiment turns a positive outcome into a negative one, it will be likely that the positive results stemmed from phenomena other than the one the experiment was actually designed to detect.

The Force of Negative Results: Negative results count more against a claim than positive results count for it. This is especially true if negative results continue over time, even if they are few in number compared to the positive results. If the phenomenon under investigation is real, those studying it should eventually reach a point where they can reliably demonstrate it to be so.

Non-Experimental Testing

Although it is very important, experiment is not absolutely essential to science. We have already noted that field work is necessary in some sciences. Until recently, experiment was simply not possible at all in astronomy on account of the size and distance in space and time of the phenomena being studied.

Many famous scientists have used non-experimental techniques to advance knowledge. Copernicus and Kepler revolutionised our understanding of the solar system using evidence derived from observations frequently contributed by other scientists, and neither performed experiments. For his most revolutionary discoveries, Charles Darwin recorded his extensive observations in notebooks, adding speculations about them.

In recent years developments in the study of mathematical statistics have provided scientists with a powerful array of techniques which allow them to disentangle the influence of the different variables in a situation without recourse to experiment. The use of computers has made the application of such techniques comparatively easy. Thus, increasingly, studies are being conducted without actual experimentation of the traditional kind, substituting mathematical computer models instead.

When scientific hypotheses cannot be directly tested by experiment or observation at all, scientists readily resort to other criteria of judgement.

- **Consistency with Accepted Theory**: We expect a new hypothesis to be consistent with the general picture we have of the way in which the world works. We are attached to these pictures or paradigms, since what we have previously learned is in some way based upon them. Thus we are right to feel some confidence in them, and right to be reluctant to give them up. Consistency with accepted theory therefore makes a hypothesis more acceptable to us than one which is not.

  When evidence against the truth of an accepted theory begins to build up, as more and more hypotheses inconsistent with the theory begin to find acceptance, then a new theory is sought. However, the old theory is still retained until something better is available to replace it, and this may take some considerable time. It may even continue to be a useful tool when a new hypothesis has replaced it.

- **Fruitfulness**: One hypothesis may have more predictive power than do others. More can be explained by it than by a rival theory. e.g. Newton's Law of Gravity is a very fruitful theory in that it allows us to explain why things fall to the earth, why satellites orbit in space, why we are thrust outwards when we travel round a bend fast, why the tides flow, etc.

- **Simplicity:** If two theories purport to explain the same phenomena, and neither can be tested directly, then the simpler of the two is usually considered preferable. It is a more elegant solution to the problem because it achieves its result more economically. This preference for simplicity is referred to as the application of the **Principle of Parsimony** or **Occam's Razor**. William of Occam (or Ockham) stated, about the process of explanation, that "Entities should not be multiplied beyond necessity." A complicated theory seems a contrived, *ad hoc* attempt to find some formula which will provide a verbal explanation of the phenomena, but which will not actually be true.

There is a catch in this word "simplicity" however. J.B.S. Haldane put it thus:

"It is really an aesthetic canon such as we find implicit in our criticisms of poetry or painting. The layman finds such a law as $dx/dt = K(d^2x/dy^2)$ much less simple than "it oozes," of which it is the mathematical statement. The physicist reverses this judgement, and his statement is certainly the more fruitful of the two, so far as prediction is concerned. It is, however, a statement about something very unfamiliar to the plain man, namely, the rate of change of a rate of change."

Case Study: Ptolemy versus Copernicus

For a thousand years our understanding of astronomy was governed by the picture of the universe provided by the Alexandrian Greek astronomer Ptolemy (c.90-168 AD) in his "Almagest." According to this view, based upon the physics of Aristotle, the earth lay at the centre of the universe, with the sun, moon and known planets moving around it in orbit. The stars were fixed in an outer crystal sphere. This accorded well with our naive intuitions that we are at the centre of things, and that the earth on which we stand is stationary.

There were problems however, on this theory, in accounting for the observed movements of the planets at certain times. But this was provided for by the device of epicycles: smaller circular orbits based upon a notional moving position on the planet's original orbit around the earth. If it was assumed that a planet was moving in epicycles, its position as observed could be satisfactorily accounted for. By the time of Copernicus, seventy-seven such circles were required to explain the movements of the sun, the moon and the five known planets.

Copernicus argued for an alternative, first proposed in ancient times by Aristarchos of Samos, that the sun, rather than the earth, is the centre of the universe, with the earth and other planets orbiting the sun, and the moon orbiting the earth. Copernicus assumed (incorrectly) that the heavenly bodies all moved at a constant rate, and that their orbits formed perfect circles, and so, to account for the observed position of the heavenly bodies, he also had to rely upon epicycles. But his heliocentric hypothesis accounted for the observed positions of the heavenly bodies on the basis of only thirty one such circles.

His theory was considered preferable because he had significantly reduced the need for so many epicycles. Thus he argued for this theory, in part at least, on the basis of its greater simplicity; and it was in part for this reason that his theory received a degree of acceptance.

We have already seen what characteristics a hypothesis must have to function adequately as a scientific hypothesis. In order to be a *good* hypothesis, it must also possess the following features:

- It should be successful in making correct predictions.
- It should provide additional evidence to buttress existing theories.
- It should require fewer auxiliary hypotheses or hypothetical entities to explain any failures to predict successfully than any existing rival hypothesis.
- It should generate new ideas for research.

The Results of Scientific Enquiry

The results of successful scientific work are traditionally called laws and theories.

Scientific laws are generalisations, which encapsulate regularities, principles or patterns found in nature.

The use of the misleading terms "scientific law" or "law of Nature" originated in an analogy with the "law of the land." In ancient times a king issued laws enjoining certain kinds of activities, such as paying taxes, and prohibiting others, such as theft and murder. Since he was a mere human being, however much his subjects were in dread of his power, it was necessary to employ officers to enforce his laws, and courts to punish breaches of them. This concept of law was then projected "into the heavens" by the belief that the gods, or God, also issued laws. Although God was much more powerful than a human monarch, it was still possible for human beings to break God's laws, since it was believed that He had given to mankind the power of free choice.

However, in addition to the commands which God gave to free humans, it was believed that he had also, at the creation, issued commands to everything else in the universe, inanimate and animate. Since these were not endowed with free will, they were in no position to break His commandments, but are obliged to observe them forever.

It was believed that those commands, which God issued to animate and inanimate nature at the creation, can be discovered by observing the regularities of nature in the world around us. Acorns always develop into oak trees and never into elephants, and the moon circles the earth every twenty-eight days and never sixty, because they have been commanded to do so by God, and, lacking free choice, they cannot do otherwise.

Thus the early scientists of the Renaissance, who sought to plot the regularities which underlie the diversity of phenomena, saw themselves as laying bare the laws imposed by God upon his unfree creation, the "Laws of Nature." In doing this work, the early scientists believed that they were laying bare the mind of God.

Today scientists would characterise the laws they seek merely as regularities which underlie the diversity of nature. Scientific laws are no longer thought of as *prescriptive* but as *descriptive*. They do not say how things *must* behave or *ought to* behave, but rather how, as a matter of fact, they actually *do* behave.

Some Scientific Laws

Newton's Third Law of Motion: For every action there is an equal and opposite reaction.

The Law of Conservation of angular momentum: The angular momentum of an object remains constant if there is no external, unbalanced torque acting upon it.

The Second Law of Thermodynamics: The entropy of an isolated system never decreases.

The Law of Conservation of Energy: The total energy of an isolated system remains constant.

Avogadro's Law: Equal volumes of gases contain the same number of molecules under the same conditions of temperature and pressure.

Mendel's Law: Every inherited characteristic is controlled by a pair of factors, of which only one can be represented in the germ cell.

By contrast with laws, **scientific theories** aim to be *explanatory*. They are wide ranging hypotheses, which purport to provide explanations of all the laws in some particular field in terms of some single over-arching principle or mechanism. Thus Darwin's Theory of Evolution explains the evolution and diversity of the various forms of living beings in terms of natural selection and the survival of the fittest.

Flaws in Theory

Failure to Develop: Theoretical knowledge should develop as experience increases. In the 1960s molecular biologists were able to make only vague claims about the role of DNA in guiding the development of organisms. Today this process can be explained in some detail; the explanations being backed up by reference to the results of countless of experiments.

Evasive Predictions: As experimental and theoretical work progresses, more sound evidence for the phenomena the theory predicts should be gathered. If the phenomena predicted by a theory remain in doubt as research progresses, then the theory itself should be regarded as suspect.

Failure to Consider Alternatives: Often the results claimed for a novel theory are accounted for equally well by existing well-founded theories. Those alternative explanations need to be investigated first, and the effect of their operation barred by stringent controls in future experiments.

How to Evaluate Scientific Research

We need to consider the researchers:

- Do they have the expertise required to conduct the research?
- Do they, or their sponsors, have any personal stake or bias in the outcome of their research?
- Are they honest?

The hypothesis:

- Is it empirically falsifiable in principle?
- Is it precisely formulated?

The experimental procedure:

- Is it adequate? Have the variables been properly separated. Has a control been used if appropriate? Have uncontrolled variables been properly excluded?
- Is sufficient data considered?
- Is the data what it seems?
- Has there been a real debate on the significance of the evidence?
- Would the procedure employed by the researchers allow the hypothesis to be falsified in practice?

The Results:

- Are the results firmly based upon the data?
- Are there any fallacies in the reasoning (e.g. confusion of correlation with causation)?
- Is there independent confirmation of the results? Have other researchers independently duplicated the experiments and obtained the same results?
- Would other explanations account for the data equally well?
- Are the results consistent with established scientific theories?

---

3. The Scientific Method

It is clear that in the process of "doing science" scientists actually do many different things: making observations, advancing speculations, conducting experiments, taking measurements, drawing conclusions, publicising their findings, etc. None of these activities is unique to science. These are all things which we do in everyday life in appropriate contexts. The presence of no single one of them explains, of itself, the success and prestige of science, or justifies the claim that science provides especially reliable knowledge.

Traditionally therefore, science has been thought to excel on account of some special overall "Scientific Method" which is used to attain to truth which incorporates and employs all the various activities we have considered in some single master plan. But exactly what that this method consists of is a subject of controversy.

Science as Generalisation from Facts

The common view of science among those who are neither scientists nor philosophers, and one generally held by everybody as late as the nineteenth century, is called the **inductivist** account. In his book, *Novum Organum* (1620), Francis Bacon advised that facts be collected and assimilated without bias to reach a conclusion, using the method of generalisation, or induction, as a basis from which future predictions could be made. This approach was most fully set out in John Stuart Mill's *System of Logic*.

Science is said to begin with the unprejudiced observations of individuals. These are expressed in the form of singular statements:

(1)   The water in my beaker at sea level boiled at a temperature of 100^0C.

On the basis of what is observed, expressed in a large number of singular observation statements, a **hypothesis** or provisional generalisation is proposed; so that out of an apparently disorderly mass of facts a general statement or **scientific law** which reveals the order underlying the apparent variety of phenomena will emerge. These generalisations result in universal statements:

(2)   Water at sea level boils at a temperature of 100^0C.

Such generalisations involve inferences of the form known as induction by simple enumeration. To be considered acceptable, such generalisations must conform to the following conditions:

- There must be a large number of observation statements upon which to base a generalisation.
- The observations must have taken place under a wide variety of conditions.
- No observations which conflict with the generalisation must have been made.

Using these hypotheses, scientists are able to make predictions that under certain conditions, certain phenomena will occur.

(3)   Water at sea level boils at a temperature of 100^0C.

   The water in this beaker, which is at sea level, is to be heated to a temperature of 100^0C.

   Therefore, the water in this beaker will boil.

The first premise states the hypothesis. This, taken together with the initial conditions expressed in the second premise, enable the deduction of the proposition asserting the predicted phenomena. Such predictions are used to test the hypothesis.

After some period of during which it is tested by many scientists across the world, such a hypothesis comes to be considered confirmed, and is regarded as a scientific law. Several scientific laws, discovered in this manner, may themselves be gathered together and related to each other under wider generalisations known as theories.

The law (or theory), together with the conditions which assert its application to particular circumstances, allow us to deduce the particular operation of the law predicted. In this way, laws and theories are said to *explain* phenomena.

Thus scientific predictions and explanations take the form:

Law or theory

Particular conditions

Explanation

This is called the **covering-law model** of explanation:

These laws and theories, once discovered and confirmed by repeated observations, are definitively and finally established as true.

Science is said to proceed incrementally, building up data arrived at by observation and experiment from which to generalise to laws, and building up laws to generalise to theories. The future task of science is to discover further laws, and subsume the laws already known under further laws of yet wider application. The ideal is to gather and relate together in this way all significant general knowledge about the universe in laws, and related these to each other under theories. Thus scientists can look forward to a day when a comprehensive body of knowledge will be accumulated which may be used to settle all disputes. Unfortunately, there are several acute problems with this interpretation of scientific method.

The value of scientific knowledge is held to lie precisely in its grounding in individual sense experience. Yet in generalising beyond individual experience, scientific reasoning would appear to make claims which are necessarily beyond the evidence. As we have already seen, inductive reasoning involves making a leap beyond the evidence available to a conclusion which asserts more than the premises will sustain, since by moving from the particular to the general, or from the less general to the more general, we make claims which go beyond our available evidence. For this reason, the evidence presented in the premises of inductive arguments is always inadequate to support their conclusions. For no matter how many instances have been observed in the past, and under how great a variety of circumstances, it always remains possible that the next instance will turn out to be different. This is known as the **Problem of Induction**.

One attempt to evade this problem was by appealing to a general principle to the effect that nature always behaves in a uniform manner. This is known as the **Principle of the Uniformity of Nature**. It may be used as a premise in a valid deductive argument in which the other premise asserts our experience of the past, while the conclusion is that that experience will be continued in the same way in the future. Thus:

(4)   Nature always behaves in a uniform manner.
        We have always observed water to boil at 100^0C at sea level.
        Therefore, We shall continue to observe water to boil at 100^0C at sea level.

The problem with this approach is that we will need to justify the assertion that nature always acts in a uniform manner. The fact that laws are successfully used to make predictions suggests as much. But we could only arrive at such a conclusion either after observing the whole of nature, or by making a series of generalisations from our experience. The former alternative is not possible, so the truth of the Principle of the Uniformity of Nature could only be established on the basis of inductive arguments. But as the philosopher David Hume pointed out, we cannot use a conclusion based upon inductive arguments to justify the practice of employing inductive arguments, since that would involve a vicious circle in our reasoning.

No inductive generalisation can be finally confirmed, and no inductive argument leads to conclusions which are other than probable. Although confirmatory evidence, evidence which supports a generalisation, is never sufficient to provide is with a conclusion which is immune from being overturned in the future, it may confer some greater degree of probability upon the conclusion. In this case scientific reasoning can be summed up as having the form:

(5) If large numbers of instances of x have the property Φ under a wide variety of conditions, and if no instances of x failing to have the property Φ have been observed, then all xs probably have the property Φ.

However, this is not much help in science, where we require justification of our claim to knowledge of the truth of universal statements.

There are also other problems concerning the vagueness of the process of confirmation of scientific laws. It is not clear how many observations are required, or over how wide a range of varying circumstances, to justify resting on our conclusion.

But there is worse to come. The strength of science was thought to lie in the fact that it was squarely based upon objective observations of the world, made by unbiased people, which could be checked. The philosopher Karl Popper pointed out that there are no observations unbiased by any theory at all. As we have already seen, observation always takes place against the background of our desires, intentions, beliefs, hopes, and expectations. We always contribute something to what we see.

This means that the scientist always makes his observations against the background of existing theories, even if these are merely those which lie embedded in the "common sense view of the world" generally accepted within our society. For example, early scientists investigating the properties of electricity reported that electrically charged rods became "sticky." This was because, as *we* should say, they were observed to attract pieces of paper and fluff to themselves. Scientific observations are inevitably influenced and guided by, and interpreted in the light of, existing theories. These theories will determine which of the many factors in the situation will be attended to and which will be ignored.

Thus scientific observations do not have the theory-free objectivity attributed to them in this account

Science as Conjectures and Refutations

The traditional view of the scientific method was criticised by Karl Popper in *The Logic of Scientific Discovery*. There, he proposed an alternative account of what happens when scientists are typically doing science.

He was heavily influenced by the belief that there are no pure, theory-free observations. All observation is theory-laden. This can be seen in the difficulty involved in trying to construct a **crucial experiment** to test which of to rival hypotheses is the better one. Since experiments cannot be disentangled from the theoretical preconceptions of those who perform them and interpret their results, it is usually possible for a scientist to interpret an experiment in different ways, depending upon the theoretical background he brings to it.

Case Study: Priestley versus Lavoisier

During the 1770s, both Joseph Priestly and Anton Lavoisier heated various metallic ores in closed containers. Both realised that the effect of this was to change the

---

characteristics of the air immediately above the ore. Things would burn in it rather better than usual.

Priestly interpreted what he saw it terms of the accepted theory of the time. Combustion and respiration were then generally explained by appeal to the behaviour of an invisible substance called "phlogiston." Ordinary air was thought to become saturated with phlogiston when it could no longer support life or combustion. So Priestley explained the results of his experiment by saying that phlogiston had moved out of the air and into the ore, leaving the air "dephlogistonated" and so better able to support combustion.

Lavoisier looked at what happened in a totally different way. He concluded that the ore, which he later called an oxide, gave off a new substance upon which the process of combustion depended. He called this new "oxygen."

Acknowledging that positive proof in science is simply unattainable, Popper portrays instead a process of trial and error. Scientific hypotheses are tentative solutions to problems, which are then subjected to a process of rigorous testing, which weeds out any which are then shown to be false, so that they can be replaced with better hypotheses.

Popper attacked the idea that a scientific conclusion could be established by a process of verification. One problem is that if we are convinced of the truth of a hypothesis, verification is easy to find, although it may not be worth very much.

"Once your eyes were . . . opened you saw confirming instances everywhere: the world was full of verifications of the theory. Whatever happened always confirmed it. Thus its truth appeared manifest; and unbelievers were clearly people who did not want the manifest truth; who refused to see it... ."

This is because "Observations, and even more so observational statements and statements of experimental results are always *interpretations* of the facts observed . . . *in the light of theories*." Thus Priestley simply interpreted the results of his experiment in terms of the theory to which he was already committed. Popper continued: "This is one of the main reasons why it is always deceptively easy to find *verifications* of a theory, and why we have to adopt a highly critical attitude towards our theories if we do not wish to argue in circles: the attitude of trying to falsify them." He added what we have already considered, that no amount of cases of x being P could ever establish that all x's are P. Because of the nature of induction, such universal statements are impossible to establish conclusively.

The process of testing, he argued, should not be seen as designed to pile up support for a hypothesis, but rather to find evidence which counts *against* it, evidence which would *falsify* it. Although it is impossible to amass sufficient evidence to support a universal empirical claim, he pointed out that it is often possible conclusively to establish that such a claim is *not* true. This is because, although in principle universal statements are not provable, they are easily disprovable by a single contradictory instance. Thus the proper object of the testing procedures of science should be to aim to disprove the hypothesis being tested rather than to establish it, i.e., it should be directed towards **falsification** rather than confirmation. Scientific investigation should be focused upon a search for negative instances which disprove the hypothesis being tested.

If the attempted refutation succeeds, then we should discard the hypothesis for a new one. If it does not, we adopt the hypothesis provisionally, i.e. until something even better comes along, that is, until such time as it is falsified; although the longer a hypothesis survives attempts to falsify it, the more **corroboration** it is said to have.

Popper calls this, "the critical method of error elimination." Far from being certain, scientific theories are merely provisional. They have such force as they have only until something better comes along; and the scientist always aims to replace existing theories with better ones.

In practice, falsification is not usually a simple or straightforward process. This is because our beliefs tend to be related to each other in networks. Any hypothesis we may wish to test will never stand entirely alone, but will be accompanied by other hypotheses which we will tend to take for granted.

For example, the hypothesis that the earth is flat could be falsified if, from the top of a cliff, we could see a ship disappear in the distance from the bottom upwards over the horizon, rather than gradually fade from view in the distance as a whole. This is what we do see, so that its mast or funnels is the last thing to disappear from view. But attempting to falsify the hypothesis that the earth is flat in this way assumes the truth of certain *other* hypotheses, such as that light always travels in straight lines; for if light rays bend over a few kilometres, that might itself explain the phenomenon of the ship disappearing from the base upwards. We always inevitably test auxiliary hypotheses along with the particular hypothesis we wish to test, so we can never be sure that we have falsified the hypothesis itself. This problem is known as **Duhem's Irrefutability Thesis**.

Popper himself admitted: " . . . no conclusive disproof of a theory can ever be produced; for it is always possible to say that the experimental results are not reliable, or that the discrepancies which are asserted to exist between the experimental result and the theory are only apparent and that they will disappear with the advance of our understanding."

Several stratagems are available for avoiding immediate falsification of a hypothesis in the face of contradictory evidence:

- We may refuse to accept the reliability of inconvenient experimental results. A single contradictory observation is logically powerful enough to overthrow any hypothesis. But in practice it is better to wait and see if it is followed by other observations which support it before discarding the hypothesis. It may be that the first observation was due to an error of some kind.

- We may refuse to accept that the observations which seem to contradict the hypothesis really do have that force, and seek some manner of reconciling them.

- We may introduce *ad hoc* amendments to our hypothesis in order to preserve it from falsification. *Ad hoc* amendments are modifications of the hypothesis designed merely in order to evade the problem of falsification. They themselves throw light upon nothing.

Case Study: Galileo and the Mountains of the Moon

According to Aristotle, the heavenly bodies should be perfect spheres. However Galileo's observations of the moon revealed what were clearly irregularities on its surface: mountains, craters and plains. It would appear that Aristotle's theory had simply been falsified by Galileo's observations.

A defender of the traditional theory, however, proposed to save it by arguing that the observed surface of the moon was enveloped in an invisible substance which filled in all the craters and covered all the plains to a height equal to or greater than the highest mountain peak. The surface of this invisible substance was the true surface of the moon, and it was perfectly symmetrical. Therefore, the moon, contrary to appearances, was a perfect sphere after all.

This idea of an invisible substance was manufactured only to avoid the falsification of Aristotle's theory by Galileo's observations. It served no other purpose, and was of no other use. It was entirely "ad hoc," and for that reason, unacceptable.

Galileo's response was to agree that the moon was covered by an invisible substance, but to argue that it was distributed equally over the moon's surface, so that the mountain peaks were raised over the plains by the same height as had been thought on the basis of observation. This response was offered in a jocular spirit, but it illustrates clearly the dangers of ad hoc modifications of theories to preserve them from falsification.

Popper calls modifications of a hypothesis designed to protect it **immunising stratagems**. Not all immunising stratagems are *ad hoc* modifications. Some are independently testable. As such they may be acceptable as improvements of the original hypothesis, making it a more sophisticated and powerful theory.

In addition to proposing falsification as a strategy for testing scientific hypotheses, he also proposed that the possibility of empirical falsification in principle be regarded as a necessary characteristic of any scientific theory. This is because it shows the hypothesis to be genuinely empirical. If there is something which someone could experience, which, if it actually happened, would prove a theory false, than that theory is a genuinely empirical theory. It genuinely says something about the world around us, and is not an empty, merely verbal claim. If there is no state of affairs, such that if it occurred, the hypothesis would be shown to be false, then its immunity from falsification shows it not to be a genuinely empirical hypothesis at all.

Case Study: Philip Gosse and the Past Which Never Was

Philip Henry Gosse was a leading naturalist of the late nineteenth century. As such, he was very much aware of the evidence being assembled by geologists for the gradual evolution of the earth's surface over a vast period of time, and of the fossil evidence which pointed to the gradual evolution of living things over a large time scale. At the same time he was a deeply religious man, committed to the literal truth of the Bible, and to the belief that the world had been created during six days in 4004 BC. He attempted to reconcile his beliefs with his observations by explaining the latter as (false) evidence of a fictitious past produced by God during the process of creation.

In his "Omphalos" he argued that everything which we experience in nature is cyclic. The question "Which came first, the chicken or the egg?" is an unanswerable one because the existence of a egg requires a chicken to have laid it, while the existence of a chicken requires that of an egg from which it came. Eggs do not make sense without chickens, and chickens do not make sense without eggs. In principle, you can not have one without the other. When God chose to create the world, he had to break into this, and other, natural cycles at some point, in order to bring both chickens and eggs into being. But at whichever point he did this, from that point the rest of the cycle might be inferred. Everything God created was thus necessarily created with traces of a past which had not actually occurred.

This seemed to throw light upon a burning controversy which had long excited some of the most brilliant minds of previous centuries, as to whether Adam, according to Scripture the first man, did or did not have a navel. Since he had been created by God, he had not been born of a woman; yet he could hardly be said to be a genuine man without a navel. According to Gosse, although Adam had never been carried in a womb, and therefore had never been nourished by means of an umbilical chord, he would have carried the remains of one in the form of a navel from the very first moment of his creation, just as though he had been born of a woman.

In just the same way, at the moment of creation there instantaneously sprang into being igneous rocks formed by volcanoes which had never erupted, and layers of sedimentary rock which had never actually been laid down as sediment, which contained fossils of plants and animals which had never lived or died. According to Gosse, the world had been created by God during a very brief period of time, but it had been created together with traces of a long history which had never actually taken place.

There are many problems with this hypothesis, but the most important is that if it were false, there would be absolutely no way of detecting it. All the appearances of past ages could simply be explained away by asserting that they had been created by God at the moment of creation. Thus Gosse would not have been at all embarrassed by the modern evidence of residual traces of the Big Bang in the form of background radiation. He would simply have said that it was all thoughtfully laid down by God at the creation in order to give the appearance of some long previous cosmic explosion. But a hypothesis which cannot be tested is, for that very reason, useless as a contribution to empirical study like science, which purports to provide knowledge of what the world is actually like.

Discussion: Which of the following propositions are empirically falsifiable?

1. The dry cleaners are closed on Saturdays.
2. President Chirac is Head of the French State.
3. Either it is snowing or it is not snowing.
4. Five added to five makes ten.
5. Dogs are fond of bones.

There would appear to be two major problems with a falsificationist approach to science. The model assumes that there is a simple "one cause - one effect" situation to be considered. But usually most phenomena are caused by the coming together of a number of variables, so that simple hypotheses would almost always be falsified due to some failure of the presence of relevant variables. Thus if Popper's standard of falsification had been applied in a simple manner, many well-established theories would never have been accepted. Newton's Theory of Gravity would never have survived discrepancies in the orbits of the moon or Uranus. They did, which suggests that Popper's paradigm of the scientific method is not the one which correctly describes scientific practice.

Scientific Advance as Intellectual Revolution

T. S. Kuhn has argued in *The Structure of Scientific Revolutions* that neither the traditional nor the falsificationalist views of the scientific method account for the radical discontinuities which are such a prominent feature of the history of science.

He has argued that scientific theories are patterns or **paradigms,** which, like Gestalts, dominate our perceptions of reality. They are not so much created *out of* the facts as they give meaning *to* the facts. All genuine scientific thinking operates within such paradigms or theoretical frameworks. The paradigms are "universally recognised scientific achievements that for a time provide model problems and solutions to a community of practitioners."

Where no paradigm has been created to bind together in a single perspective the various problems and data of a field of study, then Kuhn says that no true science yet exists. Such a field is in a state which he calls **pre-science**.

When a wide-ranging theory is proposed which unifies all the elements in the field, which explains the facts known to date, and which solves the problems currently troubling experts, then a true science has come into being. He has in mind such theories as that of Newton in Physics and Darwin in biology. These function as paradigms, determining what counts as a problem in that branch of science and what does not; what can count as a hypothetical solution to a problem and what can not; what can count as evidence for such a hypothesis and what can not.

For long periods of time scientists operate entirely within, or from the standpoint of, a given paradigm, by solving puzzles while working within the terms of existing theories. The paradigm determines what count as problems, and the parameters for solving them (i.e. what it is permissible to do towards solving them and what would count towards solving them). During this period, scientists assume the truth of the paradigm and seek to determine its implications. This state of affairs he calls **normal science**.

However, over a period of time, anomalies which the existing paradigm is unable to explain build up. Moreover the accepted paradigm begins to lose its capacity to generate new problems for the scientists to solve, so that scientists find working within it increasingly restrictive and uncomfortable. This gradually builds up to a crisis or breakdown of confidence in the paradigm. These comparatively brief periods, Kuhn calls periods of **extraordinary science**.

Eventually a new paradigm emerges which is powerful enough to explain everything previously explained by the previous paradigm, and which will also dispose of the anomalies. It comes to replace the existing paradigm, setting new parameters for determining what counts as a problem; what can count as an acceptable hypothesis; and what can count as evidence for such a hypothesis. Moreover, the new paradigm fruitfully generates new puzzles for the scientists to solve. This paradigm shift, Kuhn terms a **scientific revolution**.

During a scientific revolution, the existing paradigms are rejected for an alternative paradigm which presents a new *Gestalt*. A new pattern is adopted in preference to the old one.

Case Study: Three Theories and Two Revolutions

According to Aristotle there are four terrestrial elements or forms of matter, earth, water, air, and fire, each has a "proper" place in the universe where it is naturally found, and to which it would naturally tend to return if it were not already there unless hindered in some way. The natural place for earth is in the centre of the universe, i.e. at the centre of the earth, and earthy things tend to travel there (i.e. downwards relative to ourselves). The

---

place of water is above this, on the surface of the earth, where watery things naturally gather. The airy region lies above both; while fire naturally tends (upwards) towards the outer part of the universe.

The "natural" situation for every body is to be at rest in its proper place in the universe. If that is the case, or if a body is moving towards its proper place, then no other explanation of its movement is necessary, (although in the latter case we need to explain why that body was previously out of its proper place). It follows that if a body is at rest in some other part of the universe, we need to find an explanation for what is preventing it from returning to its proper place (falling to earth). Any motion of a body which does not tend directly towards its proper place in the universe is also in need of explanation.

Everything is made up of different combinations of these elements in different proportions. The more earth a body has the heavier it is, and the more urgently it will tend towards the centre of the universe, i.e. the faster it will fall).

This theory of Aristotle's dominated physics until modern times. It took Galileo Galilei to demonstrate by experiment that in fact heavier objects do not fall faster than light objects (excluding the effect of air resistance, which delays the fall of a feather proportionally more than that of spherical lead shot). This showed that there was something wrong with Aristotle's theory. Important predictions from the theory are not borne out by experience. Following this development many new laws concerning the motions of bodies were formulated, such as Kepler's three Laws of Planetary Motion. These described in compact form all the motions of planetary bodies, and enabled predictions of their observable behaviour to be made, but they did not in any way explain them. They were merely generalisations about what happens, not explanations of why it happens. They help us to "map" the world, but not really to understand it.

It was Isaac Newton who was able to provide a single over-arching framework into which these laws, and many others, could be fitted, and which would explain them, i.e. allow us to make sense of them, with his Theory of Gravity. Newton saw that all the scientific knowledge of his time concerning the motion of bodies could be explained in terms of the operation of a single force - gravity.

This theory was vindicated by the success of its predictions. When it was observed that the path of the planet Uranus deviated slightly from that predicted in Newton's theory, it appeared that this might be evidence that the theory was untrue. But then Leverrier calculated that the apparent discrepancies could be explained by the existence of another planet with an orbit outside that of Uranus, which exerted a pull upon the former planet. The discovery of the planet Neptune by Galle, who focused his telescope upon the region of the sky suggested by Leverrier, spectacularly confirmed the reliability of Newton's theory. Distant double stars, unimagined by Newton himself, move predictably according to his theory.

Up to the beginning of the present century Newton's Theory of Gravity was universally regarded as the ideal scientific theory. It was the paradigm case of what a good scientific theory should be, and therefore it was a paradigm of scientific knowledge. Other scientific theories could be disparaged insofar as they failed to achieve comparable predictive value and explanatory capacity in their own fields, and valued insofar as they approached the Newtonian model. Truly it seemed that: "Nature and natures laws lay hid in night; God said: "Let Newton be," and all was light."

It was easy to think that Newton had overthrown the old Aristotelian theory of matter for the simple reason that his Theory of Gravity was true and could be shown to be true in a hundred thousand applications. It accorded with common sense and provided a framework for the mechanistic understanding of the universe which was dominant in scientific thought. Thus it was believed that we could rest content that whatever else developed in science Newton's theory would still hold firm. Newton's Theory of Gravity displayed, more than any other, what was best about scientific knowledge, its immutable objective certainty.

Yet by the end of the nineteenth century it was becoming clearer that there were problems even with this theory. There were certain oddities about gravity. Unlike all other radiant forces known at that time it seemed to act instantaneously, and unlike all other forces no barrier to it could apparently have any effectiveness. Light acts only at 186,000 miles per second. The light acting upon the earth left the surface of the sun some eight minutes ago. The same is true of all other forms of radiant energy. There are substances which stop the passage of heat, light, x-rays, electricity, etc., but nothing acts as a barrier to gravity. If it did, we should have a marvellous means of almost energy-free locomotion useful for many purposes from moving very heavy objects to saving people who fall off cliffs to space travel.

The planet Mercury, like Uranus, did not quite behave as Newton's theory predicted. Leverrier, who had prompted the discovery of Neptune under similar circumstances, naturally proposed a further planet within the orbit of Mercury, the gravitational pull of which would account for the discrepancy in its orbit. This hypothetical planet was sought for, and was even confidently given the name Vulcan. Several observers claimed to have spotted it at various times, but their observations could never be replicated. They might have confused sunspots with what they were seeking. The planet Vulcan never turned up.

During the first decade of the present century Albert Einstein proposed an alternative theory which made sense of the dimensions of space and time in terms of Reimannian geometry. He considered space and time not as independent realities, but as related dimensions of a four dimensional universe. Gravity was no longer thought of as a force. A four-dimensional universe which is governed by Riemannian geometry will exhibit a form of curvature in the neighbourhood of matter. The perceived effect of this is what we call gravity. The planets do not move in the way that they do because of the force of gravity acting upon them, but because, in Reimannian space, they are moving in what is for them a straight line. They are following the path most "natural" to them.

The new theory explained everything explained by the theory it replaced. In addition, it threw light upon the problems associated with the older theory. Thus it accounts exactly for the observed path of the planet Mercury, and makes it clear why the hypothetical planet Vulcan was never discovered. It explains why no barriers can be erected against the force of gravity, since gravity is not a force but a dimension of space.

This theory , like that of Newton before, has been spectacularly confirmed by observation. Einstein predicted that during an eclipse of the sun light from distant stars would be deflected as they passed the sun to the extent that stars which should have been blocked out by the sun's mass would be visible. This was confirmed by the Royal Astronomical Society during a solar eclipse in 1919. The theory suggested that atoms in an intense gravitational field would vibrate more slowly than normal, and hence predicted that atoms on the sun would vibrate more slowly than atoms on earth. This would be shown by a shift of the light from such bodies towards the red end of the spectrum of visible light. In 1925, W. S. Adams was able to confirm the presence of a shift towards the red end of the spectrum in their spectral lines. Other confirmation has followed.

A Synthesis

No single account of the scientific method has so far provided an adequate account of the complexity and diversity of what scientists actually do. Imré Lakatos has tried to explain why it is that scientists seem sometimes to behave as Kuhn suggests and sometimes as Popper suggests. He argues that the **research program** within which scientists work at any given period is made up of a "hard core" of basic assumptions together with a "protective belt" of auxiliary statements or hypotheses. The two are made up of radically different kinds of scientific theories: **programmatic theories** and **subsidiary hypotheses**. The programmatic theories, which constitute the hard core, are fundamental, wide-ranging theories which behave like Kuhnian paradigms. They provide a framework for subsidiary hypotheses, which purport to explain how the programmatic theory works out in practice. These subsidiary hypotheses may be treated in accordance with Popper's account, although in practice attempts at confirmation tend to be more important than falsification.

Lakatos recommends that Popper's falsificationism should be understood as not directed so much at trying to prove hypotheses false, as seeking to establish the limits of their applicability, by determining those points at which the hypotheses no longer work.

Talking Point: Risk and Advance in Science

Some conjectures are more risky and daring than others, given the state of background knowledge at the time. A. F. Chalmers points out that science advances with the confirmation of bold conjectures and the falsification of cautious conjectures; not the other way around. The falsification of a bold conjecture merely shows that another crackpot idea will not ride; while the confirmation of a cautious conjecture shows that an unproblematic idea has been unproblematically applied once more. A bold conjecture confirmed makes it likely that an idea considered improbable will establish some new discovery; while a cautious conjecture falsified shows that things are not as we had imagined them to be.

Talking Point: Do scientists deal with the Real World, or an Ideal World?

When the geometer draws diagrams of circlesand triangles in order to illustrate his proofs, he is not really dealing with ordinary visible circles and triangles, which not only do not have the properties he ascribes to circles and triangles but which, in the strict sense of his terms, are not circles and triangles at all. The mathematician deals with an ideal world. Does the employment of laboratories, and the use of *ceteris paribus* clauses, show that the descriptions of scientists are as ideal, and therefore as unreal, as those of the geometers? Do scientists also deal with an ideal world?

Is there a Scientific Method at all?

The controversy over the nature of the scientific method has led to many insights into the way in which scientists have actually behaved, but it has not resulted in any paradigm of scientific method which is applicable to all scientific enquiry. The history of science shows that none of the paradigms of the scientific method fits all cases of advance in science. Moreover, by confusing the quest to discover what scientists *actually* do with laying down a pattern which all scientists *ought* to follow, the search for *the* scientific method has confused the issue. In consequence, some philosophers and scientists have stated that there is no distinctive scientific method at all. They have argued that the idea that science can, and should, be run according to fixed and universal rules, is unrealistic. It takes too simple a view of the processes of scientific investigation, and too narrow a view of the ingenuity of the investigators.

One of the reasons for the widespread belief in a general scientific method may be the way in which results are presented for publication in research journals. The standardised style universally followed makes it *appear* that scientists follow a standard research procedure. For this reason, Sir Peter Medawar called the scientific paper a fraud, since a final journal report rarely outlines the actual way in which the problem was investigated. In his Nobel Lecture (1966) Richard Feynman observed: "We have a habit in writing articles published in scientific journals to make the work as finished as possible, to cover up all the tracks, to not worry about the blind alleys or describe how you had the wrong idea first, and so on. So there isn't any place to publish, in a dignified manner, what you actually did in order to get to do the work."

Some philosophers who have studied scientists at work have come to the conclusion that no research method is applied universally. Instead, scientists approach and solve problems in the same way in which we all do: using imagination, prior knowledge and hard work. However, they self-consciously seek academic respectability for their procedures.

4. The Reliability of Scientific Knowledge

For Karl Popper, this overthrow of Newton's Theory in favour of Einstein's is the most illuminating development in the history of science if we wish to understand what science is. Newton's theory had been the most adequate and successful of scientific theories in history. It allowed the most detailed and precise predictions of future events. No theory in science could claim to have been more firmly established. Then along came Einstein's theory, which explained everything which Newton's theory explained, and more besides, and did so employing a radically different picture of reality from that of Newton's theory. According to this new theory, there is not (and never was) any force of gravity; instead gravity is an aspect of the four-dimensional Reimannian space-time continuum. If Einstein's account of reality is *true*, it follows inexorably that Newton's was false. And it had been false during all that period when it had been thought to be the most prestigious, most reliable, most accurately *true* scientific theory. And it remains false even though, for many practical purposes, we can still behave *as though* Newton's Theory were true when making predictions: " . . . it means that we were mistaken about scientific knowledge; that scientific theories always remain hypothetical; that it was always possible even for the best established scientific theory, to be superseded by a better one."

It seems to follow from this that:

- We are never entitled to say that a scientific theory is the final truth.
- Scientific theories are merely **provisional**. At best, they are simply the best thing we have until something better comes along. However well-established they may appear to be, they are

always liable to be overthrown in favour of a better theory which may describe the world in terms incompatible with the former theory.

- Scientific theories are never certain. "Scientific knowledge is a body of statements of varying degrees of certainty - some most unsure, some nearly sure, none *absolutely* certain." (Richard Feynman)

The reasons for this are:

- Scientific observations are subject to all the limitations of human observation in general. Those dependent upon instruments are further subject to the truth of the theory which the use of the instruments presupposes.
- Limitations of the methods used may influence the results.
- Universal conclusions based upon limited, and always incomplete, evidence are always subject to the possibility of revision in the face of future counter-evidence.
- We can never predict the future with total certainty, since the slightest imperfection in our understanding of initial conditions will affect the outcome in unpredictable ways.
- There may be ultimate limitations upon our powers of observation and understanding which will ensure that reality remains forever beyond our total grasp. This is suggested by the Heisenberg Uncertainty Principle.

  "Science is the attempt to make the chaotic diversity of our sense-experience correspond to a logically uniform system of thought ... . The sense- experiences are the given subject-matter. But the theory that shall interpret them is man-made ... hypothetical, never completely final, always subject to question and doubt." (Albert Einstein)

Popper argues that scientific theories do not simply correspond to the truth or fail to do so, they should be thought of as having **verisimilitude**, the property of approximating more or less closely to the truth in terms of their consequences. Scientific theories are all partial truths. Truth, in the sense of correspondence with reality, is an ideal which they will approach but never quite attain. A theory has only an approximation to the truth, or verisimilitude. What is sought in new theories is greater verisimilitude than the currently accepted theory.

We should think of a scientific truth as a picture of reality being brought into ever-greater focus. In its initial stages, when we see through a great fog, we may have radically to revise our perceptions of what this picture is telling us, as with visual illusions. In time it will become clearer.

Scientific knowledge is also limited in that it never deals with the full truth about anything.

- Scientific knowledge is *modular*. Scientists slice up complex phenomena into separate modules and deal with each separately. This leads to different types of explanation being offered of the same phenomena. Thus biologists might offer explanations of the human lungs in terms of:
  - their structure: how they work;
  - their function: what they does for the body, e.g. in taking oxygen into the blood-supply;
  - in terms of their development from cells in the sperm and egg;
  - their development by evolution in the species.

(These are known as "Tinbergen's Four Why's." Today each one constitutes a distinct discipline within biology.)

- Scientific knowledge is *abstract*. Typically, scientific explanations function by subsuming the less general under a more general law. This inevitably involves a process of reduction.

Unfortunately, it is easy to pass illegitimately from "*x* is scientifically explicable in terms of *y*" to "*x* is nothing more than *y*"; e.g. From "Beethoven's *Ninth Symphony* is explicable by physicists as a series of complex vibrations of the air" to "Beethoven's *Ninth Symphony* is nothing more than vibrations of the air"; from "Human thought is explicable in terms of stimulation of neurones" to "human thought is nothing more than the stimulation of neurones."

This leads to a form of reductionism exemplified by such unjustified claims as that only scientific explanations of the world have validity, and that if science cannot deal with something, then in some way it is not fully real.

Science and Ideology

Scientific thinking not only aims at academic respectability, it has been most successful in achieving that status. Thus scientific thinking should exclude dogmatic and ideological approaches to knowledge. However, sometimes ideology slips in, and when it does so, it is doubly dangerous, since it is ideology in disguise, which carries with it the respectability and authority of science.

Scientism

Paul Feyerabend argued that science has an ideological character, like a religion. There is an orthodoxy or "true faith" which scientists must accept and conform to, or be branded as heretics, mavericks or cranks. Ideas are rejected out of hand if they do not fit in with accepted dogma. Yet, he argues, science is no more privileged than any other discipline to claim that it is the way to the truth. It is on a level with astrology, witchcraft and traditional medicine. The claim he makes is that science is just another "belief system" enforced by dogmatism and social conditioning. It is just another ideology.

It could be argued, however, that this view fails to take account of the way in which hypotheses are systematically tested against experience in science, and in the end stand or fall on their own merits. Science is a self-correcting process. It has a public self-correcting machinery built into it in a fundamental way, which makes it different from dogmatic belief systems, in particular, the requirement for the independent repetition of experiments.

Also, science works; and does so in a unique way. To take an example from the very beginnings of science: it can be used to predict when there is going to be an eclipse of the sun, today it can do so for a thousand years in the future and with an accuracy better than to the nearest minute. In this sense, science demonstrably works better than anything else does. Newton-Smith points out that "lazing in the sun reading astrology is unlikely to lead to the invention of a predictively powerful theory about the constituents of the quark. Even if one did hit upon this theory in such a pleasant manner . . . one certainly could not come to *know* that one had done so."

Is Science Dogmatic?

Although we have argued that open minds are necessary in order to arrive at the truth, it often seems to observers that scientists actually have closed minds. New ideas are often received by fellow scientists with extreme hostility, and it is true that many of the great names of science were initially regarded with suspicion and contempt by their colleagues. Notoriously, Edison was accused of a hoax when he invented the electric light bulb. As it was considered to be an established scientific fact that heavier-than-air machines could not possibly fly, the achievement of the Wright brothers was simply ignored for some time. A frequently cited example of scientific obtuseness is the reception originally given to the now generally accepted Theory of Continental Drift originally proposed by Alfred Wegener.

Case Study: Alfred Wegener and the Theory of Continental Drift

Many people, beginning as far as we know with Francis Bacon in the 1620s, have remarked upon the curious way in which the coastlines of the continents on either side of the Atlantic seem roughly shaped so as to fit into each other like the pieces in a jig-saw puzzle. The huge indentation on the American side in the Caribbean may be filled by the westward extension of Iberia and North Africa.

In 1911, Alfred Wegener came across a scientific paper which listed fossils of identical plants and animals found on opposite sides of the Atlantic. Intrigued, Wegener began to seek, and find, more cases of similar organisms separated by great oceans. At that time such coincidences were explained by arguing that land bridges, now sunken, had once connected the distant continents. But in view of the close fit between the coastlines of Africa and South America, Wegener began to consider that these continents might have been joined together at one time.

On investigation, Wegener discovered that large-scale geological features on separate continents often matched very closely. The Appalachian mountains of eastern North America matched with the Scottish Highlands, while the distinctive rock strata of the Karroo system of South Africa were identical to those of the Santa Catarina system in Brazil. Wegener also found that the fossils found in a certain place often indicated a climate utterly different from the climate it enjoys today: for example, fossils of tropical plants are found on Arctic islands, while coal is present under the Antarctic icecap.

In 1915, Wegener published his theory of continental drift in *The Origin of Continents and Oceans*. He claimed that about two hundred and fifty million years ago the continents had formed a single mass, which he called "Pangaea." This original continent had split apart, and its fragments have been moving away from each other since that time.

Reaction to Wegener's theory was hostile. The problem was that Wegener had no convincing mechanism for how the continents might move. He thought that they were moving through the earth's crust like icebreakers ploughing through ice sheets, powered by centrifugal and tidal forces. Opponents argued that ploughing through the oceanic crust would distort the continents beyond recognition, and that centrifugal and tidal forces were far too weak to move continents anyway.

Wegener's ideas were not taken seriously until the 1960s, by which time evidence in favour of the idea that the continents are the result of the splitting and drifting of fragments of an originally unified granite land mass had accumulated impressively, due to increased exploration of the Earth's crust, especially the ocean floor. By the late 1960s, the theory of plate tectonics was well accepted by almost all geologists. Wegener's theory had been shown to be wrong in that the continents do not plough through the ocean floor. Instead, both continents and ocean floor form solid plates, which "float" on the underlying rock, which is under such tremendous heat and pressure that it behaves as an extremely viscous liquid. Also, the "fit" of the coastlines of the continents on either side of the Atlantic, Wegener's original stimulus, is not relevant, since that depends upon the sea level at the present time. It is the fit of the continental shelves which is the appropriate comparison, and that is a good one.

There is a long period of about fifty years between the proposal of Continental Drift and its general acceptance. This delay is often portrayed as evidence of dogmatic conservatism among scientists, and by implication to suggest that any wild hypothesis which is rejected by the scientific community today is similarly likely to be accepted in the distant future.

In fact the objections of the scientific community were not directed at the idea of continental drift as such, but rather at the mechanism which Wegener proposed to account for it. The idea that the granite land masses could plough through the underlying basalt was found unlikely since basalt lacks the necessary fluidity to function as an "ocean," as it was supposed to do in Wegener's original hypothesis.

After the Second World War undersea exploration led to the discovery of the Great Global Rift, thin fault lines in the earth's crust which in places separate the tectonic plates upon which the continental land masses ride. The plate boundaries coincided with regions of seismic activity, such as earthquakes volcanoes and hot springs. Thus in 1960 H. H. Hess and R. S. Dietz proposed that convection currents in the magma under the earth's crust actually push the plates about.

Thus the theory accepted fifty years after Wegener's first proposal is one in which continental drift is explained by a different mechanism.

Paul Feyerabend thinks that scientists should seriously consider any hypotheses which are proposed to them, however unlikely or outlandish they may appear. This is unreasonable. Limited resources of time and laboratory space should be given only to hypotheses which are serious contenders for success.

It is wholly appropriate for scientists to behave in a cautious, conservative and sceptical manner. New ideas appear all the time, and most of them are faulty in some way. It would be very inefficient to take all these new ideas at face value and treat them seriously, expending precious resources of manpower and money on testing ideas which are almost certainly going to turn out to be false. The initial scepticism of the scientific community provides a good preliminary means of sorting out which ideas may be dismissed without further consideration. A flawed theory with useful aspects may be reworked to take account of this scepticism, improved and resubmitted to the scientific community for its approval. A good theory will survive on its own merits sooner or later, as the history of the theory of continental drift shows.

Is Scientific Knowledge Objective?

Scientific knowledge is frequently contrasted with other forms of knowledge in that it is objectively based, and not merely a matter of subjective opinion. It aims at truth, that is, at a depiction of objective reality as it is independent of ourselves. Certainly, scientists are required to be careful in the analysis of evidence and in the procedures applied to arrive at conclusions.

It is sometimes argued that genuine objectivity is impossible in principle. All observation is theory-laden. Scientists, like all observers, hold a myriad of preconceptions and biases about the way the world operates. These, held in the subconscious, affect everyone's ability to make observations, so that it is impossible to collect and interpret facts free from any possibility of bias. There have been countless cases in the history of science in which scientists have failed to include particular observations in their final analyses of phenomena, not because of deliberate fraud or deceit, but because their prior beliefs entailed that they were unimportant.

Both Thomas Kuhn and Imré Lakatos have shown that scientists always work within a particular tradition of research. This tradition is said to provide pointers as to the questions worth investigating, dictate what evidence is admissible and prescribe the tests and techniques that are appropriate. Although the paradigm provides direction to the research it may also stifle or limit investigation, and anything that confines the research endeavour necessarily limits objectivity. It does seem likely that some new ideas in science are rejected because their significance is hidden by the current paradigm. When research reports are submitted for publication they are reviewed by other members of the discipline, and ideas from outside the paradigm are liable to be eliminated from consideration as crackpot or as poor science, and so never appear in print.

More serious is the charge made by some of the followers of Thomas Kuhn that scientific paradigms are strictly **incommensurable**. It is argued that a new paradigm may have no place at all for entities necessary to the previous one. Statements which were true within the sphere of influence of the old paradigm may not make sense in the light of the new. Theoretical terms in different paradigms mean completely different things. Thus in Newtonian physics mass and velocity are independent concepts; whereas in Einstein's theory a body's mass changes with its velocity. They would say that "mass" and "velocity" mean different things in the two paradigms. However most physicists would see Newton's theory simply as a special case of Einstein's, namely one that deals with bodies in the range between the molecular and the galactic, the range that most concerns us. That is why, despite acceptance of Einstein's new paradigm, Newtonian physics is still taught in schools and still applied successfully.

Although Kuhn is rather vague about the consequences of his theory of scientific revolutions, many philosophers and scientists have concluded that scientific advances are merely the substitution of one self-contained framework for another, and that there is no way that we could ever compare a paradigm with reality in order to measure scientific progress. They argue that scientific knowledge is relative to our frameworks, and not to absolute truth. This view is known as **scientific relativism**, and it is closely related to other forms of relativism.

Yet, despite the fact that we are necessarily influenced in making our observations by existing ways of looking at things, it seems clear that we are perfectly capable of so attending to reality that we are constrained to alter our beliefs and our existing presuppositions fundamentally.

Case Study: Röntgen and X-Rays

Sir William Crookes made a tube, in the narrow end of which he had fixed a cathode or negative pole, and in the bulbous end an anode, or positive pole. Having created a partial vacuum in the tube, he passed an electric current between the two. Something was beamed between the two since the cross formed a shadow on the glass. He thought that this was light until he placed a magnet near the tube, and the beam was deflected from its path. This suggested that a stream of particles was passing along the tube. These particles were too small to be ordinary matter. Crookes thought he had discovered a "fourth state of matter."

Wilhelm Röntgen repeated the experiment enclosing the tube in black card to exclude all light. He was doing this one day, when he noticed that a sample of salts some twelve feet away from the tube were glowing in the darkness. Years later, when he was asked what he thought when he saw this unexpected phenomenon, he replied: "Thought! I did not think. I investigated." He then tested the invisible rays with photographic plates, and so discovered x-rays.

Röntgen's discovery of x-rays was made in spite of the fact that there was no conventional theory in terms of which they could be understood. The phenomenon was observed regardless of the lack of a theory, and the observation led to a fundamental change of scientific paradigm. The phenomena dictated the paradigm, and not the other way around. Reality as perceived was not entirely determined by existing theory; existing theory had to be modified to account for the observations made. Reality dictated the paradigm, and not the other way around, as the relativists would have us believe.

5. Pseudoscience

We frequently come across theories and systems which, although claiming to be "scientific," use only the external trappings of science, while avoiding the rigours and checks built into the scientific method, and the scrutiny of disinterested fellow researchers and experts. In his *Fads and Fallacies in the Name of Science*, Martin Gardner calls these "pseudosciences." Pseudoscience is not science at all, not even bad science. It is fantasy deliberately dressed up to look like science. It is a form of intellectual confidence trick.

Case Study: Alchemy

With origins in ancient China and Hellenistic Greece, alchemy was considered to be a respectable branch of knowledge in Europe and the Islamic world for one thousand five hundred years. The theoretical basis of medieval European alchemy was Aristotle's physics. In all physical objects he distinguished the matter or stuff of which it is made, which makes it "something", from the particular form which is imposed upon that matter, which makes it "something in particular" which may be grasped by the intelligence and referred to in language as e.g. a chair or rabbit. Alchemists sought to isolate the formless stuff or "prime material" out of which everything is made, which might then be transformed into literally anything by the addition of an appropriate form.

The three practical ends of alchemy were the discovery or creation of:

- The elixir of life - a substance which would give to all who imbibed it everlasting youth.
- The universal panacea - a substance which could be administered to cure all ailments.
- The philosophers' stone - a means of transmuting base metals into gold.

Surprisingly, alchemy is not dead. It is alive and flourishing in the USA. In 1994 at Texas A&M University there was a controversy over the work of the electrochemist John Bockris. He was approached by an investor prepared to pay him $200,000 to investigate the possibility of transmuting base metals into gold by firing radio waves at them, and by mixing them with potassium nitrate, carbon and various salts, and then heating them to very high temperatures. Small amounts of gold were alleged to have been produced, but this could not be replicated by other researchers in Bockris' laboratory.

Evidence in Pseudoscience

In pseudosciences the probability is that the "researcher" worked backwards from his conclusion until he came up with possible "support" for his claims. Since he started with the results, his own belief in them does not rest on any support. He believes the evidence because of what it is supposed to support. The "evidence" is merely a means to convince others of what the pseudoscientist already thinks that he "knows."

Much pseudoscience rests upon personal testimonials. People claim to have witnessed levitating holy men or seen auras around people. They are one of the most popular and convincing forms of "evidence" presented for beliefs in the paranormal and pseudoscientific.

Such evidence is often very persuasive, because:

- It is anecdotal. Stories can be very vivid and detailed, making them appear credible.
- The people who tell the stories may appear to be credible. They often seem enthusiastic, trustworthy and honest, with no apparent reason for deceiving anyone.
- They may have the appearance of some sort of authority, say, a university degree.
- People may want to believe them, because if the stories were true the world would be a safer or more interesting place.

But testimonials and anecdotes are of little value in establishing the probability of the claims they are used to support because:

- They are liable to be influenced by all sorts of motives, such as a desire for attention, fame or excitement.
- They cannot be tested. There is this no way to tell whether the experience ever happened, or if it did, whether it was a delusion. The testimonial of "personal experience" has no scientific value. If others cannot experience the same thing, there is no way to determine the reliability of the experience. If there is no way to test the claims made, there is no way to tell if the experience was a delusion, or was interpreted correctly. Only if others can experience the same thing under the same circumstances is it possible to make a test of the testimonial and determine whether the claim based on it is worthy of belief. Therefore, testimonials are of no more value than alleged quotations from the letters of "satisfied customers" in advertisements.

In particular, since extraordinary claims require extraordinary evidence to support them, and since personal testimonials are a very weak form of evidence anyway, they will not suffice to support the claims of pseudoscience.

How to Identify Pseudoscience

The pseudoscientist may usually be recognised by certain characteristics:

- He works in isolation from other scientists.
- He submits his work to the judgement of the public rather than to that of his fellow scientists.
- His publications tend to be defensive, consistently interpreting criticism of his theories, hypotheses, or data as personal insults. Pseudo-scientists fall into the trap of considering disagreement and criticism as personal conflict, and so resist the kind of criticism that is necessary to test hypotheses. They may consider colleagues to be hostile, and even become paranoid about them; directing bitter invective against those considered opponents.
- Pseudoscientists consider orthodox science to be fundamentally mistaken: "Everybody is out of step except our Johnny." They may use the word "Science" pejoratively. Their ideas are supposed to be supported by evidence, but it just happens not to be of the kind accepted by "conventional science."
- Despite this anti-scientific bias, there may be free use of key scientific terms such as "quantum," "force," "entropy," "field," "quantum," "the uncertainty principle," etc. to

give a scientific appearance to the pseudoscientist's work. These may be combined with other words in unusual, end even nonsensical, ways, e.g. "quantum psychology," "democratic entropy." They may use an invented technical language and all the paraphernalia of real scholarship.

- The pseudoscientist is certain he has the final truth about some great mystery which he is willing to share. His conclusions are not held provisionally. They function as dogmas.
- Pseudoscientists sometimes found organisations to assist them in the propagation of the message. These are frequently hierarchical, evangelical and secretive, and themselves paranoid and hostile to criticism.
- Pseudosciences usually offer something to the public: health to the incurably sick, success to the unsuccessful, a slim body without effort to the fat, or just the thrill of being one of those in the know, who know "The Full Truth."
- The pseudoscientists' ideas are presented simply, using all the devices of advertising. Publications are propagandist in tone, using coloured language and all the range of fallacies of informal logic, together with bitter invective against opponents.
- Proponents of pseudosciences are armed with ready-made excuses for why they have such meagre evidence of their beliefs. These range from "no one funds us" to "there is a conspiracy against us." These excuses would not be needed if there were good evidence for their theories. The fact that these excuses are offered is almost an admission of a lack of good evidence. If it were otherwise, the pseudo-scientist would focus on the evidence.
- Failure is covered up by special pleading.
- There may be simple fraud and chicanery involved. At some point money usually changes hands: to buy the book, to join the organisation, to attend the lecture, to take the course, or as an offering. The wealth of the "scientist" may be concealed. A small salary may be reported, while the non-profit organisation or church owns the house, car, etc. It is just that the pseudoscientist has full use of them.

When finally cornered, the pseudoscientist is likely to assert that his claims were never intended to be taken seriously, but were only intended to get their readers to think, or as entertainment.

Glossary

ad hoc hypothesis: a hypothesis with no genuine explanatory value, one merely contrived to preserve the hypothesis from falsification by contradictory evidence.

ceteris paribus clause: a clause added to a scientific law stating that the law assumes that all relevant factors have been accounted for and uncontrolled variables excluded.

confirmation: the establishment of the acceptability of a law or theory.

control experiment: an experiment which involves comparing two populations, one which is manipulated in some manner, and another which is not.

corroboration: the support a hypothesis indirectly receives by repeatedly failing to be falsified.

covering law model: explaining an event by subsuming it under a general law.

crucial experiment: an experiment designed to decide between two rival theories.

dependent variable: the variable in an experimental situation which is determined by the independent variable.

Duhem's Irrefutability Thesis: the view that no scientific hypothesis can be definitively falsified since auxiliary hypotheses are also simultaneously tested, and we can never be sure where the failure lies.

experiment: the deliberate manipulation of factors being investigated to examine the relationships between them.

extraordinary science: according to T. S. Kuhn, the state of a branch of science when an existing paradigm is seen to be unsatisfactory.

falsifiable: a proposition is falsifiable if there is a logically possible observation statement, or set of observation statements, which are incompatible with it; ie. which, if true, would show the original statement to be false.

falsificationism: the view that hypotheses are genuinely scientific only if they have empirical consequences which are falsifiable.

hypothesis: a proposition about nature which is testable, but which has not yet been tested to the point of general acceptance

hypothetical entities: entities proposed as existing in scientific theories, but not directly accessible to sense experience.

immunising stratagems: stratagems adopted by scientists to preserve their hypotheses from falsification.

independent variable: the variable in an experimental situation which is manipulated by the experimenter.

induction: the process of inference from the particular to the general, or from the less general to the more general.

inductivism: an account of scientific method as based upon induction from observations and resulting universal laws and theories which are confirmed as true.

law of nature: an archaic term for a scientific law.

normal science: the state of a branch of science according to T. S. Kuhn, when securely dominated by a paradigm.

Occam's (Ockham's) Razor: the practice of always preferring the simpler of two rival hypotheses; also known as the Principle of Parsimony.

paradigm: a model or pattern; according to Thomas Kuhn in science it is a framework theory which determines the fundamental viewpoint and limitations of scientists in a particular field during an era.

pre-science: the state of a branch of science according to T. S. Kuhn before the emergence of a paradigm.

prescription: saying what *must* be or *ought to be* the case, rather than what actually *is* the case.

Principle of Parsimony: the practice of always preferring the simpler of two rival hypotheses; also known as Occam's (Ockham's) Razor.

Principle of the Uniformity of Nature: the principle that nature always behaves in a uniform manner, cited as a justification of induction.

Problem of Induction: the problem of justifying the acceptance of the conclusions of inductive arguments, which all systematically go beyond the evidence upon which they are based.

programmatic theories: according to I. Lakatos, the core of framework theories basic to research programmes, comparable to Kuhn's paradigms.

pseudoscience: false science; "research" having all the external trappings of science, but subject to none of its rigours and checks.

research programme: according to I. Lakatos, a tradition of scientific research dominated by a programmatic theory.

scientific law: a statement describing how some phenomenon of nature behaves, based upon generalisations from data obtained by particular observations, of regularities and patterns in nature, usually limited to particular phenomena.

scientific realism: the view that theoretical terms in science refer to real entities, even if these are not directly accessible to perception.

scientific relativism: the view that scientific knowledge is not, and cannot ever be, true or known to be true, since it is never possible to compare scientific knowledge with the facts.

scientific revolution: according to T. S. Kuhn, the overthrow of one paradigm in favour of another.

subsidiary hypotheses: according to I. Lakatos, auxiliary hypotheses which effect the application of the programmatic theory in a research programme.

theory: a model (usually mathematical) which links and unifies a broader range of phenomena, and links and synthesises the laws which describe those phenomena.

uncontrolled variables: factors outside the control, and perhaps the knowledge, of the experimenter which may affect the outcome of an experiment.

variables: factors to be considered in an experimental situation which undergo some sort of change.

verification: establishing a theory as true.

verisimilitude: a degree of approximation to the truth

13. THE HUMAN SCIENCES

"The proper study of mankind is man." (Alexander Pope).

1. What are the Human Sciences?

The human sciences are disciplines which are directed towards the systematic objective study of social and individual human behaviour. They include:

- Psychology: the study of human behaviour.
- Anthropology: the study of human cultures.
- Sociology: the study of human groups and societies.
- Political Science: the study of political systems and institutions.
- Economics: the study of the behaviour of individuals and groups in the production, exchange and consumption of goods and services.

The human sciences originated at the end of the eighteenth century when science seemed to have spectacularly extended our knowledge of the material world around us. Some scholars began to ask whether the same methods could extend our understanding of human affairs. This led to the attempt to study human nature and behaviour in a manner which would produce "respectable scientific knowledge."

However, the major problem with this enterprise is that study of human behaviour must at some point take account of human consciousness and its contents. Because no one can directly observe what is in a person's mind, these are necessarily not directly amenable to empirical observation and testing. Thus the social sciences span an area between the natural sciences and the humanities.

This has lead to a wide spectrum of approaches. At one extreme are those who share common ideals of explanation and prediction with their colleagues in the natural sciences, and who would wish to follow the same rigidly formalised procedures that the natural scientists are sometimes thought to follow, expressing their data and findings in mathematical terms wherever possible. They adopt the view that there is only one scientific method which all sciences must follow. This is called methodological monism. Thus Karl Popper, in The Poverty of Historicism, argues that: "all theoretical or generalising sciences make use of the same method, whether they are natural or social sciences."

In criticism of this approach, Alan Chalmers points out that: "The false assumption that there is a universal scientific method to which all forms of knowledge should conform plays a detrimental role in our society. . . . This is especially true in the domain of social theory, when theories that serve to manipulate aspects of our society at a superficial level (market research, behaviourist psychology), rather than serving to understand it and helping us to change it at some deeper level, are defended in the name of science."

At the opposite extreme are those who argue that the most important institutions and events in human society are unique; and that science, which properly deals with recurrent events, is incapable of treating the unique. These may adopt what is called a hermeneutic approach: that is, they see the social sciences as enhancing human self-awareness and understanding, assimilating them to the humanities. These researchers may often write like novelists or preachers.

Workers favoring a **hermeneutic** approach argue that the student of mankind must use an empathetic approach to his subject matter, usually termed *Verstehen*. In order to understand some group of people, it is claimed that the investigator must achieve some sort of ability to put himself in their place and see things from their viewpoint. Only in this way will he understand what is going on, and what he has to explain. This is impossible for the natural scientist because he cannot imagine what it would be like to be a magnet, an acid or a dead rat. The need for sympathetic insight forms a major distinction between the natural and human sciences.

Those who object to this argue that this deliberate lack of objectivity must undermine the reliability of disinterested hypothesis testing, and therefore any claim to scientific status for the human sciences. Empathy and Verstehen may suggest suitable hypotheses for the human sciences to consider, but this approach will obstruct and undermine the necessary objectivity of the process of hypothesis testing and justification.

In between these extremes are those who argue that the special subject matter of the human sciences requires the adaptation of existing scientific methods and the development of new approaches. For example, because of the nature of what he is studying, by contrast with a researcher in the natural sciences, a worker in one of the fields of human science is more likely to bring to his work biases and prejudices which may distort his perception and cloud his thinking. Because of his background, an economist may have a strong allegiance to capital or labour; a sociologist to one social class rather than another; and a psychologist for or against people of differing personality type or sexual orientation.

In general, economics seems to encourage the "hard" "scientific" approach, since economists do deal in quantities, mathematical models, and general laws with predictive capability. Anthropologists tend to favour the "soft" hermeneutic approach. It is in psychology, that both approaches clash most obviously.

The psychological school of **behaviourism** most thoroughly and most consistently seeks to assimilate psychology to a natural science. One of the most famous, John Watson, argued: "Psychology as the behaviourist views it is a purely objective experimental branch of natural science. Its theoretical goal is the prediction and control of behaviour. Introspection forms no essential part of its methods, nor is the scientific value of its data dependent upon the readiness with which they lend themselves to interpretation in terms of consciousness."

Behind this diversity of approaches lies an important difference of opinion about whether the study of the way people actually think, feel and act can in any fashion be conducted in terms which are appropriate to the study of physical and chemical processes. Behind that in turn lies a fundamental disagreement about whether social and mental phenomena can, or can not, be reduced without residue to physicochemical terms.

There are three main positions on the last question, corresponding to the three different approaches to their work adopted by scientists in this field:

- Human thoughts, feelings and values are nothing more than complex products of physicochemical forces, especially the physiology of the human brain, and can only properly be studied by the methods appropriate to the study of physicochemical processes. This is a form of reductionism, claiming that phenomena of type a are wholly reducible, without residue, to phenomena of type b.

- The way people think, feel and act cannot be reduced to physicochemical processes without residue, and so they cannot adequately be studied using the methods appropriate to those disciplines. Only a hermeneutic approach is appropriate.

- Social systems and processes possess a kind of complexity which physical systems do not possess, so that new theoretical frameworks and procedures are required for effective investigation. However, the differences are not so great that the study cannot be recognisably "scientific," in the sense that standard scientific procedures may be adapted to the new field of investigation to produce "scientifically respectable" findings.

Actions and Movements

The human sciences are concerned with human actions and behaviour, that is, with things that people do. This marks them off from the natural sciences.

Although the word "action" may be used of things in their interrelations, such as "the action of acid upon metal," it is usually reserved for the doings of human or other living agents. The actions of living things are distinguished from what happens to them. They are also distinguishable from the bodily movements of those same agents, such as involuntary ticks.

That actions are quite different sorts of things from bodily movements was explained by the philosopher Gilbert Ryle by distinguishing between a blink (a bodily movement) and a wink (an action). A blink of the eyes is an involuntary movement. It is something which happens to someone rather than something which someone does. No one regards a blink as of social significance. A blink may be a sign of something, such as the one who blinked seeing a sudden bright light, but it does not convey intentions. By contrast, a wink is something which someone does. A wink is intended. Thus we are regarded as responsible for our winking in a way that we are not generally regarded as responsible for any consequences which may follow upon our happening to blink.

The difference between bodily movements and human actions can be further shown in that:

- A particular action may be performed by using quite different bodily movements. Calling a taxi can be accomplished by waving a newspaper, raising the arm, or a combination of these movements.

- A particular set of bodily movements can constitute many different actions, e.g. signing a cheque, signing a contract, signing a death warrant, giving someone an autograph, etc.

- Different methods are usually employed in order to explain why certain bodily movements took place as opposed to why certain actions were performed. We explain the occurrence of bodily movements by giving their causes. By contrast, we usually explain actions by giving the reasons why they were performed.

Humans as Animals

It is clear that whatever special complications and difficulties may arise in dealing scientifically with humans, we are, whatever else we are, animals.

- We are related to the rest of the animal kingdom on the tree of evolution.

- We are subject to the same laws governing genetics, survival and evolution as are our fellow species. Humans and chimpanzees are about ninety-eight percent genetically identical.
- The same biological processes, ingestion, evacuation, reproduction, are found in us as in similar animals.
- We display many of the behavioural traits of all living things. The automatic responses to stimuli called by biologists tropisms, e.g. the plant turning towards the light, the moth flying into the light source. We yawn, blink, sneeze.
- When babies, we are subject to imprinting or fixing upon our parents or other carers as are other animals.

Sociobiologists study human behaviour in precisely the same ways in which naturalists study the behaviour of other animals.

This gives rise to the question as to whether such explanations are appropriate, and if appropriate, whether they could ever be adequate. Again, three positions tend to emerge:

The veneer of civilisation is said merely to hide the animal nature of human beings. Since human beings are animals, we may explain their behaviour in exactly the way in which we explain the behaviour of other animals. Some have argued that all broad patterns of behaviour are the result of adaptive processes of evolution and have, or at one time had, survival value. This approach has been adopted Desmond Morris in books such as The Naked Ape.

Others argue, frequently on religious grounds, that human beings are not animals at all, and that explaining their behaviour in terms appropriate to animal behaviour is always inappropriate. This flies in the face of all the evidence of man's animal nature, as listed above.

A third approach is to accept man's animal nature, and the insights that understanding human behaviour as a species of animal behaviour can bring, while recognising that human beings are unique in the animal world in that, due to the possession of language, we live in a world of meanings.

Human agents attach meaning to their actions. In The Idea of a Social Science, Peter Winch argues that since meaning is not open to causal analysis, where human actions are at issue explanation of social events must not be in terms of physical causes and effects, but of the motives and intentions which lie behind human actions. Knowledge of human behaviour can only be from inside, where those meanings can be understood.

For this reason, any explanation of human behaviour in terms of animal behaviour will be appropriate, but that any attempt at a complete explanation of human behaviour in those terms will necessarily be inadequate.

2. Method in the Human Sciences

The human sciences sometimes take the approach of abstraction from the complexity of human affairs in order to achieve what is seen as methodological rigour. Economists have traditionally favoured this approach.

John Stuart Mill wrote:

"What is now commonly understood by the term "Political Economy" . . . makes entire abstraction of every other human passion and motive; except those which may be regarded as perpetually antagonising principles to the desire of wealth, namely, aversion to labour, and desire of the present enjoyment of costly indulgences . . . Political Economy considers mankind as occupied solely in acquiring and consuming wealth; and aims at showing what is the course of action into which mankind, living in a state of society, would be impelled, if that motive, except in the degree in which it is checked by the two perpetual counter-motives above adverted to, were absolute ruler of all their actions . . . The science . . . proceeds under the supposition that man is a being who is determined, by the necessity of his nature, to prefer an greater to a smaller portion of wealth in all cases, without any other exception than that constituted by the two counter-motives already specified. Not that any political economist was ever so absurd as to suppose that mankind are really thus constituted, but because this is the mode in which science must necessarily proceed . . . But there are also certain departments of human affairs, in which the acquisition of wealth is the main and acknowledged end. It is only of these that Political science takes notice."

He abstracts from reality twice: once by considering only the economic sphere of man's existence, and indicating that he is ignoring a other aspects of human life; and again by only considering the operation of economic motives (such as the desire to maximise wealth) as opposed to non-economic motives (such as custom and habit) in understanding what happens within this narrow range. This abstraction is known as "economic man." Is economic man merely an abstraction from "real man" or is he "fictional man?" Mill thought that he had abstracted a set of motives that actually generate economic activity. Some economists, such as J. M. Keynes, agreed. Other philosophers and economists have disagreed.

Experiment

Controlled experiment is not always possible in the behavioural sciences. Where it is possible, there are often severe ethical problems:

▪ The necessary process of abstraction is impossible because the memories, perceptions and motivations of the subjects of the experiments may colour their responses. It has been argued that a laboratory experiment in psychology with human subjects is like a chemist conducting his research with dirty test tubes.

▪ All science involves the testing of hypotheses by observation and experiment. When the subjects of observation or experiment are human beings. This involves special ethical problems.

▪ Observation may involve an intrusion into the subjects' privacy.

▪ Subjects of experimental research may undergo physical or psychological stress, possibly resulting in permanent harm or damage. This applies where drugs or other treatments which may have damaging side-effects are being tested.

▪ In order for an experiment to be successful, it may be necessary to deceive the subjects undergoing the experiment.

▪ Some subjects may not be genuinely free to choose to participate or to refuse to participate, e.g. members of the armed forces, prisoners, patients in hospitals for the mentally ill or mentally subnormal. This also applies when there payment is offered for participation in research, since some people will be under such financial pressure that they will have little effective choice. This is especially likely since college students are the usual experimental guinea-pigs.

▪ Researchers who are trying to establish that a particular treatment will benefit patients, will administer it to some and withhold it from the control group. If the condition is potentially fatal and the treatment effective, then the means to save their lives is knowingly being denied to the members of the control group.

The use of animal subjects seems to have advantages over the use of human beings:

▪ The environment of the animals can be better controlled and monitored;

▪ It is generally felt that it is less unacceptable to risk stress and damage to animals than to human beings.

Increasingly, however, animal rights groups are arguing for the view that animals also have rights and that we should respect them.

In assessing the likely outcomes of policies, the need to test claims is crucial. Unfortunately, it is difficult to test political hypotheses due to the near impossibility of arranging for any controlled experiments. Suppose, for example, we wish to evaluate the effectiveness of income redistribution in reducing poverty. We cannot create two identical societies, giving one a placebo income tax and the other a real one in order to compare the outcomes. Moreover, the political process affects all members of a community, so that there are no disinterested observers to evaluate the outcome. Instead all that we have is the imperfect alternative of making comparisons between different cities and nations, and treating them as poorly conducted experiments in social organisation. Although these experiments lack controls, and take long periods of time before they produce measurable results, they are the best source of information on the effects of political policies which we have.

Observation

Because of difficulties in using human beings in experiments, observation is frequently used not merely to collect data but also to test hypotheses.

Observers may simply watch the subjects being investigated, avoiding intervention, or they may try to blend in with a group and act as a member of it. Non-participant observation, is probably more prevalent in psychology. By contrast, participant observation is more common in anthropology, when the investigator lives for some time among the people he is studying.

The observation may be naturalistic or controlled. Naturalistic observations are made when the investigator takes advantage of what occurs in the normal course of events without his intervention. Controlled observations are made when the investigator attempts to influence the behaviour of those he is to observe, e.g. by asking questions.

The setting of the observation may be a natural one, or it may be a contrived one such as a laboratory. **Field observation** in normal surroundings is usually necessary when the researcher wishes to know how some individual or group behaves and interacts with others under normal circumstances. Researchers have, in the interests of science, immersed themselves in situations involving some inconvenience and danger to themselves in order to make their observations. They have deliberately sought admittance to mental hospitals as patients, or to street gangs as members.

If he is an active participant in the group he is observing, the researcher may learn more about his subjects, but he is also more likely to lose objectivity. In addition, active involvement may be unwise and unethical if criminal activities are being monitored. Moreover, field observation may be inconvenient and difficult in the sense that a lot of waiting around may be necessary in order to observe the behaviour under investigation.

Since human behaviour is frequently difficult to classify, coding systems are necessary to allow systematically classification; for example, it may be necessary to decide what is to count, for purposes of the investigation, as an aggressive response.

Problems remain with the use of such methods, however:

- The fact that there is no such thing as totally unbiased observation is more important in the human than in the natural sciences, since what is observed is more likely to be the subject of strong feelings and prejudice.
- In order to record what he observes, the researcher has to make decisions, such as what counts as interaction between his subjects. This may be inherently difficult to do.

Case Study: Talking Chimps and Gorillas

In recent years, researchers have attempted to teach near human primates American Sign Language (ASL). A chimpanzee by the name of Washoe was deliberately raised much as a child in a deaf community would be - surrounded by ASL. At the age of four, she could allegedly make eighty-five signs, and combine them into two-word "sentences." This compares with most human children at the age of about two years. A similar study on Koko, a gorilla, led to her trainer making the claim that Koko learned several hundred signs, composed sentences of varying length, and was fond of jokes, puns, and metaphors.

However, both of these experiments were criticised for lack of proper scientific controls. Record-keeping was not extensive, and others who wanted to examine the studies found it hard to obtain any raw data.

A research team led by psychologist H. S. Terrace, composed of people who firmly believed that the previous studies had demonstrated language ability in primates, set up a more controlled experiment with a chimp they named Nim Chimpsky. This study included a program of careful record-keeping and regular videotaping. The results were not what the researchers had expected.

At first, the experiment was encouraging. Nim produced his first ASL sign after just four months. However, at the end of four years, he had learned one hundred and twenty five signs by the most optimistic count, while another member of the team, suggested that he may actually have learned as few as twenty-five. And while he put them together into "sentences," with a varying number of signs in each, the researchers were disappointed to find that the content did not get more complex as the number of signs increased. Moreover, Nim never showed any sign of understanding or using the grammar of ASL. Then the team began looking at the data from the other experiments, and found no clear indication that the other primates had done better than Nim.

One problem was that the vocabulary counts were usually made by people who were not themselves fluent in ASL. The Washoe team did have one native signer, but this person's count was apparently excluded from their statistics. She complained: "Every time the chimp made a sign, we were supposed to write it down in the log . . . They were always complaining because my log didn't show enough signs. All the hearing people turned in logs with long lists of signs. They always saw more signs than I did... The hearing people were logging every movement the chimp made as a sign. Every time the chimp put his finger in his mouth, they'd say "Oh, he's making the sign for "drink,"... . When the chimp scratched himself, they'd record it as the sign for "scratch." ....When [the chimps] want something, they reach. Sometimes [the trainers] would say, 'Oh, amazing, look at that, it's exactly like the ASL sign for "give." One experienced worker with primates commented, that she recognised all of Mim's "signs" as gestures chimpanzees make in the wild anyway.

Other than the Nim experiment, the primate signing studies have not been very scientific. The Nim study was set up to counter criticism of the poor methodology of the earlier studies. The team that worked with Nim now work to expose the inadequacies of the other sign-language studies. Steven Pinker reports that those involved in the original studies "have distanced themselves from the community of scientific discourse." They now prefer popular science television shows and mass-market magazines to serious scientific journals publicise their work. They have descended into pseudoscience.

Non-Participant Observation: In non-participant observation, the researcher just watches, either in the laboratory or the field, or by recorded videotape. It is sometimes felt that only in this way will the investigator see behaviour in its true form in a non-controlled situation. It is for this reason that naturalists observe the behaviour of animals in their natural habitats, rather than as conveniently captive in zoological gardens.

Unfortunately, if the observation is known to the subjects, or if they know that they are being observed, they will probably change their behaviour. They will become more self-conscious, with the result that they may become either uncharacteristically inhibited or uncharacteristically exhibitionist.

It is sometimes possible to take measures to avoid this in laboratories by the use of two-way mirrors or hidden cameras. In the field the problem is more difficult. The construction of "hides" in imitation of naturalists is hardly possible when studying human behaviour. In any case, secret scrutiny raises ethical problems.

Participant Observation: In this case, the researcher becomes a member of the group he is studying and observes it from the inside. For the observations to be of use it is usually, although not always, necessary for the researcher to disguise the fact that he is observing the group. Thus William F. Whyte learned Italian and joined an Italian slum gang in Boston during the mid-fifties, engaging in all its activities.

This method is not without its problems:

- It is very difficult to keep records while effectively a participant "in disguise."
- The researcher may find himself losing his dispassionate perspective and so his objectivity. One such observer later remarked "I began as a non-participating observer. As I became accepted into the community I found myself becoming almost a non-observing participator."
- The researcher may also be in some danger of getting drawn into illegal or dangerous situations, particularly in sociological or ciminological research.

Case Studies: A case study is the description of some individual person or persons, group or organisation over a period of time. These are important for situations which are rare and complicated, e.g. the study of rare physiological or psychological disorders.

There many problems with this approach:

- Being limited in its focus on a single individual, group or organisation, case studies constitute an inadequate basis for generalisation.
- Because a case study frequently depends upon the memory of the subject, which is inherently faulty, it is less reliable than a test or experiment.
- It is very hard for a researcher to maintain a dispassionate approach towards an individual studied in depth over a long period of time. The researcher gets to know his subject in such detail and so closely that genuine impartiality would seem almost impossible.

The Comparative Method: As a substitute for controlled experiments, in many of the human sciences, in particular in sociology and anthropology, comparisons are made between different groups or societies in some particular respect, such as some social institution or practice, e.g. the roles of married women; or sets of facts or statistics, e.g. suicide rates together with degree of social cohesion.

The comparative method relies upon observation and upon interviews. To the extent that it depends upon the latter it is weak, for the reason that people may mislead us.

Case Study: Margaret Mead and the Samoans

Margaret Mead was an American anthropologist who went to live among the Samoans to observe their way of life. She wrote a record of her observations in "Coming of Age in Samoa." There she described a society where the young were allowed total sexual freedom and at the same time seemed to experience few of the traumas associated with adolescence common in western societies and got involved in far less crime. Her book became a classic text in anthropology.

Mead herself deduced that her work was of value in judging what might be wrong with Western society and suggesting ways in which our own problems might be solved. But anthropologist Derek Freeman later showed that Margaret Mead's data was fundamentally flawed. She had been misled by mischievous informants, who simply told her what they thought she wanted to hear.

Surveys

Surveys are a method for getting information by questioning a large number of people. Much of the data for the some of the human sciences is obtained from surveys of particular groups. These surveys may be conducted by means of interviews, either face-to-face or by means of the telephone, or through the filling in and returning of questionnaires.

Great attention has to be paid to the design of the questions, which are usually given a preliminary trial on a smaller sample of the population as a pilot study.

The questions may be closed or open-ended. The closed-ended question provides the respondent with a limited number of optional answers to choose from. These are easier to handle since responses can be immediately and unequivocally sorted into a limited number of groups. Unfortunately most interesting questions are not susceptible of being treated as though they had a finite (and very small) number of possible answers; there are usually "buts" and "howevers" to take into account. Open-ended questions may produce more accurate responses, but they may be very difficult for the researcher to classify afterwards. In addition, a response to an open-ended question may not make sense, or may be vague or ambiguous.

The use of surveys raises severe problems:

• Surveys provide information about verbal responses, not about behaviour, i.e. they do not report behaviour, only people's accounts of their behaviour. Many researchers go to great lengths to try to detect self-deception and lying, but these cannot be foolproof, and the data may be systematically biased.

▪ Even if the subject is honest, if he is required to report on his past behaviour, he may have forgotten, and then imagination is likely to substitute for memory.

▪ Great care has to be taken over the wording of the questions asked. Subjects may misunderstand or misread the questions put to them. The way in which questions are phrased might lead respondents to prefer to make one possible response rather than another.

▪ Subjects may be influenced by a desire to please the researcher, and so give the answer thought to be most acceptable. This may be influenced by the culture of the subject, since in some societies great emphasis is placed upon giving a polite answer to please a questioner, rather than a truthful answer. In other cultures, "I don't know" is never an acceptable alternative to any question. It is likely that a respondent will give that answer which is most socially acceptable, and which seems to depict him in the best possible light. This is called the Hawthorne Effect.

- The researcher may influence the response by subtle bodily attitudes or by what he says. He may assist the respondent who hesitates by encouraging him along lines which the interviewer, perhaps falsely, thinks are the lines along which the respondent is struggling. This factor is further complicated by the fact that many different interviewers may be used.

Sampling

Surveys almost always require extrapolation from data gathered on a sample of the population. There are various methods of taking a sample:

Haphazard sampling involves simply stopping people who happen to be passing by and obtaining their responses. The problem with this is that if the sample chosen is not typical, in relevant ways, of the population as a whole, and it is not likely to be, the results cannot be extrapolated to the whole population, and so the survey would be misleading and worthless.

An attempt to rectify this is usually made by choosing a sample that reflects the numerical ratios of various subgroups in the population as a whole by e.g. gender, age, socioeconomic class, etc. This is called quota sampling. It is an improvement on the practice of haphazard sampling, but there is no restriction on the choice of individuals within the various subgroups.

Simple random sampling involves selecting a sample in such a way that every member of the population has, in principle, an equal chance of being chosen. This is not the same as standing in the street and accosting passers-by. The latter method would bias the sample towards the sort of people who would be likely to pass the chosen interview locations during the period when the survey was being conducted. This may be biased in that certain groups may not frequent those parts of town during that period for various reasons. Telephone random sampling may rely upon computer-generated random telephone numbers, although this biases the sample towards those having telephones, and excluding the poorest classes.

Random sampling may be combined with quota sampling in stratified random sampling. Random sampling methods are applied within the various subgroups created by quota sampling.

Although professional organisations, including those that specialise in election forecasts and university research centres, are able to engage effectively in sophisticated sampling techniques for their surveys, the great disadvantage of adequate stratified random sampling is its cost.

A realistic inspection of a sample usually reveals that the actual sample used in a survey is narrower than the population which is the subject of the research, not merely numerically but by subgroups. Thus research on the adult population of a city which involves telephone interviews should more accurately be described as research on a sample of the population of that city having access to a private telephones who are not ex-directory. The realistic description of the actual sample is termed the sample frame.

It is important to know, when evaluating a piece of research based upon a survey, how the sample was chosen. Many surveys depend upon people bothering to fill in questionnaires and return them. In itself, this may skew the sample significantly. An accurate sample is particularly important if the purpose of the survey is to describe a population.

A pilot trial of a questionnaire or experiment will often be conducted in order to discover in advance any snags or design errors so that they can be ironed out in advance of the main study. Observations made to test hypotheses must be made under the conditions with all other variables except those under consideration constant. This ceteris paribus assumption simplifies the situation, allowing the researcher to concentrate on the matters he is interested in. Unfortunately, in the world outside the laboratory things are changing all the time, and there is nothing the researcher can do about it. As a result, his results will necessarily be less certain, and less precise in their application, than results in the natural sciences.

Measurement

Measurements of differences between individuals and groups by means of mental tests takes place for a variety of reasons, to detect competency of various types, to diagnose problems, etc.

There are special problems involved in assigning measurements to social and psychological properties. In the natural sciences we only observe the relevant functional relationships from the outside, and generalise on the basis of our observations. If we were to apply this to the phenomena of social life, we should simply fail to understand what we were dealing with. In particular, the mere manipulation of statistics will lead us only to an external appreciation of phenomena whose essential character is only revealed in relation to inner meanings and values. Moreover, while the natural scientist can usually measure his data with some precision, the social scientist deals in concepts which are inherently vague or imprecise: "aggression," "morale," etc. It undermines the claim to measure some quality precisely when that quality cannot adequately be defined.

Prediction

Prediction is extremely difficult in the human sciences, since people are much more complex than weights on pulleys, copper sulphate crystals or dead rats. Moreover, the very making of a prediction about human beings may alter the outcome of events. Popper has called this the **Oedipus Effect**. If people know that they have been predicted to behave in a certain way, that may tend to make them behave in that way, and so increase confirmation of the prediction. Conversely, it may influence them deliberately to change their ways so as to falsify it.

Laws

Workers in the human sciences seek for regularities underlying the diversity of individual behaviour and social phenomena, which will allow them to make predictions, and so assist us in the both the understanding of and the control of our human environment.

The human sciences have been very disappointing in that they have not, in general, been fruitful in the production of laws. There do seem to be some established laws, but not many.

Some Laws of the Human Sciences

First Law of Supply and Demand: A rise in the demand for a commodity causes an increase in the equilibrium price and quantity.

Law of Diminishing Returns: When increasing quantities of a variable factor are used, in combination with a fixed factor, both the marginal product and the average product of the variable factor will eventually decrease.

Durkheim's Law: The rate of suicide varies inversely with the degree of social integration characteristic of a group.

There are several reasons for this apparent failure. Laws isolate significant correlations in a complex situation, and the phenomena of social life are so complex and intermeshed that it is very difficult to isolate single pairs of concomitant variables. Some have felt that the development of mathematics will in time enable these complexities to be mastered.

There is, however, a much more fundamental reason why genuine scientific laws are not to be found in the human sciences. Laws of the scientific kind are generalisations. But we do not accept generalisations as explanations of human behaviour. In order to explain human behaviour, reference to mental states, such as hopes, fears, desires, intentions, etc. is necessary. Even if we do seem to have found a generalisation which covers the behaviour in which we are interested, a further explanation of why the generalisation obtains, and one couched in mentalistic terms, is always necessary. (Consider Durkheim's Law above).

John Searle argues that for there to be laws of the behavioural sciences, there must be a systematic correlation between social and psychological phenomena and the phenomena recognised by physics. The former are defined by the attitudes people take, since this of itself creates psychological and social realities. "What counts as money or a promise of marriage is what people think of as money or a promise of marriage." These categories are open-ended in that an indefinite number of physical situations could count as money or a problem of marriage. Thus we cannot establish correlations between psychological and social phenomena and physical phenomena.

3. What is a Person?

The human sciences are distinguishable from the natural sciences because they concern human beings. This is where their difficulties lie. In order more fully to understand why knowledge about persons is problematic in many special ways, we need to consider what it is to be a person.

Traditionally, a person has been thought of as a body, together with a mind or soul. The terms of the problem were set by the mind/body dualism of René Descartes. According to his view, the mind is an independent immaterial soul which can exist independently of, but which interacts with the body. This reflects the religious beliefs of many people that we have, or better, essentially are, a soul which "temporarily occupies" a body.

In support of this view is the belief we all have of an inner identity of which we are directly conscious. In The Cerebral Symphony, William Calvin describes this as a "unity of conscious experience." He says that we are aware of a kind of "narrator" of our inner life. We usually call this our mind or soul.

Perhaps the nearest thing we have to evidence for this view consists of the near death experiences which many people claim to have had. One of the two typical types of near death experience is an "out of body" experience, in which people claim to have seen their own bodies as though from a vantage point of floating above them. Oxygen starvation in the brain is a more mundane explanation of such experiences provided by scientists.

In *The Concept of Mind,* the philosopher Gilbert Ryle characterised the view that the mind is some sort of entity which has experiences and performs actions, which operates the body from within like a pilot in the cockpit of a plane as that of a "ghost in a machine."

Mind and Body

One of the chief problems which this mind/body dualism gives rise to is understanding what the relationship between an immaterial soul or mind and a material body could possibly be.

It seems clear that, if we think in these terms, mind and body influence each other intimately. Physical events influence, and may even cause, mental events. If someone's appendix bursts, he feels pain. In their turn, mental events influence physical events. If we feel fear, our hearts beat faster. We decide to leave the room, and our body duly moves outside.

It is clear that the brain plays a key role in mental life, since when the brain is altered or injured in certain ways personality and consciousness may be changed or impaired

In 1861 a French surgeon, Pierre Paul Broca, demonstrated that patients suffering from the inability to understand or use speech (aphasia) usually suffered from damage to a particular area of the left cerebrum, now called Broca's convolution. The implication is that the impediment to the functioning of the mind had been caused by the physical damage to that particular part of the brain.

Case Study: The Horrible Accident of Phineas Gage.

Phineas Gage was a young worker employed on building a railroad in nineteenth century England. He was said to be courteous, honest, popular with his colleagues, and an industrious and dependable worker. One day in September 1848 he accidentally set off an explosion while handling blasting powder for an explosive charge. An inch-thick metal rod was blown through his left cheek, destroying his eye. It passed through his brain and out of the top of his skull, landing a few yards away.

Although Gage was knocked over, he almost immediately stood up and spoke to his shocked fellow workers. They put him on an oxcart and took him to a nearby hotel, where a doctor dressed his wounds. Although the doctor was able to stick his fingers into the holes in Gage's face and head until they met, Gage continued to talk, and asked when he would be fit to return to work.

Two months later he had apparently made a complete physical recovery. Yet he had also undergone a strange character change. He had become an aggressive, foulmouthed and ill-mannered liar. His friends said that he was "no longer himself."

When Gage died during an epileptic fit thirteen years later, the doctor who had attended to him persuaded his family to donate his skull to medical research, and deposited it in the Warren Medical Museum at Harvard. He believed that the change in Gage's personality had been due entirely to damage to his brain.

Two scientists of the University of Iowa later examined Gage's skull in the light of modern neurological knowledge. They used computer modelling and neural imaging techniques to determine the path the rod had taken when it passed through Gage's brain, determining that it had avoided the regions of the frontal lobes which govern language and motor functions, but that it must have passed through the area of the frontal lobes called the ventromedial region. Today, patients whose ventromedial region has been damaged by tumour, accident, or surgery, exhibit the same sort of personality change that had been observed in Gage.

Evidence of this nature has accumulated to such an extent that it is clear beyond reasonable doubt that many mental disorders have physical causes.

The use of drugs to alter states of mind also demonstrates the dependence of the mind upon the chemistry of the brain. Today psychopharmacology has an array of medicines capable of altering specific personality traits. Drugs may change a personality by removing tendencies to over-anxiety, inability to focus, over- impulsiveness, shyness and hypersensitivity. Today many mental illnesses seem to be little more than chemical disorders of the brain.

Recently, the practice of stimulating various parts of the brain and noticing which muscles respond has enabled scientists to discover which parts of the brain relate to specific functions. By such means a motor area, controlling bodily movement, and a sensory area, processing incoming sensations, have been mapped. Later work has identified, for example, in the hypothalamus, areas which control appetite, the sleep-waking cycle and the appreciation of pleasure.

PET (positron emission tomography) scanning enables observers to locate the part of the brain involved in different types of thinking. Radioactive water is injected into a patient's bloodstream. Since active regions of the brain use more blood than inactive ones, the parts of the brain being activated by particular mental tasks can be detected by the level of radioactivity they display.

Several approaches have been adopted to explain these findings:
- On the face of it, there seems to be a network of causal relations between mind and body, which are seen as two substances which interact with each other. This position is called interactionism.

The problem with this position is that it is not possible to see how something physical could be caused by something which is not physical, or something not physical be caused by something physical. Moreover, it is by no means clear what sort of entity the non-physical thing is.

- Some philosophers have sought to explain all mental events in terms of physical events, arguing that sensations and thoughts are nothing more than physical events in the brain. This is known as materialism.

- A milder form of materialism is known as epiphenomenalism. According to this view, consciousness is not itself physical, but it is a mere accompaniment or side effect of physical events. Epiphenomenalists argue that while physical events may cause mental events, mental events can never cause physical events. They are like the froth on the surface of the ocean, highly visible to us but ultimately of no significance. It is the waves beneath the surface which move things.

Epiphenomenalism, however, runs counter to the powerful intuition we all have that when we decide to pick up a glass, and our hand subsequently reaches out and grasps it, that the mental event in some way caused the physical event which followed it, and not the other way around.

Both materialism and epiphenomenalism are forms of reductionism, since they involve arguing that one of the two types of event occurring together can be seen as nothing more than a manifestation of the other.

- An alternative viewpoint is to regard mind and body as both aspects of a single entity, the person. But this does nothing by itself to answer the question as to how mental events affect the physical world.

- A further proposed solution is to argue that mental and physical events are identical. In some cases the terms "mental" and "physical" have different sense but identical reference, (like the terms "morning star" and "evening star" discussed in Chapter Seven).

Consciousness

One problem in attempting to understand how mind and body relate is that one of those terms, "mind," is itself not well understood. At present there are many theories competing to explain the nature of mind:

- According to behaviourism, consciousness is either fundamentally unreal or scientifically irrelevant. Mind is simply a term for certain categories of behaviour, disposition, or performance.
- The brain is a "**black box**," that is, a structure the internal features of which can be ignored. We must limit ourselves by studying only its input and output.
- There are always some physical processes or mechanisms which are the physical correlate of what we experience as consciousness. (Reductionist materialism)
- The Oxford mathematician Roger Penrose thinks that the explanation of consciousness is to be found in the non-deterministic features of quantum mechanics, perhaps in some theory which will unite classical and quantum mechanics. This is a non-explanation, or at best a pointer to where (hopefully) an explanation may one day be found.
- According to Francis Crick, in *The Astonishing Hypothesis*, consciousness is a by-product of the simultaneous high-frequency firing of neurones in various parts of the brain. The coming together of these frequencies in some way generates consciousness.
- Consciousness is a form of emergence of something radically new from a physical system, CF the emergence of a symphony from the physical constituents of the separate notes.
- The philosopher Colin McGinn argues that our brains have inherent limitations in their ability to know and understand because they are products of evolution. No understanding of the phenomenon of consciousness itself may be possible.

As yet, there is no generally accepted theory capable of answering this question.

The Self

In answer seeking to answer the question: What is a person? It is our sense of self which must be considered central.

Today there is evidence that the brain is responsible for our perception of self. An unfortunate young woman suffering from extremely severe epilepsy had her corpus callosum severed. This is the bundle of neurones which links the two halves of the brain. The result was two centres of consciousness. When asked if her left hand felt numb she was unable to give a consistent answer, repeatedly contradicting herself. When faced with a sheet of paper with the words "yes" and "no" written on it on being asked to point to the correct answer, she pointed at a different answer with each of her two hands.

Case Study: Split-Brain Patients.

While the brain is roughly symmetrical, the left and right sides performing different tasks. The left hemisphere typically specialises in language, while the right excels in non-verbal spatial abilities, facial recognition, and music.

The two hemispheres communicate by a cable of connections called the corpus callosum, and normally this communication is beneficial. But in a certain type of epilepsy, one seizure can provoke another on the opposite hemisphere. The seizures stimulate each other backwards and forwards across the corpus callosum. For this reason, since the late 1950s, some epileptics have had their corpora callosa severed surgically, halting their seizures but leaving the patients with two disconnected hemispheres.

The neuroscientist Roger Sperry was awarded a Nobel Prize for experiments on such patients. In some he fed information to only one hemisphere, while in others he fed different

---

information to each side simultaneously. His results showed that the hemispheres could function separately, with distinct analytical strengths. Sperry's experiments suggested that each hemisphere could learn, remember, reason, have opinions, initiate behaviour, be self-aware, feel time pass, imagine the future, and generate emotions. This raised the possibility that there might, in such cases, be two individuals occupying one skull. It even raised the possibility that normal people may consist of two separate individuals, yoked together by the corpus callosum.

Psychologist Julian Jaynes considered this possibility in his book, "The Origin of Consciousness in the Breakdown of the Bicameral Mind." He argued that a coherent sense of self, a well-bounded ego, developed only three thousand or so years ago. Before that, he wrote, the brain was "bicameral" (that is, two-chambered), with the two hemispheres barely integrated. One hemisphere spoke, either metaphorically or literally, and the other obeyed, attributing the voice to the gods. Jaynes asserted that the modern sense of ego represents a breakdown of bicameralism, although schizophrenics remain bicameral.

Unlike Jaynes, Sperry rejected the notion that there were two individuals inside anyone's head, and most scientists agreed with him. While split-brain patients could be manipulated into displaying two independent cognitive styles, the underlying opinions, memories, and emotions of both were the same. This could be explained anatomically. Even though the corpus callosum was cut, deeper structures of the brain critical to emotion and physiological regulation remained connected. Split brains are not really split into two but instead form a "Y." There might be two separate consciousnesses, one navigating through the town by remembering names of streets, the other by remembering a spatial map of the appearance of the town, yet it was still the same individual doing the navigating.

The issue of how many selves can reside within a single body is raised by the existence of multiple personality disorders. In normal people different facets of our person-ality tend to dominate in different settings: we may act like "a different person" when with a boss instead of a subordinate, or with a woman instead of a man. But we are not literally different people. In individuals with multiple personality disorder, however, separate per-sonalities seem to take full control of the person's behaviour at different times. Most mental health professionals agree that there are individuals in whom the different facets of person-ality are so disjointed and dissociated as to constitute a disordered state of the personality. Often these patients describe having suffered horrific childhood abuse, and some theorists think the compartmentalising of the different personalities evolved as a protective strategy. But it is not clear whether the non-overlapping identities truly represent different personalities.

One problem is that some clinicians report hundreds of such patients and believe in the reality of the disorder, citing studies showing that when personalities shift, so, for example, do eyeglass prescriptions. Others dismiss such claims, insisting that a true multi-ple personality patient shows up extremely rarely. Generally most authorities have taken the latter view. Today the diagnosis of this condition no longer implies the "existence" of multiple personalities, instead it is held to indicate the "presence" of "distinct identities or personality states," and is known as "dissociative identity disorder." A patient with this condition identifies himself in multiple ways, but the experts refuse to say whether those identities constitute genuine personalities.

Talking Point: How do we know that other people have minds at all?

We think of experience and the objects of experience as two mutually exclusive categories. We can never have other peoples' experiences. Their minds are not available to us. If all our knowledge is communicated through the senses, and we have no direct access to anyone else's consciousness, then the question arises, how can I ever know that anyone else has a consciousness like mine? Clearly we do. But this raises the questions: how does this happen, and how could we justify our claim to this knowledge?

The standard way in which we can say that we know that other people have minds is by way of analogy. I know that my inner mental states are connected to external bodily signs. I feel happy and I smile. Later I see you smile, and so infer by analogy that you are likewise happy. I step on a nail and feel pain. I screw up my face and exclaim. Then you step on the nail, you screw up your face and exclaim. I assume that, like me, you also feel pain. Hence, I infer that you also have consciousness.

Between the ages of about two years and four and a half children begin to attribute feelings, desires and intentions to others. Initially, these are the child's own feelings, intentions and desires. Then at about four and a half they begin to realise that other people can have feelings, intentions and desires different from their own. They are said to have developed what is called in Psychology a "Theory of Mind." Then the child comes to realise that other individuals have their own feelings and thoughts about himself. These insights are necessary for a proper social life.

Autistic children are distinguishable from normal children because they consistently fail to develop these insights. They lack the ability to put themselves in someone else's shoes, and so see the world from someone else's point of view. Being completely unaware of someone else's needs and feelings, they treat them merely as physical objects. Their relationships with others is condemned to remain at best superficial.

Could Computers Think?

Some have sought to understand the brain by comparing it to a computer. Computers are certainly like the brain in some ways. Like a digital computer, the brain essentially consists of numerous interconnected units capable of transmitting, or of not transmitting, an electric current.

These similarities have led some scholars to consider that the brain is nothing more than a computer, and what we call the mind or the intelligence consists of software programs. A consequence of this would seem to be that it is in principle possible to build an artificial intelligence indistinguishable from a human mind. The comparison has been made more appropriate since, in 1995, Leonard Adleman of the University of South California has used DNA molecules in a test tube to solve a simple computing problem, thus creating a biological computer.

Computers are different from human brains in many ways, however. This is true not only of their physical constituents but also of their functions.

▪ A computer may contain some five thousand units, a human brain will have more than a hundred billion neurones.

- In a computer, each unit is connected to two others. In the brain, individual neurones may connect to thousands of others, with over a hundred trillion connections in all. This is more than the number of galaxies in the known universe.
- The memory of a computer is normally cleared after a run, and it starts each new task afresh. The brain goes on accumulating new information throughout its lifetime, and can use any of this information in tackling any problem.
- The memory of the human brain exceeds that of machines. It has been estimated that if the information in an adult human brain were printed on magnetic tape in ways currently possible, an area the size of the surface of the earth would be necessary to accommodate it.
- The brain initially wires itself, and can rewire itself during life to accommodate changing demands.
- The human being not only thinks, he also feels. These feelings are also embedded in the memory.
- The operations of a digital computer can be fully specified purely formally or syntactically. By contrast, minds have semantics. That is they think *about* things.

According to Alan Turing, a machine could be regarded as thinking if and only if it could be so flexible in its responses to questions that its interrogators were unable to tell from the responses whether they were dealing with a human respondent or not. This is known as the **Turing Test.**

In order to illustrate the difference between brains and computers, John Searle designed a thought experiment. A number of computer programmers have designed a computer to simulate the understanding of Chinese. If a question is posed to the computer in Chinese, it will search its data banks for the appropriate reply in Chinese. Those who consider the mind to be a computer would, presumably say that the computer "understood" Chinese if its answers were such that a person who genuinely understood Chinese would also have given.

Now suppose a human being who did not understand that language was locked in a room with a basket of Chinese symbols and a rulebook, written in English, for manipulating those symbols. Unknown the man inside the room, the symbols being handed into the room are questions, and those he returns in accordance with the book of rules are the answers to them. Suppose that he correctly reads his rule book and manipulates the symbols so as to "answer the questions" he is being posed? Clearly he does not "understand" Chinese, because he does not know what the symbols mean. Yet his position is identical to that of the computer, which also does not understand its own "responses."

Mere manipulation of symbols according to rules does not of itself constitute understanding. In order to have understanding, we must know what the symbols we use mean. We must have access to their meanings. For this reason, computers can never really think, however much they may be programmed to provide the *illusion* that they are thinking.

Talking Point: How is Introspection possible?

We can observe our own states of consciousness. We can catch ourselves thinking certain things, observe ourselves reasoning. But how can we divide ourselves into two, so that one part of our self is able to observe the other at work?

---

4. Free Will and Determinism

Do We Have Free Will?

In addition to the problem of understanding our nature, mind/body dualism poses in its most severe form the problem of how we interact with the world. In particular, how we can possibly have the freedom of choice which most of us believe we have.

The problem of free will arises because of the incompatibility of two of our most basic beliefs. On the one hand we explain human behaviour by providing causal explanations of it in the human sciences. In explaining something we show why it is as it is, and not otherwise. On the other hand we have a deep-seated intuition that most of our actions are free. Our own choices and decisions, and the deliberate acts which follow from them, are among the facts of experience we are most familiar with. For this reason we are also conscious of the characteristic unpredictability of human behaviour.

This is a very important problem since it is because of our belief in our freedom of choice that we ascribe responsibility to people for their actions. Without freedom of choice all ethical judgements would be misconceived.

We explain anything causally by showing that, given the preceding conditions, no other outcome was possible. It was long held to be self evident that every event has a cause, and that to provide a cause is to provide an explanation of why an event happened as it did, and not in some other way. Only on this assumption is the world intelligible to us. Thus every event has a cause why it is as it is.

This belief, known as **determinism**, has been expressed in its most extreme form by Pierre Simon Laplace: "We ought to regard the present state of the universe as the effect of its antecedent state and as the cause of the state that is to follow. An intelligence knowing all the forces acting in nature at a given instant, as well as the momentary positions of all things in the universe, would be able to comprehend in one single formula the motions of the largest bodies as well as of the lightest atoms in the world, provided that its intellect were sufficiently powerful to subject all data to analysis; to it nothing would be uncertain, the future as well as the past would be present to its eyes."

The mere explanation of the movements of the physical particles which make up the human body pre-empts the possibility of our bodies moving in any way other than the way that they in fact do move. This rules out the action of our minds in the exercise of free choices influencing the movements of our bodies.

Determinism, Fatalism and Predestination

Determinism should not be confused with two other related, but different, concepts: fatalism and predestination.

Determinism is the belief that all events are effects necessitated by their causes.

Fatalism is the belief that whatever a person does, his end is inevitable: "Whatever will be, will be."

Predestination is the belief that every event in the universe is known in advance by God and, ultimately, brought about by his power.

Determinism is held on different levels of generality. Hard determinism is the view that human beings are, like everything else in the physical universe, matter in motion. That matter moves according to the laws of motion and gravity discovered by Newton. Pierre Simon Laplace concluded that if an observer knew the position mass and velocity of all the particles in the universe at any one time he could, in principle, work out the exact state of the universe at any time before or since. That would include the location and movements of all human beings.

More narrowly, determinism may simply involve the claim that personality and behaviour are determined by genetic or environmental factors.

Increasingly the human sciences are laying bare the causes of our behaviour. For example: It has long been noted that men are more violent than women. It is largely men who commit crimes of violence and who fill prison cells. This suggests that human violence may be due to something on the X-chromosome. Men are prey to genetic diseases which do not affect women because women have two X-chromosomes, so that an imperfection in one will be countered by the other. Men have no such protection, and so damaged chromosomes may give rise to conditions among males which are absent among females. Dr. Han Brunner has isolated the damaged section, and suggests that an imbalance of the substance serotonin may lead to aggression.

If such studies are well-founded, then violent crime seems to be to some extent caused by physical conditions over which the perpetrator has no control. But if he has no control, how can he be regarded as morally responsible for what he does? And if this is true, is it right to punish him?

Many drugs may appear to alter the personality. Prozac, which helps the brain maintain its level of serotonin, alleviates depression, violent mood swings, panic attacks and obsessive-compulsive disorders. When taking a pill can change your mood and the way you interact with others, it is difficult to resist the conclusion that who people are is largely chemically determined.

There is, however, some evidence which points in the opposite direction. There is evidence that behaviour may actually influence the chemistry of the brain.

Case Study: The Chemistry of Obsession

Therapy for obsessive-compulsive disorder changes not only behaviour, but the chemistry of the brain itself.

Obsessive-compulsive disorder (OCD) afflicts millions of people who repeatedly wash their hands or check that they have in fact switched the cooker off, or locked the door behind them. These obsessions can be so overpowering that they interfere with people's work performance or social or family relationships. Obsessives usually know that their behaviour is irrational, but they cannot do anything about it.

Drugs help relieve the symptoms, but most people relapse when the drugs are withdrawn. Behavioural therapy is more effective. The therapist encourages his patients to expose themselves to a situation that provokes the obsessive response. The patients gradually learn how to lengthen the amount of time they can ignore their compulsion. Eventually their urges subside.

A team of psychiatrists and psychologists at UCLA used brain-imaging techniques to show that key brain structures, whose activity is abnormal in obsessive patients, operate normally after therapy. Thus behavioural therapy changes not only the obsessive's behaviour but also his brain chemistry.

Jeffrey Schwartz and his colleagues used positron-emission (PET) tomography scans

---

to examine patients before and after ten weeks of therapy. Injections of radioactively labelled glucose, by revealing which parts of the brain are taking up the most glucose, enable PET scans to show which parts were active. Schwartz's team focused on four areas involved with OCD. They found that before treatment, all of the regions they studied ate up glucose at very high rates, but that the absorption of glucose dropped in the patents who responded to the treatment. A person in behavioural therapy learns to tolerate the warning messages his brain receives, and in doing so, he somehow also changes his brain chemistry.

This shows that the brain remains plastic much later in life than people previously thought, and is capable of fundamental change throughout life.

Before considering proposed solutions to the problem of free will, we need to consider the view that there is really no genuine problem of free will, since science has recently shown that determinism is not true.

According to the Heisenberg Uncertainty Principle, we cannot know both the position and the velocity of a subatomic particle. Our knowledge of subatomic particles is thus limited to statistical knowledge. We can know that over a certain period of time a certain percentage of events will take place, but we cannot predict an individual event. This is sometimes held to show that the determinist thesis that every event in the universe has a cause is false, opening the door for human freedom of choice.

This is a misdirected argument, since although the Indeterminacy Principle allows statistical indeterminacy at the level of particles, it does not make any difference on the level of larger objects, on the level of things that matter to human beings.

An alternative position is presented by C. A. Campbell, who argues that acts are free if they are determined by their subject, and if the subject could have done something different from what he actually did do. This view, called libertarianism, is incompatible with determinism.

Many existentialist philosophers have been very concerned to stress that what makes human beings human is their freedom of choice, which is unavoidable. According to Jean-Paul Sartre, we are "condemned to be free." We may be pressured by internal desires, but they are never more than a factor in the situation. It is *always possible* for the student to give up seeing that favourite television show, to miss that important sports fixture or to cut that much-anticipated party, in order to study for a test. It is always possible for a starving man to refuse food, perhaps as part of a hunger strike.

When faced with opposed positions of this type, a good practice is to see whether or not the alternatives are, in fact, genuinely incompatible. The standard resolution of the dilemma is to say that freedom and determinism are not genuinely incompatible. This view is known as **compatibilism**.

A rather blunt and unsatisfactory attempt to do this was provided by the German philosopher, Kant. He argued that we adopt radically different approaches towards the world depending upon whether our interests are theoretical or practical. When our interests are theoretical, that is to say when we are concerned with obtaining knowledge, we must adopt the standpoint that everything is determined in order to understand the world by means of causal explanations.

"Actions of men are determined in conformity with the order of Nature, by their empirical character and other causes; if we could exhaust all the appearances, there would not be found a single human action which would not be predicted with certainty."

On the other hand, when we turn to practical matters, when we are deciding how to act, we necessarily adopt the view that our own acts of will are the causes of our actions, and that we could act other than we do. We act in a way which implies the falsity of determinism.

The problem with this approach is that it assumed a fundamental bifurcation between what we know of the world and how we behave in it. In a sense it leaves the dilemma of freedom and determinism unresolved.

More usually, compatibilists approach the problem by investigating what is implied by saying that an act is free.

It is usually argued that to say that our actions are determined is not to deny that they are free. It is only to deny that they are constrained. That is, it rules out that they are determined in certain ways, but not that they are determined at all. Free acts are rather like the flow of water. If it is not impeded water flows according to natural laws, but we say that it flows freely. An unfree act is like an impeded flow.

When we claim that our actions are free we mean that they are not:

- Actions determined by forces outside us, i.e. performed under overwhelming external compulsion. Thus Moritz Schlick stated: "The question of whether man is morally free is altogether different from the problem of determinism. Man is free if he is not compelled, and he is compelled only when he is hindered from without in the realisation of his natural desires."

- Actions determined by unusual overwhelming internal forces. Actions performed while under the influence of post-hypnotic suggestion would be of this type. Under hypnosis a patient may be told that at a certain point after coming out of hypnosis he will perform some trivial task. For example, he is told that when the clock strikes noon he will go to the window and look down into the street. After coming out of hypnosis he may be engaged in casual conversation when the clock strikes. He will then go to look out of the window. Asked why he did it he will, apparently quite unconsciously, invent some plausible reason for what he did, such as "I thought I heard something down in the street." The action may have appeared to be the result of a typically "free" choice, but the observers know that in fact it was predetermined.

Similarly, someone who threw himself out of an upstairs window while trying to fly, who was found to have been under the influence of the hallucinogenic drug LSD at the time, would not be deemed to have performed a free act.

- Actions performed in ignorance. If I choose to open a door when, unbeknownst to me, someone is behind it standing on a ladder, and if in doing so I knock him off the ladder and he is injured, I could not be said to have freely injured him.

When we say that human actions are free, we do not deny that they are caused. If our actions were uncaused they would be inexplicable to us, and in that case, we should not claim them as free acts anyway. We should deny that they were truly actions of ours at all. To claim that human actions are free is to specify that they have *a certain kind of cause*, namely: motive, intention, decision, etc. On this view, to assert human freedom is not to deny determinism, just to deny that human actions are fully determined by certain sorts of causes, such as mechanical causes.

Another attempted solution has been offered by the philosopher Donald Davidson. He argues that we can think of events only in terms of their outward, physical descriptions, such as "my arm moving upwards." But there are some events which are capable of bearing essentially different descriptions: "my moving my arm up." The first is a physical description of a bodily movement, the second is a psychological description in terms of my intention or will. Similarly, a given event might be described as the pulling of a trigger of a gun and killing someone, or as an act of murder. The first is a physical, the second moral description.

Now, if the different descriptions of an event were such that they could not be translated into each other in an automatic way, then it would be possible for events to be related deterministically, as cause and effect, under the physical description, but not under their moral description. If we choose to talk of human actions in moral terms, then we can assume free will, and avoid any conflict with determinism.

5. Ideology in the Human Sciences

If ideology can creep into the natural sciences, it is certain that it will make its way into the human sciences.

Case Study: Abnormal behaviour and Mental Illness.

Today we are used to the idea that if someones' behavioiur is bizarre and unusual, he is suffering from a psychiatric disorder or mental illness. yet many people think that the concept of a mental illness involves an illegitimate intrusion of ideology into science.

Psychiatrists make "diagnoses" of mental and behavioural conditions, and offer "treatments" of the "mentally ill" in "mental hospitals," by analogy with the diagnoses and treatments of the physically ill in normal hospitals. The core of this system of ideas is the concept of "mental illness."

There are some diseases which can affect the brain, such as syphilis, resulting in disorders of thinking and behaviour. These are strictly diseases of the *brain*, however, not the mind. Yet by wholesale extension of this idea, all apparent disorders of thinking and behaviour now tend to be attributed to some as yet unknown biological cause, such as a neurological defect. This licenses us to create a shadow or counterpart of all the apparatus of medicine and the medical profession to deal with abnormal behaviour.

Mental illnesses are understood as bodily illnesses which manifest themselves in mental disorders. But all disorders of thinking and behaviour then tend to be attributed to biological causes. Yet these may be caused by the stresses and strains of living: by events in the patient's life, or a patient's unfulfilled psychological needs.

The blame for such disorders is placed in the wrong place. Psychiatrists blame the body for disturbed behavior, rather than the society of which he is part. It diverts attention from the social environment, no matter how much psychological disorder it causes.

Opponents of standard psychiatry point out that it effectively redefines social deviance as a medical problem. In so doing, it transforms social norms, which are relative and political, into medical norms, which are supposed to be objective and scientific.

Those who wish to defend the concept of mental illness argue that they sometimes run in families, so that it may have a genetic, and therefore biological, cause. But this argument does not prove that anything. It has been pointed out that membership of particular religious groups runs in the familly, yet no one proposes that there are Catholic or Protestant genes. In spite of this, belief that behavioural problems such as alcoholism are inherited is widespread today. Robin Murray, a leading expert in the genetics of alcoholism, found no difference in rates of alcoholism for identical and non-identical twins.

This would seem to eliminate a genetic, and therefore biological, hypothesis.

We do, as a society, find it convenient to use the concept of mental illness. But this is because turning social deviance into a medical problem allows society to take coercive measures against people whose behavior deviates from what is considered desirable. For this reason, psychiatry has redefined a great deal of normal human behavior as medically deviant by categorizing as ill people who are socially marginal.

- In the days of slavery in the USA, slaves who tried to escape their masters were classified as mentally ill: their irrational desire for freedom being considered a symptom of a mental disease called drapetomania.

- Before 1974, homosexuals were categorised as mentally ill, homosexuality being defined by the American Psychiatric Association as a mental disorder. This licensed barbaric attempts to "cure" people of homosexual desires.

- In the USSR in the 1970-80s, political dissidents were defined as schizophrenic simply because they opposed Communism. ("They must be mad!")

Being different and standing out lie at the core of "mental illness." But "abnormality" not an objective statistical matter of falling outside the normal range of distribution; it is a socially constructed category. Notions of the normal and the abnormal are value concepts which come from society, or rather from its politically and economically powerful elites, and which are therefore written into the dominant ideology.

Thus what "counts" as normal, or abnormal, behaviour varies from culture to culture. Behaviour which, in medieval Europe, might get someone the reputation of a saint, would today get him committed to a mental asylum. Similarly, much of the behaviour considered normal, or even desirable, in our culture, would be regarded as pathalogically abnormal in others. The desire of the successful businessman to spend the rest of his life getting even richer, something considered as "natural" and even praiseworthy in the modern USA, would have been seen in ancient Greece as shameful and unbalanced, as lacking in self-control and a sense of what is appropriate.

Marginal behaviour is stigmatised in our society as mental illness. Such people can be locked up in padded cells, and given electric shock "treatment" - for their own good, of course! In the early part of the century they might have received a lobotomy, (having part of their brain removed). The surgeon would open several small holes into the brain and insert a wire knife, severing some fibres with sideways movements. Later the knife would be inserted after making an opening in the roof of the eye orbits. In 1945 a simpler technique was developed. A common ice pick was inserted into the brain by tapping it with a hammer to sever the prefrontal lobe. The patient would need just a local anaesthetic, although experienced neurosurgeons sometimes fainted when watching it. Between 1939 and 1951, more than 18,000 lobotomies were performed in the United States. In Japan, most of the patients were children who exhibited problematic behavior or who produced poor results at school. Political radicals were treated as mentally deranged and lobotomised. In other societies they might have been called "heretics" and burned at the stake.

In consequence many say that there is no such thing as psychotherapy, the curing of psychiatric disorders. Like the mental illness it is supposed to cure, it is a myth based upon a metaphor. It is a pseudoscience.

6. Pseudoscience in the Human Sciences

Pseudoscience is a much more common phenomenon in the field of the human sciences than the natural sciences. There are probably several reasons for this:

- Because "science" has become an honorific title, those working in the human sciences are tempted to make claims beyond what heir subject matter and methods will properly permit.

- Because they are concerned with people, the human sciences promise knowledge of great personal importance to people. This gives the pseudoscientist an opportunity to make money out of his practice.

Case Study: Measuring Character from Bumps on the Head

In the eighteenth century one the most powerful methods of investigating brain function, the observation of persons suffering from neurological disabilities due to localised lesions of the brain, such as tumours, was still in its infancy. At that time, the main source of knowledge about the brain came from dissections performed on the dead bodies of animals and humans. Localisation of function in the brain could only be inferred only from the fact that there are many different-looking anatomical structures in it, which perhaps could be responsible for different faculties of the mind.

The Austrian physician Franz Joseph Gall pioneered the notion that different mental functions are located in different parts of the brain. In doing so, he created phrenology. Initially greeted with enthusiasm, it was later castigated by scientists as a pseudoscience.

In his book, *The Anatomy and Physiology of the Nervous System in General, and of the Brain in Particular*, of 1796, Gall argued that man's moral and intellectual faculties depend on the brain. He argued that the brain is composed of many different "organs," each one of which is related to, or responsible for, a specific mental faculty. The relative development of mental faculties in an individual would lead to a growth or larger development in the organs responsible for them. The external form of the cranium reflects the internal form of the brain, and therefore the relative development of the organs within the brain causes changes of form in the skull, which can be used to diagnose the particular mental faculties of individuals.

Gall carried out numerous and careful measurements of the skulls of his relatives, friends and pupils in order to correlate particular mental faculties to bumps and depressions on the surface of the skull in particular regions.

He identified thirty-seven mental and moral faculties which were thought could be represented in the exterior surface of the skull. These faculties were divided into several spheres: intellectual, perceptiveness, mental energy, moral faculties, love, etc. Most of them dealt with personality traits, such as firmness, cautiousness, spirituality, constructiveness, destructiveness, individuality, self-esteem, idealism, affection, etc. He produced a complete map of the location of the organs relating to these, and therefore of the areas of the cranium where their development could be detected.

The theory quickly captured the public imagination. The precision and scientific assurance of its terminology and cranial maps seemed authoritative and rational.

Eventually however, phrenology was itself attacked by the scientific establishment, which could not corroborate Gall's theory with concrete findings. In 1808, an investigating committee of scholars set up by the Institute of France declared that phrenology was not a

---

genuine scientific theory.

Gall's belief on localised brain functions was not based on experimentation or clinical observation, even though it turned out to be correct anyway. The concept that the brain organs grew accordingly to the development of corresponding mental faculties was also not based on scientific evidence, and could not be empirically tested at the time. His idea that the external topography and dimensions of the skull have something to do with the shape of the brain inside was also false. This is known today, when PET scans have revealed the anatomical relations between the two structures in great detail.

But Gall's map of the skull, which located regions where the bumps and depressions related to the thirty-seven faculties could be measured and diagnosed, proved a useful device for quacks to employ for the commercial exploitation of gullible persons, very much like astrology, palm-reading, and tarot card reading. Phrenological Parlours sprang up across Europe and the USA during the 1820s and 1830s. People consulted phrenologists for hiring employees, selecting partners for marriage and diagnosing mental illness.

Phrenology has spawned many other pseudoscientific branches based on the quantitative analysis of facial and cranial features, such as craniology, anthropometry and psychognomy. Even today there are self-appointed experts who work, talk, teach and write on the "science" of phrenology, and there are a lot of people who believe in its tenets or make money out of it.

One of the offshoots of phrenology was craniology, which advocated the use of precise quantitative measurements of cranial features in order to classify people according to race, criminal temperament, intelligence, etc. Craniology became influential during the Victorian era, and was used by the British to justify the colonisation and dominance of "inferior peoples," such as the Irish and the black tribes of Africa. Racial types were classified by their degree of prognathism (advancement of the jaw in relation to the mandible). "Inferior" races were said to be prognathic, being similar in this respect to apes and monkeys, so that they were considered to be more kin to these animals than the majority of European people.

An Italian named Cesare Lombroso, in his *Criminal Anthropology* (1895) associated certain craniofacial features with criminal types. For instance, Lombroso thought that murderers have prominent jaws, while pickpockets have long hands and scanty beards. Lombroso was a highly influential figure in the Italian police and judicial systems. Anthropometry was in use as late as the 1930s, when many judges were still ordering anthropometric analyses of defendants in criminal charges, which would be used against them by the prosecution in trial procedures.

Anthropometry was used by Nazi-inspired anthropologists and physicians, who sought to place the distinguishing of Aryans and non-Aryans on a scientific basis, using measurements of the skull. Official craniometric certification became required by law, and measurements were carried out in hundreds of institutes. Many people were sent to the death camps or denied marriage or work as a result of their "measurements."

Even today reputable companies use equally dubious pseudosciences such as graphology, the interpretation of handwriting, to sift through job applicants. They might as well use astrology or the reading of coffee grounds or tea leaves.

Glossary

behaviourism: a reductionist view that all human thoughts, feelings and values can be reduced to nothing more than complex products of the physiology of the human body, and can only properly be studied by the methods of the natural sciences.

black box: a methodological device for studying something without reference to its internal structure or features.

bodily movement: a movement of a human body which is a reflex, and is not under conscious control.

case study: a detailed description over an extended period of time.

coding system: a method of giving consistency to observation in the human sciences by establishing objective criteria for the occurrence of certain types of behaviour.

comparative method: making comparisons between various human societies and situations as an alternative to comparing the variables with the constants in an controlled experiment.

compatibilism: the view that philosophical determinism and what we call free will are in some way compatible.

determinism: the view that every event follows necessarily from other events.

empathy: an approach by which the investigator puts himself in the place of his subjects and tries to see things from their viewpoint.

epiphenomenalism: the view that mental events are a by-product of physical causes, themselves unable to act upon the physical world.

fatalism: the view that a person cannot take action to determine his own fate.

field observation: observation in a natural setting.

haphazard sampling: the practice of obtaining responses from people who happen to be passing the investigator.

human action: something performed by a person, consciously and deliberately, as opposed to a physical tic or reflex movement of the body.

interactionism: the view that physical states of the body affect mental states, and mental states affect the body's physical states.

libertarianism: the view that human actions are not determined but may be the result of unfettered free choice.

mind/body dualism: the view that a human being consists of a material body and a separate, substantial soul or mind which is the *real* person.

non-participant observation: observation in which the observer avoids intervention in the situation he is observing.

Oedipus effect: making a prediction about people may serve to alter their future behaviour so as to fulfil, or falsify, the prediction .

participant observation: observation in which the observer becomes part of the situation he is observing.

predestination: the view that everything which happens has been foreseen and predetermined by God to happen in the way that it does.

quota sampling: an attempt to choose a sample that reflects the numerical ratios of various sub-groups in the population as a whole by e.g. gender, age, socio-economic class, etc.

random sampling: selecting a sample in such a way that every member of the population has, in principle, an equal chance of being chosen.

sample frame: the realistic description of an actual sample.

stratified random sampling: the application of random sampling methods within the various sub-groups created by quota sampling.

Turing Test: a test to distinguish a mind from a machine.

Verstehen: the view that human sciences must be grounded in first-person knowledge intelligible to us as human beings, and not third-person knowledge resulting from mere experimentation.

14. HISTORY

"Everything is the sum of its past, and nothing is comprehensible except through its history." (Pierre Teilhard de Chardin)

1. What is History

Before we can begin to look at some of the problems involved in the enterprise of history we shall need to be clear about the meaning of the word. "History" may refer either to:

- The past, as in "what happened in history."
- Accounts of what happened in the past.
- The academic discipline which seeks to construct accounts of what happened in the past, and to provide explanations for what happened.

The word will normally be used here in the third sense.

History in this sense is something created by historians. This involves:

- Seeking out the *evidence* for what happened. This consists in *locating* relevant printed and documentary sources in archives, libraries and in private possession, and collecting data in the form of non-documentary evidence from other researchers, such as archaeologists;
- *Selecting* from the sources the evidence relevant for a particular investigation;
- *Evaluating* the authenticity, reliability and usefulness of that evidence.
- Constructing an *account* of the past on the basis of the evidence. This entails making inferences from the evidence.
- Providing *explanations* for what happened. This involves using the evidence to place the topic studied in a wider *context* in order to understand it better.

Historical Evidence

Among the evidence which a historian may use to help him reconstruct and explain the past we may find any of the following:

- Written reports of events made by eyewitnesses.
- Written reports of oral traditions handed down from the past.
- Private Documents: letters, diaries.
- Legal documents; e.g. grants of estates and land, reports testimony in court cases, business contracts.
- Administrative documents: tax records, estate accounts, memos of government departments.
- Records: registers of births, baptisms, marriages, deaths, burials; ships logs.

- Newspaper reports and articles.
- History books and articles in historical journals.
- Literature: novels, popular ballads.
- Photographs and film archive.
- Sound radio recordings.
- Oral eyewitness reports by living witnesses
- Oral traditions handed down from generation to generation by word of mouth
- Inscriptions on buildings and tombs
- Material remains of the past: buildings, paintings, utensils, coins.
- Features of the landscape, e.g. evidence of past settlement, terracing of hillsides.
- Place-names may also be used to tell their story, e.g. Newcastle, Abbot's Bromley.

Documentary Evidence

The historian is chiefly directly concerned with *documentary* evidence of the past. Surviving evidence for ancient and early medieval times is usually very sketchy. Sometimes it is good, sometimes it is entirely lost. The chief problem lies in finding it and interpreting it. By contrast, the evidence for recent history, particularly in the developed world, is overwhelming in its amount. The administration of each recent US President has produced about 20,000,000 pieces of paper. President Ford was in the US White House for only two years. On leaving it took nine trucks to carry away over 16,000,000 pieces of paper. In 1973 all the paperwork of the US Federal Government was estimated to occupy nearly 30,000,000 cubic feet of space. The chief problem lies in sorting through this mass of evidence to get a clear picture of what was happening.

Written sources are divided by historians into primary and secondary sources. **Secondary sources** are historical writings: articles or books attempting to reconstruct or interpret the past. Clearly not all our accounts of the past can rest upon the work of previous historians, simply repeating in different words what earlier historians have written. Historians need to consider direct evidence about the past. The written source material which constitutes direct evidence is referred to as **primary sources**.

A historian needs to gather primary sources for the period he is studying, but merely collecting them is not enough. He will need to ensure that his source is **authentic**: that it is what it purports to be, and is not a forgery. This is often a very technical matter.

He will also need to ensure that the source is **reliable** for the purposes for which he is using it. T. E. Lawrence wrote: " . . . documents are liars. No man ever yet tried to write down the entire truth of any action in which he was engaged." A document is just the material upon which the historian needs to get to work; it does not speak for itself.

In order to work out what a document tells him, the historian needs to establish the nature of the document: What sort of a document is it? Who is its author? For what readership was it originally intended? Documents differ in their reliability depending upon the *sort* of documents they are. Private letters and diaries can show how individuals were affected by events, and how they interpreted them at the time. Memoirs are likely to be accounts of "what I wish I had said at the time," rather than "what I actually said". They will tend to be self-serving reconstructions of the past with the purpose of vindicating the author, showing all his actions in the most favorable light and imputing to him exclusively the best and noblest of motives. They will stress the deviousness and perfidy of his enemies and the incompetence of his subordinates. Public speeches of politicians will provide evidence of what the politician wished the public to think at the time, rather than what he actually thought.

Some documents which purport to be records of past or contemporary events may be little more than exercises in creative fantasy. The scholarly ninth century "historian," bishop Agnellus of Ravenna, who wrote a series of biographies of his predecessors, described his method of research as follows: "Where I have not found any history of any of these bishops, and have not been able by conversation with aged men, or inspection of the monuments, or from any other authentic source, to obtain information concerning them, in such a case, in order that there might not be a break in the series, I have composed the life myself, with the help of God and the prayers of the brethren."

In addition to asking what information a document was *originally* intended to convey, he must also ask what information it also *incidentally, or* unwittingly conveys.

In general, written sources do not give even and complete coverage of the past. They are usually concerned with the rich, powerful and literate classes. We may have also possess written evidence of unimportant things, and yet none of much more important events, due to the accidents which have affected the preservation of the records. Sometimes the sources may be too few, too sketchy or too uninformative to give us any reliable information, or to allow us to make reliable inferences from them. On the other hand the written data may be so abundant that it is necessary for the historian to trawl through them to find material relevant to his purposes.

In addition to considering his primary sources, the historian may rely upon the work of a large variety of experts: palaeographers, archaeologists, chronologists, numismatists, etc. Traditionally, most non-written evidence has been provided by archaeologists. They have supplied information about the nature of the sites they have excavated, and of artefacts which may have been recovered from them.

Increasingly, science is being employed in the service of the historian in order to glean more evidence from the findings of the archaeologists. For example, an examination of the bone structure and teeth of skeletons may help determine whether they died a violent death, their health and diet. Pollen grains buried with them may determine the vegetation cover in the vicinity at the time of burial. The same care has to be taken over the interpretation of non-documentary data as over the use of documentary sources.

Statistical evidence is increasingly being exploited by historians. The registers of baptisms, marriages and funerals kept in parish churches in England go back to the reign of Queen Elizabeth I, and have been supplemented by state produced registers of births, marriages and deaths since the nineteenth century. Increasingly, data such as medieval ordination lists and modern census returns provide material for statistical analysis by historians.

The Authenticity and Reliability of Images

Care also has to be taken in interpreting what might appear to be the most modern and reliable evidence: that on photograph and film, since even this may be deceptive. As we have already seen in Chapter Five, with a little help from the photographer, the camera *may* lie.

It is well known that governments systematically doctor photographs and create propaganda films, e.g.

- Photographs of the Soviet leadership were frequently "reissued" during the period of Stalin's purges, with leaders who had fallen out of favour removed. Over the years, some of those photographs became successively emptier and emptier.
- Hitler had propaganda film of the supposed persecution of Germans in the Sudetenland of Czechoslovakia shot in Germany using actors.
- A dramatic scene frequently screened, showing the planting of the Red Flag on top of the *Reichstag* by victorious soldiers of the Soviet Army, was a re-enactment. The original film showed a soldier wearing several watches, which he had obviously looted, so the moment was recreated for the cameras on the next day with more acceptably attired actors.

- Clips of Lindburgh's first non-stop solo flight over the Atlantic in the *Spirit of St. Louis,* usually presented as scenes from the flight itself, were actually taken afterwards.
- Some of the action scenes in the Oscar-winning film made for the British Ministry of Information *Desert Victory: The Battle of El Alemein,* were shot in the Pinewood Studios in Buckinghamshire. Others were filmed in North Africa, but behind allied lines before the battle had begun.
- Realising that it might be difficult to ensure an adequate film record of the D-Day landings in Normandy for showing to the public, a rehearsal on the south-west coast of England several weeks before the real landing was filmed instead. This is often shown today as archive footage of the invasion.

Facts and Explanations

In the past it was often thought that the function of a historian was simply to get at the facts and present them to the public. Marcus Tullius Cicero set out this ideal of absolute objectivity in the first century BC when he said: "The first law for the historian is that he shall never dare utter an untruth. The second is that he shall suppress nothing that is true. Moreover, there shall be no suspicion of partiality in his writing, or of malice." The nineteenth century German historian, Leopold von Ranke, saw it his duty as a historian to "show it how it really was." Sir George Clark contrasted "the hard core of facts" with the "surrounding pulp of disputable reality." This is what E. H. Carr referred to as the nineteenth century view that history consists in "the compilation of a maximum number of irrefutable and objective facts."

It is now clear that such simple objectivity is not possible for several reasons:

Selection: Firstly, history is based upon a *selection* of the facts. We mostly know of the history of ancient Greece from the Athenian viewpoint. We have no Theban, Corinthian or Spartan chronicle of the Peloponnesian War to compare with Thucydides' account. In ancient history, where sources are scarce, assessing the bias inherent in the range of surviving sources is important.

In modern history, where evidence is overwhelming, the process of making a selection from the sources is crucial stage in the creation of history, and any bias of selection of sources to work from will be the direct responsibility of the historian.

Point of View: The British historian A. J. P. Taylor confessed that ". . . no historian starts with his mind a blank, to be gradually filled by the evidence." But this is not peculiar to historians, it is something which we have found in every other branch of human knowledge and in our everyday life. History is always written from some particular point of view. As we have seen, evidence is always collected, evaluated and interpreted in terms of a preexisting theory which guides research. The danger is that an interpretative pattern will be imposed upon the data, determining which evidence is considered significant, and worth taking into account, and which is not.

In each age people become interested in new aspects of the lives of earlier peoples, and in new aspects of problems which have interested previous generations. Each generation brings to the task of understanding the past its own distinctive techniques and insights, making history ever richer than before.

Historians who surprise their colleagues by proposing a new interpretation of events, with new explanations of their causes, are called revisionists. **Revisionist history** is a new interpretation of some period or topic in the past based the collection of new evidence or a new interpretation of the old. The causes of the Cold War have traditionally been attributed to Stalin's aggression after the end of the Second World War. Recently, many historians have adopted the view that the main cause was the aggressive imperialism of US policy. This view is frequently called revisionist, and because of this, in the US the term has acquired for some a negative character.

R. G. Collingwood argued that this showed that there is no objective viewpoint. He argued that there are no "pure" facts. They all come to us through the mind of the one who records them. "My first answer to "What is history?" is that it is a continuous process of interaction between the historian and his facts, an unending dialogue between the present and the past." For this reason, history is constantly being rewritten.

However, just because something looks different from different viewpoints it does not follow that we cannot say anything objectively true about it. In any case, a historian must have some capacity to rise above the limitations of his own society and place in history. Moreover, there is a large body of historical knowledge about which dispute is not easily possible, e.g. that Great Britain and France declared war on Germany on September 3rd 1939. This knowledge may be referred to as "historical fact" without anyone being mislead. Such "facts" are indispensable to any study of the past.

Historical Explanations

Russian novelist Leon Tolstoy expresses the puzzlement which we often feel when attempting the explanation of some great historical event when, in *War and Peace,* he seeks to know how the Napoleonic wars began. He muses:

> "What led to this extraordinary event? What were its causes? Historians, with simple-hearted conviction, tell us that the causes of this event were the insult offered by the Duke of Oldenberg, the failure to maintain the continental system, the ambition of Napoleon, the firmness of Alexander, the mistakes of the diplomatists, and so on . . .
>
> The causes of this war seem innumerable in their multiplicity. The more deeply we search out the causes the more of them we discover; and every cause, and even a whole class of causes taken separately, strikes us as being equally true in itself, and equally deceptive through its insignificance in comparison with the immensity of the results, and its inability to produce (without all the other causes that concurred with it) the effect that followed . . .
>
> And consequently nothing was exclusively the cause of the war, and the war was bound to happen, simply because it was bound to happen. . . .
>
> Although in that year, 1812, Napoleon believed more than ever that to shed or not to shed the blood of his peoples depended entirely on his will (as Alexander said in his last letter to him), yet then, and more than at any time, he was in bondage to those laws which forced him — while to himself he seemed to be acting freely, to do what was bound to be his share in the common edifice of humanity, in history."

It is clear from this passage the concept of a cause, as used in history, has some peculiarities. Historians usually seek for multiple causes, and they seek to order these in some form of hierarchy of priority.

They will usually distinguish:
- Underlying conditions which render the effect probable.
- Abnormal antecedents which are unusual factors which intrude in an otherwise comparatively stable situation and precipitate the effect.
- The motivation which lies behind the free and deliberate acts of conscious, responsible agents.

In arranging their causes in a hierarchy, historians distinguish between deep, underlying causes and surface causes; between long-term causes and short-term causes, and between cause and immediate cause or trigger.

Shallowness: causal explanations of events may fail because shallow or short-term causes only are cited. These usually fail to explain adequately why the event occurred.

Case Study: Herodotus and the Causes of the Ionian Revolt

In 500 BC Aristagoras, the tyrant of Miletus, launched a revolt of the Ionian Greek states under Persian rule in Asia Minor. Herodotus gives two reasons for the revolt.

Firstly, Aristagoras was acting as tyrant for Histiaeus, who had been taken to Susa, ostensibly to advise the king, but really so that the Persians could keep an eye on him, as the Persian satrap did not trust him. Becoming bored and discontented, Histiaeus had sent a message to Aristagoras calling for a revolt, by cutting a slave's hair off, tattooing a message on his scalp, allowing his hair to grow again, and sending him to Miletus. In this way he hoped that a revolt would break out there, and Darius would allow him to return home to restore order.

It so happened that the message was well-received at Miletus, since Aristagoras was at that time in a quandary. He had concocted a plan to use a Persian army to help capture Naxos on behalf of some discontented aristocrats, but the plan had failed. Aristagoras had been held responsible for this costly failure, and financially responsible for the expenses incurred. But since the expedition had failed, he had no plunder with which to pay them. The revolt promised him a way out of his difficulties with the Persian satrap.

Accordingly, Aristagoras met with the leaders of the many Greek states of Ionia, and they decided to launch a revolt.

As an explanation of the outbreak of the Ionian Revolt, this is obviously inadequate. It might explain why two important persons might have *desired* a revolt, but it fails entirely to explain why they Aristagoras was able to raise one. For the other Ionaian states to join in so readily there must have been some *general* discontent which rendered them amenable to Aristagoras' appeal.

For this reason, modern historians have been forced to seek for underlying causes of the revolt. Some have argued that the problem was a tribute of four hundred talents a year the Persians raised from the Greeks of Asia Minor; others have suggested discontent with the reigning tyrants, who were seen as puppets of the Persians; while others have proposed a general discontent caused by a widespread decline in economic activity.

A causal explanation needs to be powerful enough to generate the effect it is supposed to be explaining. If it is not, we need to look further. Children's history books are full of obviously inadequate "explanations," the sole merit of which is their brevity and simplicity, e.g. that the First World War was "caused" by the assassination of Archduke Franz Ferdinand in Sarajevo.

Hindsight: In understanding the past we must not forget that the intervening period of history, with all its developments, was unknown at the earlier period. We must not look back on a particular period with our knowledge of what happened subsequently, and assume that people at the time knew what we know, yet *still* acted as they did. For them the immediate future was still unknown.

Case Study: Hitler and the Policy of Appeasement

"Appeasement" is the policy of giving way to force or the threat of force. It is most frequently used to describe the policy of the Western powers towards the dictators, and particularly towards Hitler, during the years 1929 to 1939, when a series of breaches of international agreements and acts of aggression by the dictators failed to provoke any firm response from the Western powers until war was unavoidable.

Soon after he came to power, Hitler reneged on several agreements and obligations laid down by the Treaty of Versailles at the end of the First World War. For example, in March 1935 he announced that it would no longer abide by the limitations on Germany's armed forces set out in the Treaty. These breaches culminated, in March 1936, in the occupation of the Rhineland, an area demilitarised by the terms of the Treaty. Not only did the Western powers fail to respond to this challenge to international order, they proceeded to connive at ignoring German and Italian intervention in the Spanish Civil War.

Early in 1938 Hitler sent German troops to occupy Austria and incorporated it into the *Reich*. He then hd his agents provoke disturbances among the Germans of the Czech Sudetenland, and complained that they were being persecuted. In May 1938 the British and French leaders pressured the Czechs to make concessions in order to avoid war. Instead of being satisfied, Hitler promptly increased his demands and prepared for invasion. At an emergency summit in Munich it was agreed that the Sudetenland should be handed over to Germany immediately, in return for a guarantee of the independence of the rest of Czechoslovakia. Yet in March 1939, after provoking a split in the country, German troops occupied the rest of that Czechoslovakia. Several weeks later, the town of Memel, in Lithuania, was similarly swallowed up. On 1st September 1939, after concluding a secret deal with the USSR to divide the smaller nations of Eastern Europe between them, Germany invaded Poland.

On 3rd September 1939, Britain and France finally declared war on Germany. The USSR would not join the war until itself attacked by Hitler in June 1941, and the USA only when, after the bombing of Pearl Harbor by the Japanese in December 1941, Hitler himself declared war on that country.

Winston Churchill, who had vehemently opposed the policy from the start, pointed out that every successful move by Hitler had brought him new resources and strategic advantages, making the inevitable war, when it came, much more difficult than it would otherwise have been. he was accused of being a "warmonger."

With the benefit of hindsight, it is easy to condemn the Western leaders as shortsighted and cowardly, and to wonder at their lack of insight into Hitler's long term aims. But *they* did not know at that time that each demand made by Hitler was going to be followed by another. They did not know anything about future Nazi invasions, war crimes or the extermination camps, because for them those things still lay in the future.

There were warning signs. One only had to read Hitler's book *Mein Kampf* to realise what he was about; and some people, like Churchill, read the signs correctly. But if we are to understand why certain decisions were made in the past, we must understand that those who made them did so in ignorance (blameworthy or not) of what was to happen later. What is knowledge of the past for us was speculation about the future for them. Unlike ourselves, they did not have the benefit of hindsight.

3. History as Myth and Propaganda

"Who controls the past controls the future; who controls the present controls the past."
(George Orwell)

There is in many countries a large gap between:
•   History as an academic subject, as studied in universities: rigorously and in accordance with the normal standards appropriate to serious academic work.
•   History as taught in schools and as popularised in the media: sometimes little more than nationalist propaganda.

In many countries, the purpose of history as taught in schools is to initiate the young into the prevailing ideologies. In National Socialist Germany, this was nationalism and Nazism; in Soviet Russia it was Marxism-Leninism; and in the USA today, it is a potent mix of liberal monopoly capitalism, nationalism and imperialism.

> **WHEN IDEOLOGY IS ALL-PERVASIVE
> WE TAKE IT AS THE NORM**

Case Study: A Dismal Subject - US High School History

History is generally not a popular subject in US high schools, and in consequence, the average US citizen's knowledge of history is not impressive. In *Lies My Teacher Told Me: Everything Your American History Textbook Got Wrong*, James Loewen charges: "College teachers in most disciplines are happy when their students have had significant exposure to the subject before college. Not teachers in history. History professors in college routinely put down high school history courses. A colleague of mine ... sees his job as disabusing his charges of what they learned in high school. In no other field does this happen. Mathematics professors, for instance, know that non-Euclidean geometry is rarely taught in high school, but they don't assume that Euclidean geometry was mistaught. Professors of English literature don't presume that "Romeo and Juliet" was misunderstood in high school. Indeed, history is the only field in which the more courses students take, the stupider they become."

Many see the problem as lying in the bland nature of the standard high school textbooks. Loewen examined twelve, ranging from seventh grade to first year college levels, and noted that:
•   Many events, from the origin of Thanksgiving to the causes of the American Civil War, are shrouded in myth and legend. Much of the detail is actually incorrect.
•   Some historical events are presented with virtually no historical antecedents or context at all, e.g. The Japanese attack on Pearl Harbour is not usually presented as a conflict caused ultimately by the conflict of the developing imperial ambitions of the USA and Japan in the Far East. We have already noted this absence of historical context in connection with the news, but to find it in history books is truly amazing.
•   The narrative is pervaded by pervasive, flattering stereotypes of the American

character. An absolute nobility of intention is always imputed to US actions. Failures are attributed only to blunders, usually arising from the simplemindedness of the pure, good and innocent.

• The standard myths of the dominant contemporary ideology are propagated as historical fact: e.g. "America, the land of opportunity."

• Conversely, the history of U.S. intervention in many parts of the world is missing from the curriculum, or recounted only briefly or in sanitised or whitewashed form. Usually left out of such books is a critical examination of how the United States has used - and continues to use - military intervention to control other lands and peoples for the economic interests of its dominant classes.

As president, George Washington ordered his army to burn and destroy Native American villages in New York. Since that time virtually every U.S. president has ordered the U.S. military to intervene in at least one foreign country or territory. It is a story usually neglected. Those U.S. interventions that do make it into school textbooks are usually described from the professed perspective of the policymakers who ordered them.

Ideological history can be seen for what it is when we compare it with what actually happened - the simple verifiable facts.

The following is a list of SOME of the wars, invasions and military interventions engaged in by the USA. Most never make it into US high school textbooks, while those that do are usually defended, rather than explained. A full list would be much too long to include:

1846 - The United States invaded Mexico, and after the war, forced that country to "sell" nearly half its territory to the United States. 1890 - Argentina; 1891 - Chile; 1891 - Haiti; 1893 - Hawaii; 1894-5 - China; 1894-6 Korea; 1895 - Panama; 1896 - Nicaragua; 1898-1900 China. 1898 - Spanish-American War: The United States took Cuba, Puerto Rico, Guam, and the Philippines from Spain, the former colonial power. Many in those countries looked forward to independence. In the Philippines it took 75,000 U.S. soldiers fighting for three years to defeat the Filipinos. 1898 - Nicaragua; 1899 - Samoa; 1899 - Nicaragua; 1901-14 - Panama; 1903 - Honduras; 1903-4 - Dominican Republic; 1904-4 Korea; 1906-09 - Cuba; 1907 - Nicaragua; 1907 - Honduras; 1908 - Panama; 1910 - Nicaragua; 1911 - Honduras; 1911-41 - China; 1912- Cuba; 1912 - Panama; 1912 - Honduras; 1912-33 Nicaragua; 1914 - Dominican Republic; 1914-18 - Interventions in Mexico; 1914-34 - Haiti: U.S. troops invaded and stayed for nineteen years, killing an estimated 78,000 people; 1916-24 - Dominican Republic; Cuba - 1917-33; 1918-22 - Russia: The United States joined forces with other nations to invade Russia following the 1917 revolution. They did not want a non-capitalist form of government to be successful. U.S. Secretary of State Robert Lansing said that the Bolsheviks were appealing "to a . . . class which does not have property but hopes to obtain a share by process of government rather than by individual enterprise. This is of course a direct threat at existing social order in all countries." 1918-20 - Panama; 1919 - Panama; 1920 - Guatemala; China 1922-27; 1924-5 - Honduras; 1925 - Panama; 1927-34 - China; 1932 - El Salvador. Many of the interventions in Central America were during elections. Many of these interventions were made during a period of supposed isolationism.

Richard Barnet of the Institute of Policy Studies estimates that since the Second

World War the United States intervened abroad on the average of once every six months, either overtly with troops, or "managing" operations fought by the forces of client governments against their own people, or entirely covertly, using the CIA and local collaborators to overthrow hostile governments or to prop up client governments in trouble. e.g. Taking over from the British in Greece, the USA supported a regime containing former collaborators with the Nazis, presided over fraudulent elections, brutal concentration camps, largely for ex-resistance fighters, and masterminded a vicious counterinsurgency campaign. In Chile in 1973, it was to overthrow a democratically elected government because it was "Communist." In 1969-75 it was to bomb Cambodia, precipitating a crisis in which two million were killed. In 1971-73 they carpet-bombed Laos. But the US was at war with none of these countries.

The aim of intervention was always portrayed by the USA as necessary "to defend itself," "to defend the free world," "to help the people" actually being attacked, or to "spread democracy and freedom."

Yet if the aim was supposed to be to help the people being attacked, and to spread democracy and freedom, why did the USA offer friendship, weapons and millions of dollars in aid to repressive regimes such as Franco's Spain, Suharto's Indonesia, apartheid South Africa, the Shah's Iran, and Sharon's Israel.

Moreover, it is by no means clear why it is precisely the best armed and militarily most powerful nation on earth which has so frequently been "forced" to invade other countries to "defend" itself. The USA now spends about as much on defence and weapons as all the rest of the world put together. The best armed and militarily most powerful nation on earth should be *least* vulnerable to attack.

Curiously, two wars which always do get written up, and do so as vital crusades for civilisation, are the First and Second World Wars. Yet the USA, always ready at the drop of a hat to go to war against relatively powerless countries, entered those wars only tardily: the First World War in 1917 after the sinking of the *Lusitania*, and the Second World War when attacked by the Japanese at Pearl Harbour in 1941.

• Some very important forces are almost entirely absent from US history books, such as the important role of business corporations in the determination of US foreign policy.

The need to feed corporate interests helps explain the long list of US military interventions. In his *War is a Racket*, memoirs written in retirement in 1935, US General Smedley Butler confessed: "I helped make Mexico safe for American oil interests in 1914. I helped make Haiti and Cuba a decent place for the National City Bank boys to collect revenues in. I helped in the raping of half a dozen Central American republics for the benefit of Wall Street. I helped purify Nicaragua for the International Banking House of Brown Brothers in 1902-1912. I brought light to the Dominican Republic for the American sugar interests in 1916. I helped make Honduras right for American fruit companies in 1903. In China in 1927 I helped see to it that Standard Oil went its way unmolested." Butler went on: "I spent most of my time being a high-class muscle man for big business, for Wall Street and for the bankers. In short, I was a racketeer, a gangster for capitalism . . . Looking back on it, I could have given Al Capone a few hints. The best he could do was to operate his racket in three districts. I operated on three continents."

Social class is also avoided. There is no indication in the school history books that

U.S. workers were very late in getting the rights enjoyed in other industrial societies, and that the struggle in the USA for those rights was much more violent than in Europe. Several hundred American workers were killed by security forces in the early part of the twentieth century. Right up to the outbreak of the Second World War, workers were still getting killed by the police and the army during strikes. Nothing like that was happening in Europe. Nor is the roll back of those rights after the 1970s covered.

• There is a systematic lack of balance. For example, during the Cold War, the reader is encouraged to consider the Soviet Union as a repressive state, and the USA as the champion of freedom. In support of this, much is made about the repression of dissidents in the USSR and its satellite states. Yet if we consider the facts, if Lech Walensa had been a dissident in a US client state like Guatemala, we would never have known his name. He would have been summarily killed by a death squad, led by a graduate of the School of the Americas in Florida, long before he had a chance to become famous. Nor is detailed information on the repression of Soviet dissenters and the maintenance of hegemony over the Soviet Empire balanced with information about the repression of US dissenters, or the maintenance of hegemony over the US Empire.

• Seldom is the past used to illuminate the present. High school history classes rarely cover much after the 1960s anyway.

In Loewen finds three reasons why US history textbooks are so bad.

• The first is that they choose to promote patriotism rather than critical understanding and enquiry. That is to say, ideological considerations are paramount.

• Secondly, this is what the small committees of volunteer watchdogs who control the choice of textbooks used in the classroom in many states prefer. In consequence, this is what publishers produce for them. Speaking to Loewen, one author called his own textbook "a McDonald's version of history - if it has any flavour, people won't buy it." In some states, for example, the slightest reference to social class inequalities will provoke accusations of "Marxism" which are fatal to a book's prospects.

• Thirdly, teachers themselves seem afraid to adopt a critical approach to the subject. In the sort of "intellectual" climate depicted above, this is perhaps not surprising. Teachers have been fired for daring to use books with what passes in the USA for "controversial" content. In *Classrooms in the Crossfire*, Robert O'Neil pointed out that "Teachers have been fired for teaching *Brave New World* in Baltimore, *One Flew Over the Cuckoo's Nest* in Idaho, and almost everything else in between."

Loewen reported that US teachers are even afraid to teach open-endedly. A study reported in Black's *The American Schoolbook* showed that 92% of American teachers never initiated a discussion of controversial subjects; 89% avoided discussing them even when students brought them up; and, most alarmingly, 79% did not believe that they should. In this totalitarian atmosphere, there is little chance for critical thinking or for ideology-free history.

TAKE YOUR "BULLSHIT DETECTOR"
TO HISTORY LESSONS

A Fresh Look at Recent History

When the ideological spectacles fall off, and people see the difference between ideological truth and real truth, the effect can be shocking, as in the example below:

"We had been taught since childhood that the cold war, including the Korean War, the Vietnam War, the huge military budgets, all the foreign invasions and overthrows of governments — the ones we knew about — we were taught that this was all to fight the same menace: The International Communist Conspiracy, headquarters in Moscow. So what happened? The Soviet Union was dissolved. The Warsaw Pact was dissolved. The East European satellites became independent. The former communists even became capitalists. ... And nothing changed in American foreign policy. Even NATO remained, NATO which had been created — so we were told — to protect Western Europe against a Soviet invasion, even NATO remains, bigger than ever, getting bigger and more powerful all the time, a NATO with a global mission. The NATO charter was even invoked to give a justification for its members to join the US in the Afghanistan invasion.

"The whole thing had been a con game. The Soviet Union and something called communism *per se* had not been the object of our global attacks. There had never been an International Communist Conspiracy. The enemy was, and remains, any government or movement, or even individual, that stands in the way of the expansion of the American Empire; by whatever name we give to the enemy — communist, rogue state, drug trafficker, terrorist . . ."

(William Blum *American Empire for Dummies*, a talk given in Boulder, Colorado.)

How to Detect History as Propaganda

- Is the story of your nation presented as one of continuous progress, where wise statesmen solve successive problems, and labour to improve the lives of everyone?

- Is your nation always presented as the victim, and never as the aggressor, in conflicts?

- Do unexplained "problems" appear in the history you have been taught, apparently out of nowhere, and with no past?

- Is there balance and objectivity in the descriptions of rival power centres?

- Is your society presented as united in its aims and goals, without any fundamental conflicts of interest?

If these things are true, then either your country is a heaven on earth, peopled by saints, or you have received, and perhaps absorbed, a "sanitized" and propagandist account of your nation's history.

- Is there a *systematic* inconsistency between what you were taught and the ascertainable facts. (Check to see).

4. The Borderlands of History – and Beyond

Some representations of the past do not qualify as history at all.

Historical Fiction

Historical novels falsify events by adding fictional padding in the interests of dramatisation. This practice has a long past. Ancient historians, such as Herodotus, used to invent dialogue and speeches to make their accounts more readable. For example, Herodotus records a long conversation between Darius and his wife Atossa while they were in bed. (One wonders how he got his information).

Yet despite this limitation, well-researched historical fiction may convey much about the past even though the people, the situations, even the particulars of the time and most of the places may be wholly made up. A well-written historical novel may convey something of the spirit or *Zeitgeist* of a culture and an era through the imaginative and empathic insight of the author.

Movies made of historical events, however, are usually extremely unreliable:

- They are often based upon very poor historical research.
- They may present only one among several possible interpretations of the events they portray.
- They may give a distorted interpretation of events in the interests of the nation by and for whom the movie was primarily produced.
- Many movies apparently based upon history, concoct unhistorical events and customs, and impose them on the historical truth: e.g.
  - The Patton Museum frequently receives enquiries from the public about when and where General Patton addressed the Third Army as shown the opening of the film, *Patton*. But he never actually did; the speech is a composite of things he said, or might have said, at various places and times. Yet the movie scene has created a historical event in popular mythology.
  - In *Fat Man and Little Boy*, a film about the building of the first atomic bomb, the central character is a physicist who opposed the use of the bomb and died of a radiation over-dose just before the test. Although the character is based on a real person, the historical figure did not oppose using the bomb, and died almost a year after the test.

Whether intending to deceive or not, such films create the danger of leading people to confuse the realities of particular events with artistic constructs.

The producers of such films would not usually claim that what they were creating was anything other than entertainment; on the other hand audiences will nevertheless absorb a distorted or incorrect view of history from seeing the film. In this way, the products of Hollywood have systematically distorted the public's understanding of history, for example, by:

- Disguising the systematic genocide of native Americans in the USA;
- Leaving the impression that the war against Hitler was somehow won by American and Allied troops invading Europe from the west, and deliberately ignoring the main theatre of fighting, and the most onerous burdens of war, borne in the east by the Soviet people and the Red Army.

Even though movies have been around for almost a century, there is still widespread disagreement, where historical subjects are involved, about acceptable purposes for making such films, and the standards of accuracy which should be observed. Despite the reputaion which they may enjoy as films, some are crudely inaccurate, while others are little more than propaganda.

Despite the fact that historical fiction is sometimes historically accurate in its details, it is never history.

Pseudo-History

- According to Erich Von Daniken in *Chariot of the Gods* and other books, astronauts from other planets visited ancient civilisations on earth in their spacecraft, and are responsible for the creation of many ancient monuments.
- A secret society of initiates has for centuries guarded the knowledge that the kings of France were descended from Jesus Christ.
- The ancient Greeks learned all their philosophy and science from the ancient Egyptians, who were black.

We frequently come across theories which, although claiming to be "historical," in fact use only the outer trappings of academic history, while avoiding the rigours of the checks built into its methods and the scrutiny of disinterested fellow researchers and experts. Following Martin Gardner's coining of the term "pseudoscience" these may conveniently be called "pseudohistory." Just as science is imitated by pseudoscience, so history is mimicked by pseudohistory.

The trappings of serious academic work adopted to disguise its spurious nature include:
- Publishing in formats that ape scholarly journals or documentary film-making;
- Exaggerating the credentials of individuals it cites as authorities;
- Adopting jargon-filled prose or speech to sound erudite
- Seeking to immerse the reader/audience in obscure detail and convoluted argument to give an aura of exhaustive knowledge, while making it more difficult to detect and discard pseudofacts and nonsense.

Pseudohistory may be recognised by the following marks:
- It tends to be uncritical in its reading of ancient historians, taking their claims at face value and ignoring contrary empirical or logical evidence.
- It is selective in its use of ancient documents, citing favourably those that fit with its agenda, and ignoring or interpreting away those which do not fit.
- It has a mission to support some contemporary national, religious or religious agenda, rather than find out the truth about the past.
- The assumption is frequently made that if something is possible, and is in accord with the mission of the writer, then it is probably true.
- It is sometimes denies that there is such a thing as historical truth, on the grounds that only what is absolutely certain can be called "true" and nothing is absolutely certain. If nothing is true, every claim is as good as any other, including the writer's.
- It is sometimes maintained that history is nothing but mythmaking and that different histories are not to be compared using traditional academic standards of accuracy, empirical probability, logical consistency, relevancy, completeness, fairness, honesty, etc., but on moral or political grounds.
- It is often maintained that there is a conspiracy to suppress its claims because of racism, atheism or ethnocentrism, or because of opposition to its political or religious agenda.
- It betrays a preference for the spectacular, such as megaliths and pyramids; the mysterious, such as the Templars or Freemasons; or the legendary, like Atlantis or King Arthur. These it tends to treat as literal truth.

Case Study: Holocaust Revisionism
During the 1950s and 1960s, there were one or two people on the extreme right in

---

the USA who suggested that the Holocaust, the attempted extermination of European Jews by the Nazis during the Second World War, was a fiction. One such was Austin App, a Pennsylvania college professor, who claimed that the Holocaust was a fantasy promoted by Zionists.

The Revisionists were given a veneer of academic respectability by Arthur Butz of Northwestern University in his book *The Hoax of the Twentieth Century*. In it, he made a deliberate effort to appear scholarly, impartial, and reasonable, unlike previous literature which had been filled with hate propaganda. Butz' book contained the reference notes and bibliography characteristic of scholarly works, quoting many prominent historians who worked in the field and thanking a number of legitimate research centres and archives for their "assistance." In appearance it was a respectable academic study, and it was possible to imagine that Butz had arrived at his conclusions as a result of his research findings, and not because of anti-Semititic prejudice.

The *Journal of Historical Review*, published by the respectable sounding body the Institute for Historic Review, founded by Willis Carto, a wealthy California business-man, became a vehicle for Holocaust Revisionism in the early 1980s. This publication carefully copied the style and format of mainline scholarly publications, while including articles of allegedly sophisticated photo-interpretation and documentary analysis which were supposed to discredit key evidence for the crimes committed by the Nazis. Besides the overwhelming weight of evidence to the contrary, the telltales clues that this was fraudulent were the irrelevance of the credentials of the "experts" who wrote the articles, and the excruciating contortions and ridiculous assumptions required to explain away the familiar and overwhelming evidence for the Holocaust.

Glossary

archive: a place where documents are stored.

authenticity: the genuineness of a historical document, that it is what it appears to be or claims to be.

critical apparatus: footnotes or endnotes which attribute the content of a book or article to sources which can be independently checked.

hindsight: the benefit of being able to understand events by looking back on them afterwards.

historiography: the writing of history.

primary source: written material, not itself created as history, used as a historical source

provenance: the history of a written source: its origins and transmission.

psychologism: the attempt to explain historical developments in terms of the psychology of key figures.

revisionist history: a fresh interpretation of the past, based upon new evidence, or a new interpretation of existing evidence.

secondary source: the work of previous historians considered as a historical source.

15. VALUES

"Not everything that can be counted counts, and not everything that counts can be counted." (Albert Einstein)

1. Normative and Descriptive Language

It is always important to distinguish between descriptive language and normative language.

Descriptive Language reflects the way the universe actually is (facts about the world):

(1)   France is a member state of the European Union.

(2)   The A1 motorway connects London and Birmingham.

(5)   The sun is approximately 93,000,000 miles from the earth.

Note that a proposition does not have to be true to function as a descriptive proposition; it has merely to be *intended* to describe. The following are (false) descriptive propositions:

(6)   Cheshire is in Scotland

(7)   Spiders are insects.

By contrast, normative Language reflects the way we want the world to be. It expresses our preferences, desires, or ideals.

(8)   The view from the top of Mount Everest is awe-inspiring.

(10) Driving dangerously is unacceptable behaviour.

(11) Spending on the state health service is more important than giving more special tax concessions to the wealthy.

Exercise 15

Are the following statements descriptive or normative?

1.   It is difficult to draw an accurate map of Norway freehand because of its indented coastline and many small islands.

2.   Surfing is a more worthwhile sport than skateboarding.

3.   France has the best national soccer team in the world.

4.   Jason prefers listening to Pavarotti than to the Spice Girls.

5.   China is the most populous country in the world.

Descriptive and normative propositions perform radically different functions. Descriptive language is used to depict the world as it really is, or as we suppose it to be. Normative language, on the other hand, expresses our values; it helps us form a concept of what we want our lives to be, or the meaning we wish to find in them. We use normative language to express our values.

2. What are Values?

Some have regarded the capacity to be dominated by values as a distinguishing characteristic of the human race. Whenever we make choices we prefer one alternative to another. This involves making a comparison against some standard or other. Some alternatives are thought to be better and others worse.

Values should be distinguished from facts. Facts are what *is* the case. Values appear in judgements of whether something is good or desirable.

Value is ascribed to very different kinds of things: to individual objects or collections, such as a work of fine art or a collection of such works; to a quality of something such as someone's kindness or ability to score goals; and to states of affairs, such as the signing of a peace treaty.

Values are of different types, and different types of value may be ascribed to the same object. We may consider, in addition to the economic value of a sports car, its recreational value, the trips we can make in it; its value in getting us dates; its aesthetic value, if it is a sleek, well-designed vehicle. In a capitalist society we tend to regard monetary value as of great importance.

Values may be instrumental or they may be intrinsic. Things which have only **instrumental value** are not valued for themselves, but only as means to something else. They are valued as a means to some **extrinsic end** — some end which is different from the means adopted to reach it. We recognise extrinsic value when we value something for its usefulness. This is most easily understood in relation to practical utility. We value some things because of what we can do with them: tools, medicines, etc.

Things which have **intrinsic value** are valued for themselves and not for anything else. The action of preparing a meal is not something we generally do because we enjoy preparing meals, it is done in order to eat. It is a means to an end which is different from itself. It has only instrumental value. By contrast, eating the meal may be an end-in-itself, if we eat the meal just because we enjoy eating. In such a case, the meal has intrinsic value.

Of course some people may prepare meals for the sheer hell of it. In *that* case, preparing the meal would also have intrinsic value. Sometimes we may even deliberately eat only in order to have the energy to carry on doing something else. In that case eating the meal would have extrinsic value. Thus in any individual case we need to look at the intention of the actor to know whether his act has instrumental or intrinsic value for him. Some things which we do not *usually* think of in terms of usefulness may nevertheless be valued by many people because of their usefulness. Scientific theories may be useful in helping us understand the world around us. Moral codes may be valued for their power to bring order to society and to discourage antisocial behaviour.

Theories of Value

Subjectivism: Both aesthetic and ethical values are often described as being merely subjective, and as having no objective validity. This is the view which people in our society normally take when they first consider the matter. It is claimed that:
* All value judgements are equally valid since they assert no objective truth.
* Value judgements do not refer to the objects which they purport to refer to, instead they refer to the subject. Thus "*x* is good" means "I approve of *x*" or "I find *x* pleasant".

This is sometimes called the "Boo-hooray theory." It is based upon the fact that much of our use of language is expressive. It is not so much intended to convey information as to express our feelings.

Our emotional attitudes towards things determine our tastes and preferences.

Consider the two propositions:

(14) Jason is a husky.

(15) Jason is a cute dog.

The first is clearly a statement of alleged fact which may be shown to be true or false. The second would normally be described as a statement of opinion. There will perhaps be many people who would agree with this proposition, but it is equally likely that many would not. Some people may not find huskies cute at all. There may be some people for whom no dog is ever cute, perhaps on account of some experience involving a dog and teeth which rules out for ever their appreciation of canine cuteness.

The difference is underlined by the differing ways in which those who advance the two claims would respond if they were challenged. The person advancing claim (14) would point to the size, shape, colour of the coat nose, and the behaviour of the dog, pointing out that these were all distinguishing characteristics of huskies. By contrast, the person advancing the claim embodied in (15) would probably just respond "Well, *I* think he's cute, anyway."

There is an important difference between the two types of proposition. Proposition (14) is an assertion about a dog; it is a characterisation of the dog. Proposition (15) is an assertion about the dispositions of the speaker. Proposition (14) is a statement about an externally observable and verifiable fact. Proposition (15) is about the internal state of mind of the person who made it.

Proposition (15) is an expression of *preference* based upon the speaker's taste. The speaker liked dogs, especially huskies, and that husky in particular. Other people might prefer cats, and find them cute. Some may even prefer gerbils or alligators!

From this it follows that if I say "X is good" and you deny it, we are each asserting different facts about ourselves. I find it pleasant and you do not. I like it and you do not. There is no contradiction in this, merely a difference of taste. We can quite properly dispute about matters of fact, but there is simply no point in disputing about matters of taste. I may prefer raspberries while you prefer strawberries, and that is all there is to it. As the Latin phrase has it: *De gustibus non disputandum* (there is no arguing about taste).

Of course I might decide that it would be selfish of me to keep what I know about raspberries to myself, and hence I might try to persuade you to join me. I might try to persuade you of what you were missing by going on endlessly about the delights of raspberries and ice cream, raspberry tart, and raspberry crumble. I could, if I liked, write poems in honour of the divine Raspberry, fruit of the immortal gods. But if you still persisted in declaring that you just did not like raspberries, it would not make sense for me to argue that you were wrong. Assuming that you were being honest with me, and not merely falsely claiming not to like raspberries for dramatic effect, perhaps to gain a reputation as a person of independent tastes, I would have to content myself with pitying you - and your raspberryless existence.

I might argue that my preference is healthier than yours, enumerate the many virtues of the raspberry as a support of health and safeguard against disease and old-age; while speculating on the dangerous properties of strawberries. But that not be relevant to the matter of taste as such at all.

If all value judgements were like this, then there could be no special aesthetic or ethical senses. Neither could there be any question of expertise in these fields. One person's opinion will always be equally valid with someone else's, since each person has privileged access to what he is talking about, namely his own feelings and judgements. There can be no question either of "art experts" or of "moral leadership."

It is clear that we do make subjective value judgements, and we do express them carelessly in the form of what appear to be objective judgements. We do not always say:

(16) I do not like spinach,

or   (17) I like liver

We are liable to say:

(18)   Spinach is awful,

and   (19) Liver is marvellous.

This *may be* what we do with aesthetic and ethical value judgements.

Moreover, the aesthetic or ethical quality of something does not seem to be a simple element in our sense-perception. It makes sense to say that I can see the number, the size, the shape and the whiteness of the columns of the Parthenon, whereas what we call its "value" would appear to be a result of my reaction towards it or a judgement which I make after I have seen it.

Similarly, when some terrible wrong is committed, I may hear the piteous cries for help and afterwards see the inert corpse, the blood on the floor and the grieving relatives. But the "wrongness" of the act is not part of my visual or auditory field, it seems to be a reaction towards, or a judgement made *about* what I have heard and seen.

In any case, value judgements differ greatly, both between individuals within a society and between societies. The ancient historian, Herodotus, observed that "Fire burns in both Greece and Persia, but men's ideas of right and wrong vary from place to place." Hastings Rashdall wrote:

"There is hardly a vice or a crime (according to our own moral standard) which has not at some time or in some circumstances been looked upon as a moral and religious duty. Stealing was accounted virtuous for the young Spartan and among the Indian caste of Thugs. In the ancient world Piracy, i.e. robbery and murder, was a respectable profession. To the medieval Christian religious persecution was the highest of duties, and so on."

Despite these facts, it is sometimes pointed out that value judgements do not differ all that much. Murder is regarded as wrong in most societies. It may be claimed that this is only because we use the word *murder* to refer to killing people on precisely those occasions when we thing killing people is wrong. We would then have to rephrase the point in order to say that "killing people without good cause is regarded as wrong." This is no doubt true as far as it goes, but there will be great disagreement from society to society about what counts as good cause. The apparent agreement is to some extent merely verbal.

What agreement exists in such matters can in any case be explained by reference to our common nature and situation. Despite great individual differences, we humans all have broadly the same needs and interests. Thus we can be expected to have, in general, the same preferences. This is paralleled by the fact that, with the same physiology of nose, tongue and digestion, despite differences in taste, we all tend to like sweet things and to dislike bitter things.

However, things may not be as simple as the subjectivists would like us to think. What "x is good" means is simply not the same as "I like x." This can be shown from the fact that it makes sense to assert both propositions of the same thing. I could decide that I appreciate that Richard Wagner's last opera *Parsifal* is a great work of art, but also at the same time assert, correctly and truthfully, that I personally do not like it, and would not want to sit through it because I would find it depressing. Similarly, I might decide that I would really like to rob my local bank, an action which I recognise would, alas, be morally wrong.

What this means is that subjective judgements of taste and preference are simply not the same as value judgements in aesthetics and ethics.

Objectivism: Objectivists believe that some types of value judgement are universally valid. They may be firmly grounded upon knowledge and embody truths about the world.

If people are specifically asked to explain the basis of aesthetic or ethical judgements in general they are likely to be initially nonplussed, and then to assert that there is no way of making objective judgements. However, if you watch the way in which they actually behave, you will find them frequently making value judgements in a way that would not make sense unless they believed themselves to be making judgements which had objective validity and which ought to be binding upon others. If challenged, most people would claim to be subjectivists or relativists; yet when not self-conscious, they behave like objectivists.

Objectivists do not claim that *all* values are objectively based. They distinguish between:

- Totally subjective **preferences** which involve no judgement about the properties of what is being valued. These are entirely expressions of personal taste, and relate wholly to our desires. We may properly infer things about the tastes of the subjects who make preferences, but nothing about the objects of preference. Preferences are most clearly expressed in statements of the form "I like *x*", although confusingly, as we have seen, they may be expressed, obliquely and misleadingly, in statements of the form "*x* is good."
- Much evaluation relates to what is necessary to us for the attainment of some goal or end we are striving for. The thing we value is valued not for itself, but for something else, to which it is only a means. These values are closely related to objective reality, in that whether we can successfully use them to attain our ends depends upon their natures and not upon our preferences. We value them for the properties they possess, which, as a matter of fact, we believe, will assist us in attaining our ends.
- Finally, although we value some things as means to extrinsic ends we could not value *everything* merely as a means to something else. Some things must be valued as ends-in-themselves. These things have intrinsic value. They are valued for what they are in themselves, objectively.

These things may or may not be objects of our preference. They are the things we *ought* to value.

To enter upon the Enterprise of Knowledge itself commits one to certain values, for the Enterprise is itself saturated with value:

- The value of Truth in itself.
- Values instrumental to the search for knowledge, such as the value of taking a fair and impartial stance towards evidence; and of persevering in the quest for truth in the face of difficulties.
- Value judgements are necessarily made in the process of organising and communicating knowledge: judgements of consistency, clarity, economy, elegance, etc.

3. Aesthetic Judgements

Aesthetic judgements are judgements of the beauty of natural objects or works of art.

Discussion

What demonstrates the value of a work of art:

- Its popularity with the majority of people?
- Its popularity with experts and professional critics?
- Its popularity over a considerable period of time?
- The amount of money it will fetch if it is placed on the market?
- The moral purpose of the artist?

- Its usefulness in conveying some truth or insight of the artist?
- The degree to which it holds up a light to some aspect of reality?
- The degree to which it expresses the emotions of the artist?
- The degree to which it evokes emotions in us?
- Its ability to make us think about some aspect of life?
- The qualities of balance and harmony which it displays?
- The value of the message it teaches?

Accounts of Aesthetic Judgements

Today, many philosophers argue that aesthetic judgements cannot be objective. They point out that if there were general agreement between different peoples about aesthetic judgements, we would be inclined to regard them as objective. But this is not so. Different peoples make very different aesthetic judgements. What is considered beautiful in some societies is counted ugly in others. Aesthetic judgements seem to be relative to individual taste and to culture. We have no right to assume that our own values are uniquely objective.

In support of this view, it must be noted that weighty "authorities" have passed negative judgements on works of art which we today tend to regard as of great value:

- In 1814 Lord Byron said "Shakespeare's name, you may depend on it, stands absurdly too high and will go down."
- L. Rellstab, reviewing Chopin's *Mazurkas* in 1833, wrote: "Had he submitted this music to a teacher, the latter, it is to be hoped, would have torn it up and thrown it at his feet."
- The verdict of the reviewer employed by the *New York Tribune* on 27th December 1900, on Puccini's new opera *La Boheme,* was "silly and inconsequential."

There are various subjectivist or relativist accounts of aesthetic judgements:

- To say that something is of high artistic value is to express an individual judgement of preference which is just a matter of taste.
- Aesthetic judgements are essentially about appearances, and appearances are subjective, limited to the mind of each observer.
- Historical, social and cultural factors condition the aesthetic judgement.
- A further possibility, suggested by Kant, is that aesthetic judgements are subjective, in the sense that they are founded upon the individual subject's reaction to what is perceived, rather than upon what is simply "out there." On the other hand, since all our individual subjectivities have a common nature, these judgements may command universal assent. Our aesthetic judgements could be universally acceptable, and yet also remain subjective.

However, over the course of history, most philosophers have held that some aesthetic judgements are objectively based: " . . . those who have practised more arts than one, in a greater degree even than those who have appreciated many, are aware that in every picture, in every art . . . beauty is unequivocally beauty." (E. F. Carritt)

Various accounts have been offered of *how* objective aesthetic judgements may be possible:

Aristotle says that "Beauty consists in a certain size and arrangement of parts." According to this traditional view, beauty is the conjunction of the many parts of an object in an adaptation to the form as a whole. This view has been described by De Bruyne as "the oldest, most persistent and, within its limits, the most successful."

It has been taken up again in the twentieth century by **formalism** as a reaction against the idea of art as a vehicle of knowledge, moral betterment or social improvement. Formalists do not deny that art is capable of functioning in these ways, but they believe that the true purpose of art is subverted by being subjected to such ends. Art is to be enjoyed for the perception of the intricate arrangements of lines and colours, of musical tones, of words, and combinations of these. Aspects of the world can be represented and emotions expressed; but these are irrelevant to the principal purpose of art. It is claimed that art is much less adapted to the telling of a story or the representation of the world than it is to the presentation of colours, sounds, and other items in the art medium simply for their own sake.

It is harmony of parts within the whole, when realised to an eminent degree, which is said to compel our recognition and admiration. The Indian philosopher Ananda Coomaraswamy explains that in the Pali language there is a special word, *samvega*, for the shock of wonder felt by the perception of beauty of a high order. But the attractive power of a work of art is not merely the power to arouse strong feelings, but it also involves cognitive appreciation. The philosopher and novelist Iris Murdoch argues that in this attractive power, the beautiful object is drawing our attention to "what is" independently of ourselves, and at the same time, in doing so, it "makes us more vividly alive than we otherwise know how to be."

Characteristics which provide objective standards of beauty in something include:

- *Unity* and integrity. Aristotle pointed out that the unity desired in works of art is like the unity of the higher organisms in which every part functions not independently of the others but interdependently with them; and it is this interdependency of the parts that constitutes an organic unity. Take away one part, and the remainder of the parts fail to function as before. The interdependency of parts often achieves a state of such perfection that it could often be said, of a melody or a sonnet, that if this note (or word) were not there, in just the place that it is, the effect on the totality of the melody or poem would be disastrous.
- A balance or *harmony* of the parts within the whole.
- The *suitability of the medium* (materials or means) chosen to achieve the ends desired.
- A technique which produces *success* in the achievement of ends
- *Economy* in the achievement of ends.
- *Elegance* in the achievement of ends.
- The work of art holds up to us or highlights some aspect of experience or reality in a way which powerfully *commands our attention*.

Our experience of beauty depends upon a knowledge of the object in which beauty is seen. It is absurd to suppose that someone could be presented with an object and expected to judge whether it was beautiful before knowing what it was. This is because features which we should regard as beautiful in one context would be regarded as ugly in another. Function governs our perceptions.

In favour of the view that there may be objectivity in aesthetic judgements, it is argued that:

- Despite obvious disagreements, there is in fact a considerable amount of agreement on matters of aesthetic judgement. We all tend to agree that the ruins of the Parthenon, on the Acropolis of Athens, are beautiful, and that the Pompidou Centre, in Paris, is not. But of course there is also considerable agreement on matters of taste. We all tend to agree that the taste of chocolate is nice, while that of sand is not. This is simply due to the common structure of our sense organs and to the common expectations and pressures we experience as part of a particular common culture.
- There are experts in art, who teach courses to communicate their expertise. At least some of them seem to be genuine experts and not charlatans. Therefore it could be argued that there must be some genuine objective knowledge which they have mastered. This must be based upon objective aesthetic judgements.

- It does seem that we can educate our taste, so that we come to appreciate what before we had been ignorant of or blind to.

Non-Aesthetic Judgements of Art

Art may be judged by non-aesthetic criteria. It may be judged as an agency of morality by the extent to which it reflects, upholds and endorses the system of morality which is adhered to at the time. In societies where this happens, then any art that does not promote moral influence of the conventional kind tends to be viewed with suspicion.

Yet art is also able to implant unorthodox ideas. It can help breaks the fetters of provincialism in which people have been brought up. Thus works of art are sometimes created out of rebellion or disenchantment with the established order. Art may contribute to undermine beliefs and attitudes on which, it is thought, the welfare of society rests and so may be viewed with suspicion by the guardians of custom. When art promotes questioning and defies established attitudes, it tends to be viewed as insidious and subversive.

The Comparison of Forms of Art

In addition to comparing individual works of art, judgements of the comparative value of entire forms of art, e.g. ballet and basketball, are sometimes made.

These are often implicit in the judgements made by governments whether to spend national revenue obtained from taxation on supporting one art form or another. Governments have limited budgets, and may support this art form rather than that one, e.g. drama rather than bridge, athletics rather than chess.

Sometimes these judgements are based upon a desire for national prestige, e.g. to gain gold medals in the Olympic Games, to sustain a prestigious opera house. But often they are based upon a feeling that some art forms, say opera, are too valuable to allow them to struggle unaided in the marketplace. In such cases, judgements of comparative worth have been made. A government may well say that if people do not want to pay to watch chess competitions, then chess competitions can, as far as they are concerned, die out. But they may intervene to save opera from extinction because of lack of public support. This implies that opera, in their opinion, is more valuable, more worthwhile, than the game of chess.

High Art versus Popular Art: When the terms "fine arts" and "work of art" are used it is medieval gothic cathedrals, renaissance murals, Chinese vases and grand opera which we tend to have in mind, rather than comic strips, soccer matches, acid jazz, or television soap opera. The former we might term "high art" and the latter "popular art."

Clearly there is a difference between the two. We usually behave as a society as though the former were more "worthy" than the latter. The basis of this comparison might be explained in several ways:
- High art is generally more popular with those who wield economic and social prestige and power in society, popular art with the masses. The former go to the concerts at famous opera houses, while the latter settle down in front of their television sets to watch soap operas.
- In the past the former were generally more costly to produce, although this may no longer be true. A Hollywood spectacular such as *Waterworld* or *Titanic* will cost much more than a lavish opera production.
- High art requires more effort from the observer. Popular art is designed to be enjoyed at

leisure, in small doses. Everything is done to ensure that the observer is not fatigued by the length, or by the difficulty of understanding what is going on. If the performance is a long one, as in an epic movie, efforts will be made to ensure constant excitement in order to compensate. Before high art the observer is given no quarter. He has to put himself out to get his enjoyment. He has to think. In this way he has to make a contribution, and cannot enjoy the art while remaining passive, slumped in an armchair half-conscious and half-sober. High art requires a certain intellectual level of sophistication, while popular art can be appreciated by anyone capable of understanding speech, of responding to a simple drumbeat or to the sight of a custard pie slammed into someone's face.

In this last sense, popular art is said to be cheap and shallow by comparison with high art.

Talking point: What is the difference between the Value of an original Work of Art and a Copy?

Is a copy of a work of art e.g. a forged copy of a painting, a photograph of a painting, a recording of a performance, itself a work of art in its own right?

The most obvious reasons for regarding a forgery as of less value than its original are non-aesthetic:

- We like to have relics of the past and of the great: Handel's harpsichord, Elvis Presley's guitar, etc. The work of art has been produced by a famous artist and so it provides a physical link with him.
- Because of the previous preference, a work of art will fetch more in a sale than a forged work. It is economically more valuable.
- For both of the above reasons a genuine work has greater "snob value" than a forgery. Many people would feel prouder to own, or to be associated with, the original than a copy.

None of these addresses the real problem. If someone were to produce a hitherto unknown work by Mozart, which experts agree is in his style, and not inferior to anything which he has produced, it would be greeted with great fanfares of jubilation in the world of classical music. It would be performed all over the world. Yet if it were then exposed as a forgery it would be dismissed as worthless and never performed, except as a curiosity. Would it then have suddenly become artistically worthless? If that same piece had been by Mozart it would be regarded as an expression of his unique genius. Is it any less an expression of genius if that genius is not Mozart but Jim Burton, the skilled composer of music in Mozart's style?

A forgery is not a forgery because it looks different from an original. Insofar as it is effective, a forgery will resembles its original exactly. Forged hundred dollar bills are not worthless because they fail to look like real bills; they are worthless because they lack the backing of the national bank behind them.

In response, it might be argued that a work of art can be judged on the basis of how effectively the artist communicates what is in his mind. In this case, the forger had an unworthy intention, while the artist who produced the original had a noble one. But there are serious problems in understanding what constitutes an artist's intention. Perhaps the original artist was not aware of the significance of his actions himself. In any case, modern critics tend to judge a work of art on the basis of what can plausibly be read into it, rather than on what its creator's intentions may have been. The work of art is treated in isolation from the intentions of its creator, as a public object existing in its own right, and valued as such.

4. Beauty in Mathematics and Science

Mathematicians are often conscious of the beauty of what they discover or create. J. B. Shaw claims that the mathematician is fascinated with the marvellous beauty of the forms he constructs. Godfrey H. Hardy points out that "A mathematician, like a poet or a painter, is a maker of patterns." Bertrand Russell referred to: "A stern perfection such as only the greatest art can show," and James A. Sylvester to "The music of reason."

This aesthetic aspect of mathematics will be most clearly seen in the desire of the mathematician to create the most economical fashioning of his means to his ends, so as to produce the most elegant proofs possible.

Similarly, there is frequently said to be an aesthetic aspect to the work of the scientist. This may be most clearly seen in the scientist's desire to secure the simplest and most elegant method of testing a hypothesis, and in preferring the simplest hypothesis if empirical testing is impossible.

There are, however, great differences between the arts and mathematics and science.

*   The arts are intensely personal, reflecting the nature and feelings of the artist; while mathematics and science are constrained by the need for self-consistency in the former case, and fidelity to the phenomena under investigation in the latter.
*   Works of art are rich in meaning and capable of many different interpretations; while the products of mathematics and science are pinned down by the need for precision and a strictly defined meaning.
*   Artistic creations are usually about the particular and unique, while mathematics and science are about what is general.
*   Artistic creations may have moral concerns inbuilt into them, while mathematics and science are value free.
*   Something of the artist goes into his work of art; while the personality of the mathematician and scientist is irrelevant to an appreciation of his work.

Glossary

descriptive studies: studies concerned with how things are.

ends: the goals for which something else is done.

evaluation: a judgement or determination of the worth or quality of something.

extrinsic end: an end which is different from or other than the activity which is directed towards the attainment of it.

instrumental value: the value of something which is valued for something else to which it is a means, rather than for itself.

intrinsic end: an end which is not different from or other than the activity directed towards the attainment of it.

intrinsic value: the value of something which is valued for itself, rather than its use for the attainment of some other end.

means: that which is done to achieve some end.

normative studies: studies concerned with how things ought to be.

policy: courses of action.

preference: choice in favour of or against something.

relativism: the view that there are no absolute values.

subjectivism: the view that all values are subjective.

value: the worth of something.

16. ETHICS

"Everything has been figured out, except how to live." (Jean-Paul Sartre)

1. What is Morality?

We all know that some actions, like murder and torture, are morally wrong, while others, like saving a drowning child from perishing, are morally praiseworthy. Such knowledge is more frequently disputed than knowledge such as, say, that Ulan Bator is the capital city of Mongolia, or that vipers are poisonous snakes. There exist serious disagreements on many ethical matters, such as the right of a woman to have an abortion, or the right of the state to administer the death penalty. There is not so much of a consensus on moral truths as there is on factual propositions. It is therefore necessary to consider, in general, how we justify our claims to know moral knowledge. In order to do this, it is necessary to consider the nature of moral propositions, and the grounds on which we can claim to know them to be true.

Moral actions involve a person, the "moral agent," doing something or performing an act of some kind, and persons (or things) which are the "recipients" of the action. The recipient may occasionally be the same as the agent, as for instance when someone commits suicide.

Usually, the most basic ethical choice we make is about which actions of ours should be subjected to moral judgements. We sometimes seek to evade criticism by restricting the range of what we consider to be matters which fall within the sphere of morality. Each of the following areas is considered by some people to lie outside the consideration of morality:

- Politics: This may be seen as an area where only expediency counts; alternatively one can think of the public actions of politicians as moral or immoral, like those of other members of society.
- Business: Some people seek to exclude their business dealings from the area subject to moral judgements; others take the view that business needs a basis of morality in order to operate successfully.
- Certain groups may be deliberately excluded from the area of morality because they are considered to be wicked, enemies, or subhuman. They adjust the definitions of their terms in such a way that certain actions lie outside morality: for example, if some races are not quite human, then there may not be anything wrong with using them as slaves.
- Some exclude the damage we inflict on animals on the grounds that perhaps they "don't really suffer."
- Minor actions which "don't really count," such as jumping a queue, are often excluded. Alternatively one can think of all actions as moral or immoral, and as revealing (or even

constituting) a person's moral character.

- Others have exclude the damage we inflict on the environment. Alternatively one can take the view that we are responsible for all foreseeable consequences of our actions, including those from which we or future generations may suffer.

In *The Road Less Traveled*, M. Scott Peck points out that each and every one of us is lazy. This has nothing to do with the number of hours we work or our level of activity. In Western societies we are encouraged to be workaholics, and many people internalize this compulsion. But we fail to contemplate the reasons for, and consequences of, our actions. We are ethically lazy. And if we fail to grow up and out of this ethical laziness, the survival of our species on this planet may not be possible, and even if it is possible, the conditions of life may be such that it will hardly be desirable. We not only assert our rights, but also assume our ethical responsibilities.

3. The Grounds of Moral Judgements

The central question of ethics is: What are the grounds of moral judgements and values? On what basis *in general* do we say that murder is wrong and helping people good. In approaching this problem it is helpful first to consider, and discard, ways in which this cannot be done.

Inadequate Grounds of Morality

Subjectivism

It is sometimes claimed that ethical judgements are merely subjective. They express our preferences, our personal likes and dislikes. To say that something is "right" is simply to express approval of it; to say that something is "wrong" is nothing more than to express disapproval.

But this is based upon a confusion between moral judgements and preferences. The confusion arises because we like some courses of action and approve of them; while we disapprove of others, which we dislike. On the whole, we dislike murder and approve of unselfishness. But to say that murder is wrong or unselfishness right is to say more than that we dislike murder and like unselfishness.

As we have seen, personal preferences take the form "*A* likes apples and *B* does not. *B* likes oranges and *A* does not." The claim that *A* likes apples does not contradict the claim that *B* does not. They are logically independent claims which can both be true together. There is no conflict between them. The statement "*A* likes apples and *B* does not" is in no way inconsistent. Moral claims, however, are just not like this. If *A* believes that euthanasia is morally justifiable, and *B* believes that it is essentially wrong, then there is a genuine conflict.

Moreover, there is no point in asking for people to justify their personal preferences or feelings, because it is just a matter of taste. But there is point in asking someone for the reasons for his moral judgements.

Moral Authorities:

One way to avoid making moral judgements is to pass the buck by an appeal to authority.

Parental Authority: Children are considered insufficiently mature to make moral judgements of their own, and properly look to their parents to make judgements for them. But that is a state they are expected to outgrow as they mature, and learn to make moral judgements of their own. However, some adults never develop moral autonomy. Instead they remain dependent by leaning upon some other authority as a substitute.

The Law: Some people seek to hand over their moral judgement to the state, and declare "It is always wrong to disobey the law." They say: "Murder is wrong because it is against the law."

In doing this, they confuse two quite different things: what is morally wrong and what happens to be against the law of their country. We can see that the two do not necessarily coincide if we consider the that there might be something morally wrong which is not against the law of a country, and that something might be against the law of a country which is not morally wrong.

Unjust laws forbade slaves to leave their owners, imposing harsh punishments upon them if they tried to escape. These laws condemned something which we would not regard as immoral. On the other hand, many people would regard it as immoral for children not to help their parents if they are in need, but it would not usually be against the law for them to do nothing to help.

Much of the advance of civilisation has been by amending or abolishing laws which had come to be seen as immoral; while many of our backslidings into barbarism have been assisted by the enactment of immoral laws. The law and morality are simply different.

Public Opinion: Humans are gregarious animals, like sheep, and so many put their trust in what the majority of their fellow citizens think.

But what we believe to be right, people in other cultures today may believe to be wrong. Egyptian pharaohs were expected to marry their sisters. A young Sioux was not counted as a warrior until he had killed someone. Even within our own culture, the majority now differs in its judgements from the majority in previous ages. If the majority was wrong then, it can be wrong now. Public opinion is simply what people *happen* to think here and now, and it may be wrong. Whether what people believe to be reasonable or right is reasonable or right is another matter entirely.

Religious Authorities: Religious believers sometimes seek to substitute God for their parents as the moral authority they appeal to settle all ethical questions for them. They assert that a religious book, teacher, community, tradition or organisation, has all the answers.

Sometimes religious groups have courageously offered alternative sets of values from the ones generally accepted in a particular society. But generally, religion has usually served to give an extra weight of authority to those views and judgements already traditionally and generally accepted by society, and religious groups have usually been the most resistant to any questioning of them. The US Declaration of Human Rights declared that all men are created equal, although popular opinion in the southern states was strongly in favour of slavery. This was a major issue of the American Civil War, after which Abraham Lincoln signed a proclamation emancipating all the slaves of the US. The Supreme Court later ruled that the practice of racial segregation was illegal. Yet all through this period the influential Southern Baptist Church argued in favour first for slavery, and later, as a rearguard action, for segregation. Only in 1985 did the church decide formally that this support had been wrong. In Afghanistan the Taliban, Muslim fundamentalists, sought to take women back centuries by depriving them of rights regarded as normal in modern society. Generally, religious organisations teach the morality of their own society, although they usually represent the most morally conservative sections of their societies.

Religious people may argue that it is not their organisation, teacher, or holy book which they accept as their moral authority, but rather God himself. It is not clear, however, what the will of

God is supposed to be. Some Christians would rely upon the Bible, others upon the Church. Both are frequently inconsistent, both with each other and within themselves. Those who claim to found their moral values upon the expressed will of God usually disagree about what that will is.

From what we have considered above, it is clear that, except as a special provision for small children or the mentally subnormal, morality cannot be a matter of blindly following some authority. The German philosopher, Immanuel Kant, argued that morality is a matter of doing what is right precisely because it is right, and avoiding doing what is wrong precisely because it is wrong. It cannot, therefore, be a matter of obedience to authority. Morality essentially involves the autonomy of the moral agent, who thinks out which authority to accept and which authority to ignore, what to do and what to avoid doing.

Conscience: Some people believe in an inner voice, called "conscience," which is an infallible guide to behaviour. In any circumstance everyone is said to be "instructed' by this inner voice how to behave.

But we certainly have no infallible inner guide, for if we did, we would never be puzzled about what is the right thing to do, and we often are genuinely puzzled. If we are not, that is usually a sign of stupidity, prejudice, dogmatism, lack of insight or thoughtlessness, rather than the possession of an infallible inner guide.

What we call conscience is nothing more than an internalisation of the voices of parents and other figures of authority, or our peers. What it tells us to do is what they would have wished us to do. Thus "conscience" will usually reflect the values of parents, friends or current fashions of society. In one society a young person will tend to feel shame if he indulges in premarital sexual activity, in another he may feel shame if he does not. In some societies a girl will feel shame if she is not a virgin, and a boy if he is.

Rules

Some people like to think of morality as a simple matter of obeying rules. However, for the same reason that morality cannot rest upon authority, neither can it merely be a matter of obedience to a set of commands or prohibitions.

Rules, like authorities, are not self-justifying. Faced with a set of moral rules, we should ask the question "Why is it right to observe those rules, and not others?" The response must be either one of the approaches listed above and rejected, or an explanation as to why the conduct enjoined is good, and the conduct prohibited is bad. Whatever that explanation might be, *that* would be the reason for doing some things and not others, not mere conformity to the rules.

Moreover, no finite set of rules can cover every contingency adequately. Rules tend to be vague or ambiguous. Legislators have great difficulties making the rules which we call laws, wording them so that they unambiguously cover every eventuality. For this reason the courts of law deliver judgements on whether, in particular cases, the law has or has not been infringed. Even so, laws frequently have to be amended. Amendments of moral rules must have some rational basis, but this rational basis, which would enable us to make such decisions, is itself the basis of morality. The rules are thus not necessary except as rough guides.

How to Make Moral Judgements

The criteria for making moral judgements must be provided by reason. The following criteria effectively define the conditions for any moral judgement at all:

Deliberateness: A moral judgement cannot be made unawares. It is an intentional act.

Freedom: Some genuine choice must be available to the agent, so that he could have chosen to have done otherwise. A true moral judgement cannot be compelled; it is essentially a voluntary act.

Conceptual Clarity: We cannot think rationally if we have only a vague idea of what we are thinking about, if our concepts are not well-defined or lack clarity.

Rationality: Our thinking has to be consistent, avoiding logical fallacies and errors.

Coolness: Good judgements can only be made in a calm, detached atmosphere, free from strong emotions. Otherwise they will be biased, on account of the influence of prejudice. We need to be aware of the possibility of importing bias in our choice of our language when we formulate the problem.

Information: In order to make moral judgements, correct information may be necessary about, for example, the consequences of particular sorts of actions. This is often of an everyday kind, but sometimes expert knowledge is required; e.g. to know whether an embryo can feel pain, whether someone in a coma is completely beyond the power of recovery.

Well-Grounded Moral Principles: Moral principles are principles which prescribe conduct for all moral agents.

The philosopher David Hume argued that a serious mistake occurs when the attempt is made to deduce ethical obligations from exclusively factual statements.

> "In every system of morality, which I have hitherto met with, I have always remark'd, that the author proceeds for some time in the ordinary way of reasoning . . . when of a sudden I am surpris'd to find, that instead of the usual copulations of propositions, *is*, and *is not*, I meet with no proposition that is not connected with an *ought* or an *ought not*. This change is imperceptible, but is, however, of the last consequence. For as this *ought* and *ought not*, expresses some new relation or affirmation, 'tis necessary that it shou'd be observ'd and explain'd; and at the same time that a reason should be given, for what seems altogether inconceivable, how this new relation can be a deduction from others, which are entirely different from it."

The view that ethical precepts can be deduced from facts is now called the **naturalistic fallacy**.

For this reason, ethical arguments were said by Aristotle characteristically to take the form of a **practical syllogism,** composed of:
- an ethical principle or norm
- the facts of some particular situation
- the evaluation or decision about what to do.

Impartiality: This is of the essence of moral judgements, since it carries the force of their claim to be "right" and to have a claim upon us. The judgement of a reasonable person must apply to all *genuinely similar* situations, regardless of person. If something is wrong for one individual under certain circumstances, then it will be wrong for all other individuals *under the same circumstances*. The application of double standards is thus excluded. The philosopher Kant expressed this principle by saying that we should so act that the maxim of our action could be willed as a universal law. He called this the "categorical imperative." Philosophers sometimes express this by saying that an ethical judgement should be "universalizable.

This secures that the judgement is made out of a sense of duty rather than out of desire, and so does not merely reflect narrow self-interest.

The Status of Persons: Persons must be treated as ends, not means. Kant said, "So act as to treat humanity, whether in your own person or in that of any other, in every case as an end, never as a mere means." This involves a concept of the dignity of each person as a person.

Utilitarianism

This is expressed by the Principle of Utility, which states that the supreme good is that which tends to the greatest good of the greatest number. This "good" is understood as the maximization of pleasure and the minimisation of pain. An act is said to be right insofar as it tends towards the attainment of that ideal, and wrong to the extent that it tends away from it.

A simple application of this principle, that we should always act in such a way as to maximise the greatest good of the greatest number, called **Act Utilitarianism**, to practical situations can lead to bizarre results.

Case Study: Melville and the Surgeon who was an Act Utilitarian

Melville, a high school senior, was admitted to his local hospital with a broken leg. He had been playing rugby football and had met with an accident. but he was otherwise very healthy.

Many of the other patients in the hospital suffered from far more serious conditions. Two had lost the use of an eye in accidents. Two had failing kidneys. One required a heart transplant, and so on.

Now it so happened that the chief surgeon was an act utilitarian. 'If,' he mused, 'I act in such a way as to maximise the greatest good of the greatest number, I should use my healthy patient as a source of spare parts for the others. In addition, there is a shortage of blood since donors have not been forthcoming recently, I can add his blood to the blood banks. Of course Melville is young, and most of the patients he will be helping will be older. But if I add up the extra years of life which his death would give to them, the general advantage would clearly be served by cannibalising his body for spare parts.'

Philosophers have therefore made the principle more sophisticated by applying it not to individual acts but to rules of action. We have to decide whether, if everyone behaved in a certain way, it would serve the greatest good of the greatest number. This is simply a matter of using the principle of utility in conjunction with that of universalizability. In this form, it is known as **Rule Utilitarianism**:

Discussion: How adequate would you consider each of the following as moral justifications for doing, or not doing, something?

1. My parents would not like it if they knew about it.
2. We would all be in a bad state if everyone did that kind of thing.
3. It would harm someone else.
4. I would not like someone doing that to me.
5. I might get caught and punished.
6. I would feel bad about it afterwards.
7. It would be a selfish thing to do.
8. It would be against the law.
9. People might find out, and then I would be ashamed.
10. People like me do not do that sort of thing.

Failure of Moral Judgement

We may fail to make adequate moral judg,ments for several reasons.

Lack of Moral Autonomy: We may surrender our autonomy to authority, as when we blindly condone or condemn something simply because our parents, the laws of our country, public opinion, or our the teachings of our religious group, approves or disapproves of it. In such cases, we have not really made a moral judgement at all, we have simply passed our responsibility over to others. To that exent we are no longer functioning as autonomous moral agents.

Conceptual confusion: We may be confused about some of the concepts we are using to thinking with. We may wish to treat persons with respect, yet not be aware of what counts, and does not count, as a person. This may not be an easy matter to decide. For example, the question whether abortion is or is not morally permissible depends upon when a person starts to exist. Some say that a foetus is a person, others that it is something which has the *potentiality* to become a person if it were to survive, but that it is not yet a person.

Ignorance of the Facts: We may make a wrong moral judgement because we are no aware of all the facts relevant to a situation, or we are mistaken about them. For example, in the past we were ignorant of the fact that people who appear to be in a comatose state, yet who show some signs of life and emotion over many years, may in fact be brain dead, and incapable of recovery.

Over-heated Judgement: Sometimes our judgements are made precipitately, and without cool, rational appraisal, as when we read something that makes us angry. Sometimes, for example, we are outraged at a horrible crime which we have read about, and demand harsh penalties. Yet we may know very little of the situation, and if we did, we might change our opinion. For example, we may be outraged to read of someone being brutally murdered in his sleep by his son. Yet we might not know that the son and his mother had been kept a prisoner by the father over many years, and very brutally persecuted, and that the son had reason to believe his father was about to kill his mother.

Prejudice: Most often, our moral judgements are skewed because we are prejudiced, and so thinking aprioristically. This prejudice is usually present for the usual reasons: it is to our advantage; we are deluded by our allegiance to an ideology, etc.

Discussion: Blaming the Victim

Psychologists have noted an unexpected prejudice in most people towards blaming the victim of any crime. We seem to need to hold onto an illusion that life is fair and just, since if we did not, it would generate more anxiety than we could tolerate. We would have to think: "No matter how good I am, something terrible could happen to me." To maintain this illusion, we have to distort our understanding of other people's undeserved bad fortune by arguing that they "must have" deserved it in some way.

This attitude is used to "justify" injustice. If someone's home was burgled, then he was probably careless and deserved it. Is someone was raped, then she should not have been where she was at the time. If homosexuals or Jews were persecuted then there must be something wrong with them.

4. Two Ethical Issues

Euthanasia

Euthanasia is killing someone or allowing him to die in order to ease his suffering and allow him a "good death."

Although Jewish and Christian societies have condemned euthanasia, many others have not. In the ancient world, infanticide, suicide and mercy killing were all tolerated if it was felt that the circumstances permitted it, i.e. to avoid extreme suffering. Thus the Roman philosopher Seneca wrote:

> "I will not relinquish old age if it leaves my better part intact. But if it begins to shake my mind, if it destroys my faculties one by one, if it leaves me not life but breath, I will depart from the putrid or the tottering edifice. If I know I must suffer without hope of relief I will depart not through fear of the pain itself but because it prevents all for which I would live."

The great eastern religions, Buddhism, Confucianism and Shintoism all allowed for mercy-killing. In the west, some advocates appeared who actually went beyond this to urge euthanasia in certain circumstances. Sir Thomas More, later to be made a saint in the Catholic Church, wrote in his *Utopia:*

> "When any is taken with a torturing and lingering pain, so that there is no hope either of cure or ease, the priests and magistrates coma and exhort them that, since they are now unable to go on with the business of life, are become a burden to themselves and all about them, and they have really outlived themselves, they should no longer nourish such a rooted distemper, but choose rather to die since they cannot live but in such misery."

As a result of the spread of utilitarianism, more and more people came to favour euthanasia, and in Britain the Voluntary Euthanasia Society was founded in 1936. Similar groups were set up in other countries. The Netherlands became the first country to legalise euthanasia.

A typical case where Euthanasia might be considered would be the following:

Case Study: A Case of Terminal Cancer

Gerald was dying of cancer. Although he was given a pain-killing injection at regular intervals, his body had built up a resistance to it over a long period of treatment. The pain could no longer be controlled for more than a few minutes after each injection. He knew that he was going to die anyway, since his cancer was incurable and had spread throughout his body. Since he did not want to linger in pain, he asked that his doctor end his life with a lethal injection. His family were in agreement.

The patient was incurably ill, in pain, and both he and his relatives wished to have his life terminated.

Gerald was able to express his opinion and so his would have been a case of *voluntary euthanasia. Involuntary euthanasia,* euthanasia administered against the wishes of the patient, is not a live issue. It would generally, and properly, be regarded as murder. However, sometimes the patient is not in any state to express an opinion, and almost certainly never will be again. Many cases will be like this.

Case Study: A Fatal Overdose

Alexander was a popular high school student, on the honour roll and the school basketball team. For some weeks he had, unknown to his parents, been experimenting with illegal narcotics. One night he took cocaine which had not been properly mixed, and went into an immediate coma. On being rushed into hospital he was found to have serious brain damage and was put on an artificial life-support system. The doctors believed that he would never come out of the coma, but that he could be kept alive indefinitely so long as the machines were never switched off. His family, realising that there was no possibility of any real future life for their son, asked the doctors to switch off the life-support system.

This would be a case of *non-voluntary euthanasia*, since the patient could not give consent, and his parents wished to act on his behalf.

A further useful distinction can be drawn between various types of euthanasia in relation to the action necessary to cause death. Although Gerald was dying, intervention by the doctors would have been necessary to cause his death, i.e. they would have had to take the step of administering some lethal poison. On some occasions all that would be necessary would be for the doctors to *refrain* from doing what they would normally do to keep someone alive.

Case Study: A Hopeless Case

Irene had just suffered her third heart attack. A ninety-three year old diabetic, she was suffering from various other ailments, some of them serious. She was senile, incontinent, losing her eyesight, unable to look after herself, and had no known living relatives. Then it was discovered that she had pneumonia. This would be fatal if antibiotics were not administered quickly.

In this case the doctors need only refrain from doing something to allow her an easy death as an alternative to struggling in ill-health and semiconsciousness until death finally intervened.

Cases where positive action needs to be taken to end a life, are termed *active euthanasia*, while those where only inaction is required are called *passive euthanasia*. Passive euthanasia would have been sufficient to end Irene's life, while Gerald's case would have required active euthanasia.

It is important to note that judgements about one form of euthanasia might end with a different verdict than judgements of another.

Arguments against Euthanasia

- Killing is always wrong, therefore mercy killing, however laudable the intentions of the killer, is always wrong.

  Firstly, this often repeated slogan is almost always never accepted by those who put it forward. Almost everyone admits some exceptions to the rule that killing is always wrong: self-defence, under certain circumstances during wartime, in cases of capital punishment, etc. If exceptions are permitted, then perhaps this is a justifiable exception also.

Secondly, those who advance this rule generally make no attempt to explain why anyone should accept it. It is just put forward as self-evidently true, which it certainly is not.

- Although a cure may seem hopeless, we do not know what the future will bring. There are cases where a patient has recovered his health even though the doctors had given up all hope. For those people to have been killed or allowed to die would have been a tragically unnecessary loss of life.

However: It does not follow from the fact that occasionally doctors have been wrong in their judgements that no doctor's judgement is to be trusted in the future. While it is prudent to be very careful about such judgements, and always to err on the side of caution, it is nevertheless true that it is possible to say with reasonable certainty that someone *cannot* recover from some illness because of the nature and degree of the damage done to the vital functions. It is possible to say that someone is effectively brain dead, and will never recover from a coma.

Arguments for Euthanasia

- Euthanasia is justified because it relieves unnecessary suffering.
- Applying the rule that we should always do to others as we would have them do to us, it is clear that most people would, under certain circumstances, choose euthanasia for ourselves if we could. Consider the position Jason found himself in.

Case Study: The Fate of a Drunken Driver

Jason had been a lively, sociable college student. One night returning from a party, where he had been drinking, he had crashed his car into a tree by the side of the road. The petrol line was broken and the car was soon engulfed in flames. Surprisingly Jason was not injured, although he was trapped between the steering column and the seat. Because of the distortion of the car chassis caused by the crash, he was not able to open the doors of the car, and was in immediate danger of being burned alive where he sat. He pleaded with passers by to kill him by hitting him on the head before the flames reached him.

It seems clear that if we were to find ourselves in his position most of us would hope that people would put us out of our misery.

Euthanasia and the Law: While it may be possible to argue that euthanasia can be morally acceptable, it would not necessarily follow from that conclusion that it ought to be allowed by law. That is quite a different question. It is possible to argue that euthanasia is morally acceptable, but that to make it legal would be dangerous to the lives and liberties of the sick, the old and the helpless.

Animal Rights

There are various estimates of the number of animal species sharing the planet with us, but it is not clear even how many species have been identified. Estimates of this vary from 1,400,000 to 1,800,000. Obviously no one has any remotely respectable assessment of how many individual animals are riding spaceship earth with us.

We use animals for many purposes: antibiotics, brushes, buttons, candle wax, cosmetics, detergents, engineering coolants, fertiliser, food, hair treatments, inks, insecticide, insulin, leather, margarine, paint, soap, vitamins." During the later years of the twentieth century people began to wonder whether we had obligations towards animals which were essentially the same as those we have towards other human beings, i.e. moral obligations.

Since philosophers use the term "person" to denote something having moral rights and towards which we have moral obligations, the key question is: are animals persons? This is a question parallels those we have already considered regarding human foetuses and people who are kept alive on artificial life-support systems. In order to answer it we need to take into account the information we have about the sort of things animals are.

Do Animals Have Minds? René Descartes denied that animals have minds. Man is unique, he argued in having an immortal soul which is responsible for all our inner life, our feelings and thoughts. He argued that animals, among which he did not include the human species, are like machines. They are "natural automata." The sounds and movements they make are more complicated than those of human machines, such as clocks, but that is only because animals are machines made by God. They have no interior life and no consciousness. Although they make bodily movements, they cannot perform actions. They cannot suffer.

A consequence of this doctrine, and one which aroused considerable opposition at the time it was first proposed, is that there can be no such thing as cruelty towards animals. They cannot be said to have any rights; and we cannot be said to have any obligations towards them.

In order to preserve the truly scientific character of animal science, many scientists have been reluctant to deal with animal subjectivity or consciousness at all. They have tended to follow the lead of Conwy Lloyd Morgan, who formulated what has been termed Morgan's Canon, which says that the action of an animal should never be interpreted as the outcome of the exercise of a higher psychical faculty if it is possible to interpret the action as the outcome of a lower one. This is an application of Occam's Law to evolving species. The adoption of Morgan's canon leads inevitably to the behaviourism of John B. Watson and B. F. Skinner in animal sciences, the idea that all behaviour is explicable without reference to consciousness.

Those who favour this approach accuse opponents of anthropomorphism in attributing distinctively or exclusively human characteristics to animals. Anthropomorphism became the most heinous sin which an animal researcher could commit.

Today the sceptical view is sometimes stated, that we simply do not, and could not, know whether animals suffer. In his more cautious moments, Descartes himself professed this view: "But though I regard it as established that we cannot prove there is any thought in animals, I do not think it thereby proved that there is not, since the human mind does not reach into their hearts."

This position is quite absurd. It rests upon the idea that pain is a private thing and that I cannot feel your pain and you cannot feel my pain. Therefore, we only know if someone else feels pain if he can tell us and describe it to us in such a way that we can each recognise our own experience in that of the speaker.

However, we do know what causes pain. We know that sensitivity to pain has is the result of the presence of a particular biological mechanism. We have a common origin with other species. We share with them a nervous system, a function of which is to enable the animal to avoid contact with sources of danger. It does not make sense to suppose that this nervous system has a radically different function in all other animals from that which it has in man.

In humans pain is caused by excessive sensory stimulation. We have sensitive eyes; thus a very bright flash will cause pain. If we see equally sensitive organs in animals we should expect that a similar input would produce similar pain. If the animal's sense organs are more sensitive than our own, such as a dog's nose or a hawk's eyes, we should expect greater liability to suffer pain than is experienced in humans.

When we see, in creatures unable to communicate with us in language, that which in us would be a response to pain, we ought to assume that they too are feeling pain under analogous conditions to the pain felt by humans. Thus if an animal gives every indication of suffering pain, such as howling or squealing, there is no reason at all to take the stance that we should not bother about the way we treat it because we do not know whether they are capable of feeling pain or not. The presumption must be that they do, and indeed, every evidence is that they do.

In fact we can learn that animals have an inner life, and we can do it in much the same way that we learn that other humans have an inner life: by analogy between their behaviour and our own.

There is good evidence that this inner life is more sophisticated than we had previously assumed. Recent work by Elizabeth Brannon of Columbia University, New York, has shown that monkeys can count up to nine. She said: "This finding is important, because it shows that monkeys know things about number that we haven't taught them."

All that is missing is language. Animals cannot tell us that they are in pain in a language. But being unable to speak a true language is no barrier at all to the communication of such simple matters. Most animals are quite capable of expressing the fact that they are in pain, and they do so in the very clearest of terms.

Case Study: Dreaming Monkeys

We have all seen pets make noises, twitch and pump their legs in their sleep. When humans do this we say that they are dreaming, and excitations of the brain recorded by electroencephalograph machines record the characteristic brain-wave patterns of human dreaming.

Dr. Charles Vaughan of the University of Pittsburgh placed rhesus monkeys in cages in front of screens and trained them to press a bar every time they saw an image on a screen in front of them to the point where it became an automatic reaction to the appearance of an image.

The monkeys were then attached to electroencephalograph machines and allowed to fall asleep. When the monkeys began the twitching associated with dreaming in humans, they began to press the bars in their sleep, while at the same time the EEG recorded traces of brain-waves characteristic of dreaming.

Vaughan concluded that the monkeys seeing images on the screen of their minds, which triggered the automatic response in them of pressing the bars. They were dreaming.

Recent studies have established beyond reasonable doubt what should be immediately obvious to any intelligent observer, that at least the higher animals not only feel pain, but also have emotions such as fear, anger, anxiety, and affection. They may suffer from stress. Social animals, such as dogs, may suffer from loneliness, and bereavement.

Of course in general the further we get away from human beings in the evolutionary chain, the less do we tend to perceive those signs, but then the less similar is the biology and behaviour of the creature. Although signs of intelligent behaviour are sometimes to be seen in animals very distantly related to us, for example, in octopuses.

Many animals communicate with each other and with us non-verbally, since we share many characteristics of body language with other species. It is not necessary to have a doctorate in animal psychology to know when a guard dog is warning you to stay out of his territory.

Animals display forethought in achieving their ends in various ways. Some use tools. Thus chimpanzees will use twigs to lever termites out of their nests.

Case Study: Animal Medicines

The Navaho Indians have a legend that the bears taught the tribe the medicinal properties of a certain plant which is useful against bacterial infections, worms and stomach ache. They still use the plant for this purpose. Shawn Sigstedt, an ethnobiologist, investigated the reactions of bears in captivity to this plant, and found that they would enthusiastically chew it, rub it into their fur in sensitive areas, and then swallow it.

In 1987 researchers studying the behaviour of chimpanzees in Tanzania's Mahale Mountains National Park observed a sick chimp drag itself away from the group to a bitter shrub which the chimps always avoided when seeking food. This plant is used by Tanzanians as a cure for gastrointestinal disorders. The chimp chewed the bitter shoots, drinking the juice but spitting out the pith. Within twenty-four hours she was cured and had rejoined the group in all its activities. The chimp's activity seemed clearly intelligently goal-directed rather than random.

Following up this clue primate researchers have come up with at least fifteen plant species which seem to be used as medicines, and which they refer to as the "pharmacopeia of the apes"

It seems clear that animals can think. But they may also think about what other animals are thinking. In that case, they may be said to be aware of their own identity, i.e. self-conscious. Examples of deception seem to show this. The piping plover is noted for walking away from its nest and pretending to be injured when a predator approaches. By darting forward and renewing its act as injured it gradually leads the predator away from the nest. By contrast, the plover will dive bomb cows, which are only dangerous since they may inadvertently step on the nest. Monkeys have been observed to practice deception in a variety of circumstances.

Behaviourists will argue that such behaviour is due to natural selection. But while that may be so, that does not rule out that it is also self-conscious. Much human behaviour is also explicable by natural selection, but it may also be both conscious and self-conscious.

Scientists seek regularities of behaviour. But signs of intelligent thought are best seen by original one-off behaviour conveyed in anecdotes. The use of scientific methods, therefore, predisposes the scientist to focus precisely upon those aspects of behaviour which are most automatic and repetitive, and therefore which are innately conditioned.

Do Animals Count?

The problem with animal consciousness and self-consciousness is that, for the higher animals at least, the conclusion must be that they are "persons." They may have rights and we may have duties towards them. They become part of the world properly governed by ethical considerations. We can no longer abuse and exploit them without guilt.

Buddhists and Jains have long believed that all living beings have souls of fundamentally the same kind, and that these souls transmigrate after death into bodies of other species. Since they also believe that it is wrong to take life, this is prohibition extended to all living things.

If higher animals may count as "persons" many ethical issues are raised: For example: Is factory farming morally unjustifiable? This is a system of livestock production in which the animals: calves, pigs, hens, are kept indoors in crowded conditions in which their movements are very severely restricted. These conditions are frequently horrific. The animals may never be taken from their cages until it is time for them to be killed. Thus there are calves which have lived their entire lives without ever walking on a meadow, and hens which die after a long life of egg-laying without ever having picked grubs out of the earth. This system of animal "husbandry" allows for large-scale production within a very restricted area, and is done primarily in order to maximise the farmer's profit, although it also incidentally has the effect of allowing the production of cheaper meat and eggs.

Glossary

act utilitarianism: the view that we should always act in such a way as to maximise the greatest good of the greatest number.

anthropomorphism: attributing to animals inner states, thoughts and emotions which are proper only to human beings.

conscience: a supposed faculty of moral intuition possessed by everybody which, according to popular opinion, infallibly allows us to distinguish in any situation what is right from what is wrong.

consequentialism: the view that an action should be judged by its consequences.

deontology: the view that an action should be judged by its relation to our duty.

hedonism: the view that pleasure is the ultimate good.

moral principle: a general proposition asserting what ought (or ought not) to be done.

Morgan's Canon: the principle that the action of an animal should never be interpreted as the outcome of the exercise of a higher psychical faculty if it is possible to interpret the action as the outcome of a lower one.

naturalistic fallacy: inferring what one ought to do from a set of exclusively factual premises.

practical syllogism: a syllogism in which the major premise consists of a moral principle, the minor premise consists of the facts relating to some particular situation, from which a conclusion is inferred concerning a decision about what should be done in relation to it.

rationality: that which conforms to principles of good reasoning, shows good judgement, is consistent, logical, and relevant.

rule utilitarianism: the view that we should always act in such a way such that, if everyone behaved this way, it would serve the greatest good of the greatest number

universalisability: the principle that if some act is right (or wrong) for one individual under certain circumstances, then it will be right (or wrong) for all other individuals under the same circumstances.

utilitarianism: the moral principle that one ought to act so as to maximise the greatest good of the greatest number.

17. POLITICS

"The highest morality must be the preservation — and wherever prudent, the accretion — of American power." (Robert D. Kaplan)

1. What is Politics?

Consider the following situations:

- The Trade Ministers of several neighbouring states meet together to attempt to solve a problem which has arisen over tariffs.
- The National Parliament passes a new law lowering the age of consent for homosexuals.
- An environmental organisation demands an end to the tipping of industrial waste in a river.
- Teachers threaten to go on strike for more pay.
- After a dispute, a famous pop group decides to split up.

The first two concern the operations of government; the third and fourth show large organised groups striving to achieve their goals; while the last records a disagreement within a small group. All are political, for we may talk about world politics, the politics of a nation, and the politics of small groups, such as those employed at a particular workplace. Politics is concerned with conflicts of interest between groups and within groups, and the way that these are resolved. We usually think of political matters on the national or international level, but there is also local politics, the politics of the workplace the church and the social club.

Aristotle said, "Man is a social animal, therefore he is also a political animal." We live in communities in which we are all, to some extent, depend upon each other. This community of interdependent individuals is known as "**society**." Thus in addition to the ethical relationships we have with other individuals, with their reciprocal rights and obligations, we also have relationships within society, in the form of the various communities of which we are part. Politics is not merely concerned with *means*, it is also about the choice of ultimate *goals*, since the decision as to which policy we ought to follow depends upon the sort of society we are aiming at.

Considered as knowledge, "politics" may refer to one of three different branches of human knowledge:

- The study of what political institutions and activities used to be like. This is part of the study of History.
- The study of what political institutions and activities are actually like today. In this sense,

politics is a branch of sociology. Political science is one of the human sciences. Both of these studies are *descriptive*.

▪ The study of the way political institutions and activities *ought* to be ordered.

This is *normative* politics. It is concerned with "the moral phenomena of human behaviour in society." It is about what are good and bad policies, and therefore with political ideals. It is with politics in this last sense that we are concerned in this chapter.

The importance of this subject cannot be underestimated today since the level of organisation of human societies has increased so much that no one, certainly in the industrialised world, can be ignorant of the influence which political institutions and decisions have upon almost every aspect of our lives. This influence may stretch from how much tax we have to pay, to whether and how we try to halt and redress the deterioration of our environment, to whether we go to war.

2. The Basic Problem of Politics

Politics is concerned with choices. Pierre Mendes-France, once Prime Minister of France, said: "To govern is to choose." There are two general principles which can be adopted towards the making of those choices.

● The medieval Italian political philosopher Niccolo Machiavelli argued in *The Prince* that: political choices should always be made in one's own self-interest. On this view the political world is a naked struggle for survival, in which some will be successful because of their might, cleverness and luck. That is all there is to it.

● Aristotle proposed an alternative view, namely that political choices and actions should be governed by law. Aristotle saw politics as "ethics writ large" - the application of the methods and principles of ethics to public life. Politics, on this view, is the intentional pursuit of the improvement of the human condition by organised means - the building of "civilisation."

The issues are seen most clearly in the history of ancient Greece, where an unusual level of philosophical self-consciousness led to these issues being debated in the context of events of the time.

Case Study: Massacre on Melos

During the late fifth century BC the cities of the Greek world found themselves involved in a period of general warfare which lasted for almost thirty years. Two rival alliances of cities, one led by Athens and the other by Sparta, fought for dominance of the Greek world. In this war, the inhabitants of the tiny island of Melos sought to remain neutral. Then in 416, during a period of truce in the fighting, a powerful Athenian fleet arrived in the harbour of Melos and demanded that the islanders join the Athenian alliance, or face the consequences. The islanders pointed out that they had not in any way harmed the Athenians, and wished only to remain neutral and to be left alone. The Athenians retorted that they would not tolerate this, because it would set a bad example to their other "allies." To remain neutral and to avoid harming the mighty was not acceptable. They must be obedient servants.

A lengthy debate ensued about the rights and wrongs of the situation, recorded by Thucydides. The ambassadors of Athens asserted: "You know as well as we do that right, as the world goes, is only in question between equals in power, while the strong do what

> they can and the weak suffer what they must . . . of the gods we believe, and of men we know, that by a necessary law of their nature they rule wherever they can." i.e. Might is right. On this view, politics is not subject to moral judgement.
>
> The Melians refused to submit to the arbitrary will of the Athenians, were besieged, and forced to surrender during the winter of 416-415. The Athenian assembly met to decide their fate, and voted to put all the men to death, and to enslave the women and children. This was done.

The central issue of politics is simply this: do we live in a world in which the strong do as they will, or do we all live in a world in which the Rule of Law prevails, one in which all parties, however powerful, are equally bound to observe the Law.

THE MAIN ISSUE IN POLITICS:
DO WE LIVE IN A WORLD IN WHICH
THE POWERFUL DO WHAT THEY WILL?
OR DO WE LIVE IN A WORLD IN WHICH
ALL ARE UNDER EQUAL OBLIGATION TO OBEY THE LAW?

This question can be raised on two levels: within the state and in relations between states. Within the state it becomes the question: Do the governors govern in accordance with the Law, or by arbitrary will? This is the difference between constitutional and unconstitutional government.

As it concerns relations between nations, it becomes the question: Do the powerful nations observe International Law and treaty obligations, or do they simply do what they will.

During the nineteenth and twentieth centuries a concept of International Law was developed, and organisations like the United Nations and the International Court of Justice set up. Unfortunately, for fifty years the superpower rivalry called the Cold War took precedence over matters of right and wrong. But when the collapse of the Soviet Union removed any significant rival to the USA, it was anticipated that the bloodiest century in world history might be succeeded by a New World Order, in which International Law would replace national rivalries. This would have been timely, given the need for international cooperation to deal with the imminent threats to the ability of the planet to continue to support life. The issue which confronted the world at the end of the twentieth century was whether the USA would use its unprecedented lone superpower status to reinforce civilisation and the Rule of Law, or whether it would use its massive military superiority over the rest of the world to enforce its will by force in the interest of its own ruling class.

By now the answer is clear. The latter path has been chosen. For publicity purposes, US government spokesmen still sometimes seek to make a moral case for their government's actions, but it is clear that US policy is not in any way motivated by considerations of morality.

This has been so since 1945, when the USA first became, in reality, an unrivalled super-power. In Russia after the death of Lenin the leaders of the revolutionary government expected that Trotsky would try to seize power, and they watched him carefully. While they were doing so, Stalin quietly gathered into *his* hands all the reins of power. In the same way, while the nations of the world feared insane German ambition to "rule the world," the USA quietly moved into that position. Even after it had *done* so, it managed to convince much of the world that the danger lay with the Soviet Union, a fabrication which flattered and suited the Soviets themselves, until they could no longer keep up the pretence.

Long ago, Dean Acheson instructed the American Society of International Law that no "legal issue" arises when the US responds to a challenge to its "power, position, and prestige." A similar doctrine was invoked by the Reagan administration when it rejected World Court jurisdiction over its attack on the state of Nicaragua. State Department Legal Adviser Abraham Sofaer explained that most of the world cannot "be counted on to share our view" and "often opposes the United States on important international questions." Accordingly, we must "reserve to ourselves the power to determine" which matters fall "essentially within the domestic jurisdiction of the United States" At that time, the USA actually vetoed a UN Security Council resolution calling on all governments to observe international law.

The choice made by the USA is now evident in many ways. The Government of George W Bush has peremptorily rejected nuclear arms agreements it had previously entered into, the biological weapons convention, environmental protection agreements, such as the Kyoto Treaty, anti-torture proposals and the International War Crimes Tribunal. It has always preached free trade where and when it has the advantage, and practiced protectionism where and when it does not. It supports dictatorships like Uzbekistan's, which tortures prisoners; terrorist governments like Ariel Sharon's; and terrorist organisations which torture and mutilate and murder, like many military and paramilitary forces in Central and South America. It holds several hundred captured Taliban soldiers at Guantanamo Bay, in Cuba, in violation of that Geneva Convention from which its own troops have so often benefited. US Secretary of Defence Donald Rumsfeld has said that these prisoners will not be released, even if they were tried and found to be innocent. It has waged aggressive war against Iraq, justifying it with claims it knew not to be true. It makes economic threats against those who do not readily co-operate with every twist and turn of US policy.

The main problem for the nations of the world today is how to deal with this unprecedented threat to international order and justice.

2. Political Ideologies

Much political thinking is not appropriate to the modern approach to knowledge at all, but harks back to older, outmoded, dogmatic ways of thinking. This is true of the thinking and decision-making dominated by political **ideologies**, such as conservatism, liberalism, socialism, and anarchism.

Ideologies provide a perspective, a set of assumptions about society, and especially about human nature, the purpose of political activity, and the nature of economic activity.

According to its own adherents, each ideology is unique. Conservatives often claim that conservatism, unlike its rivals, is not an ideology but rather the systematic application of simple common sense. Liberalism was seen by its proponents as the "rational" ideology, to be contrasted with the uncritical acceptance of authority and tradition characteristic of conservatives. Marxism is seen by its supporters as uniquely "scientific," because it is supposedly alone based upon an objective and true "scientific" analysis of society.

The claim to unique possession of the truth leads to divisions of opinion within an ideology being regarded as outbreaks of "heresy," e.g. differences between social liberals and the Reagan-Thatcherite New Right; and between Leninists and Trotskyites, Maoists and Revisionists among those normally labelled communists.

Those who rule a society and enjoy its greatest privileges control the rest of the population in two ways: by obtaining their consent to their rule, or by imposing their dominance by force. The former is always preferable, since the latter is inherently unstable. The way in which consent is generated is chiefly by the propagation of an ideology which *justifies* the powers and privileges of the ruling class.

The prevalent ideology within any society usually supports, and purports to justify, the existing socioeconomic arrangements, particularly as these benefit the dominant groups in society, who will be those who enjoy most of the benefits of the existing arrangements. Karl Marx pointed out that ideologies are systems of propaganda designed to support the ruling class in its exploitation of all other groups. He showed how exploited and disadvantaged groups are conditioned to accept a value system which justifies both their being exploited and the enjoyment of the rewards of the privileged who exploit them.

These are **implicit ideologies**. They may rarely be explicitly documented in a scholarly manner, but they permeate society, and their values will saturate the mass media.

An implicit ideology is a mechanism for convincing exploited people that their poverty is sacred, rational, just or necessary. Power legitimizes itself by showing itself to be "necessary" or "natural," by implying that "there are no alternatives." Thus the ideology of conservatism, now in abeyance almost everywhere, arose in a society dominated by a hereditary aristocracy. It sought to show that those who inherit privilege have a right to do so, why an aristocratic society is a truly just society, and why envy of the privileges of the aristocracy is wrong-headed, since the only alternative would be chaos. The ideology of liberalism, now dominant almost everywhere, arose among, and was fostered by, a mercantile industrial class of capitalists. Accordingly, liberalism attempts to show that those who have acquired money have in general done so justly, and have a moral right to the privileges which this buys for them, that a capitalist society is a truly free society, and that envy of the rich is wrong-headed, and that any other way of organising society fails to take account of "human nature."

By contrast, many **explicit ideologies,** i.e. those consciously adopted, provide a critique of existing society, detailing what is inadequate about it and what ought to be changed. Those that do usually also set out a body of objectives to be attained if society is to be just, a picture of what an ideal society would be like, and sometimes also a programme for getting there.

Thus many explicit ideologies are **utopian**. They present a blueprint, usually a very vague one, which is the model of what society *should* be like: an ideal society. When that is achieved, it is argued, all will be well. For these ideologies a set of prescriptions is necessary, laying out the practical steps required to get from society as it is at present constituted to society as it should be. Change, sometimes violent change or revolution, is seen as the only way to bring about the utopia envisaged.

Ideologies and Parties

The words used here to name political ideologies (conservative, liberal, socialist, etc.) refer to ways of thinking, and should not be confused with specific political parties. Over a period of time political parties often gradually change their outlook. Dominant groups within them change their ideology in order to gain, or retain, power. For example, during the nineteenth century the British Conservative Party evolved from a genuinely conservative party into a liberal party, and in so doing, deprived the Liberal Party of much of its support base in the population. During the 1990s many socialist parties in Europe have adopted a new form of liberalism. For this reason, the current name of a political party is often an indication of its ideological position in the past, rather than its contemporary outlook.

Neo-Liberalism

Neo-liberalism is associated with the rise of Reagan and Thatcher in the early 1980s, and it has boomed as a global phenomenon since that time. The basic tenets of Neo-Liberalism are:

• The dominance of a deregulated market: Private enterprise must be freed from all bonds of the state. There should be total freedom of movement for capital, goods and services. This is supposed to be because "an unregulated market is the best way to increase economic growth, which will ultimately benefit everyone." This is known as "trickle-down economics."

This decreases any limitations to the already existing advantages, in almost every aspect of the market and life, which accrue to those who already have most wealth. It enables employers to move work to other regions to take advantage of low wages and poor regulation, and so reduce wages and safety standards by eliminating workers' rights. Absence of price controls also enables monopolies to raise prices at will. Government regulation of everything that could diminish profits, including the protection of the environment and the ensuring of safety on the job for workers is reduced or removed.

• Pubic expenditure on social services, e.g. health, education and infrastructure maintenance should be reduced. This does not apply to government subsidies to corporations and tax benefits for businesses, as they create a "healthy" economy. This also includes large indirect subsidies to defence contractors through keeping the international temperature high enough to justify defence spending by the government (i.e. the taxpayer). This is one of the chief means of transferring wealth from the less wealthy to the more wealthy.

• State-owned enterprises, goods and services should be sold off to big business. This includes key industries, railroads, toll highways, electricity, schools, hospitals, and even the prisons and the water supply. This is supposed to be in the pursuit of greater efficiency. This is a form of looting of public resources, which have been built up over many years at the expense of the taxpayer, for the benefit of those able to purchase them. Privatization has the effect of concentrating wealth even more into a few hands, and making the public pay even more for its needs, since enterprises paid for by the taxpayer are sold at relatively low prices to corporations and wealthy individuals. As a result, they are run for private profit rather than the public good.

• The concept of the public good is replaced with "individual responsibility." This replaces any concept of social solidarity with a situation in which it is "every man for himself." This, of course, benefits those who are wealthy and powerful, because they are protected from ill-fortune by their wealth. The entire onus of finding solutions for the need for health care, education and social security is thrown onto the poor and those generally lacking in resources. If they fail, as they are most likely to, they will be castigated as "lazy," and therefore deserving of their fate.

Today, neo-liberalism is the dominant ideology over most of the developed world. It is being imposed upon the entire world by powerful financial institutions like the World Trade Organisation (WTO), the International Monetary Fund (IMF), the World Bank and the Inter-American Development Bank. Supposedly each of the World Trade Organisation's member countries have an equal say in determining its policies. In practice, decision-making is dominated by the USA, the European Union, Canada and Japan. Since 1995, the WTO has ruled every environmental policy it has reviewed to be an illegal trade barrier that must be eliminated or changed; and, with one exception, it has ruled against every health or food safety law it has reviewed. Nations whose laws were declared trade barriers by the WTO, or that were threatened with WTO action, have, under pressure, changed their policies to meet WTO requirements.

It could be argued that neo-liberalism is a threat to the poor, to freedom and democracy, and to the sustainability of life on the planet.

Nationalism

Nationalism has proved one of the most pervasive and powerful ideologies of the nineteenth and twentieth centuries; and this is probably still true today.

The ideology of **nationalism** must be distinguished from certain sentiments which are frequently confused with it. Patriotism is the sentiment of love of one's country, its landscape, its people, its customs and institutions, its little idiosyncrasies. Sometimes this can turn into chauvinism, an aggressive, competitive "My country right or wrong" attitude, similar to the loud, but unthinking, support of his team by a soccer fan.

By contrast: nationalists believe that:

- Mankind is somehow naturally divided up into distinct nations. Every individual human being is born into, and belongs to, a nation. Each nation constitutes a distinctly identifiable group of people.
- Each nation has the right to a separate homeland: its national territory, identifiable by its distinct colour on the map.
- Each nation has the right to self-government.
- The only legitimate form of political organisation for the nation is the nation state. Multinational states are anomalous. The only legitimate government of a state is a national government.

So deep is the influence of this ideology that to many people the points set out above will seem self-evident. In fact they are modern beliefs, products of the French Revolution. Before this period, the world was dominated by dynastic states, thought of by analogy with property as the proper possession of their ruler. While we might find patriotism, and even chauvinism, it was generally believed that it was right for rulers to have control over the areas they had inherited or won by conquest, irrespective of the ethnic origins, languages, religions, customs, or even the wishes, of the people who lived there.

Within a nation state, various groups will disagree about how it is to be organised. Conservatives, liberals and socialists will argue about the proper form of its political, social and economic organisation. For this reason, nationalism is said to be an **incomplete ideology**. It needs something else to supplement it, so nationalists are usually also either conservatives, or liberals, socialists or fascists as well.

Yet the existence of nations is a myth, only maintained by carefully avoiding focusing clearly upon the obvious difficulties inherent in the view. This can be seen by asking precisely what the distinctive characteristics of any nation are, which distinguish, or mark it off, from all other nations, by virtue of which you can decide whether someone is or is not part of that nation. There are various ways in which a nation could be defined: but each of these must be rejected, because counter-examples for each kind of definition can be cited which do not satisfy those conditions.

- During the nineteenth century race was generally considered to be the foundation of national unity. Common descent, referred to by the Nazis ominously as "blood," was what conferred nationality upon any individual.

Even a slight acquaintance with history will reveal that this is nothing more than an illusion. Virtually all states contain people who are of very diverse genetic origins. In the United Kingdom are found the descendants of the ancient Celts, thought to form the majority in Northern Ireland, Scotland, Wales and Cornwall, and the descendants of the invading Angles and Saxons forming the majority in England. Added to this mix are descendants of the Danish and Norwegian invasions of the Dark Ages, and the Norman invasion from France in 1066.

The extensive intermarrying with immigrants since that time, with Flemings during the Middle Ages, with French Huguenots, Jews and Commonwealth immigrants in more modern times, have further clouded the mixture.

The United Kingdom lies off the continental mainland, occupying islands which have not been successfully invaded for nearly a thousand years. It is clear that continental nations which do not enjoy this geographical isolation must be equally, if not much more so, a product of mixed racial origins. We are all mongrels.

It is clear in any case that human populations are rarely clearly distinguishable as biologically distinct groups, so that the concept of "race" is not a useful one. The human species is highly diverse, with individuals and populations varying in observable traits such as body size and shape, skin colour, hair texture, facial features and certain characteristics of the skeletal structure. Populations also differ in respect of other genetic traits. This variation is a product of evolutionary forces operating on human groups as they have adapted to different environments. But throughout history, whenever different groups have come into contact, they have interbred. As a result, all populations share many features with other, neighbouring groups. Variations in any given trait tend to occur gradually rather than abruptly over geographical areas. In addition, genetically there are greater differences among individuals within large geographic populations than the average differences between them. Thus any attempt to establish lines of division among biological populations is both arbitrary and subjective.

- A nation is sometimes defined as the inhabitants of the territory administered by the national government. The main problem with this is that in the past national governments have repeatedly claimed the right to acquire and control territory beyond their borders in order to "liberate" their nationals living in other states. Notorious examples include Hitler's claims on Austria and the Czech Sudetenland. Even today, many nations claim territory as "rightfully theirs" for precisely this reason. But it would be inconsistent to claim that a nation is defined in terms of those living on its territory, while at the same time claiming territory outside one's own borders on the grounds that one's own nationals live there.

- A nation may be thought of in terms of those who share a common language. But it is rare to find a nation in which all the nationals born in the country speak the same mother tongue. Many states contain significant linguistic minorities, such as the Bretons of France and the Magyars of Rumania. In addition, the inhabitants of some states, such as Switzerland and Belgium, have no common language.

- Today national identity would more usually be associated with culture: a vague term including language, religion, characteristic customs, outlooks and ways of life. Once more, many so-called "nations" exhibit a disconcerting variety within themselves which a nationalist would find hard to explain away. The French way of life and customs differ greatly from the Pas de Calais to Provence. The way of life of each of its *pays* or distinctive regions, depends upon its climate and geography, and differs from region to region. Moreover the culture of Lorraine shares much in common with the German Rhineland it borders, while that of French Flanders has much in common with Belgian Flanders across the frontier.

- Many of the most successful states of the modern world are not, in any of the above senses, nation states, e.g. USA, Switzerland and Singapore.

Since nations exist only in the minds of their members, they are said to be "imagined political communities". Nationalism is based upon fantasy. In *The Devil's Dictionary* Ambrose Bierce defined a political boundary as "an imaginary line between two nations, separating the imaginary rights of one from the imaginary rights of another." He might better have defined it as "an imaginary line between two imaginary nations, separating the imaginary rights of one from the imaginary rights of another."

Despite its basis in fantasy, nationalism is not a harmless fiction. It provides a prime example of the very real dangers posed to real people by false beliefs which are held dogmatically. Nationalism has been one of the main sources of terrorism, war and genocide in the modern world, as leaders seek to force reality to fit their fantasies.

- People separated by national boundaries from minorities speaking the same language as themselves in neighbouring countries have seen it as their duty to "liberate" their fellow "nationals." This was an excuse for Hitler's invasion of Czechoslovakia in 1938.

- Countries with distinguishable minorities within their own borders have deliberately oppressed them, treating their minorities as second class citizens. Occasionally, they have attempted to exterminate them, as the Turks exterminated over a million Armenians during 1915-17 in an effort to create a modern state for the "Turkish nation."

- Societies have been faced with significant terrorist activity launched by members of minority groups who consider national independence their birthright, such as members of the Basque terrorist organisation ETA in Spain.

- Members of nation states tend to read the existence of their nation back into the very different conditions of earlier history, and then to identify themselves with past "glories." They may then lay claim to all territory once occupied and controlled by people they identify as their ancestors at its very widest extent. This is a recipe for international disputes and wars. Thus Mussolini sought to recreate the Roman Empire in the twentieth century.

- Before the rise of nationalism, warfare was considered to be a struggle between rulers conducted by professional soldiers against professional soldiers, and not involving civilians. Crimes by soldiers against civilians were punishable. With the rise of nationalism, wars came to be thought of as a struggle between nations, in which everyone was necessarily involved. Among the consequences of this were the introduction of universal military conscription, the harnessing of all the resources of the nation to fight wars, and the treating of civilians as proper targets of war. This led directly to the concept of "total war" exemplified in the two World Wars of this century. Hiroshima and Nagasaki are direct consequences of nationalism.

- Independence movements in the old colonial territories of the third world were motivated by nationalist sentiments. Each colony of the Europeans demanded independence as a nation state in its own right. But the colonial boundaries often reflected no realities on the ground; they were sometimes nothing more than the outcome of compromises reached in conferences between rival powers scrambling for territory during the nineteenth century – sometimes literally by drawing straight lines on a map in a drawing room in Europe. These imposed boundaries might leave some tribal peoples living on one side of a colonial border, and other members of the same tribe on the other. Under colonial rule this meant that some members of the tribal people lived under say, British colonial rule, while their fellow tribal members lived under the French. With the coming of independence, each group was expected to somehow integrate itself into the new nation states which were brought into being; members of a tribe on each side of a border becoming members of different nations.

  Naturally this has led to mutual suspicions; to the oppression of minorities which did not renounce their traditional loyalties and contacts with their kinsfolk across the border; to civil wars within the new nation states; and to wars between neighbouring states.

- Nationalism reduces the ability of governments and people to work together for common goals, necessary for the survival of the planet, and diverts attention from the real problems we face: the growing power of multi-national corporations and the "war" of the rich against the poor.

Case Study: The Former Yugoslav Republic of Macedonia

Communist Yugoslavia was described as "a country with six republics, five cultures, four languages, three religions, two alphabets and one party." Until his death in 1980, it was kept together by the "one party" under the firm control of Joseph Tito, a popular Communist partisan resistance leader who had resisted Stalin's attempt to gain control over Yugoslavia after the Second World War.

With the break up of Yugoslavia, an area in the south of that country, which had been named "Macedonia" by Tito, originally as a basis for staking future claims on Greek territory to the south, found itself an independent entity. An area without clearly-defined natural boundaries, inhabited by Slavs speaking a dialect of Bulgarian, but with a large Albanian minority, the new government felt obliged to create and foster a new national identity for their state. Thus they adopted the name "Macedonia," historically a vaguely defined area, the heartland of which lies to the south of the new state, around Thessaloniki in Greece. As its national symbol the new state adopted the Macedonian star, recently discovered on the tomb of King Philip II, father of Alexander the Great, which had been excavated at Vergina, in Greece. As a consequence of their "nation-creating" activities, some enthusiasts began laying claim to the history of the Greek Macedonians: and to the achievements of figures such as Philip II and Alexander the Great. The absurdity of trying to create a nation by borrowing the history and symbols of a people living beyond their borders was then compounded by some nationalists by making claims to the territory of Greek Macedonia and the port of Thessaloniki. This was justified on the grounds that if these places were in any sense "Macedonian" then they must rightly belong to the "Macedonian nation."

The problem would not have arisen if those concerned had not been bemused by the false idea that every state must be the political form and expression of a single "nation," with its national identity rooted in history; and if they had not followed the usual policy, when no genuine identity could be found, of promptly manufacturing or "borrowing" one.

If nationalism is a fiction, why it is fostered? Like most political ideologies, nationalism appears to support the interest of ruling groups, since it pulls together the majority population in a state in an emotional bond on the same side as their rulers and against all other groups. It does this by exploiting the feelings of home, community and belonging that attach us to where we come from. It also blinds us the fact that exploitation of the poor by the rich usually takes place *within* a state. Poor Germans at the beginning of the twentieth century were not kept poor by the efforts of poor Frenchmen. If they were kept poor at all, it was because their labour was being exploited by rich Germans. Nationalism disguised this and turned anger outwards.

Case Study: Manifest Destiny

US nationalism receives its full expression in the notion of Manifest Destiny. In an attempt to explain the thirst for expansion of the USA, and to present a defense for its claim to new territories in 1845, John L. O'Sullivan wrote:

".... the right of our manifest destiny to over spread and to possess the whole of the continent which Providence has given us for the development of the great experiment of liberty and federative development of self government entrusted to us. It is right such as that of the tree to the space of air and the earth suitable for the full expansion of its principle and destiny of growth."

The concept to which O'Sullivan gave a name was much older. It was originally the idea that the rightful destiny of the white settlers of the United States was to spread over the continent of North America, to take, control and populate the country as they saw fit "from sea to shining sea." A corollary was the belief that the white man had the right to destroy anything and anyone who got in his way. In practice, this necessitated the mass destruction of tribal life and organization, the confinement of Indians to reservations, and at times, genocide. Later, when settlers in the USA came into contact with other settlers, it was to mutate into a belief that America had a mission given by God to expand its borders with no limit.

It was an idea which had originated centuries before, and was an appropriation, by the white settlers, of the Old Testament belief of the Israelites that they were God's chosen people, and had the right to settle the land of Canaan and displace, or exterminate, the inhabitants: "When the Lord your God brings you into the land which you are entering to take possession of it, and clears away many nations before you . . . then you must utterly destroy them; you shall make no covenant with them, and show no mercy to them . . . For you are a people holy to the Lord your God; the Lord your God has chosen you to be a people for his own possession, out of all the peoples that are on the face of the earth." (Deuteronomy 7:1-7)

Among several American religious groups, most notably the Mormons, the idea that somehow the white American settlers were God's Chosen People, took root in the USA. Manifest Destiny is a more secular version of the same ideology, claiming unique status for white Americans, and not merely a right, but a duty, to expand into the land of others, and dispossess or kill them.

James Monroe in 1822 echoed the idea in his famous Monroe Doctrine when he warned Europe and the rest of the world to "Stay out of the Western Hemisphere," already designated as "America's Empire." Manifest destiny was adopted by those desiring to secure Mexican land in the Southwest (the Oregon Territory and California), and, in the 1850s, Cuba. Following the Spanish-American War, members of Congress called for the annexation of all Spanish territories in America. Some newspapers even called for the annexation of Spain itself. By the end of the century, expansionists were employing quasi-Darwinist reasoning to argue that because its "Anglo-Saxon heritage" made America supremely fit, it had become the nation's "manifest destiny" to extend its influence beyond its continental boundaries into the Caribbean and Pacific, towards Asia and the Far East, bringing it into inevitable conflict with Japan, which was similarly expanding.

With the rise of the USA as a world power, Manifest Destiny has transformed itself into an ideology justifying an American claim to dominate the globe. Long ago, Albert T. Beveridge rose before the U.S. Senate and announced: "God has not been preparing the English-speaking and Teutonic peoples for a thousand years for nothing but vain and idle self-admiration. No! He has made us the master organizers of the world to establish system where chaos reigns... He has made us adepts in government that we may administer government among savages and senile peoples." Theodore Roosevelt, John Cabot Lodge, and John Hay, each endorsed the view that the Anglo-Saxon [Americans] were destined to rule the world. President Wilson noted that "the U.S. was involved in a struggle to command the economic fortunes of the world."

Today, this ideology, originally fashioned to justify aggression, theft and genocide in the North American continent, is as much threat to all the peoples of the world as it was to the Indians of North America centuries ago.

How to Detect Dangerous Nationalism

We must suspect ideological thinking when we come across the following:
- The prominent display and parading of flags and other national symbols, with an exaggerated, quasi-religious respect shown towards them. In its most extreme form, special acts of submission or allegiance may be offered to them. Leading statesmen will hardly ever appear on television without an array of flags diplayed prominently behind them.
- The belief that *we* are "special," not merely to ourselves, but objectively. In its most extreme form this will result in claims that one's own country has to be the "greatest," "first" or "best" in the world in some way, without any genuine consideration being given to whether this is *actually* true, and without any genuine knowledge of the other countries to which one's own is being compared.
- The attitude that one's own government always acts from the purest motives and for the good of all; especially when the evidence, on face value, points most clearly to the opposite conclusion.
- The systematic application of double standards to the actions of ones own government and those of the governments of other nations, and towards one' s own compatriots and foreigners. These double standards may be built into the language used in the media.
- The "built-in" justification, in advance, of any apparent expansionism or aggression on *our* part by some sort of mission or duty, imposed upon us by a higher power, or by the inevitability of historical forces.
- The attitude that one's own head of state or head of government may never be directly questioned or criticised, or even subjected to the normal requirements of the law.
- One's own military is invariably referred to in exaggerated terms of respect, and rarely subjected to criticism. Their motives and conduct are assumed to be always of the highest standard under all circumstances. Exaggerated respect is also shown towards important individual military figures. Extreme hostility is directed towards any suggestion that they may not always be blameless in their actions, and towards any attempt to treat them as responsible for their actions, and to subject them to the impartial judgement of the law.

3. Making Sense of Some basic Political Concepts

Political concepts may at first sight appear to possess a clarity which, upon closer investigation, they lack. We shall analyse four such concepts: "distributive justice," "democracy," "terrorism," and "responsibility."

Distributive Justice

One third of the world's population lives in poverty, and according to UNICEF, nearly 33,000 children die each day of malnutrition-related diseases. This would lead one to suppose that there is not enough wealth, in the form of food, in the world. Yet the world today produces enough grain alone to provide every human being with 3,500 calories a day - enough to make most people fat. This does not even take into account many other foods, such as meat, fish, vegetables, root crops and fruits. Abundance, not scarcity, best describes the world food supply, as increases in food production during the past thirty-five years have outstripped the world's population growth by about sixteen percent.

In a 1997 study, the American Association for the Advancement of Science (AAAS) found that 78% of all malnourished children under five in the developing world live in countries with food surpluses. Many of the countries in which hunger is a major problem export much more food than they import.

Clearly, the world has an urgent problem, and that problem does not lie in the amount of wealth in the world, but rather in its distribution. The pattern of wealth distribution and its recent evolution, is surprising. In 1960, the richest twenty percent of the world's population had seventy percent of the world's wealth. Today they have eighty-five percent. In 1960 the poorest twenty percent of the world's people had 2.4% of the world's wealth, and today they have just 1.1%.

Statistics comparing rich and poor countries do not, however, reveal the full story. In each country a small handful of the population both controls and benefits from the lion's share of its wealth.

In the United States, just one percent of the population owns forty percent of the country's wealth; while the top ten percent controls eighty percent. Since the 1970s, the top one percent of households have doubled their share of the national wealth to forty percent, and have more wealth than the entire bottom ninety-five percent.

Financial wealth is even more concentrated. The top one percent of households enjoy nearly half of all financial wealth. But this disguises the fact that wealth is sharply concentrated at the top end of the top one percent. The richest 0.5% of households enjoy forty-two percent of the financial wealth of the country. In 2001 the average CEO's pay was more than $11,000,000. Twenty years ago the average CEO was paid forty times more than the average employee, now it is more than five hundred times. Many CEOs make more in a year than their employees will make in a lifetime.

This is true of the world as a whole. The assets of the world's top three billionaires are more than the combined Gross National Product (GNP) of all the least developed countries of the world and their 600 million people. Twenty-eight billionaires own more than the population of half of the world's countries.

Moreover, it should be remembered that apart from a few very famous entrepreneurs, this small fraction of society which enjoys most of its wealth neither produces anything nor performs any useful services. Insofar as they perform any "work" at all, that work consists in creaming off the greater part of the fruits of their labour from those who actually do work.

Something is radically wrong with how the world's resources are distributed. Something is radically wrong with the structure of the global economy.

Yet every time weaker nations have attempted to reallocate their resources and undertake land reform to feed starving populations, powerful interests in the rich world and its multilateral corporations have thwarted their efforts, often by violent means. They have imposed economic strangulation, sent in proxy armies, or simply invaded, as the peasants of Chile, Nicaragua, Vietnam, El Salvador, Cuba and Haiti, among many others, know only too well. The goal of the wealthy: '. . . is not, and never was, to feed today's undernourished or starving millions, but to perpetuate poverty and dependence." It is to their advantage. They profit from it.

Distributive justice is a very important and urgent issue. Each of us has only one life. The quality of that life depends, to a great extent (although, of course, not entirely), upon the amount of wealth that we enjoy. This can be seen in many ways.

One person who was going to make herself lunch drops an egg on the floor. She first has to clean up the mess, then gets another egg to cook. Another person, poorer than the first, drops an egg on the floor, cleans up the mess and resigns herself to missing lunch altogether, since she has no more, and cannot afford to buy another. A third, richer than either, simply calls the maid to clean up the mess and cook another one for her. A fourth person in the Third World may only dream of having an egg to break. For each person, a simple thing like dropping an egg on the floor is a profoundly different experience.

It might be said that some things cut across such differences, such as health. But being ill is equally, or more, different for people of different levels of wealth. One person feels very ill and has to make a long and arduous journey to get into the nearest town by public transport to see a doctor. There he will queue a long time before being cursorily treated. A second will be able to drive to the surgery. A third will make a call and wait for a visit. Both will be decently treated by the doctor. A fourth will have a call made on his behalf, and the doctor will rush to his residence, wringing his hands at the thought of a fat fee, and be eager to be as helpful and kind as possible. A fifth, in the Third World, will have no chance of seeing a doctor at all. For the first man, the bill for medicines will be an added worry. For the third it will be of no concern almost whatever the cost. The last will never get any medicine anyway. Yet the last man probably produces something by his work, tea, fish or even gold. The fourth man probably does nothing except gather into his own ownership wealth which other people have created by their labour.

If they break the law, there will be similar differences. For stealing food, one poor worker may be summarily imprisoned by curt law officers. For stealing a small but significant amount of money from his employers another may be given a fair trial and imprisoned by polite but firm law officers. For stealing millions via shell companies in the Caymans, a powerful businessman/politician may be asked to repay some of it, or have to pay a bribe, or if brought to trial, will have the inconvenience of having to hire a top lawyer to get him off. Moreover, it is the rich man who is usually regarded as a pillar of the community, someone deserving of respect. Only if his crime is very crude and the legal system reasonably uncorrupt, will he pay any penalty. And if he does, we can be sure that he will not be sharing a cell with the first man, nor even the same type of cell.

The issue of distributive justice is the choice of a principle in accordance with which it would be just to distribute wealth. There are several possibilities:

• Wealth should simply be left to whoever has it. The principle of distribution should be based upon what one can acquire. Everyone gets what he can. As we say: "Possession is nine-tenths of the Law."

• All wealth is created out of raw materials by work. These raw materials are natural substances which we find about us. The work involved in turning them into wealth is performed by workers. The raw materials were not created by anyone, they were just there: the common heritage of all beings on the planet. Yet the richest one percent, who own so much, do not do any work, in the sense of creating wealth, nor even in the sense of performing services to others. They employ their capital to create more money for themselves. They do not even organise the workers to create wealth. They employ lieutenants to do this. Yet the workers who actually produce wealth and perform services for others, each at present enjoy comparatively little of the profits. This suggests a more just solution: that wealth should be distributed in proportion to useful work. "He who does not work will not eat."

Democracy

In relation to knowledge, certain forms of government seem privileged. For the enterprise of knowledge to succeed we need:

- a society which functions well enough to allow people to engage in acquiring and transmitting knowledge. This requires:
  - a state of law and order, where people are safe and secure enough to pursue their goals;
  - a state of reasonable prosperity, so that the luxury of the pursuit of knowledge for its own sake can be followed – and this is increasingly expensive as science requires more and more expensive training and resources.
- an open society, where information is allowed to circulate without impediment.
- a society where no authority is allowed to interfere in the ability to disagree and criticise generally accepted opinions.
- a belief that reason should be dominant over authorities and emotions.

There are, however, many problems in establishing such a society, theoretical as well as practical, and there are many different forms which democracy may take. In ancient Athens, where democracy was invented, all citizens met together to make specific decisions, and political power and responsibility was spread as widely as possible.

Case Study: Athenian Democracy in the time of Pericles

The Assembly of all free male citizens, held supreme power. It decided upon matters of peace and war and foreign alliances. It appointed and received ambassadors. It controlled military affairs. It determined the size and composition of forces, authorised campaigns, appointed generals and heard their reports.

Each year five hundred men, fifty from each of the ten tribes, were chosen by lot to serve on the Boule. The Fifty chosen from a single tribe would meet every day for one tenth of the year. These would form the effective government of the country. They would prepare agenda for the meetings of the Assembly.

Each day the Fifty would elect one of their number as chairman for the next day. For twenty-four hours he would function as the head of state. If there was a meeting of the Assembly, he would preside over it.

Magistrates were appointed to perform particular duties, such as supervising markets and keeping the roads clean. These were chosen by lot, and worked in boards of ten, each member having equal powers with the others, with no one acting as permanent chairman.

For deciding cases in the popular courts each tribe provided each year six hundred jurors chosen by lot from among those who had submitted their names. These jurors determined the verdicts, while the law laid down the penalties. The officials were confined to presiding over the courts.

> Among the basic principles which underlay the system were:
>
> - Choice for office by lot: ensuring that fame, popularity or bribery did not secure election.
> - Limitation on re-election: Since no one could serve on the Boule more than twice in his lifetime, and no one could be chosen as chairman more than once during a single tenth of the year, it seems clear that during the course of a normal lifetime, most Athenian citizens would have had the experience of serving in the Boule, or government, and each would have acted as head of state at least once during his lifetime.
> - Giving responsibility equally to boards of officials: No permanent chairman was appointed, so that no single person might dominate their meetings.
> - Providing pay for service to the state: Only in this way was it possible to ensure that poorer citizens could actually afford to give the time to serve the state and so were actually able to exercise their democratic rights.
>
> In this way the Athenian constitution provided what Pericles called a "school of democracy," enabling all the individual citizens to develop and exercise their political experience, skills and insight. It did not, however, lead the citizens to wish either to extend their rights to their women or slaves, nor did it lead them to extend to other states at their mercy the rule of law under which they lived in their own society.

This form of government is known as direct democracy. Today only the citizens of the self-governing cantons of Switzerland enjoy similar rights. In most modern democracies: the voters usually have, individually, very little power or influence. They can vote every four or five years. (In many countries the result will be known beforehand as a foregone conclusion.) They can write to or see their Member of Parliament or Congress; they can vote in state or local elections, and serve on a jury. Politicians make the decisions in Parliament. Citizens simply choose the set of politicians (usually in practice one out of two) who will make those decisions for them. This is known as representative democracy.

Discussion: Compare the two following accounts of democracy. In the first, Pericles speaks abou the democracy of the ancient Athenians in his own day. In the latter, Leslie Janka,a deputy White House press secretary under President Reagan, explains what US democracy was like in the 1980s.

> *"Our constitution is called a democracy because power is not in the hands of a minority, but of the whole people. When it is a matter of settling private disputes, everyone is equal before the law; when it is a matter of putting one person before another in positions of public responsibility, what counts is not membership of a particular class, but the actual ability, the man possesses. No one, so long as he has it in him*

to be of service to the state, is kept in political obscurity because of poverty. And, just as our political life is free and open, so is our day-to-day life in our relations with each other. We do not get into a state with our next-door neighbor if he enjoys himself in his own way, nor do we give him the kind of black looks, which, though they do no real harm, hurt people's feelings. We are free and tolerant in our private lives, but in public affairs we keep the law. This is because it commands our deep respect." (Pericles in Thucydides)

"The whole thing [The administration of US President Ronald Reagan] was PR. This was a PR outfit that became President and took over the country. And to the degree then to which the Constitution forced them to do things like make a budget, run foreign policy and all that, they sort of did. But their first, last, and overarching activity was public relations."(Leslie Janka)

The Contemporary Crisis of Democracy

Today there is an unprecedented crisis of democracy. Many of the world's leading democratic politicians are regarded by large numbers of their own people, and by the rest of the world, with unparalleled contempt. The elected heads of government in several countries which are supposed models of democracy: the United Kingdom, Australia, Italy, Spain, etc. have demonstrated that they find it easier to do what the White House demands of them, for example, in supplying troops or other support to fight US wars, than to follow the clearly expressed wishes of their own electorates. Massive popular opposition to the US-led attack on Iraq in many countries, whose governments nevertheless give in to the demands of the Bush White House and offered some form of support, has raised the issue of how genuine democracy (and independence) is in those countries.

After the lies surrounding the weapons of mass destruction [see Chapter 5], people no longer trust their governments. They should not have been so trusting in the past. US Presidents Kennedy, Johnson and Nixon covered up the deliberate waging of war in Indo-China over many years, and repeatedly lied about their actions, leading Senator Fulbright to say: "The biggest lesson I learned from Vietnam is not to trust government statements." And so on . . .

Real power is, in any case, passing from governments to multinational corporations. These are totalitarian institutions, run from the top, relatively unaccountable, and interlinked in various ways. Their first and most important interest is immediate profit. Their second is to construct a public of uncritical, industrious workers and avid, but stupid, consumers.

These corporations have achieved an unparalleled position of wealth and power. Today, there are 63,000 transnational corporations worldwide, with 690,000 foreign affiliates, but they are related together in various ways. Ninety-nine of the hundred largest are from the industrialized countries; three quarters are based in North America, Western Europe and Japan. Over half of the world's top one hundred economies are corporations, rather than nation states. If we compare the revenues of a corporation with the Gross Domestic Product (GDP) of a country, Royal Dutch Shell is bigger than oil rich Venezuela, WalMart is bigger than Indonesia, and General Motors is roughly the same size as Ireland, New Zealand and Hungary combined. (Statistics from Corpwatch)

It is often assumed that democracy and capitalism somehow go together. The Cold War was usually portrayed as a struggle between the capitalist "free world" ("good") and communist totalitarianism ("evil"). In fact many would argue that democracy and capitalism are actually incompatible. *Chicago Tribune* economics correspondent R.C. Longworth writes " . . . democracy's priorities are equality before the law, the right of each citizen to govern the decisions that govern his or her life, the creation of a civilization based on fairness and equity. Capitalism's priorities are inequality of return, profit for the suppliers of capital, efficiency of production and distribution, the bottom line." Economist Lester Thurow, writes that "democracy and capitalism have very different beliefs about the proper distribution of power. One believes in a completely equal distribution of political power, 'one man one vote,' while the other believes that it is the duty of the economically fit to drive the unfit out of business and into extinction. 'Survival of the fittest' and inequalities in purchasing power are what capitalist efficiency is all about. Individual profit comes first and firms become efficient to be rich. To put it in its starkest form, capitalism is perfectly compatible with slavery. Democracy is not."

History shows that in any case the large corporations actually prefer authoritarian dictatorships. Wages tend to be lower in dictatorships than in democracies, and there are bans on labour unions. There tend to be easier environmental and safety protection laws, which can in any case be bypassed by bribery. Even in democracies, the corporations have spent the last fifty years consolidating their power and insulating themselves from democratic control.

In many countries, politicians use their legal powers to protect themselves from criminal prosecution, and their time in office to fill their pockets, obtain "jobs for the boys," or secure a comfortable future for themselves after leaving office. This is frequently by acquiring promises of well-paid non-executive directorships of large companies for whom they have performed "favours" of some sort.

Many states have two-party systems of government, in which the electoral system is so designed that any third party finds it almost impossible to break in and have a chance of winning an election, so nobody votes for it. Leaving the field to the two main parties. In any case, getting elected requires large amounts of money. In many such states, one party openly represents the interests of wealthy and privileged elites, while the other professes to represent all those who are not privileged. The wealthy and privileged then use their wealth and influence effectively to bankroll and control the leadership of the second party. Thus whichever party gains power, it will serve the interests of the same wealthy and privileged minority.

During election campaigns, politicians go through the motions of making promises, which they break as soon as they get installed in power, in the interests of their sponsors who helped pay for their election. Many elected leaders seem to expend most of their energy when in office either repaying the debts incurred in getting elected, or in raising money to get re-elected.

All these things lead to a profound cynicism and voter apathy. This also is in the interests of the privileged, who prefer that government be left to them, by an electorate which feels that political action is futile, and which is content to work dutifully, consume avidly, and spends its free time watching spectator sports and television.

In such societies, "political activist" is actually turned into a term of reproach. We can compare this with Pericles proud boast: "Here each individual is interested not only in his own affairs, but in the affairs of the state as well: even those who are mostly occupied with their own business are extremely well informed on general politics . . . we do not say that a man who takes no interest in politics is a man who minds his own business; we say that he has no business here at all."

Terrorism

Which of the following counts as terrorism?

- During the night of 21-22nd April 1997 Muslim fanatics burst into the farming community of Haouch Boukhelef-Khemisti, some fifteen miles south of Algiers, and massacred ninety-three people, nearly half of them women and children. The dead, many of whom had been mutilated, were savagely hacked to death using knives, shovels, pickaxes and farm implements. The death toll would have been higher had not the security forces interrupted the massacre. The assailants were unknown, but were thought to have been Islamic militants.

- The Ibrahim Mosque in Hebron is popularly reputed to contain the tombs of the Biblical patriarchs Abraham, Isaac and Jacob. During the month of Ramadan, a period set aside by Muslims for prayer and fasting, worshippers crowd into the mosque everyday at dawn for the prayers which mark the beginning of the daily fast, which lasts from sunrise until sunset, and like Muslims everywhere at worship, they kneel forward, touching their foreheads to the ground. On one such morning in March 1994, a fanatical Israeli, Benjamin Goldstein, entered the mosque and opened fire on the kneeling worshippers indiscriminately. The Israeli government later claimed that thirty-nine people had been killed, but Palestinians counted fifty-two dead, together with another seventy wounded.

- On 13th December 1943 occupying German forces gathered 1436 males over the age of fifteen in the centre of the hill town of Kalavryta in southern Greece, shot them all and then burned the town.

- During August 1945 the US dropped two atomic bombs on Japan. Perhaps 190,000 Japanese died almost immediately. Many died prematurely during later years of radiation sickness. Hiroshima was targeted because the city, lacking significant military targets, had previously been deliberately preserved from damage by bombing, so that their destruction could be clearly observed, and would send the starkest possible message to the world about the awesome power of America's new weapon.

"Terrorism" is a term of disapproval. Supporters are more likely to use the term "freedom fighters." To be useful, the term has to be used with clear specifications. The following is suggested: the deliberate and indiscriminate killing of civilians to achieve political goals. This would have the following consequences:

- Terrorism is directed at civilians rather than soldiers in an army. This rules out guerrilla action during wars.

- As indiscriminate violence, aimed at terrorising the general population, it rules out the specific assassination of leaders.

- The justice of the cause is irrelevant. Thus terrorism directed against the white population of South Africa by groups opposed to apartheid was terrorism, despite the justice of their cause.

- Terrorism remains terrorism even though the terrorists are successful, and may come to be leaders of states. During 1946-8 Israeli terrorists massacred Palestinian villagers and assassinated British soldiers in Palestine. Many of those actively involved later became leading politicians of the state of Israel. When they held positions of power, they regularly condemned terrorism as though it was something that only Palestinians engaged in, and in which they had no part.

- Regular armies can commit acts of terrorism during a war, as for example the Japanese during the "Rape of Nanking."

- Rulers and governments can commit acts of terrorism. Joseph Stalin sought to terrorise the population of the USSR by widespread arbitrary and random arrests and executions during the purges of 1936-8 and afterwards. In general, governments which engage in terror tactics against their own citizens, such as those of Israel, Turkey and Indonesia, are far more effective than non-state organisations such as the Basque terrorist group ETA, in Spain or the Irish Republican Army in Northern Ireland.

- States may also aid and sponsor terrorist groups, such as the Iranian sponsorship of anti-Israeli groups in the Middle East, and US sponsorship of terrorist groups in Cuba.

In the past, the tendency of the Western media has been to confine the word "terrorism" to those hostile to the policies of the USA. In the case of nations to be undermined, e.g., Nicaragua, Cuba, the governments were called terrorist and the insurgents labelled democratic. In the case of countries supported against indigenous liberation movements, e.g., El Salvador and the Philippines, the governments were called democratic and the insurgents labelled terrorists. It is not surprising that many consider the USA itself to be the world's leading "rogue" or terrorist state: "The most salient truth will remain taboo. This is that the longevity of America as both a terrorist state and a haven for terrorists surpasses all. That the US is the only state on record to have been condemned by the World Court for international terrorism and has vetoed a UN Security Council resolution calling on governments to observe international law is unmentionable." John Pilger "The Truths They Never Tell Us," *New Statesman,* (Nov. 26th 2001)

Today, more usually, "terrorism" is confined to acts of violence and intimidation carried out by individuals and small groups. In fact terrorism has always been associated primarily with governments. Only states use systematic torture as a method of intimidation, and the scale of their acts of violence makes the terrorism of individuals and small groups look relatively insignificant. The reason for this change in meaning is to define as terrorism, and therefore as unacceptable, any form of warfare waged by those who cannot afford F-16s or cruise missiles, i.e. the poor or dispossessed.

Responsibility

While the other concepts we have examined have been frequently discussed, the important concept of responsibility has been ignored. This is itself significant. The issue of responsibility in a democracy can be considered in respect of the great power-wielding corporations, the representatives of the people, the press and the people themselves.

The most obvious form of responsibility avoidance found today is the limited liability corporation. It is a device whereby debts can be repudiated without penalty to those who incur them, and whereby executives can extort corporate assets from boards of directors in the form of "compensation packages." These have become so huge that the ratio between the highest and lowest paid employee in some corporations has reached a level of six hundred and fifty to one. They allow a few highly paid executives to abscond with these assets when all the other employees lose everything, often as a result of executive mismanagement.

The most obvious form of corporate irresponsibility, however, is towards the environment. Gore Vidal says: 'Although AIDS can be discussed as a means of hitting out at unpopular minorities, the true epidemic can never be discussed: the fact that every fourth American now alive will die of cancer. This catastrophe is well kept from the public by the tobacco companies, the nuclear power companies and other industries that poison the earth so that corporate America may enjoy the freedom to make money without the slightest accountability to those they are killing."

In *The Turning Point,* Fritjof Capra writes: "The numerous horror stories of corporate behaviour in the Third World which have emerged in recent years show convincingly that respect for people, for nature, and for life are not part of the corporate mentality. On the contrary, large-scale corporate crime is today the most widespread and least prosecuted criminal activity."

Among the most heinous of corporate crimes is that of "dumping." Products such as drugs or pesticides which have been ruled as unsafe for public consumption in the USA are exported by their manufacturers or others to the Third World, often with the active support of the State Department. Space limits us to three examples:

• Children's garments treated with a fire retardant were withdrawn from sale in the USA by the Consumer Product Safety Commission (CPSC) after it was found that the retardant caused cancer. Seeking to make at least a small profit from them, several million were shipped overseas and sold cheaply in the Third World. No one knows how many children have developed cancer as a result of wearing these clothes.

• A certain design of baby pacifiers was discovered to cause choking deaths, and a ban was imposed by the CPSC. Several manufacturers subsequently exported over 400,000 to the Third World.

• Depo-Provera is a contraceptive which is injected. It was banned for such use in the United States because it caused the development of cancer in beagles and monkeys in experiments. Yet it has been exported to seventy other countries, where it is used in U.S.-sponsored population control programs.

Case Study: The World's Worst Industrial Disaster

Union Carbide has been involved in numerous industrial accidents and environmental contaminations throughout its 80-year history, but none as dramatic as the tragic leak at the company's poorly maintained facility in Bhopal, India, in 1984.

A carbon company founded in 1886, Union Carbide moved into the manufacture of poison gases and chemicals during World War I. From World War II, until 1984, it was a contractor to the US government's nuclear weapons programme. It became the world's largest manufacturer and distributor of industrial chemical products, producing trash bags, anti-freeze and batteries, among other things. It employed over 11,500 people and had facilities in 40 countries.

It was also responsible for several large-scale industrial accidents and pollution incidents. In 1934, it was caused the USAs largest, at Hawk's Nest Tunnel in West Virginia, when nearly 2,000 workers died of exposure to silica dust. In 1981, it was responsible for spilling over 25,000 gallons of a cancer-causing chemical, in the Kanawha river in West Virginia. In 1984, over four hundred employees in their battery factory in Indonesia were suffering from kidney diseases. The company doctor was asked not to tell the workers that there was mercury in their drinking water, lest they "become anxious."

In the early hours of December 3, 1984, five tons of poisonous methyl isocyanate gas from the pesticide plant in Bhopal, India, leaked into the air. Water had entered the storage tank of this highly toxic chemical, and the reaction produced a cloud of poisonous methyl isocyanate (MIC), hydrogen cyanide, and other toxins.

Engineers tried to turn on the plant refrigeration system to slow the reaction, but it had been drained of coolant weeks before as part of a cost-cutting exercise, in order to save $40—50 a day. They tried to route expanding gases to a neighboring tank, but its pressure gauge was broken, indicating that the tank was full, when it was really empty.

They tried to purge the gases through a scrubber, which was designed for flow rates, temperatures and pressures a fraction of what was escaping from the tank. Then they tried to route the gases through a flare tower to burn them away, but the supply line was broken, and had not been replaced. They tried to use hoses to spray water on the gases so that they would settle to the ground, but they were escaping at a point one hundred feet above ground, and the hoses would only reach to forty feet. Then they fled. The management learned of the leak at 11:00 pm. The factory alarm was started by a worker at 12:50 pm, but the management turned it off within minutes. They also delayed the sounding of a public siren until 2:00 am. By that time the gas had leaked out into the surrounding heavily populated area.

Within hours, as many as 100,000 people poured into nearby hospitals, their eyes and lungs burning, with urine and faeces running down their legs. The doctors in the government hospital nearby had no information on the leaked gases, or how to deal with the effects of exposure to them. When they rang the factory, the medical officer assured them that the leaked gases were similar to tear gas, and that people simply needed to wash their eyes.

Up to eight thousand people died on that night. Forty percent of the women pregnant at that time aborted. The horror continues. Some ten to fifteen people still die each month from gas related illnesses, so that the death toll has now topped 16,000, and it continues to rise. Nearly one-fifth of the exposed population of 500,000 today suffers from a whole host of maladies: lung fibrosis, impaired vision, bronchial asthma, breathlessness, loss of appetite, severe body pains, painful and irregular menstrual cycles, recurrent fever, persistent cough, neurological disorders, fatigue, weakness, anxiety and depression. Cancer and sterility are above normal levels, while the incidence of tuberculosis in the affected population is more than three times the national figure. Researchers have found chromosomal aberrations in the exposed population, indicating a strong likelihood of congenital malformations in future generations.

The pesticide factory had been built to produce and store one of the most deadly chemicals, in an area where over 100,000 people were living within a two kms. of the factory. A safety team had noted, in May 1982, a total of sixty-one different hazards, thirty of them major, including the strong possibility of the accident which actually occurred. As part of the Corporation's policy on cost-cutting, the work force had been halved, with obvious consequences for maintenance and safety. The position of maintenance supervisor had been eliminated for the work shift on duty at the time of the disaster; and the period of safety-training for workers reduced from six months to fifteen days. At the company's West Virginia plant all the vital systems had back-ups, and were automatically linked to computerised alarms and crisis control systems. At the Bhopal plant there was a single manual alarm, which had been switched off so as not to alarm people "unduly."

Warren Anderson, Union Carbide's CEO, flew into Bhopal after the tragedy in December 1984 for a three-day visit. Both civil and criminal charges were filed against him, including a charge of culpable homicide. Anderson and other Indian company officials were arrested, but the officials were lodged in the company's luxury guest house, while Anderson was released on the same day on bail. A subsequent summons from the Bhopal court drew no response from him. In March 1992 the Chief Judicial Magistrate issued a non-bailable arrest warrant. Effectively, the U.S. government refused to honor its extradition treaty with India.

The Indian Government took upon itself the sole power to represent all the victims, and filed a suit for upwards of $3 billion. Four years later, and without informing the victims, it settled for nearly $470 million, which amounts to a few hundred dollars each of the victims. Union Carbide officials refused to show up in court in Bhopal.

The company failed to provide either just compensation or appropriate medical care. Yet the company was able to pay its shareholders a $33 bonus dividend plus $30 a share from the sale of its battery business, and gave its top executives a total of $28 million in "golden parachutes." After news of the court settlement, Carbide's stock increased $2 a share. The then chairman, Robert Kennedy who owned 35,000 shares in the company, personally benefitted $70,000.

In 1995 Union Carbide announced: "we believe the corporation has consistently acted in a humane and decent fashion toward the victims over the eleven years since the Bhopal tragedy, and that most people examining the facts will reach the same conclusion." Yet for years, none of the victims had access to any sustained affordable medical care. Union Carbide never released complete information about the chemicals released, or the results of tests they had conducted on the health effects of the chemicals, even though such information could have helped thousands of people by facilitating improved treatment and appropriate care. The reason given was that they were trade secrets. Meanwhile the corporation did have the finance to set up a propaganda website "bhopal.com," to put out its own version of events: that the disaster had been deliberately caused by an (unidentified) disgruntled worker. In addition, Union Carbide refused to clean up the site.

The abandoned factory continued to leak toxic contaminants into the surrounding area for some time, contaminating the soil, ground water and wells in the vicinity. Spontaneous fires from combustible chemical waste would sometimes break out. In May and June 1997 the factory was dismantled. At that time, toxic chemicals stored in tanks were let out, causing panic in the neighbourhood. The local people had wanted to convert the factory into a museum, to preserve the memory of what had happened there.

In a report entitled "The Bhopal Legacy," published in 1999, Greenpeace showed that the site was still extensively contaminated. The levels of mercury found in a sample in May 1999 within the factory, were between 20,000 and 6 million times higher than levels expected in uncontaminated soils. Several other chemicals likely to cause damage to the respiratory system, kidney and liver, and two carcinogens, were found in the soil and ground water. Over seven hundred metric tonnes of toxic waste lie hidden under layers of mud, and during the monsoon flood they leak into an open sewage drain. This waste has trickled deep into the earth, polluting the water table. Local people have to use this water. Nearly two-hundred and fifty handpumps have been marked in red as not for drinking. Water from these pumps smells like insecticide and irritates the skin when rubbed on.

Dow Chemical, which acquired Union Carbide in 2001, refuses to admit any liability for Carbide's actions, and has pressured the Indian government to reduce the charges on Anderson and others from "culpable homicide" to "hurt by negligence," a non-extraditable offense. In an unbelievable turn of events, Dow also persuaded the government to divert part of the compensation for victims to cleaning up the area. In fact even that did not happen, for funds earmarked for environmental rehabilitation were used for building roads, street lighting, etc., in areas not affected by the disaster.

Anderson could never be located by the US authorities. They claimed they were unable to find him so he never appeared in court to face charges for crimes in Bhopal. So, in August 2002, Greenpeace members, accompanied by a posse of journalists, paid him a visit - at his home in Long Island, New York - and served him with a citizens' arrest warrant. "This came after an Indian court had rejected a plea to reduce charges against him, and had asked New Delhi to press for his extradition. They added: "We call on the U.S. State Department to arrest him immediately, now that his address is known, and to extradite him to stand trial in Bhopal for culpable homicide."

The original accident, the failure to assist the victims, and the contaminated condition of the site, are startling examples of corporate irresponsibility. But guilt must also be shared with the Indian government, which showed more interest in courting foreign corporations than in the health of its own citizens, and with the US government, always ready to protect the wealthy heads of U.S. corporations, no matter how disgusting their actions.

The sole goal of business is the generation of the maximum profits at minimum cost in minimum time. This is the only reason for existence of the modern corporation. Any activity undermining or conflicting with that goal is not, in corporate terms, justifiable. Thus it can be said that the corporations are essentially amoral, inhumane and psychopathic titans - powerful, morally blind giants; despite some expensive advertisements which claim the contrary, they have no capacity for compassion and remorse towards the suffering of their victims. Only this can explain such behaviour as that narrated above.

Our elected representatives may also have blood on their hands without ever wielding a gun or machete themselves. The more power they have, the greater capacity for committing crimes, and for doing so while appearing to have clean hands, because other people do the killing, raping and stealing for them. They may launch wars, impose economic sanctions, and so on, for their own reasons, while their public relations agents and subordinates spin high-sounding "justifications" out of thin air.

Case Study: A Bloodthirsty Politician

After the First Gulf War, the USA pressured the United Nations to impose economic sanctions against Iraq until it proved that it was not engaged in a program to produce weapons of mass destruction like nuclear bombs or poison gas. These sanctions meant that Iraq was not allowed to buy or sell almost anything from other countries in the world. It could not get spare parts to repair water purification plants damaged by bombing during the war. It could not get either spare parts for medical equipment or medicines. Iraq claimed that it had allowed inspections from the United Nations, but the US government was not satisfied. According to the United Nations, perhaps a half a million children have died as a result of the sanctions. It is clear that the US government knew that Iraqi civilians were dying as a result of these actions.

> Former US secretary of state Madeleine Albright, when asked in a television interview if the deaths of 500,000 children in Iraq as a result of the American-driven sanctions were a price worth paying, replied: "We think the price is worth it."

The press also has its responsibilities. In December 2003 the International Criminal Tribunal for Rwanda jailed three Rwandan journalists for inciting the 1994 genocide that killed 800,000 people. On what became known as "hate radio" they had preached ethnic hatred and encouraged the majority Hutus to massacre Tutsis. This is the first time that the press has been held responsible for its actions since the organisers of Nazi propaganda were judged at the Nurnberg War Trials.

The Western press helps create the conditions under which the public accepts its leaders' desire to wage wars of aggression, and helps hide the consequences?

Case Study: Chemicals and Baby Milk

Within hours of the bombings of the US embassies in Tanzania and Kenya in August 1998, the *Wall Street Journal, New York Times* and other prominent voices in the American news media began calling for military retaliation. Before any serious investigation had even begun, editorials appeared in major newspapers suggesting the Clinton administration should consider taking action against a number of Middle Eastern countries. Potential targets suggested included Iran, Iraq and Libya. Syria and Islamic fundamentalist groups based in Egypt, Afghanistan and Yemen.

On 21st August 1998, bombing attacks on the Sudan and Afghanistan were launched. The target in Sudan was declared to be a chemical factory producing chemical weapons. Later it became apparent that the factory produced fifty percent of thr medicines and baby milk powder used in the country. Its deztruction led to many deaths.

During the Iraq War, (launched to destroy Saddam's Weapons of mass destruction which the Western leaders already knew did not exist), US military spokesmen repeatedly declared: "We don't do body counts." Medact, the British affiliate of International Physicians for the Prevention of Nuclear War, published a report that estimates the number of Iraqi civilian deaths during the invasion to range from 5,708 to 7,356. The report estimates that the number of civilian deaths after May 1, when Bush declared an end to major combat operations, ranges from 2,049 to 2,209. Another study released last month by the Project on Defense Alternatives, based in Cambridge, estimated that the number of Iraqi civilian deaths in the first month of the war to be between 3,200 and 4,300. In June, the Associated Press estimated the number of Iraqi civilians killed in the invasion to be 3,250. The AP report said, "hundreds, possibly thousands of victims in the largest cities and most intense battles aren't reflected in the total."

War crimes tribunals have been set up to try those on the losing side guilty of atrocities in Germany after the Second World War, and during the wars in the former Yugoslavia. Slobodan Molosevic and others are on trial, and others are being sought. Yet when the international community set up a permanent International War Crimes Tribunal to try all those guilty of war crimes, the US Government not only withdrew from it, but has put political and economic pressure on over a hundred countries to promise never to agree to send US military, or former US military or politicians to trial. The reason given is that people could accuse US personnel "for political reasons." But this is true of anyone. And anyway, the innocent would have nothing to fear. This strong-arm policy looks like nothing so much as clear evidence of consciousness of massive guilt.

ONLY THE LOSERS ARE TRIED FOR WAR CRIMES

Citizens also may avoid their political responsibilities by abdicating their citizenship to their "representatives." If a democracy is a genuine one, then the citizens of the state are obligated to take some responsibility for the actions of their government, insofar as they elected it and tolerate it.

When it is a matter of going to war, US citizens seem to be concerned to know how much it will cost, and how many American soldiers may be killed. Yet most have not been equally demanding that their government tell them how many people they intend to kill, are killing, or have killed, in their name. Moreover, the issue of whether going to war on some particular occasion is ethically justifiable, as opposed to tactically advantageous, is hardly ever discussed - and the US public seems, for all its public adherence to religion, to want to keep it so.

4. The Politics of the Environment

Case Study: The Devastation of Easter Island

One of the greatest mysteries of human history is posed by the strange statues which are found all over Easter Island in the South Pacific Ocean. European visitors asked who had erected the strange structures, and where had they gone to?

Only sixty-four square miles in area, Easter Island is the world's most isolated habitable land. It lies more than two thousand miles west of South America and one thousand four hundred miles from Pitcairn, the nearest habitable island. It has a mild climate and fertile soil, yet when discovered by Europeans it was covered with barren grassland, and there were no trees or bushes over ten feet in height. The native animals included only insects and rats, with no land birds, or reptiles. The only domestic animals were chickens.

The human population of some two thousand Polynesians were ignorant of the skills of seamanship. Only three or four canoes were seen on the island, so that it was difficult to see how the islanders could have got there. When "discovered," the inhabitants of Easter Island were unaware that other people existed.

Yet more than two hundred stone statues standing on massive stone platforms lined the coast. At least seven hundred more were found in quarries, or on roads between the quarries and the coast. Some were sixty feet tall and weighed between two and three hundred tons, while the platforms on which they stood were up to five hundred feet long and ten feet high, with some slabs weighing up to ten tons.

The first Western travellers who reached the island could not understand how it was possible that such impoverished people had been able to erect such massive images. They had neither wheeled vehicles nor draft animals. Thor Heyerdahl argued that Polynesia must have been settled by advanced societies of American Indians, who in turn must have received their civilisation across the Atlantic from ancient Egypt. The Swiss writer Erich von Daniken believed that the statues of Easter Island were the work of extra-terrestrial beings who had been temporarily stranded there, before being rescued in a space ship.

Today these fanciful speculations have been replaced by the evidence of archaeology, palaeontology and pollen analysis. The earliest evidences of human activity have been radiocarbon dated to AD 400 to 700. Pollen samples taken by boring out columns of sediment from swamps and ponds shows that before the first humans arrived, and during the early years of settlement, Easter Island was covered by a subtropical forest of trees and bushes. Bones of fish and porpoises, many species of seabirds and land birds, rats and seal, showed what had been cooked in ovens fired by wood from the island's forests.

The first Polynesians to arrive must have found themselves in an island paradise. But the evidence of the pollen grains and the bones shows that destruction of the forests was well under way within a few centuries of their arrival. Earth samples revealed a layer of charcoal from wood fires, while pollen of palms and other trees disappeared, to be replaced by grass pollen. The fifteenth century marked the end of the forest. People cleared land to plant gardens. They felled trees to build canoes, to transport and erect statues, and to burn. Rats devoured the seeds from the trees, while the native birds that had pollinated them and dispersed their fruit died out. Every species of native land bird became extinct. Porpoise bones disappeared from garbage heaps; no one could harpoon them anymore, since the trees used to construct seagoing canoes had died out. The colonies of more than half of the seabird species breeding on Easter Island were wiped out. To replace these meat supplies, the Easter Islanders became cannibals.

This ecological disaster was closely related to the mysterious statues. The Polynesians began by erecting modest stone statues on platforms. Over the years statues and platforms became larger and larger, as rival clans tried to surpass each other with ever more spectacular displays of wealth and power. Eventually, the growing population began cutting the forest more rapidly than it could regenerate. As the forest disappeared, the islanders ran out of timber and rope to transport and erect their statues. Springs and streams dried up, and wood was no longer available for fires. Crop yields declined, since deforestation allowed the soil to be eroded by rain and wind, dried by the sun, and its nutrients to be leeched out. Statuettes showing sunken cheeks and visible ribs suggest that people were starving.

By around 1700, the population began to crash toward between one-quarter and one-tenth of its earlier level. Many people took to living in caves for protection against their enemies. Rival clans started to topple each other's statues, breaking the heads off. By 1864 the last statue had been thrown down.

Easter Island is planet Earth on the small scale. Today, across the globe a rising population confronts shrinking natural resources. If we continue to follow our present course, we shall soon exhaust the world's major fisheries, tropical rain forests and fossil fuels in just the way that the Easter Islanders exhausted the resources of their island, and in so doing, polluted and destroyed their own home.

Pictures of the planet earth sent back from the first manned space vehicle have started a revolution in the way we think of the earth and its resources. Previously we tended to regard it as indestructible, and infinite in its resources. The photographs of a frail blue sphere spinning alone in the hostile vastness of space gave mankind a new perception of its home. We are now aware that our planet is finite in resources, and is surrounded by a fragile membrane bearing an ecosystem which has supported mankind for quite a short time, but which may not support him for much longer. This new way of looking at Earth is encapsulated in the phrase "spaceship earth."

Signs of danger to the fragile ecosystem are to be found around us even now. They include the following:

- The rate of human population growth has increased to the extent that it endangers the survival of the ecosystem. During the 1830s the human population reached one billion. By the 1930s it had doubled. In 1986 it reached five billion. If human population growth continues at the same rate we shall soon be doubling the population of the earth every twenty years.

- Due to the increased human population, the desire of people to improve their material standard of living and the greed for a quick profit sanctified by capitalism, the usable resources of the planet are being depleted at an increasing rate. In the last fifty years, the USA alone has consumed more of the world's resources of minerals and fossil fuels than all of humanity in its previous history. If every country came to share the standard of living of the USA achieved in 1979, it would become necessary to increase world industrial production one hundred and thirty times. The Club of Rome forecast, using computer predictions based upon present trends, that world resources will be seriously depleted early in the twenty-first century.

- Pollution of the land, sea, rivers and air is increasing. Acid rain is killing off the forests of Europe. In 1983, 8% of West Germany's forests were affected. By 1988 the proportion was 50%.

- The extinction of natural species follows the runaway growth in human population, the increasing exploitation of natural habitats for human use and increased pollution of the environment. Species are being killed off at such a rate that we are living in the sixth age of extinction, the last being that of the extinction of the dinosaurs, probably caused by a huge meteor strike. This is particularly noticeable and harmful in the burning of the world's remaining species-rich rain forests.

- The ozone layer which insulates the earth from the harmful effects of ultraviolet radiation has been damaged. A recurring hole in the ozone layer over the South Polar region during the winter was discovered during the 1950s, but its significance was not realised for some time. In 1987 the first signs of a similar development over the North Pole were first detected. In the same year it was established that the cause is the presence of chlorofluorocarbons in the atmosphere. These substances are used in air-conditioners, refrigerators and aerosol sprays. If the ozone level in the atmosphere declines by twenty percent, then two hours in the sun would blister exposed skin.

- A process of global warming has been detected, radically altering the climate, and with it many other features of our planet. Six billion tons of carbon dioxide are pumped into the atmosphere every year, mostly from 350 million motor vehicles. The result is a cloud of brown smog over cities from Bangkok to Los Angeles. The use of fossil fuels for industry and transport, together with the destruction of the rain forests, is dramatically changing the composition of the earth's atmosphere. Since the late nineteenth century, the level of carbon dioxide has increased by 25%.

Since carbon dioxide allows incoming heat energy from the sun to pass unhindered, but traps outgoing heat, it has the effect of raising the world's temperature. This is called the 'greenhouse effect'. Since the advent of the industrial revolution, the earth's temperature has already risen by about 0.5^0 Celsius. Increasing carbon dioxide in the atmosphere will increase the world's temperature at an increasing rate. Current estimates suggest an increase of between 1^0C and 4^0C by the middle of the twenty-first century.

The effect of this has already destabilised the world's weather system, causing record summer temperatures and devastating floods. It is melting the ice at the poles, and will cause the flooding of low-lying land.

Science is able to provide us with knowledge of our environment, and of the probable consequences of our own behaviour. It may draw attention to something which is not evident to us, such as the disappearance of the ozone hole. Without science we should have had to wait for the effects of increased ultraviolet radiation to become obvious in the form of increased cancer. But political judgements are required in order to determine how we should behave towards the environment.

The situation in which we find ourselves at the end of the twentieth century shows that we need to expand the concept of ethics to include all living things. We need to learn how to live together in order to avoid mutual destruction with nuclear, chemical or biological weapons. But we need to learn to live not merely with each other, but also with the other inhabitants of "spaceship earth," in order to preserve, rather than destroy, our common home.

Among issues proposed to prevent ecological disaster are:

- Population control by means of family planning and contraception. Yet this is opposed by powerful religious groups, such as the Roman Catholic Church. Thomas Robert Malts argued in his Essay on the Principle of Population that if such voluntary "preventive checks" to the growth of the population do not take place, then "positive" checks, such as famine, will do the job.

- Protection of natural habitats, such as the tropical rain forest, now threatened by mining and farming interests. This is opposed by those powerful corporations which see the pursuit of immediate profit and the operation of unbridled capitalism as the highest values of mankind.

- Control or elimination of pollution of the environment. This is costly, and again, is frequently opposed by powerful business interests.

- We need to reduce consumption and end the drive for economic growth in order to develop a self-sustaining society. We must reorient ourselves so as to end the demand for more and bigger material possessions. E. F. Schumacher, in Small is Beautiful, argues against the worship of large scale economic activity and argues for a small scale economy as less environmentally damaging and so sustainable. This may seem idealistic, but if it is the only alternative to the fate of the Easter Islanders, it is also realistic.

- The use of recycled materials may help to slow down the depletion of natural resources.

- Some technology e.g. the bicycle, the computer, is not dangerous to the environment, and should be encouraged and developed, in preference to environmentally destructive technology, such as the internal combustion engine.

- There should be a fundamental change in the way that we look at the world, and our place in it, an end to selfish anthropocentrism, whereby we see all things as of value only insofar as they are of value to us, and the earth as simply something provided entirely for our own use. The belief that animals are there to be eaten, to charm or divert us, or for laboratory experiments, is a dangerous one. It has led to the present perilous situation, and must be replaced with a new bio-centrism, which sees the non-human world as of value in and for itself.

Unfortunately, the outlook is not good.

- Neo-Liberalism, currently the most influential politico-economic ideology, opposes all government imposed restrictions on profit-making to save the environment, in order to protect and maximise the profits of the wealthy.
- Since it was created in 1995, the WTO, which imposes Neo-Liberal policies on governments world wide, has ruled that every environmental policy it has reviewed is an illegal trade barrier that must be eliminated or changed.
- It is necessary that the USA, the world's largest polluter, lead the way. Yet the USA is the most powerful champion of Neo-Liberalism, and by its repudiation of the Kyoto Agreement on reducing pollution from fossil fuels, (because it did not include sufficient special "get out" clauses to exempt US corporations), has shown itself to be unprepared to play any constructive role in helping meet the most important threat to life on the planet.

5. Ethics, Politics and Technological Developments

Today the ability of science to create technology which may prove a monstrous threat to the world is of a character and magnitude which made the fears expressed in the tales of Frankenstein and Dr. Jekyl and Mr. Hyde seems almost cosy by comparison. At the same time awareness of the imminence environmental catastrophe has been awakened. Most recently, developments such as genetic engineering and the use of mind-altering drugs raise new fears.

The blame for all this has been placed by many squarely upon the shoulders of technologists and scientists. Developments in technology increase the choices of action available to us. In doing so, they create new problems concerning the proper limits of our actions. They present new problems in individual ethics and for political decision-makers. Unfortunately, our wisdom does not seem to have kept pace with the knowledge explosion. Advances in science and technology have not yet been sufficiently paralleled by advances in ethics and politics.

Case Study: Engineering the Personality

Many drugs have the ability to change the personality. Pharmaceutical companies have developed a range of drugs to cope with mental illnesses, such as schizophrenia and chronic depression. Psychopharmacology is based upon the following:

- Every feeling or expression of personality originates in neurontrasmitters, chemical signalling molecules in the brain.
- Particular areas of the brain become activated during particular mental states.
- The neurotransmitters which are activated for particular mental activities may be identified.
- Mental illnesses are seen as imbalances in the functioning of these neorotransmitters.
- Chemical interference in the brain by administering drugs to the patient can restore the "correct" balance.

Increasingly, lesser personality disorders, quirks or eccentricities are seen as differing only in degree from mental illnesses. They are only called "illnesses" when the person becomes dysfunctional, and cannot live a normal life in society. Thus the difference between someone who is always suspicious of other people and someone who is paranoid is only a matter of degree.

Psychiatrist Donald Klein of Columbia-Presbyterian Medical Centre in New York observed that the withdrawal of a shy person is like the withdrawal symptoms suffered by an amphetamine user. He reasoned that what must be happening in shy people is that the brain is not producing enough of its natural stimulants. With Michael Liebowitz he began to treat hypersensitive patients with Nardil, a substance which blocks the destruction of the brain's natural stimulants, and claimed positive results after only six weeks treatment.

Shyness may be socially debilitating if it is extreme, but in moderate amounts it can be an attractive personality trait. But the possibility arises now to programme shyness out of the personality. It seems likely that with the medication available, pressure may be put upon people to "conform" to a stereotype of a "normal" personality in regard to shyness. This would, of course, be in the interests of the companies producing the drug. But it would be an invasion of individual liberty, and no less so if it were to be imposed upon individuals by the weight of public opinion rather than by a dictatorial government. It would also impoverish society if we were deprived of those variations of personality which ensure the variety and richness of our society.

Should Some Knowledge be Forbidden

The ancient Greeks told a story about a time when men lived on earth without problems. There was no need to work. All the various diseases and cares which make man's life a misery had all been imprisoned inside a jar in the care of a certain Epithemeos. Although he had been strictly warned never to accept presents from the gods, when they presented him with a woman, Pandora, he accepted the gift. Out of insatiable curiosity she drew the lid from the jar and all the evils which had been trapped inside flew out, scattered across the face of the earth. They remain at large to punish mankind today. This story of Pandora's box illustrates the threat which arises from the advance of scientific knowledge.

But the ethical and political problems arise out of the *application* of knowledge rather than as a consequence of the existence of the knowledge itself. Thus it is claimed that science and scientists cannot be held responsible for whatever uses the knowledge they have acquired is put to by others.

Science has been blamed for the current threat to the environment; whereas in fact this is due to selfish and short-sighted policies implemented by politicians, to unrestricted exploitation of the earth's resources by capitalism (including the state capitalism of the so-called communist countries), and to general greed. It is not the fault of science that we all choose to put our convenience and pleasure before the environment when choosing to drive a car. We prefer the privacy, convenience and sense of power a car gives to relying upon, and paying for, a well-organised public transport system. Politicians have supported this line because if they had not, they would not have held office for long. We mostly get into trouble because of our own short-sighted selfishness. Science will be needed if we are ever to seek seriously to put things right.

Yet there is some knowledge which may be so dangerous that its very existence is a threat to us, in that some group somewhere will always be so criminally stupid or ruthless as to use it. Those people may be terrorists, or they may be members of a lawfully constituted and internationally recognised government. The lesson of history seems to be that if weapons exist, then at some time or other they will inevitably be used. The facts are clear. Twice in this century, a President of the United States of America has ordered the dropping of atomic weapons on cities.

Case Study: The Atom Bomb

The knowledge which made possible the atom bomb was the discovery of the Hungarian physicist, Leo Szilard. In 1933 he was walking through the streets of London when he was forced to stop for crossing lights. By the time they had changed, he had realised that the release of vast amounts of energy might be possible if a nuclear chain reaction could be generated which would break up the structure of the atom. In 1938 he discovered that uranium had just those powers which might trigger such a chain reaction.

In 1939 Szilard persuaded Albert Einstein to write a letter to President Truman explaining the potential of this discovery. With the conquest of much of Western Europe by the Nazis in 1940, Roosevelt told the Pan-American Scientific Congress that if Western scientists did not help develop weapons to defend their freedom, then it might be lost. He assured them that he would be responsible for whatever uses their work would be put to. In the next year the project of constructing an atomic bomb began at Los Alamos in New Mexico.

By the beginning of 1945 it was clear that the Axis powers would lose the war. Szilard became concerned because, despite this fact, the Americans were still continuing work on the atomic bomb. He argued that the USA could claim a strong moral position when it was struggling to preserve freedom, but when victory was in sight and there was no longer any danger of the enemy developing such a weapon, that position had been eroded. He argued that for the USA to possess the bomb would lead to a nuclear arms race in the future, and suggested it be put under international control. He persuaded Einstein to write another letter to President Roosevelt to persuade him to call off the projected testing of the bomb

It was the new president, Truman, whose Secretary of State, James Byrne, replied. He argued, among other things, that Congress would insist upon some return for the money it had invested in the project, and that testing it would render the Russians "more manageable."

The bomb was successfully tested on 15th July, 1945. On 6th August a bomb was dropped on the people of Hiroshima, immediately killing over 60,000 people and causing many more to die painful deaths subsequently over many years from radiation sickness and cancers. Although the Japanese had approached the Soviet government with a request to mediate an armistice, three days later, another bomb was exploded over the city of Nagasaki, ahead of schedule.

The justification given was to save US lives which would have been lost during an invasion of Japan, although the figures given for those saved were sometimes greater than the numbers of the planned invasion force. In any case, it was evident that Japan was about to surrender. The only sticking point was that the US demanded unconditional surrender, while the Japanese government wanted guarantees that the emperor system would be retained. In fact the Japanese government still insisted on this condition after Nagasaki, and the emperor system was in fact retained.

In the years that followed, when the deadly after-effects of the explosions were becoming more and more obvious, the atom bomb was not placed under international control and, as Szilard had feared, a nuclear arms race followed.

Scientific knowledge was essential for the development of the bomb and its production was a feat of technology. It was a political decision to produce and test the bomb. Scientists by themselves could never have produced the bomb because they did not have the material resources to do it. It was essentially an ethical/political question whether to use it or not. That decision was not made by scientists, it was made by President Truman — twice.

Two considerations emerge from these events:

• Once the knowledge to build the bomb existed, it was almost impossible for that knowledge to "disappear." Humanity could not return to a state of innocence.

• Once the ability to create and use the weapon existed, it was both made and used — twice. The private justifications were economic and stategic: to provide a return for the resources invested, and to threaten Stalin and the USSR.

Glossary

descriptive politics: the study of how societies are ordered and governed.

direct democracy: a form of democracy in which the citizen is directly involved in the processes of political decision-making and in the activities of government.

explicit ideology: ideologies consciously developed against the prevailing ideology of a particular society.

implicit ideology: the prevailing ideology of a particular society.

neo-liberalism: a contemporary revival of a primitive form of the liberal ideology.

normative politics: the study of how societies ought to be ordered and governed.

political ideology: a theory which provides an account of man and society and a set of values.

representative democracy: a form of democracy in which the citizen elects representatives to make political decisions and exercise the powers of government on his behalf.

society: a group of people living in interdependence.

terrorism - deliberate indiscriminate violence against civilians to achieve political ends.

utopianism: the wish to reconstruct existing society in accordance with some blueprint or ideal pattern.

18. PHILOSOPHY

"Wittgenstein used to compare thinking with swimming: just as in swimming our bodies have a natural tendency to float on the surface so that it requires great physical exertion to plunge to the bottom, so in thinking it requires great mental exertion to force our minds away from the superficial, down into the depth of a philosophical problem." (George Pitcher)

1. What is Philosophy?

While everyone is aware of the sort of things which astronomers study, even though they may have themselves read no serious books about astronomy, there is often a sense of mystery about what philosophers do. The easy way to answer the question "What is philosophy?" is that it is what you have already been doing while you were reading this book and thinking about its contents, or discussing the questions raised in it in class. You were probably doing philosophy.

Philosophical thinking is something which we all do occasionally during the course of everyday life when we ask questions such as the following:

- Can we know anything for certain?
- Is a person his soul, mind, body, or something else?
- Do we have free will?
- How can we really know what happened in the past?
- Is it possible to say for certain what is right conduct and what is wrong, independently of our preferences?
- Can it be proved that God exists?

Academic philosophy is a much more rigorous version of the same thing. The source of philosophical knowledge is reason, and the tools of philosophers are tools are language and logic.

Considered historically we can say that philosophy is the name for the knowledge that people have sought by using reason as part of the Enterprise of Knowledge. Philosophers deal with those questions which cannot be settled by empirical means.

These are frequently questions about the appropriateness of the methods used in other disciplines to deal with the subject matter, the coherence of the basic concepts employed, and the general nature and reliability of the conclusions reached.

One way of understanding this function of philosophy is to describe it as a "second-order discipline." If we refer to our thinking about the world, for example, in physics or history, as first order thinking, then philosophy may be defined as *thinking about* this first order thinking, as **second-order thinking**. This reflective second-order thinking about the nature and limitations of the various disciplines is usually labelled as "philosophy of . . ." There is a philosophy of science, a philosophy of history, a philosophy of religion, etc.

When engaged in doing any absorbing task it is worthwhile occasionally to take a break, to draw back from the details and get a general overview of the whole enterprise. Then it is appropriate to ask, "What am I trying to do?" "Is it worth doing?" "Could I possibly succeed in what I am trying to do?" "Am I on the right lines?" If the people engaged in the minutiae of the task cannot spare the time, or have not the qualifications to do this for themselves, then it is better if someone else should do this for them. In this world of increasing specialisation of function this might be desirable, even if in this case the *special* function is to take a *general* overview of things.

This is what the Philosopher does in relation to the Enterprise of Knowledge. The philosopher takes a look at all the special knowledge, codifying and evaluating, in general terms, the concepts and methods used, and the type of results obtained. In this sense, Philosophy is a *critical* discipline.

Provisionally the philosopher may use the knowledge obtained by the specialised disciplines, or even everyday knowledge, to help throw some light upon the more general questions which cannot be dealt with by the special methods. In doing all this, he uses reason. This is rational man's inspection of the foundations of the various forms of knowledge, and his reflective overview of the significance of all knowledge.

In addition, philosophy is still concerned with those most fundamental and general questions which may be asked, and which no special methods have been devised to answer other than the use of reason: "What can we know?" (**Epistemology**), "What are values?" (**Axiology**) and "What (in most general terms) exists?" (**Metaphysics**).

In this book we have been engaged in Epistemology at a very elementary level. Yet the distinctions between Epistemology, Axiology and Metaphysics are rather artificial. In order to answer questions about what we can know, it is necessary to ask questions which are really metaphysical and axiological. In asking whether we can know about other people's minds, we needed to consider what minds are. This is a metaphysical problem. In asking whether we can know that an action is right or a painting is of high quality we need to know whether there are objective standards of ethics and aesthetics. These are the most important questions of axiology.

How is Philosophy Done?

When we look at what philosophers actually do in using reason to answer to the questions they ask, we find that they usually do one of two things: they either analyse concepts or they advance or criticise arguments.

Conceptual Analysis

The concepts which we operate with are expressed in language. Frequently a single word in a language has to represent several different concepts. If these are unrelated or insignificant as far as knowledge is concerned, little of consequence will result. If, however, a single word stands for a series of related concepts, perhaps concepts which are difficult to disentangle because they are so closely related to each other, and if moreover these are key concepts in some field of enquiry, then major confusion may be generated. Sometimes two related concepts expressed by two different words are nevertheless confused by us, because we are not clear about the difference between them.

In Chapter Two it was necessary to distinguish between several different senses of "knowledge." We distinguished "knowledge" followed by a direct object from "knowledge that" and "knowledge how." We made a distinction between personal knowledge and objective knowledge. It was also necessary to investigate the relationship between the concept of "knowledge" and other closely related concepts such as "belief," "experience" and "certainty." This was conceptual analysis.

If the basic concepts we operate with are confused, then all that is based upon them will rest upon shaky foundations. Confusions will occur and misleading standpoints will be adopted. This may happen in the field of everyday knowledge and equally in the specialised subject areas.

One result of conceptual confusion will be the struggle to answer unanswerable questions. Some questions themselves involve hidden nonsense, so that attempting to answer them leads only into a morass of problems, e.g. "What is the meaning of life?"

One of the initial tasks of the philosopher is to help clear up these confusions.

One way of clearing up conceptual confusion is by means of a **thought experiment**. The thought experiment is a means of exploring a problem by considering a specific situation which is set up so as to throw in high relief those features relevant to the problem. The interactions of the various elements in the situation are themselves matters of common knowledge and unproblematic relative to the issue at hand, but they are used to highlight salient features of the problem. In a thought experiment, as in a scientific experiment, we are able to eliminate irrelevant and complicating factors in order to focus our attention upon the matter about which we are interested.

Thought experiments may throw light upon the assumptions we unconsciously make about our everyday experience. They may reveal aspects and features of concepts which were hidden from us. Examples of thought experiments include the Prisoners' Dilemma in Chapter Eighteen and the Mysterious Gardener in the Appendix.

Philosophical Arguments

The vast bulk of philosophical writing consists of arguments, which are based either upon conceptual premises or upon very general, and usually uncontroversial, empirical premises. These arguments are generally employed to attack or support general positions about the various fundamental issues considered in Philosophy.

In previous chapters, we have considered many philosophical arguments.

3. Truth

When we seek to know, we claim that what we seek to know is the truth. But what the truth is, is a question that many wise men have tried to grapple with.

A tiny number of philosophers have been sceptics, claiming that we can know nothing. This view is wrongly attributed to Socrates by Lord Byron in his poem, *Childe Harold's Pilgrimage*:

"Well didst thou speak, Athena's wisest son!
'All that we know is, nothing can be known.'"

This view *cannot* be true because it is self-refuting. Socrates' Paradox reveals precisely this. If we could know nothing, how could we know that we could know nothing?

Having ruled out **scepticism**, there are three main theories about the nature of truth, the correspondence, coherence and pragmatic theories.

Truth as Correspondence with the Facts

The everyday notion of truth is expressed by the correspondence theory. A proposition is true if it corresponds with the facts, and false if it does not. The facts are states of affairs which actually obtain, independently of our perceptions of them, or our beliefs about them.

Unfortunately, talk about facts seems clear until we start to ask precisely what constitutes a fact. Is it a different fact, if Yuri is the father of George, that George is Yuri's son, or that George is descended from Yuri? Are there negative facts, such as George not being Yuri's daughter?

It is also difficult to understand exactly how statements "correspond" with the facts. The philosopher Ludwig Wittgenstein once thought that they in some way "pictured" the facts. But how they could do this he never made very clear, and this view has almost no support now. He gave it up himself.

The correspondence theory of truth also leads to paradoxes, e.g. A piece of card has

(1)   The sentence written on the other side of this card is true

written on one side, and

(2)   The sentence written on the other side of this card is false

written on the other side. If (1) is true, then (2) must also be true; but that would make (2) also false. If (1) is false, then (2) must also be false; which would make (1) also true.

The logician Alfred Tarski showed that such problems could be avoided, when we are talking about the truth or falsity of sentences in some language, by distinguishing between two types of language, language used of objects and language about the language itself. If we are to talk about the truth of the sentences of a particular language, we need another language in which to do so. This he termed a metalanguage. A sentence must be in one or the other languages; it cannot be in both. Thus (1) cannot both refer to and be referred to by (2). In this way the paradox disappears.

More significant is the observation that the correspondence theory implies that the truth of a single proposition can be assessed in isolation from the truth of all other propositions. But it is charged that this is not possible, since the significance of any proposition depends upon theories which we hold. The US philosopher John Dewey argued:

> "To assume that anything can be known in isolation from its connections with other things is to identify knowing with merely having some object before perception or feeling, and thus to lose the key to the traits that distinguish an object as known . . . The more connections and interactions we ascertain, the more we know the object in question."

Truth as Coherence

This criticism suggests an alternative view, according to which a proposition is true if it is consistent with all the other propositions we hold. Coherence theories of truth imply that statements are true if and only if they fit in with the vast interrelated system of statements which constitute our general view of the world. If they do not cohere with this view then they are false.

Thus Robin Horton, in *African Traditional Thought and Western Science* drew attention to the parallels between modern western scientific thought and the belief systems being observed and recorded by anthropologists. Horton noted that just as traditional societies tended to explain the common sense phenomena of life in terms of hidden forces and entities operating "behind" the world which we experience, so modern science posited its own unobserved forces and entities to explain the world, such as gravity, genes, viruses, electrons and the unconscious.

If this theory were true, then you might have two entirely inconsistent belief systems, both of which were internally coherent, and yet the propositions of each system would be true within that system. A particular proposition might cohere in one system and not with the other. It would thus be at once both true and false; true for the adherent of one system and false for the adherent of the other. Thus to accept a coherence theory of truth as a complete account of truth is to accept that truth is essentially relative.

Truth as "What Works"

It has also been argued that the purpose of our beliefs in practice is to help us get on with life by enabling us to predict future experiences. If they succeed in doing this, they are accepted; and if they fail, they are rejected. A statement is true not merely because it coheres in some belief system, but because it coheres in a belief system which works. That is, it is true if it has positive predictive value, and false if it does not.

This belief that a belief is true if it works is known as **pragmatism**.

Pragmatists are also committed to the view that truth is not absolute, but modified as discoveries are made, and that it is therefore relative to time and place and purpose of inquiry.

However, a belief could have predictive value yet, as a matter of fact, it could be false.

Relativism

The coherence and pragmatic theories of truth are both relativist theories, in that each denies the possibility that we can reach some objective truth about the world. If such theories were true, there would be no such thing as truth and falsehood as such, only truth or falsehood within a certain conceptual system, or truth or falsehood in certain circumstances.

The French philosopher Michel Foucault argued: "Each society has its regime of truth, its "general politics" of truth: that is, the types of discourse which it accepts and makes function as true; the mechanisms and instances which enable one to distinguish true and false statements, the means by which each is sanctioned; the techniques and procedures accorded value in the acquisition of truth; the status of those who are charged with saying what counts as true."

Nietzsche writes: "There are many kinds of eyes. Even the sphinx has eyes—and consequently there are many kinds of "truths," and consequently there is no truth." Thus people say: "Everyone has a right to his own opinion; for every opinion is just as valid as any other".

But anyone who thinks about this for more than a few minutes will realize that it cannot be true. If every opinion were as valid as any other, then contradictories could be true at one and the same time. But this is absurd.

The nature of relativism can be better understood if we borrow the concept of a *blik* from R. M. Hare. He told a story about a lunatic who thought that the dons (teachers) in his university were trying to kill him. His interpretation of his experience takes this a starting point and uses it as a constant standard of reference. His interpretation of his experience is always such as to be consistent with this belief. Whenever it is necessary, the lunatic makes adjustments to his beliefs so that nothing which happens will be allowed to count against his basic belief or *blik*.

Not all *bliks* are equal, however. It is important, so far as it is possible, to have the right *blik*, which will include:

> " . . . the continued ability of the road to support my car, and not gape beneath
> it revealing nothing below; in the general non-homicidal tendencies of dons; in
> my own continued well-being (in some sense of that word that I may not now
> fully understand) if I continue to do what is right according to my lights; in the
> general likelihood of people like Hitler coming to a bad end."

Relativism is also subject to paradox, since it asserts that all is relative while necessarily excepting itself, as a belief, from the general curse of inescapable subjectivity.

False Paths to Truth

There seem to be three main false paths or blind alleys which we can turn into when engaged upon the Enterprise of Reason:

- Overvaluing one particular form of knowledge, and asserting that its methods alone can achieve truth. In the past it was usually religious beliefs which were elevated above all others. Today the belief thatt one form of knowledge is superior to all others usually takes the form of **scientism**.
- Attempting to reduce one form of reality to another, or **reductionism**, e.g. mental states to bodily states, tunes to aggregates of sounds, societies to aggregates of individuals, etc. The basic fallacy involved is the assumption that if some form of explanation of some phenomena p_1 can be given in terms of some simpler phenomena p_2, then simply in virtue of that fact, p_1 is *nothing more than* p_2.
- Regarding all theories and positions as equally valid, i.e. **relativism**.

Reductionism

As we have seen, science necessarily chops the complexity of phenomena into manageable slices in order to deal with its subject matter adequately. This means systematically ignoring certain aspects of the world. This is fine, and is one of the reasons for the success of science. But it is a fatally easy move from that to assert that what is ignored does not exist.

- Much of the success of modern science in understanding nature has been by the application of mathematics to provide precision and accuracy. But mathematical categories are not equally applicable to all aspects of reality. The initial attitude of the early modern scientists was to concentrate upon those aspects of reality which could be handled numerically, and to ignore the rest. As a practical proposition for a scientist, this is an unobjectionable move. But from arguing that the non-measurable aspects of reality should be ignored in their work, many scientists moved to arguing the quite different proposition that what is not measurable is in some way not real.
- Alternatively, there has been a tendency among workers in the fields of human science to include within their research field those aspects of reality which can not properly be handled numerically, by doing so anyway. This involved professing to measure qualities and properties which are inherently incapable of being treated in this manner. In this way they hoped to acquire the honorific label "science" for their disciplines.

The problem with this approach is that things are almost always, in some sense, greater than their parts due to the emergence within the whole of new properties. A machine, a living creature and a symphony all have properties which their parts severally do not possess. This is even true of what at first sight appear to be mere aggregates. The skilful speaker knows that a crowd will react in quite a different way from the way in which the individuals of which it is composed would react if each were addressed separately. Explaining **emergent properties** in terms of their parts should not be thought of as "explaining them away" as emergent properties.

Relativism:

Relativism is a position we have encountered in relation to factual knowledge and values: science, aesthetics and ethics. In its most extreme form, **cultural relativism** states that people from different cultures inhabit different worlds. With different languages, and so differing sets of conceptual tools, with different Logics and different concepts of causation, they construct different worlds to live in. Consequently, the *experience* of the world each has within his own culture will be different. It follows that the beliefs, values, institutions and customs of one culture can never be objectively or validly judged superior to those of any other culture. For this reason, no genuine dialogue between people of different cultures is possible. There is nothing objectively common to which they can appeal in translating from one the terms of culture to those of another.

Case Study: Magic and the Azande.

During the late 1920s a young anthropologist, E. E. Evans-Prichard, went to live among the Azande of the southern Sudan, in order to study their way of life. He recorded a society dominated by the idea and practice of witchcraft.

All unexpected or unwelcome events were explained as the work of witches: "If blight seizes the groundnut crop it is witchcraft, if the bush is vainly scoured for game it is witchcraft . . . if a wife is sulky and unresponsive . . . it is witchcraft . . . if . . . any failure or misfortune falls upon anyone at anytime . . . it may be due to witchcraft."

Bewitchment was not a matter for special wonder but was accepted as an everyday liability. By use of oracles, the Azande would learn who had bewitched them, and secure punishment of the guilty and compensation for the injured party.

There were contradictions in this system. It was believed that the power to bewitch was inherited from fathers to sons. Yet when a man was accused by an oracle of witchcraft, his sons and brothers would all strenuously assert their own innocence.

The system was, however, workable. Living among them, Evans-Prichard said, "After a while I learned the idiom of their thought and applied notions of witchcraft as spontaneously as themselves in situations where the concept was relevant." He behaved like a member of the tribe, and found their belief system "as satisfactory a way of running my home and affairs as any other I know of."

The Azande belief in witchcraft was, in practical terms, a coherent and useable belief system. Living the form of life of the Azande, Evans-Prichard was never forced to confront the question of its truth or falsity. Neither were the Azande. It was simply a belief system which worked for the society which accepted and used it.

The Azande world picture determined the limits of what was possible for them: "In this web of belief every strand depends upon every other strand, and a Zande cannot get outside its meshes because this is the only world he knows. The web is not an external structure in which he is enclosed. It is the texture of his thought, and he cannot think that his thought is wrong." An Azande could criticise various fragments *within* the system, such as the effectiveness of a particular witch doctor, but there could be no questioning of the system as such. In particular, the basic defining beliefs of the Azande world picture, such as belief in "witchcraft substance" were considered by the Azande themselves to be incontrovertible.

Evans-Prichard himself criticised the Azande beliefs from his "scientific point of view," which he believed to have a unique relation to objectivity. Judging the Azande world picture by the criteria of this scientific worldview, he found the former to be wanting, in that it failed to pass the test for veracity. But other scholars fastened upon his words to argue that this judgement was fundamentally mistaken. They have claimed that science cannot provide us with a concept of objective reality, since the term "objective reality" lacks any meaning outside the system of beliefs in which it is used. P. C. Almond put it thus:

> ". . . expressions like "agreement with reality", "independent reality" and "objective reality" cannot be explained by reference to, for example, the scientific realm of discourse, since these expressions gain their meaning from such a realm of discourse; to explain them in terms of that realm is to beg the question."

It might be thought that any system of beliefs is open to a test for coherence which is not relative to it. But philosopher Peter Winch claims that: " . . . there comes a point where we are not even in a position to determine what is and what is not coherent in such a context of rules, without raising questions about the point which following those rules has in society."

On this view, a system of thought is not subject to criticism or judgement "from outside" at all. Systems of thought are not subject to any external criteria of intelligibility or veracity. This is because "...the criteria of logic . . . arise out of and are only intelligible in the context of, ways of living or modes of social life as such."

Back to Correspondence Again

That there is something fundamentally wrong with this view can be seen if we consider another example of human cultural diversity:

Case Study: The Blood Sacrifices of the Aztecs of Mexico

When the first western adventurers landed in the country now called Mexico, they were appalled to discover that the holy places of the Aztecs were regularly the scene of gory human sacrifices, during which the victim's hearts were torn out of their bodies in order to ensure the continued functioning of the powers of nature.

According to Aztec belief, the birth of the sun, at the beginning of time, had been accomplished only by an act of self-immolation. The gods had gathered at Teotihuacan, where a leprous god, one whose body had been covered in boils and sores, threw himself into a huge fire, the blazing coals of which were transformed into the sun by the power in his blood. This sun was, however, initially motionless; and before it could be made to move, other gods were obliged to offer up their own lives. In order to keep the Sun moving, and in order to prevent darkness overwhelming the world for ever, human beings later had themselves to take over the role of the gods by providing the sun with the nourishment of blood it needed to continue functioning properly.

The regular practice of human sacrifice was believed to be necessary to maintain the course of the world; without it, everything would come to a standstill, and the world would be plunged into everlasting darkness. For this reason, man's first and most important duty was to feed the sun with human blood. What was believed to be true of the sun was thought also to be true of all those other forces of nature upon which humans depend. All required the nourishment of human blood.

Usually, the victim offered to the Sun was held down by his arms and legs over a slightly convex stone altar by four priests, while a fifth ripped open his chest with a flint knife and tore out the still beating heart. Sometimes a warrior was tied with a rope to a huge stone disc, known as the temalacat, and, armed only with wooden weapons, he would attempt to defend himself against attackers bearing real arms. At the moment he was killed, his heart would be torn from his body.

Women had their heads struck off as they danced to the earth goddesses. Children were drowned as offerings to the rain god. Others, destined to be sacrificed to the fire god, were first drugged on hashish and then thrown into a blazing fire. On certain occasions the flesh of the victims was eaten as an act of communion with the gods they represented.

At special ceremonies mass human sacrifices would be held in which hundreds of

---

victims would be immolated at the same time. It has been estimated that at least twenty thousand persons a year were killed by the Aztecs over a period of several centuries, just by having their living hearts torn out of their bodies.

Truth as a Regulative Concept

The relativist would have to say that this conceptual scheme worked for the Aztecs – at least, the ones who survived — in the sense that their cosmology enabled them to organise their lives. The sacrifices were duly performed, and the Sun did not stop moving. By the standards of coherence and pragmatism, their beliefs were true – at least, for them. We have a different cosmology and different values, so that their beliefs are false and their practices unacceptable – to us.

But we *know* that the movement of the Sun is governed by laws which are quite unaffected by blood sacrifice, and always have been. In any society which believed otherwise, we might feel obliged to enlighten them. We also *know* that sacrificing people in religious ceremonies to maintain the powers of nature is not merely misconceived but also morally wrong. In any society where that was practised, we should feel morally obliged to persuade them to end the practice. Of course, some of our own ideas about the nature of the Sun and about the morality of sacrifice may be false, but if so, they will be judged at the bar of reality. They may need to be revised in the future. But if so, this revision will be by reference to the reality towards which our beliefs are increasingly conformed.

Relativism involves a fundamental confusion between our representations of the truth and the truth itself. The coherence and pragmatic accounts of truth depict our representations of the truth rather than the truth itself. When some matter is straightforward and noncontroversial, we apply the standard of correspondence with the facts, as determined by our experience. When matters are more theoretical, and we cannot do this, we fall back upon coherence and pragmatism as provisional measures.

When considering a propositions such as:

(3)   The dog is at the door and wants to be let in

uttered by a friend, we would simply go out and check with the facts. It is true that it is we ourselves who divide the world up into classes that include dogs and cats. It is also true that if we had no interest in them at all then we might have failed to distinguish them in our language or thought. In that weak sense, our categorisation is arbitrary. But the distinction between dogs and cats is a real one, whether we make it or not, because objectively, i.e. in reality, dogs are different from cats. The categorisation is one which corresponds with the facts.

If our friend says:

(4)   There is a little green man from Venus at the door

we have the option also to go and check with the facts. However, he is much more likely to say:

(5)   That was a little green man from Venus at the door, but he has gone now.

In that case, we could not check. Under those circumstances we would appeal to our system of beliefs as a whole in order to decide between there being little green men living on Venus and paying a visit, despite that planet's apparent inhospitability to life and the general absence of reliable information about previous visits to Earth, together with the unlikelihood of ourselves being given the honour of a personal call, and our friend's having a strange sense of humour. The latter coheres with them; the former do not.

Coherence and practical utility are two ways of determining truth in the absence of anything better, but they should not be confused with the truth itself. The coherence and pragmatic theories of truth point to important ways in which we sometimes arrive at the truth, when the process is not straightforward, and important limitations upon our approach to the truth.

"Truth" is a regulative concept. It may be compared to "accuracy" as an ideal never fully realised. Truth itself is not relative, although our representations of it always are.

Discussion: State how, and in what terms, you would defend the truth of each of the following propositions. In which cases would you tend to use each of the above approaches to truth?

1. It is right to help those in need of help.
2. I am here and not just dreaming that I am here.
3. The boiling point of water is 100 °C.
4. Flying saucers do not exist.
5. Health is the most important thing in life.
6. Cows are animals.
7. Alexander the Great died in 323 BC
8. I have a headache.
9. Water has the chemical composition H_2O.
10. Five added to five makes ten.

Glossary

axiology: the philosophical study of values.

conceptual analysis: the disentangling and mapping of complex concepts or of related concepts so as to avoid confusion.

critical philosophy: philosophy which consists of analyses of the basic assumptions and concepts of everyday life and of the various academic disciplines.

cultural relativism: the view that there is no objective standard of truth independent of particular human cultures.

emergent properties: properties of things which are not properties of any of the several parts of which they are constructed, or into which they may be analysed.

epistemology: the philosophical study of what (generally) can be known, and under what conditions and limitations.

foundational knowledge: knowledge upon which all other knowledge is built up.

Hume's fork: a (controversial) method for separating meaningful from meaningless theorising.

metaphysics: the philosophical study of what ultimately or most generally exists in order to create a general and systematic account of reality.

pragmatism: the belief that something is true if it is helpful to us to believe it to be true.

pseudoquestion: a question which is strictly unanswerable because the formulation of the question itself involves some conceptual confusion.

psychological certainty: feeling certain.

regulative concept: a concept which serves as an ideal to be aimed at and as a measure of performance.

relativism: the view that all truths are relative to culture, that there are no absolute truths.

second-order thinking: thinking about the nature and limitations of the other disciplines of knowledge.

speculative philosophy: philosophy which consists of an attempt to develop a synoptic view of all forms of knowledge, and an overview into which the various forms of knowledge may be fitted.

thought-experiment: considering a possible situation in which the elements and relations are matters of common knowledge in order to work out some conceptual point.

truth: correspondence with reality.

19. THE FUTURE OF THE
ENTERPRISE OF KNOWLEDGE

"Business now stands as a guard dog at the gates of perception." (George Monbiot)

At the end of the second millennium, the enterprise of knowledge has come a long way from its first beginnings among our early ancestors. Although some would place the origins of the Enterprise far before that time. In *A World of Propensities* Karl Popper writes:

"The origin and the evolution of knowledge may be said to coincide with the origin and the evolution of life, and to be closely linked with the origin and evolution of our planet earth. Evolution theory links knowledge, and with it ourselves, with the cosmos; and so the problem of knowledge becomes a problem of cosmology."

Certainly, we benefit from our predecessors. Isaac Newton wrote to Robert Hooke: "If I have seen further it is by standing on the shoulders of giants."

The achievements so far have been truly great. Today we know more about the physical nature of the universe and our own history than any generation before us. But the achievements have not been limited to the area of facts. Advances have taken place in our understanding of values as well. Today we are aware of prejudice and ideology, their causes, their nature and the harm they do, as never before. Parallel with the fruits of developments in factual knowledge, such as new medicines and more efficient means of communication, we have developed new insights into the rights of women, children, indigenous peoples, and homosexuals. We have even come to see that animals may have rights. Many of these new insights have already been written into law.

At the present time the enterprise of knowledge is not only ongoing, it would, in some ways, seem to be gathering pace in a most exciting way, as there are ever accelerating developments in our ability to store, manage and transmit information.

At the same time, the opening years of the twenty-first century can give no one cause for optimism. If the Enterprise of Knowledge seems successful as never before, it is also threatened as never before. And past history shows that the progress of this Enterprise is by no means inevitable.

Globalization

The term "**globalization**" was first coined in the 1980s, but the concept of economic globalization goes back to the middle on the twentieth century, when, at the end of the Second World War, the USA found itself by far the dominant economic force in the world, and with its "open door" policy sought to remove all protectionist barriers against investment and trade. This move was resisted in various ways, but in the 1980s it was resumed in earnest.

For owners of significant amounts of capital, this is udoubtedly a good thing. Vigorous trade has made for more accessible raw materials and markets, and a ready supply of cheap labour. Supporters of globalization say it has also promoted the exchange of information, led to a greater understanding of other cultures and allowed democracy to spread to new areas of the globe.

Yet despite these benefits, the drawbacks seem by far to outweigh its benefits.

The poor are under threat. The share of global income enjoyed by the poorest people in the world has dropped from 2.3% to 1.4% in the last decade. In many parts of the world, the standard of living and life expectancy is actually falling, and has been for several decades. But even in the developed world, many have suffered, rather than benefited, from globalization. There is increased insecurity in the workplace. Workers in the developed countries are under threat as companies shift their enterprises to countries where they can get away with paying low wages, where workers have few, if any, rights, and where companies have few, if any, obligations. Thus many of the branded goods enjoyed by consumers in the developed world are manufactured by child labour under sweatshop conditions not seen in the West for a century or more. Moreover, the capitalists' option to relocate work is being used to roll back workers' rights in the developed world, which is already beginning to result in a return to conditions even there.

The progress of knowledge requires as a precondition an open society. Open societies flourish in areas where power is not concentrated in a few hands, like ancient Greece, with its tiny city states. Ideally it requires democracy for its efficient development. Yet today, power is concentrated in fewer hands than ever before in the entire history of mankind. Today, the world is dominated by a single imperial superpower, apparently anxious above all to show that its enemies have nowhere in the world where they can hide from American vengeance.

Moreover, the future of the Enterprise of Knowledge is wrapped up in the future of democracy. And democracy itself is under question when many leaders of the so-called democratic states have demonstrated that they find it easier, to follow the wishes of an unelected "planetarch" in the White House, than the clearly expressed wishes of their own peoples. At the same time, huge multinational corporations, more powerful and influential than democratically-elected governments, put their shareholder interests above those of the communities they dominate, and the customers they are supposed to serve.

A few corporations are, in effect, private armies. Private Military Contractors (PMCs), frequently run by retired military generals, do the dirty work previously carried out by mercenaries. They provide stand-ins for active soldiers, engaging in everything from actual fighting and battlefield training to logistical support and military advice at home and abroad. And they are under no effective government control.

The very engines of knowledge, the universities, are under threat from a corporate takeover in the interests, as always, of immediate profit. In *The Long Revolution,* Raymond Williams points out that ". . . it is necessary to break through to the central fact that most of our cultural institutions are in the hands of speculators, interested not in the health and growth of the society, but in the quick profits that can be made by exploiting inexperience."

Our very culture and its values are under threat. R. Cronk points out, in *Consumerism and the New Capitalism* how "the traditional cultural values of Western society are degenerating under the influences of corporate politics, the commercialization of culture and the impact of mass media. Society is awakening from its fascination with television entertainment to find itself stripped of tradition, controlled by an oppressive power structure and bound to the credit obligations of a defunct American dream."

It is not only Western culture, which is at risk. The rich diversity of human cultures is under threat as globalization facilitates the imposition of US culture on the rest of the world. Thomas Friedman wrote: " . . . globalization is in so many ways Americanization: globalization wears Mickey Mouse ears, it drinks Pepsi and Coke, eats Big Macs, does its computing on an IBM laptop with Windows 98." Additional forces destructive of local cultures are the spread of satellite television and international media networks, and the development of mass tourism.

As if that were not enough, the very global environment itself is under threat as powerful corporations show almost total disregard the well-being of our common environment in the stampede for mega-profits and market supremacy. To save the environment, we need to defend it from the corporations, and the governments in their pockets.

The Dominance of an Infantile Culture

The idea of cultural relativism has been rejected in this book. All cultures are *not* equal, although all *may* have something valuable to teach us. In such matters, only experience can tell. We have to study them to find out what they can teach us. But if they are destroyed, we will never know.

The danger today is that a single infantile culture is being propagated at the expense of all others. Its immediate attractiveness is that it promises instant gratification at the lowest levels at the expense of depth and seriousness. It is cheap (in quality if not in cost) and nasty. It is the enemy of the rational scientific culture of "Old Europe," as it is of all genuine cultures. Because it is immediately and effortlessly assimilable, it destroys what it replaces and impoverishes those it who assimilate it. Essentially incomplete and ultimately unsatisfying, it generates a desire for dogmatism, which is soon found in ideological politics and religion. It is a homogenised mass culture created by big business to serve its own interests.

During the mid-twentieth century the existing popular cultures in the Anglo-Saxon world were gradually replaced by a single mass culture. Localities were robbed of their distictiveness, so that today the Anglo-Saxon world is a uniform environment, defined by the sameness of our high streets or shopping malls, the values we absorb from the media, and our distinctive patterns of behaviour and our social interrelationships.

Advertising has been a powerful tool in this process. It has made possessing and consuming what the corporations have to sell the standard of social success. It propagandises for commercialism and consumerism in an indirect fashion. It functions as propaganda for neo-liberalism by insinuating the values of consumerism into people's day to day life, including their most personal relationships and values. Today, for example, it is considered an essential way of showing appreciation of someone to buy them something on particular occasions determined by the market (Christmas, Mothers' Day, etc.). Failure to spend money on these occasions is seen as an indication of a profound lack of personal appreciation.

This new mass "popular culture" is essentially debasing and trivialising. The gaudy and flashy are used to catch the attention of the public, who, increasingly dependent upon this "fix," show a degraded ability to pay attention to anything with substance for more than a few minutes at a time. Culture is understood chiefly as "entertainment." It is something which, ideally, should be capable of being appreciated without any effort at all. Thus the serious arts are too difficult to be of interest to any but a minority, and are the preserve of an eccentric few, like a private hobby. It has been replaced by a crude chauvinistic **Philistinism**.

In *Where the Stress Falls: Essays*, Susan Sontag dreaded "the ascendancy of a culture whose most intelligible, persuasive values are drawn from the entertainment industries" and which spell the "undermining of standards of seriousness." But that day has already arrived. We are becoming dutiful consumers and workaholics for the greater good of the corporations, and the

0,5% of the US population who own and direct most of them.

No better symbol can be found for the destruction of ancient and insightful cultures by the new, shallow, violent, Philistine mass culture which is engulfing us all than the smashed Sumerian pottery and cuneiform tablets, and the burning of priceless medieval manuscripts, in Baghdad in 2003; which recalls the destruction of the library of Alexandria in 686.

An inevitable consequence of this cultural impoverishment is the "dumbing down" of education. "Child-centred" and "activity-centred" teaching methods, originally adopted for young children with learning difficulties, are now increasingly considered appropriate for older children, even for young people about to enter university. At the present rate, by 2050 university students will be playing games to make learning more fun, and unable to read any book with more than a few pages in it, which does not have some coloured pictures to break the monotony and make learning easier. As the pill is increasingly sugared, there is less and less "pill" in the pill. Education, like politics and almost everything else (e.g. news, religion, sports), is being assimilated to the consumer product called "entertainment."

We are increasingly left with a uniform consumerist culture which has been manufactured by business corporations in their own interests, and propagated chiefly by the mass media, but also now, increasingly, by schools and colleges.

The Threat to Democracy

Democracy is necessary for the efficient development of the Enterprise of Knowledge. Yet democracy is profoundly undermined by cultural deprivation.

Noting, in a drive through the centre of Texas, signs saying: "Iraq today; France tomorrow"; "You're either with us or against us"; and "God said it, I believe it, and that settles it"; one writer observes that "in this land of fierce fundamentalism" "nuances are challenging." She goes on: "Intellectuality is not trusted in these parts. Sticking to your gainful employment, counting progress by its material make-up, and conforming to what you've been taught from childhood on is considered strong character." Anyway, the mass media are always there to divert people with professional spectator sports, sex scandals, or "personalities" and their problems. "Don't bother them with body-bags from Iraq; show them a movie star or sportsman on his way to court."

Democracy is in crisis in any case, because of the ability of US administrations to cajole, bully, or bribe most other governments to act in *their* interests, and that of their backers, rather than that of their own people, and because the prevalent two-party system is seen to be an evident farce in many countries. The end will be a depoliticized citizenry marked by apathy and cynicism, in which activism is criminalized, and the large corporations who pay for the election campaigns, and therefore for the governments themselves, do as they will. In addition, it seems that any government not compliant to the dictates of the US government can expect to be victimised, especially economically. We have already seen an unelected US president refuse to deal with an elected leader of the Palestinian people in the name of "democracy."

Democracy is in crisis even in the USA itself. There it has been discovered that in this advertisement-oriented society, voters will tend to vote for a familiar face. And since politics is now a virtually a branch of the entertainment industry, it is advisable to choose a figure from the movies. In 2003, the electors of California chose Arnold Schwarzenegger, a bodybuilder turned movie star, known to most of them primarily as a robotic killer in *The Terminator*. This multimillionaire, endorsed by wealthy backers, ran a successful campaign by promising little more than to be "the people's governor" - whatever that may mean. Perhaps the next stage will be to run, and subsequently to be governed by, "virtual candidates": say, Superman versus Mickey Mouse.

The Privatisation of Knowledge

Knowledge grows in the atmosphere of free exchange of information and criticism. It is not knowledge until it has been shown to be justified, and it is not part of the great collective Enterprise of Knowledge until it is publicly accessible. From that point on, it is part of the great tradition, and others will freely use it to advance further. As Isaac Newton wrote to Robert Hooke: "If I have seen further it is by standing on the shoulders of giants."

In the past, certain groups have claimed to possess some special right over a body of knowledge, and sought to keep it from the people entirely, or to ration it out in spoonsful as a concession. This was a feature of dogmatism, and was employed to give them special status as an elite, with the economic, social and political privileges which went with it. Most often, their claim was bogus, and they were little more than well-organised bodies of confidence tricksters.

The mystery religions of the ancient world claimed hidden, or esoteric, knowledge, which the adepts would teach to the initiates, usually for a fee. Various mechanisms of deception, such as hidden speaking tubes, were used to convince the initiates that what they were getting for their money was worth the cost.

Today the Enterprise of Knowledge is threatened as never before by a move to privatise knowledge, to consider it *property* which can be owned and traded. Since knowledge is essentially social in character, this is as absurd as a previous move to treat land as property. Yet that move succeeded; so that today millions do not find it remarkable that someone should regard part of the earth's surface as in some way his or her own private property (not to mention the fish in the pool, the worms in the soil and the plants growing out of the earth), on the strength of the possession of a piece of paper.

Such extensions of the concept of ownership benefit the few who have large amounts of free capital to invest, and they already own most things anyway.

This encroachment upon the great tradition of human knowledge is showing itself in many ways.

Increasingly, government funding for universities is being reduced, while private sources of income are being sought to make up the difference. This has several effects desired by those who support such measures. Firstly, it reduces taxes and benefits, which have tended in the past to redistribute wealth from the more wealthy to the less wealthy. Secondly, it increases the powers of corporations, as opposed to governments. Thirdly, if the costs are passed on to the students, it reduces competition for the children of the wealthy in desirable institutions. But most of all, it places the knowledge generated in the universities in the hands of the corporations, as a resource for the generation of greater private profits.

The universities have come to be not places where knowledge is generated, but places where profits are generated for their "benefactors." This in turn has several consequences:

• Science ceases to be the search for new knowledge, and becomes the search for techniques to exploit existing knowledge for the profit of the corporations.

• Extensions of knowledge, and the development of the practical benefits of knowledge, will only be exploited if there are sufficient profits to make it worthwhile for the corporations, e.g. cures for diseases of those who can pay well for them, as against cures for diseases of those who cannot.

• Scientists will no longer be able to investigate environmental hazards if they are caused by the "benefactors" of the university, or publish their results if that would prove "difficult" for them.

• While openness was characteristic of science in the past, today the corporations require "confidentiality" (i.e. secrecy), because to them, knowledge is money.

In the UK, for example, the government is in the process of effectively "selling off" much of the resources of the universities to big business; in a similar way to that in which other public resources, built up at the expense of the taxpayer, have been, and are being , sold off to those who can afford them, to be exploited by them for their private profit.

Because of the Knowledge Explosion, the body of scientific literature is vast, and it can be very hard for students and researchers to find the information they need. Today, search engines are able to search through thousands of articles and pick out the few that a scientist might need. But some publishers wish to ensure that this knowledge will belong not to the scientific community, but to themselves, so they are setting up electronic archives of scientific knowledge, and will charge for access to it. This is not knowledge that they have paid for, since the authors of the articles published in academic journals are not paid for writing them; yet the publishers insist that the authors sign over the copyright to their work to them.

Copyright used to be used to protect an author's work so that someone could not simply publish a work of his without paying him something for it. Today it has become a means of assimilating written work to property. The copyright is being extended over ever longer periods, to benefit not the author, but his heirs or estate, who probably contributed nothing to it at all.

The World Trade Organisation's agreement on Trade Related Aspects of Intellectual Property Rights has closed down the access to new technology and medical advances to many developing countries. Some countries such as India, Brazil and Thailand have developed their own pharmaceutical industries, producing generic medicines for a fraction of the cost of brand-named drugs manufactured by the Western multinationals corporations, the prices of whose drugs are far beyond the reach of most people in the Third World.

Yet the WTO aims to restrict the right of these countries to produce cheaper drugs for their own people, forcing them instead to accept the private ownership of brand-named medicines through long -lasting patents. In 1998 the WTO ruled that the Indian government must amend its national legislation in line with the TRIPs agreement to give greater rights to pharmaceutical companies.

In 1997 in South Africa, Nelson Mandela secured the introduction of a Medicines Act which would require the government to obtain the cheapest medicines to fight AIDS, tuberculosis and other infectious diseases. It required pharmacists to prescribe a cheaper generic version of brand-named drugs wherever possible, and empowered the health minister to override patents taken out by pharmaceutical companies when public health was at risk. So in March 2001, a consortium of thirty-nine drugs companies entered into litigation against the government of South Africa to force it to repeal the legislation. The drug companies insist that South Africa must fulfil its responsibilities as a member of the WTO and put the rights of the drug companies before public health.

The UN has condemned the TRIPs (Trade Related Aspects of Intellectual Property Rights) agreement as a violation of human rights.

Patenting used to be a means of ensuring that an inventor might securely enjoy some of the profits of his work. Today it is being extended to cover things which are "discovered" by employees in the interests of the corporations who employ them.

Today, some corporations have patented rights to the distant products of genetic engineering. They claim the right to royalties on crops which are "descended" from seed which they have sold.

Thus in 2000 a US company claimed to have acquired the European patent for two human genes whose mutations cause the development of breast cancer. The company warned that in future, hospitals testing for that condition would *have* to use the company's test, and of course, pay the company for the privilege.

In all, one is tempted to recall Winston Churchill's famous warning in 1940 about falling into "the abyss of a new Dark Age, made more sinister, and perhaps more protracted by the lights of perverted science."

Glossary

globalization: the abolition of obstacles and barriers to worldwide communications, trade and investment, with the increasing homogenisation of culture.

Philistinism: glorying in cultural poverty.

Appendix: Religion

"The main doctrine of a fanatic's creed is that his enemies are the enemies of God."

(Andrew White)

Some people will be surprised to see a section on religion in a book about knowledge. Others will consider that special religious ways of knowing and the content of religious knowledge are the most important forms of knowledge. This subject is bitterly controversial because religious beliefs are usually, although not always, held dogmatically or ideologically.

1. Religion and Reason

What is Religious Belief?

The claims made by religious believers are very important, since if they were true, this life might be merely the anteroom to another, more real, form of existence. If those beliefs were true, we would immediately find a new significance and meaning in life. If those beliefs are false, then there is no afterlife, and we would ourselves be obliged to create meaning and significance for our lives in this world, since there would be no meaning or value given from outside; no assistance from outside if we made a mess of things ourselves, and no afterlife either to fear or to look forward to.

Religious belief is sometimes held with aggressive **certitude**. Believers are convinced that they are in possession of the final truth. In this it is unlike belief in science, in that in science we know that theories are provisional, always liable to be overturned by fresh evidence or insights.

Religious belief is usually a form of ideology. Its followers begin any investigation or discussion with the presumption of its truth, and adjust their interpretation of their experience so as to support their belief. For this reason, they are particularly liable to delusions. They are inclined to use propaganda in order to persuade others of the correctness of their beliefs. (The term "propaganda" comes from the former name of a department of the government of the Roman Catholic Church charged with the propagation of the faith.) Religious people are also inclined to regard all disagreement with their own views not merely as wrong but wicked, to censor opposing views, and to punish those who put them forward wherever and whenever they have the power to do so.

For this reason, an open and critical treatment of this topic is not feasible in some societies. In others, no rational discussion of religious issues will be possible at all, and an attempt to initiate one would be dangerous. In some, discussion would only be possible if everyone's arriving at the "correct" conclusions could be guaranteed in advance.

Fanaticism

Because religious belief is usually ideological, intolerance is fundamental to many faiths. If a religion teaches that it is the only valid spiritual path, then people of all other faiths must logically be in error. Believers will tend inevitably to infer that other religions have no merit whatsoever. Some will then, equally inevitably, come to regard all other religions as demonic. Some of these will take the next logical step, when they get the chance, moving beyond mere intolerance of attitude to actively seeking to persecute followers of other faiths. God is understood to want us to defend and protect our religion, and to bring its blessings to everyone else – whether they want them or not. Rival religions, unbelief and scepticism will not be tolerated. Ultimately, the forced conversion and even the mass murder of outsiders will no longer be considered crimes at all. Instead, such acts will demonstrate a praiseworthy depth of commitment and effort.

Religious believers have to face this aspect of what they are involved in. Generally, the closer a believer is to the literal interpretation of his faith (**fundamentalism**), and the more seriously he takes it (**zealotry**) the more likely he is to express negative and destructive sentiments towards all who disagree with him. This is because these sentiments seem to lie at the very heart of many faiths.

Islam is a faith, born among a warlike desert people, and *jihad,* or holy war, is said to be the highest duty of a Muslim. The *Qur'an* says: "But when the forbidden months are past, then fight and slay those who join other gods with Allah wherever you find them; besiege them, seize them, lay in wait for them with every kind of ambush . . ." (9:5) "When you encounter the unbelievers, strike off their heads, until you have made a great slaughter among them . . ." (47:4) "Make war upon such of those to whom the scriptures have been given as believe not in Allah, or in the last day, and who forbid not what Allah and his apostle have forbidden . . . until they pay tribute . . ." (9:29)

One of the chief wellsprings of intolerance is the belief, characteristic of cult members, that their particular group is an elite, chosen out of the general run of mankind, which possesses the Full Truth, which is engaged in the only truly Righteous Mission, and which is accredited by God himself. The Jewish scriptures claim, and orthodox Jews today still believe, that the perfectly good God who created the universe decided to choose one single group of people out of all the inhabitants of the earth to show them especial favouritism.

On the basis of this belief in their status as "God's Favourites," the ancient Israelites felt authorized to behave with extreme intolerance towards their neighbours.

"If your brother, the son of your mother, or your son, or your daughter, or the wife of your bosom, or your friend who is as your own soul, entices you secretly, saying, 'Let us go and serve other gods,' which neither you nor your fathers have known, some of the gods of the peoples that are round about you . . . you shall not yield to him or listen to him, nor shall your eye pity him, nor shall you spare him, nor shall you conceal him; but you shall kill him; your hand shall be first against him to put him to death, and afterwards the hand of all the people.

"You shall stone him to death with stones, because he sought to draw you away from the Lord your God, who brought you out of the land of Egypt, out of the house of bondage. And all Israel shall hear, and fear, and never again do any such wickedness as this among you." (*Deuteronomy* 13:6-11)

Being chosen by God justified not only extreme intolerance towards those who thought or worshipped differently, it was also held to justify genocide.

"When the Lord your God brings you into the land which you are entering to take possession of it, and clears away many nations before you . . . then you must utterly destroy them; you shall make no covenant with them, and show no mercy to them . . . But thus shall you deal with them: you shall break down their altars, and dash in pieces their pillars, and hew down their Ashe'rim, and burn their graven images with fire. For you are a people holy to the Lord your God; the Lord your God has chosen you to be a people for his own possession, out of all the peoples that are on the face of the earth." (*Deuteronomy* 7:1-7)

In Saint Luke's Gospel Jesus is recorded as saying, in the course of a giving a parable: " . . . the Lord said unto his servant, Go into the highway and hedges, and compel them to come in, that my house may be filled." (14:28) This is advice which his followers have not been reluctant to adopt, although today this is something of an embarrassment, and the *Catholic Encyclopedia* says: "Instances of compulsory conversions such as have occurred at different periods of the Church's history must be ascribed to the misplaced zeal of autocratic individuals."

The arrival in the New World of Christopher Columbus in 1492 opened up the Americas to Christian missionary work. Wherever he landed, Columbus planted a cross to claim the island for Catholic Spain. If the Indians objected, he would threaten them: "I certify to you that, with the help of God, we shall powerfully enter in your country and shall make war against you ... and shall subject you to the yoke and obedience of the Church." On the island of Hispaniola alone, due to Columbus' landings, some fifty thousand natives died. The survivors became victims of rape, murder, enslavement and Spanish raids. One conquistador wrote: "So many Indians died that they could not be counted, all through the land the Indians lay dead everywhere. The stench was very great and pestiferous." The Indian chief Hatuey fled with his people, but was captured and burned alive. As he was being tied to a stake a Franciscan friar urged him to accept Jesus Christ so that his soul might go to heaven. Hatuey replied that if heaven was where the Christians went, he would prefer to go to hell. An eyewitness reported:

"The Spaniards found pleasure in inventing all kinds of odd cruelties . . . They built a long gibbet, long enough for the toes to touch the ground to prevent strangling, and hanged thirteen [natives] at a time in honor of Christ Our Savior and the twelve Apostles . . . then, straw was wrapped around their torn bodies and they were burned alive."

Eventually all the native inhabitants of the island were exterminated, so that the Spaniards had to import slaves from other islands. In less than a single normal life-span, an entire culture of millions of people had been exterminated. Then the Spaniards turned their attention to the main-land. The slaughter had barely begun.

The same genocide was to be witnessed in North America. The first settlers would have perished during the first winter after they landed if they had not received the help of the Indians. In response, John Winthrop, first governor of Massachusetts Bay Colony, saw his duty as being to " . . . carry the Gospel into those parts of the world . . . and to raise a bulwark against the kingdom of the Anti-Christ." When some two thirds of the native population died of the smallpox, brought by the settlers, this seemed to them a great sign of "the marvelous goodness and providence of God." The Governor wrote in 1634: "they [the natives] are near all dead of the smallpox, so as the Lord hath cleared our title to what we possess."

Today many problems are defined by religious differences. Religious people tend to say that it is not religious but racial, economic, social, or political differences which are the *real* cause of the problem. They seem to argue that religious differences never cause or exacerbate any problems. However, while such conflicts usually have complex origins, in which all the above play a role, it is often the religious differences which give them much of their bitterness, and which justify, in the minds of the parties to the conflict, their self-righteousness and cruelty; and it is sometimes religious differences, fortified by fanaticism, which prevent solution to the problems.

IN A WORLD OF WEAPONS OF MASS DESTRUCTION
RELIGIOUS FANATICISM MAY BE
A LUXURY WE CAN NO LONGER AFFORD

---

2. Religious Ways of Knowing

Religious believers usually claim to be in possession of a special source of knowledge which has a unique authority, although they differ on what this source is, and what it says.

Faith

Some religious people may claim to know "through *faith*", which they think of as a special form of knowledge open only to those who possess the "gift" of unquestioning commitment. In practice, the only test of whether someone has this faith is whether his beliefs coincide with that of those believers who also claim to know in this way. If you do, you have faith; if you do not, you are dismissed as in error.

This seems to be a simple case of claiming some special status for one's own beliefs by inventing a mysterious source of knowledge only available to oneself, or those who agree in every respect with oneself. People who hold their beliefs in this way usually have very little time for other people who hold perhaps very slightly different religious beliefs, which they may also claim to be equally based upon faith. There is no more reason for accepting one claim on this basis than any other.

Religious Experience?

Some people claim to have extraordinary experiences which, they say, are like meeting someone: like a confrontation with some person or force, yet which are quite different from all normal experiences. The medieval Frenchman, Saint Bernard, explained it like this:

"It is not by the eyes that he enters, for he is without form or colour that they
can discern; not by the ears, for his coming is without sound; nor by nostrils,
for it is not with the air but with the mind that he is blended."

According to Evelyn Underhill in *Mysticism*, this claim is not to be understood as merely metaphorical: "Innumerable declarations prove it to be a consciousness as sharp as that which other men have, or think they have, of colour, heat or light."

This claim to a direct experience of the divine, not mediated by any sense-experience, is called **mysticism**.

Mystics do not generally claim to have had some experiences or "feelings" which they later went on to interpret as confrontation by God, rather they claim a direct, unclouded experience which is more like

(1) I met *x* today

than

(2) I had a feeling of meeting *x* today.

In short, they claim knowledge of God by acquaintance (See Chapter Two).

There are, of course, many problems associated with such claims.

Unfortunately, no one can check a claim to some special religious experience. Since it is essentially private, there is no way of checking its authenticity. Therefore it is a claim which can safely be made by anyone who wants to become an object of attention, or anyone who wishes to start a religious movement with himself as head, messiah or guru, with no foundation at all. Since such claims cannot, in the nature of things, be checked, it is difficult to see what value they can have.

It is sometimes said by those who support such claims that they can be vindicated by the life-style of the persons making them; but no one's life-style can be assessed until it is over, and he is dead. Much of what is reported by those who claim mystical experiences is similar to the experiences of those who take hallucinogenic drugs, or those who suffer from mental disorders, such as schizophrenia. Moreover, mystical experiences are given different interpretations in the different religious traditions. Such an experience may be assigned by a polytheist to the approach of a god; by a Christian as the "beatific vision" of the one, true God; and by a Buddhist as the abolition of the self in Nirvana.

The Scottish philosopher, David Hume, points out that if we consider the differences between religious believers about the objects of their belief, then we can see that there is virtually nothing which they have in common which might constitute an object of such an "awareness."

"What true or tolerable notion of deity could they have, who acknowledged and worshipped hundreds? Every deity that they owned over and above one was infallible evidence of their ignorance of him and a proof that they had no notion of God, where unity, infinity and eternity were excluded. To which if we add their gross conceptions . . . and other qualities attributed by them to their gods; we shall have little reason to think that the heathen world, i.e. the greater portion of mankind, had such ideas of God in their minds as he himself, out of care that they should not be mistaken about him was Author of."

Revelation

"Sacred Speech"

Individuals sometimes claim to speak with the authority of God. This claim may take several forms. People have sometimes claimed that a god actually speaks through their bodies, using their voice boxes in the way in which, during a spiritualist seance, the medium claims that a spirit speaks through her body using her vocal chords. Usually these people utter what appears to be nonsense. Then that person later, or someone else at the time, claims to provide an interpretation of the sounds. Common among Christian Pentecostalists, this is called **glossolalia**.

The practice goes back to pagan times, and was used in the ancient Greek religion by the oracle of Apollo at Delphi. The *pythia*, an old woman, would sit on the tripod, chew laurel leaves, breathe in smoke from a chasm, go into a trance and utter nonsense sounds. Priests would then turn this into Greek verse for the visitors who had paid to consult the oracle.

"Sacred Books"

When writing was invented it was thought to be magical, in that marks on stone or papyrus could hold a meaning not apparent to others, which different people could nevertheless unlock at different times.

Thus religions whose formative period of development took place during periods when elites in their society first became literate, often possess a body of sacred writings which they claim embodies a special revelation of the truth from God. The Hindus have the *Bhagavad Gita* and the *Upanishads,* the Parsees revere the *Vedas*, while the Sikhs have the *Granth Sahib*. Three of the worlds great religions, Judaism, Christianity and Islam, are known as the "religions of the book" because of the importance which believers attach to their Scriptures. These are believed to describe the most important events in the story of God's dealings with mankind, and to provide a guide for living in accordance with his will. For Christians this book is the Bible; for Jews it is what Christians call the *Old Testament* together with the *Talmud;* while for Muslims it is the *Qur'an*.

In its most extreme form, **fundamentalists** claim that their own holy book is, in every claim and in every respect, literally true, because it is the work of God, not man.

Biblical fundamentalists believe that their sacred books contain the Full Truth about mankind and the world he lives in, and the Key to How to Live. As such, their authority, they claim, is unquestionable. As a Protestant fundamentalist explains: "The Bible is the very utterance of the Eternal; as much God's own word as if high heaven were open and we heard God speaking to us with human voice." Similarly, the *Qur'an*, is considered by Muslims to be the true word of God, the ultimate authority available to man, and in all respects infallible. Every part of it is believed to have had a supernatural origin, down to its punctuation, since it is the earthly copy of an original written in heaven on uncreated stone tablets. Even to question its authority would be a grave sin.

When asked to justify their claim that their Sacred book is beyond all possibility of error, biblical fundamentalists, whatever their religion, tend to use three types of argument.

Firstly they may quote from their Scriptures in support of their faith in their Scriptures. Christian fundamentalists tend to refer to: "All Scripture is given by inspiration of God. . ." taken from the *Second Epistle of Timothy* (3:16). If a Mormon is asked for proof that the *Book of Mormon* is true he may point to the promise given in *Moroni* 10:4-5: "And when ye shall receive these things, I would exhort you that ye would ask God, the Eternal Father, in the name of Christ, if these things are not true; and if ye shall ask with a sincere heart, with real intent, having faith in Christ, he will manifest the truth of it unto you, by the power of the Holy Ghost." This reasoning, however, is circular.

Biblical fundamentalists may also appeal to the vast mass of believers who have in the past drawn inspiration from their belief in the inerrancy of their Scriptures. But this is a mere appeal to opinion. Moreover it conveniently ignores the counter-evidence which is provided by the vast mass of believers in the inerrancy of the Sacred Scriptures of *other* faiths than their own.

Fundamentalists may appeal to a feeling which a person may have when reading their scriptures, which is said to authenticate their contents, showing them to have a divine origin. For Mormons the "truth" of their Scriptures is said to be demonstrated by a physical sensation called "burning in the bosom"; spiritual confirmation which authenticates a conviction that something is true. Again this is merely a "feeling," and psychological states do not necessarily tell us anything about the world outside the subject.

There are insuperable problems attached to fundamentalist claims. Sacred books arose in prescientific societies, and contain material which is inconsistent with modern scientific knowledge. They are also frequently internally inconsistent. What is asserted on one page may be inconsistent with, and may even directly contradict, what is asserted on another. Biblical fundamentalists have to explain how the presence of such false information and inconsistencies are possible if God is the author of their Scriptures.

In response to such difficulties as these, they may assume that just so long as they can suggest some theoretically possible interpretation of a problem passage which would technically remove the contradiction or discrepancy, then they have preserved their inerrancy doctrine; no matter how far-fetched or unlikely that interpretation may be, and no matter how frequently they are forced to do this. They may argue that just so long as the interpretation they present is not absolutely impossible, then it *must* have happened like that. The trouble with this sort of *ad hoc* reasoning, so common in pseudoscience and pseudohistory, is that at every step the fundamentalist's position becomes less and less credible,

The contents of such books can usually be explained by the normal methods of historical research. In any case, such books appear to be of limited help in leading believers to the ultimate and final truth. First of all there is disagreement between religious believers about what the scriptures *are*; then those who agree on sharing certain scriptures usually disagree over the precise interpretation of them.

3. Reason and Religious Belief

Some religious traditions have denied that reason has any place in religious belief at all. The early Christian Tertullian gloried in the irrationality of his beliefs: "After Jesus Christ no need for speculation, after the Gospels, no need of research . . . My first principle is this: Christ laid down one definite system of truth which the world must believe without qualification." Not only did he think it unnecessary to subject religious dogmas to rational scrutiny, he actually asserted of his faith: "I believe because it is absurd." The Protestant reformer, Martin Luther declared: "Whoever wants to be a Christian should tear the eyes out of his Reason . . . Reason must be deluded, blinded, and destroyed." The same hostile and defensive attitude towards learning can sometimes be found in Islam. A famous Muslim teacher said: "We do not enter into vain talk about Allah nor do we allow any dispute about the religion of Allah . . . When our knowledge about something is unclear, we say: 'Allah knows best'"

Many believers, like the Danish theologian, Soren Kierkegaard, have argued that religion is an essentially irrational activity which requires acceptance of doctrines which are contrary to reason. This position is called **fideism**.

Of course, ideological thinking and fanaticism are not *inevitable* accompaniments of religious belief. It has also been claimed that by the use of reason man can arrive at knowledge of the existence and nature of God and therefore support theism by reason. It has also been claimed that by the use of reason we can never know whether God exists or what he is like (**agnosticism**), and also that we can know that he does not, or could not, exist (**atheism**).

During the Middle Ages many philosophers were pulled in opposite directions by their reason and their religious faith. Reason told them one thing, and faith another. This is true for many in today's world, where they are torn between what they learn at school or from the media or from the use of their own powers of reasoning, and what they are expected to believe by parents who are religious believers, or by the dogmas of the sect to which they belong.

One way of dealing with the conflict between science and religion is to place them in intellectual compartments as completely distinct modes of understanding, and assign to each a completely different set of rules. Many followers of the Arab philosopher Averröes argued for the idea of "Double Truth", that there were two truths which were mutually contradictory, one shown by faith and one discovered by reason.

Some thinkers maintain that the role of science is to provide us with facts, and the function of religion is to promote values. Such a proposal ignores the fact that religion can function to its devotees as a source of genuine moral inspiration only if they take its vision of the world to be fundamentally *true*. For this reason, many religious people cannot accept the view that science and religion have nothing to do with each other.

The medieval Catholic theologian Thomas Aquinas firmly rejected the idea of "two truths." He that there may be two *paths* to truth, but that there must be a single truth to which they both lead. Thus we may use reason or faith to reach the truth, but both "truths" ultimately cannot conflict.

Arguments for Religious Belief

The Argument from Morality

It is frequently claimed that religion is necessary to underpin morality. Pope Pius XII wrote: "As you know, once religion is taken away there cannot be a well ordered, well regulated society." This warning encapsulates a fear that many have had over the centuries, that religious belief is all that stands between civilised life and the brute state of nature, in which the Law of the Jungle reigns supreme. Religion is thought to be the foundation of morality, the source of our ethics. Remove the religious foundation, and the superstructure of morality will collapse — with the terrifying consequence that mankind will regress into barbarism. The Russian novelist, Dostoyevsky said: "If God does not exist, then anything is permitted.

Case Study: The Man who became a God

In his *Erewhon Revisited*, Samuel Butler told the following story:

A man named Higgs spent some time in a remote part of the country before leaving in a balloon. After a gap of some twenty years he returned to find that the people there had adopted a new religion in which he was worshipped as the "Sun Child" who ascended into heaven. The annual feast of his Ascension was about to be celebrated. Full of indignation Higgs approached Hanky and Panky, the high priests of the new religion and threatened to expose them by revealing that it was himself who went up in the balloon and that he was just an ordinary man. But Hanky and Panky restrained him, saying: "You must not do that, because all the morals of this country are bound up with this myth, and if they once know that you did not ascend into Heaven they will all become wicked." Persuaded by this argument Higgs quietly left the country.

The belief that religion is necessary to underpin morality is an ancient belief. The Roman geographer Strabo wrote: "The great mass of women and common people [!] cannot be induced by mere force of reason to devote themselves to piety, virtue, and honesty. Superstition must therefore be employed, and even this is insufficient without the aid of the marvellous and the horrible."

However it can be argued that religion is not a suitable foundation for morality. In his *Notebooks of Lazarus Long,* Robert Heinlein observed: "Men rarely (if ever) manage to dream up a god superior to themselves. Most gods have the manners and morals of a spoiled child." In this he follows the observation of Xenophanes of Colophon, made centuries before, that: "Ethiopians have black, snub-nosed gods, and Thracians have blue-eyed, red-haired gods . . . If cattle and horses and lions had hands, or drew with hands, or did such works as men, they would have drawn the shapes of gods like them, horses like horses, cattle like cattle, and made their bodies like the ones they have."

The God of the Bible is certainly recorded as regularly condoning crimes committed by his favourites and as equally regularly demanding the massacre of the enemies of his favourite people. Moreover, by keeping people at a low level of moral development, that of blind obedience to authority, religious-based morality prevents the growth of a mature, autonomous rational morality among believers. Historically, it could not really be said that intensely religious societies have demonstrated a superior morality to those whose religion is less strong, let alone that strong religious belief ensures morality while lack of it ensures barbarism.

Arguments Against Religious Belief

Arguments from Known Causes.

During the nineteenth century the birth of the human sciences prompted attempts to explain the phenomenon of religion scientifically. One way was as an attempt to answer fundamental questions about the world, man and his place in it, by methods which are naturally congenial to us, such as stories. As such, religions are thought to be forms of prescientific thought.

If this were true, religious explanations should have systematically retreated before the advance of scientific explanations, and this seems to be what has happened. Initially all sorts of natural phenomena received religious explanation, from the thunder as the weapon of Zeus to the rainbow as God's sign that he would never destroy the world by flooding again. As scientific explanations of these phenomena were provided, religious people comforted themselves with the claim that the complex nature of the living world was scientifically inexplicable. When this was largely explained by Darwin, the fact of life itself was held to be the problem which still required reference to divine creativity. With the discovery of the DNA and of the nature of life, only the origins of the universe itself remained as the scientifically inexplicable. With the advent of the theory of the Big Bang, even that need has disappeared, leaving only the existence of anything at all as apparently scientifically inexplicable.

This phenomenon, of using "God" as a means for explaining whatever, at some time, is inexplicable by any other means, has been referred to as the "God of the gaps." God is used as a convenient *ad hoc* hypothesis to plug any gaps left by scientific explanation. When we can explain something scientifically, we do so. When we can not explain something, we substitute a pseudo-explanation. We say: "God did it."

Other psychological and sociological explanations of religious belief have been proposed. Thus Marxists have argued that religious belief is part of an ideology imposed by, and in the interests of, the governing classes. Its doctrinal and ethical teaching serves to justify the possession of wealth and privilege by those who in fact hold it. God made the rulers rulers, and to question them shows lack of proper humility. We should all be content with the station in life in which God has seen fit to place us. Religious belief in an afterlife, "pie in the sky when you die" for those who have no pie in this life, helps make life bearable for the oppressed. Its rituals bring colour into otherwise drab and impoverished lives. These things made life more bearable for the oppressed and exploited masses, but serve to discourage them from taking the steps necessary to win their freedom.

The problem with all of these theories is that they show what may be the *origins* of religious belief, the reasons why religious belief is propagated and maintained, and *causes* of religious believers' actually holding their beliefs. They do not show whether those beliefs are in fact true or false. Arguments against the truth of religious beliefs should properly be directed at the *grounds* of those beliefs, not at their *causes*. Many or even all of the explanations of religion given above could be true in whole or in part, yet it could also be true that nevertheless there exists an all-powerful, all-knowing and all-good God.

The Argument from Mutual Incompatibility

A major problem with religious beliefs is that they usually come as a package, which one is required to accept or reject in entirety. To be a Muslim one must accept the existence of a God of a certain nature and character, that he revealed himself to Mohammed, and that therefore all the requirements of the *Qur'an*, the record of that revelation, are true. To be a Roman Catholic one must accept a God of a certain nature and character, the belief that God revealed himself in Christ, that the requirements of the New Testament and the Church though the ages is true. Each of these commits the believer to a mass of propositions which must all be accepted as true: that it is a duty imposed upon all believers to visit Mecca at least once in a lifetime, that the Pope is the successor of saint Peter, etc., etc., etc. This is often a huge and very specific commitment.

Each such package is only as strong as its weakest part. The truth of any package, as a package, falls if one element within it, considered essential, fails. This in itself renders the truth of any religion extremely unlikely. Of course, if one element in a particular package comes to be thought of as obviously false or no longer acceptable, it tends to be relegated to the status of inessential, even if it had previously been assumed to be essential.

Moreover, each package, considered as a package, is inconsistent with all the others available. If the Jains are right, then the Buddhists, Jehovah's Witnesses, Mormons, the Muslims, the Christians, and the Hindus are all wrong. The truth of *any* one package would count against the truth of all the others.

4. The Existence of God

Those who feel that no arbitrary exceptions can be made to protect certain ideas from the light of reason, and that the same critical approach must be applied here as in all other branches of knowledge, have attempted to settle the major questions of religion, especially whether God exists or not, by using reason. The reasons on both sides have resolved themselves into a series of arguments for or against the existence of God.

Arguments against the Existence of God

The Argument from the Existence of Evil
The argument from evil is directed not against belief in any gods or god, but against the most influential form of theism, the **ethical monotheism** of Jews, Christians and Muslims. These religions propose a god who is, at one and the same time, **omnipotent** (all-powerful) and also unreservedly good. At the same time, all three religions not only recognise the existence of evil in the world, they make its existence a matter of crucial importance to their faith.

If God is omnipotent, he will be able to do whatever he likes. If he is perfectly good he will always and in every respect wish to do what is best. If he *can* do what is best and will always *wish* to do what is best, there is no reason at all why the best does not obtain in the world. But clearly it does not. We can all imagine a world better than the one which actually exists; e.g. one in which there was no HIV virus, or wars, or theft, or road accidents, or rotten apples.

Thus these three beliefs: that God is omnipotent and perfectly good and that evil exists, are not mutually compatible. If there is evil and suffering, as undoubtedly there is, then God, if he exists, cannot be all powerful or all good. He may be all good and wish to avoid all evil, but powerless to do so. He may be all powerful and able to avoid all evil, but unwilling to do so. But He cannot be both all-powerful and perfectly good. Therefore if he exists at all, he must be very different from what most religious people have imagined.

Various attempts, sometimes called '**theodicies**' have been made to reconcile these incompatible beliefs.

It has been said that suffering is part of "God's plan." It is the means whereby he is preparing us for the next life. The problem with this is that the use of means to achieve our ends is something which we limited creatures need to resort to, but not something which an all-powerful being would require. If he wished, he could have created us in a state of readiness for the next life, with no need to spend some time suffering on earth in preparation for it.

Perhaps the most popular response to this problem has been to attribute all evil to the misuse of human free will. It is said that God could have created a world without evil if only all the beings within it were mere automata, lacking in free will. But God wished to create beings like himself, enjoying free choice, even though, inevitably, some would choose to do evil. This was because he valued this freedom and independence of some of his creatures greater than the loss engendered by the necessary entrance of evil into the world.

This might seem to explain the evil which is due to human free choice: murder, theft, rape, warfare, child neglect, etc. It would not explain natural disasters, unless these were due to human actions in some way. While that may be true today of floods caused by excessive destruction of forest cover, or dust bowls created by short-sighted over-farming, it is not true of most natural disasters: earthquakes, volcanic eruptions, floods and hurricanes. Even in everyday life there are unhappy accidents which are genuinely nobody's fault, such as that of "Peter and a Small Patch of Oil on the Road" on page 233.

The traditional way to evade this difficulty was to propose that there are non-human spirits created by God which have free will and misuse it, i.e. devils, and these are responsible for all unfortunate occurrence in nature which cannot be accounted for by the abuse of human free will. This is not a view which would gain much credence today, however.

Saint Augustine argued that evil is not something real, but rather a lack of some kind. Just as blindness is a lack of something we expected to be there, namely sight, so evil is the absence of goodness we expected to be present. However, someone being tortured in a Turkish jail might well resent the idea that the pain he was suffering was merely to be an absence of the pleasure and well-being he had been expecting.

The philosopher Leibniz took a more direct and robust approach to this problem. He argued that in any world imperfection is logically necessary (See Chapter Twelve). This is because a created world is by definition finite, and finitude is imperfection. Even an omnipotent God cannot create something perfect. What a good omnipotent creator would do is create the best of all possible worlds. Therefore, if God exists this must be the best of all possible worlds.

We can, of course, imagine that any single evil or group of evils were absent from our world, thereby apparently showing that there can be better worlds than this one and disproving the thesis that this is the best of all possible worlds. For example, we could imagine a world exactly like this one, but in which one disastrous earthquake had not occurred, say the one which killed 30,000 people in Lisbon. This happened during the time for worship, so that most of the churchgoing population of the city was in the churches when the quake struck. In *Candide*, Voltaire used this as an example to show that Leibniz' theodicy was absurd. But Leibniz argues that to be possible, states of affairs have to be **compossible** with other actual states of affairs. An ordered universe would be governed by the **Principle of Sufficient Reason**. This states that for everything which happens, there must be a sufficient reason why it happens as it does and not in some other way. In such a universe, to change any single state of affairs would be necessarily to alter others in all sorts of ways. The abstraction of any particular evil from the actual world would, he argues, make the world *in total* worse than it is. Using modern scientific knowledge, he would have argued that the stress on the tectonic plates would have built up so much without an earthquake at Lisbon at that particular time, that without it a worse one would have occurred subsequently, and that would have been a greater evil.

The Argument from the Incompatibility of Omniscience and Free Will

If God is all-knowing or omniscient, then he knows now everything which will happen in the future. But in that case the future must develop exactly in accordance with what God knows it will be. But if the events of the future must happen in this way, and not otherwise, then the future is already determined. If the future is determined in this way, then we do not make genuinely free choices, since we have no alternative but to choose what God, in advance, knows that we will choose.

This has consequences unacceptable to religious people, who make much of the moral choices which God allows us, and the rewards or punishments he has in store for us in the next life, depending upon how we have used those choices. If we are not free to do other than what we shall do, then we are not responsible for our choices, and there is no justification for reward or punishment, heaven or hell. Since God does reward and punish us for choices over which we have no control, his action is arbitrary and irrational, and in the case of sending sinners to hell, immeasurably cruel.

Saint Augustine attempts to evade this dilemma by pointing out that God's foreknowing what someone will do does not, of itself, cause them to do what they do. Since God knows what will happen, then what will happen is necessary, but since God did not cause the person to make the choices he will make, that person will make those choices freely.

The Argument from Unfalsifiability

Many modern philosophers find fault both with the things which are claimed about God (that he is invisible, intangible, everywhere, perfectly good, etc.) and with the way religious people respond when challenged about their beliefs. John Wisdom illustrated their response using a modern "parable."

Case Study: The Elusive Gardener

Two travellers stumbled upon a clearing in the jungle, where many beautiful flowers and many weeds were growing. One of the travellers expressed his belief that someone was tending the flowers in the clearing. The other disagreed. Extensive enquiries were made of people living nearby, but no one had ever seen anyone tending it.

They decided to keep a watch over the place to determine which of them was right. They took various measures to detect the presence of an elusive visitor, such as setting up a fence, electrifying it, patrolling it with bloodhounds throughout the night. No gardener was ever seen; nor were any indications ever spotted which might suggest an intruder.

Yet the traveller who believed in the gardener continued to cling to his belief. He now claimed that the gardener must be invisible, inaudible and intangible. Completely undetectable, he maintained, he nevertheless turned up regularly to tend the garden. The then sceptical demanded to know what was the difference between the believer's belief in a totally undetectable gardener and there being no gardener at all.

Wisdom's point is that the religious believer so qualifies his belief to avoid its being shown to be false, that what remains is no different from an imaginary God, or no God at all. After all, a ten thousand dollar note which is invisible, which gives off no sound when rustled, which is intangible, which gives off no smell or taste, which exists in no particular place or time but which is always present everywhere, and which no bank machine or teller can ever detect, is the same as no ten thousand dollar note at all.

So treated, the claim that God exists "makes no difference" because it has no content. This is equally true of other religious claims. For the claim "*x* loves you" to have some content, it has to make some difference in the world. But is, for example, it does not rule out dying slowly of lung cancer, drowning when the ferry boat sinks, or being run over by a truck, what does "God loves you" actually mean?

The Argument from the Meaninglessness of Religious Language

In general, words can be used to mean more or less whatever we choose them to mean. But it is argued that in the context of religious language words are frequently stretched beyond breaking point.

For example, Christians say that there is one God but that he is three persons: Father, Son and Holy Spirit. Each is God, yet there are not three gods but one God. They assert that Jesus, who was born as man, and who was therefore time-bound and limited in power and knowledge, was also God, who exists outside time and is infinite in power and knowledge.

Many philosophers hold that such use of language is simply nonsense. In general words mean what we want them to mean, but they cannot mean just anything at all. In particular, if our use of words involves us in contradictions such as those above, then we are just talking nonsense. Our language gets its meaning from our sense-bound existence, and cannot be applied to something which is supposed to be totally beyond that world, or **transcendent**.

Arguments for the Existence of God

Arguments from Design

It is argued that the order we see in the world around us, and which is a necessary condition of our existence, could not have arisen by chance; that it is necessary to postulate an intelligent designer in order to make sense out of it. It is also claimed that we may infer from the nature of the creation that it has a single designer. From the vastness of the universe, we can infer that he is omnipotent. From the way in which everything is adapted to our existence, we may conclude that he is good.

This argument is based upon an analogy between the universe of our experience and a mechanism produced by intelligent human design. William Paley expressed the argument thus:

> "In crossing a heath, suppose I pitched my foot against a stone, and were asked
> how the stone came to be there; I might possibly answer, that, for anything I
> knew to the contrary, it had lain there for ever: nor would it perhaps be very easy
> to show the absurdity of this answer. But suppose I had found a watch upon the
> ground, and it should be inquired how the watch happened to be in that place;
> I should hardly think of the answer which I had before given, that for anything
> I knew, the watch might always have been there."

The reason for the difference is that the watch is a complex entity made up of different parts which are arranged together in such a configuration that the watch will perform a function, namely to indicate the time, which could not be achieved if any of the parts were missing, or if the parts were arranged in a haphazard manner, or in any other way than they in fact are arranged. This subordination of arrangement of parts within the whole to some purpose is what shows the watch to be the product of intelligent design.

It is argued that if we consider a natural organ like the eye, we can recognise a similar subordination of the several parts, and their arrangement relative to each other, to a purpose, namely that of enabling the possessor of the eye to see. There is a transparent cornea which protects a focusing lens, a light sensitive retina at the focal plane of the lens, and neural circuits which detect colour motion and depth. The iris changes diameter in order to control the amount of light admitted. There are muscles which move one eye in tandem with the other. The parts in this case are not cogs and wheels, they are made of tissue rather than of metal. But the principle is the same. The eye seems designed precisely for sight, and for nothing else.

But if the existence of the watch requires a watchmaker to account for its existence, then the existence of natural objects no less requires the hypothesis of a maker to explain *their* existence. The maker of natural objects we call 'God'.

Unfortunately, arguments based entirely upon analogy are inherently weak, and this one is no exception. The analogy can be turned upon its head. The evidence of our experience of the design and order we seem to experience in world may be said to better support an alternative conclusion. Although we experience everything apparently working towards some unified purpose, we also experience apparent the opposite of this. There is pain and suffering and useless waste. This suggests that the creator is not good or is not all-wise. It might even be held to support the view that there is no single creator; rather the universe was created by a group, with a strong minority working at cross-purposes with the others.

The argument is sometimes stated as though there were only two alternatives: the hypothesis of God as a designer or sheer accident. Certainly accident is an untenable hypothesis. It is as wildly improbable that the various parts of the eye should have come together by chance, and come together in such a way as to enable a creature to see with it, that is, incorporated into the body of an animal, as it is for a hurricane blowing through a builders yard to erect a functioning office building. But these alternatives are not the only ones available. Charles Darwin showed how objects of improbable complexity serving definite functions could arise from a long process of natural selection. This theory does not require a god to explain such phenomena as the eye, only the familiar world working as we can observe it working today. That theory, moreover, like all truly scientific theories, is falsifiable. It would be falsified by the appearance of a feature of an animal which appeared to be designed but which did not appear at the end of a series of evolutionary development, or a complex organ which would have no survival value in intermediate form but only when fully developed.

All this talk about design in nature is in any case begging the question. To refer to something as exhibiting the properties of "design" implies that there is a designer. That is what we are supposed to be trying to establish. What we actually perceive is order, regularity and function. This *resembles* the results of design, and some people have *claimed* it to be design, but whether it is design is something which the believer has to establish. And this argument certainly does not do that.

Arguments from Dependency

The arguments from design move from particular experiences of the world and its apparent design to the existence of God. Cosmological Arguments express a sense of what the theologian Paul Tillich called "ontological shock" in the face of the startling fact that the universe exists at all.

The simplest form of this argument is based upon the idea that everything which exists has a cause of its existence, otherwise it would not exist. We might call this the **Law of Universal Causation**. The existing state of the universe is to be explained in terms of the laws of nature and its preexisting states. But this causal sequence cannot recede into infinity, for without a First cause there would be no subsequent causes or effects. This First cause is the ultimate cause of the existence of the universe, and it is what people call 'God'.

One problem with this argument, and there are many, is that there is a contradiction within it. On the one hand it is stated that every event has a cause; on the other there must be an uncaused First Cause. The argument "takes off' from the Principle of Universal causation, but the conclusion denies that Principle. Either the Principle is valid or it is not. If it is we cannot admit an uncaused God, and the regress of causes must be infinite. If we admit an exception to the principle, why should that exception be God, why should not matter be equally regarded as the uncaused first cause.

Bertrand Russell pointed out, just because every event has a cause, it does not follow that the universe, considered as everything which exists has a single great Cause. This no more follows than that because every rat has a tail there must exist a single great Tail for every rat. However, Russell was not aware of the recent theory that the universe originated in a "Big Bang." If this theory is true, then it is appropriate to treat the universe as a unity in such arguments.

A more sophisticated version of this argument depends upon the Principle of Sufficient Reason. We have already met this principle in connection with the philosopher Leibniz' response to the problem of evil, but we now need to consider it in a more refined form. As formulated by Leibniz, this states that there is, in principle, an explanation of every contingent event: why it is as it is, and not otherwise. (A contingent event is one which might not have occurred; see Chapter Twelve). We may never be able, as a matter of fact, to discover what that explanation is, but we must work on the assumption that it is so. An infinite regress of explanations of the contingent states of the universe is not possible, since without a terminus in something non-contingent, nothing would be explained. That non-contingent, or necessary being must be one for whom existence is an essential property (or it would itself be contingent). This necessary being is what men call God.

One response to this argument would be to challenge the Principle of Sufficient Reason itself. Yet we normally behave as though it lies behind the attitude we adopt towards explanation. We sometimes may take the line that we have no hope of finding an adequate explanation of something. We may on other occasions decide that seeking for an explanation is not worth the trouble. But we never say that there is simply no explanation to be found; nor do we act as though we believed that to be possible. Accepting this, the Principle might be interpreted as making no claim about the way things are, but rather understood merely as an ideal to be aimed at. It would then be a regulative principle that we should always be prepared to seek explanations, without giving any guarantee that explanations are there to be found. As Russell pointed out: "A man may look for gold without assuming that there is gold everywhere; if he finds gold, well and good, if he doesn't he's had bad luck." Again, the Principle of Sufficient Reason may be regarded simply as an expression, albeit oblique, of a feature of human psychology, namely that people are so disposed as to expect to find adequate explanations for things, and are ill-disposed to brook exceptions to this" "explanation, like peanuts, nourishes a desire for more of the same."

In order to support an argument for the existence of God the Principle needs to be more than the name of an unattainable ideal or a psychological drive, it needs to be true. Against this John Hospers argues that all explanations necessarily terminate in unexplained brute data. Thus Z may be explained in terms of Y, which is not explained. In turn Y may be explained in terms of X, which is unexplained. Anthony Flew concludes from this that a series of explanations must terminate in brute data, proving the Principle of Sufficient Reason false. But W. L. Rowe points out that what it proves is that in the giving of actual explanations there is always some fact left unexplained by us. It does not prove that in such cases there is no explanation to be given.

In fact Hospers' analysis of explanation is faulty. The proposition
(1) "Triangle ABC has three sides"

is sufficiently explained by the proposition

(2) "Having three sides is an essential property of a triangle."

Explanatory series may be terminated by necessary truths which are self-explanatory. In such cases Z is explained by Y and Y by X. The demand to explain X is incoherent since X could not be otherwise.

It is one thing to say that the PSR is possible, but is it true? R. Taylor writes:

"...if one thinks about it, he is apt to find that he presupposes it in his thinking about reality, but it cannot be proved . . . If one were to try proving it, he would sooner or later have to appeal to considerations that are less plausible than the Principle itself. Indeed it is hard to see how one could even make an argument for it without already assuming it. For this reason it might be called a presupposition of reason itself."

Oddly enough, it can be argued that now that the big-bang theory has come to be generally accepted by cosmologists, this approach has been vindicated, since we can no longer assume that matter is eternal or that the universe has an infinite past. Science has brought home to us, in a startlingly fresh way, the radical "contingency," or non-necessity, of the cosmos. This universe, it now seems, did not have to exist at all, nor did it have to possess the peculiar traits that allowed for the evolution of life and consciousness. But since there is no eternal necessity for this particular universe existing at all, it is appropriate to ask why it does.

Stephen Hawking's answer is that even though we must now admit that the universe is finite, we are not compelled to agree that it had a clear beginning. Time could have emerged only gradually out of a purely spatial matrix that had no well-defined temporal beginning itself. An initially non-temporal universe, Hawking asserts, does not require any creator: "So long as the universe has a beginning, we could suppose it has a creator. But if the universe is completely self-contained, having no boundary or edge, it would have neither beginning nor end: it would simply be. What place would there then be for a creator?"

However, it is difficult to see how anyone can talk coherently about a universe "emerging" from sheer spatiality without this process of "emergence" taking place in time. In any case, Hawking misses the point, since "creation" refers primarily to the believer's sense that the universe *whether it had a "beginning" or not* is necessarily always grounded in and sustained by a transcendent God.

The concept of a necessary being leads to the attempt to prove the existence of God from a purely conceptual argument.

Arguments from Logic

This family of arguments stems from an insight which struck Saint Anselm, the archbishop of Canterbury, during vespers on Christmas Day 1100. Meditating upon the phrase of the Psalmist "The fool says in his heart 'There is no God,'" he wondered just why the atheist is a fool. This, he saw, was because the denial of God's existence is self-contradictory. Merely by examining the concept of "God" we can understand that the nonexistence of God is impossible.

Expressing his thought in more modern terminology we can say that the idea of God is that of a something which is the greatest logically possible being, ("greatest" here being understood in terms of mode of existence). If a being were proposed as God, yet was supposed to exist in such a manner that he might not have existed (i.e. he exists contingently) then that being would not count as God, for we could propose a "greater," namely a being which existed in such a manner that it could not fail to exist. To suggest that God might fail to exist, or exists in such a manner that he might not have existed, would contradict the notion of the greatest logically possible being.

In other words, when we examine the concept of God, we find it involves us in self-contradiction even to suppose the logical possibility of his nonexistence.

This**Ontological Argument** has seemed to many to be too good to be true. It usually leaves a suspicion that a rabbit has been pulled out of a hat which must somehow have been concealed prior to the performance. A monkish opponent of Anselm's argument, Gaunilo argued that you cannot argue things into existence in this way. He (Gaunilo) could imagine an island so great that one could not conceive of its nonexistence. Anselm was able to respond that the argument would not work with an island, since an island is by nature something limited and contingent. This argument applies only to one unique concept.

Glossary

agnosticism: the belief that we cannot know whether God exists or not.

atheism: the belief that we can know that God does not exist.

biblical fundamentalism: the belief that a book or collection of books contains the final revelation from God; that its contents, interpreted literally, have ultimate authority in all things; and they it contains the answers to all the important questions of life.

cosmological argument: an argument that the mere existence of the universe demands an explanation in terms of the existence of a First Cause or Creator.

dualism: the belief that the world is governed by two gods.

fideism: the belief that religious faith is irrational and must not be subjected to the demands and tests of reason.

fundamentalism: believing literally in the fundamentals of the faith.

glossolalia: the practice of uttering nonsensical combinations of sounds which are then interpreted as the voice of the Holy Spirit.

Law of Universal Causation: a statement of the view that every state of affairs has some cause.

miracle: a special act of God which demonstrates his power by altering the normal working of Nature.

mysticism: the view that direct experience of God or ultimate reality is possible in a manner not mediated through any outer senses, and that in this way alone can ultimate reality be truly known.

numinous: the sense of being confronted with something "wholly other" and awe-inspiring.

omnipotence: the power to do anything.

ontological argument: an argument that understanding of the concept of God shows that his non-existence is logically impossible.

Principle of Sufficient Reason: Leibniz' statement of the view that there is, in principle, an adequate explanation of every contingent state of affairs: why it is as it is, and not otherwise.

religious experience: some special experience of God or other experience which confirms religious belief.

revelation: a special communication from God to man, e.g. the Bible, the *Qur'an*, the *Book of Mormon*.

theism: belief in the existence of a single good, omnipotent God who creates and maintains the universe in being.

theodicy: an attempt to reconcile belief in the existence of an all-good omnipotent God with our experience of evil in the world.

theology: the systematic study of God and his attributes.

zealotry: fanaticism in support of the faith

Further Study/Discussion/Essay Questions

Sources of Knowledge

Which source of knowledge do you find to be most compelling, and which most reliable?

Testimony

Is accepting something on authority ever rational behaviour, or is it always an abdication of a person's independent power of judgement?

Is all education propaganda?

Is the use of propaganda designed to warn people against the dangers of cigarette smoking, the use of illegal narcotics or Aids a bad thing?

"The camera cannot lie." How true is this today?

Is the television news a "window on the world" or a distorting mirror?

Reason

Do we know that the sun will rise tomorrow?

How can Logic help us attain truth?

Explain how analogy is fundamental to thought.

Language

On what grounds can someone be censured or corrected for departure from the standard rules of his language in speech or writing?

Can one language be better than another as an instrument for acquiring and communicating knowledge?

Could the sum of human knowledge be expressed in any *one* language?

If we cannot say something, can we know it?

Do differences in language lead to the experience of different "worlds" by their speakers?

Mathematics

Is mathematics discovered or invented?

How is it that mathematics "fits" the real world?

Is mathematics about truth or validity?

"No human investigation can be called real science if it cannot be demonstrated mathematically." (Leonardo da Vinci) Are there any problems associated with this outlook?

Can everything be expressed in mathematical terms?

"Strange as it may sound, the power of mathematics rests on its evasion of all unnecessary thought and on its wonderful saving of mental operations." (Ernst Mach) Is the knowledge provided by mathematics empty?

The Arts

Are plumbing, cookery and soccer arts? If so, in what senses of that term?

What is "great art", and how does it differ from popular art? Is it, for example, that great art requires intellectual sophistication, whereas popular art can be appreciated by a half-inebriated, half-asleep simpleton?

What is meant by saying that a work of art is true? How is this "truth" different from that sought in other disciplines?

Is true that only the creator of a work of art really understands it?

Can art or music ever be wholly abstract?

In what sense is a fictional work of literature false, and in what sense may it be true?

Facts and Explanations

Are all explanations of why something happened of the same type? Give examples.

What counts as a good explanation?

"No observation can tell us whether one event was the cause of another." Is this true? If it were true, ought we to abandon the notion of a cause?

To explain is to predict, and to predict is to explain." Is this true?

We often explain things by reference to their functions: thus the practice and institution of marriage might be explained by pointing to its function in providing security for children. Do such explanations confuse the *effect* of something with its *cause*?

What is wrong with *ad hoc* explanations? Give examples.

The Natural Sciences

Is scientific knowledge uniquely secure or certain knowledge?

"Scientific evidence is only as objective as those controlling it allow it to be." Is this true?

"Mathematics is the queen and servant of science." Explain how this may be said to be true.

"If I have ever made any valuable discoveries, it has been owing more to patient observation than to any other reason." (Isaac Newton) Is this likely to have been true?

"Research is to see what everybody else has seen, and to think what no one else has thought." (Albert Szent-Gyorgyi) What, if anything, does this quotation teach us about advances in science?

Why is physics often regarded as the paradigm of knowledge?

"Scientific observation is dependent upon theory, and can therefore never be neutral or objective." Discuss.

Is science chiefly a body of knowledge or a method?

"The scientific method, as far as it is a method, is nothing more than doing one's damnedest with one's mind, no holds barred." Is this true?

What bearing does the problem of induction have upon the practice and assessment of scientific knowledge?

Compare the laws of science with the laws of games and states. In what sense are they true?

What purpose do scientific theories have?

"The more falsifiable a theory is, the better it is." Is this true? If so, why?

What is the value of falsificationism?

"Science . . . is attuned to the basic human characteristic of fallibility." Explain how this is so.

What is the difference between scientific and pseudoscientific knowledge claims?

It is sometimes said that the use of experiment is what distinguishes science from non-science. Discuss this with reference to several of the following: astronomy, astrology, alchemy and natural history.

Konrad Lorenz defined truth in science as "the working hypothesis best suited to open the way to the next better one." Is this true?

When Alfred Wegener proposed the theory of continental drift, he was ridiculed. So as Thomas Gold when he proposed the theory that pulsars are spinning neutron stars. Both theories are accepted today, and have become part of orthodox science. The most interesting thing about crackpot theories is that when the next great breakthrough in science occurs, it will look exactly like a crackpot idea. What does this tell us about scientific knowledge?

Is astronomy more reliable than astrology? Can you explain how?

The Human Sciences

What differences do you detect between the subject matter of the natural sciences and the subject matter of the social sciences? What are the implications of the similarities and differences for the study of the social sciences?

Are the so-called "social sciences" genuinely sciences?

Do we know how we ought to organise society? If so, how do we know?

Are political judgements moral judgements "writ large"?

If we are not prepared to tolerate those who are intolerant, are we no more tolerant than they are?

Should researchers be forbidden from investigating certain hypotheses?

Is there some knowledge so dangerous that it should be suppressed?

"Ours is a world of nuclear giants and ethical infants. We know more about war than we know about peace, more about killing than we know about living." (General Omar Bradley) What does this teach us about the future direction of the Enterprise of Knowledge?

Is it possible for the social sciences to provide knowledge of people's behaviour in the same sense that physics, chemistry and biology provide knowledge?

"How do I know what I think until I see what I say?" (E. M. Forster) Is this an adequate characterisation of a behaviourist approach to psychology? How useful do you consider such an approach to be?

What special difficulties are faced in dealing with data in the social sciences?

Is man a "naked ape?" What implications does your answer have for the human sciences?

Does "empathy" have any place in scientific work?

Why is the problem of "action" central to the question of whether or not the human sciences can properly be called sciences?

Why are "laws" so rare in the human sciences?

What is the difference between our knowledge of our own pain and our knowledge of other people's pain?

It is sometimes said that the use of experiment is what distinguishes science from non-science.

Discuss this with reference to several of the following: economics, parapsychology and psychology.

Are the human sciences capable of achieving truth about human beings?

History

What problems are posed for the historian in using as evidence any three of the following written sources: diaries, memoirs, accounts of judicial proceedings, internal government memoranda?

What problems are posed for the historian in using as evidence any TWO of the following: buildings, portraits, cartoons?

Do historians depend too much upon written evidence of the past?

Contrast the characteristic problems faced by historians studying the recent past with the problems of those studying the distant past.

What problems are faced by historians in trying to understand the religious beliefs and practices of past societies?

How useful to the historian are the notions of "progress" and "class conflict""?

Do historians fail to make an adequate distinction between reasons and causes?

Why is history continually being rewritten?

Ought historians to be more scientific?

Could there ever be historical laws?

Can there ever be a "true" account of the past?

Is it possible for a historian to escape theory?

"Nothing changes more constantly than the past; for the past that influences our lives does not consist of what happened, but of what men believe happened." (Gerald W. Johnston) Is the function of history to provide us with knowledge of the past, or to influence our understanding of the present and our conduct in the future?

How, and for what reasons, can the past be distorted?

Is a value-free history possible, and if so is it desirable?

"Just find out what happened and tell it as it was." Is this good advice to give a historian?

Is history the creation of historians?

Are there any historical facts?

Value

Is the worth of anything a measure of its usefulness?

Is argument about the value of conduct or art always futile?

Is beauty in the eye of the beholder?

Do you make any difference between a book, song or movie you like, and a book, song or movie being good? If so, what are the differences?

Is it an objective fact that Michaelangelo was a great painter, or that Wagner was a great composer? *(Substitute other names if you feel more comfortable with them).*

Why is the music of Bach superior to that of Bon Jovi, and Mendelssohn superior to Megadeath? *(Substitute other names if you feel more comfortable with them).*

Does the evaluation of works of art raise problems of knowledge in the same manner as other pursuits of truth?

Is what is beautiful always the same in every society?

Can a dangerous animal or an evil person be beautiful, or a corrupting novel, play, film, or other work of art, be a great work of art?

Is beauty, or artistic merit, in the eye of the beholder?

Is everyone an equal judge with everyone else in the arts?
Are there aesthetical values in mathematics and science?

Ethics
What reason is there to behave morally?
Does anyone ever behave absolutely unselfishly?
Is it futile to argue about moral issues?
Do moral issues raise problems of knowledge in the same way as other attempts to reach the truth?
Is morality relative to culture, or is there an absolute set of moral standards or principles by which we can judge whether the values and moral codes of our own society are right or wrong?
Can there be a moral right to disobey a law?
Should moral actions be judged by rules, principles, motives or consequences?
How may moral dilemmas be resolved?
"Integrity without knowledge is weak and useless, and knowledge without integrity is dangerous and dreadful." (Samuel Johnson) Examine the part played by knowledge in making moral decisions.
What is the weight of emotion, reason, conscience, tradition and religion in making moral judgements?
Do we know how we ought to organise society? If so, how do we know?

Politics
Are political judgements moral judgements "writ large"?
If we are not prepared to tolerate those who are intolerant, are we no more tolerant than they are?
Should researchers be forbidden from investigating certain hypotheses?
Is there some knowledge so dangerous that it should be suppressed?
"Ours is a world of nuclear giants and ethical infants. We know more about war than we know about peace, more about killing than we know about living." (General Omar Bradley) What does this teach us about the future direction of the Enterprise of Knowledge?

Philosophy
What is truth?
Is any knowledge beyond rational doubt?
How would you define the phrases "reasonable doubt," "firm conviction," "moral certainty," and "mathematical certainty"? Does it make sense to attach probabilities to these phrases, such as "at least a 90% chance of being true"?
Who is likely to know most about childbirth, a qualified male gynaecologist or a woman who has given birth to twelve children?
Does the increasing amount of information about necessarily lead to greater wisdom?
Is the worth of anything (an idea, argument, theory, work of art, moral code, or person) a matter of how useful it is?
How does the certainty of our knowledge relate to its sources and the ways in which we organise it?
Does all knowledge depend upon the recognition of patterns and anomalies?
According to the sceptic, only one thing is certain -that is, that nothing is certain. Is this true? If so, is it not also false? If so, what does this tell us?

Religion

"It was as if I were surrounded by a golden halo of light. I had only to reach out my hand to touch God himself, who was so surrounding me with his love." Experiences such as this one are sometimes claimed to prove the existence of God. Do they?

Is the existence of God compatible with the existence of AIDs?

Is religious belief rational?

Is religion a delusion?

What is religious faith? Is it a form of knowledge or belief, or is it distinct from either?

"*Proof* of the existence of God is irrelevant. What matters is *faith*." Is this true?

Can the existence of God be known?

"Arguing with a person's faith is like chasing them around a big empty parking lot. You can keep backing them up, and backing them up—but you never actually corner them." (George Weilacher) Is this a fair description of religious believers, and if so, what does it tell us about religion?

Could any developments in Science ever count for, or against, the existence of God?

What would have to happen to convince you of God's existence, or of his nonexistence?

Is the concept of God like that of gravity?

Is the scientist's faith that the world is governed by unchanging laws comparable to the religious believer's faith in God?

Discuss the view that proof of God's existence is irrelevant, and that what matters is faith.

Expressions such as "God exists" and "God is love" are frequently said to be at best peculiar or paradoxical and at worst meaningless. Discuss how such expressions are peculiar or paradoxical, and whether they are meaningless?

Is there a necessary conflict between science and religion?

General

Are there "scientific facts," "historical facts and "mathematical facts?" If so, what is the difference between them?

In what sense may logic, mathematics and the arts be said to be languages? Compare them with each other and with ordinary language.

When a teacher gives an answer in a mathematics class, he may stand to be corrected by his students. Are teachers of other subjects in the same situation. If so, why? If not, why not?

What is the difference between the use of symbolism in logic and mathematics on the one hand, and in the arts on the other?

How do scientific theories compare with political and religious ideologies as knowledge?

Which form of knowledge do you find to be most compelling, and which most reliable?

Is there any knowledge which no person could reasonably doubt? T What values are implicit in the Enterprise of Knowledge? T Does scholarship trivialize experience?

What sorts of things can, and what sorts of things cannot, be proved?

What is meant by the elegance or beauty of mathematical proofs and scientific theories? Should this count in mathematics and science?

Compare the role of a scientist in acquiring truth to that of a historian or artist.

Is censorship ever acceptable?

Does the scientist or artist have any responsibility to society?

"Few people are capable of expressing with equanimity opinions which differ from the prejudices of their social environment. Most people are even incapable of forming such opinions."

(Albert Einstein) If this is true, what hope is there for the Enterprise of Knowledge?

"The most beautiful thing we can experience is the mysterious. He to whom this emotion is a stranger, who can no longer wonder and stand rapt in awe, is as good as dead: his eyes are closed." (Albert Einstein) Is this true, or is it mere mumbo-jumbo?

"These days people seek knowledge, not wisdom. Knowledge is of the past, wisdom is of the future." (Vernon Cooper) Do you agree?

"Everyone takes the limits of his own vision for the limits of the world." (Arthur Schopenhauer) How does reflection upon our knowledge counteract this tendency?

"To say that a man is made up of certain chemical elements is a satisfactory description only for those who intend to use him as a fertilizer." (Hermann Joseph Muller) In order to understand a man, what else do we need to take into account in addition to what the natural sciences say about him?

Thomas Jefferson once said that he would rather believe that Yankee professors could lie than that stones could fall from heaven. Is this a reasonable approach towards claims of bizarre or impossible events?

"I often say that when you can measure what you are speaking about, and express it in numbers, you know something about it; but when you cannot measure it, when you cannot express it in numbers, your knowledge is of a meagre and unsatisfactory kind." (Lord Kelvin) Is this necessarily so?

Do we have anything to learn from the study of the myths and folklore of primitive and ancient peoples?

Who knows most about you, yourself or other people?

Suggested Activities for Oral Presentations

The following are a few general ideas, which provide a form within which students can insert and develop their own individual or group presentations with reference to their own specific interests.

Sources of Knowledge

Two people take up opposing positions about one of the dubious "alleged" sources of knowledge and argue their case.

Sense-experience

Enact a short play in front of the class. Then hand out a questionnaire designed to find out what the audience observed, and how they interpreted what they observed. What does this teach about sense-experience?

Testimony

Take a recent news story which you feel is covered in a biased manner, then systematically alter it so that the roles are diametrically opposite. Either swap the names of the two opposed countries and their leaders, etc. around, or substitute the names of fictional countries and leaders. Hand it out to the class. Does this expose a double standards routinely applied to the story in the media?

Compare the treatment of a news story in two different newspapers (photocopy them) or on two different television channels (video them).

Show how "labelling" is used to skew news coverage of a particular story in one particular direction.

Find, map and explain an example of the systematic application of double standards in a news story.

Video a discussion on a controversial news topic. Explain how the choice of speakers, attitudes and questions of the chairperson seems calculated to favour one side rather than the other.

Reason

Show how closed-system reasoning can be of use in a particular situation. Explain *why* it is useful.

Language

If you know well a language which the others in the class do not know, explain how certain words and phrases cannot be translated, except with difficulty into the language used by the class, and what problems this might give rise to.

If you come from a culture different from that of most people in your class, explain any gestures which have different meanings in your own culture, and the problems that might give rise to.

Mathematics

Take a report based upon statistics and examine the use which is made of the statistics. What questions would you want to ask about the way in which the data was gathered and the statistics presented?

Arts

Take a work of art and present it, a copy of it, or part of it, to the class, e.g. five minutes from an opera on video. Show how knowledge is conveyed by this work of art in various ways: e.g. the drama, music, choreography, stage set design, etc.

Natural and Human Sciences

Explain and illustrate a case of the forgery or misrepresentation of the results of a scientific investigation.

Detect, present and explain the presence of ideological thinking in a work purporting to be science.

Detect, present and explain a work of pseudoscience. (If it is a book, photocopy some quotations, if a television programme, video a section).

History

Show by reference to a textbook you have used in the past, how the teaching of history in your country is ideologically influenced, perhaps in the direction of nationalism, and your reactions towards it at the time.

Show clips from a historical film, and explain where it is misleading and inaccurate.

Detect, present and explain a work of pseudohistory. (If it is a book, photocopy some quotations, if a television programme, video a section).

Ethics

Invent a particular situation which raises a more general ethical problem (like the case studies in the chapter on Ethics). Have several people adopt different approaches towards the solution and argue their points of view. Pay attention to how claims are justified.

Politics

Several people adopt different political ideologies and debate on a problem of contemporary relevance from the point of view they have adopted. Pay attention to how claims are justified.

The Future of the Enterprise of Knowledge

Take an old (more than twenty years) edition of a newspaper or magazine and compare it with today's edition. What does this tell you about comparative interests and standards of literacy? Examine their subject matter, layout and language.

Form a group to role play research students, university officials and corporate benefactors of a university in a situation where the research students have discovered that the manufacturing processes or products produced by the benefactor harms the environment or the customer.

Religion

Several students "adopt" a different religion, and debate on a problem of contemporary relevance from the point of view they have adopted. Pay attention to how claims are justified.

General

Several people representing different areas of knowledge (e.g. mathematics, arts, sciences, etc.) take an object of some sort and explain how it may be understood or treated from their particular point of view.

Answers to Exercises

Exercise 6.1
1. command
2. question
3. statement
4. exclamation
5. statement

Exercise 6.2
1. argument (Foreign students have a harder time at college than those who are studying in their own country)
2. not an argument
3. not an argument
4. argument (Customers benefit from advertising)
5. not an argument

Exercise 6.3
1. appeal to undesirable consequences
2. argument from silence
3. argumentum ad hominem
4. appeal to pity
5. argument from force
6. incoherence

Exercise 6.4
1. begging the question
2. complex question
3. tautology
4. argument by redefinition
5. double bind

Exercise 6.5
1. incompatible
2. not incompatible
3. not incompatible
4. incompatible
5. not incompatible

Exercise 6.6
1. false
2. true
3. undetermined
4. true
5. undetermined
6. undetermined
7. false
8. true

Exercise 6.7
1. denying the antecedent: invalid
2. denying the consequent: valid
3. denying the consequent: valid
4. denying the antecedent: invalid
5. denying the consequent: valid

Exercise 6.8
1. true
2. false
3. false
4. false
5. true
6. false
7. true
8. false
9. true (some" carries no implications about "all")
10. true

Exercise 7.1
1. vague
2. neither
3. indefinite
4. indefinite
5. vague
6. vague
7. vague

8. vague
9. indefinite
10. neither

Exercise 7.2
1. equivocation
2. slippery slope
3. equivocation
4. division
5. slippery slope
6. amphiboly
7. division
8. equivocation
9. accent
10. meaningless claim

Exercise 7.3
1 .figurative
2. too wide
3. too wide
4. negative
5. too narrow

Exercise 7.4
1 .persuasive
2. precising/persuasive/theoretical
3. operational
4. theoretical
5. persuasive

Exercise 11.1
1. fact
2. fact
3. judgement
4. fact
5. judgement
6. opinion
7. judgement
8. fact
9. judgement
10. judgement

Exercise 11.2
1. neither necessary nor sufficient condition
2. sufficient condition
3. necessary and sufficient condition
4. sufficieent but not necessary condition
5. necessary but not sufficient condition

Exercise 11.3
1. *post hoc ergo propter hoc*
2. single cause
3. genetic fallacy
4. magical thinking
5. anecdotal
6. *post hoc ergo propter hoc*
7. single cause
8. magical thinking
9. magical thinking
10. *post hoc ergo propter hoc*

Exercise 11.4
1. necessarily false
2. contingent
3. necessarily true
4. necessarily false
5. necessarily true

Exercise 15
1. descriptive
2. normative
3. normative
4. normative
5. descriptive

Select Bibliography

Barnes, B., *About Science*, (Oxford, 1985)

Berger, John, *Ways of Seeing* (London, 1972)

Bogart, Leo, *The US Information Agency's Operating Assumptions in the Cold War*, (New York, 1976)

Bryson, Bill, *Mother Tongue: The English Language*, (London, 1990)

Carr, E. H., What is History? (London, 1990)

Chalmers, A. F., *What is this thing called Science?* 2nd ed. (Milton Keynes, 1978)

Chomsky, Noam, *Deterring Democracy* (London, 1992)

Chomsky, Noam, *Necessary Illusions*, (New York, 1988)

Chomsky, Noam, *Rogue States: The Rule of Force in World Affairs,* (New York, 2000)

Close, F., *Too Hot to Handle: the race for cold fusion* (Princeton, NJ, 1991)

Cytonic, Richard E., *The Man who Tasted Shapes* (London, 1994)

Dennett, Daniel, *Darwin's Dangerous Idea* (London, 1996)

Dunbar, Robin, *The Trouble with Science* (London, 1995)

Fiske, John & Hartley, John, *Reading Television* (London, 1978)

Flew, Anthony, *Thinking about Thinking* (London, 1975)

Gardner, M., *Science: good, bad and bogus* (Oxford, 1983)

Glover, Jonathan, *Causing Death and Saving Lives* (London, 1977)

Glover, Jonathan, *Utilitarianism and its Critics* (New York, 1990)

Golding, Peter & Elliott, Philip, *Making the News* (London, 1979)

Ground, Ian, *art or bunk?* (London, 1993)

Harrison, Ross, *Democracy* (London, 1993)

Herman, Edward S., & Chomsky, N., *Manufacturing Consent*, (New York, 2001)

Hertsgaard, Mark, *On Bended Knee: The Press and the Reagan Presidency* (New York, 1988)

Hick, John, *The Existence of God* (New York, 1964)

Hofstadter, Douglas R. & Dennett, Daniel C., *The Mind's I* (London, 1982)

Hood, Stuart & Tabary-Peterssen, Thalia, *on television,* 3rd ed revised (London, 1997)

Kitcher, P., *Vaulting ambition* (Camb. Mass., 1985)

Kuhn, D., *The Skills of Argument* (Cambridge, 1991)

Leowontin, R. C., *The Doctrine of DNA: Biology as Ideology* (London, 1993)

Lipstadt, Deborah, *Denying the Holocaust: The Growing Assault on Truth and Memory* (London, 1994)

Loewen, James W., *Lies My Teacher Told Me: Everything Your American History Textbook Got Wrong,* (New York, 1995)

Maltese, John Anthony, *Spin Control*, 2nd ed. (Chapel Hill, NC., 1994)

McChesney, Robert W., *Rich Media, Poor Democracy: Communication Politics in Dubious Times* (New York, 2000)

Mitchell, Basil, *The Philosophy of Religion* (Oxford, 1971)

Monbiot, George, *Captive State: The Corporate Takeover of Britain* (London, 2001)

Mueller-Hill, B., *Murderous Science* (Oxford, 1988)

Nagel, Thomas, *Mortal Questions* (Cambridge, 1999)

Neill, Alex & Ridley, Aaron [eds] Arguing about Art (New York, 1995)

O'Shaughnessy, Nicholas, "Political Marketing and Political Propaganda," in *Handbook of Political Marketing,* ed. Bruce I. Newman, (Thousand Oaks, Ca., 1999)

Parker, Ian *et al, Deconstructing Psychopathology*, (London, 1995)

Paulos, J. A., *Innumeracy* (New York, 1988)

Philips, Peter & Project Censored, *Censored 1997, The News that Didn't make the News: The Year's Top Twenty-Five Censored Stories*, (New York, 1998.

Philo, Greg, *Seeing and Believing: The Influence of Television* (London, 1990.

Pilger, John, *Hidden Agendas* (London, 1999)

Pinker, Steven, *How the Mind Works*, (London, 1998)

Pinker, Steven, *The Language Instinct: The New Science of Language and Mind,* (London, 1995)

Plantinga, Alvin, *God, Freedom and Evil* (London, 1975)

Priest, Stephen, *Theories of the Mind* (London, 1991)

Purtill, Richard L., *Moral Dilemmas* (Belmont, Ca., 1985)

Rampton, Sheldon & Stauber, John, *Weapons of Mass Deception: The Uses of Propaganda in Bush's War on Iraq* (London, 2003)

Roberts, R. M., *Serendipity* (New York, 1989)

Ross, Colin A. & Pam, Alvin, *et al, Pseudoscience in Biological Psychiatry (New York,)*

Sacks, Oliver, *An Anthropologist on Mars* (London, 1995)

Sacks, Oliver, *Seeing Voices: A journey into the World of the Deaf* (London, 1990)

Sacks, Oliver, *The Man Who Mistook His Wife For a Hat,* (London, 1985)

Sahlins, Marshall, *The Use and Abuse of Biology: An Anthropological Critique of Sociobiology* (London, 1977)

Scheuer, Jeffrey, *The Sound Bite Society: Television and the American Mind* (New York, 1999)

Schick, Theodore Jr. & Vaughn, Lewis, *How to think about weird things: Critical thinking for a new age* (Mountain View Ca., 1995)

Selby, Keith & Cowdery, Ron, *How to Study Television* (London, 1995)

Shaw, Patrick, *Logic and its Limits*, 2nd ed. (Oxford, 1997)

Shermer, Michael, *Why People Believe Weird Things: Pseudoscience, Superstition and other Confusions of our Time*, (New York, 1997)

Singer, Peter, *Practical Ethics* 2nd ed. (Cambridge, 1993)

Sutherland, Stuart, *Irrationality: The Enemy Within*, (London, 1992)

Swinburne, Richard, *The Coherence of Theism* (Oxford, 1977)

Swinburne, Richard, *The Existence of God* (Oxford, 1979)

Taubes, G., *Bad Science* (New York, 1993)

Wolpert, Lewis, *The Unnatural Nature of Science*, (London, 1992)

INDEX

Parting Message:

THINK

THINK CRITICALLY

and don't forget that

"BULLSHIT DETECTOR"

For up-to-date information about Anagnosis books:
visit our website: **www.anagnosis.gr**
email: anagnosis@anagnosis.gr

Anagnosis, Harilaou Trikoupi 130, Kifissia, 14563 Athens, Greece
fax: ++30-210-62-54-089
telephone: ++30-210-62-54-654